PENGUIN BOOKS
THE ARMCHAIR DIPLOMAT ON EUROPE

The Armchair Diplomat on Europe

Your Opinionated Guide to the Hot Shots,
Hot Spots and Incendiary Issues

MELISSA ROSSI

PENGUIN BOOKS

PENGUIN BOOKS

Published by the Penguin Group
Penguin Books Ltd, 80 Strand, London WC2R 0RL, England
Penguin Group (USA) Inc., 375 Hudson Street, New York, New York 10014, USA
Penguin Group (Canada), 90 Eglinton Avenue East, Suite 700, Toronto, Ontario, Canada M4P 2Y3
(a division of Pearson Penguin Canada Inc.)
Penguin Ireland, 25 St Stephen's Green, Dublin 2, Ireland
(a division of Penguin Books Ltd)
Penguin Group (Australia), 250 Camberwell Road,
Camberwell, Victoria 3124, Australia (a division of Pearson Australia Group Pty Ltd)
Penguin Books India Pvt Ltd, 11 Community Centre,
Panchsheel Park, New Delhi – 110 017, India
Penguin Group (NZ), cnr Airborne and Rosedale Roads, Albany,
Auckland 1310, New Zealand (a division of Pearson New Zealand Ltd)
Penguin Books (South Africa) (Pty) Ltd, 24 Sturdee Avenue,
Rosebank 2196, South Africa

Penguin Books Ltd, Registered Offices: 80 Strand, London WC2R 0RL, England

www.penguin.com

Published in Penguin Books 2005
1

Set in 8.5/12 pt Frutiger 55
Typeset by Rowland Phototypesetting Ltd, Bury St Edmunds, Suffolk
Printed in England by Clays Ltd, St Ives plc

ISBN-13: 978-0-14102-146-1
ISBN-10: 0-14102-146-2

Contents

To Mel and Ellen for passing on their thirst for travel and learning

Acknowledgements

So many people helped in the creation of this book that it is impossible to name them all. However, here are but a few to whom I will be eternally grateful. Miss Laura Milan for diligent research; Roxanne Rowles for chronic insights; my wonderful research assistant Sophie Cotter for everything; Katherine Dunn for being the most gracious person on the planet; Melik Boudemagh for his all-purpose brilliance; Anne Pramaggiore and the Pramaggiore clan for wonderful vacations; Karl Abramovic for being; Liliana Cabal, Nils Petersen and Judith Wienerrother for digging up articles; Sarah Jane Kincaid and Enrique García Lozano for general kindness; Erin and Marcello, Stefano the shoemaker, Katya and Lucca, and Paula and Roberto for Italian insights; Max, Marina, Sofia and Bill for wild nights across Europe; Iposa for fab lunches; Christoph Kirsch for croissants; Guiliano Smaldino for surprises; all my flatmates (especially Lotte, Katrina and Karsten) for being so helpful; Edit, Kata, Peter and Robert and the Hungarian Tourism Board for peeling back Hungary; Latvian President Vaira Vike-Freiberga and her assistant Aiva Rozenberga for welcoming me to the presidential castle; Prime Minister Juhan Parts and his assistants for meeting with me in Tallinn; Ritums Ivanovs, Andris Vitolins, lovely Maria, and Asnate Smeltere for showing me Riga; Lee Anthony Courchesne and Brenden Murray for Barcelona's multicultural magnet Andu; Anne 'Lingling' Millereau for making Brussels fun; Keith Bellows, Sheila Buckmaster, Jayne Wise and all the others at *National Geographic Traveler* for sending me across Europe; Michael Meyer, Chris Dickey, Stryker McGuire and Ginny Power for eye-opening *Newsweek* assignments; Catherine and Sam Couplan for Monday dance-a-thons; Philippe Herzog and Gypsy for all-night Parisian tours; Esther Gomez and Pilar Vico for helping me to better understand Spain; Ricky Burdett, Christina Roosen, Luis Afonso, master musician 'Don G', puppeteer PJ and Mifalda of Portugal for enlightening interviews; Davil for showing me Denmark; Sue of Raval for letting me take over her dining room; Peter Lemeer and all the Peters in Maastricht who helped put together the pieces of the puzzle; Air Baltic for making travel to the Baltics easy; the particularly helpful tourism boards of Spain, the Netherlands and Belgium, and all European tourism boards (except for those in the UK and France) who kindly donated pictures; the hundreds of Europeans whom I interviewed on planes, trains and in cafés; Carlos Mundy for being the maestro of the kitchen; the assorted MEPs and thinktankers who provided invaluable info; Andrew Henty and the crew in production, Richard Duguid and John English for their thoughtful copy editing; Elisabeth Merriman for diligently pulling together copy; and above all my fantastic agent Bill Gladstone and my brilliant editor Helen Conford who patiently guided me through this.

Preface

This book was born on yet another rainy night in Maastricht, my former home in the Netherlands, when I received a phone call from Florence, Italy. On the line was the artist Erin Murphy who always keeps abreast of international affairs. 'Melissa,' she said, sounding vaguely troubled, 'exactly what is the EU?'

I didn't miss a beat. 'The European Union is a supranational umbrella that makes laws concerning the economic, agriculture, transportation, energy, judicial and environmental affairs in member countries. Members pay dues to the EU, which in turn allocates money back to countries for such things as agriculture and infrastructure. Many of its members use the shared currency, the euro, and the EU represents the biggest trading bloc in the world.'

There was a long pause.

'Erin, did that make any sense?'

'No,' she replied. 'I don't understand what the EU is and I don't even understand what Europe is any more. Can you figure it out and let me know?'

I promised to get back to her. A year later, I called back.

During that year, which I spent travelling across Europe, writing articles for *Newsweek* and *National Geographic Traveler*, interviewing residents, analysts, journalists and politicians, and drawing information from government documents, think tanks, NGOs, newspapers, websites and numerous insightful publications, I realized that Erin certainly isn't alone. Most Europeans are baffled about what contemporary Europe is and how it fits into the EU. And from confusion springs apathy – and if citizens become apathetic and kiss their power away, then democracy goes with it and EU citizens might as well call up Brussels and tell the EU they can do whatever they want because nobody understands and nobody cares.

That's why I wrote this book: to offer Europeans an opinionated guide that provides the basics for an understanding of European affairs. In a way this is a geopolitical travel book, and as with travelling, two things hold true: you can't make sense of the terrain without a map, and it helps quite a lot if you know the basics of the language. That's what this book provides: a general map and language guide to the countries that are part of the European Union, plus Switzerland and Norway. By map, however, I mean more than just physical layout: this book also pulls in the histories, grudges and defining issues and tries to show how the separate pieces of Europe fit together. And it also gives you the basic language, in the form of names and places that are necessary vocabulary to put together the puzzle these days.

I hope as you delve into this book that it makes you laugh, makes you cry, that it empowers you, makes your mouth drop open in disbelief, and that it helps you understand the relevant issues that are defining Europe today. Most of all, I hope it piques your interest, and makes you want to learn more about the amazing part of the world that calls itself Europe.

Melissa Rossi
Barcelona
November 2004

Introduction

Europe is at the most awkward moment of its history. Certainly there have been more violent times, when emperors, kings and knights launched battles and wars that left the ground blood-soaked and scorched. There have been more volatile eras, when ideas and ideals brewed up revolutions that had heads rolling in the streets. And there have been more repressed periods, as when half the continent was forced into communism and the other half turned its back and tried to forget.

> *Eight of the ten countries that came into the European Union in 2004 were communist for over four decades after the Second World War; seven of those were Soviet republics or satellites.*

But in most of modern Europe's momentous periods – and this indeed is one – most Europeans could tell you what Europe was and who was running the place. Now many Europeans are scratching their heads about what 'the continent' is. It apparently stretches to Cyprus, which dangles forty miles from Syria, but somehow skips Turkey which lies along the way; Romania and Bulgaria may be part of it, but it often excludes Russia and the Ukraine. It extends nearly to Africa since it now includes Malta, but there's debate about whether Britain and Greenland can really be part of Europe.

And while it requires experts to ascertain what Europe is geographically since the fall of the Soviet Union, politically the matter grows even more confusing. Although most Europeans can at least tell you who is heading their country, no one seems quite sure what to make of the union to which most European countries now belong. To most people, the European Union is apparently some drab building in Brussels that every so often pours euros out of a slot and issues a new law about the size of potatoes. As to which twenty-five countries are members of the EU, until recently many Europeans were quite convinced that Turkey was among

the ten new countries to enter in 2004; in a recent survey 7 per cent of the British listed the United States as part of the EU.

In short, Europe and Europeans are utterly mystified. And who can blame them? The media, except for a short spate of reporting about the ten new countries entering the European Union in May 2004, has done a deplorable job explaining what the EU is and the increasingly significant decisions being made in Brussels. And the EU itself, despite making an official goal of becoming more citizen-friendly, seems to be going out of its way to obscure what it is and to keep the people in the dark. Heaven forbid that they could circulate a brochure round all EU households explaining their institutions, the countries that are EU members and such important events as the expansion in size from fifteen countries to twenty-five, with more at the back door. Instead, the EU boasts that it has a website (http://europa.eu.int) – and indeed they do, although you need a team of lawyers to decipher what the voluminous information written in Eurocratese actually means. (See Glossary for basic information about the European Union institutions.)

> ***Explaining itself, often poorly:*** *The good news is that the EU has a new question-answering service – Europe Direct (tel: 00 800 6 7 8 9 10 11; http://europa.eu.int/europedirect/) and several helpful publications including* Europe on the move *about the recent enlargement (download it at http://europa.eu.int/comm/publications/booklets/move/41/index_en.htm). The bad news is that apart from that, much information on the website is indecipherable. Take, for example, this baffling beginning of a Question and Answer 'explanation' of the European Commission's opinion about the draft European Constitution: 'Q In insisting on reopening the composition of the Commission, are you not encouraging those who wish to reopen the whole institutional package? Hence, is the Commission not undermining the Conventions test and jeopardizing the IGC as a whole?'*[1]

And besides, until recently most people regarded the European Union as a topic more boring than taxes, the understanding of which was as daunting as unravelling the DNA molecule. 'The EU doesn't affect me,' Europeans said with a shrug, while the EU was passing laws about the types of food that Europeans eat, how it is cultivated and how much Europeans pay for it, what power source fuels European electricity, the airlines, ships and lorries that come in to European countries, property sales to foreigners and how minorities are treated. The EU decides how much funding is available for road and bridge improvement, dam construction and education, not to mention whether Europeans can, or can't, easily move to another EU country to live and work. About the only things the EU doesn't affect is when Europeans eat, if Europeans floss, their churchgoing habits, when holidays are celebrated and their sex life.

> *Media stars: Currently there are only two publications that provide first-rate coverage of the EU: the* EU Observer *(euobserver.com) and the* Economist *(economist.com). Both are essential reading for those who care about the changing face of Europe.*

Suddenly, however, the EU got much more interesting as its soap-opera potential came to light. In 2003 Europe and the EU divided over the issue of Iraq, with France and Germany leading the contingent that opposed it and the French president Jacques Chirac telling those who supported it to 'shut up'. That year, a proposal for an EU constitution wasn't passed, when Spain and Poland defiantly blocked it. In 2004, when the ten new members from the East linked arms with the West, EU residents realized they had little idea about where Estonia, Latvia and Lithuania were, much less about the history and politics there and how Russia keeps threatening to destroy them; they realized that Slovenia and Slovakia were actually two different countries, and that over a decade ago Czechoslovakia had broken apart. They came to see that new EU member Cyprus is a powderkeg and that the possible entry of Turkey to the EU in the future is laden with controversy: while the *Economist* demands from its front-page story 'Why Europe must say yes to Turkey',[2] major players in the EU believe that to admit Turkey would be 'the end of Europe'.[3]

Turkey

No country wants to be part of the European Union more than Turkey, which belongs to most of the other European-based clubs, including NATO. In fact, Turkey has been promised entry into the Brussels-based Union – by the United States, which last time we checked has absolutely no right to make such promises. However, the possibility of Turkey – where Islam is practised by most of its 69 million residents – becoming an EU member is highly controversial for several reasons. Although there are some 12 million Muslims living in European countries, Europe is indeed a Christian club, even if it tries to deny it. Most of the anti-immigration parties are targeting Muslims and Africans; while they may be racist and xenophobic, there is no denying that there are social stresses between the locals and immigrants of these groups, as evidenced by the emergence of these populist groups. If Turkey entered it would be the largest member of the EU in terms of area – dwarfing even France – and its population would overtake Germany's 83 million by 2020 or so, making it the most populous member. Turkey is poor: some 18 per cent live in poverty, and about 10 per cent are unemployed, meaning that many would probably wish to migrate for work. While Turkey has EU membership as its cherished goal, what it most needs is an economic boost. The EU could and probably should uplift Turkey's financial situation, with among other things increased trade and foreign investment. Whether full membership is desirable remains to be seen, but it will be a source of loud debate for years to come.

Another touchy issue: Russia, not part of the EU, is not pleased that so many countries formerly under its control have said 'dostvidanya' and turned an icy shoulder. Russia continually lambasts the Baltic Countries in particular, threatening to obliterate them and bring them back under Moscow's rule.

What's more, plenty of leaders of these new EU countries walked in steamed up about everything from agricultural subsidies to matters historical. President Kwasniewski of Poland asked Western Europe to apologize for not coming to the Poles' aid during the 1944 Warsaw Uprising; Czechs are angry that the West didn't intervene when the Soviet Union rolled in to stamp out 1968's Prague Spring; Hungarians are hurt that Western Europe didn't help during the 1956 revolt against the communists. Many in Eastern and Central Europe are just plain resentful that Western Europe skipped the painful decades of Moscow control and that the West is now far richer. And there are border disputes and issues being tabled that go back to the First World War.

Europe has a headswirling number of long-held grudges, some over territories, some over wars and violent acts, and many going back to the Versailles Peace Treaty of 1919 and before. In fact there are so many festering wounds and historical beefs that Europe might do well to adopt a new two-day holiday: 'We're Sorry Day' – during which every country's leadership apologizes for the numerous horrendous acts committed by their forefathers – followed by 'You're Forgiven Day' – during which every country's leadership formally accepts the previous day's apologies.

Meanwhile, a host of wild characters charged into the European Parliament – many of them Eurosceptics voted in to take their countries out of the EU. Italy sent in former *Playboy* centrefold Alessandra Mussolini – grand-daughter of *il Duce* and a staunch defender of women's rights – who is now taking a seat alongside Robert Kilroy-Silk whose avowed intent during his five-year stint in the European Parliament is to 'wreck it'. Poland voted in the farmers' party, which is best known for throwing spuds at EU officials; Hungary sent in its first Roma representative and Austria's delegate Hans-Peter Martin must have a pretty free social calendar since he blasted to fame after videotaping MEPs checking in at the Parliament building and then promptly heading back to the airport.

Europe offers more opportunities for women to enter politics than any other place in the world, partly because of national laws mandating female representation, partly because of young leaders who appoint women as heads of ministries, and in part because alpha-dog males are being lured into the more lucrative, less risky private sector, creating a power vacuum that motivated women can fill.

In short, Europe is anything but a snooze these days and what happens over the next few years will either see Europe rise as a unified superpower or see it collapse and implode. In the pages that follow you can glean insight into the players, the histories, the issues and the dynamics involved in what some are calling 'the greatest peacemaking project in history'[4] and what others regard as a huge socio-political and economic gamble that not only is redefining what Europe is, but could ruin it.

How Big is Yours? EU by Population, Area and Income

	POPULATION*	AREA (sq. km)	INCOME† ($ per capita)
1. Germany	82,425,000	357,000	27,600
2. France	60,425,000	547,000	27,600
3. United Kingdom	60,271,000	245,000	27,700
4. Italy	58,058,000	301,000	26,700
5. Spain	40,281,000	505,000	22,000
6. Poland	38,627,000	313,000	11,100
7. Netherlands	16,319,000	37,000	28,600
8. Greece	10,648,000	132,000	20,000
9. Portugal	10,525,000	92,000	18,000
10. Belgium	10,349,000	31,000	29,000
11. Czech Republic	10,247,000	79,000	15,700
12. Hungary	10,033,000	93,000	13,900
13. Sweden	8,987,000	450,000	26,800
14. Austria	8,175,000	84,000	30,000
15. Slovakia	5,424,000	49,000	13,300
16. Denmark	5,414,000	43,000	31,100
17. Finland	5,215,000	338,000	27,400
18. Ireland	3,970,000	70,000	29,600
19. Lithuania	3,608,000	65,000	11,400
20. Latvia	2,307,000	65,000	10,200
21. Slovenia	2,012,000	20,000	19,000
22. Estonia	1,342,000	45,000	12,300
23. Cyprus	776,000	9,000	19,200‡
24. Luxembourg	463,000 ·	3,000	55,100
25. Malta	397,000	316	17,700

* All population figures are estimates from July 2004, according to the *CIA World Factbook 2004*.
† Income: per capita. All per capita GNP figures are for 2003 unless otherwise marked and reflect the commonly used economic measure of purchasing-power parity, which factors in exchange rates and weights goods in countries to give a common base of comparison. (Source: CIA.)
‡ Income figure for Cyprus is Greek Cyprus 2003 estimate; $5,600 Turkish Cyprus.
(Sources: *CIA World Factbooks 2003* and *2004* and *Oxford Handbook of the World* by Peter Stalker, New York: Oxford University Press, 2000.)

Part One
Old Europe

Old Europe – Introduction

You can call it 'Old Europe', you can call it 'Western Europe and Greece', you can call it 'the EU-15 (plus two)'. But whatever you call it, this is the energetic power centre of Europe, the industrial heartland, and the population core of what is now the European Union.

Except for two countries – Norway and Switzerland – all of Western Europe is in the EU.

Old Europe

France: Most land, most pushy, biggest food producer
Germany: Most people, biggest economy, most anxious
United Kingdom: Most aligned with US; least likely to use euro
Ireland: Best example of how EU can turn a place around
Belgium: Most eurocratic: headquarters of EU and 'capital of Europe'
Austria: Most vehemently antinuclear; first to start immigration debate
Italy: Most embarrassing head of government; best political soap opera
Spain: Most fun, highest unemployment rate
Portugal: Most behind, highest illiteracy rate
Greece: Most easterly; most tied up with Cyprus
Netherlands: Most tired of being ignored
Luxembourg: Most small, most rich
Denmark: Most surprising: anti-immigration, anti-euro
Sweden: Most likely to suffer mysterious political assassinations
Finland: Most gung-ho of Scandinavian countries about EU
Norway: Most happily independent of EU
Switzerland: Most unlikely to ever join EU

Language lesson: EU-15 is Eurocratese for the fifteen countries that were part of the European Union prior to the 2004 enlargement.

A dense assemblage of diverse cultures, ethnicities and languages, these are the nations that laid the foundations – roads, maps, religions, language and socio-political ideas and governmental frameworks – for what Europe is today. These are the countries that kept alive the concept of an organized land mass for millennia, as the Roman Empire, Holy Roman Empire, Napoleonic Empire, Third Reich or European Union.

Of all the EU-15 countries, only three don't use the euro: Britain, Denmark and Sweden.

And outside occasional alliances, for most of the years these nations have been existing side by side they have been sniping, taunting, clobbering and slaughtering each other, doing it so well, in fact, that it took years, sometimes decades to put everything together again after the military run-ins that sometimes lasted over a century. The Second World War took it to a new extreme: were they to go through a more advanced version of that again they might as well commit collective suicide.

These are now the richest, most developed countries of Europe – and they are among the most affluent in the world – for three reasons. They had a multi-billion dollar loan from the United States in the form of the Marshall Fund to rebuild themselves after the war, and they had sixty years to heal from the devastation – both physical and emotional – of the war. And in the course of recreating themselves they devised a novel method to lessen the likelihood of so thoroughly destroying themselves again. Sharing resources, dividing power, creating an expanding trade market, and redistributing income, they cobbled together what would evolve into the EU.

Another factor that kept cohesion: shared military. While NATO served the purpose of militarily uniting most of these countries since the Second World War, new European military alliances are being created: the EU has its own forces but some members are aligning separately.

Even with most of Old Europe joined as a loose union that abides by the same trade rules and laws and (mostly) shares the same currency, these countries still occasionally bicker and snarl at each other, and there is plenty of discontent within the union. With growing Eurosceptic parties within most EU member countries, who knows? The EU could unravel if certain countries decided to back out. Without EU membership, however, they risk being a lone weak voice against a united whole.

With most of Western Europe linked together as part of the EU, they opened the door to the East in 2004, for a number of reasons. But while they welcome the new states, they haven't yet welcomed their workers: in most EU-15 countries, citizens of the ten new EU countries cannot legally work in Old Europe until 2012.

Why the EU-15 Opened the Door

- Create a political-socio-economic power that can rival the US
- Take advantage of cheap labour
- Increase available resources
- Expand market and foreign-investment opportunities
- Stabilize Europe and keep it from warring
- Minimize risk of Russia again moving west
- Expand strategic influence
- Guilt

The hesitation among Western European countries to allow the new countries' workers to enter hints at the most looming problem for all the EU-15 at the moment: immigration. While new workers are indeed needed, in many countries increasingly powerful groups have risen, questioning the social impact of foreigners living in their lands. And while many countries are now shutting the door, they will not be able to do so for ever.

In the meantime, Old Europe finds itself at the most interesting, complicated and intense moment of its history; never before has there been such a massive, voluntary union of this sort across Europe. US Secretary of Defense Donald Rumsfeld used the term 'Old Europe' to signify a rusty, decaying Europe, but the poor man was misguided. For all the stresses involved in stitching together most of Europe in an 'ever-closer union', the end result is a reinvigoration of both old and new.

1. France: The Individualist

Fast Facts

Country:	French Republic; République Française
Capital:	Paris
Government:	republic
Independence:	486 (unified by Clovis)
Population:	60,425,000 (2004 estimate)
Leaders:	Head of State: President Jacques Chirac (1995)
	Head of Government: Prime Minister Jean-Pierre Raffarin (2002)
Elections:	President elected by universal suffrage for 5-year term; Prime Minister nominated by House of Representatives
Name of Parliament:	Assemblée Nationale
Ethnicity:	Celtic and Latin, with Teutonic, Slavic, North African, Indochinese and Basque minorities
Religion:	83% Roman Catholic; 10% Muslim; 2% Protestant; 1% Jewish
	(Note: these are estimates, since the government can't legally ask a citizen's religious affiliation.)
Language:	French (but of course)
Literacy:	99% (2001 estimate)
Exports:	machinery, cars, oil, aircraft
Per capita GDP:	$27,600 (2003 estimate)
Unemployment:	9.4% (May 2004 Eurostat figure)
Percentage in poverty:	6.5% (2000)
EU status:	founding member (EEC member since 1957)
Currency:	euro
Known for:	baguettes, bad moods, breaking rules

Standout Qualities

Wine: World's best (they say)
Whine: Known for moodiness
Will: Known to stomp foot and stomp off

Résumé

The land synonymous with silky wines, glossy chocolates and thick, buttery accents, France is all wrapped up with food. Whether you're nibbling on creamy cheese bursting out of the rind, chewy baguette thickly spread with pâté, duck-rich cassoulet served in a copper pot, or salad Niçoise studded with tiny black olives, comestibles and the art on the plate are as integral to France as fashion and perfume.

Shooting Stars: France, the land that popularized the word 'restaurant' – it means 'restored' – was also the country where food criticism was born in 1803 with the review guide Almanach des gourmands. *Since then, the matter of the discerning palate has become even spicier as pernickety sorts make or break dining establishments with the stroke of their pens. The Michelin Guide –* Le Guide Rouge *– which serves as the culinary bible is now one of the world's mightiest books for its prestigious listing of the best places to swallow and swirl, awarding a maximum of three rosettes for those that most make critics swoon. The list that has swelled chefs' heads – and ballooned the price lists – has also apparently cost the gastronomic creators their sanity: Bernard Loiseau, chef at France's La Côte d'Or, killed himself in 2003, fearing that Michelin would dock one of his rosettes, and others have threatened the same.*

More edibles push up and plump out in France than in any other country outside the US: with over half of French land covered in pastures, vineyards, orchards and fields, agriculture yields over €26 billion a year and nearly a quarter of EU food originates here. The extraordinarily diverse landscapes – the silvery olive groves and lush vineyards that spread out in the Mediterranean south, the fishing villages strung along the rocky shores of Brittany and the fields of wheat swaying across the middle – produce more than pretty postcards: the variety of fresh food on display in the sprawling French markets provides the basics of the cuisine that has had visitors cooing for centuries, and is but one reason why France is the number-one tourist destination every year.

The French Paradox

Is it the flaky croissant, the stone houses amid lavender fields, the location nudged up against an ocean, two seas and the Alps that draw some 75 million foreigners to France every year? Is it the history of the cliff-perched castles, glittering Versailles and marble-tabled cafés, where creators once tipped back absinthe, or the lure of haute couture and the perfume houses that beckon with scents pressed from flowers and oils? Is it the romance that seems to ooze from the ground and spill over lips, the stylish culture that surrounds or the happy sounds of the lilting 'Bonjour' and 'Merci'? While the symbols of France are well stamped in the mind – the woven metal of la Tour Eiffel, the Louvre where Mona Lisa wanly smiles, the seaside villages where Impressionists filled canvases with dots and flecks – who really knows what France really is, except an ephemeral, sometimes playful, sometimes grumpy, geographical state of mind that is perhaps best defined with a smug shrug? France is a contradiction, a moody artist of a nation that creates vibrant masterpieces then dwells in dark conspiracy theories, a popular bon vivant whose soirées marvel but whose bluntness offends, a thinker who triggers ideological revolutions but who never fathoms contentment, a country that swells with nationalistic pride but where plenty of regions want to secede. The country that penned Europe's first declaration of human rights was one of the world's most brutal colonizers; the country that loudly demands responsible international action is tainted by shady backroom deals; the country that dishes out criticism of everyone else is secretly sensitive and easily wounded. Politically, too, the country is a paradox: its unusual cohabitation system – wherein the president and prime minister are often from different parties – keeps the powerful president in check but frequently blocks any progress, and the French people, in between whingeing, so love France and the perks that come with it that they rebel every time any privilege is whittled away, even if it is for the nation's own good. But like a distant lover, whose mannerisms and smells are alluring, but whose true thoughts are rarely revealed, the appeal of France is its moody mystique and its inimitable style, which along with the omnipresent culture and history that seep in from every corner, keep the romance with France alive, and the tourists coming back for yet another fling.

The geographical giant of Western Europe, with towering leaders to match, France is the mightiest EU country alongside former foe Germany, with whom it revs up the financial–industrial motor of the continent. The two countries have the largest economies and populations, and form the 'Franco-German axis' of the EU: they pay the most dues, they get the most agricultural subsidies back (France alone pulls in some €10 billion)[1] and they pretty much dictate what direction the EU is going in: it was France and Germany, for example, who pushed the EU's recent 'enlargement' and it was France and Germany who insisted that EU countries couldn't run more than a 3 per cent national deficit, a rule which they both ignore. If the two think they run the club, it's understandable: their postwar partnership laid the foundation back in 1950.

> France and Germany actually got the EU ball rolling when their post-Second World War governments linked the resources most needed for war and postwar reconstruction – coal and steel – thinking by doing so they might be less likely to knock each other flat again. That led to a free trade area and an independent authority – the European Coal and Steel Community – that set prices of the resources starting in 1952; over five decades, it snowballed into today's EU.

French Standouts

- Largest EU country by area
- Biggest EU food producer (grain, cheese, wine, beef, poultry)
- Most EU agricultural subsidies (€9.75 billion in 2002)[2]
- Launched EU (inadvertently) with Germany
- World's top travel destination
- Most nuclear power in Europe (56 plants)
- One of the two EU countries with nuclear arms (other is Britain)
- Second biggest European economy (second to Germany)
- Stood up most brashly to US over Iraq (well, somebody had to)
- Language most suited to love (makes 'ticket, please' sound sexy)

That France is even deemed to be part of the Brussels club speaks to the power derived from belonging, since for most of modern history La République was a rather egotistical free spirit that considered itself the most influential country on the continent – and indeed often was. Even when France wasn't directly lording it over the outlying areas as it did during Napoleon's reign, the prevailing political ideas and the creativity brought to life here sparked movements and revolutions in far corners of the known world, not to mention romantic notions and longing looks in the direction of Paris. So crucial was the knowledge of Français, the language of *les beaux arts* and international diplomacy, that even Yanks and Brits bothered to learn it.

> *Some speculate that French lost its power as a global tongue, and its weightiness on the world stage, in 1964, when English was officially adopted as the common language of international pilots and air-traffic controllers.*[3]

So alluring was this country, so exalted was the image of France that anybody who could afford to get there hopped on a horse, a ship or a train and moved right on in. Chopin took up with George Sand, Gertrude Stein discovered Picasso, the Fitzgeralds drank too much, Jim Morrison died, Henry Miller got lice and George Orwell was down-and-out here, being but a few of the foreigners who ploughed into the scene. France was so edgy it was leading the avant-garde before the term had even been thought up and any description of the culture was usually superlative-happy. French chefs were the world's most sublime, French designers the world's most adored, French intellectuals the most closely studied and chased after.

> *The Intellectuals Terribles: Brainy twentieth-century philosopher-writers Simone de Beauvoir and Jean-Paul Sartre thrived on triangles. Feminist writer de Beauvoir, a professor at the Sorbonne, frequently seduced her students – typically teenage females – and threw them into the lion's den with insatiable existentialist Sartre. Some lasted a few months, some a few years, and some worked their way into 'the family', a band of fawning sycophants who surrounded the intellectual duo. No third party challenged the comfortable arrangement more than their friend of nine years, the writer Albert Camus, who didn't partake in their ménage à trois: 'Imagine what she [de Beauvoir] would be saying on the pillow afterwards – how awful, what a chatterbox,' he confided to a friend. Camus, like the rest, ended up an object of their mockery after he wrote an article against Communism which the political fashionistas had adopted after the war: not only did Sartre's paper savagely attack Camus' piece in 1952 – so brutal was the review*

that Camus and Sartre never spoke again – de Beauvoir also went in to skewer him in her book The Mandarins.

Contemporary France, typically the narcissistic muscle of the Continent, however, has grown frankly flabby and is now painfully examining its lumpy form in the mirror. Creativity is stymied, the government sector is bloated – providing a quarter of French jobs – and the formerly state-dominated economy is bilious, with unemployment, albeit lower, still hovering around an unappetizing 10 per cent. Tourism has shrunk, wine sales are sagging, and in the latest show of across-the-Atlantic passive aggressiveness, the US (still steamed up about France's lack of support on Iraq) banned imports of French foie gras mumbling something about facilities being unclean. The corruption that was once as acceptable as wine with lunch is suddenly unpalatable, and courts keep throwing the book at unsavoury politicians and corporate heads for cooking theirs. The government's belt-tightening measures, and gestures towards private firms to swallow up formerly government-run companies, are more moves unsuited to French tastes, eliciting protests, blockades, stampedes, and blackouts as workers demonstrate their great dislike of change or anything that threatens to chisel away at their quality of life that includes free health care and prescription drugs, a maximum 39-hour working week and a paid five-week vacation each year.

Taking it to the Streets

In France, where rhetoric is part of schooling and the favourite hobby is debate, the large-scale illustration of disagreement – protests – are an often-exercised national right. Rising fuel prices, pension cuts and duties on cheese are just a few issues that have recently prompted fishermen to block ports, lorry drivers to block highways and farmers to let bulls charge through government buildings leaving steaming 'calling cards' in front of photocopying machines. In June 2004 the protests amped up considerably: when the government announced plans to part-privatize state-owned electricity and gas utilities, factory workers – worried about potential job losses – cut off power to the Eiffel Tower, government buildings, train lines, the homes of the president and prime minister, and large parts of cities – even switching off transmissions to England and Spain – to show how bright an idea they thought any potential utility sell-off was.

Surprisingly, in a country that's always been ballsy, what most defines France today is sheer fear, a recent social phenomenon so well known that the media simply call it 'l'insécurité'. Although France is nowhere near as dangerous as the UK, crime and violence are rising – murder rates alone jumped 26 per cent in 2001[4] – and politicians are among those dodging knives and ducking bullets. The year of the last presidential election – 2002 – was particularly heinous, which explains how one of the country's loudest racists, Jean-Marie Le Pen, ended up in the last stretch of the presidential race.

Bad Year: 2002

In March a 38-year-old father was beaten to death by a gang of youths whom he'd asked to stop bullying his son; in April an activist in Nanterre sprayed bullets across a city council meeting, killing eight and wounding twenty; in June a neo-Nazi gunman took aim at President Jacques Chirac during a Bastille Day parade; in October Paris Mayor Bertrand Delanoe was stabbed and that same month 17-year-old Sohane Benziane perished when a boy of North African descent doused her with lighter fluid – and forced her to drink it – and then set her on fire. Even though half of the perpetrators of those high-profile attacks were white Frenchmen, it was another group that came most to symbolize encroaching danger: Le Racaille – the so-called rascals – roving gangs of second-generation Algerian, Moroccan and Tunisian youths, who live in *les banlieues*, the dilapidated, seedy suburbs that are home to millions of poor immigrants. They usually don't speak Arabic and while their parents may be Muslim, typically these kids are not practising. Meeting for violent rumbles in parking lots, the boys torch cars for fun – sometimes setting over a hundred ablaze in a night – and are the group best known for street mugging, pick-pocketing and robbing tourists on trains. More alarming: their violent attacks on young women, typically those who live in their banlieues. Gang rape is a rite of membership, and numerous cases are being reported – one 13-year-old girl was sexually assaulted by 88 boys[5] – and hardhitting books and movies documenting the common phenomenon (reports of which are said to increase 20% a year) have rattled the country.

Strained relations between French and Arab Muslims have their roots in the Algerian War of Independence that ended in 1962, but recent events have triggered a new wave of emotions, most of them fearful. In 1994 Algerian Islamists hijacked an Air France flight intending to plough it into the Eiffel Tower, and the next year French-Algerian radicals let loose a wave of bomb attacks on the Paris Métro, killing eight and injuring hundreds. The September 11 2001 attacks on the US, the allegations against French-Moroccan Zacarias 'the twentieth hijacker' Moussaoui for his involvement in that plot, and the fact that failed 'shoe bomber' Richard Reid boarded his flight in Paris haven't helped matters either. However, some French-Arabs have also soared to national hero status in recent years: in 1988 the footballer Zinedine Zidane scored France's two winning goals in the World Cup Final, making the French-Algerian athlete the country's most popular man. (The French team that year was made up almost entirely of first- and second-generation immigrants. Jean-Marie Le Pen blasted the victors, saying they weren't really French.)

Bombarded, as they were in 2002, with sickening news of a society that appeared to be curdling before their eyes, French voters were furious that the government hadn't tackled the problem. Radical rightwinger Jean-Marie Le Pen of the National Front galloped into the front line. The problem, he said (as he has been saying since the 1970s), was simple: North Africans and other immigrants had overrun the place. France's policy of allowing in foreigners is 'fatal to our country',[6] he told fans. 'Massive immigration has only just begun. It is the biggest problem facing France ... We risk being submerged!'[7] There was only one way to solve it, said the self-made millionaire, who has grown even wealthier after inheriting oodles from several rich supporters. 'I pledge an immediate end to all immigration and to send three million immigrants home!'[8] In the first round of presidential voting in April 2002, Le Pen snatched a shocking 17 per cent of the vote, giving him a shot at the presidential seat – even if it was a long one. His showing shoved aside Socialist candidate Prime Minister Lionel Jospin and put Le Pen head to head against President Chirac for the second round – the first time since the Second World War that a hardcore nationalist had made it so close to the Élysée Palace. Most French people were open-mouthed with new horror at the thought of Le Pen running their show.

'I'm just the thermometer for the political malady of France' –
Jean-Marie Le Pen in an interview on RMC-Info radio in April 2002.
Thermometer, yes, but for which orifice?

Mad Jean-Marie Le Pen

Given his doughy face, glass eye, and tightly drawn snake of a mouth, 76-year-old Jean-Marie Le Pen, who made a fortune selling recordings of Nazi marching tunes, hasn't soared in popularity from looks alone. Nor does the man who is prone to explode at friends and colleagues exude an easy-going charm or a camera-friendly slickness that beguiles TV viewing masses. What has propelled Le Pen from obscure leader of the National Front, which he started in 1972 using the slogan of the Nazi-collaborating Vichy government – 'Work, Family, Fatherland' – to the bête noire of French politics is his contagious rage, much of it stemming from matters Algerian. A paratrooper in the Algerian War of Independence, Le Pen is accused of torturing militants then – a charge he denies – although he makes no bones about his belief that granting Algeria's independence was one of France's biggest mistakes; many of his supporters are from the OAS, a secret right-wing military group that tried to assassinate De Gaulle for cutting Algeria free. The Algerians, and other North Africans who emigrated to France, says Le Pen, milk the system and (along with other immigrants) are singlehandedly the cause of France's unemployment and crime – an idea endorsed by the young neo-Nazis who flock to his rallies. No more mosques should be constructed in France, says Le Pen, armed border controls should come back as should the death penalty; abortion should be criminalized and France should dump the euro and return to the French franc. So rabid are his speeches that violence often breaks out: in 1995 a group of skinheads left his rally and promptly killed a Moroccan, pushing him over a bridge, then one of his campaigners, while flyposting for Le Pen, murdered a black youth – a move that Le Pen defended. His son-in-law landed in prison for a violent attack on the campaign trail, and Mr Le Pen himself is no pacifist: he temporarily lost a seat in the European Parliament after he physically assaulted a female Socialist in 1998, and he lost his eye in a brawl with a Communist. Now Le Pen, who tries to confuse his image with that of Joan of Arc – official patron saint of his party – is protected by his own 300-strong paramilitary force, some of whom are neo-Nazis and some former members of the army.[9]

Ultimately Le Pen never really had a chance: over a million rallied across France in protests against him, and voters turned out in huge numbers to throw their support behind the incumbent Chirac, who won with 82 per cent of the vote, even though many grumbled that the choice was between a thug and a thief. But Le Pen's popularity did starkly illustrate the anxiety that has gripped the French people, and it kicked the Chirac administration into action, forcing the government to take high-profile steps to address the unease. Interior Minister Nicolas Sarkozy unveiled a new crime bill that increased numbers of police, broadened their search rights, banned youth loitering, and cracked down on prostitution – and formed an official government board to discuss issues with Muslims. And Chirac took the hard line and supported the controversial ban on head-scarves in school, as a gesture that Muslims would not inflict their culture on secular France.

Veiling the Issue

It began in 1989: two schoolgirls in Creil, a suburb of Paris, were sent to the principal's office not for selling drugs, or mouthing off to their instructors, but for wearing headscarves – an obligation for many Muslims, who discourage the public display of a woman's hair. The state school system, which officially forbade the headscarves, suspended the scarf-wearers and went on to expel hundreds more – acts that caused widespread fury among Muslims. A government-commissioned report released in 2003 recommended upholding the ban, saying the blatant display of religion challenged France's secularism. Or that was the official take when the ban was signed into law, which also forbade the wearing of oversized crosses and Jewish skullcaps. Many Muslims, however, viewed it as a crackdown on their faith and any show of fundamentalism; analysts saw it as a high-profile way to calm the French masses, stirred up by political rightwingers shrieking that Muslim immigrants were swamping the country. The passage of the law caused a huge stink – thousands protested and human rights groups condemned it for curtailing freedom of expression and freedom of religion. As for Muslim women in France, more supported the ban (49 per cent) than opposed it (43 per cent).[10]

In March 2004 the French government and French embassies in Muslim countries received letters threatening terrorist acts in retaliation for the headscarf ban. The abductors of two French journalists in Iraq also demanded the headscarf ban be overturned.[11]

Ah oui, there are issues domestically, but France has retained a powerful role in Europe, and under Chirac the country cut a more striking profile on the international scene than it has in decades. Although France fought with the Yanks against Iraq in the 1991 Gulf War, in 2002, when the Bush machine began making loud noises about militarily running Saddam Hussein out of Iraq – claiming that he still had weapons of mass destruction – Chirac stood up in loud protest. Backed by Chancellor Gerhard Schröder, the French president was the most vocal critic of the plan, refused to endorse it and went on to block US moves to solicit UN approval for the impending invasion. The vast majority of French people supported his stance, but his position fractured Europe, where some leaders – including Britain's Prime Minister Blair as well as some who wanted to be in the good graces of the American money bags – supported the Bush administration's 2003 invasion of Iraq.

'The consequences of war would be considerable in human terms. In political terms, it would destabilize the entire region ... A war of this kind cannot help giving a big lift to terrorism. It would create a large number of little Bin Ladens' – President Jacques Chirac, 16 February 2003[12]

'We are not pacifists. We are not anti-American either ... But we feel there is another option, another way, another more normal way, a less dramatic way than war ... I am telling my American friends: beware. Be careful. Think it over seriously before you make an act that is not necessary and that can be very dangerous, especially in the fight against international terrorism that we are really working hard on together' – President Chirac, 16 March 2003[13]

'The United States has just issued an ultimatum to Iraq. Whether, I repeat, it's a matter of the necessary disarmament of Iraq or of the desirable change of regime in that country, there is no justification for a unilateral decision to resort to war' – President Chirac, 18 March 2003[14]

The Bush government was stunned at the French and German questioning of their stomping into the Middle East, clearly annoyed when the European duo challenged the pyramidal power structure that had the United States cast as world dominator. The Yanks were also displeased when France and Germany, both NATO members, recently linked arms with Belgium and Luxembourg to form a separate military alliance that functions independently of the US-dominated NATO; it would be an army of 'chocolate makers', the US State Department snorted in response.[15]

Transatlantic Hostilities

Never mind that President Chirac was entirely justified in not backing President Bush's attack on Iraq. And never mind that Chirac's actions may have been motivated as much by France's oil investments in Saddam's country as by his prescient knowledge of the political instability and violence that the invasion would unleash. When he condemned the US-led Iraq war in 2003, blocking any American move to gain UN approval and lashing out at European countries that gave it a nod, Chirac's disapproval let loose a fierce anti-France movement in the United States that is still reverberating on both sides. Unnerved by the September 11 attacks, many Americans had believed Bush's portrayal of Saddam's hypothetical weapons of mass destruction as an immediate threat to their country and easily swallowed the reality-blurring propaganda linking the Iraqi leader to al-Qaeda, creating a fictional 'Osadama bin Hussein'. America's pensioners felt particularly betrayed by Chirac's chastisement: thousands of Americans had died when the US fought for France in the world's two biggest wars – how dare France not help take down the twenty-first-century face of evil who (their president warned) was about to attack them with biological weapons? Millions of bottles of champagne and French wine were poured away, Americans boycotted French restaurants, French water, French cheese; one senator even proposed that US troops who had died during the wars be freed from French cemeteries and sent home. In one of the more ludicrous moments of US history, the furious Americans renamed French fries and French toast – calling them 'freedom fries' and 'freedom toast' – although they stopped short of officially referring to deep osculation as 'freedom kissing'. The French, American pundits announced, were nothing more than 'cheese-eating surrender monkeys' – an epithet taken from *The Simpsons* – and even the *Wall Street Journal*'s editorial page hurled insults, calling Chirac, among things, 'a rat'.[16] More significant was the effect: in the following year American imports of French wines dropped 20 per cent, the wave of American tourists to France dried up, and the US continually growled about crippling the French economy. Meanwhile, anti-American sentiment swelled up again in France (and across Europe), where boycotts of American products were launched and conspiracy theories flourished – helped along by a best-selling French book that stated the 9/11 attack on the Pentagon was a hoax.

Despite the occasional move towards rapprochement after the fallout over the Iraq war – the frosty smile for the TV camera and the lukewarm words about the two countries' long mutual friendship – the Bush administration is still hacked off at France, most recently when Chirac blocked US moves to bring NATO in to babysit the Iraqi soap opera that the US action created. The bigger issue, however, is that France is trying to restructure the global power dynamic: the world's only superpower hasn't stopped hissing that France will pay.

History Review

In the beginning was France. No country has inadvertently shaped the current state of modern Europe more than France, where prevailing thoughts can sweep through as forcefully as the remorseless Mistral wind. Although Clovis, king of the Franks, first lassoed the northwestern land together as a kingdom in 486 CE, it was another Frankish king, Charlemagne, who took it much further in 800: with the Pope's blessing he roped together most of Western Europe, forcibly creating the Holy Roman Empire – which would last in one form or another for the next thousand years.

A hotbed of Catholicism in previous centuries – it's still nominally Catholic now – France has been the backdrop for plenty of religious conflicts. The Catholic church even turned on itself here, during the Western Schism. For thirty-nine years, from 1378 to 1417, the world had two popes: one in Rome and another in the former papal head-quarters in Avignon, each calling the other the 'anti-pope'.

Historical Hotshots: The Cathars

The French aren't nearly as fervent in their Catholicism as they once were: historically, their beliefs fuelled battles and massacres, among them the sixteenth-century Wars of Religion that ran Protestant Huguenots out of France. Catholicism also spelled doomsday to the Cathars, a liberal Christian sect once living in the southwest Languedoc region, where chestnut forests, limestone caves and clifftop castles hold clues to their lost past. Originating in the Balkans, the group who arrived in France around the seventh century CE believed the physical world was Satan's playpen, although God ran the soul. They worshipped outdoors, pushing the ideas of reincarnation, equality between the sexes and vegetarianism, while shunning serfdom and taxes. Although the Cathars saw sex as a devilish temptation, they thought marriage was worse, since it gave the illusion that copulation was God-approved; thus they had liberal attitudes about the romping of singles and some say the concept of romantic love grew out of here. They regarded the material riches of the church as evil, the Pope as corrupt, and refused to tithe to the Catholic church, and preached that Jesus didn't die on the cross, but was hanging out with their ancestors, to whom he passed such mementoes as the holy grail. Such notions didn't play well in Rome, and in 1209 Pope Innocent III hired mercenaries from Northern France to permanently shut up the heretical sect. Nobles and knights in Languedoc (many wary of the church) honoured the Cathars, opening their castles to them and fighting battles in their name – the anti-Cathar crusade destroyed most of their fortresses. Over 20,000 Cathars were burned at the stake or driven off cliffs in the next year; the last practitioner, dragged forward in 1321, was killed by the Inquisition. Cathar relics – coins, pliers, jewellery – are still found today, and thanks to a flurry of books, tens of thousands of pilgrims now travel to Albi and Carcassonne to search out the treasures that some say are still hidden there.

Planting the seeds for Anglo-French hatred: In the tenth century Vikings (aka Normans) so ravaged the north-west coast of France that King Charles III finally handed over the region to the marauders – called Normandy by the Norman invaders – under the condition that they became his loyal subjects. Viking chief Rollo duly respected the royal wishes, going on to wed the king's daughter. William the Conqueror was a descendant of that French–Viking matrimonial union.

Since then there's rarely been a dull moment, although plenty of them were violent. In its earliest years much of the kingdom's energies were directed at the foe across the water, England. The two countries' mutual dislike heated up in 1066 when French William the Conqueror sailed over and lived up to his moniker on English soil. France and England would go on to lash out at each other militarily for the next eight centuries, including during the 100 Years War, which, stretching from 1337 to 1453, actually lasted 116.

If the French led neither the Renaissance nor the scientific revolution, they were stars (along with the British) of the eighteenth-century Enlightenment when such concepts as original sin were questioned, the pursuit of the rational was idealized, and the corruption of clergy was a source of loud outrage. (During this heady era, France and England even began getting along.) As critical encyclopedias came rumbling off the printing presses, and essays talking about the possibilities of liberty for one and all fell into the hands not just of the elite but the growing middle class, the charged air and the push for change were nearly palpable. Inspired by ideas such as all humans are created equal and quoting the likes of Jean Jacques Rousseau – 'Man is born free, and everywhere he is in chains' – commoners rose up over such issues as unfair salt taxes and income taxes and demanded change.

A Few Influential French Idea Pedlars

- René Descartes (1596–1650): The mathematician is often considered the father of modern philosophy for his famous *Cogito, ergo sum* – 'I think, therefore I am.'
- Denis Diderot (1713–84): His controversial 28-volume encyclopedia, pulling together entries from dozens of Enlightenment thinkers, raised the blood pressure of the church (which condemned it) and the state (which burned it). The critical encyclopedia hinted at the ascent of man from ape, and questioned such mainstay practices as slavery, church corruption and absolute monarchies.
- Charles Louis de Secondat Montesquieu (1689–1755): He mocked the French obsession with religion in his 1721 novel *The Persian Letters*, and his 1748 *Spirit of Laws* surveyed the world's political systems for those that most

offered liberté; advocated separation of church and state and abolition of slavery.

- Voltaire (1694–1778): Best known for his satirical novel *Candide* about the hazards of naive optimism, playwright, essayist and political activist Voltaire decried corrupt clerics and championed human rights, including those of Protestants.
- Jean Jacques Rousseau (1712–78): A believer in the inherent virtue of mankind, the Swiss-born dreamer laid out a radical new idea in his 'social contract' – that government should serve the people and not vice versa.

The defining moment of the country's history was the king-toppling French Revolution, a dramatic display of the power of the people which resulted in the First French Republic in 1792, although a few more kings and dictatorial types would be back. The 1789 revolutionary uprising, triggered in part by shortages of bread, was the largest and most dramatic in European history, and would inspire revolts, revolutions and formations of new countries for centuries to come.

The French Revolution

Poverty, hunger, unfair taxes, lack of representation and the novel idea that every human had rights all planted the seeds for a revolution that was the most monumental ever to rear up in Europe. In 1789 French king Louis XVI, strapped for cash and losing power, called for a revival of the Estates General, a loose version of parliament. Representing three classes – the clergy (First Estate), nobility (Second Estate) and peasants, middle class and all the rest (Third Estate) – the meeting was hijacked by the Third Estate, representing 98 per cent (about 25 million) of the population. The bourgeoisie wanted more say, and formed the National Assembly, inviting the other two estates to join: Louis, not pleased about the development, tried to stamp out their fire by preventing them from meeting. Instead they gathered in an indoor tennis court – and issued the Tennis Court Oath, vowing to write a constitution that would address such issues as liberty, equality and freedom. Louis again was not happy, and amid rumours that his army would quash the rising power of the National Assembly, mobs stormed the Bastille, the prison that stood as a symbol of monarchical oppression. From there, chaos broke loose as 'the people' put in their own claim to rule and violence reigned for the next decade. The Declaration of the Rights of Man – guaranteeing liberty, freedom of expression, and equality – was approved on 17 August 1789, but it apparently didn't apply to the royal class or the rich, many of whom were soon rounded up and marched to the guillotine. The constitution was finally penned in 1791; though that draft granted rights for a limited monarchy, the king was brought to Paris, but a later constitution declared France a republic, and Louis XVI, who was caught trying to sneak out, was ultimately pushed under the National Razor. Political clubs and zealous leaders, including the Jacobins headed by bloodthirsty Robespierre, vied for power, killing thousands in their newfound liberté and much of Europe called for war on France or vice versa. The struggle, that killed at least 450,000 in assorted uprisings, counter-revolutions, massacres and meetings with the executioner, continued until 1799 when General Napoleon Bonaparte galloped into Paris to seize the reins and clean up the revolutionary mess.

For all its lofty ideals, the Revolution opened the door to mayhem: the rich and powerful were killed, then those who killed the rich and powerful were killed, as group after group struggled to fill the power vacuum created by the absence of an absolute monarch. Napoleon appointed himself as leader to slap the country back into shape – initially as First Consul and in 1804 by declaring himself emperor. His administrative ideas were so detailed and brilliant that many of the changes he effected – including his legal code – are still in place today. And that is one reason, say some in France, why the country is currently stalling.

Napoleon 1769–1821

Short, balding and suffering from haemorrhoids – a factor, some say, in his final battlefield performance at Waterloo – Corsican Napoleon Bonaparte ravaged Europe, with up to five million dying during his military campaigns.[17] However, he had a benevolent effect on many areas of European life, including permanently pulling the plug on the violence that exploded after the French Revolution. The emperor extended the French border from Portugal to Poland, snatching nearly all of Europe save the British Isles, and established administrations (usually led by his relatives) that showed his more humane side: the legal code he imposed didn't allow much room for speaking one's mind, and thousands of political prisoners soon sat behind bars or were snuffed out by secret police, but his laws did formally abolish serfdom, separate church from state and guarantee freedom of religion and equality for all. More important still was his policy of universal education that often included women and the poor. The man whose memento from battles in Egypt was the Rosetta Stone – the key to hieroglyphics – inadvertently triggered the call for independence in South America, by so upsetting Spain when he invaded in 1808 that much of the Spanish military was called back; he also gave Poland (brief) independence from Russia, Austria and Prussia. The Napoleonic Code he devised, that created a heavily centralized government, is still the basis for law in France and countries as far away as Peru. The territories he stitched to France, however, soon unravelled. The Congress of Vienna of 1815 ripped the new acquisitions away and whittled France down to a size smaller than it was before Napoleon swaggered in.

The Congress of Vienna – the meeting where European powers decided France's post-Napoleonic fate – re-established the French monarchy with the Bourbon king Louis XVIII, brother of the not-long-before guillotined Louis XVI. He was followed by Charles X, who changed France's destiny when he claimed Algeria as French territory.

After thirteen years of unbridled successes, Napoleon slipped up when he invaded Russia in 1812. His army was knocked out cold by the brutal Russian winter. Barely a fifth of the 300,000 whom he marched towards Moscow limped back, and many deserted; after the next year's defeat at Leipzig he abdicated in 1814 and was shipped off as an exile to the Mediterranean island of Elba. That didn't last long: while European leaders were in Vienna, toasting the downfall of Napoleon and dividing up his empire, the exile sneaked back to rule France for another 100 days. That brief reign ended with the battle of Waterloo, to which he arrived late, some say because of his 'piles', and where British general Wellington put an end to Napoleon's rule. Another Bourbon king was placed on the French throne, while Napoleon was packed off to St Helena – far out in the Atlantic – where he worked on his memoirs and complained that the British were poisoning him. Indeed when he died six years later in 1821 –

probably from stomach cancer – there were high levels of arsenic in his body, although the toxic substance was also used to treat syphilis, which some believe Napoleon had contracted.

Legacy: Napoleon's long-lasting laws forbade mutilations to one's body, a category which now includes vasectomies. French men can be snipped only for medical reasons and must freeze some of their seed prior to shutting the family jewel box.

Never mind that the first thing Napoleon had done upon seizing power was declare that the French Revolution was over: it wasn't. The questioning spirit and the search for balanced government that had prompted the uprising at least had not been extinguished: they continued to redefine France numerous times throughout the tumultuous nineteenth century. Monarchs returned, and were toppled, the power of the common man was ripped away and restored, the church regained tremendous power and lost it, and France was in such upheaval that in the 1800s it called a second, then a third republic. France also continued on its colonization kick, claiming new territories in Asia, the Americas and Africa.

Algeria and the Swat that Led to Colonization

Until the nineteenth century, Algeria, that Mediterranean-edged African land of sinewy mountains, thick stands of date palms and sweeping Saharan dunes, was, for the French, little more than a pirate-infested coast where they could buy wheat. Decades after huge shipments of grain had been shipped out to feed Napoleon's soldiers in Egypt, France hadn't shaved much off the resultant multi-million-dollar bill. The lingering debt led to a showdown: in 1827, after being told that the imperious French king Charles X couldn't be bothered to answer Algeria's letters requesting payment, the enraged Algerian leader Hussein Dey called the French Consul in Algiers a number of unflattering names – then slapped him with a flyswatter and booted him from the palace.[18] King Charles settled the dispute by sending in the military and announcing that Algeria was a French colony. Given the clash of cultures – Algeria was mostly Arab–Berber, Muslim and heavily tribal – it would probably never have been a happy cohabitation, but it started on an excessively violent note. The French, who claimed to be on a 'civilizing mission', raped the local women, robbed the state treasury, pillaged villages, defaced cemeteries and looted mosques[19] – and sequestered the best agricultural lands for the colonial farmers they soon sent in. Not only was Algeria an agricultural annexe, the French also shipped troublemakers off to the seemingly faraway land which was considered part of France proper. The locals had few rights, although eventually they were offered French citizenship if they renounced Muslim law, which few wanted to do. Although many of the colonial 'pieds noirs' fell in love with the exotic land, few Algerians were in love with the French, and it would all lead to a major blow-out when Algeria tried to shake off France 130 years later, and the French wouldn't let go.

Of all France's nineteenth-century post-Napoleonic rulers, Napoleon III – nephew of Napoleon Bonaparte – most changed the country, and not all for the better. After several unsuccessful stabs at presidency, the man initially known as Louis-Napoleon landed the seat at the Presidential Élysée Palace in 1848, where by law he could sit for only one term. Stupid law, thought Louis, who changed not only the law (with a military coup in 1851), but also his name (to Napoleon III) and title (emperor) when his legal term expired.

'Because we have had Napoleon the Great, must we have Napoleon the little?' asked Victor Hugo in 1851 from the National Assembly, where he held a seat until uttering those words. Presented with an arrest warrant by Napoleon III's police, Hugo fled to Belgium, then England, where he wrote Les Misérables *as well as sarcastic poems about the new emperor, predicting (correctly) that he would bring France down.*

Although generally a well-meaning chap, Napoleon III was a dilettante and dabbler in international affairs. He signed France's military on to help Italy's Count Camillo Cavour sew up the patchwork of Italian kingdoms as one – and then thought better of that and pulled out his forces after one battle, nearly sabotaging Cavour's unification idea. In between various military and political dalliances, Napoleon III sent French troops to conquer Mexico in 1863, another move that backfired. His worst blooper: succumbing to a ploy from Prussia's Otto von Bismarck, who tricked him into declaring war, which it was obvious (at least to Bismarck) that France couldn't win.

The Lure: General Bismarck leaked a doctored telegram from the Prussian king Wilhelm to the press. The so-called Ems telegram, heavily edited by Bismarck, made it sound as if the king was furious with the French ambassador, and that he would try to install a German on the vacant Spanish throne, an idea intolerable to the French.

In July 1870 Napoleon III foolishly declared war on the German state of Prussia and was soon captured. The Prussians laid siege to Paris for four months, cutting off food supplies and thus forcing the residents to eat cats and rats, while Leon Gambetta, the minister who was supposed to be running the place, floated out of town in a hot air balloon.[20] Napoleon III lost not only France's valuable agricultural and resource-rich region Alsace-Lorraine to the Germans but was forced to throw down his crown and flee his throne; like his namesake, he left France tinier than when he stepped in. It was also financially crippled: France was forced to pay Germany €800 million worth of war reparations.

Napoleon III left an enduring legacy: he hired Baron Haussmann to redesign Paris, ushering in the wide boulevards lined with department stores and Mansard buildings that are its trademark today. Haussmann also called for the capital's first modern sewage system.

The constant clash of political forces, the occasional bloody revolt, and the ideas batted around at salons, cafés and literary restaurants launched an era of decadence, helped along by absinthe, opium and laudanum. Predictably, the creative crowd was at the front of finding new edges to fall over – the impressionist painters shocked the art world when they unveiled works of subtly flecked images, and plenty of artists frolicked in brothels, many contracting syphilis, the AIDS of the day. But French wordsmiths took it even further and redefined raunchiness with wanton delight. Baudelaire had caused an uproar with the publication of *Les Fleurs du Mal* in 1857 – although scarcely pornographic, its timid allusions to sex caused the book to be banned; Flaubert likewise kicked up a ruckus the same year with the publication of *Madame Bovary* and her affair – never mind that adultery was common, it wasn't acceptable to admit to it in print. But the bad boy poets of the 1870s blazed the most scandalous trail of all.

'Dark and wrinkled like a violet carnation/It breathes humbly lurking in moss . . .' (from 'Sonnet to an Arsehole' by Arthur Rimbaud and Paul Verlaine)

The Cursed Poets

It began with a letter: inside the post to the Parisian poet Paul Verlaine, 27, were poems that revealed an extraordinary talent, and unflinching brilliance. The accompanying letter from Arthur Rimbaud, a 16-year-old from north-east France, with its request for a meeting, held the seeds for Verlaine's undoing. 'Come, dear great soul', Verlaine replied, enclosing the train fare. 'We await you; we desire you.'[21] When Rimbaud arrived, his hypnotic blue eyes swirling with drunkenness, head covered in a tousle of honey-coloured curls, mouth letting loose unnerving insights and childish laughs, both would sink into an abyss of hedonistic pleasure that still has the world talking. Verlaine's wife didn't like Rimbaud from the start – he was rude and he smelled – and Verlaine's friends found Rimbaud peculiar as well, particularly when they found him naked, bellowing on the roof. He was even too much for the 'Nasty Boys' – a society of poets known for raucous nights of recitations: one night Rimbaud stabbed a poet (well, it was a small knife). But Verlaine was taken by him, left his wife and infant son, and sailed off to live with Rimbaud in London on a rampage that left broken furniture, scorched friendships and body lice in its wake. Verlaine loved absinthe; Rimbaud delved into opium, hashish, and morphine, believing it the poet's duty to make 'himself into a seer by a long, involved, and logical derangement of the senses. Every kind of love, of suffering, of madness . . . he exhausts every possible poison so that only essence remains.'[22] Stumbling drunk through shadowy, predawn alleys, spending long nights looking at life from the other side of the bottle, indulging in S&M, the two had a rare artistic communion: they pulled back the layers of the mind, unlocking the language of the subconscious that spoke in dark hypnotic images. The duo became leaders of the Symbolist movement, even though they lost works, and torched others. After a few months, Verlaine staggered back to his wife, but Rimbaud pleaded for another rendezvous: 'Come back, come back, dear friend, only friend, come back. I promise to be good.' The meeting in Brussels soon descended into debauched violence: when Rimbaud slashed Verlaine's hand with a knife, Verlaine shot him in the wrist. Rimbaud called the police and Verlaine spent the next two years in a Belgian prison – during which his wife divorced him, Rimbaud abandoned him, and Verlaine found God, spending his remaining life writing religious poems, while suffering cirrhosis of the liver and syphilis. As for Rimbaud, after writing a *Season in Hell* about his time with Verlaine, he gave up poetry at the age of twenty-one and travelled to exotic lands from Cyprus to Somalia, working as merchant mariner, gun-runner, even circus performer. Rimbaud too had syphilis, although the cause of his death at the age of thirty-seven was gangrene.

By the mid-nineteenth century France and Britain were actually getting along – well, as much as they ever do. But the former anxiety about the enemy over the channel was replaced by a new reason to twitch: the rapid industrialization of neighbouring Germany, newly unified under Bismarck. The anxiety was well founded: Germany pounded France three times between 1870 and 1940. The First World War devastated France, killing or injuring 11 per cent of the population[23] – in part because of the questionable orders of Philippe Pétain, who in 1916 directed French soldiers to block the Germans and protect the strategically worthless fortress of Verdun. The French and Germans dug in for the next year, in one of the war's most remarkably stupid and violent meetings that killed a total of 600,000 on both sides.

If there was one good thing about the Great War it was the wave of creativity – celebratory, questioning and cynical – that it unleashed. France exploded in *Les Années Folles* – 'The Crazy Years' – an over-the-top era of decadence, dance halls and disposable spouses, when cultures and classes mixed in the cafés of St Germain-des-Prés and the bars of Montmartre near the Moulin Rouge, and new art forms – jazz, journalizing, and automatic writing among them – emerged. Intellectuals and iconoclasts from all corners (Marc Chagall, René Magritte, Salvador Dalí, Ernest Hemingway, George Orwell are but a few) flapped towards the creative flame of Paris and the renowned École des Beaux Arts, and 'Lost Generation' Americans arrived en masse after 1920 when Prohibition dried up their alcohol-guzzling muses. Josephine Baker can-canned in the buff save for a belt of bananas, Picasso designed costumes and sets for experimental Jean Cocteau ballets produced by Diaghilev, choreographed by Massine, and set to the typewriters and siren music of Satie that had audiences hissing, and the newborn Surrealists rioted during plays, brandishing guns, swinging from chandeliers and erasing the lines of sanity with their exercises to tap the subconscious. Travellers such as André Malraux brought the Orient to their writing, Colette penned tales of bedroom romps with foppish lads, Anäis Nin captured her steamy escapades with Henry Miller (and his wife June) in her diaries, Céline depressed the hell out of everyone with the monsters he unleashed in books, and the status of mail pilots soared when Antoine de Saint-Exupéry wrote *Night Flight*, made into a Clark Gable flick. The Great Depression of the 1930s may have drained wallets and bank accounts, but not the vitality of the Crazy Years.

A Few Creative Standouts

Colette (1873–1954): Her husband locked her in a room and took credit for the *Claudine* series she wrote; once she dumped him, she flitted between more husbands and women, writing more than four dozen novels, including *Gigi*, her most famous.

Jean Cocteau (1889–1963): He gallivanted with everybody and delved into opium, which unleashed all forms of expression including plays, ballets, films and novels, including *Les Enfants terribles*, *Orphée* and *La Belle et la bête*.

André Breton (1896–1966): Wrote the manifesto for Surrealism, and became unofficial dictator of the movement. Among his exercises was 'automatic writing' – free-flowing spilling of words guided by the subconscious – which produced *The Magnetic Fields* with Philippe Soupault, whom Breton later ejected from the group.

André Gide (1869–1951): Driven by a search for self and later for God, he wrote psychological novels (*L'Immoraliste, Les Caves du Vatican*), many exploring morality. Won Nobel Prize for Literature in 1947.

André Malraux (1901–76): Adventurer, champion of human rights, brilliant novelist and art critic, overachiever Malraux was also a flamboyant Minister of Culture (1958–69).

Were they too drunk or simply in denial? France was slow to respond to the renewed threat of Germany in the 1930s, believing that any attack from the east would be stopped by the Maginot Line, underground fortifications inspired by the static defensive strategy of the Great War. At least one person knew that France was in a vulnerable position: Brigadier General Charles de Gaulle.

Charles de Gaulle (1890–1970)

With huge, bulbous nose and sad brown eyes that seemed to reflect the battlefield misery he had witnessed, towering Charles de Gaulle was Nostradamus and Napoleon rolled into one. Like the sixteenth-century mystic, De Gaulle was a seer, although his predictions, many of them uncannily accurate, were derived through intuition, military strategy and Machiavellian logic. As early as 1905, he was obsessed with the impending rise of Germany, writing papers about another Franco-German war, and short stories in which the 15-year-old cast himself as 'General Charles de Gaulle'. Like Napoleon – to whom he was derogatorily likened by his professors at military school – he was arrogant, autocratic, pushy and a skilled strategist – and would become a profoundly powerful leader. And like the nineteenth-century general, he would leave a lasting legacy on his country – and one that France should probably now shed. De Gaulle's vision was mostly a frustrating gift, since nobody would listen. After fighting in the trenches of the First World War, he foresaw how military encounters would soon change. The military planners relied on a static strategy: a head-on, stagnant exercise, with fighters entrenched at the same spot for years. Future military clashes, he reasoned, would be multi-front blitzkriegs using the new vehicles of war, tanks and fighter planes, that would bombard from land and sky. Not only did France need to modernize its one-dimensional war thinking, he warned in the 1920s, it had to prepare for another invasion; Germany, he predicted shortly after the Great War ended, would be back.

An instructor in France's national military school and as assistant to Marshal Pétain, De Gaulle continued a fervent one-man campaign right up until 1940: he wrote books on the need for France to revamp its armed forces and battle thinking; he gave lectures, he dashed off memos, he bent the ears of whoever he thought might effect a change, but it only gave him a reputation of being a strident doomsayer.

In 1940, when Nazi Germany rolled in with tanks, using the exact methods and routes that he had long predicted, De Gaulle was promoted to brigadier general, helping to draw up war plans. Even then the French military was slow to employ coordinated attacks using tanks and bombs dropped from overhead. On one occasion, however, De Gaulle led a battle that duly demonstrated how to aggressively use tanks and a multi-strike force and forced the Nazis to retreat. It marked the only military victory for France in the entire war.

Without adequate forces or a modernized army, France couldn't hold its territory, and some generals advocated continuing attacks from Algeria; others suggested politically aligning with Britain, and running the war from there: 'Non,' said Marshal Philippe Pétain, who was wheeled out to conduct the war. He instead negotiated an armistice.

Pétain and Vichy

Elegant Marshal Philippe Pétain was a grandfatherly sort whose valour in directing millions of French soldiers to fight at the same battle line for a year led to his nickname 'the hero of Verdun'. Twenty-two years later, Grandpapa Pétain was half batty. But a mighty symbol he was, so they whisked him out to lead the country in May 1940 when it was under Nazi attack. Pétain engineered France's quick surrender, handing over the north of France for Nazi occupation and setting up his government in the resort town of Vichy for which he was cheered as a hero, who by cooperating had saved France from Poland's terrible fate. The man who personified kindliness, and whose beaming likeness hung from store windows with the party slogan 'Work, Family, Fatherland' was in fact busy writing up anti-Semitic laws (unbidden by the Nazis) that forbade Jews from setting foot in cinemas or public pools, banned them from senior jobs, and even stripped them of radios and bicycles. He let loose a vicious secret police, the Milice, and deported 75,000 Jews starting in 1942 (13,000 were rounded up on one day that June) and lived a luxurious life, feasting in grand Burgundian style, while his people (subjected to strict food rationing) went to bed hungry. By the time the Allies and De Gaulle's Free French forces liberated France in August 1944, 150,000 political hostages had been shot, 750,000 workers had been sent to factories in Germany, and 270,000 had been deported on the basis of political conviction, religion or race. Tried and convicted of treason in 1945, Pétain's sentence read: 'The death penalty and national disgrace.'[24] He was spared execution by President Charles de Gaulle, who commuted the punishment to life imprisonment, and Pétain spent the next six years looking out over the Bay of Biscay from his cell. When he died in 1951 his death certificate was supposed to have said 'Philippe Pétain, without profession.' A last-minute change allowed it to read as he would have wanted: 'Philippe Pétain, Marshal of France.'[25]

The news that France had so easily surrendered came as a shock, particularly to De Gaulle, who had just negotiated a deal with the British to continue the war from there, only to discover that Pétain was signing an armistice. De Gaulle turned on his heel and ran back to England.

In London, De Gaulle appointed himself the saviour of France and set up the Free France resistance. He encountered several problems: first, he had few forces to command, and second, the Allied leaders couldn't stand him. Prime Minister Winston Churchill found De Gaulle so arrogant and dictatorial that he often ignored him; President Franklin D. Roosevelt also found the pushy man distasteful, and went on to recognize Pétain as legitimate leader of France. Frustrated, De Gaulle finally bolted to Algeria in 1943, where he set up the French Committee of National Liberation; the British and American leaders refused to recognize it. They didn't even tell him about the planned landing in Normandy until hours before it was launched.

> The Anglo-American snubs continued after the war: De Gaulle was not invited to attend the 1945 Yalta Conference, where the fate of Germany was decided.

De Gaulle's moment finally arrived in 1944: on 26 August he led the liberation march down the Champs-Elysées to the cheering masses. Soon appointed provisional president, the general set about creating the Fourth Republic starting with the penning of a new constitution. De Gaulle envisaged a reorganized government that would reduce parliamentary power and bolster the presidency. When his plan was shot down, De Gaulle stormed out after a mere six months in office. De Gaulle had to wait for nearly fourteen years before he was summoned back to the Élysée Palace.

His resignation did spare De Gaulle one heartbreak: in the years following the war France lost most of its colonies, including Morocco, Tunisia and Guinea. The French had no desire to give up their strategic hold in Indochina (today's Vietnam) which had been wrested away by the Japanese during the war. But they ultimately had little choice: despite superior equipment and financing from the US government (which did not want to see Indochina under communist rule), 58,000 Frenchmen died in the eight-year war (1946–54) to keep hold of the land. After the Viet Minh devastated French fighters at Dien Bien Phu in 1954, the French finally granted independence, packed their bags and slunk home.

The French military was soon deployed again, this time to Algeria,

Africa's second largest country, a substantial provider of France's food and a symbol of French colonial greatness. Its ego battered by the Second World War and Indochina, France wouldn't let go of this last vestige of its superiority without a fight. And a fight they got – one that would drag out over seven ugly years.

Algerian War of Independence

Just after midnight on 1 November 1954 the calm of the Algerian night was shattered by a series of loud explosions as dozens of bombs simultaneously ripped apart police stations, knocked out communication towers and electrical utilities, blew up French stores and businesses. Within minutes fires blazed across the land and a message soon crackled over the radio calling for independence from the French and 'the restoration of the Algerian state . . . within the framework of the principles of Islam'. French interior minister François Mitterrand responded the next day: 'The only possible negotiation is war.' And thus one of the most savage episodes in postwar history was launched. Begun by the militant Algerian group FLN – made up of former officers in the French army – the call for independence was not initially strongly supported by most Algerians, although many had lost their lands to the French, were living in dire poverty and working as slaves. But as the French military brutally rounded up civilians from villages, and as stories about the French use of torture – the electrodes attached to testicles and eyes, the suffocations and the drownings – began to circulate, many Algerians did indeed want to shake free of the French. Most of the million *colons* – French, Spanish and Italians – who had settled there to work on French farms, were opposed to independence. Whenever a colon village was raided or another colon was found hanging in the street with the trademark 'Kabyle smile' – a slit throat – vigilantes would launch another *ratonnade* – or 'rat hunt' – when they'd massacre Algerians, sometimes over a thousand a night. By 1955 almost half a million French troops had descended, erecting electric fences along borders with Tunisia and Morocco, slaughtering villagers whom they thought were hiding rebels, rounding up poor mountain farmers into concentration camps; by 1957 two million Algerians were living in the squalid French camps where many starved to death. Algerian guerrillas continued raids on colonial villages, exploding bombs at restaurants, blowing up buses, ritualistically dismembering army men – averaging thirty bombings and attacks every day – and even taking their battle to France, where rivalry with another Algerian independence group turned vicious: over the next seven years, some 5,000 in France would die in the bombings and machine-gun attacks in brutal 'café wars'. By 1958 the French military in Algeria threatened a coup d'état unless General Charles de Gaulle was brought back. Not only did they think that the powerful general could resolve the conflict, they thought he would back them in an Algérie française.[26] They were quite wrong.

De Gaulle strode back into the presidential palace in 1958, finally realizing his hour. He wrote a new constitution, creating a top-heavy power pyramid with greatly strengthened presidential powers and weakened parliament, and called for a new republic – the Fifth. He strengthened the country's role in the European Economic Community, obtaining huge agricultural subsidies for France, and he nationalized French industry and utilities – creating such powerful enterprises as French petrol giant Elf (and authorizing for it a multi-million-dollar black box to give bribes). He called for a new school to educate future politicians and a polytechnical institute, he made France a nuclear power, and internationally he forged a new independent identity for the country, as one that would rather sulk alone than be a team player. But for many Frenchmen, De Gaulle is remembered most for what he did in Algeria: he gave it away.

De Gaulle officially granted the African colony independence in July 1962, although he kept the French ties to the country for oil exploration. At the news of Algerian independence, France erupted in riots.

Nuclear Matters

If there was one lesson De Gaulle took away from the Second World War, it was that to be a world power a country had to have nuclear arms, and as early as 1944, when he served as interim president, De Gaulle formed the French Atomic Energy Commission to investigate exactly how to do it. When he re-entered the political arena in 1958, President de Gaulle accelerated the research into both nuclear arms and nuclear energy as a domestic power source, constructing a uranium-enrichment plant, developing surface-to-surface missile capabilities, and building nuclear submarines and a squadron of bombers. In February 1960 France announced it was a nuclear power, backing up the statement by testing a nuclear bomb in the Sahara. The international community was outraged, in part because a nuclear test ban was in effect, but also because the United States had discouraged France from developing any nuclear capabilities. The move into the nuclear arena was more than just a defence matter: it was as much about recreating national pride after the country's humiliating defeats in previous decades. Unlike most Western Europeans, the French even now remain relatively unconcerned about any hazards posed by nuclear plants, and almost three-quarters of French electricity is provided by nuclear power.

Of all his achievements, De Gaulle's actions in foreign affairs were his most important, even though the effects weren't all positive. First of all he forged a closer relationship with Germany, realizing that the two countries together could most forcefully influence Europe. He also negotiated a dominant role for France in the newly formed European Economic Community. Relations were not so warm with Britain or the US. De Gaulle, snubbed by the British and Americans during the war, bore a grudge. Suspicious about American involvement in European matters, he frequently griped about its influence on the British and he routinely sniped at the growing dominance of the 'Anglo-Saxons', as he called the Anglo-American bond.

Twice he blocked Britain's entry into the EEC, in 1963 and 1967 – partly to ensure that Britain could not interfere with the agricultural subsidies for France then being discussed. And in 1966 De Gaulle – furious both with NATO for softening its plans on how to deal with a potential Soviet invasion, and the US for entering the lost French territory of Vietnam – not only minimized France's commitment to NATO, but demanded that NATO close its Paris headquarters and kicked the military alliance out of France.

De Gaulle wasn't keen on NATO membership from the start. One early indication of the future problems: in 1958 a French general, working with NATO, would not divulge the location of NATO's nuclear warheads in France. De Gaulle ordered all of NATO's nuclear weapons out of France.

Ironically, after surviving numerous assassination attempts, what ended the show for Charles de Gaulle were the riots of 1968. When millions of students protested about overcrowding in colleges and millions of workers protested about the low minimum wage in May, the country shut down for thee days. Valiant De Gaulle looked like a wimp when he fled the presidential palace, while Prime Minister Georges Pompidou stayed on in Paris and toughed it out. Even though De Gaulle negotiated the end of the protest – promising improvements at universities and a higher minimum wage – he never fully regained his confidence or power. The following year, when a referendum he initiated about senate and regional reforms failed, De Gaulle, who had made France an international heavyweight, resigned.

Notable Moments in Franco-American Relations

The Franco-American relationship was founded in friendship, but it's been on the rocks lately. A review:

- 1770s: France loans so much money to the American revolutionaries who fight British rule that it nearly goes broke, a factor leading to the French Revolution
- 1860s: France's vineyards are plagued by phylloxera, a grape blight that rots the vines: US sends over disease-resistant grape stalks that save the wine industry
- 1884: France sends Statue of Liberty to New York, a symbol of their mutual love of *liberté, égalité et fraternité*; originally it was designed for Egypt
- 1917: France slaughtered in First World War; US enters the war and evens the score
- 1941: US and British leaders loathe De Gaulle, refuse to recognize as legit
- 1944: Allied forces (US, Brits, Canadians, Aussies, New Zealanders) liberate France from Nazi occupation
- 1947: US offers Marshall Plan aid to Europe to rebuild after Second World War
- 1966: President Charles de Gaulle gives NATO marching orders out of France
- 1984: French and US scientists battle over who isolated the AIDS virus first
- 1986: President François Mitterrand refuses use of air bases for refuelling when US fighters fly over to attack Libya; US aircraft 'accidentally' drops a bomb while flying over France

- 1991: France fights alongside US against Iraq in Persian Gulf War
- 2003 (February): President Jacques Chirac declares opposition to war in Iraq and intention to veto any UN Security Council resolution approving an invasion; US threatens economic reprisals and tries to delete 'French' from its vocabulary and wine cellars
- 2003 (June): President Jacques Chirac and President George Bush meet in Evian and smile for the cameras, pretending that everything is *très fantastique*

De Gaulle was succeeded by his former PM Georges Pompidou, whose only lasting contribution was the Pompidou Centre – an impressive cultural hub boasting modern art museum and library – encased, alas, in a post-modern architectural monstrosity. But it was when François Mitterrand took the stage as president in 1981 that France really put on its modern face to the world, in every way.

François Mitterrand (1916–96)

With his affairs, political changes of heart, and the hiding of his health problems, Mitterrand always seemed to be leading a double life, and there are two takes on his two-term presidency as well. On the one hand, Mitterrand – who'd switched from the right wing to the left in the 1970s – brought fresh hope to France, being the first Socialist in power since the Second World War – and in many ways he delivered. Mitterrand abolished the death penalty, nationalized ailing businesses and revved up the economy with his €3 billion *Grands Projets* – Great Projects – programme putting tens of thousands directly and indirectly to work building monuments across Paris, in the city's biggest, most dramatic facelift since the days of Baron Haussmann. Among the standouts: I. M. Pei's pyramid blocking the front of the Louvre, the huge Bibliothèque Nationale, the Bastille Opera House, Museum of Science and Industry, and the Arab World Institute (the last built with Arab donations). Mitterrand forged a strong bond with Germany – he was good mates with Chancellor Helmut Kohl – and he not only pushed for EU enlargement, but a separate, non-NATO armed force for Western Europe as well. On the downside, Mitterrand was a notorious control freak, and his government was involved in assorted shady deals in Africa, many concerning national oil company Elf, including arms running, bribery and misuse of government funding. During the Mitterrand years, France was slapped with two of its biggest scandals ever. In 1985 the *Rainbow Warrior* – flagship of Greenpeace – sank off New Zealand, after two bombs exploded. The French government admitted it was behind the bombing. That same year, thousands of French were exposed to HIV from tainted blood supplies: the French government had opted not to use an American test for the virus, waiting for a French lab to develop a blood test. While his presidency started out as gangbusters, Mitterrand slipped in his final years, probably because he was dying of prostate cancer – another issue he kept from the public. After fourteen years in the power spot – making him France's longest lasting twentieth-century leader – Mitterrand was succeeded by Jacques Chirac and died six months after he left the Élysée Palace.

Quick Tour

From the boulder-strewn shores of Normandy to the palm-swaying French Riviera, from grand boulevards sweeping past mansard-roofed mansions to country roads twisting through pale silver olive groves, France may be lovely but it has always been the cranky individualist of the Continent – thinker, artist, hedonist and, like its infamous emperor Napoleon, never appearing really content with what it is or possesses. The country is forever pulled in a struggle between joie de vivre and ennui, self-aggrandizement and self-loathing – and that chronic discontent has through the centuries unleashed a flood of novel ideas. Whether you're talking about the 'Enlighteners' harping about the shackles that barred liberty, the Impressionists rebelling against the use of the paint brush as camera, or existentialists condemning the country's colonial ways, that constant dissatisfaction has spurred France into powerful new directions, as thinkers and creators launched movements without even trying.

A Few Movements Launched in France

- Symbolism: Whether in painting, poetry or literature, the late nineteenth-century Symbolists – known to mine the unconscious with opium and hallucinogens – rejected concrete realism and wove images as expressions of something else: a rose is not a rose, but a metaphor for passion and perhaps thorny love. Leading exponents in literature: Edgar Allan Poe, Charles Baudelaire, Arthur Rimbaud; in painting: Odilon Redon, Gustave Moreau, Paul Gauguin.

- Impressionism: Born in the 1870s with Claude Monet's *Impression: Sunrise*, the rule-breaking Impressionists rejected historical and biblical themes and often painted out of doors, capturing light in wispy flicks of unmixed colours and coaxing dreamy sensations of nature and everyday life onto their canvases. Other leading Impressionists: Édouard Manet, Pierre-Auguste Renoir, Edgar Degas.

- Pointillism/Neoimpressionism: Late nineteenth-century technique that gave precision to Impressionism with exact pinpoints of colour, as in the picnic and circus scenes of Georges Seurat.

- Fauvism: Meaning 'wild beasts', this 1905 movement epitomized by Henri Matisse, Georges Rouault and Raoul Dufy emphasized dramatic strokes of vibrant non-naturalistic colour over realistic portrayal of subjects.

- Post-Impressionism: Late nineteenth- and early twentieth-century style that gave solid form to airy Impressionism by using dramatic, thickly applied strokes, as exemplified by Paul Cézanne, Vincent Van Gogh and Henri de Toulouse-Lautrec.

- Cubism: Created in 1907 by Georges Braque and Pablo Picasso, this style of fragmented lines and broken angles gives multiple perspectives and an idea of what life looks like to a fly. Initially often still lifes of wine bottles or musical instruments, later Cubist works involved layered collage and sculpture.

- Art Deco: Jazz-age interior and architectural style that draws from tropical nature (jungle foliage and zebras), 'native' (Aztec and African) cultures and the streamlined style of the machine age, the movement got its name from the 1925 World's Fair in Paris which included an expo of 'Arts Décoratifs et Industriels Modernes'.

A few other French contributions to contemporary culture: per-
fume, portable cameras, department stores, haute couture, haute
cuisine.

Or at least that's how it used to be. Culturally France seems to be slipping,
and – gasp – hovering near the dreaded zone of passé. English has flicked
French aside as the international lingua franca, Milan and London are
epicentres of haute couture, and critics now claim that the world's greatest
chefs are in Spain. Today's most popular songs in French are sung by Italian
Carla Bruni; Ireland is the home of the most controversial French writer
Michel Houellebecq and France's most popular person – soccer legend
Zidane – plays for Real Madrid. France's best known icons these days aren't
intellectual heavyweights who sniff at Nobel Prizes, but graceful athletes
who butt heads on the field and DJs who spin repetition-happy lounge
music and peddle €40 CDs; the songs of gravel-voiced Serge Gainsbourg
may still float through stone-walled bistros where diners dig into garlicky
escargots, but the kids outside are blasting hip hop, as they head to McDo.
The artiste lost in swirls of Gauloise smoke at the pavement café gazes out
not just at the light dancing upon elegant Parisian domes but at the cold,
glassy angles of La Défense looming over the city, and that milky coffee
in a bowl now competes with Starbucks' paper-cup café au lait to go. And
these days the French ensure that their films and songs are heard through
'the cultural exception': a high percentage of films shown and music heard
over the broadcast waves must be 'made in France'.

Comeback: French cinema, too, has plunged from its peak during the
1950s and 1960s when the likes of François Truffaut, Jean-Luc Godard
and Louis Malle took turns calling 'Cut!' During the 1980s when big
hits included less-than-lighthearted art film Betty Blue – *the highlight*
is when terminally depressed Betty pokes out her eye – some French
filmmakers called it a wrap for that market and fled to Hollywood. In
film, however, France scored a recent victory with the smash hit Le
Fabuleux destin d'Amélie Poulain, *a feel-good fairy tale about a sweet-*
hearted Montmartre waitress who works magic on all whose lives she
touches; too bad Amélie didn't have a chance to touch the world of
one-eyed Betty, back when Mademoiselle Blue had two. So adored
was Amélie, *the flick that lifted the heavy-hanging veil of depression,*
that the movie not only won the Best Film award at the 2002 Césars:
it was the biggest moneymaker in the history of French film.

The glamorous Césars – France's prestigious film awards – turned ugly in 2004, when actress Agnès Jaoui lashed out at the Minister of Culture for 'absurd laws' cutting unemployment benefits for artists; so furious was the creative crowd in 2003 with the government's squeeze on funding for culture that they cancelled such beloved celebrations as the summer theatre festival in Avignon.[27] Even the deification of the French chef was hauled out for questioning when in 2004 the former Michelin restaurant inspector Pascal Remy wrote a tell-all casting unsavoury aspersions at the little red culinary bible and those mighty Michelin rosettes. (He claimed that the guide uses only a handful of critics to review 10,000 restaurants in France alone, and hinted that perhaps some of the eateries didn't earn their rosette ratings simply by stellar cooking.) And a whole bevy of finger-pointing books flew off the printing presses – among them Nicolas Bavarez's La France qui Tombe (France is Falling) – condemning the French government's inability to address the country's economic malaise, and triggering a national debate about France's decline, while only darkening the mood further.[28] No wonder that so many French people have made anti-depressants and anti-anxiety pills a crucial part of their daily diet.

> The French take more mood-altering medications – anti-depressants, sedatives, and anti-anxiety pills – than any other country in the world. At least a quarter of the French population is on anti-depressants, and the French toss back two to four times as many happy pills as any other Europeans.[29] French social security pays for nearly all medication, so most patients leave the doctor's surgery with prescription in hand.

But all the whingeing and hand-wringing is just part of a national process that is pointing to one thing: France needs to change. The cornerstones of the Fifth Republic – top-heavy presidency, centralized government, state-run economy, heavy subsidies and built-in bribes – just aren't working as well in the twenty-first century. And no administration proves it more than that of Jacques Chirac, a neo-Gaullist, who seems to be ticking off the boxes of De Gaulle's checklist, but without getting the same results.

The state-run enterprises born under De Gaulle are being sold off; the too-powerful presidency that his Fifth Republic constitution created is now typically balanced by ineffective 'cohabitation' with a prime minister from a different party; the bribes that De Gaulle literally factored into the budget don't cut it in an era that demands transparency and that could use those billions for social programmes. And as economists are warning, the heavy subsidies dished out for everything from agriculture to art, only weaken the economy and hinder France's inherently competitive nature.

Rotting in the Fridge

Granted, it's hard to find a squeaky-clean company anywhere that powerful humans tread, but lately France is looking particularly sooty. Corruption is so endemic it's almost laughable. Votes are routinely rigged – with some 5 per cent of votes in some Parisian arrondissements considered fraudulent, and wives and lovers have a way of showing up on payrolls, often for doing nothing: Xavière Tiberi, wife of former Paris mayor Jean Tiberi, collected some €40,000 for a 36-page typo-ridden, childishly-written paper on countries that speak French; some say that she never even turned in the paper until someone questioned what the cheque was for. The formerly state-owned bank Credit Lyonnais cooked its books in the 1990s[30] and so thoroughly messed up operations that $20 billion of taxpayers' money was needed to keep it afloat. Elf – the national petroleum company – was prosecuted for using millions of euros of taxpayers' money to grease the palms of politicians and executives in arms and oil deals – all with government approval: the ensuing scandal that rattled the country in 2003 brought 33 of its employees to the witness stand where 15 were convicted of embezzling about €300 million, including three top executives (they all escaped their five-year prison terms on grounds of ill health). Vivendi, the national water company turned international water corporation/multinational entertainment empire, was busted in 2002 for accounting sleight-of-hand that made its multi-billion-dollar debt look like profit; the US Securities and Exchange Commission hit the company with a 50-million-dollar fine and class action suits are in the works.

Dipping into the coffers and misusing funds isn't just a private problem: more than 500 politicians have been charged with or investigated for corruption since 1994. Chirac himself is facing corruption charges, but he is immune while sitting in the presidential chair. Chirac's good mate former prime minister Alain Juppé, the man previously thought most likely to be Chirac's successor, was convicted on charges of graft for using public money to finance party positions during the 1980s and

1990s, when his bon ami Chirac was Paris mayor. The city government promptly announced that it plans to sue.

The nuclear-energy programme launched by De Gaulle may keep France more independent for its energy needs, but its numerous plants are high-risk targets in an era of terrorism. That characteristically Gaullist 'we'll play our way or we won't play at all' mentality now risks sidelining the country and is setting it up for an upset in the EU, where ten new countries are now eyeing France with suspicion. And the schizophrenic attitude towards immigrants, particularly Algerians, has backfired: by ignoring the fact that most immigrants weren't integrated, France has only created and made itself vulnerable to the violence. However, slowly, that is changing as the young second-generation immigrants become more active members in French society – and using their creative talents is one way to bring them into the mainstream.

> *The foreign-born and second-generation immigrant population is one of France's richest creative hotbeds, with its own language – verlans, that sticks the first syllable on the end – the name 'Melik' becomes 'Likme' for example: popular French rap, R & B and 'rai' – Arab-pop – is now blasting out of the rough immigrant neighbourhoods, as are works of some of France's hottest young filmmakers and writers. Whereas the first wave of creativity was often tough, hard-hitting exposés of the banlieue – La Haine by Mathieu Kassovitz, being one example – banlieue art lately is lightening up. One of the most successful standup comedians in France, for example, is Jamel Debbouze, known for his tough-guy beur humour.*

For, all the grumpiness and bumpiness of contemporary France, the country isn't exactly on its knees. The place definitely needs some tending to, and its economy is currently out of whack: its 3 per cent budget deficit in 2003 is a black mark that has the EU snapping that France better pull itself together – admonishment that the French government is prone to ignore, even though it insisted that EU members produce balanced budgets. Oh well, no one ever said the French play by the rules, even if they wrote them; such behaviour is just part of the French paradox. For its nerve, and its verve, its independent streak and its style, France may annoy, perplex and positively enrage, but often enough it's adored or at least secretly admired, albeit with a shrug, a roll of the eyes and a sigh, 'Oh the French!'

Future Forecast

France and the United States will battle it out economically and France will continue (with Germany) to insist that the world needs more than one superpower. The Franco-German dominance in the EU will be tested with the arrival of ten new countries, and domestically France's immigrants may prove to be the spark that lights the country's cultural fire again.

Hot Spots

Paris: The City of Light has had a few dark moments lately: explosions on the Métro, bomb scares at Sacré-Coeur, warnings about the Eiffel Tower being a terrorist target, the shooting of a suburban city councillor and the stabbing of the city's mayor may make the paranoid want to cower in the wine cellar permanently. French people who live elsewhere are not necessarily enamoured of the capital and the way Paris in the minds of many is synonymous with all France, yet the city's perfume houses, well-watched catwalks, stellar subway and, of course, the Louvre, can be addictive if you don't mind tossing out €5 for a café.

Paris: a showy marriage of old and new, as seen at the Louvre.

Corsica: The lovely island of lavender and wind-battered cliffs is Napoleon's birthplace and France's hottest spot of dissent. Separatists are only 20 per cent of the islanders, but they're furious about land development, taxes and France's mismanagement, and claim to have been behind three thousand bombings in the past three decades. Also believed to be the hand behind the recent assassination of the French Prefect Claude Erignac, who was trying to clean up the island's corruption.

Eurosatory: Every spring, Paris puts on the world's biggest international exhibition of land armaments, showcasing the latest and greatest ways for humans to kill and mutilate each other. Well attended, of course.

> *Arms that blast legs: France is one of the world's leading arms pushers, with landmines being a speciality; the French didn't sign the treaty banning use of the limb-ripping devices.*

Superphénix: Located near the Swiss border in Creys-Malvill, the much-touted Superphénix was the world's largest breeder reactor; now it's the world's largest soon-to-be-decommissioned breeder reactor. Numerous problems and leaks forced the French government to announce it would shut down the once-respected facility – decommissioning is to start in 2005.

> *Breeding problems: France was the showcase for the much-hyped self-sustaining breeder reactor that produces lots of nuclear waste, which is then used to fuel the reactor. Developed during the 1960s and 1970s when it was wrongly believed that the world would soon run out of uranium, the make-your-own-future-fuel concept is unpopular now because it's so hazardous and problematic.*

COGEMA La Hague: Perched atop the cliffs at Normandy, this ticking time bomb recycles and reprocesses nuclear waste – producing weapons-grade plutonium and uranium, and emitting plenty of 'enriched' effluent that radioactivates the English Channel along the popular coastline, a favourite with tourists. French scientists have reported that children who go to the beach more than once a month are three times more likely to develop leukaemia;[31] who knows what such contamination might mean for the seafood from the area. On one thing the French government seems clear: the facility, commissioned in 1976, is now a security risk. Just after the September 11 attacks on the US, an anti-aircraft missile system was installed to protect this site that has become a national hazard. Even the 'virtual tour' on the facility's website was shut down.

Marseille: The Mediterranean port city nearly seems a country of its own with a predominantly Arab population that keeps its men and women segregated: cafés and squares are filled with the former, while the latter can be found in huddles talking on the streets in between. Some adore Marseille for its markets, sea urchins, bouillabaisse and exotic flair, others find it positively seedy. The wealthy pull up in their yachts and smugglers pull in with drugs in this city known for its underworld links.

On the road: The south of France is a magnet for jetsetters – and thieves who follow them along the French Riviera. Stories abound of cars pulled over by faux police, who mug the occupants and take their jewellery and riches: it even happened to Salvador Dalí.

Eiffel Tower: Built to showcase the marvels of modern engineering, the Eiffel Tower was to be but a temporary display in the 1889 Universal Exhibition in Paris. Was scheduled to come down around 1914, but the First World War saved it: it was put to use as a radio tower, intercepting enemy messages. The 300-metre (984-feet) tall Tour Eiffel is now the symbol of Paris, and as such has been a target in assorted planned terrorist attacks. The tower caught fire in 2003, and nearly 400 have taken a suicidal plunge there. It's said that one such attempt was foiled when the woman landed on top of a car; legend has it that she married the car's owner.[32]

'We, the writers, painters, sculptors, architects and lovers of the beauty of Paris, do protest with all our vigour and all our indignation, in the name of French taste and endangered French art and history, against the useless and monstrous Eiffel Tower' – petition signed by 300 French creators and presented to the city government in 1887

Grasse: Since the sixteenth century this perfume capital outside Cannes has been pressing essential oils from jasmine, violets, roses, geraniums, cedar and spices, and the scent of flowers from the nearby farms – Chanel owns one – hangs in the air. Hard to believe Grasse was once a stinking town of leather tanneries; when they took to scenting the leather gloves during Louis XVI's reign, the French perfume industry was born.

During the French Revolution it appeared that the perfume industry might permanently evaporate, but the habit of spraying and dousing oneself with sweet-smelling concoctions was revived by Napoleon's wife, Josephine, who adored the stuff. It's said her favourite scent was musk, which he reviled; after he ditched her, legend has it she made sure his royal abode reeked of musk before she handed back the keys.

Bookstores: Controversy and conspiracy make their home here with plenty of critical books by French authors, including *The Frightening Fraud* by thinktank president Thierry Meyssan, who says the plane that slammed into the Pentagon during the September 11 attack didn't really exist.

The cheese shop: It's said that the average French person consumes over 24 kilos (50 pounds) of cheese every year. EU regulations may try to impinge on French cheesemaking, which often uses raw milk. As if the French would listen if the EU tried to influence the production of their beloved cheese.

Toulouse: Thriving southern city, headquarters of Airbus.

Basque country: The Basque separatist issue isn't unique to Spain: ETA and some other Spanish Basques want to merge with Basque areas across the French border on the other side of the Pyrenees. French Basque country – in the southwest of France – is a hiding spot for Spanish Basques on the run.

Alsace-Lorraine: Snuggling up against Belgium, Luxembourg, Switzerland and Germany, this north-eastern region is actually two: Alsace spreads along the River Rhine, and Lorraine tumbles down from mountains to meet it. Containing Strasbourg – now one home of the European Union's Parliament – the region is important for the industry and trade links from the Rhine; but mostly it's adored for its history and for the natural beauty that is likened to a continuous garden. When the Germans snatched the region in 1871, it was a French national tragedy. Although the French got it back following the First World War, German speakers still dominate Alsace; French speakers are the majority in Lorraine, which is famous for quiche.

Provence: Overhyped by writer Peter Mayle and his beloved Provence series, the southern region does have charms – Roman ruins, open-air markets, and vineyards to name but few – but the sight of eerie cooling towers between towns isn't one of them. Van Gogh went loopy here, and cut off his ear; he really would have gone nuts if he could see what's happened to the property market: prices for houses have shot through the roof since Mayle began his cooing. It's said among those in Provence that the writer's entire French vocabulary consists of 'Vin rouge'. Well, it's a start.

Strasbourg: Assorted EU agencies have offices here – and since 1992, the European Parliament meets here every month, mostly because France insists on it even though it's not at all practical. In fact, it's such a drain, using €200 million[33] (about half of the Parliament's budget) in commuting expenses alone, that there are frequent calls to make Brussels the one and only parliamentary home. Another reason to consider staying in Belgium: Strasbourg is a crime haven, known particularly for torchings of VIP vehicles: over 1,300 cars were set ablaze by young punks in 2002 alone, and the little darlings are now moving into carjacking.[34]

UN Security Council: France is one of the Five Big Boys with veto power.

Père Lachaise cemetery: Almost everybody who was anybody lies here in the site turned into a Parisian cemetery after Napoleon bought it in 1803: Gertrude Stein, Edith Piaf, Molière, La Fontaine, Sarah Bernhardt, Colette, Bizet, Georges Seurat, Oscar Wilde and Chopin (minus his heart) are but a few of the 100,000 dead whose lives are remembered with vaults, tombs, sculptures and sepulchres. Among the most popular places: the tomb of journalist Victor Noir, which features a life-size ornament of a man lying on his back: infertile women have nearly rubbed off his crotch, believed to be a fertility aid.

> *Jim Morrison's grave: Ever since 1971 when Morrison's fire flickered out, thousands of Doors fans heap love letters, albums and booze bottles across the singer's grave, trampling and trashing the plots of the dead neighbours in the Père Lachaise cemetery in the process. Under pressure from families whose kin were buried there, cemetery officials considered moving Paris's most popular grave in 2001, when its thirty-year-lease ran out; however, they decided to let sleeping Doors lie.*

Chunnel (aka the much sexier *le tunnel sous la Manche*): They'd been talking about it since 1802, but history was finally made in May 1994 when Folkestone, England, and Calais, France, were connected by this thirty-mile rail tunnel under the English Channel, and wannabe immigrants found a new way to get in: walk underwater. The project cost a mere $21 billion (€17 billion) and took three years to dig.

> *Water woes: France has been hit twice by recent oil spills: a thick carpet of oil washed up on French shores in 1999 after the Erika went*

down; the Prestige, *which sank off the coast of Spain, layered more petro-goo upon French coasts in late 2002. The Seine may be oil-free – and lately the Parisian government has been piling sand to make beaches along it – but it's far too skanky for swimming.*

Brittany (Breizh): Settled by Welsh and Irish missionaries, the land whose name means 'Little Britain' has a Celtic-linked culture, and a language not unlike Welsh; until the early twentieth century, public use of the language was formally banned. Swallowed up by the French kingdom in 1532, Bretons have been demanding autonomy ever since. The Breton Revolutionary Army, a small separatist group, which is linked to Basque separatists ETA, has vandalized or bombed government buildings in hundreds of attacks since 1960, but in April 2000 they planted a bomb at a McDonald's; one worker was killed.[35]

La chambre: 'Go to bed!' the state is telling young couples. The government is offering new incentives to help boost the falling birth rate, including tax cuts and lower rents but, thus far, they don't seem to be working as aphrodisiacs. Perhaps a bedside picture of Jerry Lewis would do the trick.

Bureaucrat school: It's tough to get into this school, l'École Nationale d'administration, that teaches students how to be bureaucrats and administrators, and it is tough to survive the course, but those who do are the crème de la crème, being virtually guaranteed top positions in government.

Hot Shots

'I've known the US for a long time. I visit often, I've studied there, worked as a forklift operator at Anheuser-Busch and a soda jerk at Howard Johnson's. I've hitchhiked across the whole United States . . . I love junk food and I always come home with a few extra pounds. I've always worked for and supported transatlantic solidarity. When I hear people say that I'm anti-American, I'm sad, not angry, but really sad' – President Jacques Chirac, interview with Time *magazine*[36]

Jacques Chirac: French President 1995 to present, centre-right Union for a Popular Majority: so what if he's allegedly corrupt, wears a hearing aid, and can't seem to get through EU summits without knocking back a bottle of wine. The man who started out his presidency by controversially testing nuclear bombs in French Polynesia will go down in history for being right about Iraq. Despite his age (he'll be 75 in 2007), may run for a

Nicolas 'Sarko' Sarkozy:
eye on the presidency.

third presidential term – if only to avoid being tried on corruption charges.
Nicolas Sarkozy: Head of Union for a Popular Majority; former minister of interior; former finance minister; former friend of Chirac. Political mover Sarkozy, who loves the media and vice versa, steals the show. He doesn't hide the fact that he wants the presidential chair, and to many French, the second-generation Hungarian–Frenchman smells sweet in a system that stinks more by the day. New head of Chirac's Popular Majority party, the conservative who dated Chirac's daughter, is no longer chummy with the Chiracs, since he made his ambitions known. Chirac's daughter has said Sarkozy is too short to be the leader of France – apparently forgetting about Napoleon.

Laurent Fabius: Once superstar of the Socialist party and the youngest prime minister – he was a mere 37 when appointed by Mitterrand in 1981 – Fabius was hurt over the HIV-tainted blood scandal during his term. Now making a major comeback and looking likely to be the Socialist candidate in the next presidential election.

Jean-Pierre Raffarin: French Prime Minister 2002 to present. Grandfatherly type who may soon go flying, since he is ineffectively dealing with issues of the day.

Dominique de Villepin: Foreign Minister 2002–4; interior minister 2004 to present. Debonair, right-leaning diplomat of Chirac's UMP who has been foreign affairs whiz in assorted roles since 1980, Villepin is said to be able to seduce with his words. Well, no wonder: in his spare time, he's a poet.

Valéry Giscard d'Estaing: President 1974–81. When he was president, Giscard d'Estaing tried to send immigrants back, offering them money to leave, but the plan wasn't successful. Active in EU affairs, he chaired the convention that penned the EU draft constitution and handed over the document in 2003, with directions not to change a word in his masterpiece. Widely considered quite pompous and arrogant.

> '*It would be the end of Europe*' – *Valéry Giscard d'Estaing in 2002, on what would happen if Turkey enters the European Union*[37]

François Mitterrand: See box on p. 38.

Bertrand Delanoe: Mayor of Paris 2001 to present. He's often referred to as 'green and gay', and Paris's openly homosexual mayor is certainly one to party: elected in 2001, he has made the city of romance even more fun. At his request, the river Seine turns into a balmy beach each year: part of its right bank is covered in over 2,000 tons of sand come summer and dotted with planted palm trees, hammocks and cafés, where millions soak up the sun and enjoy outdoor concerts. On Valentine's Day, he beckoned the city's residents to gather in front of the Hôtel de Ville for a collective reenactment of Robert Doisneau's famous photo 'The Kiss', and he's battling London to make Paris the home of the 2012 Olympics. In 2002, he threw an all-night event for Parisians – with art shows, concerts and parties all over town, but paid for it with more than a hangover: a homophobic French–Algerian stabbed him in the abdomen in the midst of the merry-making at City Hall, but Delanoe quickly recovered. Parisians adore their first liberal mayor in 130 years, except for one thing. He wants them to stoop so low as to pick up their dogs' poo. Predictably, the city's dog owners barked loud protests.

> *In canine-friendly Paris, the pavements are covered in some sixteen tons of dog dirt every day.*

National Front (FN): Jean-Marie Le Pen founded this ultra-rightwing nationalist party in 1972, which in the 1980s began a formidable rise: FN mayors presided over several prominent French cities, and the party earned enough votes for seats in the National Assembly and European Parliament. However, the FN has splintered lately: after a rift, Le Pen's heir apparent

Bruno Megret, who is far brighter and more radical than Le Pen, started his own party in 1999. Le Pen's daughter Marine, who now heads the party, is causing a split by pushing a more modern take on abortion, which she doesn't want criminalized. Due to the internal squabbling the party certainly isn't as vital as it was in the 2002 elections, but it took 10 per cent in the 2004 European parliamentary elections.

Jacques Barrot: European Commissioner for transport policy from 2004.

Médecins Sans Frontières (Doctors without Borders): Founded in 1971, this independent emergency relief agency is the world's largest, swooping in to give free medical care during emergencies, disasters and epidemics and entering war zones that few others dare touch.

Nostradamus (1503–66)

Physician to plague victims by day, astrologer and mystic Michel de Nostredame had another passion at night: clad in a robe, surrounded by candles, and clasping a magic wand of laurel,[38] he peered into water-filled copper bowls and glass orbs to coax visions that unveiled the future. Apparently Nostradamus did indeed have soothsaying skills – or so thought his physician father and grandfather as well as Catherine de' Medici, who protected him from Inquisitors after he foretold the death of her husband in a joust. Nevertheless, the seer whose nanny had been burned for being a witch wrapped his visions in code, using anagrams, enigmatic writing and symbols in four-line rhymes that have had the masses scratching their heads for more than four centuries. His book *Centuries*, ultimately filled with some one thousand predictions, was first published in 1555, and some believe it has foretold everything from the invention of the guillotine and the rise of Hitler to the assassination of President John F. Kennedy and the fall of the Twin Towers. However, some metaphysicians say that editions since 1940 may be riddled with errors: they claim British intelligence, knowing that Hitler studied the Renaissance mystic, inserted fake lines prophesying that Hitler would fall.

Michel Houellebecq: Genius, peddler of porn, misogynist, bigot, reactionary, racist, the most significant modern French writer: novelist Houellebecq – called all that and more – knows how to whip up the masses with his nihilistic themes that are so cold they become satires. The style isn't complex, but his books (*Whatever, Atomized, Platform*) are best avoided by the faint of heart: gang rapes, brain-spilling murders, sex tourism, and kitty killings are just a few topics that have made him reviled for darkening the world or adored for mucking about in the shadows already there. Slapped with a lawsuit for inciting racial hatred for his unflattering portraits of Muslims and for calling Islam 'the stupidest of religions', he replied that he was taken out of context: he'd said all monotheistic religions are dumb.

Victor Hugo (1802–85): The 1800s are often described as 'The Century of Victor Hugo', reflecting the immense power of the man of letters, who ran one of the era's most raucous salons (attendees often wore medieval costumes while puffing cigars) and whose best known works are *Les Misérables* (the dense novel about a convict and a jailer in post-revolutionary France, begun in the 1840s, finished 1862) and *The Hunchback of Notre-Dame* (which he'd signed a contract to deliver in 1828, and finally began writing two years after the deadline). Elected to the National Assembly in 1848, he had to flee in 1851 for his criticisms of Napoleon III, but was allowed back several years later, and served again in the National Assembly from 1870 to 1876. Poet, painter, playwright and politician Hugo had a libido as big as his impact: even into his seventies he insisted on taking on a lover a day for his insatiable 'lyre' – and is said to have gone through dozens of new ones in the course of a typical month.[39]

Marcel Proust (1871–1922): For a man who spent most of his life in bed – suffering from asthma and hypochondria – Proust made up for lost time when he ventured out, charming Guy de Maupassant, Emile Zola, Edgar Degas and Sarah Bernhardt at the literary salons and dinner parties of Parisian high society, gallivanting through the Ritz with fashionable friends in tow and paying butlers to detail the soirées that he had missed. His first two novels flopped, but it was the notebooks he filled with his detailed observations of the elite that held the potential for his greatness. Eating little but ice cream and beer in a soundproof room lined with cork, he painstakingly reworked the notes into a staggering 3,000-page, thirteen-volume masterpiece that is considered by many the most brilliant novel of the twentieth century. Called *A la Recherche du Temps Perdu* (In Search of Lost Time or Remembrance of Things Past), the first volume appeared in 1913; the second volume, published in 1914, was such a rage that it received the prestigious Prix Goncourt and prompted him to write five more volumes; a further six came out after his death. In fact, the obsessive scribe hadn't finished editing the final chapters, leaving it to his publisher to sort out what the man who was known to edit at the printing press actually had intended.

Hero: Jean Monnet (1888–1979)

Economist, thinker, diplomat Monnet, a one-time cognac salesman with only a high school education, profoundly affected France and Europe, arguably more than anyone in the twentieth century. The first Secretary General of the League of Nations (precursor to the United Nations), Monnet later worked with traditional foe Britain in uniting the two countries against the Nazis, and convinced the United States to sell arms to the Allies: his actions are credited with shaving at least a year off the Second World War. He helped Romania and Poland stabilize their economies, aided China in revamping its ailing railway system, and helped kickstart the postwar French economy. His most influential contribution: the realization that France and Germany would function more harmoniously through joint economic ventures. Monnet was the architect of the Schuman Plan and the resultant Coal and Steel Agreement of 1950 that led to the European Economic Community and, ultimately, the European Union. 'There is no future for the people of Europe other than in union,' Monnet pronounced. His humanistic visions propelled the many countries of Europe towards more cohesion than any before dreamt possible.[40]

Media star: *Le Monde Diplomatique* – decidedly a voice of the left, but you can find articles here that nobody else will touch. Some articles free, others subscriber only: www.Mondediple.com

2. Germany (Deutschland): Reinventing Itself

Fast Facts

Country:	Federal Republic of Germany; Bundesrepublik Deutschland
Capital:	Berlin
Government:	federal republic
Independence:	1871 formation of united Germany (Second German Reich); 1990 East and West reunified
Population:	82,425,000 (2004 estimate)
Leaders:	Head of State: President Horst Koehler (2004) Head of Government: Chancellor Gerhard Schröder (1998)
Elections:	President elected by Federal Convention (Parliament and delegates) for 5-year term; Chancellor elected by absolute majority in Parliament for 4-year term
Name of Parliament:	Federal Assembly; Bundestag
Ethnicity:	91.5% German; 2.4% Turkish; 6.1% Serb, Croat, other
Religion:	34% Protestant; 34% Roman Catholic; 3.7% Muslim; other or none 28.3%
Language:	German
Literacy:	99% (1997 estimate)
Exports	machinery, cars, chemicals
Per capita GDP:	$27,600 (2003 estimate)
Unemployment:	9.8% (May 2004 Eurostat figure)
EU status:	founding member (EEC member since 1957)
Currency:	euro
Known for:	rearranging the continent

Standout Qualities

Heavy: The brains
Heavy: The history
Heavy: The guilt

Résumé

The land of deep brooding thinkers such as Kant, Hegel and Nietzsche may be the brainiest country on the planet, and without question, no other country has rearranged the world more. Gutenberg revolutionized communications when he turned a wine press into a printing press in 1455, Martin Luther shattered sixteenth-century Europe by nailing his ninety-five theses to a church door. Karl Marx planted ideas for a societal makeover with his nineteenth-century utopian delusion that mankind would selflessly toil together as one and Albert Einstein and Max Planck decoded the keys to the universe. And no single person caused a more extensive restructuring of the world order than Hitler when he launched his war – the event that most defined the twentieth century, with effects that still shape the world today. Among those effects: Germany has been sitting in the corner ever since.

> Because the Germanic states were sewn together as a country only in 1871, many of what are history's great Germans would not have identified themselves as Germans at all, but as residents of assorted kingdoms. Kant was a Livonian, Hegel a Schwabe, Luther and Nietzsche were Saxons, Gutenberg was a Frankfurter, Marx a Prussian by birth. Born a German Jew, Einstein became a naturalized US citizen in 1940, Planck was a German, and as for Hitler, he was born an Austrian.

World War II: Expensive in Every Way

When someone mentions Germany, Mercedes Benz, Boris Becker and Becks beer might pop to the forefront of your mind. But the three things still often associated with Germany are Hitler, concentration camps and the violent rise of the Aryan nation that horrified the world. It matters little that the ugliest chapter in human history closed six decades ago: the loss of life, the devastation and the genocidal atrocities unleashed on Jews as well as Roma, Communists and anybody else deemed undesirable were so cruel and on such a huge scale that Europe is still feeling the psychological effects: of all the military showdowns across the Continent, that one was so nightmarish that it rattled the long-running assumption that humankind is basically good. With 60 million dead and most of Europe in ruins, the atrocity that resulted when Hitler attempted to take over the planet required billions of dollars and decades of rebuilding; the emotional scars still remain. But what is often overlooked is that Germany suffered too, and not only because not all Germans supported Hitler or shared his maniacal plan. Almost all of Germany was flattened during the last months of the war, when the Allied forces tried out new weapons that sucked off roofs and torched entire cities, their mostly civilian residents suffocated and charred in giant fireballs from the sky. Twelve million Germans were pushed out of east European lands in repatriations after the war, and two million died in violent reprisals along the way. Germany lost a quarter of its previous territory when Allies redrew the map, and then that land was politically severed, with a third of Germany lost to Moscow-aligned Communists for the next forty-five years. Germany paid out billions in war reparations, and sixty years later Germany is still paying – for Holocaust victims, for slave labour, for damages and looted riches and art. But perhaps the heaviest payment for Germans is the intellectual burden and guilt that still weighs upon the masses, most of whom were born after the war. Over the past sixty years, while it feverishly built up a solid economy, Germany was forced to dissociate itself from what it had been and construct a whole new Germany and German image. With the postwar political fracture between West and East Germany and the need to jump into a new future, Germans lost their identity and their past and the ability to have any national pride. To refer to almost anything that happened before 1945 with anything except extreme shame is *verboten*.

In addition to the $5 billion Chancellor Schröder approved in 2002, Germany has paid over $64 billion to victims of the Second World War, including to families of the six million Jews killed in concentration camps and to those subjected to forced labour. Germany also repaid $1.1 billion to the United States for $1.3 billion of Marshall Plan aid and donated $75 million to Harvard University to start a foundation promoting better understanding between the United States and Europe. Germany spends billions on foundations that foster international appreciation and world peace.[1]

The unrivalled population giant of Western Europe, all the more since the 1990 surprise reunification of West and East Germany, Deutschland has long been the financial locomotive of the European Union, whose substantial dues – it shovels in more money than anyone else – help keep the rest of the place chugging along. There's a reason why modern Germany found itself in the Mr Moneybags role, besides the obvious one that it has a bigger economy that any other EU player. The underlying dynamic that has shaped German–European relations since the war is the unspoken rule that if Germany wanted an active role on the Continent, it had to pay up, shut up and play by the rules, dictated mostly by the US and France.

Germany and the Guiding Hands of the US and France

The United States was the most dominant force in the rebuilding of West Germany, and for several decades after the war hundreds of thousands of Americans, many of them military personnel, lived in West Germany overseeing the birth of the new nation. US funding helped reconstruct it, the US guided the hands writing the new constitution, the US influenced decisions from industry to energy, the US inflicted its values and the US brought Germany into NATO. But the country that really guided Germany back into Europe was France, which approached Germany in 1950 with a plan to pool their resources. As with the US, their move to bring Germany back into the loop wasn't altogether an altruistic gesture. The motives were threefold: first, if France and Germany shared the resources needed for war – coal and steel – they would be less likely to go to war again. Second, France saw that with Germany on its side it would have more power in international dealings and throughout Europe. And third, France was about to go bankrupt from payments to farmers: German funds could be used to bail it out.[2]

France and Germany now form a formidable partnership in the European Union. Often referred to as the Franco-German axis, their bond is usually the driving force of the EU and they definitely like to throw their collective weight around. Roles have truly changed from half a century ago: now Germany is the soft-spoken half of the power duo alongside its one-time victim France, which every so often kicks Germany around. But who knows how long the current situation will last? Germany's economy is shaky at the moment, and the entry of ten new countries may indeed rattle the EU power structure, which was teetering before the new kids even walked into the room.

Guilt-ridden by the events of the Second World War and saddened by the loss of East Germany to the Soviet bloc in 1945, West Germany did more than hook up with France and other European countries in the European Economic Community. In the decades after the war, Germans plunged into their jobs with zeal, turning the country into a workhorse and transforming the economy into Western Europe's most productive. The German Economic Miracle that made the country one of the world's wealthiest, however, took a sharp blow in the 1990s: once the engine-room of Europe, Germany is now hailed as the Continent's Sick Man. The reason: a sudden reunification with East Germany that saw Germany's population shoot up by sixteen million overnight. By 2003 over €640 billion had been sunk into gluing the two halves together and still East Germany is lagging behind.

'As far as I know, this enters into force . . . immediately, without delay' – Communist party leader Gunter Schabowski, during a 1989 news conference announcing East Germans could travel into West Berlin[3]

So Happy Together?

It was actually a misunderstanding. When East German leader Erich Honecker approved a policy change on 9 November 1989 that East Germans would be allowed to cross through to West Berlin, he didn't mean the wall should come down. He meant they could go on holiday to West Berlin. But his message, issued at night by a bureaucrat, was misunderstood. The guards not only allowed the tens of thousands who rushed towards Brandenburg Gate to cross over into West Germany, they didn't stop those who appeared with picks and began hacking at the concrete and barbed wire wall that had split Berlin since 1961 – and symbolically cleaved Communist Eastern Europe from the West. Geysers of champagne spilled in the streets, everywhere revellers were hugging and crying, and the West German government soon handed out a small welcoming packet of cash to the incoming East Germans. Fifteen years have passed since the joyous family reunion, East and West still don't fully function as one, and resentment now hangs heavy in the air. Wessies (as West Germans are now nicknamed in Germany) are still paid about 25 per cent more than Ossies (East Germans), and the Ossies have a much higher unemployment rate (around 18 per cent); living is cheaper in the East, but many of the young Ossies are heading West. Despite the government moving the capital from Bonn to its previous home in Berlin, many Ossies say that the reunification has resulted mostly in their culture being absorbed into the West's – and their dreams about the happiness of living in the West have been trampled, particularly as their city centres are becoming dilapidated and the young are moving away. Many Wessies are annoyed at the hundreds of billions of euros in costs borne mostly by them of bringing the two halves together and the draining effects on the economy, which until the two reunited was charging full steam ahead.

After the fall of the wall, Honecker kept a low profile, trying to elude West German officials who wanted to try him for the deaths of 162 people killed while attempting to escape over the Berlin Wall that Honecker had been in charge of erecting in 1961. They finally caught up with him, but when he stood trial in 1993, he was released due to poor health. He died the next year of liver cancer.

Now the German unemployment rate – nearly 10 per cent – is one of Europe's highest, and Germany (like France) keeps running budget deficits that violate the rules for the eurozone. The collective mood is anxious, as Germans, always worriers, wonder where the economy is heading. Relations between Ossies and Wessies are still stressful in the reunited Federal Republic of Germany, where the East is playing catch-up and the West is plain weighted down.

History Review

For most of its history, Germany wasn't Germany: it was hundreds upon hundreds of fiefdoms, kingdoms and principalities headed by German-speaking nobles, kings and knights, all of whom fell under the umbrella of the Holy Roman Empire. Supposed to heed the authority of the emperor, many gave him little more than a tip of the hat and the assorted territories generally had their own laws and levied their own taxes, making travel across them a deeply confusing affair. Just as confusing were the boundaries which were always going in new directions depending on the whims of knights and the merchants who followed them as they won new towns: at points they extended east into today's Baltic States and Poland, north into today's Denmark, south into today's Switzerland and west into today's France.

Where traders go, riches follow – this seemed to be the case in expanding Germanic settlements. One example of the fabulous wealth of German merchants can be seen in Riga, Latvia, where much of their fifteenth-century architecture built by the wealthy German merchant class still stands.

Comrade Chic

Those from the five new eastern *Länder* (states) sometimes feel their culture was shoved under the rug, but it has recently come back into vogue. There's a veritable 'Ostalgie' trend in Germany now – a nostalgia for the East that's reflected in everything from propagandistic art and posters to Communist-era music and sweets. Now at Ostalgie clubs, it's campy for the partygoers to sport 'People's Army' jackets, Soviet badges and Young Communist uniforms. *Goodbye Lenin!*, a film by Wolfgang Becker released in 2003, also spurred on the nostalgia movement. The plot: an elderly East German woman falls into a coma in the late 1980s; when she recovers, Germany has been reunified, but her son, not wanting to shock her, recreates life in East Germany as it was when his mother (and country) fell. More than fashion statements and films, there is a true nostalgia in some Ossies for the old days, when at least everybody had a job and knew their place in the world.

Despite the geographical mayhem, the German principalities garnered a reputation for several things. From the twelfth century on, German speakers became famous as traders, forming the immensely important Hanseatic League that shuttled goods across northern Europe from today's Poland to Sweden, Germany and Russia. The maritime trading group would carry on – and expand – into the sixteenth century. Moreover, from the fifteenth century the German heartland was the publishing hotbed of Europe, with Frankfurt its epicentre, pulling in thousands with its twice-yearly book fair. (Frankfurt still holds its book fair – the world's biggest – but now this highly attended event takes place only once a year.) German merchants, developing into a powerful middle class, hauled Gutenberg's presses to other cities and soon Strasbourg, Basel and Venice were hubs of the new publishing industry. So hungry were people for something to read (besides the Bible), and so profitable were book sales, that by 1500 up to 20 million books were spread around Europe – far more than had ever been previously accumulated in the history of mankind. Broadsheets also fluttered across the Continent, bringing news and novel ideas to those who were literate or knew someone who was.

The German territories were also the first battlegrounds for religious war. The criticisms lodged by Martin Luther in 1517 against the corruption of the Catholic church stirred up such a reaction that, within a few years, battles were waged against the 'heretical' ideas and for the freedom of expressing them. Even though Pope Leo X condemned Luther in a papal bull – Luther responded by burning it – the Lutheran religion (and other Protestant variants) flourished in the northern German states, while the southern German states mostly remained Catholic. The religious conflict spread like a raging venereal disease and was just as deadly. Almost all of Western Europe was soon engulfed in the Thirty Years War, which knocked out much of the European population but nowhere more so than in these parts. A third of German-speaking people had died by the time that war fizzled out in 1648.

> In 1774 the German writer Goethe published the novel The Sorrows of Young Werther. So heart-wrenching was this story of unrequited love that young men across Europe were swept away in the melancholy and killed themselves. Goethe, however, was more than just a powerful novelist: he wrote lyrical poetry (sometimes set to music) – the dramatic epic work Faust being such a famous example that Faustian came to mean the dilemma of selling one's soul to the devil. A scientist intrigued with metals, optics and the study of animals, a philosopher fascinated by the possibility of evolution, a conductor, a lawyer and a professor, Goethe was such a well-rounded expert and influential figure that he was eventually invited to live at the ducal castle at Saxe-Weimar, where he became the resident duke's top political adviser and theatre director.

The same themes continued over the next few centuries – expansion, trade, mercantilism, religious conflicts and territorial battles – and boundaries kept moving not only in Germany but across the entire Holy Roman Empire. By the time Napoleon arrived on the scene and dismantled the empire, there were over 300 German kingdoms, principalities and states. The 1815 Congress of Vienna, the meeting of European leaders which rearranged the lands once held by Napoleon, whittled down the number of states in the newly formed German Confederation to thirty. The entire Austrian empire run by the Habsburgs comprised one huge state alone.

Prussia, a northern state that included part of Poland and territory along the Rhine, was the number two state in terms of size and population in this new Confederation of German States. Run by the Hohenzollern dynasty, militaristic Prussia had no intention of being overshadowed by Austria, which by then was militarily flabby and politically weak. Or rather, Prussian Chancellor Otto von Bismarck had no intention of riding in the German passenger seat.

'Laws are like sausages. It's better not to see them being made' – Otto von Bismarck

Rarely has the world known as brilliant a statesman and strategist as Bismarck, who became Imperial Chancellor (Prime Minister) of Prussia in 1871. An expert in manipulation, Bismarck played psychological chess, while the rest of Europe's leaders were at the level of marbles. His strength was that he knew exactly what he wanted, and knew just how to get it. His first priority was getting Austria out of the Confederation of German States. Realizing it would be ineffective merely to ask them politely to leave, Bismarck inveigled them into a quick war with the Danes over Schleswig and Holstein, small northern duchies. The war was easily won, but Bismarck found a technicality in the agreement with Austria – which had first wanted to run part of the conquered land, but then didn't – and used this ruse to declare war on Austria. Prussia won in a few short weeks, and Bismarck's condition for peace was Austria leaving the Confederation; Prussia also annexed surrounding lands – including Frankfurt, Hannover and Hesse-Kassel.

The Alsace-Lorraine region so important to both Germany and France would bounce back and forth between them. France lost it in 1871, regained it after the First World War, lost it during the Second World War and regained it at the end of that conflict in 1945.

Then Bismarck's eyes turned to the west, where France was holding on to the Elsass-Lotharingen region (which they called Alsace-Lorraine) that the Prussian Chancellor coveted for its coal mines and access to the River Rhine. For this he had to trick Napoleon III (nephew of the Corsican general) into starting a war. That too was wound up in a matter of months, and annexing the region as a new Prussian land, Bismarck proceeded to stage three of his plan: in 1871 he announced the unification of Germany as the German Empire, with Prussian king Wilhelm I as its royal head and Bismarck as political leader. From then on Bismarck contented himself with statesmanship and alliances, fine wines and cigars and with rare exception until 1914, Europe – at least Western Europe – found itself in deep peace.

Bismarck had created a new type of war: brief, with minimal damage and a specific, attainable goal in mind. For the next four decades, European leaders were under the false impression that all future wars would be the same: quick and relatively painless. The Great War would shatter that belief.

In the late nineteenth century the newly formed country Germany was at a high point. The German industrial machine was churning and the standard of living was improving for many as they moved from farmland to city. Urban areas were expanding and being upgraded in a methodical, well-planned order that brought modern plumbing to the masses. Hermann Hesse was publishing his first works, Nietzsche was the controversial philosopher of the hour and the operas of Richard Wagner underscored the classical genius of German composers in a tradition going back through Beethoven, Schubert, Handel and Bach. In 1885 Karl Benz unveiled his new machine – an automobile powered by an internal-combustion engine – and Gottlieb Daimler invented the gas-powered motorcycle the same year; chemist Heinrich Hertz soon invented aspirin and helped alleviate the headaches from the new urban racket. Contact lenses, X-rays and Zeppelins were but a few more German creations of the times.

In 1888 the headstrong and dramatic Kaiser Wilhelm II began wearing the German imperial crown. Seeing Bismarck as a threat, he forced the Chancellor to resign, only the first of the Kaiser's many mistakes.

While few were doubting the brilliance of the German mind, not all were trusting it. Many were suspicious of the country's new stability and growing military might; trains were now crisscrossing the country and shipyards were delivering so many ships that Germany for the first time rivalled Britain's might. Responding to this threat, in 1906 the British unleashed their new weapon: HMS *Dreadnought*, a terrifying warship which with its weapons, size and speed had the potential to blow everybody else's navies out of the water. And from then on the great arms race was under way as all the military powers vied to have their own Dreadnought or something better.

Peace was slowly unravelling: conflicts brewed up in Africa, and, starting in 1912, the volatile Balkans erupted in several wars over nationalism and territorial squabbling. Armies were building up, revving their motors. And cocksure Kaiser Wilhelm II kept shooting off his mouth and further destabilizing an already weakening scene. Whenever he tried to assure other countries that he was a dove, he instead planted ideas that Germany very much had war on its mind.

> 'You English are mad, mad, mad as March hares. What has come over you that you are so completely given over to suspicions . . . I am a friend of England, but . . . the prevailing sentiment among . . . my people is not friendly to England. I am, therefore, so to speak in a minority in my own land . . .' – German Emperor Wilhelm II in 1908 trying, unsuccessfully, to calm British fears about Germany's arms build-up[4]

The Kaiser was hunting in Norway in 1914 when he heard that Austrian Archduke Franz-Ferdinand had been shot by a Serb. His advice to the Austrian emperor Franz Joseph, the archduke's uncle, was to put the Serbs in their place. The Kaiser was, after all, itching to take his new weapons for a spin. On 28 July 1914 Germany and Austria invaded Serbia. Little did the Kaiser know that he was setting off a chain of events from which Germany still hasn't fully recovered. The First World War had begun.

It wasn't just that the war that had been dubbed 'the summer war' when it started dragged on for four dismal years, nor was it the physical destruction, loss of life and financial drain that the 'war to end all wars' caused to European economies. What hurt Germany, seen as the instigator of the most brutal military showdown then known to man, was the wrath that the war stirred up. When it came time to settle matters, the victors – Britain, Russia, France and the US – made sure not only that Germany paid, but that it was utterly devastated.

> 'They [will] be shunned and avoided like lepers for generations to come' – Woodrow Wilson's vision in 1919 on the future of the German people after World War I[5]

Germany lost not only all of the territories briefly gained in the war, but other important holdings too. Alsace-Lorraine went to France; East Prussia and the port of Danzig went to Poland along with the coal mines of Silesia; Sudetenland went to Czechoslovakia; Schleswig to Denmark; the cities of Malmedy and Eupen to Belgium. And if that didn't hurt enough, then there was the war-reparations bill: $33 billion (about €27 billion) and the paring down of Germany's military and arms so that it emerged a weak police force.[6] Another requirement: never again would Germany be allowed to pair up with Austria politically, economically or militarily.

It's estimated that, ultimately, Germany paid only about $4.5 billion (€3.6 billion) of its First World War reparations bill.[7]

Bertold Brecht (1898–1956)

Leftie poet and playwright, Brecht is best known for shaking up theatre with his 'alienation effect' (wherein actors show the audience that they are merely acting) and by writing politically themed works that demand that the audience think. His *Threepenny Opera* (1928) – a cabaret-style satire with catchy melodies (composed by Kurt Weill) that jabs at the corrupt Weimar Republic – was the most popular play of 1920s Berlin (and Weill's opening tune was adapted as Louis Armstrong's 'Mack the Knife'). Due to Brecht's devotion to Marxism, Nazis banned his works in the 1930s and shut down his plays, and Brecht fled to Scandinavia, where he wrote *The Resistible Rise of Arturo Ui* (about a cauliflower-obsessed gangster who symbolizes Hitler) and *Mother Courage and her Children* (using the Thirty Years War as a parable about fascism). He later moved to the US, where he was so harangued by the 1950s communist-squelching House Unamerican Activities Committee that he left. He set up in communist East Germany, ran a Marxist theatre company (the Berliner Ensemble), became disillusioned with Soviet communism and physically went to seed: he looked so skanky that guards once prevented him from entering a state gala held in his honour.[8] For his clever writing and revolutionary techniques he goes down as one of the innovators of twentieth-century theatre.

In 1919 the Weimar Republic was established as part of the new revised Germany. It was destined to fail, starting unsteadily and soon slipping into chaos marked by violent uprisings and strikes. Germans were crushed by the war debt, and the mood wasn't helped by food and fuel shortages. Worse, the currency soon became worthless as a result of hyperinflation: the value of the mark dropped from 4.2 marks per dollar before the war to 4.2 trillion marks to the dollar.[9] Germans had to push wheelbarrows of cash to the shop to buy bread. Some simply used the marks as fuel for their ovens.

The United States loaned the Weimar Republic some $2.5 million (€2 million) between 1924 and 1929, which helped the economy to a limited extent. Nevertheless the German mood was ominously dark as the people wondered how they would ever dig themselves out of the black hole brought on by the world war and the 1919 Treaty of Versailles.

In 1923 a little-known Austrian who headed a new political party invaded a beer-hall meeting of the Bavarian prime minister with a grand plan to take over the Bavarian government. Police were called in, the attempted take over failed and Adolf Hitler – who had masterminded the beer-hall putsch – spent the next year in prison, dictating his memoirs to his cellmate Rudolf Hess. It was published in 1925 under the name *Mein Kampf*, and although it would later become a best seller and a set school textbook – nearly every household had one – it's said that very few ever read it. Book sales alone made Hitler a millionaire.

Hitler originally gave his autobiography the pithy title of 'Four and a half years of Struggle Against Lies, Stupidity, and Cowardice'. For some reason, the editor changed it. In the Netherlands and Czech Republic to own a copy is illegal, whatever the title.[10]

The Depression of 1929 gave the rest of the world a hint of what Germany had been suffering for the previous decade, but it only worsened life in the Weimar Republic when it hit the next year. But amid the heavy gloom one ray of hope beamed through for the weary people. A rousing orator had appeared on the scene, coaxing Germans out of their collective depression and vowing that Germany would soon return to greatness. And little by little Germans started listening.

Adolf Hitler (1889–1945)

The offspring of a government employee and his second cousin, Adolf Hitler – whose father changed his last name from Schicklgrüber – was coddled as a child, and led to believe he was brilliant. Orphaned at the age of 18, he moved to Vienna, where Hitler fancied his calling was to be an artist, but the Art Academy didn't agree, rejecting his application several times. Moving to Munich, he fought in the First World War – for Germany – and was temporarily blinded after the British dropped mustard gas. He heard of Germany's defeat in a hospital bed, blaming Jews for his blindness and the war that Germany had just lost. Believing Jews to be the root of all evil, Hitler vowed to deport them from Germany. After the war he was transferred to German military intelligence. His assignment: spread anti-Semitic feelings and infiltrate the German Workers Party, one of several nationalist groups.[11] On leaving the army in 1920, he took over the party, added 'National Socialist' to the beginning of the party's name, and within three years led a failed military takeover in Munich that landed him in jail. Released in 1924, Hitler returned to find the party had crumbled in his absence, but he patiently rebuilt it – complete with a propaganda department. Although he didn't appeal to the intellectuals, the rich, or the well educated – and he was generally loathed in Berlin – the budding politician noted that while the masses didn't respond well to a simple attack on Jewry, they swallowed his anti-Semitic propaganda when he threw in jabs against the ailing Weimar Republic as well. In 1930 the Nazis took 18 per cent of the vote in elections, becoming Germany's second most popular party. In January 1933, due to back-room compromises of the weak government, Hitler was appointed to sit in the Chancellor's (Prime Minister's) chair. Over 29 and 30 June 1934 dozens of Hitler's political enemies died, killed by his henchman Heinrich Himmler. On 2 August the President happened to pass away as well. Hitler absorbed that role into his new one – Führer. Within weeks, all political parties other than the Nazi party had been banned, thousands were arrested, tens of thousands of books by Jewish writers were blazing in main squares and the government was calling for a boycott of all 'non-Aryan' goods and posting storm troopers outside Jewish stores alongside signs imploring 'Germans defend yourselves! Buy only at Aryan stores!'[12] Hundreds of thousands of Germans – including half the German Jewish population – soon fled, their properties promptly seized by the government. And meanwhile, most of the world looked at the strange little man as a passing fad, a non-threat, a joke.

Hitler escaped at least seventeen attempts on his life, the first in November 1939. Austrian officers tried to kill him, Nazi officers tried to kill him, so did Erwin Planck, son of the esteemed German scientist Max Planck. Although some who had opposed Hitler's policies left Germany in the 1930s – during the Nazi years, Germany suffered a huge brain drain – there was an anti-Nazi resistance movement underground in Germany during the war. One of its leaders was Willy

Brandt, who became Chancellor of West Germany in 1969. Another resister who was arrested was communist Erich Honecker, later to become leader of East Germany.

Kristallnacht

By then, Hitler had already stripped away Jews' citizenship and their rights – for example, to marry non-Jewish Germans, to hold government or high-ranking jobs – and he had already begun to deport some out of the country, although not to camps. On 7 November 1938, when Herschel Grynszpan – a German Jew living in Paris whose family had been deported to Poland and whose pleas to the German embassy were ignored – shot embassy secretary Ernst von Rath, Hitler had an excuse to take his anti-Semitic policies one step further. For that bullet in Paris, Jews across Germany would pay dearly. During 'The Night of Broken Glass' – Kristallnacht in German – the government forces launched a pogrom. Over the next two days of rioting, amid the crashing of windows of Jewish businesses, homes and synagogues, 30,000 Jews were rounded up, some bludgeoned to death and the rest sent to concentration camps. The Holocaust had begun.

Hitler had no interest in following the rules of the Treaty of Versailles and announced (and demonstrated) his intentions to make that treaty null and void: he rearmed the military this time with mighty Panzer tanks; he built a new navy; tested his new fighter planes and fire bombs in practice runs in Sweden and real battles in Spain. Nobody in the international community said anything. He annexed Austria – expressly forbidden by the Treaty of Versailles – but the only country formally to protest at the move was Mexico. He demanded the Sudetenland in north-western Czechoslovakia, and the leaders of Britain and France handed it to him. Eyebrows were raised when he took all of Czechoslovakia in March 1939. But it wasn't until the Nazis marched on Poland on 1 September 1939 that the world really sat up and took notice. Two days later, Britain, France and Australia declared war.

'Now what?' Adolf Hitler to his foreign minister on 3 September 1939, upon hearing that Britain had declared war. The Führer, having dealt with appeasement-happy Prime Minister Neville Chamberlain, had not believed that Britain would enter into the fighting.

From there it was dominoes falling: in April 1940 Germany invaded Denmark and Norway, followed in May by Belgium, the Netherlands, Luxembourg and France. In September the blitz on England began. And soon millions of Jews and war prisoners were being shipped to concentration camps; by 1942 some camps had chambers where they would probably be gassed, in others they would be worked to death.

Hitler is held responsible for the deaths of between 45 million to 60 millions.[13]

That the war dragged on for six years was helped along by the fact there were too many arms, too many sophisticated weapons and too many people willing to use them. The nadir of human existence finally ended – through exhaustion of resources and a whole new level of sophisticated destruction: the Allies tried out their new firebomb weaponry on Germany, and the United States dropped two nuclear bombs on Japan. And in February 1945 the Allied leaders met at Yalta to figure out how to crawl out of the black hole of war and make a transition to what was hoped would be a better world.

Hitler is believed to have committed suicide on 30 April 1945 in a bunker not far from the Brandenburg Gate. Details of the death are sketchy – including whether it was by cyanide or by a shot from a pistol – since the Soviets were the first on the scene. They said they cremated the corpse.

From 1945 to 1949 West Germany put many remaining Nazis on the stand in the highly publicized Nuremberg Trials, finding most of them guilty.

The Berlin Airlift

When exactly the Cold War began is hard to say, but many point to Berlin in 1948. All of Germany was then divvied up and occupied by the Four Powers – the United States, Britain, France and the USSR. Capital Berlin, located in Soviet-controlled East Germany, was divided into four occupied sections as well, with the Soviets occupying East Berlin, and the other three countries occupying quadrants on the West. The troubles began when West Germany introduced a new currency, the deutschmark, to stabilize the economy. Stalin responded by closing all roads across East Germany that led to West Berlin, cutting off all food and energy. The only way to get in the needed goods was by dropping them from planes over the city. The Soviets, assuming that the Allies would just let West Berlin fall, looked on open-mouthed as food drop missions continued for the next 462 days. Expensive, inefficient and dangerous, the airlift was the only way to keep West Berlin (surrounded as it was by Soviet occupied territory) from becoming engulfed by communism; so potent a symbol was the city that it was deemed worth it.

In 1949 East Germany, under pressure from Moscow, declared itself a communist country that would remain separate from the West.

The United States took an active role in West Germany, lending money through the Marshall Aid Plan and giving advice on everything from industrial redevelopment to the writing of the Constitution. The Soviet Union greatly influenced East Germany, establishing the model of the communal household for numerous families and monthly work plans and requiring that East Germany join up in the armed alliance of communist countries, the Warsaw Pact. East Germans weren't happy with their conditions: during the first twelve years, 2.5 million sneaked over the border. To halt the drain on the work force, the East German government in 1961 quickly erected a thick, high, fortress-like 43-kilometre-long wall topped with barbed wired, lit up by floodlights and patrolled by guards and dogs.

In 1953, the East German government announced that all quotas for work production would be increased by 10 per cent. The people were already hungry: their food-rationing cards couldn't buy fruit – there wasn't any – nor was there much meat. The reaction to the call for high efficiency was loud and defiant: across East Berlin and other industrial cities, hundreds of thousands of workers rose up in protest, demanding a return to democracy, free elections and the West. Hours later, Soviet tanks rolled in. At least fifty died, and another thousand were imprisoned.[14]

Vocabulary Review

German Democratic Republic: former East Germany (run by USSR)

Federal Republic of Germany: former West Germany (mentored by US) and continuing name for the reunified country

Länder: states. There are sixteen in Germany, including five new *Länder* in the Old East, each with its own parliament and a fair amount of power

68ers: the protest generation that ushered in the new, more open Germany and are in power today

Ostpolitik: Willy Brandt's policy of opening up to East Germany

Lebensraum: living room – Nazi term for acquiring new land

Drang nach Osten: Pushing towards the east – Hitler's expansion eastward

As West Berlin was located in off-limits East Germany, to get to West Berlin from the West travellers had to fly, or drive along the highway without exiting before reaching their destination.

Initially West German policy was to refuse to acknowledge the government of East Germany and demand that all Allies do the same. However, Willy Brandt thawed the ice and began talks with the East German leadership in 1969. West Germany also began giving financial aid to their doppelganger on the other side of the wall – and East German leader Erich Honecker, for one, eagerly accepted it, if only to give the appearance that the East German economy was robust. In retrospect, Honecker was merely milking the West, with no intention of opening up the East, much less unifying. Even after Gorbachev took power in Moscow and instructed Soviet republics and satellites to open up, Honecker refused to honour the demands. Through the late 1980s the unification of East and West looked about as likely as the bulldozing of the wall, which is to say not likely at all.

In the 1970s West Germany was besieged by terrorism: Palestinians broke into the 1972 Munich Olympics, killing eleven Israeli athletes and hijacking a plane, causing an international uproar. Some local extremists were just as violent: members of the urban guerrilla group Baader-Meinhof and the related Red Army Faction (RAF) kidnapped businessmen, assassinated politicians, lawyers and industrialists, robbed banks and attacked US air force bases, killing at least fifty and causing German public buildings to transform into fortresses. On a happier note, during that decade, Chancellor Willy Brandt made diplomatic connections with East Germany and the West German economy roared.

Pressure was building to open up the East. In the summer of 1989 Soviet satellite Hungary lifted its shoot-to-kill policy, allowing holidaying East Germans (and others) to flee from Hungary into Austria. Honecker's gesture of 9 November 1989 finally to allow Germans to travel to West Berlin was misconstrued by border guards to mean that the countries were no longer divided. Both sides were equally surprised when the wall came down, and the process of politically uniting was immediately tabled. On 3 October 1990 what had long seemed impossible became real as both East and West, after fifty-one years, came together as one.

After German reunification, nearly all of East German industry simply shut down. Inefficient and polluting to begin with, the East's industrial machine fell apart when Soviet funding dried up – and 75 per cent of East Germans soon found themselves out of a job. As money from the Federal Republic pumped up the East's industrial system, more East Germans went to work, although still almost one in five are unemployed. Even among the working there have been numerous strikes and walkouts because East Germans, even after substantial increases in real wages from the Soviet years, still earn 20 per cent less than West Germans working in comparable jobs.[15] Some say the income gap is closing, as is the psychological divide. More West Germans are going to college in East Germany and more young people are seeing themselves simply as Germans rather than Ossies or Wessies.

Quick Tour

Deutschland is underrated: the hilly land pushed against the Alps is awash with glittering cities and tiny wine towns, folded with steep hills and deep forests, and home to numerous spas with water believed to have great restorative powers which one may indeed need after a few nights of oompah-pahing in the beer halls.

Germany is up in tourist popularity: in 2003 it was the tenth most visited country in the world with 18 million visitors. Locals say part of the reason tourists often love it there is that they have such low expectations when they arrive – and then are very pleasantly surprised.

Like the country itself, Germans are under-appreciated. Often well edu-cated, well travelled and thoughtful, the 'new Germans' are frequently Europe's most informed and most open minded, and despite popular perception can be drily hilarious. Even if Germany is not known as a home for wacky comedians – slapstick Jerry Lewis was not born here – it does have its lighter side: after Italy's minister of tourism complained in 2003 that Germans were louts who clogged up Italian beaches, a local magazine sent over a group of models to sunbathe in front of the Italian embassy in Berlin – in the buff. You may take your lunch break in the nude in a park in downtown Munich – and Germany is where you will find the annual Love Parade, the biggest open-air techno bash on the planet. Not to mention how loopy the place gets during the Oktoberfest.

In Germany each region has its own special beers, all made according to particular legal requirements called Reinheitsgebot, *which specify what must be and can't be included. Regulations call for purity: water, hops, yeast and malt are the only acceptable ingredients.*

Few – especially Germans themselves – cut them any slack for their twen-tieth-century history even though most of today's Germans were born after the war and nobody has tried to atone for the past more than the current generation. Modern Germany's leaders are now mostly pensive and soul-searching – many of them protesters in the 1968 marches who grew up bearing the heavy weight of a past that they had nothing to do with: this generation has tried to heal the wounds with European countries with apologies, grants, reparations and compensation to survivors of camps. Recent German politicians have also pushed forth an idea to unite Europe as one, being the strongest proponents of EU expansion.

The Social Revolution of 1968

It started out as just another protest in an international wave of anger against the United States' involvement in the Vietnam War, but what the demonstrations of 1968 really marked was the beginning of a new Germany. Hundreds of thousands of German students and youths took to the street, bringing the worst violence and unrest in the postwar era, and demanding that Germany face its past, present and future. The ire was nearly palpable as the idealists – many born during or just after the war – rebelled against the establishment ('the swine system') for linking arms with the militaristic US and NATO; their wrath turned against the older generation as well, for following Hitler's mad dream and then cloaking their actions in silence. The positive results of the 1968 demonstrations, which are regarded as a social revolution by many, are more educational freedom, more honesty and a heartfelt desire to improve Germany's image in the world; even women's liberation came out of that era. The most vehement 68ers, as that generation is known, tended to go on to achieve fame: some became politicians – Chancellor Gerhard Schröder and Foreign Minister Joschka Fischer among them – a few others became vicious radicals, such as Baader-Meinhof, who terrorized Germany for the next twenty years.

A popular reality TV show in Germany is called I'm Sorry *wherein guests call former friends, lovers and family members and ask forgiveness.*

Granted, nobody knows how to get in a funk better than Germans and, given their concerns about the economy (and the cultural ban about saying much about the past), they seem like they are heading towards another collective bad mood. The country known for its schedules – breakfast at 8, lunch at 1, dinner at 6 – is predictably organized about the latest showing of dissent. Protests are on Mondays, in the afternoon, and lately they're 60,000 strong and more. The impetus: cuts to welfare spending. Dental care may be a thing of the past, and a new labour reform programme – dubbed 'Hartz IV' after its designer, VW head Peter Hartz – slashed unemployment benefits from about €800 a month to about €600. Additional money will be available, but at a small hourly wage – if the unemployed get out and work.

Many of Germany's unemployed are highly educated and skilled, but find it more lucrative to take the monthly unemployment benefit than accept work they don't want. The government recently launched a scheme to boost small businesses, but Germans say that to qualify for help one must jump through numerous hoops.

Most Germans are comfortable at the moment, although with many paying nearly 50 per cent income tax, some are wondering where their tax money is going. With over four million Germans out of work and the country's financial motor stalled, anxiety hangs in the air and the topic of conversation always turns back to the economy. Chancellor Schröder, who promised tax cuts, is instead trying to raise taxes, while pushing unpopular social welfare reforms that among other things slash the period during which the unemployed can receive government help from three years to one. Few are rallying behind Schröder, who came into power after the Christian Democrats were hit with a weighty corruption scandal which tipped the balance in his own party's, the Social Democrats', favour. Not only does he have to fight against the opposition party that holds the majority in parliament, he battles against the left wing of the Social Democrats, who are loath to cut worker benefits.

Keep working! *In 2003 economic experts suggested that to lighten the load on state pension plans, Germans should stop retiring in their fifties. The experts no doubt caused a few grey hairs to sprout with their suggested retirement age – 67. Workers will have plenty of time to get used to the idea of working longer. The experts suggest that the new practice kicks in by 2035.*[16]

New, New German Film

In the 1980s Wim Wenders brought the intensity of Berlin to the big screen with *Wings of Desire* – a surreally beautiful film about angels watching over the living – and Rainer Werner Fassbinder focused on the corruption in a society trying to readapt after both world wars. Now there is a whole new wave of 'New German' film. Wolfgang Becker blended humour and nostalgia in the hit *Goodbye Lenin!* about life in East Germany and Tom Tykwer showed the hand of fate with *Run, Lola, Run* – the same scene shown with four different endings. Other big names of the German big screen: Dieter Buck – who brings a strange folk tale to life in *Karniggels* – as well as Andreas Dresen and Caroline Link.

So many of Germany's issues at the moment tangle around the same word: reunification – between East and West, between past and future, and between Germany and Europe, where it wields economic power but is forced to talk very softly even when it's getting screwed. While reunification was always the dream when the two halves of Germany were split, the costs of sealing up the geographical fracture have made West Germany's formerly steadfast economy start to crack. Also draining the country's vitality and coffers: the generous welfare provision and the hefty annual dues to the EU, larger than any other country's.

In September 2003 Prime Minister José María Aznar of Spain sniped that Germany should live up to its EU commitment to balance its budget, just like Spain had. Chancellor Schröder accurately retorted that Spain's healthy economy was a reflection of the money Germany had pumped into it via the EU.

Meanwhile, the United States is still fuming over Germany's lack of support for what Chancellor Schröder dismissed as an 'adventure' in Iraq. So what if he was right? The Americans don't want to hear it in a German accent too. The US responded to Schröder's lack of support by relocating many US troops from German bases, where they had greatly bolstered local economies, to bases in Poland.

The chilly Washington wind that blasted in the direction of Berlin in 2002 after Schröder's remark didn't warm up a bit when Germany's minister of justice Herta Daubler-Gmelin attacked President Bush: 'Bush wants to divert attention from his domestic difficulties. That is a popular method. Hitler has done that before.' She resigned a few days later. Schröder took the bull by the horns and wrote a September 2003 op-ed in the New York Times*, articulating Germany's stance, underscoring the gratitude towards the US in helping it rebuild after the war and pointing out that, while Germany disagreed with the US over Iraq, Germany is 'willing to shoulder more responsibility' in the future.*[17]

Another problem that lurks in the background: the country has yet to confront its own frail self-esteem – a tightly wound, extremely sensitive issue. Decades of war guilt have created a society that, even when its economy soars and everyone should be comfortable, still feels vaguely uneasy; any expression of satisfied pride sets off the alarm bells and fears of a rekindled nationalistic pride. When leaders opine that today's Germans shouldn't feel guilty any more the comments seem cold and insensitive to all the suffering that German military exploits once caused. Germany has apologized, Germany has paid – although everyone knows that the death, destruction and pain can never be erased with money or words. Then again, nearly sixty years after Hitler's death, maybe it's time for the world to forgive Germany, starting with Germany forgiving itself, knowing full well that no one will ever forget.

Upcoming issue: The twelve million Germans kicked out of Czechoslo-vakia, Hungary, Poland and elsewhere in the years following the Second World War. Approved by the Allies' Potsdam Conference on how to divide Germany after the war, the forced exodus of Germans from surrounding countries was supposed to be orderly and humane. Rage from the war was vented on the exiled Germans, two million of whom died during the journey back to Germany; those who made it were also resented in Germany since there was no housing or work for them. Now some of the pushed-out Germans want their old land back or compensation: in March 2004 seventy-seven exiled Sudeten-land Germans filed suit against the Czech Republic in the European Court of Human Rights. The Czech Republic is the only European country that has received no money for Nazi war victims because it won't discuss the exile issue.

Future Forecast

Increasing uneasiness. Poland is petrified that Germany will someday snatch up all its land, and the Czech Republic doesn't want to touch the issue of the Germans it shoved out after the Second World War, not to mention the lands in Sudetenland that some exiled Germans want back; Slovakia and Hungary aren't keen on discussing the postwar German exiles either. The arrival of assorted formerly German-occupied countries, including the Baltic States, may open new wounds, but maybe it's best to get all the grievances and grief out in the open one last time and then make an attempt to evolve.

Hot Spots

Berlin: The Eye of the Kaleidoscope

Nobody can accuse Germany of being stuck in a rut. Over the past century, the country – like a hot-to-trot clotheshorse heading out to a singles' bar – has tried on more looks, personalities and agendas than any other country in the world. And no place better epitomizes that kaleidoscope of national identities than Berlin, the city split by the River Spree, that has undergone more mood changes than even Paris. The nineteenth-century capital of Prussia, Berlin became the new capital of a united Germany in 1871, when the mammoth Brandenburg Gate – topped by a winged chariot – was erected as a symbol of peace. It was soon to became a symbol of militaristic expansion. The opulent centre of opera and finery in the early twentieth century transformed into a city of poverty after the First World War, but that era also was Berlin's most raucous and risqué, when smoky cabarets with husky-voiced women and transvestites overflowed with debauchery. That period ended with the emergence of Berlin as headquarters of the Nazi war machine – artists mostly fled or were killed – and most of Berlin was rubble after the firebombs of the Second World War. Occupied and divided, Berlin was permanently cleft in a tug of war between East and West Germany – a split underscored by the 1961 erection of East Germany's concrete wall that penned in those on the communist side. But with the German reunification thirty years later, Berlin again bloomed as the German capital, starting in 1999. Now it's a city of renovation, creation and cranes. Cheap rents and a slew of cool bars drew arty types from designers to DJs, novelists to playwrights – and the city, although nearly bankrupt, explodes with culture and art. Over 150 museums and galleries, three opera houses, dozens of theatres, a nightlife that pulses, chic restaurants, an underground arts scene, second-hand clothing stores (and those with original fashions that merely look second-hand) are just a few reasons alternative types – looking for the unmined creative hot spot of Europe – are donning thick coats and setting up here.

More Turks (2.5 million) live in Berlin than in any other city except Turkey's largest urban area, Istanbul. Many were invited in a few decades ago as guest workers.

The Jewish memorial: It's been in the planning process for years, but the €26 million 'Monument for the Murdered Jews of Europe' still isn't quite done. Consisting of 2,000 columns of varying heights spanning more than 6,000 square feet, the memorial in central Berlin will include a museum with photos and biographies of the 6 million Jews killed in concentration camps during the war; it will also be treated with a graffiti-resistant coating – when it is completed. In fact, the coating is the latest delay in the monument that has been on the boards for well over a decade. The problem: the manufacturer, Degussa, was linked to the manufacture of the gas that killed millions of Jews.

Hamburg: Elegant, dotted with parks and boasting a wild bar scene, the

Schwarzwald: one of Germany's tucked-away treasures.

city has plenty of touristic charm, but that probably wasn't the lure for alleged 9/11 ringleader Mohammad Atta who studied engineering and urban design here and worked for the city planning office. He was known to employers at the city office as kind, hard-working and devout: he had a prayer rug at his desk and would give his thanks to Allah five times a day.

Prussia: The powerful kingdom that brought Germany together was dissolved as a geographical entity in 1934, and is now rarely referred to except in historical documents; it's viewed by many Germans shamefully because of its militaristic past.

Bavaria: Best known for the Oktoberfest when its beer halls are even more festive than usual and for rigid Edmund Stoiber (whom you won't see at the beer halls), heavily Catholic Bavaria is the overachiever of Germany, with the lowest unemployment rate and the scariest ideas: the Bavarian government recently proposed 'tagging' Roma as a way to identify them. This didn't go down well with anti-discrimination groups.

The Rhine: Europe's busiest waterway and, until recently, the biggest sewer in Europe, the Rhine provides both drinking water and an industrial dumping pond. Now it's being cleaned up and aquatic life is returning, as are the fishermen. Eel anyone?

> *Green-friendly: Germany is one of the world's environmental heroes, and its popular Green Party keeps an eye on sustainable development. Recycling is second nature – of course there is kerbside collection of glass, metal and paper – the once-polluted waterways are vastly improved, the public transport is excellent and all of Germany's nuclear plants are to be phased out by 2020. And, by and large, Germans simply don't litter.*

Military bases: Rumoured to be home to plenty of NATO's nukes, a programme begun under Chancellor Helmut Schmidt in the 1970s and reinforced by Chancellor Kohl in the 1980s.

Dresden: This beautiful city in eastern Germany seems jinxed: it was fire-bombed by the US and Britain at the end of the war, with 35,000 civilians suffocated or incinerated in the citywide inferno while the German army was out fighting the Red Army. After it was rebuilt to its original plan and unveiled in stately splendour in 2001, the floods of 2002 ravaged it, but Dresden has been shined up yet again.

Frankfurt: Rising along the River Main, the financial heart of Germany has a stunning skyline of skyscrapers that resembles New York, hence its nickname Mainhattan. Dripping with culture and museums, the city is also home to October's Book Fair, the world's largest and most significant.

The ground: The Second World War left another legacy: Allied bombs – often weighing in at 500 pounds, occasionally 2,000 pounds, are still embedded in German soil. Almost 2,000 have been unearthed in Berlin alone since 1945: some have been 'live' and killed those who stumbled across them. It is believed there are still 15,000 more to find in that city. Now over 2,500 people work trying to search them out across the country, digging up about 20,000 tonnes of the explosives every year.[18]

Desks: Chips and chunks from the Berlin Wall now serve as paperweights all over the world. Those not already owning their own Berlin Wall paperweight best not bother now: so many fakes have been peddled that it's said the wall has been sold three times.

Dreams Come True

Mad King Ludwig (1845–86) of Bavaria had the grandiose dream of building enchanting mountaintop castles that would capture music in architectural form. Tributes to his favourite composer Richard Wagner, Ludwig's castles are splashed with scenes from his operas and even caves are built into the spindly-towered fantasies. From a security point of view they were pretty worthless, and in fact they may have cost Ludwig his life: he was found mysteriously drowned in Starnberger Lake. His family, livid about his extravagant follies that were eating up all their money, was suspected of plotting his death. Ludwig's castles, particularly ornate Neuschwanstein, turned out to be a brilliant investment: today they are Germany's biggest tourist draws.

Oder–Neisse Line: The border between Poland and Germany was drawn in 1990, but ethnic Germans on the Polish side want to reunite, and that makes Poland nervous. The land indeed used to be part of East Germany, but Stalin, who wanted a strip of eastern Poland to join with the USSR, shoved the Polish borders to the west. Look for friction here.

Schools have been in the limelight lately: in a recent international survey comparing student scores from different countries, Germany did not come out at the head of the class, falling about midway, a bit under Brazil. More alarming: in 2002 a freshly expelled 19-year-old high school student in Erfurt whipped out a gun and took aim at classmates and teachers, killing fifteen. The German parliament passed a new weapons control act within two hours.

Garching reactor: While Germany plans to phase out all nuclear reactors for electricity, it has no current plans to shut down a 20-megawatt nuclear research reactor, fuelled with enriched uranium, at the Munich Technical University. This sort of reactor flies in the face of non-proliferation agreements, and some worry that it could be used to build nuclear bombs.[19]

Nuremberg: the city where Hitler pushed through legislation to strip Jews of their legal rights was also where Nazi war criminals were tried.

After the war, in addition to the international war tribunal in Nuremberg, West Germany tried a further 80,000 suspected Nazis.

An International Phenomenon

The Germans are often believed to have invented the notorious concentration camp, but such 'enemy camps' were first put into active use by the British during the Boer War in 1899, when thousands of Dutch and German settlers died, mostly from starvation and disease. The Russians were also early advocates, spelling death to millions – particularly Balts, Poles and dissident Russians – who were shipped off to Siberia to work in the gulag labour camps. The United States hauled off many Japanese during the Second World War to internment camps, which are rarely mentioned in history books. Even Egypt has concentration camps in the desert where the Muslim Brotherhood was sent in the 1950s. The German camps differed in that their concentration camps sometimes had gas chambers and crematoria added later, as the corpses piled up.

Autobahn: Twelve thousand miles of mostly speed-limitless highway, the Autobahn – the world's first interstate – was commissioned by Hitler in the 1930s to give jobs to the Depression-era unemployed. Polish Jews and POWs ended up completing it in 1941, but the armed forces didn't use it much, since the asphalt couldn't support their tanks.

Hot Shots

Gerhard Schröder: Chancellor, 1998 to present. Born during the war – his war-widowed mother eked out a living selling charcoal – Social Democrat Schröder was part of the 1968 generation that rose up in social revolution. Another rallying point for the so-called 68ers was Germany's close involvement with the US military machine; although Schröder sent troops to Afghanistan in 2001, he has distanced himself from American war-mongering recently and rode to re-election victory in 2002 partly by just saying no to Iraq. In 2004 his unpopular economic reform package prompted thousands to turn in their Social Democrat cards and Schröder stepped down as party head that year. Unfairly blamed for all that ails the country, Schröder is sensitive to jibes from the press: he sued the publication that reported he dyed his hair.

Schröder was chastised by US Secretary of Defense Donald Rumsfeld, who said the Chancellor had 'poisoned'[20] the relationship with the US,

Former cabbie Joschka Fischer is now Germany's most popular politician.

although Rumsfeld hasn't exactly sweetened it, listing Germany as part of 'Old Europe', which in Rumsfeld's book was meant as a barb. Innocently drawn into a diplomatic scuffle in summer 2003 when Italy's Prime Minister Silvio Berlusconi likened a German member of the European Parliament to a Nazi and an Italian tourism minister called Germans 'hyper nationalist blond louts', Schröder cancelled his summer vacation plans to Italy that year.

Horst Koehler: President 2004 to present. Christian Democrat Koehler might be able to help the hurting economy: after all, until taking the presidential seat he was head of the IMF.

Red Army Faction (RAF)

Among the protesters marching in 1968 was a wealthy young man named Andreas Baader and an intellectual, somewhat sickly, young woman called Ulrike Meinhof. The dismay and rage felt by the two was extreme and contagious. By 1972 they had lured a few dozen into their urban guerrilla group – Baader-Meinhof – all frantic that Germany was becoming part of the US-guided military–industrial machine and all sure that only they could stop it and only with violence.

The Red Army Faction (RAF), as Baader and Meinhof later renamed the group, took aim at the military and industry, targeting both Germany and the United States in their attacks. Their most impressive year was 1977: in a mere six months RAF assassinated a German federal prosecutor and two of his colleagues, downed the president of a bank, killed four high-placed business consultants, kidnapped and killed an industrialist, and hired Arab guerrillas to hijack a Lufthansa plane, an ordeal during which they held passengers hostage for days and killed the pilot. By 1988 the group was mostly dead, imprisoned or missing, although after Germany reunited ten RAF members, presumed living in the Middle East, turned out to be living just in the East, on the other side of the wall. Some believe that East Germany's secret police was heavily involved with the group.

Baader-Meinhof – the final chapter: After a botched ransom attempt to gain his release, Andreas Baader supposedly killed himself in prison, as part of a suicide pact, although details are sketchy. Meinhof also supposedly died by suicide in 1976, but there was soon a battle over her brain. Her family wanted to bury it, but scientists kept it for years exploring inconclusively if previous surgery for a brain tumour had kicked off her violent streak; her family finally won back the grey matter.

Joschka Fischer: Foreign Minister 1998 to present. A former taxi driver, Germany's most popular postwar politician – and one of the top ten in Europe – now leads the Green Party, but during 1968 was more radical. In 2001 *Stern* magazine ran photos of him looking rather aggressive during the peace marches, including one where he appears to be attacking a policeman. The former activist apologized and says he's changed his ways (giving up drinking and taking up running for starters). The policeman says he's forgiven Fischer, and the voters apparently did too. Fischer's book about turning teetotaller became a bestseller. Maybe he can write a follow-up about divorce: after two marriages that lasted three years, and a third that ended after twelve years, he's now on wife number four, who is twenty-one years his junior. At least the man is honest: when asked if he'd ever smoked pot, he quipped that not only had he inhaled, he'd enjoyed it. Initially a major proponent of a more powerful EU, Fischer has stopped singing that tune ever since the Iraq war revealed the headstrong wills of the individual EU members. He may be tapped to be the EU Foreign Minister if the draft constitution passes and the position is created.

> *The unflattering photos of Fischer published in* Stern *had been peddled by the daughter of left-wing radical Meinhof; she accused Fischer of 'selling out'.*

Johannes Rau: President 1999–2003. Although German presidents wield little power, Social Democrat Rau delivered a few unforgettable speeches in February 2000; when he apologized for the Holocaust to the Israeli Parliament, there was hardly a dry eye in the house. His farewell speech was a cracker too: he lectured corporate heads, businessmen and politicians about their greed at a time when workers face an uncertain future, and expressed concern about the current mood in the country, asking, 'Have we put ourselves down so much that we don't believe in ourselves any more? Are we getting into a kind of collective depression?'[21] Well, he should talk: in 2001 he said Germans could not be proud about being Germans – albeit a common opinion these days in Deutschland.

Edmund Stoiber: Minister–President of Bavaria 1993 to present. White-haired and super-tanned, Stoiber doesn't like beer, but he apparently adores living up to the image of the Super-German Type A, working eighteen hours a day and encouraging others to keep up with his pace. The work has apparently paid off: the popular Christian Democrat from Bavaria has helped make his state Germany's wealthiest, and in Bavaria unemployment is a mere 5 per cent. Stoiber ran unsuccessfully against Schröder in 2002; next time he could get it. One snag: many in the rest of the country aren't fond of Bavarian politicians, typically the country's most conservative. Stoiber is no exception. Another potential problem: he supports the Sudetenlanders who want their land back. If he seriously waves the Sudetenlander banner, things could get tricky.

> *Rising Star: From East Germany, the conservative head of the Christian Democrats Angela Merkel had to clean up the mess left over from the slush-fund damage to the party. She has her eye on the chancellorship – and might get it. Women have considerable power in German politics, currently holding nearly a third of the seats in the federal parliament.*

Also in her favour: the Christian Democrats are currently in the majority.[22]

Neo-Nazis: The recent appearance of neo-Nazis, said to number around 30,000 – mainly in the East – presents a tough problem. The government deprogramming school for neo-Nazis hasn't attracted many, and courts have ruled that it is unconstitutional to ban the neo-Nazi parties. In 2000 the young neo-Nazis were behind the murder of an African man and a bomb explosion in Düsseldorf, but now many think they are heading to France and Sweden.

Armin Meiwes: A computer handyman from Kassel, Meiwes turned stomachs around the world when it was discovered that he had cannibalized fellow German Bernd-Jürgen Brandes in March 2001. Meiwes had advertised on the Internet for a 'well-built man, 18–30, who would like to be eaten by me'. Meiwes claimed that over 200 responded, but only Brandes, a software developer, was serious. During the January 2004 trial the court saw the videotape of Brandes acknowledging he wanted to be food for Meiwes; the court also heard Meiwes' description of how he butchered, stored and ate Brandes meal by meal – sometimes as a sandwich, sometimes fried up with eggs – and noting that the body tasted like pork and was particularly delicious when washed down with South African wine.[23] Meiwes, sentenced to eight and a half years' imprisonment for manslaughter, might never have been discovered had he not posted another Internet ad requesting another willing victim. An alert Austrian turned him in.

Helmut Kohl: Chancellor 1982–98. Portly four-term Chancellor, powermonger Kohl was a heavyweight in almost every way: he approved deployment of NATO nuclear missiles at German army bases, headed the republic when the Berlin Wall fell and oversaw the reunification between the two halves of Germany. He lost to Schröder in 1998, largely due to votes from dissatisfied East Germans, and he fell hard: he was implicated in a scandal the next year that had some calling for him to take a vacation in prison. After first denying that, as head of the Christian Democrats, he had created a slush fund to hide millions of euros' worth of campaign contributions, Kohl finally admitted that he had personally accepted $1 million (€800,000). The scandal shook his religion-tied party, whose popularity hit an all-time low, after being the power party of postwar German politics.

Shadowy dealings: Mystery still surrounds the Christian Democrat finance scandal that broke in 1999, and may have involved at least $15 million (€12 million) of unreported, illegal donations to the party during the 1980s and 1990s. Involving arms dealers, Saudi arms sales, French oil deals, suitcases stuffed with money and Swiss bank accounts, the ordeal resulted in several resignations – Kohl stepped down as honorary party chair for one – and the suicide of a former treasurer. Kohl would never admit where the money came from, but there were suspicions that Kohl's close friend François Mitterrand had tossed over a chunk of it, perhaps to influence business, perhaps because he was a strong Kohl supporter.

Scientologists: Were they trying to infiltrate the top of Germany's power pyramid? Or were they just trying to get leaders to take free personality tests? Who knows if the German press was on to something or exaggerating the numbers, but recently there was such a scare about the pseudo-religion trying to influence German politics that it turned into an international brouhaha; recent estimates put the numbers of followers at less than 10,000.[24]

Willy Brandt *aka* **Karl Herbert Frahm:** Chancellor 1969–74, Foreign Minister 1966–9. The West German politician who first unlocked the diplomatic door to the East, Brandt previously had been a Nazi-hating, radical journalist hiding in Oslo, Norway – where he first became widely known under his famous pen name that he had used to escape Germany and Hitler's death squads.[25] As West German Chancellor he returned to Oslo in 1971 to pick up the Nobel Peace Prize for his 'Ostpolitik' Cold War-thaw programme. Brandt started what Kohl finished almost two decades later, with the reunification of both Germanies. He helped smooth international relations as well: when Chancellor Brandt was led to a memorial for Second World War victims in Poland, he fell to his knees. In 1974 he was brought to his knees again, this time being implicated in a spy scandal in his office that forced him to resign.

Hitler was obsessed with the occult and fascinated by the published predictions of Nostradamus. Some occultists say that editions of the seer's vision that were published after 1939 are filled with more nonsense than the rest: the British MI6, say occultists, rewrote the books and embedded in them symbolism to suggest that Germany would lose the war.

Guenther Verheugen: European Commissioner 1999 to present. The Commissioner formerly in charge of enlargement, Verheugen now oversees enterprise and industry.

Media stars: Lots of interesting press here, including *Deutsche Welt*, one of several papers that publish in English: www.dw-world.de

3. United Kingdom (Great Britain): Playing Both Sides

Fast Facts

Country:	United Kingdom of Great Britain and Northern Ireland
Capital:	London
Government:	constitutional monarchy
Independence:	Unified 900 (established as UK in 1927)
Population:	60,271,000 (2004 estimate)
Leaders:	Head of State: Queen Elizabeth II
	Head of Government: Prime Minister Tony Blair (1997)
Elections:	Monarchy hereditary; Prime Minister is head of majority party or coalition in House of Commons, 5 years or less
Name of Parliament:	Parliament (House of Commons and less powerful House of Lords)
Ethnicity:	English 82%; Scottish 10%; Irish 4%; Welsh 2%; S. Asian, African-Caribbean, other
Religion:	Anglican (nominally) 45%; Roman Catholic 15%; assorted Protestant 4%; Muslim 2%; also Sikh, Hindu, Jewish
Language:	English (the Queen's, and heavily accented variations)
Literacy:	99% (claimed); functional illiteracy 22% (says UN)
Exports:	equipment (machine, power, electronic), fuels, chemicals, cars
Per capita GDP:	$27,700 (2003 estimate)
Unemployment:	4.7% (March 2004 Eurostat figure)
Percentage in poverty:	17% (2002 estimate)
EU status:	EEC member state since 1973
Currency:	British pound (sterling)
Known for:	fair play, being clever and respectable, usually

Standout Qualities

Bloody history: Wars with everybody who mattered
Bloody ban: No death penalty any more
Bloody hell: Where did the empire go?

Résumé

Britain is no longer the hungry imperial whale prowling the seven seas, swallowing more land than any other colonial power, nor is it currently the manufacturing heart of Europe that kick-starts important revolutions. The land whose thinkers (such as Sir Isaac Newton) unveiled the basic workings of the planet (gravitational forces for one) and whose creators introduced many of the world's most important devices (the steam engine, radar and flush-toilet among them) isn't Invention Central any more. But the island-kingdom popularly known as Britain still stands tall on the global power team. Granted, these days clout comes less from how Britain acts than how it reacts and less from what Britain is than who it knows and can pull over to its team or vice versa.

The British idea machine hasn't entirely conked out: Briton Tim Berners-Lee demarcated a whole new frontier in the 1980s when he invented the world-wide web as well as the language and codes that would run it.

Geographical Confusion: United Kingdom v. Great Britain v. Ireland

Popularly called Britain, the country officially known as the United Kingdom is made up of four parts: England, Scotland, and Wales – which all share the same island and are collectively known as Great Britain – as well as Northern Ireland, the six British-run counties on the island of Ireland to the west. All of Ireland was once part of Great Britain, but the bulk of the island became a separate, independent republic in 1921. (In this book, Britain and the UK are used interchangeably.)

The country that twice checked Germany's twentieth-century expansionist dreams (as well as Napoleon's the century before), Britain is geographically and politically the EU's odd man out – and therein lies its strength. The UK counterbalances the weight of the Continent's two most powerful forces – these days through political manoeuvres and wars of words – offsetting the 'Franco-German axis' in the EU. With the EU's third highest population, third highest total GDP, and (currently) the same number of votes as France and Germany, Britain is the country that can most effectively challenge the power duo from Paris and Berlin and question where they are driving the EU car.

Britain and America

Never mind that little flare-up back in the eighteenth century when American colonists forgot about loyalty to the king, resulting in the War of Independence (1775–83) against Britain. Throughout the past century, and into the present, Britain has been America's pet friend: clasping hands in wars and in their pursuit of globalized corporate democracy, the two Western powerbrokers are united in love of oil, arms sales and doing what is proper, especially if there's a quid or two to be made. Americans fought alongside Brits in both world wars – and without British friendship, the US may never have entered the European battle arenas where the arms it shipped and the troops it sent were crucial in evening the score. America and Britain forged such powerful alliances as NATO, standing out as the most vocal 'white hats' in the Cold War, and encouraging those under Communist regimes to rise up and rebel, although giving little help to those who did. Anglo-American activities in the Middle East, however, have been the most questionable – whether you're looking at costs, ethics, or motives. Brits fought alongside Americans in 1991's Desert Storm to drive Iraq out of Kuwait, and the Anglo-American duo continued to fly fighter planes over Iraq (theoretically to protect Kurds and Shiites) for a decade, imposing no-fly zones in that country, without international authority to do so; meanwhile, agents from both countries continued to sell Iraq weapons or the components to make them. The US and the UK jointly launched the 'War on Terror' with the 2001 bombing of Afghanistan that laid low the Taliban and let loose a wave of anarchy in its wake. But their most controversial move – ever – was the 2003 invasion of Iraq, an action insisted upon by the US and seconded by Britain, whose Prime Minister helped garner limited European support. Framed as part of the 'War on Terror' and sold with dire warnings from both President George Bush and Prime Minister Tony Blair that Iraq possessed weapons of mass destruction (WMD) that it could soon unleash on their countries, the 2003 war – launched despite international protests and millions marching in the streets – made both countries look like warmongering fools when no WMD were found and Iraq subsequently erupted in guerrilla-ridden chaos. Not only did the leaders' claims appear to be bogus, so was the packaging: Bush and Blair had been planning a regime change in

Iraq at least eight months before the September 11 attacks on the US (with which Iraq was never linked) or the 'War on Terror' was launched. A divisive issue in Britain, where the split was 50–50 on going to war, the move on Iraq triggered serious questioning of the benefits derived from loyally and consistently backing the country that was once its colony and is still viewed as best friend.

Geographically and ideologically, the UK also bridges the gap between the European Continent and the United States, Britain's good mate and fighting partner. The Anglo-American relationship rattles the European Union's elite – some hiss that Britain is 'Atlanticist' (too close to the *other* side of the ocean) – but it aptly reflects the British ambivalence about being part of the EU. The UK and Ireland are the only two of the EU-15 countries who don't honour the borderless Schengen zone and more importantly, Britain – along with Sweden and Denmark – keeps pooh-poohing the euro, which has never even made it to a vote in the UK. While the rest of the EU waits, with folded arms, to see if Britain will ever fully commit to being part of the Europe club, Britain is wondering the same.

The UK, which often calls itself Britain, thereby technically cutting out Northern Ireland, often refers to the US as America, thereby technically cutting out North America's Canada and Mexico, and all the countries that are part of South and Central America. Neither term is geographically correct, but both are so engrained in popular usage that they are widely accepted.

Isaac Newton (1642–1727)

When the BBC conducted a 2003 vote on The World's Greatest Briton, such heavyweights as William Shakespeare, Lady Di, Charles Darwin, Charles Dickens, Charlotte Brontë, Francis Bacon, James Boswell, Samuel Johnson, Jane Austen, Adam Smith, John Locke, John Lennon, John Maynard Keynes, Rudyard Kipling, Lewis Carroll, Twiggy and Posh Spice were skipped over for a scientist who, legend has it, was the first in his family of farmers to learn to read and sign his name.[1] Sir Isaac Newton, the grandfather of the Enlightenment, set the world spinning in numerous new directions with his writings and profound realizations. The boy who had showed little academic promise – he was initially considered listless and dull, although he once built 'a windmill powered by a treadmill run by a mouse'[2] – was suddenly struck by a force of brilliance in his late teens – some say his curiosity was aroused by the strange symbols in a book of astrology – that could keep him awake for days and made him a channel for revealing the hidden knowledge of the universe. In bouts of mania he invented the reflecting telescope, figured out the nature of colour, devised calculus, and established laws of physical motion and gravity – most of his realizations coming to him in the three years leading up to his 25th birthday. He explained the orbits of comets, the pull of the moon on the oceans, he had ideas and improvements to make upon everything from clocks to windmills, and in 1686 his most famous book *Philosophiae Naturalis Principia Mathematica* (*Mathematical Principles of Natural Philosophy*) was published – with wealthy astronomer Edmund Halley (of comet fame) picking up the printing tab for what was the most profoundly important book of the day. The only area in which Newton did not fully succeed (besides his social life – he was too busy for romantic dalliances and was notoriously cranky) was alchemy – a subject about which he wrote millions of words, and which so consumed him that he suffered several nervous breakdowns, believed to have been caused by inhaling toxic vapours during experiments. Nevertheless, the man who so changed human understanding of the physical world did eventually find a method of transforming his life of ideas into gold: in 1690, he took a government position as Master of the Mint, creating new coins that were resistant to counterfeiting, and becoming extremely wealthy in the process.[3]

The UK looks pretty puny now compared to the behemoth it was during the nineteenth-century Victorian era, when nearly 40 per cent of the planet's land was stitched into the British empire's tapestry, but in many ways, this is Britain's golden hour – well, at least until one peeks under the rug. Forget the 1970s and 1980s when the British economy was so shaky that the government pathetically cut the free milk scheme in schools, unemployment hovered around 14 per cent[4] and the major trade unions crippled the country with continual strikes.

That depressing period of British history triggered more than the birth of angry punk music – epitomized by the Sex Pistols (who without their band would probably never have landed a job). It was also the era when two of the country's lingering problems emerged: foot-ball hooligans – who take their football so seriously they slam people and rip up property after a match – and the anti-immigrant British National Party, linked to neo-Nazis and an instigator of ethnic violence.

The British pound now looks invincible as one of the world's strongest currencies; with unemployment under 5 per cent, the British economy is the most vibrant of the big countries in the EU and the unions are not the prickly thorns they used to be. The UK is even cooler now than when the 'Cool Britannia' concept was devised a decade ago: no other European country has so many authors, bands and celebs whose popularity catches on across the whole Continent: names such as Beckham, Coldplay and Potter are now the symbols of the UK. British leaders, previously ageing, stodgy and dour, are now often young, modern and slick, and the British media, with its wide-ranging focus, is arguably the most influential on the planet. And power-wise Britain hasn't flexed more muscle on the international scene since 1984, when Maggie Thatcher whacked her handbag on the EU table, demanding 'I want my money back' – and getting it.

Mind the CAP

Humbled after being twice prevented from entering the European Economic Community – France kept blocking the move – the UK, when it finally entered the Common Market in 1973, didn't come in with a fantastic deal. While France and Germany got plenty back for their dues in the form of Common Agricultural Policy (CAP) subsidies, Britain's relatively small agricultural sector didn't command as much. Prime Minister Thatcher rectified that with the 1984 'handbagging incident' – demanding that the EU hand over a rebate that amounts to about £3.6 billion (€5 billion) a year. The rebate has been under attack ever since – the German press is obsessed with it – but never as much as in summer 2004 when the European Commission, at the behest of German budget commissioner Michaela Schreyer (whose country has been saddled with the highest EU net dues), announced that to pay for the ten new countries coming in, the British rebate would be scrapped. That idea was not well received: Blair promised to veto the proposal, and the UK media pointed out what amounted to a grand power play, where suddenly Britain would be the biggest net contributor to the Union (the Netherlands, however, would still be paying most on a per capita basis). The European Commission tabled their proposal at the worst possible time: British scepticism about the EU has never run higher or been more heated, and the loss of the rebate made membership of the Brussels club even less appealing to those who were already banging on the door to get out.

Of course there's a flip side. The British economy appears so robust that the European Union wants to cancel Britain's annual rebate from Brussels and cast Britain in the Mr Moneybags role long shouldered by Germany. The strength of the pound buys luxury on holiday, but at home life is staggeringly expensive. The designer hotels and snazzy restaurants that helped make Britannia so 'cool', charge 10 quid for a martini and €400 a night. Even if London is Europe's cultural epicentre, house prices are so steep that only creators who've nailed the Booker Prize or have pre-sold ten works to the Tate Modern can afford anything but a (public) council flat. Clever leaders such as Tony Blair are seen as spouting fountains of misinformation and causing a national erosion of trust; even the BBC is eyed more sceptically since it was rapped in a government investigation looking into its coverage of Blair's claims about Iraq. And that constant cootchie-cooing with the US is a serious liability: thanks to Britain's always-at-DC's-side stance, radical Islamists are threatening to strike out in the UK. Many militant Muslims wouldn't have to travel far for action: they already live here, having been welcomed in under previously liberal asylum and immigration laws, and the ethnic mixing that is such a cultural plus now casts a political shadow over a society that so easily shuts the door to its own.

Bad Advertising: Abu Hamza al-Masri

Abu Hamza al-Masri lost both hands and an eye as a guerrilla fighter in Afghanistan – for which he received disability payments from the UK government[5] – but the 40-something Egyptian-born imam doesn't want pity: with his hook hand and glass eye, he seems to relish his role of the fearsome-looking leader calling on his flocks to demonstrate their belief by offering to give up their lives to radical Islam's cause. In his moving speeches, which typically drew up to two thousand to London's Finsbury Park mosque – the largest of the UK's 1,500 mosques – he praised Osama bin Laden, referred to the US as 'The United Snakes of America', and called upon the faithful to hold up banks;[6] the mosque also reportedly gave instruction to would-be militants on how to use AK-47s. 'If you do things for the cause of Allah, losing your life for it is the highest form of faith,' he has said.[7] No group is more concerned about fervent al-Masri than the Muslim Council of Britain, which diligently works for peace and Muslim integration and sends press releases disassociating itself from his acts; the Muslim Council has urged imams in the UK to work with police in terrorism investigations. But protest as the Muslim Council might about radicals hijacking their faith, mullahs such as al-Masri snatch bigger headlines. The Egyptian was seen as so incendiary and threatening in his Finsbury Park sermons that British police raided the mosque in 2003 and the Charities Commission pushed him from his post for his 'inflammatory' words. Big deal: al-Masri, playing the martyr card, continued ranting just outside the mosque doors. In spring 2004 the British government finally succeeded in stripping him of UK citizenship – gained through marriage in 1981 – and that summer the US offered to take him off their hands: after being promised that the US would not execute al-Masri, the UK arrested the mullah and extradited him to America, where he was slapped with eleven criminal charges including trying to start a terrorist training camp in Oregon, being linked to al-Qaeda and hostage-taking in Yemen. Who is worst affected by the harsh words of al-Masri and other radicals? Moderate Muslims, the vast majority forced to find new places of worship and now victims of general 'Islamophobia'.

The UK is home to some two million multi-ethnic Muslims, one-third of whom are recent converts and about 10 per cent of whom are considered radical. In January 2003 police raided an apartment in north London, arresting six Algerian men after finding traces of the poisonous gas ricin there. Richard 'the shoe bomber' Reid (a fan of al-Masri) is British, as were several suicide bombers who recently blew themselves up in Israel. Al-Qaeda also publicizes threats and admissions of guilt via al-Quds al-Arabi, a London-based Arabic newspaper run by Abdel Bari Atwan, a Palestinian living in Britain.

Meanwhile, Britain is suffering a multi-pronged identity crisis. The first issue can be mostly summed up in four words: is it Europe, really? Sidelined geographically, Britain is now pondering how committed it is to being one with the Continent, if it should ever sign on for the euro or even stay in the EU. Former prime minister Margaret Thatcher, now retired, is threatening to launch a campaign to cut all ties to Brussels, and the UK Independence Party makes ditching the EU its main thrust and 'Say no!' its battle cry. With a new, celebrity member – Robert Kilroy-Silk, previously of British talk-show fame – the Independence Party took twelve seats in the European Parliament, being voted in to the EU body with the promise of taking Britain out.

> 'Apart from oil – which was discovered, is produced and is paid for by the West, what do [Arabs] contribute? Can you think of anything? . . . What do they think we feel about them? That we adore them for the way they murdered more than 3,000 civilians on September 11 and danced in the hot, dusty streets to celebrate the murders? That we admire them for being suicide bombers, limb-amputators, women repressors?' – BBC talk-show host Robert Kilroy-Silk in his 4 January 2004 Sunday Express column. He was sacked from the BBC as a result of his words.

> 'It's a close one. The Arabs have given us numbers, the modern alphabet and the pendulum. Kilroy has given us a chat show, a newspaper column and a strangely orange sun tan' – Sunday Times columnist Roland White, 11 January 2004

Loves That Camera: Robert Kilroy-Silk

With silver hair, glistening smile and orange-glowing perma-tan, Robert Kilroy-Silk has the polished look of a TV broadcaster, and no surprise: he was one for seventeen years, from 1987 to 2003. The host of morning talk show *Kilroy* on BBC1, the sixty-something former Labour MP styled himself as a British Jerry Springer: on his drama-rich talk show guests were known to sob, yell and, on at least one occasion, drop their trousers; the host himself is famous for his on-camera jabs and off-camera punches. When he signed on with the UK Independence Party, he promised to jolt politics the same as he did with his high-voltage show.

In June 2004 the party shocked the political establishment by pulling down 16 per cent of the vote for the European Parliament – and preventing either Labour or Conservatives from taking a majority. Kilroy-Silk announced one goal for his stint in the European Parliament: to 'wreck it'.[8] The Independence Party, which Kilroy-Silk promised would 'expose the fraud and corruption and the way in which this institution and the [European] Commission and the EU are eroding our sovereignty and independence',[9] was stealing the spotlight from the minute it skipped in, and not simply because of Kilroy's fine suits and sparkling teeth. It was the things they were saying: Independence Party member Godfrey Bloom had just taken a seat on the Women's Rights committee when he announced: 'I want to deal with women's issues because I just don't think they clean behind the fridge enough.'[10]

Instead of wrecking the EU, Kilroy-Silk attacked the Independence Party. In early 2005, he dismissed UKIP as 'a joke', and split to form his own party, Veritas. How the new party holds up remains to be seen, but one thing is for sure: where the former TV show host goes, trouble (and the camera) usually follows.

'Do fish feel guilty? Laxatives have no effect? Your leg fall off? Fathered 57 children in one night? Nasal hair chokes your goldfish? Damaged by spoons? You put a nutcracker WHERE?' Online parody of Kilroy-Silk's catchy intros for his talk show, from www.robertkilroy-silk.com, a site not maintained by the politician, but by a comedian called Dogbomb.

Britain's nagging identity question is not limited only to the relationship with countries across the Channel: the UK seems unsure exactly what its role in the world should be any more. Long seeing itself as the moral backbone of the planet, Britain is now pondering how far it should go in taking the less fortunate in, as labourers or refugees. Initially welcoming workers from new EU countries in 2004, for example, the government quickly backpedalled, adding that they would not be entitled to full citizenship benefits. Nevertheless, within four months of joining the EU, some 90,000 from Eastern European countries registered to work in the UK. It's the ones who aren't registered that the Home Office worries about: thousands may be slaves.[11]

'The eyes of the world are turning to Great Britain. We now have the moral leadership of the world, and before many years we shall have *people coming here as to a modern Mecca, learning from us in the twentieth century as they learned from us in the seventeenth' – British health minister Aneurin Bevan in 1948, unveiling a revamped National Health Service and explaining why Brits should pay for immigrants' health care too.*

Allowances for asylum seekers have also been tightened and there's such a rush to get out of the country the 50,000 or so applicants rejected each year that removal centres are jam-packed. Public misperception on the issue abounds – the majority of Britons believe their country takes in a quarter of all the world's refugees, when the figure is about 3 per cent[12] – and the issue grows more volatile daily. The anti-immigrant British National Party is accused of stirring up racial hatred and the government centres for holding asylum seekers likely to be deported are sites of riots, violence and suicides.

Every country is facing the issue of those who are denied asylum but disappear into the night. Now Britain has nine 'detention centres' – usually former prisons – to house asylum seekers who seem likely to make a run for it; often they are picked up right from the point of entry and sent to the 'removal centres'. They've been in the news lately since on average there is one assault every day: detainees are starting fires, several riots have broken out, and in July 2004 two asylum seekers killed themselves within a week. Thousands marched in protests demanding that government upgrade the facilities, revamp its policies, and speed up decision making so that the foreigners need not be penned up here for months at a time. Now, like others in the EU, the British government is considering setting up asylum application centres abroad – perhaps in Croatia – to keep the unwanted from showing up at the door.

One more twist to the British identity problem: exactly what territories should be included on its map. Through the twentieth century, former colonial countries began snapping off like brittle leaves, and in 1997 even Hong Kong was lost, when it was handed back to China. Now the non-English parts of Britain – which England has long lorded over – are demanding more autonomy, and the British government has been loosening the threads that keep it tightly sewn together as one. How far the unravelling will go remains to be seen.

Scotland and Wales have had their own parliaments since 1999. As for Northern Ireland it's had one (theoretically) since 1922, but it spends years at a time shut down and non-functioning.

History Review

Romans and Vikings, druids and dragons, knights and magicians, murderous queens, loony kings and torturous deaths – British history has them all pressed into its pages along with wars with the French, wars with the neighbours, and battles against poverty and disease, which given the bone-dampening weather always seemed to be more deadly here. But regardless what the territorial holdings were that year – an island or an empire – the common thread of British history has been the monarchy, except of course when harsh Cromwell stepped in to act like the cruellest of kings.

A Few Memorable Monarchs

- King Arthur: Who knows if he really existed (there are mentions as early as 600 CE), but Arthur and his court have grabbed plenty of ink, much of the lore written at least seven centuries after the Round Table disbanded.
- King John (b. 1167; king 1199–1216): In 1215 forced to sign Magna Carta, the first document giving rights to the common man.
- Henry VIII (b. 1491; king 1509–47): Married six wives but had to yank the Church of England out of the Catholic Church to do it. Launched attacks on Ireland in order, among other things, to loot the Catholic places of worship.
- Mary Queen of Scots (1542–87): Never sat on the English throne, but Catholic Mary, a cousin of Elizabeth I, tried to snatch it from Protestant Elizabeth I: when her plot was revealed, she was beheaded, paying the executioner to make it a clean chop. Alas, he didn't.
- Elizabeth I (b. 1533; queen 1558–1603): Who knows if she was really a virgin (she so loved to flirt), but the Virgin Queen – as she was known since she never married – led a happy, stable court (well, for those times) and pointed British navigators to far parts of the globe.
- King James I (b. 1566; king 1603–25): Originally king of Scotland, when Elizabeth died he was called to sit on the English throne as well – a period

known as the Union of the Crowns, during which Scotland became more integrated with England. (The pairing was not officially consummated, however, until the Act of Union of 1707.)

- Queen Victoria (b. 1819; queen 1837–1901): Her offspring and their descendants married and/or stepped in as crowned heads all over Europe (even Queen Alexandra of Tsar Nicholas fame was related) but Victoria, the longest-reigning British monarch, is best known for Britain's colonial acquisitions and technological advances during her era. Less known: she drank marijuana tea to ease menstrual cramps.

The territory now known as the United Kingdom was mostly a patchwork of fiefdoms, villages and kingdoms, which the English had tried to dominate since the twelfth century. Even by the sixteenth century the place still wasn't functioning as one, but under Elizabeth I the kingdom first began significantly colonizing abroad, with the likes of Sir Francis Drake returning home with ships filled with stolen silver and gold that helped Britain build up an impressive navy with which to expand the empire.

Explorers: British Men Behaving Badly?

The Portuguese, Spanish and Dutch were already snatching up land all over the place when the British, under the sixteenth century's Virgin Queen Elizabeth I, headed into uncharted waters and entered into the colonization game; the expansion of the empire would continue into the twentieth century. A few of those who uncovered the long-hidden lands:[13]

- Sir John Hawkins (1532–95): Never one to foster diplomatic relations, Hawkins brought Britain into the West Indies slave trade and was the first Brit to systematically loot Spain's treasure-laden ships – acts that soon brought Spain and England to war.
- Sir Francis Drake (1540–96): A pirate and a slave trader (and no surprise, Hawkins' cousin), scallywag Drake could do no wrong by Queen Elizabeth I but was despised by the Spanish for damage to their fleet and treasury; sank the Armada when it sailed into the English Channel in 1588 (legend has it he first finished his game of bowls); was also the first Brit to circumnavigate the globe.

- Sir Walter Raleigh (1554–1618): Poet and romantic – Raleigh, legend has it, tossed his cloak over a puddle that lay in the Virgin Queen's path – he searched in vain for the fabled El Dorado where the rivers flowed gold. Explored the Americas, started a colony on the east coast of the US, hauled spuds and tobacco to Britain, turned into a royal spy, and penned books about his travels as well as world history. Fifteen years after Elizabeth died, King James I had Raleigh beheaded for treason, but the problem may actually have been royal embarrassment over his massacre of a Spanish village while he was searching for the city of gold.

- Captain James Cook (1728–79): Sailed to Tahiti to best observe Venus and calculate the size of the solar system, mapped Antarctica and the northern Australian coast, and died in Hawaii during a skirmish with natives over a stolen canoe. First to feed his crews foods rich with Vitamin C to prevent scurvy.

- Mungo Park (1771–1806): Scot who trekked through West Africa during two expeditions surveying the Niger, his obsession and curse: he contracted tropical diseases, was taken prisoner, and ultimately drowned in the river that he put on the map and vice versa.

- David Livingstone (1813–73): Missionary, physician and early slavery abolitionist who explored nearly a third of the Dark Continent over three decades. After Livingstone disappeared into the heart of Africa, the *New York Herald* sent explorer Henry Stanley to find him, which he did in 1872 after two years of searching, greeting the stranger with the famous line 'Dr Livingstone, I presume?' Even though Stanley brought medicine and supplies, Livingstone died of dysentery the next year: his heart remained buried in the land that he loved, but his corpse was carried 1,000 miles by loyal natives and shipped off to England.

- Sir Richard Burton (1821–90): Military man and spy who sought out secrets in India's souks and bazaars, Burton later explored Arabia, Egypt and Somaliland (searching for the Nile's source) while writing extensively about the exotic Muslim world hitherto unknown to Europeans.

For a nation surrounded by water, the British were slow in hopping into their ships and getting into the colonization race, entering into it mostly in the 1600s – a century later than Portugal and Spain. Their first claims were along the east coast of North America, where they set up colonies from snowy Canada to balmy Florida. From there they delved into the

Caribbean, snatching up most of the small isles, but by the time they reached South America, the Spanish and Portuguese had gobbled up almost everything: the British lassoed but one tiny tract in the north called British Guiana – and they planted the flag in several Central American countries, such as Belize, which they depleted of nearly all of its wood. By the mid 1700s they were busy colonizing whatever they could grab in Asia, including parts of India. Of the colonial holdings, North American colonies, particularly in the south, were among the most valuable. What North America (and India) offered to England was cotton – ships full of the stuff – that was processed with new, clever British technology, such as spinning jennies (invented by James Hargreaves), and steam engines (revolutionized by Scotsman James Watt). Richard Arkwright, considered the father of the modern factory, set up water-powered machines that spun cotton in the 1760s. These new inventions sparked the Industrial Revolution that brought the hordes from their cottages where they had spun by the warm hearth to cities where they sweated in factories and were literally cogs in the machine.

Predictably the inventions weren't always welcome: the inventors, some of whom died penniless, were often chased and attacked by the mobs who saw the vile new machines as taking their jobs.

When the American Revolution brewed up in 1775, Britain had no desire to part with the resources from the colonies. After eight years of fighting, Britain finally backed off, conceded defeat, acknowledged independence and set off to India to set up more cotton plantations there.

The Days of British Expansion

The powerful British navy – the world's most magnificent until the twentieth century when Germany, Japan and the US shoved it aside – was one element in expanding the land holdings of Britain. The need for raw resources and markets to sell goods, however, was just as important a reason to claim farflung corners as their own. What began as a competition with the Spanish and Portuguese over sugar, wood and gold from lands in Central and South America, ultimately took the British into North America, Asia and Africa as well. Revved up under Queen Victoria, the British colonizers touched down on every corner of the globe. By the end of the 1800s the empire's holdings included:

- Canada (now independent, but part of Commonwealth: Queen of England is still head of state)
- Australia and New Zealand (now independent, although Queen of England still head of state)
- Hong Kong (given back to mainland China in 1997)
- Cyprus (independent in 1960), Malta (independent in 1964)
- most of India and what is now Pakistan and Bangladesh (independent in 1947)
- Afghanistan (well, the British claimed to rule the lawless land during the 1800s)
- South Africa, Rhodesia (now Zimbabwe and Zambia), the Gold Coast (now Ghana), Kenya, Sierra Leone, Egypt, Sudan, British Somaliland (now Somaliland, which seceded from Somalia) (all independent in 1960s–70s)
- The Falklands, Belize, Honduras, Bahamas, Gibraltar

The nineteenth-century British military forces were formidable: it was the Brits, under Wellington, who put a stop to Napoleon's grand ambitions at Waterloo in 1815.

In 1837 the 18-year-old Queen Victoria took her place on the throne where she would remain for sixty-four years, a time when over half of the country's residents moved to London or industrial cities like Manchester and Birmingham. No era in British history was more spectacular than the Victorian era of gleaming glass pavilions and engineering marvels, when British society leapt into the future, pulling the rest of Europe along with it. The electric telegraph (invented by Britons William Cooke and Charles Wheatstone) had the impact of a rocket launched into space, so much did it open up new worlds, and Brits made gargantuan efforts stringing cables under the Atlantic and running the singing wire across the vast island of Australia. Just as revolutionary: the steam locomotive (invented by Cornishman Richard Trevithick) that crossed over massive iron bridges, turning journeys that once required days into hours, delivering more hordes of workers to the quickly populating cities, and replacing the barges on canals that had hauled coal to factories that made steel. New lands opened up to the masses with huge steam ships that plied across oceans in two weeks, and explorations into Africa and Asia brought not only more riches, but riveting adventure books: so close at hand (and so intriguing) did the world suddenly seem that it became a fashion statement among wealthy Victorians to display outlines of the new lands as wall-size ornamental map screens.

Charles Darwin (1809–82)

Charles Darwin, heir to the founder of Wedgwood pottery, could have retired to a leisurely life of flitting about collecting butterflies and plucking pansies on the moors. Instead, he triggered the biggest leap in human self-understanding when he published *The Origin of Species by Means of Natural Selection* in 1859. Invited in 1831 as the captain's companion on HMS *Beagle*, which voyaged to South America for five years, Darwin was seasick most of the journey, but threw himself into nature exploration once the ship anchored. Most interesting: the finches and tortoises on the Galapagos Islands off Ecuador, where locals informed him that you could tell which island a tortoise or bird was from by subtle differences in its markings. Back in England, Darwin became intrigued with the idea that species adapted to their surroundings, and that those with the most favourable qualities to that environment were the most likely to survive. Alas, his notes from the islands were scanty, so he borrowed the observations from others onboard,[14] and threw himself into a frenzy of writing and research, ultimately proposing that humans were not of divine origin, as the church instructed, but had evolved from primates. Realizing that his theories would be deeply offensive to the church, he sat on his manuscript for twenty years. He might never have published it, had not a letter arrived in 1858 from a scientist in Asia, Alfred Russell Wallace, laying out almost exactly the same premise as Darwin had in his unpublished book. Honourably, Darwin sent Wallace's paper for publication, but soon thereafter he finally lugged his own dusty manuscript to the printer. Predictably, the church condemned his ideas, but Darwin's book about our ancestors the apes wasn't as controversial as it might have been: his friends published reviews in prestigious journals,[15] and one, Thomas Henry Huxley, launched a lecture series about it. Darwin's ideas also opened the door to eugenics – selective breeding to emphasize positive characteristics – later an intrigue of the Nazis. The man who first peddled eugenics, Sir Francis Galton, was profoundly affected by Darwin, being his cousin.[16]

The nineteenth century wasn't the finest time to be part of the UK if you didn't live in England. In Ireland a million starved to death in the 1840s; in Scotland crofters were pushed off the land in 'The Clearances', and in Wales the earth was laid open to expose the vast veins of coal.

The Victorian era was certainly not an 'equal opportunity' period for all classes and progress was at best uneven. Toilet paper didn't catch on when Joseph Gayetty introduced it in 1857 (the masses preferred using tree leaves),[17] but the flushing toilet began appearing in the homes of the rich around that time – soon necessitating new sewage systems, since London's water company continued, for a few years, to approve the stinking effluent-clogged Thames water as fit to drink.[18]

Although variations of flushing toilets have been uncovered in numerous ancient civilizations (Greek, Roman, Arabic and Egyptian), they were reintroduced in 1596 when a water closet was built for Elizabeth I, although it never had wide popularity. A modern version was unveiled in 1851 for the Great Exhibition of London, and was a smash hit with the visitors; Sir Thomas Crapper introduced numerous improvements in the 1870s that ultimately led to wide acceptance by the masses.[19]

The era was still hazardous, particularly for the poor: cholera raged along with typhoid and assorted deadly flus. Syphilis was a common cause of death and insanity; most commoners still lived in overcrowded, rat-ridden dwellings, and the likes of Jack the Ripper made the night seem much darker even after the streets glowed with gas light, which arrived, thanks to William Murdock, in 1792.

But if parts of London were a scourge, Ireland – the largely undeveloped agricultural land that Great Britain had officially brought into its folds in 1801 – was in a far worse condition in the mid nineteenth century. A million Irish people starved to death over three years of the Potato Famine (1845–7) that turned their tubers into black mush; English landlords drove the weak people, who couldn't pay rent, off their farms. Another million Irish, realizing that their situation would not improve under the English, headed off to America on anything that would float.

England's VIPS, such as the Queen, had other things on their minds than rotting Irish potatoes, among them the Great Exhibition of 1851. Over six million visitors descended upon the Crystal Palace to roam amid statues and past huge fountains, take in life-size displays of dinosaurs and replicas of coal mines, past 13,000 exhibits of looms and harvesting machines, shiny kitchen appliances and exotic plants.[20] The event was heralded as the symbol of the world's most advanced society, although the Britain of that age could scarcely be called the most humane. And no one would epitomize the avarice and cruelty of that era more than Cecil Rhodes, the De Beers diamond magnate who was one of the first to exploit the riches of southern Africa and the people who lived there.

Cecil Rhodes (1853–1902)

Sickly son of the village vicar, Cecil Rhodes as a young man sailed to the warm climes of the Dark Continent where he recuperated from a tubercular condition at his brother's South African farm. He arrived in the middle of a diamond rush, and the young Englishman managed to acquire a hefty portion of the nearby Kimberley mines that held most of the world's most adored sparklers. Wealth, however, wasn't enough, although he had even more when he bought up regional gold mines: Rhodes wanted land, power and British domination of the world. 'I contend that we are the finest race in the world and that the more of the world we inhabit, the better it is for the human race',[21] he wrote in *Confession of Faith*, a book he penned at the age of 24. 'Why should we not form a secret society with but one object, the furtherance of the British Empire and the bringing of the whole world under British rule, [including] the recovery of the United States, making the Anglo-Saxon race but one empire? What a dream, yet it is probable, it is possible.'[22] Though he never succeeded in bringing the whole world under British domination, he certainly brought part of Africa under it, being the de facto founder of three colonies, Nyasaland (today's Malawi) as well as Northern and Southern Rhodesia (today's Zambia and Zimbabwe respectively), which he named after himself and presented to Queen Victoria as a gift. It wasn't just the brutal land acquisition by his paid armies who killed a thousand in his name that made Rhodes such a loathsome figure or even the fact that he caused the nasty Boer War (1899–1902) after a botched raid on (Dutch) Boer lands. It was his treatment of the Africans who lived near his mines that was most appalling, since he turned many of them into imprisoned slaves. The problem was that Rhodes needed thousands of workers for his diamond and gold operations, and most of the locals rejected his low pay: they wanted to keep their day jobs as small farmers living on their land. So Rhodes systematically muscled his way into politics, using bribery and murder to sway any opposition, buying newspapers along the way, and finally buying and bullying his way into the office of prime minister of the British Cape Colony. He then heavily raised taxes for blacks and banned them from owning most of the land they already owned, which he grabbed up for white settlers, effectively forcing the Africans to work in his mines. Not only did they labour for Rhodes, they had to move into heavily policed mining compounds, which they were rarely allowed to leave, even when smallpox epidemics broke out. Oh, but what fun they must have had. According to his live-in companion (Rhodes was rumoured to be gay) Dr Leander Stall Jameson, 'Cecil's favourite Sunday pastime was to go into the De Beers native compound, where he had built them a fine swimming bath, and throw in shillings for the natives to dive for'. (No word on whether he asked for the coins back at the end of the day.) Although Rhodes died of a heart attack in 1902, he left many an enduring legacy, among them the Rhodes Scholarships at Oxford, until recently exclusively for men (usually white) and the De Beers Diamond Company which still hoards most of the world's diamonds and has been charged with anti-trust activities and artificially manipulating the market. The land grabs Rhodes initiated when he was prime minister still have repercussions today: in 2002 Zimbabwe's President Robert Mugabe snatched many of the same lands back – this time taking them from the whites and giving them to the blacks.[23] One more continuing Rhodes ripple: he's now an idol to neo-Nazis.

The nineteenth-century British were typically the most benevolent of colonizers, which, granted, is not saying much. They hooked up communication systems – telegraph wires and undersea cables – built roads, schools and hospitals, introduced new agricultural crops, and planted the seeds for such concepts as parliamentary democracy and theoretical liberty. However, the treatment of indigenous peoples in the colonized lands usually ranged from hideous to heinous, with needless battles, massacres and suppression of cultures to the point of being nearly wiped out. Slavery was often encouraged, wars were purposely whipped up, diseases (inadvertently) introduced, resources were entirely depleted, religion and culture changes were forced upon the locals, certain groups were favoured over others (the British brought the Hindus back into power in India, much to the Muslims' chagrin) and most of the money and riches from the colonies went to the British Treasury or British companies. At their worst, the British imperialists were brutal: textile plants in Madras, India, were burned so India couldn't compete with Manchester's factories; opium was inflicted on the Chinese to even out the balance of trade; the (Dutch and German) Boers in South Africa were marched to the world's first concentration camps where about 20,000 died during the Boer War, which was kicked off by the discovery of gold on Boer property.

Brits in the Sands

No Europeans have more loved the Middle East than the British who began seriously mucking around in the area in the early twentieth century. Like the Dutch and Portuguese, the British had already scrambled into Indonesia, India and Malaya and China's mainland, but the regions known as the 'Near East' and the 'Middle East' – so called because it was Europeans drawing the maps – were most fascinating to the British, the first Westerners (since the tenth-century Vikings and, later, Marco Polo) seriously to explore such areas as Mesopotamia, Persia, Syria and Palestine. Of the three British explorer–spies most associated with the area, two were women, surprising given the cultures that were often openly misogynist (much of Arabia was Wahhabi land) and where no women (besides them) dared travel alone.Gertrude Bell (1868–1926) and Freya Stark (1893–1993) were forced to ride sidesaddle, travel in hats, jackets and long skirts even when crossing the desert at high noon, although both sometimes disguised themselves as men. Both spoke Arabic, Persian and assorted dialects, and both were fellows of London's Royal Geographical Society, which held the world's largest collection of maps and volunteered its services to the military. But there were differences: Freya, who showed up in 1927, was not wealthy, being the daughter of bohemian artists; initially drawn to these exotic lands by a love of their languages, she was at heart a writer, although during the Second World War she spied on the Nazis for the British government. Gertrude Bell was wealthy, brilliant, well educated, and terribly the overachiever. Extremely powerful, holding many government posts, she is credited with literally drawing the doomed boundaries that would become Iraq; it's said that in 1921 she alone convinced Churchill – then Colonial Secretary – to renege on the British promise to make Kurdistan a separate country for Kurds in what is now northern Iraq. The third name most tied up in the area is T. E. Lawrence or rather Lawrence of Arabia, who quite resembled Peter O'Toole who played him in the movie. After promising the Arabian Hashemite clan that they would run the entire Middle East if they fought with him against the Ottoman Turks, Lawrence was quite disillusioned after the First World War when his own government didn't follow through on his promise. Lawrence returned to England where he wrote *Seven Pillars of Wisdom*, and died in a motorcycle accident in 1935. Gertrude, who loudly campaigned against women's suffrage, moved to Egypt, suffered a broken heart and killed herself at the age of 58. Freya continued exploring the region well into her nineties, her love of adventure keeping her alive until the age of 100.

Due to a secret agreement during the First World War, the British and French were given 'mandates' over the Middle East after the Ottoman Empire fell in 1918. They both made a terrible mess of the area, drawing bogus maplines, bringing to power the groups that would favour their interests, and planting the seeds for unrest that still haunts the region today.

With diamonds and gold from South Africa, its tea and spices from the East, and a nasty habit of 'borrowing' treasures such as the Elgin Marbles (elaborate marble friezes taken from Greece), nineteenth-century Britain grew yet more powerful and moneyed.

Revisionist historian Niall Ferguson argues that nineteenth-century Britain actually put far more into her colonies – developing roads and setting up schools and hospitals – than it took out. It is certainly true that of all the colonial powers, Britain treated her colonies better than anyone else.

The twentieth century, however, steamrollered the kingdom's ego back to proper size – and its geographic size would soon shrink as Britain's colonies, following the examples set by the United States before, proclaimed independence. One of the more pressing matters in the new century was Ireland, the predominantly Catholic island to the west, whose problems Britain had long ignored and where starting in the seventeenth century it had been sending Protestant settlers, who weren't accepted by the Catholic Irish and vice versa. Scotland and Wales, like England predominantly Protestant, had finally backed down to English rule, and accepted their fate of being junior parts of the kingdom, but Ireland – at least Catholic Ireland – had no such intentions. The rebellions and secret societies launched after the Great Potato Famine of the 1840s only grew more violent as did acts of terrorism on both sides. By 1921 the British government gave up and accepted Irish home rule, and eventually independence, but with one condition: the six counties in Northern Ireland, where Britain had sent Protestant settlers, would remain under British rule. That arrangement has been a point of bloody contention ever since. (See Ireland.)

The Troubles, as the last territorial battle over Northern Ireland is known, began in 1968, when Catholics, who are a minority group in Northern Ireland, peacefully protested demanding more rights. They were attacked savagely by some Protestant Loyalists who wanted Northern Ireland to remain tied to Britain – which led to angry marches and showdowns between paramilitaries and civilians on both sides. The Catholic, Republican IRA (who wanted Northern Ireland to go back to Ireland) entered the scenario with suitcase bombs, typically targeting the British government, and the fighting escalated until 1998, when the Good Friday Agreement was signed. Giving government representation to both sides – and offering the possibility of Northern Ireland's freedom from Britain if decided on by a vote – the Good Friday Agreement cooled off some of the heat.

There were more nightmares ahead in the twentieth century: namely the two world wars. The First World War (1914–18) was a costly miscalculation: European leaders had thought it would last at most a summer, during which they could take their new fighting machines out for a quick run; instead it dragged on for four gruelling years, during which 750,000 Brits died. The Depression of 1929 hit Britain hard, particularly as the economy was already wobbling after the misguided tweaks of Winston Churchill, then Chancellor of the Exchequer. And then Britain under Prime Minister Neville Chamberlain went weak. Granted, nobody wanted a return to war, and nobody could really afford it. By the 1930s most leaders agreed that the terms inflicted on Germany after the First World War were too tough: the country had gone bankrupt paying war reparations, its cash was worthless, and it had had to take out a huge loan from the United States to keep afloat. Germany's territorial losses, some believed, had been too harsh as well. So when Hitler showed up on the scene in 1933, and soon began talking about taking 'lost' areas with majority German populations back into Germany, it didn't at first sound all that unreasonable, except perhaps to the leaders of the countries he wanted to take back. Austria joined on without a fuss, but when Hitler fixed his gaze on the Sudetenland, the north-western corner of Czechoslovakia, President Edvard Beneš wasn't keen to give it up. Sorry mate, was the message from Chamberlain, seconded by Daladier of France. As the countries that had helped put

Czechoslovakia together, France and Germany had few qualms about taking it apart. In what now looks like quivering appeasement, Chamberlain and Daladier simply forked the Sudetenland over to the Führer, thinking it would placate the man who was widely regarded as a harmless nut. It didn't.

> 'My good friends, for the second time in our history, a British prime minister has returned from Germany bringing peace with honour. I believe it is "peace for our time". Go home and get a nice, quiet sleep' – Neville Chamberlain, 30 September 1938, in Britain upon signing the Munich Agreement that ceded part of Czechoslovakia to Hitler. Nazis invaded the rest of Czechoslovakia within months and Poland in September 1939, kicking off the Second World War.

The Second World War hammered Britain, bleeding it economically, killing 355,000 Britons and subjecting Brits to the daily terror of being pummelled by hundreds of bomb-dropping Nazi planes that sometimes killed thousands before the day was done; during the Battle of Britain – the three months in 1940 when the country suffered the most vicious attacks – over 23,000 civilians died. Like the residents of Malta (then a British colony, where the bombing actually went on for five months straight), the British did not back down: the British Bulldog, as Prime Minister Winston Churchill was known, never seriously entertained the thought of surrender. With the newfangled device of radar (developed by Scottish physicist Alexander Watson-Watt), valiant fighters, and the resonant voice of Churchill calming the masses nightly from the radio, the Brits won the Battle of Britain, being the only European country to fight off a full-blown Nazi attack.

> 'The Battle of Britain is about to begin. Upon this battle depends the survival of Christian civilization. Upon it depends our own British life and the long continuity of our institutions and our empire. Though the fury and might of the enemy must very soon be turned on us, Hitler knows that he will have to break us in this island or lose the war. If we can stand up to him all Europe may be freed, and the life of the world may move forward into broad sunlit uplands . . . Let us, therefore, brace ourselves to our duty and so bear ourselves that if the British Empire and its commonwealth last for a thousand years, men will still say, "This was their finest hour." ' – Winston Churchill, speech in the House of Commons, 18 June 1940

Winston Churchill (1874–1965)

Pasty-faced, homely and prone to long bouts of sheer gloom, Winston Churchill so altered the fate of Britain – and Europe – that some historians regard him as the single most influential person of the past century. Scorned by his wealthy and critical father, jowly Churchill – who rarely strayed far from a fine cigar – was a correspondent for London's *Morning Post* in South Africa during the Boer War (1899–1902), when he was captured: his dramatic escape made for page-turning journalism and turned his byline into a household name. He used his fame to springboard into politics, and during the First World War became First Lord of the Admiralty, a position he was soon stripped of after ordering the landings at Gallipoli in the Dardanelles off Turkey, a fatal mistake that cost over 21,000 British lives and wounded over 52,000 British soldiers. Thereafter he was dubbed 'The Butcher of Gallipoli', and Churchill's career looked like it had but one direction: down. He slunk back into Parliament, and in 1925, after becoming Chancellor of the Exchequer, he brought back the gold standard valuation to back up the pound – another huge error that had British economist John Maynard Keynes ridiculing Churchill's policies and calling them 'feather-brained'. Churchill was right about one thing: the looming threat of the Nazis. In the 1930s Churchill's frequent tirades in the House of Commons about the dangers of Hitler so bored his fellow parliamentarians that they entirely ignored his warnings for years. By the time Britain declared war on Germany in September 1939, however, they were ready to listen and Churchill's foresight was rewarded in 1940, when Chamberlain's government crumbled and the king asked Churchill to form a new one. Appointed prime minister on 10 May 1940, Churchill proved Hitler's strongest psychological enemy and the force that simply would not back down. The prime minister's strength was never his military planning: his fire was in his words, particularly those broadcast in radio addresses to Brits and often heard across the world. His voice might as well have boomed from the heavens: so inspirational and calming were Churchill's self-written speeches heard against a backdrop of whining air raid sirens and exploding bombs that he alone came to symbolize steely defiance against Hitler. While his words helped to steady the British populace, his alignments ultimately helped win the war: the day after Pearl Harbor was bombed on 7 December 1941, he headed out on a ship for America, speaking before Congress on Christmas Eve, and pulling the United States into the European arena, where its forces (along with the USSR's) were instrumental in finally bringing Hitler down. Humiliated in 1945, when even after he'd won the war he lost his office, Churchill nevertheless accurately predicted what the Soviet Union was up to – and he coined the term 'Iron Curtain' in a famous 1946 speech in Missouri. He returned to Number 10 Downing Street in 1951, but that time worked little magic, proving he was a far greater leader in war than in peace. His speeches were not the only words for which Churchill is remembered. For his books, including *A History of the English-Speaking Peoples*, he won the Nobel Prize for literature in 1953.

'[Churchill] made it more than clear . . . that he expected England and the United States to run the world . . . I said bluntly that I thought the notion of Anglo-Saxon superiority inherent in Churchill's approach would be offensive to many of the nations of the world . . . He said why be apologetic about Anglo-Saxon superiority, that we were superior . . .' – Henry Wallace *(journalist and head of the wartime Board of Economic Welfare) writing in his diary about a 22 May 1943 lunch with Churchill*[24]

Like most of Europe, Britain built itself back up with Marshall Plan funding, almost a quarter of which went exclusively to the UK. The country's Victorian-era status and sheen, however, weren't regained for decades, until the 1990s. And part of the progress to getting there – some would say, while others would say it hindered it – were numerous right-wing Tory (Conservative Party) governments including three terms of Margaret Thatcher, the Iron Lady who made a weapon of her will, and her handbag.

Margaret Thatcher (Prime Minister 1979–90)

The grocer's daughter made the leap to Iron Lady during one of the toughest patches of modern British history: the economy in a wreck, the unions striking, and Argentines trying to snatch back the Falklands. She was tough – maybe too tough – on all counts, privatizing state-held companies such as British Telecom, sending in police to break up strikes, sending British troops to the Falklands in 1982, to battle less for the land and more for mineral rights. Nobody ever called Britain's first female prime minister (and first female leader of the Tories) a weak, flaky dame – especially not when she was wielding her handbag – and she was famously friendly with US President Ronald Reagan. She signed Britain up for the Iraq War part I in 1990 and made Britain's biggest arms deal of all times (selling $50 billion worth to the Saudis), but possibly Margaret Thatcher's most controversial move occurred after she had left office and demanded the release of General Augusto Pinochet (accused of human-rights abuses in Chile), saying he'd greatly helped with the Falklands War. The Iron Lady recently suffered a stroke, but still has threatened to return to the podium and speak out against continued membership of the EU. Fifteen years since she stepped down, Thatcher still divides Brits: some say she was the best thing to happen to the UK, the rest say she was the worst.

Quick Tour

So much of Britain is charming, if hard on the wallet, and so often plagued by grey skies and rain, but even on the most insufferable nights there's usually something bitingly good on the telly.

When the Brits do satire, they do so brilliantly, aptly displaying their lightning wit which is often directed at themselves; British news documentaries are the most moving, British news is often the out and out best in the English-speaking world and beyond, despite what Lord Hutton may think.

Food for Show

For centuries, traditional British food could best be defined by three words: greasy, tasteless and beige. Not any more, thanks to a slew of celebrity chefs that come in assorted flavours. The Naked Chef, Jamie Oliver, casts himself as the easy-going, let's-pretend-I'm-an-everyday-bloke, with his hands-on 'Mates, it's easy!' approach as he bangs around and slams drawers while chatting up viewers in faux cockney, known by his critics as 'mockney'. Control freak Gordon Ramsay whips up kitchen nightmares and adds a calculated dash of sadism, humiliating his celebrity guests when they mess up, which they do about every three minutes. 'Domestic goddess' Nigella Lawson prances around in stilettos, tossing back martinis and nipping at wine as she spices up her shows with gossip and infuses her dishes with sensual style, making British women everywhere feel wretched that they too can't juggle being beautiful, brilliant, sexy and a stellar chef. Nigel Slater is the most humdrum of them in both looks and TV style, but nobody is more passionate about food or better captures the sensation of taste in his writing: 'Next door's elderflowers tumble over my garden wall like a spilt glass of cream soda. I steal them at first light . . . then dip the frothy white heads into a light batter of beaten egg whites and flour before frying them in hot oil. Drained and dusted with caster sugar, they are the lightest of Sunday breakfasts, puffing up like deep-fried cumulus.'[25] While many extol the recent culinary leap that has proved that British cuisine extends beyond fish and chips and shepherd's pie – and some claim telly chefs have brought British men into the kitchen – celebrity cooking shows have also had an unexpected effect. Many Britons – perfectly capable of overboiling peas back in the days when that *was* the cuisine – now suffer performance anxiety. According to a report from the University of Reading, more than two-thirds of Brits have stopped throwing dinner parties due to unrealistic expectations.[26]

British TV is not only teaching Brits how to cook, to make a garden, to decorate their house, to buy and sell property. A new programme on Channel 4 called Sex Inspectors *shows them how to copulate. Viewers can actually watch couples going at it and tune into the post-coital reviews by sexologists.*

Yet how lovely is the land when you can see beyond the cleared splash from the windscreen wiper. Country villages ringed by pastures and dotted with lakes, blindingly green hills of Scotland punctuated by cemeteries and golf courses, Northern Ireland's crackling-fire inns downwind from whiskey breweries, and Wales' battered coasts are but a few things that snared tourists long before the Harry Potter craze. The British Tourist Authority is mighty thankful that J. K. Rowling's children's novels brought their country back on to the tourist radar. British tourism in 2001 was devastated by foot-and-mouth and mad cow disease, both of which trampled the economy and resulted in unsightly pyres of flaming cattle corpses. Kids tracing Harry's steps as he learns to fly in magic school have helped to make the UK the sixth most visited country in the world.[27]

Always intrepid travellers – Brits have been writing travel books since around the time paper was invented – they have even more reason to set out for faraway destinations now. EasyJet, Europe's first budget airline, is headquartered here as are a half-dozen other low-cost airlines that shuttle Brits everywhere from Slovenia to Riga. One fine reason to live in London is the ease with which you can get away.

Culture still matters in Britain, where theatre thrives, particularly in London's West End, and where the latest shows at the Tate Modern and displays at the Saatchi gallery still keep jaws flapping.

Charles Saatchi, who with his brother founded one of the world's biggest advertising firms, is patron of the arts for a controversial, terribly modern, bunch. Damien Hirst's works range from overflowing, oversized ashtrays to chunks of dead fish, but the Chapman brothers – Jake and Dinos – typically elicit the loudest rage and disgust. The two fancy buying up rare works – Goyas for example – only to deface them with crude drawings of clowns. Plastic sex dolls dipped in bronze and child-sized mannequins with plastic penis noses are the sort of sculptures that can have one running to Florence for shelter.

In Britain, books are as hot a topic as movies (in some circles, at least) and the Mann Booker Prize for fiction is as coveted as and more influential than America's Pulitzers. But in Britain, too, newspaper leadership is sliding, with Brits reading 10 per cent fewer daily papers than they did in 1990. More alarming, thought-provoking publications such as the *Guardian*, *The Times* and the *Independent* are losing readers to trashy tabloid the *Sun*: with its topless pin-up on page 3, Murdoch's paper claims the highest circulation – nearly 4 million to the 100,000 of the *Guardian* and *The Times*.

***The Times** is read by the people who run the country;*
***The Mirror** is read by the people who think they run the country;*
***The Guardian** is read by the people who think about running the country;*
***The Mail** is read by wives of the people who run the country;*
***The Sun** is read by the people who don't care who runs the country as long as the naked girl on page three is attractive, but who say they actually read it for the sports.*[28] *– Internet observation*

Cn U Rd Ths?: Literacy Matters

In the United Kingdom politicians are often persuasive debaters, whose words and delivery were crafted by years of study at fine institutions. The British media is the world's finest: sharp minds, snappy style and reporters in far-flung corners give it an edge unrivalled anywhere. The education system was historically considered one of the world's best, and such prestigious universities as Oxford and Cambridge add more lustre to the gleaming British reputation of intellectual superiority. British writers are among the world's most popular, with the elegant words of Shakespeare, Dickens, Austen and the Brontës still widely read long after the paper they scribbled on has crumbled to dust. So it was particularly alarming when reports began to emerge that actually Britain has a very high 'functional illiteracy' rate of 24 per cent, meaning that readers have difficulty with basic reading in daily life. It's believed as well that almost a quarter of the population can barely add.[29]

Forty per cent of Britons say they never read books. And overall 13 per cent of Britons say they simply never read anything whatsoever, although the number rises to 19 per cent in the North.[30]

Given a culture that to the rest of the world appears so sophisticated and sensible (at least until they realize most Brits are reading the *Sun* for their news), populated by people who are among the planet's kindest and most polite (except when they are at football matches or on stag holidays), it's hard to imagine encounters more violent than the accidental brushing of umbrellas, followed by ten minutes of red-faced apologies. ('Oh dear me, no, truly it was my fault!') Alas, that image is certainly not always the case, if it was ever the case at all, probably being an image planted by Jane Austen who was making it up even then. Nonetheless, Hugh Grant has taken the image and run with it.

Is Britain a racist society? When the BBC hired a survey firm to put the question to Britons in 2002, over 51 per cent said yes. And 44 per cent said they believed that immigration since 1952 has hurt their country.[31]

Gunning for Trouble

Some say they're coming in from the Jamaican communities, some point to the IRA, some think they're related to drugs and the East European mafia. Whoever is bringing them in, guns are showing up all over Britain and spiking the crime rate. Between 2001 and 2002, reports the BBC, over 22,000 firearm offences were committed in Britain – a jump of almost 30 per cent from the previous year.[32] Handgun ownership was outlawed in 1996, but that apparently didn't make much of a difference. A recent gun amnesty yielded over 40,000 weapons, and that's probably but a drop in the bucket. And while gun crimes are soaring, most bobbies walk around armed with little more than a truncheon.

And, despite their history of being highbrow, more and more Brits seem to care most about two things: football and/or foxhunting, both of which have become national obsessions.

Smells like BNP

Yes, it was hot. Or at least hottish for the UK. That May night in Oldham – a manufacturing town with a large Asian population in the north of England – the temperature was 18 degrees. But was it merely the heat that prompted a fight outside a fish and chip shop between a skinhead and a Pakistani that triggered a night of blazing street fighting? Or did it have something to do with the racist British National Party, which had been canvassing in the north, giving out brochures that (falsely) claimed Asians received preferential treatment and urging followers to fight immigration. Did it have anything to do with the speech BNP leaders had just given in a nearby pub or the rumours they spread that Asians – mostly Pakistanis and Indians – were putting up no-go areas to bar whites? Or was it simply that in these areas long known for segregation a rage has been smouldering for decades? Whatever the exact reasons, Oldham – like the neighbouring town of Burnley six weeks before and nearby Bradford a month later – blew up in violence through the night. Gangs of white hooligans charged into Pakistani neighbourhoods chanting 'If you hate Pakis, clap your hands,' and throwing bricks through windows and into faces. Whites and Asians hurled 700 petrol bombs at each other and at police, looted stores and torched over sixty cars – causing some £10 million (about €15 million) in damages. By daybreak, hundreds had been arrested, dozens injured, and the streets littered with scorched car shells and smashed windows looked like a war zone. Two weeks later the British National Party took 16 per cent of the vote in Oldham – their highest showing ever. Two years later, when a group was sent to prison over the riots, six of them reportedly were followers of the BNP.[33]

The government is getting more sensitive and savvy to the national divide: now reports talk about 'parallel lives' and recommend not simply dismissing anti-immigration protests as 'racist' but opening up honest discussion about multiculturalism. But while official reports may recommend breaking down the racial barriers between neighbourhoods, some estate agents are threatened if they try to find housing for foreign-born people who might bring down the property values for existing homeowners, and lawyers who work with immigrants say they receive death threats and have their offices firebombed.[34]

'Unfortunately, it is often only the extreme rightwing organizations that talk openly about race – and their agenda is divisive and politically motivated. A concerted, co-ordinated national debate [on multiculturalism and race] . . . in our view [is] even more necessary than in 2001' – from government report 'The End of Parallel Lives? The Report of the Community Cohesion Project 2004'

Britain isn't merely divided between black and white, Muslim and Christian, English and Irish, English and Scots, English and Welsh – all divisions that still cause occasional bristling. English society was based on the class system: beyond being simply a case of the upper crust being the educated who didn't need even to be paid for delving into scientific pursuits, while the poor worked long hours in heinous conditions, rarely climbing out of their inherited life station, the English class system is obsessed with details. With one's accent, one conveys one's life story, and how much money might ever be made; which university one attends, the neighbourhood one hails from and the club one belongs to – all these are the social indicators that matter. The class issue, so engrained in Victorian times, still plays out today in debates over public and state schools and the opportunities afforded to attend the country's most prestigious universities, making mobility in British society feel tightly restricted.

The class issue shows up even in football, where the team that one favours can reflect one's rank in society. Of London's six – yes, six – Premier League football clubs, for example, Arsenal appeals more to blue-collar workers, while Chelsea (recently purchased, controversially, by a Russian tycoon) is the choice of the well-heeled Westenders.

Class wars and the multicultural issue rage on, terrorism apparently looms on the horizon, and the government – which recently sent out 'Preparing for Emergencies', a brochure recommending that citizens stock up on tinned goods, bottled water, and batteries in case of a terrorist attack – passed draconian laws that allow detentions without charge and trials by secret courts. Requirements for a national ID card – with biometric indicators and Lord knows what else (tax payments, driving records, IQ and race?) – are bound to be a reality in the near future. Even if all life's stresses legitimize a night out at the pub, Brits have to slam down their drinks at top speed since the pubs close way before midnight, which only fuels the national problem of binge drinking. Plenty of Brits are responding by moving to Florida and Spain once they hit retirement age. Yet for all the problems, Britain still stands out as one of the world's powerful and important nations. The wittiest of all Europeans, Britons are among the globe's finest musicians and writers, and – hallelujah – at least some of them can now cook.

The Swinging Sixties

While Britain had firmly established herself as a literary and drama goldmine several centuries back, it appeared to be lagging in the music department – unless you count the whining of bagpipes and organ music in church – until the 1960s. Who knows what triggered it – Bo Diddley and Elvis or the underground culture of acid and pot – but never in twentieth-century music was there a more happening scene. The Beatles set poetic lyrics to loud guitar and still kept a popular touch. The Kinks added backstreet raspiness and raunch, and the Stones put it into an explicitly sexual style, complete with Mick Jagger humping the mic. Twiggy introduced minis, Carnaby Street and Biba were the places to shop, whether buying Yardley lip gloss or Mary Quant geometric-print clothes. The scene lasted into the 1970s, until drugs and religion, bad relationships and burnout seemed to drag everyone down. But in that era Britain stole the show from Paris – and still hasn't given it back.

Future Forecast

Brits will probably never kiss off their beloved crown but, grumble though they may, are likely to stay put in the EU (with or without the euro), while continuing the debate about whether or not they are really part of Europe.

Hot Spots

London: The land of designer hotels, designer martinis, designer magazines and designers is more multicultural and hopping than ever – well, for a place where the pubs close before you've had a chance to digest dinner. Hub of finances and services, London also has the most vibrant theatre world, art scene, and publishing industry but the costs are alarming. Fifty quid for a taxi to the airport, one hundred for a night on the town, and rents that force middle-agers to share (or stay put with their parents) . . . it's best to have an expense account or a hefty trust fund around here.

The North–South divide: Traditionally, the northern English were the factory workers who viewed the southerners, who were traditionally richer, as a bunch of limp-wristed intellectual softies who'd never had a tough day in their life and were far too obsessed with shopping in Harrods

London's regal Tower Bridge.

and London property prices. Southerners historically viewed the northerners, particularly those in Leeds, Liverpool and Manchester, as stinking, scrounging layabouts who talked strangely and were generally uncouth. Shadows of the historical typecasting linger on, although they've lessened since more money is coming into the North.

Northern Ireland: In the six counties still bound to Britain Loyalist–Republican flareups continue despite the 1998 Good Friday Agreement, but tourists are tiptoeing back in again. With good reason: the place is gorgeous with its rugged coasts, castle ruins and mansions turned into inns. Nevertheless, with the extra costs for police and security to keep the peace, it is a financial burden for Britain. Almost half of Brits want to cut Northern Ireland loose, but any change in its course will be decided by the residents of Northern Ireland in a vote. (*See* Ireland.)

The new problem in Belfast: violence against immigrants is raging here, with recent reports of dozens of Asian and African families being forced from their burning houses or businesses. Some say it's all about protection money, which the IRA reportedly demands, and demonstrations of what happens if you don't pay it. Others blame it on the British National Party, which is reportedly moving into town.

Scotch Whisky v. Irish Whiskey

Connoisseurs and nationalists get very upset should you confuse the best-known drink of Scotland with the version made in Ireland. The easiest way to distinguish which one is which is to note the spelling: if it's 'whisky', it's from Scotland, if it's 'whiskey', it's not. Scotsmen light up when they talk about their whisky: it draws its unique essence from the magic combo of burnt Scottish peat and Scottish water, so pure that you'd think it's an elixir the way they gush about it. 'Whisky', which derives from the Gaelic *uisge beatha*, or 'water of life', is typically made from barley (sometimes rye) dried over a peat fire that imparts a smoky taste, and is often a single malt – meaning it comes from one distillery. Irish whiskey tends to be blended – actually being a cocktail of whiskeys of different distilleries. Peat fires are normally not used in the making of Irish whiskey, and the resultant product is sweeter. Some of the finest Scotch whiskies, say connoisseurs, are Oban, Talisker and Lagavulin. One more mistake you don't want to make: never call a Scotsman 'Scotch'.

Scotland: Salt-sprayed land of kilts, bagpipes and haggis – a sheep's tummy stuffed with oatmeal and a medley of chopped guts – Scotland has its own distinct culture that has survived centuries of English domination. Once a land where Gaelic was the dominant tongue, the country that sits atop England has mostly given up the language, but the thick brogue and feisty spirit live on, despite such nineteenth-century land grabs as the Highland Clearances, when landowners with pipe dreams about creating hunting estates and sprawling sheep farms drove out tens of thousands from villages and farms. With its heather-clad moors and abundant fauna, Scotland is the nature reserve to the north – a land where the posh smoking-jacket crowd head for their deer stalking, salmon fishing and grouse shooting – and where ex-Beatles buy islands. Rich with legends and rituals, the country's most famous event is August's Edinburgh Festival when the streets and every available venue are filled with music, theatre and readings, and on the top of Castle Hill you might take in a freak show. But nothing is more festive than the ceilidh – a social gathering where Scots swirl each other around roaring pinewood fires to the traditional shoe-stamping music of fiddlers and accordion, with skirts swinging high and whisky glasses clinking. Politically, in recent decades there has been a nationalist movement to shake free of England, using money from the oil pumped off the Scottish coast as an economic base. Since 1999, when Scotland was granted its own parliament and more autonomy, the calls for an independent Scotland have receded.

Some British remark that these days heroin has more devotees among the Scots than going to a ceilidh, but perhaps that's just the powerful impression one gets from Trainspotting, *a book and film about despair in a subculture ruled by needles.*

Wales: The setting of Arthurian legend, Wales was formerly the resource storeroom of Britain with coal mines and steel mills – many now closed – and is the most isolated of the British bunch, and the quietest. But lately you can hear plenty of loud mumbling in this land that has its own language (only 20 per cent now speak it), its own church (the Non-conformists who sent the Anglicans packing), and its own history (they're still miffed that the male heir to the throne takes the title 'Prince of Wales'). The problem: sick of urban crime and spiralling house prices (a modest house in a nice area can easily cost upwards of £300,000, or €450,000), many Londoners are moving in. 'They sell their houses in London for a million pounds,' explains one Welshman, 'then come and buy one of ours, making quite a little profit in the move. Then they throw a thousand-pound cheque to the church, and more to the civic boards, and then they're sitting on the school governing bodies and all the boards and running your town.' His claim may be exaggerated, but that's why many Welsh see the movement of Londoners into their turf as another English invasion.

> *Tom Jones was discovered when he was a Welsh coal miner, Shirley Bassey while working in a factory, and Lord knows how many Welsh have to suffer their colleagues' crooning in the hope that they too will hit the big time.*

Sellafield: This sprawling complex in Cumbria is the biggest emitter of radioactivity in Europe and the site is more contaminated with radioactive waste than the ground around Chernobyl. An assemblage of half a dozen reactors, a faulty reprocessing plant, and a stockpile of plutonium, this money-sucking mini-city that employs 7,000 has been previously caught red-handed falsifying reports. Controversial since 1951 when it was opened to provide fuel for nuclear bombs and electricity for towns, Sellafield is now the object of Irish and Norwegian protests demanding that the facility be entirely shut down; the Norwegian government filed a lawsuit when radioactive crabs, lobsters and seaweed along Norway's shores were traced here. Nobody knows what to do with the untidy bundle of nuclear waste that seeps into the ground and drifts into water and air, resulting in a radioactive-toxic mess that travels as far as the Arctic and Barents Sea.[35]

House of Commons v. House of Lords

The (Lower) House of Commons, whose parties are voted in by the public, is the more powerful of the two houses in the British Parliament. The (Upper) House of Lords is a throwback to the sixteenth century and consists of 634 lords (aka peers) who inherited the position or, more commonly these days, were appointed by the prime minister. The House of Commons gets rowdy with plenty of loudly expressed dissent or approval. The House of Lords is more formal: they go through silly rituals, and are set up mostly to provide a check on the House of Commons – they can veto legislation – than to initiate anything; there's increasing pressure to drop the hereditary positions altogether.

> The uppercrust bunch kept chasing away measures to ban the fox hunt, vetoing the House of Commons' bills whenever the pesky things showed up here, but in November 2004, the Commons overturned the Lords and finally passed a fox-hunting ban. This house is a better forum for debate, where matters do tend to get more properly discussed, but it doesn't have teeth.

National Health Service: A great idea back when it was launched in 1946, Britain's socialized health care has become so substandard now that anybody who can is paying for private insurance and taking their health woes to the private sector.

UN Security Council: Britain, along with France, the US, China and Russia, is one of the five permanent members of this United Nations body that is the one that can approve international war actions, impose sanctions and demand action of countries. As with the other four permanent members, Britain has veto power which can knock proposals off the table.

Not only does Greece want the Elgin Marbles back, India is clamouring for the Koh-i-Noor diamond, which was ceded to Queen Victoria in 1849.

Falkland Islands: Argentina says the islands are theirs –and the Falklands are certainly closer to that country than the UK – but the Brits just won't give them up. The underlying reason (so to speak): the UK is exploring for oil there. With Britain's North Sea oil drying up, and the country facing the prospect of importing most of its petrol, Prime Minister Thatcher ordered the military to snatch back the islands when Argentina's junta tried to seize them in 1982: she was so determined not to lose the archipelago that she reportedly even sent over ships loaded with nuclear missiles.

Anywhere the British drew a boundary: As colonizers (during the nineteenth century the sun never set on the British empire which included land on all continents) and as babysitters (holding on to much of the Middle East after the First World War) the Brits appeared to be drawing their maplines with poison pens. Nearly every boundary that a British hand drew is now the site of major ethnic tensions and chronic problems. A few examples: Palestine, India/Pakistan, Iraq/Kuwait, Iraq/Iran, Somalia, South Africa, Zimbabwe.

Mosques: Some 1,500 of them across the UK, with Finsbury Park historically the most radical.

Trains: Everybody complained when the train companies were privatized, but the British have cause for legal complaints as well as fear. Hundreds have died in train crashes in recent years – and one pays a premium price to ride on the danger rails. A return ticket from London to the countryside an hour away can cost £65 (€100) and up.

The surprise find of North Sea oil in the 1970s was a boon, but it is running low. Now some are looking to the gusty sea for a new energy source: wind power.

Loch Ness: You know *what* they are looking for – the dragon-serpent known as Nessie that a few people may have captured in a photo with her head coming out of the loch some decades ago, even though the photos are largely dismissed as fakes. The question is *why* have so many people become so obsessed with the creature that they've moved to the Scottish loch and devoted their lives to looking for her, when there are so many more worthwhile pursuits, such as trying to communicate with extra-terrestrials. (*See* Sweden.)

Hot Shots

Tony Blair: Prime Minister since 1997, heading the 'New Labour' Party, slick Tony is an Oxford-trained barrister whose courtroom abilities have translated well to the Commons where he wows with his speeches. Self-assured and a bit cocky, he is brainy and eloquent, though one never knows whether to fully believe the words he weaves together so artfully: he promised that pubs would stay open longer than 11 p.m. if he was re-elected, yet he has dragged his feet on that revolutionary idea; he exaggerated Iraq WMD capabilities in his famous '45 minutes' speech, and he apparently told a big fib when he promised Chancellor Gordon Brown he wouldn't pursue a third term. Still popular (although now some Brits call him Tony Bliar), the Bible never strays far from his bed – he believes that all the world's questions can be answered in its pages – he is bringing a distinctly religious flavour to Whitehall with a new 'persuasion committee' that has been asked to lobby lawmakers. Blair is a modern man too: he took paternity leave in 2000 after the birth of Leo, his fourth child.

Tony – as he prefers to be called by the masses – has backed President George W. Bush on almost everything except the latter's tariff on

Former talk-show host Kilroy-Silk
wants to march UK out of EU.

*imported steel. His apparent fondness for Bush resulted in his detrac-
tors branding him a poodle, and he was spoofed in a 2002 George
Michael animated video, showing President Bush tossing a compliant
dog a bone, and Blair continually retrieving it. May have redeemed
himself when he landed a part in a 2004 episode of* The Simpsons.

Lady Diana (1961–97)

It was a little too chocolate-box to have been true, cynics said from the start. On
29 July 1981 Prince Charles, 32, and Lady Di, a blushing 20-year-old former
kindergarten teacher and daughter of an earl, captured the collective heart of
dreamy romantics everywhere with their fairytale wedding: Di looked smashing
in ivory taffeta and antique lace, her 25-foot train trailing down the aisle of
St Paul's; Charles looked regally sombre with his decorated chest dripping with
shiny medals, while 3,500 invited guests and some 750 million viewers across
the world toasted the royal matrimony that finally brought youth and modern
style into the castle. The union quickly produced two handsome male heirs –
William and Harry – and the occasional peep into the royal world that appeared

less than idyllic. Charles was distant and boring, Di was bulimic and lonely, Queen Elizabeth was as cold as a medieval stone castle on a stormy December night. The divorce that gossips had long before predicted became reality in 1996: Charles suffered a drop in popularity as a result and Di publicly embraced worthy causes such as landmine removal, and privately embraced a few men who raised royal eyebrows. Her final beau Dodi Fayed – son of Harrods owner Mohamed Fayed – died alongside her one night in late August 1997 when the Mercedes S280 they were in spun out of control in a Paris tunnel. The death was blamed on the intoxicated state of driver Henri Paul, but there have been plenty of rumours otherwise: Mohamed Fayed is but one who says the couple was murdered, and conspiracy theorists have put forth the reason as being that Di was pregnant. In 2004 the British government announced it would open an investigation into the 1997 death of Lady Di, who feared that Prince Charles was going to have her killed.

Gordon Brown: Chancellor of the Exchequer (powerful finance minister), 1997 to present. 'Beep, beep, Tony, outta my way!' he seems to be saying, sometimes subtly and sometimes not. The Scotsman, who heads the country's treasury department and is quick to point out what a fine job he's done (and largely, he has), has his eyes on Britain's highest power seat – and it's not the first time he's gazed at it: in 1994 Brown dropped plans to put his name in the hat for the Labour leadership, after Blair promised he would leave the post on turning 50.[36] Apparently the prime minister hasn't seen a calendar: his half-century birthday was celebrated in May 2003. Lacking Blair's charisma, Brown is deemed more trustworthy than the PM in opinion polls, and he loathes the idea of adopting the euro, as do many Brits. Beep, beep, Tony, beep, beep.

Jack Straw: Secretary of State for Foreign and Commonwealth Affairs, 2001 to present; Home Secretary 1997–2001. Remember that kid who sat in the front row frantically waving his hand saying, 'I know the answer!' And when the teacher called on him, he said, 'Oops, I just forgot.' That's former barrister Jack Straw, the well-meaning but bumbling foreign minister who plays the dork to Tony's Mr Slick. Oddly, just when you're about to laugh off the man who often sits behind the prime minister during televised speeches, nodding his head in literal 'yes man' agreement, Straw can surprise you – with a well-written, well-argued piece in the *Economist* about the proposed constitution perhaps, or a candid admission that British colonial history and poorly conceived boundaries set the framework for today's geopolitical problems.

> ***That's Sir to you:*** *Every so often British monarchs do look down and recognize the immense talent in the kingdom. A few who have knelt before Her Royal Highness to be knighted: Sir Roger Moore, Sir Steve Redgrave, Sir Ian McKellen, Sir Elton John, Sir Paul McCartney, Sir Terence Conran, Sir Richard Branson, Sir Mick Jagger, Sir Bob Geldof and Dame Judi Dench. There have been a few questionable calls, among them Romania's late dictator (Sir) Nicolae Ceauşescu.*

> *We all know the United States is the biggest arms dealer on the planet, but Britain is number 2, selling about €7 billion a year. Britain, along with France, is one of the two EU countries with nuclear weapons.*

Queen Elizabeth II (b. 1926): Reigning monarch since 1952 and winner of the royal big hat award, she throws the occasional rocking jubilee but has kept very mum about the assorted scandals that have hit since the marriage between Di and Charles went down the tube, except to describe the airing of the royal household's laundry in 1992 as 'an Annus Horribilis'.

Prince Charles (b. 1948): Heir Apparent, His Royal Highness Prince Charles Philip Arthur George, Prince of Wales and Earl of Chester, Duke of Cornwall, Duke of Rothesay, Earl of Carrick, Baron of Renfrew, Lord of the Isles, Great Steward of Scotland, and Knight of the Garter is beginning to look a bit tired (it must be exhausting just remembering his title) and perhaps his regalia just doesn't shine as brilliantly as it once did. But while patiently waiting for his chance on the throne, he busies himself writing articles and letters to Parliament with suggestions and now has a new hobby: organic food. Charles is behind the 1,100-acre organic farm at one of his estates, and the selling of the chem-free greens under the label Duchy Originals, with its tens of millions in profits going to non-profit organizations.[37] No wonder they invite him to head so many – 200 at the last count.

Prince William (b. 1982): Handsome elder son of Charles and Di – his mother nicknamed him DDG for 'drop dead gorgeous' – William likes to cook, it's said, but probably won't indulge in his father's habit of donning kilts for public affairs. 'It's a bit draughty,' he explained to *Vanity Fair*. One might not think he'd mind the breeze: he's been known to show the 'full monty' at parties while strutting to seventies hit 'YMCA'. Some object to the nudity, others to the song. May someday steal the throne from his father – well, at least, if it was put to public vote.[38]

Prince Harry (b. 1984): The young'un has a wild look in his eyes, is a demon on the polo field, and had a little 'cannabis incident' when he was in boarding school. Caused a furore when he showed up at a 2005 costume bash in Nazi uniform. Soon apologized (via publicist), Charles demanded he take a tour of Auschwitz.

Camilla Parker Bowles, Duchess of Cornwall (b. 1947). The stars uncrossed in 2005, when Prince Charles wed long-time lover Camilla. The couple was forced to repent publicly for their previous adultery, and the wedding might cost Charles the crown, but the prince never looked happier. The marriage was met with lukewarm response by the tight-lipped British public, mildly appeased that, should Charles ascend, Camilla won't be queen, but Princess Consort.

The Beeb

The British Broadcasting Corporation (BBC), funded by television licensing fees, sent out its first broadcast in 1922: the news, read by Arthur Burrows. If for years it was rather dull, but thorough, in recent decades it has entered a new realm with much of the edgiest comedy – *Absolutely Fabulous* (about two wine-swilling, coke-snorting career women) to *The Office* (about a megalomaniac but lonely office manager) – the hardest-hitting documentaries (about the genocide in Rwanda and the racism and violent acts of the British National Party) and the widest coverage of world news. The BBC was rapped in 2004 for broadcasts concerning Tony Blair's allegation that Iraq could unleash WMD within 45 minutes – a claim that according to the BBC had been 'sexed up'. The apparent source of the info was arms inspector David Kelly who, shortly after being called before a parliamentary investigation committee, killed himself. The Hutton inquiry criticized the BBC for shoddy reporting methods – and the slam came at a most critical time: just as the BBC was awaiting government renewal of its charter to continue broadcasting for the next ten years. It got the green light nevertheless.

Posh and Becks: reigning celebrity couple. Take a dashing footballer (David Beckham), one of the world's best, and hook him up with a luscious sexpot (Posh Spice) of pop-music fame, and what do you have: too much ink wasted on trivial matters such as what Posh packed on her trip to Madrid and with whom Becks slept last week. Apparently, however, plenty care, even though these two celebs make Madonna and hubby seem quite deep and contemplative in comparison.

Peter Mandelson: European Commissioner, 2004 to present. A most controversial appointee, Pete is Tony's good mate – and the spin doctor behind Labour's rise in the 1990s. But he screwed up twice before – once when he didn't disclose a large loan from another minister, which resulted in his resignation, and then, when Northern Ireland secretary, he was accused of bending the rules over passport applications for overseas Labour Party donors, and was again asked to leave his post. Will the third time be a charm? Doubt it.

Sir Alexander Fleming: The British biologist who discovered penicillin saved millions of lives and ended the fatal effects of syphilis.

The Tories: Losing ground and face, the Conservative Party which dominated British postwar politics is a weakling today. Even after they stuck new heads on the leadership spears they emerged with the less than mighty Michael Howard, who has been described as 'having something of the night about him'. Or perhaps they meant 'Something of the knight about him'? In either case, he's likely to restrategize the party platform – and make leaving the EU its main plank.

Anti-Nazi League: Certainly there's a need for this watchdog group, but they can get the crowd as hot and bothered as the racists they're trying to fight.

Countryside Alliance: Wealthy, powerful and conservative leaning – many are Tories – the Countryside Alliance, which has some 100,000 members, was formed in 1998 'to campaign for the countryside, country sports and the rural way of life'. In the name of preserving the right to hunt the fox, some 200,000 have marched, thousands have hounded politicians, and the group sends out private investigators to dig up dirt on opponents. In 2004, the fox hunt, controversial for over a century, became a matter of shrieks and howls: in September, when the lower house of Parliament – after hearing some 700 hours of debate on the topic – was going in for the kill and set to outlaw all hunts that use dogs, over 1,000 Alliance members rabidly demonstrated outside – and five stormed into the parliamentary chicken coop: the House of Commons. The Commons voted for the ban; predictably, the House of Lords shot it down, but they were outfoxed as the Commons invoked the 1949 Parliament Act, which allows the lower house to ignore the upper house and pass legislation on its own. The hunting ban came into effect in February 2005: the Alliance is taking the matter to the courts, and threatened to ignore the law and disrupt the general election in May.

One of the Alliance's most fervent supporters is Otis Ferry, son of pop crooner Bryan Ferry.

Animal Rights Activists: Some hardcore types are calling upon their followers to kill heads of research centres which test on animals.

Ken Livingstone: Mayor of London 2000 to present. Love him or hate him, rebel mayor Ken Livingstone stands out: his controversial 2003 'congestion charge' reduced traffic in parts of the capital by 15 per cent; he marched in protests against the Iraq War and he called George W. Bush 'the greatest threat to life on the planet' – hours before the President rolled into town. Named 2003 'Politician of the Year' by the Political Studies Association, Livingstone has been re-admitted to the Labour Party after being expelled for standing as an independent in the 2000 mayoral elections: party leaders made sure he wasn't chosen as the Labour candidate because of his leftist politics, whereupon he trounced Labour in the poll. Having seriously misjudged the mood of the capital's population, and with the prospect of Labour losing again in 2004, Labour brought Ken back into its fold: he was subsequently re-elected – by a much narrower margin.

Media stars: *Guardian* (www.Guardian.co.uk), *Economist* (www.economist.com), BBC (www.news.bbc.co.uk). Top-rate reporting, clever writing and broad scope: take a bow.

4. Italy (Italia): Fractured Beauty

Fast Facts

Country:	Italian Republic; Repubblica Italiana
Capital:	Rome
Government:	republic
Independence:	1871 (unification completed); 1946 king abdicated, republic born
Population:	58,058,000 (2004 estimate)
Leaders:	Head of State: President Carlo Azeglio Ciampi (1999)
	Head of Government: Prime Minister Silvio Berlusconi (2001)
Elections:	President elected by assembly of delegates for 7-year term
	Prime Minister appointed by President
Name of Parliament:	Senato della Repubblica
Ethnicity:	Italian
Religion:	Roman Catholic
Language:	Italian
Literacy:	98% (this statistic is questionable)
Exports:	engineering products, textiles, clothes, cars
Per capita GDP:	$26,700 (2003 estimate)
Unemployment:	8.5% (January 2004 Eurostat figure); the south has an estimated 20% or higher unemployment rate
EU status:	founding member
Currency:	euro
Known for:	Michelangelo, Leonardo da Vinci, pasta

Standout Qualities

Food: Pizza, pasta and pesto
Drink: World's largest producer of wine
Amore: Drunk with love (mostly of mama)

Résumé

Apparently the court jester of Europe, Italy is just hard to take seriously: known for switching sides mid-war, Italia is a country where leaders rarely last a year, porn stars are thrust into the senate and corruption courses through its veins like a vital nutrient. The land custom-made for a holiday poster – gliding gondolas, Roman ruins, Tuscan villas and fab food all rolled into one – isn't as light-hearted as it appears, however, especially lately. Prime Minister Silvio Berlusconi, Italy's longest-running leader since the Second World War, is a dangerous clown, the country's approach to unwanted refugees is medieval, and the land that holds many of history's architectural treasures is the target of increasingly scary terrorist threats. And let us not forget the ever-present Mafia – whose activities have been even more frightening lately.

> *'Either you dump the incompetent Berlusconi or we will really burn Italy. We are in Italy. None of you is safe'*[1] *– a message signed by the Abu Hafs al-Masri brigade in August 2004, the seventeenth in six weeks. A previous message had suggested that Muslims 'should store food for a month and make arrangements to protect themselves'. While most of the West is receiving threats, the fact that Italian police in 2002 arrested Islamic radicals who were about to poison Rome's water system only makes the threats here seem more real.*

Berlusconi – a flamboyant billionaire who owns or controls most of Italy's national TV, major magazines and book-publishing houses, an advertising agency, a newspaper and the AC Milan football team – is conflict of interest personified: the prime minister sacks journalists who criticize his laughable political performance and ensures that his many bloomers are downplayed, while his TV stations distort his impact, showing him talking to cheering crowds in auditoriums filled to the brim, when in fact he's droning on in a half-empty room.[2]

Berlusconi stands accused on several charges of corruption, including bribing judges in the 1980s to allow him to buy out a supermarket chain.

Most of the laws he has passed are in his own self-interest, including the one that granted him immunity from legal prosecution while in office (not to mention the one that made cooking financial books legal), and even the UN condemned his rants about Italy's 'mentally deranged' judicial system: his hatred of Italy's judiciary was keenly illustrated when he tried to do away with bodyguards for judges – necessary in Italy's Mafia-ridden society – effectively signing their death warrants. Even though 70 per cent of Italians opposed it, he signed Italy up in loud support of the 2003 invasion of Iraq. He sent some 3,000 troops for the postwar clean-up; he apparently paid for that and the deaths of eighteen Italians in a November 2003 Iraqi suicide bombing with a popularity plunge in the June 2004 European Parliament elections, which saw his party take only 20 per cent (down 5 per cent from 1999). But Berlusconi is best known as the prime minister whose foot more often resides in his mouth than in his shoe. A trademark of his entire reign, Berlusconi's shall we say 'lack of diplomatic finesse' was at no time more appalling than when he opened Italy's six-month EU presidency in July 2003: the very first day he likened a German MEP to a Nazi. His tourism minister, Stefano Stefani, didn't help Italy's image further when he subsequently referred to Germans as 'super-nationalistic blond louts who invade Italy's beaches', apparently forgetting that they pump billions into Italy's tourism industry.[3]

A Few Berlusconisms

- 'In Italy, they are making a movie on Nazi concentration camps. I will propose you for the role of capo'[4] – Berlusconi to German MEP Martin Schulz in July 2003. Schulz was questioning Berlusconi on his passage of a bill that made the prime minister immune to legal charges while in office.
- 'We should be conscious of the superiority of our civilization . . . [that] guarantees respect for human rights and religion. This respect certainly does not exist in the Islamic countries' – Berlusconi in September 2001, commenting on September 11 attacks.[5]
- 'Mussolini never killed anyone. Mussolini used to send people on vacation in internal exile.'[6]
- 'All citizens are equal before the law . . . [but] some citizens are more equal than others.'[7]
- 'For gathering corpses, pedalos are fine. I don't believe there were any complaints' – Berlusconi on why pedal boats were used to retrieve the bodies of drowned refugees off the Italian coast.[8]

Never mind that the whole country goes on vacation for the month of August, Berlusconi couldn't wait. He took a month off during the 2004 work year for a facelift.

Meanwhile, Italy has some serious problems to contend with. Among the most pressing: the boats of dead and dying refugees that keep showing up on Italian shores. Given its 2,500 miles of coast and location mid-Mediterranean, the country draws hundreds of thousands of Albanians and Africans, and Italy now lets very few of them in legally; the 20,000 or more *clandestini* who do slip into the country each year typically can't find a job, and must make do prostituting themselves, pushing drugs, stealing or selling toys in squares and fleeing at the sight of police. Given the thousands of ships and rafts of wannabe immigrants in Italian waters every year – one report estimates that two million would-be immigrants will soon be heading towards the peninsula – the problem is not going away. But Berlusconi's government has not made a serious effort to address it, except giving the Italian coastguard and navy the legal power to force vessels to turn back before they reach port. One prominent member of the governing coalition, Umberto Bossi, suggested that Italy deal with the issue simply by sinking any ships filled with would-be immigrants that come near.

> *'I want to hear the roar of the cannon. The immigrants must be hunted down . . . At the second or third warning – boom! Fire the cannons at them. Otherwise this will never stop' – Umberto Bossi, former reform minister in Berlusconi's ruling coalition.*[9,10] *Bossi, of the anti-immigrant Northern League, is known for his anti-immigration slogan 'more polenta, less couscous!'*

The country that was so sick of widespread corruption that it launched the *Mani Puliti* ('clean hands') movement in 1992 – with over 2,000 politicians, government employees and businessmen indicted and over 600 found guilty[11] – just doesn't seem any cleaner now with Berlusconi directing the show; besides, most of the politicians ejected in the clear-up have served their time, paid their fines and are back. The man who was a former lounge singer on cruise ships – he still loves to croon for his friends – has split an already economically and politically divided Italy even more: some see him as the self-made tycoon who has boosted Italy's image in the international arena with unwavering support of President George Bush, and who can still save the economy. Others are hitting the streets to protest – millions demonstrated against his support of Iraq, and another 200,000 marched against the law he signed letting himself off the legal hook. But plenty believe that even though Berlusconi is a buffoon, among current politicians nobody would be an improvement, a sad thought indeed.

In January 2004 an Italian court threw out the law that shielded Berlusconi from being tried while in office but as of September 2004, the status of the law was being debated by a panel of judges.

Berlusconi's coalition, at four years Italy's longest-lasting government since the war, began weakening in 2004, when Lega Nord leader Bossi quit, and finance minister Giulio Tremonti walked out. Somehow the PM won yet another vote of no confidence. Among those who wouldn't mind making a grab for the premiership seat: Giancarlo Fini of the neo-fascist party National Alliance, which is Berlusconi's main coalition partner. Former prime minister Romano Prodi, the recent ex-president of the European Commission obviously wants his old seat back, and his Olive Branch Coalition did well in 2004, taking twenty-five seats in the European Parliament to Berlusconi's Forza Italia's sixteen. Another possible contender: Alessandra Mussolini, granddaughter of *il Duce* and now an MEP in Brussels. Just another colourful character in Italy's Technicolor political cast, Mussolini is one of the few women in Italy's political arena, and unlike *La Cicciolina*, the Hungarian-born blonde bimbette porn star who sat in parliament from 1987 to 1992 and loved to whip up her shirt, Mussolini proves you don't have to bare all in porn movies to make it as a woman in Italian politics. Mussolini merely bared all as a *Playboy* centrefold.

Italy has had fifty-nine governments since 1945, and over three dozen political parties vie for power.

Although the self-made Berlusconi was voted into office in 2001 with the promise that he would exert the same golden touch on Italy's economy as he had on his personal empire, the world's fifth largest industrial economy is merely limping along: the unemployment rate is near 9 per cent, industry is not competitive, government and business alike are riddled with charges of fraud and corruption and the country's biggest corporation, the milk empire Parmalat, is mired in charges of fraud. Crime is rising, the immigration issue continues and the country is so divided in incomes and opinions that some have suggested politically sawing it apart. The land that led the Renaissance now funnels its creativity mostly into design, writing and cars, but its creative ability to solve problems is sorely lacking. Nevertheless *bella Italia* is beloved: for its food, its culture, its enduring Roman architecture and Renaissance art, not to mention its flirtatious men who are frequently mistaken for angels by those who don't speak Italian and don't know what the li'l angels are saying.

Vocabulary Builder

Three of the most important and popular phrases in melodic Italian start with 'va' which means 'it goes'.
Va bene: All goes well!
Va via: Go away!
Va fa culo: Up yours!

History Review

The chunk of strategic real estate dangling into the Mediterranean was much coveted land that frequently changed hands over the past two millennia. Until the nineteenth century the ancient Romans were the only force to unite the land, which for the 1,500 years that followed was a disunited mess; the mismatched patchwork of its history explains why it's so fragmented now.

Plenty of people had previously lived on this peninsula that kicks out into the Mediterranean – ancient Greeks being among the first to settle on the shores of what today is Italy – but the group that most put their stamp on the area were the toga-wearing, wine-swilling Romans. It wasn't just their poets and historians or their architectural skills that made them hugely important. Nor was it their fighting ability and expansionist nature per se. The most enduring legacy that the Romans left not only to Italy but all of Europe was their stone roads that for the first time connected much of the Continent as one: that all roads lead to Rome underscores not only the cohesion of the society, but the historical fact that they gave the first paved transit ways. Countries left out of the Romans' developmental loop – Ireland, for example – were left out of the European loop for centuries.

At its height, the Roman Empire stretched from England to North Africa, Portugal to Yemen, bringing much of Western Europe, the Balkans and Turkey into its territorial expanse.

Some historians sniff that the Romans weren't as great as the Greeks, merely being history's thieves – conquering ancient Greek colonies, kidnapping the culture, giving it a few twists (such as new names to Greek gods) and calling it their own. While indeed carrying on with many Greek ideas, designs and political practices, the Romans went further, both in the practices they introduced – building aqueducts and arches and constructing with cement, for example – and in the areas they conquered. Greeks were shoreline developers who relied on their ships; Romans went further inland with their marching armies.[12]

Romans established Latin as a unifying language, introduced engineering marvels from central heating to water distribution to cities, and followed social practices from public baths to drunken orgies and tossing your enemies to the lions. They advanced military organization, legal systems, urban planning and government administration. Although early Romans were polytheists – worshipping Venus and Jupiter, Bacchus and Mars – the late empire under Constantine turned Christian, leading to another of Rome's legacies: connecting Europe by Christianity. And the Romans brought real-life drama to a new height: it's amazing they could get anything done with the soap operas they were living.

Julius and Other Caesars

Julius Caesar (c. 100–44 BCE): Said to have been a Caesarian birth, this dictator-for-life started the takeover of the Greek empire, had mad fling with Cleopatra, killed in Senate by Brutus.

Augustus (63 BCE–14 CE): The first of the emperors per se.

Tiberius (42 BCE–37 CE): So paranoid that he had most of the powerful men around him assassinated, leaving only his nephew Caligula to inherit the empire; bad choice as Caligula may have been the one who killed him.

Caligula (12–41 CE): Nuttier than the rest put together, and one of the cruellest, torture and incest fan Caligula once sent his military to attack England, then changed his mind and sent them to pluck sea shells on the French seashore instead.[13] He is said to have made a legal adviser and senator of his beloved horse.

Claudius (10 BCE–54 CE): The lame stutterer, regarded by his family as daft, made it to emperor simply because he was viewed as not threatening. Went through the wives, and had his third one killed after she had an affair. Then married his niece, who poisoned him with mushrooms.

Nero (37–68 CE): Killed his mother and hated by his people, his rule was

plagued with corruption and debauchery; Rome burned down under his rule
– he was possibly the arsonist.

Hadrian (76–138 CE): Expanded the empire to its furthest reaches, notably
constructing a defensive wall in Britain.

The Romans were also fine historians, writers and poets: much modern
knowledge of the era comes from the writings of Livy, Ovid, Horace,
Suetonius and Virgil, but nature helped capture the times as well. The
explosion of Mount Vesuvius preserved the life and people of Pompeii
when it blew in 79 CE. Those who hadn't left upon seeing the first plumes
of smoke hours before were killed in a surge of heat, lava and gases, their
last acts preserved in a coating of volcanic ash that caught them huddled
together in a barn, taking a final sip from a glass or running down a street
clutching a lantern as they tried to escape the eruption that brought
sudden darkness to the afternoon sky.

The Roman Empire was split into western and eastern parts, after Constantine I (272–337 CE) founded a new eastern capital in 295. Despite the
catchy name he gave it – New Rome – it was dubbed Constantinople after
him; now called Istanbul, Constantinople soon would become the great
centre of the eastern (Byzantine) empire, while Rome would continue as
the power seat in the west. Constantine greatly affected that city as well:
after he had a vision of a flaming cross in the night sky – a sight which
drove him to accept Christianity – he donated a palace to the bishop of
Rome, who would henceforth become increasingly powerful as the leader
of the Catholic church, better known these days as the pope. More importantly, Constantine was the first Roman emperor to promote Christianity,
and hereafter most Roman settlement would be Christian – another link
that would form the foundation of modern Europe.

> *The almighty power of the Roman pope came into question on several
> occasions. In 1054 the Archbishop of Constantinople broke with the
> Roman Catholic Church, creating what would become the (Greek)
> Eastern Orthodox Church. In 1378 the Archbishop of Avignon also
> rebelled, and for thirty-nine years the world had two popes – or one
> pope and an antipope (as he was called in Rome) in Avignon.*

Although the empire limped on until 476, the fire was pretty much out by
the third century when Vandals, Visigoths and other ruffians swooped in

and took over Roman territories. And for the next 1400 years the Italian peninsula was a geographical free-for-all: Sicily and Naples (together confusingly known as the Kingdom of the Two Sicilies) were run at assorted times by Arabs and Spanish; Rome and territories to the east were Papal States, the north was a medley of Austrian and German territories; even the French staked out land at points in Italy's chequered history.

The most powerful city states were all in the north, the mightiest and most advanced for centuries being Venice. Lying at the geographical divide between West and East, and initially part of the Byzantine empire from which it shook loose in the eighth century, the city of canals was a major trading centre where Arabs sold off the spices they had hauled from the East, the architecture was a blend of Arabic and Roman, and the artistic and aristocratic society was enlightened, and known for such arts as lace-making and glass-blowing. More importantly, Venice – ruled by doges or dukes – had remarkable naval prowess, and besides extensive lands in the north, it eventually controlled the coastal territories all along the Adriatic (including today's Croatia, Slovenia and Dalmatian Islands) and the Aegean island of Crete. Known for its riches – it was the wealthiest Italian city-state and one of the most splendid kingdoms in all of Europe – Venice, land of courtesans, scholars, explorers and palaces, was a magnet for royalty and the rich from across the Continent, and such VIPs as the Medicis came here to relax whenever they'd been kicked out of Florence, which was often. Noted even earlier for its scribes, in the fifteenth century it was the publishing centre for this part of the world, including for music.

Marco Polo (1254–1324)

No name is more entwined with Venice than that of Marco Polo, the son of an affluent merchant who travelled the Silk Road into the Far East. After one journey, Marco's father and uncle returned bearing a letter from Mongolian leader Kublai Khan requesting that the Pope send him 100 Christian educators who could teach of life in the West, but they had a difficult time lining up 100 wise men, especially those who wanted to spend years in such a faraway place. The Polos instead returned several years later bearing extravagant gifts – the lamp oil of Jerusalem's Church of the Holy Sepulchre was one – as well as a letter of introduction from the Pope, and young Marco Polo. Trekking across today's

Persia, Afghanistan, the Himalayas and China, young Polo jotted down notes of the sights and the stories – stones that burst into flames, pavilions with streams of honey and wine, processions of hundreds of elephants, feasts for six thousand, money made of paper, a sophisticated postal system. Seventeen years later, the trio of Polos returned to Venice with their stories – which put them on the local version of the lecture circuit. Imprisoned for several months in 1298, Polo made use of the time by dictating the tales of his travels, which would be published as *The Travels of Marco Polo* – a book that instantly elicited a reaction of awe and disbelief. So widespread was the scepticism about such things as magic carpets and elephants being transported in the talons of giant birds that even his children thought he was making it up: as he lay dying in 1324, they begged him to recant all his wild tales and admit they were all lies. His final words were: 'I have only told half of what I saw.' Modern historians too have greeted his stories suspiciously, pointing out that for a man who supposedly travelled to China, his stories are missing important descriptions including those of chopsticks, bound feet, tea and the Great Wall.

By the fourteenth century, Florence too was rising to international stature, growing rich from the mercantile trade, and becoming a centre of banking commerce, with a strong currency, the florin, that other countries recognized. A competition in 1402 for the engraved bronze doors of the Florence Baptistry, which sculptor Lorenzo Ghiberti won (and would spend forty-eight years completing) is sometimes used as the beginning of the Italian Renaissance, and for the next two centuries, the creative spark was alive through Italy (and Europe), although the flame burned no brighter than in Florence. The sinewy marble sculptures of Michelangelo, the subtly powerful paintings of Leonardo da Vinci, the pointed writing of Dante and the domed architecture of Brunelleschi were but a few of the remarkable achievements of the cultural movement that drew from classical Rome and Greece. Funded in part by the church, which commissioned many of the most important works, the art of this golden era was very much helped along by the Medicis, bankers and de facto rulers of Florence – whose family would ultimately rule this Tuscan city well into the eighteenth century as well as producing two popes (Leo X and Clement X) and two queens of France (Catherine and Maria). Cosimo de' Medici 'discovered' Michelangelo and Donatello, and the family that fed, educated and housed the likes of Leonardo, Botticelli and others who would become the era's leading artists, also enriched the city, building churches and monasteries, libraries and academies, and making Florence the show stealer of the day.

Historical Thinkers and Creators

Galileo (1564–1642): Dropped balls off leaning tower of Pisa to deduce theories of gravity; said to have been forced to recant his theory about a heliocentric universe before the religious board.

Brunelleschi (1377–1446): Put the cap on Florence's Duomo – taking inspiration from the egg which he supposedly smashed on the table in demonstration of how he would dome the thing.

Dante (1265–1321): Caught the worst qualities of humanity and displayed them in descending levels of hell in his *Inferno*. Neighbours, friends and even the Pope were skewered in the controversial book.

Michelangelo Buonarroti (1475–1564): The Sistine Chapel and David are but a couple of his works.

Leonardo da Vinci (1452–1519): Flying machines were but one invention of the thinker/artist/designer who is best known for Mona Lisa's sad smile. Experimented with mixing his own kind of paints, alas, and now many of his murals haven't held up.

Raphael (1483–1520): Mr Madonna whose finest works hang in the Vatican's Papal Apartments.

Botticelli (1445–1510): His 'Birth of Venus' made fat beautiful, and fat women have been describing themselves as Botticellian beauties ever since.

Machiavelli (1469–1527): Advised rulers about the subtleties of power plays with his guidebook, *The Prince*.

The Medicis' power in this contentious city, always known for competing families and guilds, was not universally respected: in 1478, another powerful family – the Pazzi – with the help of an archbishop and the nod of the Pope, attacked the Medicis while in church, killing Giuliano, the co-ruler of the clan. Surviving the ordeal, Lorenzo the Magnificent (1449–92) became known as the Saviour of Florence.

The Pazzi, the archbishop and other conspirators were soon hung – and hanging: their corpses dangled from the top of the Palazzo Vecchio, as was the fashionable practice of the day.

Generous Lorenzo should never have opened his purse for the radical priest Savonarola, who turned on his patron and ran the Medici clan out of town in 1494. The righteous holy man took over as the effective dictator of Florence, closing down wine taverns and dress shops, shutting the doors of gambling houses and book stores. In 1497, he ordered that all the riches of the Florentines – and all that smacked of glamour and decadence – be destroyed. Paintings of nudes, non-religious books, splendid hats, ornate dresses, poems with secular themes, mirrors and makeup were carried to the main square, where they were torched, the wealth of the era going up in the smoke of the Bonfire of the Vanities. Florentines soon regretted that move, and within weeks, they rose up against him and his heretical ideas of religious reform. In 1497, he was excommunicated and the next year hanged, his corpse burned in the same square where he had destroyed the city's treasures.

Fickle Florence had a reputation for kicking out its main families: nearly every major road bears the name of a family that once had influence and then was given the Florentine heave-ho. Even the moneyed Medici were banished on several occasions; unlike most of the others, they just kept coming back. Renaissance Florentines also had a few run-ins with the Pope: on one occasion, so great was his ire at Florentines that he imposed a stiff tax on salt, knowing that it was crucial for bread. The Florentines weren't fazed: they figured out how to make yeast rise without it, and to this day, most Florentine bread doesn't contain a grain of the stuff.

Historical Hot Shot: Filippo Mazzei

Surgeon, diplomat, essayist, and winemaker, Filippo Mazzei from Tuscany, upon invitation from the likes of Benjamin Franklin, arrived in the American Colonies (with tailor, cook, servants, farm workers and cuttings of vines) in 1773 to start the Colonies' first official vineyard in Virginia. Thomas Jefferson urged Mazzei to take over the plot bordering his new home, Monticello, and some say that in fact suggestion-filled Mazzei came up with the name for Jefferson's digs. Mazzei soon transformed from Italian vintner into a pamphleteer and orator for the Revolutionary cause, and loaned sacks of money to Jefferson to aid the Colonists rebelling against England; two centuries later, for his dedication, he was commemorated with a US postal stamp. At the time he caused a few headaches: after a botched diplomatic venture for the rebels in Paris (Ben Franklin was finally sent over to seal the major money-borrowing deal) and a stint as a thinker for the king of Poland, Mazzei holed up in Tuscany, planning to return soon to his American vineyard. Thrilled at the receipt of a particularly feisty letter from Jefferson (in which the American lambasted George Washington and cast aspersions at the Adams government of which he was vice-president), Mazzei trotted his translation to the newspaper in Florence. The letter was picked up by the Parisian press, and then by London's, with each translation the already insult-peppered letter becoming even spicier: the next year, when Jefferson's translated letter finally arrived and was printed in the United States, the missive triggered an uproar – particularly as the newly passed Alien and Sedition Act outlawed criticism of the government, and the vice-president had been heaping it on thick. A humiliated Jefferson soon rented out Mazzei's vineyard to Germans whose horses trampled the grapes, stamping out the wine-making experiment as well as Mazzei's sole reason for ever returning. As for Mazzei's loan to the cause, among Jefferson's last words was a plea to pay back the family Mazzei, an act finally accomplished quite a few decades later.[13]

The peninsula continued in its divided fashion, with rulers from all across Europe, until Napoleon briefly pulled it together as one in 1804. That didn't last long, but the idea of peninsular unification appealed to some. In the nationalistic fervour of the mid-1800s, Count Camillo Cavour, prime minister of Piedmont and in the employ of King Victor Emmanuel II, hooked up with guerrilla fighter Giuseppe Garibaldi to cobble together the assorted states as one united country. Kicking off the drive with a war against the Austrians in 1859, the unification efforts, helped along by Garibaldi and his volunteer 'Red Shirts', was finally completed in 1871, and Victor Emmanuel II (formerly king of Piedmont) became monarch of all Italy.

Come si dice 'king'? It may have had one name – the Kingdom of Italy – but in 1871, when all the pieces came together, the people couldn't communicate. A mere 3 per cent of the population spoke Italian.[14] Still today, the country is heavily regionalized – and while most know Italian, dialects, unintelligible to those who don't live there, are the rule. Not only do they vary by region, they often vary village to village.

The Vatican was most unhappy about losing its papal state to the incoming monarchy, and issued a bull demanding that Catholics not recognize the new government. So fearful were popes of what would happen if they ever left the Vatican that not one left his confines for the next six decades, until 1929 when Mussolini granted the Vatican independence, making it the world's smallest independent state.[15]

Il Duce: Benito Mussolini (1883–1945)

History has often portrayed Mussolini as a fool, but in fact the fan of Nietzsche fancied himself an intellectual, and worked on several newspapers. As with Hitler, a frustrated painter, Mussolini too was a creator – *Il Duce* was a novelist – and one can't help wondering whether the world might be a less pained place if they'd both received (or deserved) a little more artistic respect. Although Mussolini's novel *The Cardinal's Mistress* was indeed published in 1908, it was hardly a bestseller, being a bit thin on plot (a cardinal falls in love and wants out of the church, but the Pope won't let him go and everything turns ugly) and rather purplish in style: 'Like a boy he knelt at Claudia's feet . . . ''You will be the Madonna of the temple within me. I will be your slave. Strike me, despise me, beat me, open my veins with a subtle dagger, but grant me the revelation of yourself, grant that I may speak to you, grant that I may lose myself with you in the supreme illusion.'' '[16] No doubt dismayed at the lack of sales, he got into politics, but the former socialist soon broke with that party and started up a fascist newspaper in 1914. Three years later he was drafted to fight in the First World War. Italy had been aligned with Austria and Germany but in typical Italian style switched sides and went in with Britain and France. Mussolini didn't see the battlefield: wounded in a practice drill, he returned to perfect his writing and right-wing political platform. In 1921 he took a seat in Parliament during an anxious time when the country struggled economically and was torn politically between communists and a weak capitalist system that looked like it might collapse. Although Italy had fought on the winning side in the war, the country's citizens were not happy with the results: financially handicapped from the start of the war, Italy had gone into debt buying weapons to fight it and owed about €3.5 billion as a result. What's more, the country didn't get the lands they'd been promised.[17] Mussolini stirred nationalist sentiment and boosted the sagging Italian ego. Although not as captivating an orator as Hitler, he was nevertheless rousing in his speeches and by 1922 he simply marched on Rome with his 'blackshirts', the fascist militia, and established himself as leader of the country, shutting out other parties, censoring the press, and creating the myth of *Il Duce*, a relentless work-aholic with the ability to work magic for Italy on the international stage.

So much for the magic Mussolini had promised: the dictator may be credited with making the trains run on time, but he got Italy into all kinds of trouble. His invasion of Abyssinia in 1935, when he ordered the army to use nerve gas on the defending forces, who were fighting mostly with spears, brought the scorn of Europe upon him. He also signed up with Hitler in the Second World War, but his poorly organized forces often required the Nazis to come in and bail them out.

The monarchy, always pretty flimsy, had done little to oppose Mussolini during the first eleven years of his 'reign' but in July 1943, *Il Duce*'s fascist colleagues conspired against him and worked with the typically timid king, who prised Mussolini from office and tossed him into prison. Italy immediately switched teams, suddenly supporting the Allies. Hitler was furious and the Nazis stormed in, turning wine villas into fortresses as they battled incoming Allies; they lined the roads with land mines and blew up bridges upon their retreat. Although Mussolini didn't stay behind bars for long – Nazi paratroopers helped him escape – he had lost all his popular appeal once he was free: setting up in the north, Mussolini behaved as if he was still in power, but he was heading a puppet government with Hitler pulling the strings. In April 1945, while trying to sneak off to Switzerland, Mussolini and his mistress were shot and killed near Lake Como by partisans who strung them up – upside down – letting them hang in public where their corpses rotted for days.

> An art lover, Hitler spared Florence massive destruction to preserve its Renaissance glory. Nevertheless, he ordered the bombing of all the bridges spanning the Arno river, except for the Ponte Vecchio – the old covered bridge lined with gold shops, which he demanded be saved, not suspecting that the communication wires for Florence's resistance twisted under the bridge. After the war the blown-up bridges were rebuilt just as they had been, using many of the same rocks, pulled up from the Arno.

Modern Italia wasn't really born until 1946, after Italy voted to boot out the king and become a republic. After 24 years of fascism, Italy crawled into the postwar era, one of the most impoverished and dismal countries of Europe. The new republic revived in the late 1950s and 1960s: funds from the Marshall Plan helped ignite the industrial boom in the north, where Fiat, for one, revved up the economy; funding for the south, the Mezzogiorno, however, was customarily siphoned off by the Mafia, leaving it, as usual, behind in the race. Small, often family-owned businesses emerged in the neighbourhood borgos, and still today, Italians are more likely to be self-employed or work for a small firm making clothes, leather goods, or furniture than to work in a large corporate factory.

> *Wine makers: Tuscany's wine estates were long made possible by a quasi-feudal system that started in Renaissance times and continued for centuries. Called* mezzadria, *which translates as 'halfers', the system relied on tenant workers who weren't paid in money: their wages were half of the wine, olive oil and produce from the estate, where they were offered housing and their own small plots. When the serf-like* mezzadria *system was formally outlawed by government in the 1960s, peasants headed to the cities en masse. Unable to afford to pay labourers to work in their vineyards – and believing agricultural forecasts that predicted the Italian wine market was doomed – many nobles put their estates up for sale: many northern industrialists bought them up and entered the wine game, snatching up villas for a song. Even though it is outlawed, the* mezzadria *system, say some in the wine world, is making a comeback.*

In the 1970s Italy was rocked by violence during '*Gli Anni di Piombo*' – or 'Years of Lead'. Mafia kidnappers and radicals from the right and left (including the notorious Red Brigades) began assassinating politicians, bombing trains and targeting political leaders: the Red Brigades alone are accused of killing a total of 350 people, including former prime minister Aldo Moro, kidnapped in 1978; three months later his bullet-ridden body was found in the boot of a car.

Another group kidnapped 17-year-old Paul Getty III, keeping him chained up in a cave for months. Getty's father, black sheep of the family and a drug addict, didn't have the $17 million (about €14 million) demanded by the kidnappers, and Paul's wealthy grandfather was reluctant to help. The family changed its tune when the kidnappers sent a letter containing Getty's severed ear; they might have helped sooner, except that a postal strike in Italy had delayed the letter by three weeks.

A 1980 bombing on a train outside Bologna that killed thirty hasn't been solved: fingers pointed at the Red Brigades as well as the radical right but nothing was proven. In the 1980s, the government rounded up hundreds of suspected terrorists, particularly Red Brigades members, and jailed them, spelling a final '*arriverderci*' to the group, it was hoped.

Quick Tour

From the chiselled Alps in the north to stone farm houses surrounded by vineyards, from gondolas that sail past sinking palaces to Rome's crumbling *Colosseo*, Italy is a feast for the eyes. It is also a daily extravaganza of food. While every culture values eating, they are simply obsessed with the ritual here in the land where all existence can be summed up in two words – '*Buon Appetito*' – which is uttered before every meal. As one Italian explains it, 'If you have food, and a good appetite, then your life must be all right.'

Mangia, Mangia!

Forget money, palazzos, amore, fast cars. Whether it's fiery penne arrabiata, cheesy polenta or prosciutto wrapped round melon, nothing is more important to Italians than food. This is the land where '*si mangia bene*' (you can eat well there) is the highest compliment and where proverbs exalt the dinner table as the only place where one doesn't age. What for much of the world is a joyless duty of sustenance is an act revered by shoemaker, artist and banker alike; in Italy nothing is more sacred than a good meal. Simple flavours – sweet tomato sauce or ricotta-stuffed ravioli drizzled with sage butter – reflect more than close ties to the earth: a whole system of laws, some written, some verbally imposed, guides food from garden to stomach. Heaven forbid that the beloved mozzarella di buffalo – to be served only at room temperature – comes cold or from a cow. A stale pastry at a café may warrant a ticket from food police. So dangerously aphrodisiacal are the white truffles shaved tableside over pasta that a century-old law prohibits them from being carried on trains, and your perfectly foamed cappuccino is a breakfast drink only; don't embarrass yourself by ordering one after lunch. Sprinkling cheese on a fish dish is grounds for expulsion and risotto can only be made from Arborio rice, so adored that smuggling it out of the north was once punishable by death (Thomas Jefferson risked it nonetheless). The food laws go on ad infinitum: never mix basil and oregano, don't twirl spaghetti with a spoon, wine should be bottled and grape leaves trimmed only during a rising moon. Fresh fruit is served with a bowl of water for washing the fruit, not your hands, and except for the snack grabbed at a bar, where all sandwiches are held napkin-wrapped, eating must never be rushed: it's no surprise that Italy spawned the anti-microwave, anti-processing, anti-fast food movement called Slow Food. Predictably, its symbol is the snail.

This is a culture where, like salmon returning to their spawning grounds, everyone within driving distance returns to their mother's home for the all-important pranzo on Sunday, and the travelling distance is getting shorter these days: given the state of the economy and house prices, few Italians are moving out in their twenties, and some never do.

> *Italy has the highest 'stay at home' rate in Europe: 95 per cent of adults under 30 still live at home.*[18] *The average age for an Italian to leave the coop: 34 years.*[19]

Not only does the phenomenon perpetuate a Peter Pan syndrome, it has helped trigger a drop in the birth rate: Italy now has the lowest in the world. While the Pope may be respected, few Italians – especially in the north – adhere to his papal edicts on contraception. So ignored is the Catholic church's view on family planning that abortion during the first trimester is provided free; a recent proposal to make women pay after more than one termination triggered outrage.

Shortage of public day-care centres, and the high price of child raising, have turned Italy into a society of one-child families. In 2004 the government offered a bonus of €1,000 for every newborn bambino.

Beyond just the issue of breeding, the live-at-home syndrome cultivates a restricted world view where, like a century ago, it's easy to spend your whole life within a radius of ten miles. And that partly explains why the Italians often have such a problem with immigrants who barge into their established world.

The Albanian Factor

Sitting just across the Adriatic Sea, Albania is the homeland of most immigrants into Italy. The relationship between the two countries has been strained, to put it diplomatically. Part of the tension goes back to the First World War: Albania was dangled as a promised territory at the beginning of the war, but come 1918 Italy didn't get it. Mussolini took Albania in 1939, and for a few years the countries were politically merged. But the relations have been much more tense in the past fifteen years. When Albania's communist dictatorship fell in 1991, 24,000 Albanians appeared on Italy's doorstep in three days. The government welcomed them, issuing work visas, and the president even urged Italians to adopt Albanians or at least put them up in their homes. Six months later another

15,000 showed up in Bari, on the south-east coast. This time the government sent out riot squads and they were pushed into a stadium, where food was air-dropped in. Five days later they were airlifted out and sent back to Albania. During those six months, said Italians, there had been a huge jump in crime, so much so that the government issued a statement that Italy was not a land of immigration. And in 1997 an Italian coast-guard ship ran into an Albanian ship causing it to sink and take down eight Albanians with it. The Italian vessel was accused of ramming the Albanian ship on purpose.[20] Now, however, some Italians and Albanians work closely together. Albanian-organized crime gangs and the Mafia in Puglia – the heel of the boot – coordinate shipments of smuggled cigarettes and Eastern European sex slaves.

In Italy, an outsider need not even come from a different country: some Italians still suspiciously eye those who come from a town thirty miles away. And no 'Italians' have it harder than Sicilians who many Italians will tell you aren't Italian at all. Merely to mention someone who hails from the southern island that trails off the toe of the peninsula and looks like it's being kicked by the boot will elicit the almost universal response of knocking on the table and the exclamation '*Loro sono duri*' – they're thick.

Fragmented identity: Italy is divided into twenty regions, where there is plenty of hoopla-ing about the local football teams, but it lags behind on national spirit. Disgusted by the country's many political scandals, few Italians get fired up for national elections, and according to Newsweek International, *more than 40 per cent can't identify the colours of the Italian flag.*

In fact, the whole south gets a bum rap by those in the north, who will point out that while unemployment is 9 per cent nationwide, it climbs to 25 per cent in the areas below Rome; it's 50 per cent among those under 30. Wealthy northerners are so tired of tossing money at the enfeebled south in numerous projects that seem to go nowhere except somebody's silk pockets, that there's frequent debate about splitting the two regions into separate countries.

MEP Umberto Bossi, until recently the most vocal member of Berlusconi's coalition, formed his party Lega Nord (Northern League) on the premise of sawing the country in two.

The Mob's Newest Trick

Typically known for such delightful activities as running heroin, trafficking sex slaves from Eastern Europe, operating prostitution rings, siphoning off government-funded projects and demanding 'protection' payments from businesses, the Italian Mafia has recently moved into new territory. Long involved in rubbish collection, they are now in the toxic-waste disposal business. Beginning in the 1980s, when new laws about recycling required that industries properly dispose of lead, arsenic, carcinogenic chemicals and radioactive materials, the Mafia – particularly the Camorra around Naples – saw their chance. Costs for safely getting rid of the hazardous materials were high – until the mobsters sneaked in with the proper permits and papers (provided by corrupt officials), offering to alleviate the headache for a tenth of the price that other contractors were bidding. Winning contract after contract from paper mills, tanneries and chemical companies, the Mafia loaded up their trucks with their carcinogenic cargo having no intention of taking it to a safe treatment facility. Sometimes they offloaded the poisons in municipal landfill sites, which aren't meant to hold hazardous waste, but the thugs didn't care since they owned the sites. Sometimes they dumped them into the ocean or caves and sometimes they illegally dug deep holes and filled them with the toxic waste, not concerned that it leeched into the water supply, contaminating it; to cover up their tracks, they sometimes built concrete factories over the subterranean waste dumps. Recently, however, the Mafia sank to a new low: they mixed the deadly sludge with fertilizer and posing as salesmen gave it to farmers to try out free of charge. Now thousands of acres of prime farmland are poisoned, cows and buffalo in parts of the country produce toxin-laced milk and the costs of cleanup run into billions of euros. It's alarming enough to the Italians that fresh locally made mozzarella was banned in some southern towns due to contamination of cattle; worse, cancer rates have soared – in some areas around Naples quadrupling within a few years.

Another problem: low newspaper readership – less than 40 per cent of adults in Italy read newspapers, and many of them are only reading the sport – which only emphasizes the hazards of a TV media machine that is run by the prime minister. Adding to the cause for worry is the lack of anything mildly educational on Italian TV which is, sadly, laughable. With its cleavage-baring hostesses who entertain the newscasters during the news, its singing and dancing TV hosts and cheesy light-entertainment extravaganzas, it is the Continent's worst, again something for which Italians have Berlusconi to thank. Not surprisingly, Italians don't put much faith in the tube. According to a recent Eurobarometer survey, only 37 per cent trust information they get from the Berlusconi-dominated box.

The Italians who are paying attention to their society regard it as sinking to a new stultifying low – and politically, some call it a '*disastro*'. But for many Italians '*tutto va bene*' – everything's fine, if they have Mama – and control of the TV.

Somehow, despite *i molti problemi* – the laughable politics, the regionalism that prevents the country from working as a united whole, the Mob, the disorganization that just seems to be the Italian way, not to mention the illegal immigration that adds yet another dysfunctional thread to the social fabric – Italy just keeps chugging away, finding the meaning of life in a plate of good food and amazing the 30 million tourists who visit each year, who can't fathom the chaos hidden behind all the beauty.

> *La dolce vita*: *Currently Italians can retire at 57 and begin drawing their pensions. The Italian government is pushing to delay the retirement age by a few years since pensioners are draining the system: 14 per cent of GDP goes to state pensions. Prime Minister Berlusconi recently nearly caused coronaries when he suggested that perhaps Italians should wait to retire until the ripe old age of 65.*

Future Forecast

As in the past, so in the future: whoever is theoretically in charge, Mama is really running the place.

Hot Spots

Roma: It's said here in the city of seven hills that when Rome's Colosseum falls, civilization goes with it; in the meantime the city awash with astounding leftovers from Imperial Rome is being overrun by feral cats. The capital city whence the ancient empire sprang is still one of Italy's liveliest and visitors shuttle from the Pantheon and the Vatican's Sistine Chapel to the Trevi Fountain, into which they pitch coins to ensure their return.

Milano: Fashion and finance centre, heavily bombed during the war, but

Florence: where the Renaissance lives on.

with a few bits of architectural heritage remaining. Many of the area's wealthiest live out of town, in villages to the north.

Tuscany: With red-capped Duomo, sculpture-filled squares, and the Uffizi that celebrates the Renaissance both inside (with its museum) and out (with its long-columned loggias), Florence always steals the show in this gorgeous region, but the vineyard-laden countryside where one wakes to crowing roosters and mist hanging over the valleys is one of the more heart-warming places on Earth, even if you get carsick on the curving roads there. Siena, where everything takes on a warm golden hue, is the site of the Palio, where in a much-hyped competition between neighbour-hoods, horses race in the squares as they have since Da Vinci's day. Florence and Siena have been feuding since medieval times, including over their borders; during one territorial standoff, a race between two roosters ultimately redrew the map.

Mezzogiorno: The troubled, ratty southern half of Italy is filled with half-built structures where people live (building owners need not pay taxes until the structure is finished, so they delay completion per-manently), has the highest unemployment rates, bigger families and tends to be more religious and to loathe Italy's assorted communist parties. It still has its charms: the Amalfi coast, with its high, hairpin roads, is dazzling, and chaotic, crime-ridden Naples, where every year buildings simply crumble, has a frenzied allure which may have something to do with its perfectly pulled espresso. More famous: its pizza.

Drivers in Naples are known to race through red lights. The reason, explains one Napolitano, is that the traffic lights are usually broken and permanently red, so there's no point in stopping to see if one actually works.

Sicilia: Original home of the Mafia – which some say kept order on the chaotic island – Sicily bears the brunt of Italians' prejudice, even though its cuisine – astoundingly fresh fish, handmade pasta and flowery white wines – may be the country's finest. Phoenician ruins stand among Arabesque palaces, palm trees sway from imperial squares, but a few streets off the main drags, poverty runs rampant. Sicilian women are either very clumsy or there's a serious anger-management problem down here to judge by the many broken noses.

Since 2001 the Italian police and carabinieri have cracked several militant cells, including one that planned to pump cyanide gas into the US Embassy in Rome and another plot to poison Rome's water supply.

Puglia: The heel of 'the boot' boasts some of the tastiest cooking in the country (well, except for the horsemeat), and a Mafia that is more brutal than most. The port city of Bari is an entry point for smuggling from Albania, including illegal tobacco and Eastern European 'sex slaves'. The traditional houses are strange cones called *trulli*.

Aviano air force base: This northern base has had more problems than the other dozen Italian bases that the US and NATO routinely use. In 1998, a US fighter plane accidentally sliced through the wires of a cable-car at a nearby ski slope, causing the car to crash and kill twenty. The base was also the source of a previous scandal when news leaked that the US was transporting nuclear arms via Aviano, in violation of Italy's law banning nuclear weapons on its territory.

The dinner table: Mind the rules here: nearly as important as food is the order of dishes that always begins with antipasti and ends with the salad, an eating peculiarity that along with the 'passeggiata' – that after-meal stroll – may explain why Italians are so rarely fat.

Italian Film

Federico Fellini, Vittorio de Sica and Roberto Rossellini unleashed a new genre of dramatic cinema with *La Dolce Vita*, *Bicycle Thieves* and *Rome, Open City*. But nobody in recent history has broken more hearts than Roberto Benigni who co-wrote, directed and starred in *Life is Beautiful*. The film, about a father who tries to spare his son the horrors of the Second World War, swept the Cannes Film Festival; at the Oscars, Benigni sprinted across rows of chairs to accept his award for 'Best Actor' in 1998. *Cinema Paradiso* by Giuseppe Tornatore also stirred global emotions with a double love story which could only have sprung out of Italian compassion.

Showrooms: Alfa Romeo, Bugatti, and Lamborghini put the world's slickest designs on top of four wheels, although these days with *Fratello Grande* (Big Brother) calculating kilometres per hour and snapping photos as you whiz by, it's just not as much fun to speed in them any more.

> *Countless marriages have suffered under Italy's latest attempt to enforce speed limits. Using licence numbers to track addresses, the snap-the-speeder technology sends the photo of the offending vehicle straight to the offender's house. It's not the fines for the speeding tickets that are the problem. The headaches arise from who is sitting in the passenger seat: most wives aren't happy when they see it's not them.*

Catwalks: Gucci, Pucci, Prada, Ferragamo, Armani, Valentino and Dolce & Gabbana are just a few of the names that have made Milan's catwalks and showrooms flashier and just as important and far more daring than the classic houses of Paris.

United Colors of Benetton: Giuliana Benetton had a talent for designing handknit sweaters, and in the 1950s, as a teenager, her brother Luciano used to ride off on his bike and sell them. In 1965 the siblings started United Colors of Benetton and shook up the masses when they turned casual into chic, and made fashion advertising political. Their billboards won awards and caused highway pile-ups across Europe showing, for example, a sexy nun french-kissing a monk, or a white baby nursing at a black woman's breast. Benetton shows the same subtlety with the startling photos and reportage in their moving bilingual magazine *Colors*, which captures the joys and sorrows of the world and takes readers to far corners where other magazines don't dare.

The Garden: The obsession with food may be rooted in the country's peasant past, but even the wealthiest Italians pride themselves on their green fingers. Give a man a foot of land and he'll put in a small garden and vineyard, grind pesto from smashed basil, pine nuts and parmesan, and concoct honeyed drinks from white grapes that he's dried. A good Italian, even if living in the heart of the city, has found somewhere, balcony, rooftop, or windowsill, to grow tomatoes (one kind for salads, another for sauce) and to pluck herbs fresh from the plant. Genetically modified food has no place here, where antique seeds are cultivated and saved and no gift is finer than that of olive oil with a slight scent of pine and straight from the cold press.

VinItaly

Oh it may sound like a Big Bacchanalian bash, but it's a serious business when 2,000 wine producers uncork their stuff, some 30,000 buyers swarm around for a taste and potential billions of dollars are up for grabs. That's what happens every spring in Verona, when the concrete convention centre is tarted up with plastic vines and wooden tables for VinItaly, the biggest wine sale of the year in Italia, and some say, the world. With the possibility for lucky vintners to sell out that year's entire stock in a mere 120 hours, the five-day event of swirling, sniffing and spitting is about as festive as Wall Street on a really long opening day. Despite their Latin lover façade, few Italians can be found flirting (not even with the lovely wine pourers rented out for the event), having apparently interrupted their *coitus attemptus continuus* inclinations in favour of the business at hand – that's how important it is.

The Mafia (aka *Cosa Nostra* in Sicily, *Camorra* in Naples, *Sacra Corona Unita* in Puglia, *'N Drangheta* in Calabria): Demanding protection money and cuts in public works as well as smuggling contraband, the family-bound masters of psychological terrorism still make the wheels turn, particularly in the south where, despite occasional attempts at a clean-up, the syndicate is so entrenched that some say without it things might be worse. 'Pizzo' buys 'security' in Sicilia, in Napoli it's called 'racket' and whatever you call it, many northerners don't want to invest in the south because of it. Some mobsters send roses to the widows of those victims who don't pay up; in Sicily they historically took care of the deceased man's family for the rest of time. Famous Mafia town Corleone is being cleaned up: now there's a Mafia museum, but few gangsters.

Hot Shots

Pope John Paul II: Karol Wojtyla (1920–2005)

Few popes have been more visible than Polish Pope John Paul II, who came to holy power in 1978 and spread his word all over the world from Cuba to Croatia, Mexico to Canada, speaking out against the Soviet Union, against birth control, and against the horrors of war. He named more saints than any other pope: he canonized 476 and beatified 1,320, launching more to holy status than all other popes combined. While most popes spoke from the balcony, John Paul II frequently made appearances in his papal chariot around St Peter's Square in the Vatican, waving to the assembled masses. In 1981 the Pope was the target of an assassination attempt during one of his Vatican spins. Didn't slow him down much: the next time he was taken out for a ride, his popemobile was simply covered in bulletproof glass. Didn't slow down his attacker for too long: pardoned by the Italian government, the would-be pope killer is now in Turkey where he's recently announced he's going into politics. (He'll have plenty of time to come up with campaign slogans since he's currently in prison, serving time for a previous murder.) Pope John Paul II came under fire for his links to Opus Dei, an ultraconservative faction of the church.

Silvio Berlusconi: Prime Minister 1994; 2001 to present. Despite his shady reputation, Italy's richest man first charged to power during the anti-corruption drive of the 1990s. His initial brush with the premiership in 1994 lasted only a few months, but he was back in 2001, slipping out of calls to trial on corruption charges by passing a bill that the top five leaders in Italy can't be tried while in office. The EU has cast an anxious eye at the businessman-cum-politician from the start, viewing him as 'a threat to Europe', while the media mogul attracts plenty of attention from the international media: the *Economist* (from Britain), *Le Monde* (from France) and *El País* (from Spain) are just three that have skewered him and called for him to step down. Even the Italian media presented the

MEP Alessandra Mussolini: a fascist
who fights for women's rights.

government with a 'White Paper' about Berlusconi-inspired sackings of
critical broadcasters and the censorship now imposed from within, since
directly (as CEO) or indirectly (as prime minister) he controls virtually all
of Italy's private and public TV. He ended his outrageous six-month stint
as president of the European Council by applauding the Russian president
Vladimir Putin's controversial actions in Chechnya, prompting the
European Commission to issue a separate statement saying it did not
concur with the Italian PM.

> **What a joker:** *According to* Time International, *Berlusconi tells a
> tale about a plane trip with his two children. Flying over a labour
> protest, Berlusconi pondered aloud whether he should drop a one
> hundred-euro note into the crowd, and make one person's day. The
> daughter suggested that he drop two fifty notes and make two
> people's day. The son suggested that he drop five twenties and
> make five people's day. At that point, the pilot turned around and
> suggested that Berlusconi jump out of the plane and make every-
> one's day.*

Romano Prodi: Former Italian Prime Minister (1996–8), head of left-
leaning Olive Branch Coalition and enemy of Silvio Berlusconi, Prodi

moved to Brussels and took over as president of the European Commission when it was reeling from scandal in 1999, and many expected it to sputter along greatly weakened. However, former professor Prodi kept the power in the powerhouse that makes policy on everything from beef to energy, environment to enlargement. Although he is not dripping with charm, Prodi is Italy's finest international diplomat: after Germany's Chancellor Shröder cancelled his planned holiday in Italy in 2003, Prodi dropped in to invite him personally to the opera in Verona.

> **Noteworthy:** *Oh he may be a jerk in relationships – the tenor had his secretary–lover inform his wife the marriage was over – but Luciano Pavarotti is still the national hero and you can hear his voice floating out of windows almost any day of the week. New on the opera scene: creamy-voiced Eros Ramazotti. The staggering singing of Paolo Comte (who, like Serge Gainsbourg, always sounds like he's been hitting the bottle) only gets better with time, and who would have guessed that Italian supermodel Carla Bruni would have a voice as heavenly as her face or that her French would be so polished even the French are agog.*

Giancarlo Fini: Head of the National Alliance, former journalist Fini is trying to soften the image of the neofascist, moving closer to the centre, and condemning Il Duce's version of fascism as 'absolute evil'. Seems to be working – he is one of the country's most popular politicians and he and his party are soaring in influence.

Writerly Sorts

The profound storyteller Umberto Eco, who will never be accused of being a minimalist with works such as the 800-page *The Name of the Rose*, won a Nobel Prize for Literature; left-wing satirical playwright Dario Fo, part of Italy's 'laughter culture', unleashed his humour by cracking his whip at corrupt society, and daring Oriana Fallaci may be the world's most unflinching journalist and toughest interviewer: she posed many a difficult question to world leaders, and is rumoured to have occasionally had a romantic fling post-interview. However, the former leftie appears to have done an about-face: now Fallaci harpoons Europe for allowing itself to become Arabized – Eurarabia, she calls it. In her recent book

The Strength of Reason and her post-September 11 diatribe *The Rage and the Pride*, racist statements including that Muslims 'multiply like rats' offset her insights about radical Islam's growing hatred of the West. Her books sell wildly – especially in Italy.

Umberto Bossi: Head of the right-wing Lega Norte (The Northern League), he first came to power bellowing that wealthy Milan and environs should secede and form a separate country called Padania, and soon ended up a coalition partner in Berlusconi's first government in 1994. Even though Bossi walked out that year, causing Berlusconi's coalition to fall, he nevertheless was appointed minister in the current Berlusconi administration, which he quit in 2004 after suffering a stroke. Makes some Italians shudder: his party is more of a cult with a national holiday and even a beauty contest for Signorina Padania, and his ideas for Italy's immigration policy – including, apparently, to sink the incoming ships – are just plain scary.

Alessandra Mussolini: Italian parliamentarian, MEP 2004 to present. Doe-eyed, pouty-lipped and hot-tempered Mussolini is a walking contradiction: a fascist, whose most important goal is protecting women's rights, Mussolini posed nude for *Playboy*'s centrefold in 1983; the former actress with a degree in medicine now heads her own party – the only woman in Italy to do so – after she broke with the National Alliance when its leader Giancarlo Fini apologized for Italy's activities during the Second World War. Now an MEP, she bristles at sexist comments from the UK Independence Party, while staunchly defending the reputation of dictator Benito Mussolini, her grandfather.

Mussolini, who is the niece of Sophia Loren, has called for sex offenders to be chemically castrated, has pushed for Italian mothers to be able to give their last names to their children, and protested against a rape ruling in Italy – the judge said it was impossible to rape a woman wearing jeans – by striding into parliament with other female parliamentarians, wearing jeans and waving a banner: 'Jeans: an alibi for rape.'

Media star: *Colors* is the best magazine coming out of Italy – and surprise, it's not Berlusconi owned. They cover the most basic of topics – food, water, shelter, drugs – in an innovative way that plugs readers into the distant reaches of the world. Eye-opening, award-winning and right-on: www.colorsmagazine.com

Last Word: On 19 April 2005, white smoke puffed from the chimney of the Sistine Chapel announcing the appointment of the 265th pope – one whom many had hoped would modernize the church, by among other things allowing women priests to bolster the dwindling ranks of clergy. Instead, it was Cardinal Joseph Ratzinger, 78, a hardliner from Germany, who appeared at the Vatican balcony – and he may prove even more traditional than his conservative predecessor, John Paull II. Taking the name of Benedict XVI, the new pope opposes the ordination of women, stem-cell research and gay marriage, and considers religions other than Roman Catholicism to be 'deficient'. Some raised questions about his past – he was, as was common during the Nazi era in Germany, a member of the Hitler youth group – and others speculated that his ultraconservatism would both polarize opinion within the church, and call into further question its role in the world. Even though there hasn't been a pope from Germany since the eleventh century, Germans weren't thrilled: a poll in *Der Spiegel* showed that a majority of his countrymen did not support Ratzinger's new role in the church, many believing his views are simply too rigid.

5. Belgium (België, Belgique): Falling Apart

Fast Facts

Country:	Kingdom of Belgium; Koninkrijk Belgie, Royaume de Belgique
Capital:	Brussels
Government:	parliamentary democracy under a constitutional monarch
Independence:	4 October 1830 (from Netherlands); monarchy since 1831
Population:	10,349,000 (2004 estimate)
Leaders:	Head of State: King Albert II (1993)
	Head of Government: Prime Minister Guy Verhofstadt (1999)
Elections:	Monarchy is hereditary: PM appointed by monarch
Name of Parliament:	Senate/Senaat/Senat
Ethnicity:	58% Flemish; 31% Walloon; 11% other
Religion:	75% Roman Catholic; 25% Protestant/other
Language:	French, Flemish (Dutch derivative)
Literacy:	98%
Exports:	machinery, chemicals, diamonds
Per capita GDP:	$29,100 (2003 estimate)
Unemployment:	8.6% (May 2004 Eurostat figure); *Economist* says 11% in 11/03
Percentage in poverty:	4% (1989)
EU status:	founding member (member of EEC since 1957)
Currency:	euro
Known for:	EU, chocolate, Tintin

Standout Qualities

Mixed: Flemish and Walloons
Mixed: Jews and Arabs
Messy: Waging wars with laws

Résumé

At first glance, Belgium appears to be entirely wholesome to the point of eliciting snores: known for divine chocolate, sparkly diamonds, pretty medieval towns and comic books, Belgium – where the Smurfs were invented – is also headquarters for the European Union and NATO, which only makes it sound even snoozier.

Geographical Confusion: Brussels v. Wallonia v. Flanders

Brussels is Belgium's capital and likes to call itself the Capital of Europe since most EU institutions are headquartered here; Brussels is also bilingual – with French and Flemish (Dutch derived) both official languages. In Wallonia, the industrial southern half of Belgium that also holds the heavily wooded Ardennes region, they speak French. In Flanders, the northern half that holds diamond centre Antwerp as well as Bruges and Ghent – both former textile heavyweights – they speak Flemish (although most understand French). Language is hugely important in these parts and the Flemish and Walloons are forever fighting about language and just about everything else.

Boring, however, it's not: Belgium is riddled with corruption, seediness, ethnic tensions and hair-raising scandals, at least a few involving alleged paedophilia rings, which some claim could take down the government if the details were revealed.[1] Carcinogenic dairy products, bribe-greased arms deals, hissing secessionists – not to mention the soap operas at the European Commission – are just a few things that have put this odd little country on the front pages, and just a few of the reasons the place appears to be coming undone.

Scandal Magnet

For a country of ten million – a population only slightly larger than Paris – there are a disproportionate number of scandals here in the land that was home for Agatha Christie's quirky detective Hercule Poirot; they could certainly use a real person with Poirot's skills, since so many of the country's mysteries go unsolved.

Marc Dutroux, accused in 1996 of raping six young girls and killing four of them while he was out of prison on parole (after being convicted of raping five young girls a few years before), outraged Belgians not just because of his heinous acts, and not just because of the slackness of the police (who took over a year to find him), the courts (which took over seven years to try him) and the prisons (from which he escaped – albeit briefly – in 1998), but also because he keeps hinting that he's but a part of a much wider paedophilia ring that leads to some very high places. Bizarre murders and crimes pop up with regularity – whether you're talking about Protestant minister/school teacher Andras Pandy who, along with his daughter Agnes, was found guilty of killing their family (and chopping them to pieces and dissolving them in acid),[2] or the 1991 murder of Socialist politician André Cools in Liège, or the father who allegedly pimped out his 12-year-old daughter to the local mechanic, lumberjack, antiques dealer and (again allegedly) the family doctor and a dozen others. The dioxin-laden dairy products ordeal that rattled the country in 1999 was more than just another alarming food scare right on the heels of BSE and foot and mouth disease: it became a political brouhaha when not only did the Belgian government keep it a secret for a month, they went on to order the food back on the shelves, after the EU had condemned it as unsafe. The then prime minister Jean-Luc Dehaene, Europe's longest-lasting postwar leader, so botched his handling of the affair that he was promptly voted out of office two weeks later. The foreign minister has been accused of selling passports to known East European criminals in the 1990s, a handful of ministers were implicated in a scandal over bribery and arms, a high-ranking official stepped down for attending a reunion of the Nazi SS, while the separatist group Vlaams Blok (Flemish Bloc), that wants to destroy united Belgium, is gaining momentum. No wonder that many Belgians talk about moving somewhere else.

The knottiest problems at the moment are coming out of the port city of Antwerp, Belgium's second-largest metropolis, the world's biggest distributor of diamonds and a hotbed of tension. Known as the Jerusalem of the West, Antwerp is home to some 20,000 Jews (many Hassidic, and many involved in the diamond industry) about 12,000 of whom live in the old Jewish quarter. Right next to that is the Arab quarter, residence of many of the city's 30,000 Moroccans and Turks; a new group called the Arab European League is very vocal about their rights.

> *Arab activist Dyab Abou Jahjah, head of the Arab European League,*
> *has no interest in 'assimilating' in Belgium. He thinks the government*
> *should provide segregated schools for Arabs, separate housing zones*
> *and should make Arabic an official language of the country.*

Antwerp is also the headquarters of popular anti-immigrant party Vlaams
Blok, whose main objective is for Flanders to secede. The already potentially explosive mix keeps getting more volatile. In November 2002, a
Moroccan schoolteacher was killed by a Flemish dockworker; Moroccans
and other Arabs rioted in the streets, knocking out store windows and
overturning cars. The government said that the Arab European League
was behind it and threatened to ban the group, but the League's leader
Jahjah said he was only trying to calm things down. Claiming that Belgian
police discriminate against Arabs (probably a legitimate charge), he organized an Arab European League patrol in response, who keep watch over
the city and hassle police. They have also warned Jews that if they do not
renounce Israel, they are likely to be victims of terrorist attacks. Jews are
certainly the victims of a new surge of violence: a Jewish youth was stabbed
in June 2004, and Jewish (and black-owned) businesses are increasingly
vandalized. Now Jews want the government to provide additional protection.

> *Across Belgium there's been a recent rise in anti-Semitic acts: in April*
> *2002 alone, bullets were sprayed along the wall of a Charleroi syna-*
> *gogue and Molotov cocktails exploded in a synagogue in Brussels.*
> *Jewish cemeteries are routinely graffitied with swastikas.[3]*

Vlaams Blok, which runs Antwerp's city hall and wants the country to ship
back its foreigners, is lashing out at the Arab immigrants, and pointing at
their high unemployment. At over 20 per cent, the rate in Antwerp is twice
as high as the country's average, but the case in Arab neighbourhoods is
often more extreme. Among those under 30 years of age the rate is closer
to 40 per cent.[4] And Vlaams Blok, which took a quarter of the votes in
the 2004 regional parliamentary election and is now the country's most
popular party, is under the national government's scrutiny. The Belgian
government says Vlaams Blok is racist and in late 2004 banned the party.
In the meantime, no other party will talk to them or form a coalition with
them in parliament.

> *Vlaams Blok, which is now busy reorganizing under a different name,*
> *is retaliating by airing the government's dirty laundry. Among the*

items in the 6 June 2004 issue of The Flemish Republic, *Vlaams Blok's
'newsletter explaining why Flanders is seceding from Belgium', is an
item that the government printed a booklet for high schools listing
the world's '13 major genocides'. Missing from the list: mention of
Belgium's nineteenth-century genocide of the Congo people.*

And Antwerp is but one city that illustrates the strife that runs strong in
the whole country. In short, Belgium may look pretty enough, but it's a
battlefield these days in this country where the Walloons and Flemish are
at each other's throats, the Arabs and Jews don't get along, Vlaams Bloks
wants to secede – and kick out the Arabs – and the government is blocking
Vlaams Blok. That the EU is headquartered here in a country that is ripping
itself apart may portend the future for the supranational government as
well.

History Review

Hugging the North Sea and nudged up against France, Germany and the
Netherlands, Belgium has had to tolerate all the neighbours moving in at
assorted points or traipsing across it as though it were the back door to
France. Made wealthy by textiles – woollen fabrics, delicate lace and fine
tapestries put Brussels, Ghent and Antwerp on the map – the area in the
fourteenth century was ruled by the House of Burgundy, which made it a
centre of art and gave it the still-lingering habit of the Burgundian lunch
– a blur of courses such as white asparagus, lobster tarts in buttery sauce,
partridge with port and endless bottles of wine. By the fifteenth century
the area was conjoined with the Austrian Habsburg empire, ultimately
being pulled into the Spanish Netherlands.

Peter Paul Rubens (1577–1640)

He might not be the most famous Flemish painter ever – that's Rembrandt – but
Peter Paul Rubens was nevertheless the most famous and wealthy of the
seventeenth-century crowd. For a guy whose home was Antwerp (in today's
Belgium) he certainly got around – studying for years in Venice, Genoa and
Rome, before heading to Spain and London – and made a huge name for himself
wherever he set up his easel. Best recalled for his oils – some 2,000 of them,

some of corpulent women, some with religious themes, and some now fetching upwards of €50 million – the man who was a court painter all across Western Europe, riding across countries in regal carriage and with entourage, was also a skilled diplomat: he negotiated, among other things, a peace between England and Spain, who'd been going at it off and on for five decades. That was in 1630, and the following decade of his life was not only his last, but his most productive. After marrying a 16-year-old when he was 53, Rubens was inspired to create many of his finest works, and also to sire five more children. His rich style of living came with a price: gout took him out.

Spanish Inquisitors laid claim to the land and executed thousands for perceived heresy, and for the next two hundred years what is now Belgium was pulled between the powers in Madrid, Vienna and Paris. Napoleon invaded in 1792, and sold off church property that was about half of the Belgian land; just outside Brussels he finally met his demise in 1815 at the Battle of Waterloo. Under the 1815 Congress of Vienna – the meeting of international leaders that redrew the former Napoleonic Empire and tried to prevent future invasions – Belgium, Luxembourg and the Netherlands were moulded into one country. The arrangement didn't much please any of them.

Belgian independence was triggered by an opera *La Muette de Portici*, about a revolt in Naples. So stirring was the work that it literally unleashed an uprising that began in the opera house and then spilled into the streets. Belgium proclaimed independence within weeks, and borrowed a German prince to head the new state. Under King Leopold II, whose rubber plantations in the Congo brought riches, the country prospered, but at a great cost: millions of Congolese died.

King Leopold II (1835–1909) and the Belgian Congo

Long of face, and even longer of snowy white beard, Leopold was a dreamer even before he climbed upon the throne at the age of 29, taking control of a 35-year-old country that was fraying, as it had been since his father was shipped over from Germany to run it.[5] Walloons and Flemish were quarrelling even back then, and the country was also divided between secular liberals and Catholics.

To divert himself from the problems at hand, Leopold invented and exaggerated health ailments as a reason to travel to exotic locales from Egypt to China. Independently wealthy, all the more so after investing in his French friend Lesseps' idea for the Suez Canal, he wanted one thing: to expand Belgium's boundaries. Even though his advisers tried to steer him away from such silly notions, Leopold could use his own money to make good his dream about finding a glorious colony where Belgium could raise its flag. Alas, all the ones he thought he might rent or buy – the Philippines, Angola, New Zealand among them – weren't for sale. Hearing stories about the Dark Continent's Congo river, he decided to develop it, announcing in 1876 that he would send a mission to bring the light of Belgium to the jungle and save Africans from slavery. The idea was popular with the masses, but Leopold did just the opposite: his men ravaged the people and the land, turning the locals into the most cruelly treated of slaves. Levelling villages to set up rubber plantations, the Belgians demanded that the newly homeless tribes harvest the plants at unreasonable rates, sometimes taking their wives hostage to force the men further into the jungles where wild rubber trees grew. Those who resisted were killed; those who didn't keep up with the demand had their hands chopped off. Millions of Congolese people had died before English maritime journalist Edmund Dene Morel unravelled what was going on in 1900. He discovered that the ships coming back from the Congo were loaded with far more riches than they claimed, and those that went out didn't carry trade items, but weaponry. This wasn't free trade, this was slavery, he deduced, and went on to make a huge stink about it. By the time the British government sent out consul Roger Casement to report on the situation – almost three decades after the Belgians first set foot there – most of the original population along the Congo had been wiped out. An initial report by the Belgian government released in 1905 was so damning that Leopold was forced to donate some of his land to the state to keep it under wraps. The matter stayed hushed up until the 1980s, when a Belgian ambassador discovered the report and publicized its contents and the truth finally fully came out.[6]

The Belgian government – and the royal family – had a fit when the BBC wanted to air the documentary White King, Red Rubber, Black Death *about the genocide in the Congo. The programme was broadcast – but was heavily edited.*

During the First World War, when Belgium fought against Germany, the country became a permanent front, where troops dug into trenches for four years, fighting alongside their king. During the Second World War, Germans again invaded Belgium to enter France; Nazi-occupied from 1940, Belgium had a fair share of collaborators, many of whom were executed after the war. A constitutional monarchy was established in 1950, and the strategically located country was finally a beneficiary of its geography instead of a victim of it: NATO and the European Economic Community (now European Union) both made their headquarters in Brussels in the 1950s, making the city once again prosperous, a path it will no doubt continue to follow with the enlargement of the EU.[7]

Quick Tour

Take a bunch of beautiful baroque buildings, thick forests and fantastic restaurants, throw in some swan-filled canals, add some bad seventies housing, dodgy areas, port crime, war cemeteries, bloodied battle grounds, ethnic crackling, language barriers, and graffiti – then shake it up with corruption, lack of planning, rich food and lots of really good beer – and scatter it across the land scrunched up between France, Germany and the Netherlands – and there you have it: Belgium, gorgeous in a falling-apart sort of way and totally lacking cohesion, but interesting nevertheless.

The Benefits of Being Belgian

The best things to do in Belgium are to drink, eat and sleep, and Belgians in both the north and south have excelled in providing compelling reasons to do so. The country has some four hundred beers – brewed by Trappist monks, some spiked with sour cherries, some white, gold, red, or syrupy black, and all of them best drunk in the country's many cosy pubs. Belgium boasts imaginative eateries as well: sleek oyster bars with waterfalls caught behind glass, homely inns where buckets of mussels are served up in creamy beer sauce, restaurants where you dine amid church icons; the hazard to visitors is the weight gain that seems inevitable in Belgium, particularly if one partakes of the multi-course, multi-hour Burgundian lunch. Hotels may be converted railway stations deep in the woods or castles where peacocks wander the grounds. The combination of beer, feast and snooze must be better for you than it sounds: Belgians are considered the healthiest people on the planet. Well, they certainly aren't the skinniest.

Even though the place is filled with beauty, so often the country gives the feeling that the left hand doesn't know what the right is doing, or just doesn't care. Cities, such as helter-skelter Liège, seem thrown together without any vision, a woods-hidden castle may be surrounded by industry, a ritzy shopping avenue is edged with prostitutes, a pristine lake-dotted district is riddled with crime; even in technologically savvy Brussels, you'd be lucky to find an Internet centre that isn't in the back of some rundown Pakistani deli with computers from the 1980s. Politically, the country is even more fragmented, with six individual parliaments trying to run the place in some unified manner, and every national party split into two – one representing Flanders in the north and one representing Wallonia in the south, and both sides feeling that the other is being unfair.

A 2001 train crash that killed eight was caused because the signalmen – one Walloon, one Flemish – spoke different languages and couldn't communicate. Sixty per cent of the population speaks Flemish; however, in Brussels 80 per cent of the population speaks French.

Breaking up is Hard to do: Flanders and Wallonia

They share an intense history (of being invaded from all corners), a monarch (since 1831), a capital (bilingual Brussels) – and little else. The Flemish in the north are right-leaning and are more connected with maritime trade. Wallonia in the south is home mostly of Mediterranean sorts who tend more to the left. Why the two contending groups ever decided to form a country in 1830 is more a reflection of their previous mutual dislike of the Netherlands, the last of the neighbours to hold Belgium in its sway. Wallonia, which had the country's coal (now mostly exhausted) and steel mills (now mostly closed), used to be the rich dominant half, but now it's the other way around; the wealthy Flemish are tired of subsidizing the poorer south, where in some cities more than a third are unemployed. Their squabbling has been going on perpetually, but is more heated now, and the language issue has played out in bizarre ways: now every national political party is divided into French- and Flemish-speaking branches and there are even parliaments for the different language groups, including a German-speaking minority. Flanders won't subsidize libraries that have too many French books and a school bus recently was banned from stopping in a Flanders neighbourhood because it had a name in French on its side. The Walloons have constructed pricey bridges to connect French-speaking districts, and the French speakers who live in Flanders have launched boycotts of Flemish, refusing to speak it in stores or to pay local taxes, which are written in Flemish. As trivial as it may sound, the problem has launched nationalist movements in both camps, although the banned Flemish Vlaams Blok is by far the most vehement and vocal. With a continual devolution of power to the Flemish and Walloon governments, a split seems likely sometime in the future, although Brussels would be another thorny issue to sort out.

Crime is up too, particularly carjackings of foreign dignitaries' fancy cars – and morale is low in cities of high unemployment in Wallonia such as Charleroi, where car theft is rampant. The country's much-celebrated genocide law, under pressure from the United States (which was appalled that President George Bush, Sr, Colin Powell and other American VIPs were charged with war crimes), has been watered down so much it might as well have been binned.

War Crimes Law

What became one of the world's most controversial laws started with a phone call from Rwanda. Belgian Martine Beckers had just received a terribly disturbing one from her sister then living in the African country, who said that a gang of machete-wielding Hutu had broken into her house, stolen everything, and threatened to return to finish off the family. It was the last time Martine Beckers ever heard her sister's voice: along with other villagers, Beckers' sister and family were massacred with machetes. When she discovered what had happened to her sister, Beckers called the Belgian police, thus planting the seed for what would become Belgium's most infamous law: the 1993 Belgian War Crimes Law directed Belgian courts to try cases of international genocide and attacks on civilians. The murderers of Beckers' sister were never found, but the law opened the door for trials of other Rwandans, including two Roman Catholic nuns who in 2001 were found guilty of inciting murder. From there, the number of cases snowballed. War crimes suits were filed against Israel's Prime Minister Ariel Sharon (for his role in the Lebanon massacres at Sabra and Shatila), Saddam Hussein, former Iranian President Rafsanjani and Cuba's Fidel Castro. Added to the list in 2002 were former President George Bush, Colin Powell, Norman Schwarzkopf and Dick Cheney – for their roles in the death of civilians during the 1991 Gulf War. The US administration was already unhappy with the law, when in 2003, a new case was filed against President George W. Bush, Secretary of State Colin Powell, Secretary of Defense Donald Rumsfeld, General Tommy Franks and British Prime Minister Tony Blair. In June 2003, Rumsfeld threatened to move NATO out of Belgium if the law wasn't amended, and the next month he froze the US financial contribution to building a new NATO headquarters in Brussels that carries a €300 million price tag.[8] By September, the law had been amended and now it can be used only if a Belgian citizen or longtime resident is a victim or suspect of a war crime. Charges were dropped against the US, UK and Israeli officials, but rumour has it that the US administration is still disgruntled that the law exists in any form.[9]

Belgians are legitimately frustrated at the system that can't seem to prosecute criminals effectively and is stained with corruption and ineptitude; in October 1996, in what was called the White March, 300,000 protested against the police's lackadaisical handling of the Dutroux affair, which dragged on for another seven years. The Verhofstadt administration has appeared nearly squeaky clean thus far, but in the past decade numerous politicians have fallen. One standout: three former ministers and the ex-NATO Secretary-General Willy Claes were tried for allegedly receiving and giving bribes in 1988 and 1989 to make sure huge Belgian defence contracts went to an Italian and a French firm. Over the past decade at least a dozen Belgian political bigwigs have resigned, been killed or committed suicide over assorted murky government dealings. In a country that didn't have much of an integrated national identity from the start, the scandalous crimes and government misdeeds have just frayed any Belgian identity and pride further.

Although it has been NATO headquarters since 1967 (when France kicked NATO out) and was a charter member of the organization, Belgium is starting a separate military coalition with France, Germany and Luxembourg that would act independently of NATO and the EU. The new alliance's military headquarters will also be located in Belgium.

Sometimes the only thing that seems to be holding the place together is boyish Prime Minister Guy Verhofstadt, in his fifties, who despite his goofy grin and choppy haircut is quite the thinker and diplomat: by doling out more regional powers, he's kept the country from entirely unravelling in an era when the Flemish and Walloons are snapping at each other more loudly than ever about everything from taxes to language. Despite handing out income tax cuts, he hasn't been able to conquer unemployment, which has soared nationwide to almost 12 per cent – with unemployment rates of 35 per cent in parts of Wallonia, where business in steel towns has nearly ground to a halt. Another problem he couldn't stop: the 2001 folding of national airline Sabena.

Verhofstadt, along with European Commissioner Romano Prodi, recently commissioned a task force of creative thinkers to try to give Brussels, the symbol of the EU, a warmer, snugger feel. Their recommendations weren't terribly helpful: they suggested setting up a few more institutions – including one to study the EU.[10]

Future Forecast

Sooner or later Flanders and Wallonia will stop their chronic bickering and divorce. Flanders will get Brussels out of the deal; Wallonia will get Marc Dutroux. But whatever map divisions lie in its future, you can bet that Belgium (or at least whatever part of the country holds Brussels) will remain in the European Union, since so much of the country's wealth is tied up with the EU buildings and activities centred here.

Grand' Place: heart of Brussels.

Hot Spots

Antwerp: World's fourth biggest port, and a new centre for fashion design. Antwerp is charged with tension between Arabs and Jews and Flemish secessionists. Also a major trans-shipment point for drugs, arms, sex slaves and stolen goods of all sorts.

More than gems come out of Antwerp: it is also a major distribution centre for the world supply of the drug ecstasy.

Brussels: The Capital of Europe, as it's been called since the European Union took up permanent residence here, is home to what may be the prettiest square in Europe – Grand' Place – and a patchwork of ritzy and trendy areas mixed with dicey ones. Officially bilingual, Brussels is located in the region of Flanders, but considered its own autonomous territory. Developers sparked outrage through the 1990s when they bulldozed numerous historical buildings to erect modern corporate structures, many of them for the EU. Over 12 per cent of offices in Brussels are devoted to EU institutions.[11]

Grand' Place was destroyed in 1695, when the armies of King Louis XIV of France tried to knock down the city hall. That edifice remained, but the rest of the square's buildings crumbled. They were rebuilt as headquarters for assorted mercantile guilds, all trying to outdo each other in gold-heavy baroque style. Now restaurants and museums have moved into the guild buildings, but in the nineteenth century a few distinguished guests lived on the square, among them Karl Marx, who wrote some of his Communist Manifesto *while staying in a room above the Swan Restaurant, now a favourite of the bourgeoisie.*

Liège: New life is starting to blow through this formerly rundown city, but as yet it's still a hodgepodge of dilapidated and renovated buildings.

Bruges: Once a wealthy and important textile town, the canal-happy city now seems to cram in more tourists per square centimetre than Paris.

Army bases: In 2001 Tunisian Nizar Trabelski was arrested in Belgium and admitted to plotting to blow up the Kleine Brogel military base outside Brussels.[12] Other bases are also believed to be targets for Islamist terrorists. One reason: Belgian bases, many used by NATO, are said to hold nuclear weapons.

Berlaymont (aka Berlaymonster) building: Star-shaped structure that was once the home of the European Commission and was closed in 1991 due to asbestos in its walls; at least eighteen workers in the building have died of cancer or other related illnesses. The Belgian government oversaw rebuilding, which was supposed to have been completed by 1998, but ran six years behind. Now opened, but with huge cost overruns; construction companies are facing fraud investigations. In short, an embarrassment.[13]

Democratic Republic of the Congo: Still a mess, and fingers point at Belgian occupation for planting the seeds that make the place a hotbed of violence.

Hot Shots

Guy Verhofstadt: Prime Minister 1999 to present. Intellectual economist who has helped the country immensely by giving leadership a refreshingly clean appearance. A right-leaning Liberal by political party, his coalition with the Socialists has produced some surprisingly left-oriented legislation, including legalizing euthanasia and closing down Belgium's seven nuclear plants; also considering legalizing prostitution and gay marriage. Immediately before taking over the six-month presidency of the EU's European

Dyab Abou Jahjah: wants more
rights for Arabs.

Council in 2001, he hammered out a deal giving more powers to Belgium's
regions. After likeable Guy steps aside – a big position at the EU might
await him – the whole place could collapse.

King Albert II: Reigning monarch 1993 to present. His nephew Prince
Philippe was the one who had been groomed to take over the throne, but
when Albert's childless brother King Baudouin died in 1993, politically
more adept Albert was handed the crown. Didn't exactly lead an easy life:
his mother, Princess Astrid of Sweden, died in a car crash when he was
one; six years later the royal family was deported to Germany when the
Nazis took over Belgium. As a prince who wasn't then in line for the
throne, he was a tad wild: loves motorcycles and riding them fast, to judge
by the number of times he's reportedly been pulled over – and though he
married Italian noblewoman Paola Ruffo di Calabria in 1959, he admits to
having fathered a daughter with a Belgian baroness in 1968.

Dyab Abou Jahjah: Founder Arab European League. Lebanon-born Jahjah
is handsome, bright and a thorn in the government's side. The Arab rights
activist who was once part of Hizbollah applied for political asylum in
Belgium in 1991; denied that, he gained citizenship through marriage. His
ex-wife says she was tricked and may sue him. In the meantime, the press
calls him the Malcolm X of Belgium, because he is demanding that Arabs
be treated as equals in work, law and housing. But he is simultaneously
demanding they be given special rights to their own schools and housing
developments. The government is looking for a way to send him packing.

Louis Michel: Foreign Minister 1999 to 2004; European Commissioner 2004 to present. The portly Wallonian is always good for a colourful quote, but Michel outdid himself lashing out at Austria after Jörg Haider's party made it into the governing coalition, saying, 'Europe doesn't need Austria.' Decidedly brainy, the French-speaking Liberal might not be snowy white: the Foreign Ministry's alleged selling of visas to mobsters in Bulgaria in 1997 (Michel is being sued for obstructing information about it) and sending arms to Nepal are but two things for which he is taking flak.[14] Now European Commissioner for development and humanitarian aid.

Marc Dutroux: Father of three and an electrician by training, Dutroux is best known for his nefarious activities: some say he was once a cocaine dealer at sex parties, and it's now accepted that, while receiving unemployment benefit, he dealt in stolen cars and bought seven houses. He may have also been involved with trafficking sex slaves from Slovakia. First charged with the rape of a fifty-year-old woman in 1983, whom he mutilated with a razor, but those charges were thrown out for lack of evidence. A few years later, he was found guilty of kidnapping and raping five young girls: he was released from prison on parole in 1992, after serving three years of his thirteen-year sentence. In 1996, Dutroux was charged with raping, kidnapping and torturing six other young girls, and murdering four of them. Two of the dead, both eight-year-olds, had starved to death while he was in jail for car theft. Examinations of his properties also turned up a dead colleague, whom he admitted to drugging and burying alive – apparently because he let the two little girls starve. Beneath his houses he had built cages, tunnels and concrete cells to keep his victims in. He was finally tried and found guilty in June 2004 of child rape and murder, and now faces life imprisonment.

> Some press reports have also linked the crimes to the Satanic Order of Abrasax in Wallonia. A letter from Dutroux's alleged accomplice Bernard Weinstein, whom Dutroux killed, reportedly mentions a need to hand over more girls to be sacrificed by the High Priestess of the Order.[15]

Jean-Michel Nihoul: Brussels businessman and self-proclaimed 'Monster of Belgium', he reportedly boasted that he won't be prosecuted in the Dutroux case because he can name too many government officials involved in his sex parties. He was tried in 2004, but was let off.

Vlaams Blok: Right-wing anti-immigration political party – was the most popular and had most seats in the Flemish parliament until banned for being racist. It wants Flanders to separate from Belgium, or rather, it wants

Belgium to die. This party – which some believe is linked to families of Nazi collaborators – may get its wish. It also wants to kick foreigners out. Vlaams Blok recently took a third of the vote in the Antwerp local election, and may be the next mayorship albeit under a new name.

King Baudouin: Monarch 1950–93. While the people voted for a return of the monarchy in 1950, they apparently didn't want the old monarch, Baudouin's father King Leopold III, who never could shake off rumours of collaborating with the Nazis. So violent were the protests and hateful were the riots that broke out just prior to the reestablishment of the monarchy, that Leopold offered the hot seat to his eldest son Baudouin instead. The late king oversaw the transformation of Belgium to one of Europe's richest countries.

> *One of the reasons Belgians weren't so fond of King Leopold III was that he immediately surrendered to the Germans who invaded in 1940. Not so his father King Albert, who'd ordered his subjects to fight throughout the First World War, and had fought alongside them. As for Albert's father Leopold II, that's another matter altogether.*

King Leopold II (1835–1909): Monarch 1865–1909. Belgium's second king is best recalled for opening up the Congo to Belgian development and triggering the so-called 'Scramble for Africa' in 1884, when European powers divided the Dark Continent among themselves. One of Europe's wealthiest men, by the end of his life he loved nothing more than riding around on an oversized tricycle and sneaking off to court his teenage French lover.

Victor Horta (1861–1947): Belgium's best known Art Nouveau architect, Horta co-designed the stunning Royal Greenhouse of Laeken, and went on to lend swirls and curves to buildings across Brussels, including the city's first department store, l'Innovation.

Georges Simenon (1903–89): Celebrated for being the pen behind the fictional Parisian detective Inspector Maigret, Simenon was a fiend: he cranked out at least four books a year – totalling more than 500 (plus innumerable short stories) by the time he died at 86 – in between (he claimed) having sex at least three times a day, perhaps not always with his wife: he was known as 'the man of 10,000 women'.[16] By locking himself in his study, Simenon – who wrote under numerous aliases – was able sometimes to churn out eighty pages a day, typically meeting his goal of finishing his books within two weeks. The most prolific modern writer, he once claimed: 'I have no imagination; I take everything from life.' He somehow managed to keep his interesting affairs out of his fiction, at least.

Tintin (1929–83): In 1929 Georges Rémi (aka Hergé) gave birth to the modern comic book when he inked boy reporter Tintin, fluffy canine Snowy (aka Milou), and scotch-swilling sailor Captain Haddock, who in their first adventure battled communists in the Soviet Union. Over the course of 22 volumes they and other memorable characters, like the Thompson Twins and Professor Calculus, uncovered treasures and battled evil forces everywhere from Peru to the moon. The crude caricatures of other cultures raised questions of the suitability of the comic for children before PC was even a term, and some thought it odd that Hergé was able to continue publication during the Nazi occupation as well. Nevertheless, Hergé was among the twentieth century's most beloved creators; so revered was the artist that nobody dared complete the volume he left unfinished upon his death at age 76.

René Magritte (1898–1967): He brought the absurd to the everyday and vice versa in clean, precisely captured images that always contained a slip of logic and a joke: the back of a man's head is shown, while he looks into a mirror – and sees the back of his head, or perhaps the sky is raining rigid, blank-expressioned businessmen. The Belgian art world didn't get his reality-questioning works: in 1927, Belgian critics so slayed his first show of surrealistic paintings in that country that he packed up and moved to France, where his works still weren't fully appreciated for another two decades. By the time he died in 1967, however, he was acclaimed as an innovator and the foundation stone of Pop Art.

Pieter Brueghel the Elder (c. 1525–69): Brueghel stands out as a star of sixteenth-century Flemish art for several reasons: 1) he strayed from the religious themes and portraits of the wealthy that were the common moneyspinners for artists of the day, perhaps the first to paint landscapes (like *Hunters in the Snow*) that weren't just biblical backdrops; 2) he turned his paintbrush to vibrant village life, capturing it in bawdy detail that was nearly scandalous (see *The Peasant Dance*), especially considering that the Spanish Inquisition was hanging around Antwerp where he worked, and 3) whatever corner of his paintings a viewer takes in, another vignette unfolds, telling us more of life in that day than whole books. He was the head of a whole artist dynasty, which included Pieter the Younger, Jan the Elder and Jan the Younger.

6. Ireland (Éire): Getting Its Due

Fast Facts

Country:	Republic of Ireland; Éire
Capital:	Dublin
Government:	republic
Independence:	1921 'Irish Free State' limited independence from United Kingdom; 1948 republic formed called 'Eire'
Population:	3,970,000 (2004 estimate)
Leaders:	Head of State: President Mary McAleese (1997) Head of Government: Prime Minister Bertie Ahern (1997)
Elections:	President elected by popular vote for 7-year term, Prime Minister appointed by President
Name of Parliament:	Dáil Éireann
Ethnicity:	Celtic–English
Religion:	Roman Catholic 92%, Church of Ireland 3%, other 4%
Language:	Irish (Gaelic) official; English
Literacy:	98% (1981)
Exports:	machinery and equipment, computers, chemicals, pharmaceuticals, live animals
Per capita GDP:	$29,600 (2003 estimate)
Unemployment:	4.5% (May 2004 Eurostat figure)
Percentage in poverty:	10% (1997 estimate)
EU status:	entered EEC in 1973
Currency:	euro
Known for:	jigs, wakes, IRA

Standout Qualities

Green: Forty vibrant shades of it here
Growing: The new kid on the financial big-boy block
Greenbacks: US companies helped trigger the boom

Résumé

Make way for the new Ireland: after centuries of wallowing in depressing financial and historical muck, Ireland has picked itself up, shined itself off and is now displaying itself for the sparkling gem that it is. Ireland's economy is racing, its world status is rising and for the first time in 170 years more people are moving to the island of soft folded hills than running away from it.

An unheard-of 250,000 immigrants moved to Ireland between 1995 and 2000, many of them Irish who'd long before moved away for more financial opportunity.

The good news is that the 'Emerald Tiger' has slipped out from Britain's long, oppressive shadow and is jigging with business partners all over the world. And the best news is that the heated situation in Northern Ireland has cooled off, well, sort of, pretty much, at least for the moment. And the latest news is that the *Economist* says that Ireland is the best place in the whole world to live (although the London-based magazine has not moved there yet).[1]

Ireland v. Republic of Ireland v. Northern Ireland

Ireland is a gorgeous chlorophyll-happy island that lounges between the Atlantic and the Irish Sea. The island is divided into two countries: the bulk, twenty-six counties, is the Republic of Ireland – or Éire – which became independent from Britain in 1921, and the six counties to the north-east, which are part of an entirely different country, namely the United Kingdom or as it is more informally known, Britain. While most of those living in the Republic of Ireland are Catholic, the dominant group in Northern Ireland for centuries was Protestant. Catholics live in Northern Ireland as well: their call for equal rights in the 1960s led to civil unrest between both religious groups there, although even before, relations had been testy. However, the situation is much improved since the 1998 Good Friday Agreement, which gives more power to both groups, and would allow Northern Ireland to leave Britain and become part of Ireland if the majority vote to do so.

Ireland finally opened the door to women in politics and with impressive results: former president Mary Robinson headed the UN Commission on Human Rights and is now one of the most respected politicians in the world. Acclaimed for centuries for its writers – James Joyce, Oscar Wilde, Samuel Beckett and Lady Gregory among them – Ireland has reached millions more with the music of U2, Sinead O'Connor, the Cranberries and Bob Geldof, who weave politics, folklore, society and history into song.

> ***Ireland is the EU's poster child of success:*** *No other EU country has ever used funding from Brussels to stimulate its economy to greater effect: while the other poorer countries of the EU-15, namely Spain, Greece and Portugal, boosted their per capita incomes to around 70 per cent of the Western European average, Ireland vaulted to the 110 per cent mark – meaning that the Irish are making more than most Western Europeans. Wisely spent EU money, good marketing and a surge of foreign investment – in the 1990s, IBM, Intel and other computer firms suddenly wanted a piece of the Dublin action – the Irish economy boomed, leaving Britain open-mouthed in the dust. Financially, Ireland is one of the stars of Europe, and is considered the world's most global economy, although the 2001 'dot.com crash' rather rattled it.*

The bad news is that the EU funding that helped make Ireland sparkle is about to be cut, but the good news is it probably does not really matter. The other bad news is that it's hard to imagine that Ireland will ever be fully content until its North and South are again united as one. And that just may never happen, which may be good news or bad news depending on which side you're on, and pretty much everybody takes a side around here.

> *Never has Éire been trendier, as evidenced by its earnings from tourism: in 2002 tourism kicked €4 billion into the coffers. In 1992, the figure was less than half: €1.6 billion. Now some eight million tourists touch down on the Enchanted Isle every year.*

After centuries of waiting, the luck of the Irish has finally turned up and the country's good mood and good fortune even rubbed off on the EU: during the notably well run Irish presidency of the Council of Europe – the EU's rotating summit of leaders – the European leaders managed to pass a much battled-over draft EU constitution.

As if deciding life is worth living – or perhaps that life without rules is too much fun – in 2004 the Irish enacted no-smoking measures in all public buildings, including restaurants and bars. That may be a draw for the 'we don't smoke, we drive' Americans, but we'll see what effect that has on heavy-puffing Europeans.

In short, Ireland, the name of a country that more often than not used to be said with a sad grimace, now elicits a smile and a nod.

History Review

If only the Romans had arrived in Ireland, its entire history might have been different. Though the Roman conquerors made it to England, where they built walls and roads and connected it with the Continent, the third-century adventurers never made it across the Irish Sea, leaving Ireland's environment wild, undeveloped and disconnected. The Vikings tramped through, however, starting in the eighth century CE, being keen fans of Ireland's churches. They weren't so fond of the Catholic religion that St Patrick had bestowed upon the isle a few centuries before. Rather, the Vikings liked the gold that dripped from the church walls, which they looted along with the other church treasures.

The Vikings did, however, pull Ireland more into the trading loop. Dublin, the culture-dripping city that is home to Trinity College, was originally a Viking trade post.

The English were also drawn to Ireland in part because of the church: Protestant from the sixteenth century on, the English (and Scots) regarded the Catholic Irish as superstitious savages, and apparently having not heard of the commandment 'Thou shall not steal – especially from a church', Henry VIII sent his men to plunder the gold and riches from the holy houses as well. Henry's new Anglican religion eventually set up house on the western isle where it was called the Church of Ireland, which became a huge issue, as the Irish were required to pay a tithe to the Protestant church even though they were Catholic.

Book of Kells saved: *Considering how many times the Catholic church in Ireland was ravaged, it's almost a miracle that this ornate copy of the Gospels from the eighth century still exists. With shimmering gold woven into its pages, the flowery Latin script flows between fantastical* *images of serpents and beasts, and is now housed in Dublin's Trinity College. Those who don't wish to brave the long queues can now view its 340 folios via CD-ROM.*

The English sent in thousands of Protestants to colonize the northern part of the island – and their arrival en masse and their treatment of the Irish as wild cannibals didn't go down well, leading to a fiery Irish uprising in 1641, which the English easily stamped out. Continuing on a losing streak, when the English Civil War kicked off at the same time, the Catholic Irish cast their lot for the king. The war's victor, parliamentarian Oliver Cromwell (his victory was celebrated by executing the king), exacted cruel revenge on the undeveloped backwater of Catholics, which he loathed. To solve the 'Irish Problem', Cromwell yanked away almost all Irish rights, and pushed through laws stripping Catholic Ireland of its culture, from its language and music to its jigs and traditional clothes. Catholic Irish couldn't buy houses or land, attend schools, or enter professions such as law.

Britain's treatment of Ireland was lampooned in the eighteenth century novel Gulliver's Travels *by Jonathan Swift, who satirically writes of two islands, one happy and perfect, and the second that resides under the first, receiving all the upper one's slop. The writer once complained to the English Parliament, 'Am I a freeman in England, and do I become a slave in six hours by crossing the Channel?' His best-known stab at the Englishman's view of the Irish, however, was his essay 'A Modest Proposal' in which he suggests that the Irish eat their young, thereby staving off hunger and keeping the population under control.*

To prevent future generations of Catholics, the Irish were banned from passing on the religion, and their children were often plucked from their homes and shipped as slaves to the West Indies' sugar plantations. Cromwell's army crushed any dissent, offering forgiveness to those who surrendered, who were typically executed nevertheless.

Secret words: *Although education for Irish Catholics was banned, clandestine classes, called hedge schools, were taught hidden away in the woods.*

Decade after decade there was little the Irish could do. The Protestant North politically signed Ireland to England in 1801, by which time the powerless Catholic Irish were mostly peasant farmers, renting from English landlords who ran their agricultural estates from offices in London.

The situation went from really ugly to heinous in 1845, when the potato blight struck the peasants' sole crop. The English initially didn't fathom the severity of the disease that turned potatoes to black mush overnight and they shrugged off the reports of mass starvation as just another exaggerated Irish fantasy. One lord suggested quite seriously that the starving should drink water flavoured with curry powder to substitute for real food. Many English who owned Irish estates evicted their tenants who, given crop failure, couldn't pay. The blight ruined crops for the next several years, but 1845 is the year most painfully recalled, for the million Irish who starved to death and the million who boarded unfit ships, or anything else that might float, and headed across the ocean to the United States, an exodus that led the way for millions more over the next century.

Much funding for the IRA came from the United States, home to many Irish whose families bolted during the Potato Famine.

The callous treatment by the British, who – it is hard to get around the fact – let the Irish Catholics starve (some Irish call it genocide), was made worse by the fact that there was plenty of food being shipped to Ireland during the famine: with their failed crops, the Irish Catholics simply had no money to buy it. The British finally shipped in dried corn; the Irish, however, had no mills to grind it. The Protestants in the North not only survived, some thrived, planting even more bitterness in the hearts of the Irish.

From 1845 until the prosperous 1990s, Ireland continually had been a country of emigration, as the young left the beautiful but dreadfully poor country of tiny towns, seeking their fortunes elsewhere.

The Potato Famine was the turning point. From starvation and emigration, half of the Catholic Irish population was wiped out, and those who had survived the famine had little love left for the British, whose hands grasping the Irish land now appeared as poisonous as the ruinous blight. The Irish language that had been nearly eliminated was shaken from its slumber, and the Gaelic revival was coupled with a nationalist movement demanding independence, which came to be known as Home Rule. Starting in the late nineteenth century, the land known for its forty shades of green was often splattered in red from the bloody battles fought over it, and if the Irish had once been the underdog, now their rebels were often the aggressors.

Vocabulary Builder

Gaelic, the original Celtic tongue, is also the language of Irish nationalism and its words and phrases still pepper Irish speech today, although it is most used along the west coast. Suppressed by the English and a symbol of poverty and disobedience, Gaelic was revived in the late 1800s and went hand-in-hand with louder calls for independence. Ironically, use of Gaelic is dropping in Ireland, while there's a revival of it on the west coast of Scotland.

Éire: Ireland

Taoiseach (tee-shock): Prime Minister

Dáil: the lower house of parliament

craic: laughs with friends

seanachi: story teller whose fireside tales brighten rainy nights

The secrecy that had once shrouded their schools and language was now the rule among Irish independence societies: Fenians (aka Irish Republic Brotherhood) and the Invincibles were but two of the angry, underground groups born in the mid nineteenth century. Starting in the 1860s, the Fenians kicked up revolts, attacked landlords and planted the occasional bomb, and the Invincibles claimed responsibility for the murder of British politician Lord Cavendish in 1882 – all moves that stirred up anti-Irish sentiment among the English, and anti-rebel sentiment in the Irish.

The Surreal Dimension

The wind howling through the glen sounds like muffled voices, mushrooms sprout from the rain-sodden ground almost magically, fog tangles eerily among gnarly witchy-fingered branches and the quaint stone cottages puffing smoke during the day seem scarily isolated at night: there's something about Ireland that, like the chlorophyll, seems supernaturally charged. Whether it's the remnant of folk tales implanted in young minds, or a way of explaining the unknown, many Irish, particularly those in rural areas, believe in magic – leprechauns, wood sprites and screaming banshees; across the countryside, lone undisturbed mounds rise up mid field and are thought to be fairy rings; salt is thrown into borrowed milk; dried herbs hang over doors to keep phantoms from entering. You don't have to go far to find rational-seeming people who swear that they have encountered the wee folk.

Some in London acknowledged the dirt on England's hands during its inglorious history with the Irish, and Prime Minister William Gladstone was a supporter of Irish Home Rule; in the 1860s, he eased some of the financial burdens, such as the mandatory tithes of the Irish to the Protestant church, but his efforts were mostly blocked.

The biggest battles for freedom brewed up in Dublin: during the 1916 Easter Uprising, the Irish seized the Dublin Post Office and declared Ireland independent. After the British army arrived, there was a major show-down, and 1,500 died. Initially most Dubliners, who loathed their violent methods and booed and hissed when the British paraded them to prison, shunned the rebels. But their hushed execution without trial by the British brought many Irish around to their cause and the rebels were soon seen as heroes.

In 1918, all of Ireland's elected politicians were from Sinn Fein, the pro-independence political party founded in 1905. Sinn Fein's first act was to cut ties to the English Parliament, set up their legislature in Dublin and give it a Gaelic name Dáil Éireann. And their first announcement was that Ireland was independent. Predictably, that wasn't well received in London, and a three-year on-and-off war ensued.

An Eye for an Eye, a Life for a Life

The year 1920 was nastier for Irish civilians than most, in part because the British had unleashed paramilitaries – called the Black and Tans – whose job was mainly to make life in Ireland miserable. They succeeded admirably in their goal. In the course of a few weeks:

- the IRA killed 14 undercover detectives
- the Black and Tans opened fire at a football match, killing 12
- Irish rebels killed 18 Black and Tans
- Black and Tans torched downtown Cork

By 1921, England was weary and ready to deal. The twenty-six counties in the South, which made up around 85 per cent of the land, would be given Home Rule, governing themselves and essentially acting as an independent country, though still actually part of the British Empire. The six counties in Northern Ireland – where the Protestant majority did not want to be independent – would remain part of Britain.

Poor Michael Collins: A hero of the Easter Uprising but a young, inexperienced politician, he was sent to broker the 1921 deal with the British. He is said to have scratched his name on the Anglo-Irish Treaty with a deep sigh, saying, 'I have signed my death warrant.' He was right: within nine months, Collins was dead.

Meet the Fighters

Whether they want Ireland united or to keep the North linked to Britain, most Irish and Northern Irish don't condone violence for the cause. But chances are one of their ancestors died in the never-ending battle.

Nationalists, Republicans: Typically Catholic, want Ireland and the North politically united.

Loyalists, Unionists: Typically Protestant, want Northern Ireland to stay linked to London.

Irish Republican Army: Sprang up to unify both parts of Ireland, bombing cars and buildings and typically harming civilians, to make its point. Somewhat calmer, but accused of $50 million bank heist in 2004; everybody's sick of 'em.

Real IRA: Nothing like a wayward clone to stir up some problems: this more radical cell that branched into its own group keeps on bombing as do a few other offshoots.

Ulster Defence Association, Ulster Volunteer Force, Red Hand Commando

and Red Hand Defenders: Loyalist Northern Ireland paramilitaries who are as violent as the IRA go through waves of calm and violence, and are prone to leave territorial markings in the form of the 'Ulster flag' – a blood-red imprint – on walls and buildings across Northern Ireland.

Sinn Fein: The political arm of the IRA, whose leader Gerry Adams says he has no control over the IRA, although few really believe him. *Sinn féin* means 'we ourselves' in Irish Gaelic.

Northern Irish Police: Catholics accuse these Protestant police of discrimination and targeted violence, but many police stations were the targets of intense IRA bombings, and now look like fortresses.

Ireland was (sort of) free, but Ireland divided wasn't the answer desired by the Irish masses. Nevertheless, one faction – to become known as Fine Gael – accepted the 1921 treaty. Another faction – Fianna Fáil – didn't. So fierce did emotions run on the treaty that it led to a brutal year-long civil war. The pro-treaty faction won, but the disappointment over a split Ireland has never subsided. And meanwhile, in Northern Ireland a virulent anger was festering. Although some moved to independent Ireland in the South, the Catholics who remained in the North weren't treated as equals; even into the 1970s, good Protestants were taught that Catholics (who went to different schools, lived in other parts of town, and even had their own taxi services) were civilized beasts who didn't even know how to use knives and forks.

Those Troubles

More than 3,600 people died during the three decades euphemistically termed 'the Troubles'. The conflict that began in 1969 and carried on violently for the next thirty years was centred mostly in Northern Ireland, particularly Belfast and Derry (aka Londonderry). The problems, however, stem from 1921, when the island of Ireland was divided into two parts – a Catholic-dominant Irish republic in the south and a Protestant-dominant territory in the north tied to Britain. Most of the deaths (many of which were innocent civilians) were the responsibility of two parties: the Irish Republican Army (IRA), and the equally violent Ulster Boys. The era of bombs left in briefcases at bus stops (signature IRA) and protesters being beaten with iron rods (signature Ulster thugs) was at least symbolically put to bed with the Good Friday Agreement of 1998. However, radical cells from both sides try to keep the conflict alive, as does the good Reverend Ian Paisley, whose motto, when it comes to negotiating with Catholics, is 'No Surrender!'

What inspired the Catholics in Northern Ireland to begin their initially peaceful protests: the black civil rights movement in the US.

In the late 1960s the anger exploded: the clock-turning moment was a 1969 peace march turned violent. When Catholics led a passive protest in Belfast demanding equal rights, Ulster (Protestant) militiamen attacked them with wood beams, iron rods, bottles and chains. The Troubles had begun.

A Few Troubling Moments

Bloody Sunday: 1972: The symbolic anti-British protest in Derry (aka London-derry) turned nasty; 13 protesters killed, allegedly by British troops.

Bloody Friday: 1972: Six months after Bloody Sunday, IRA sets off car bombs all over Belfast; 22 bombs explode within 75 terrifying minutes.

Orange marches: Annually: Every spring hundreds of older Protestants march to the beat of drums through Northern Ireland's Catholic neighbourhoods in a sad and aggressive display of sectarian hatred.

Ulster bombings in the South: 1974: Protestant Loyalists explode bombs in the Republic of Ireland, killing 33.

IRA assassination: 1979: IRA hits Lord Mountbatten, the Queen's uncle.

Food strike: 1981: Ten IRA prisoners starve themselves to death, including first Sinn Fein minister Bobby Sands.

Brighton Bombing: 1984: IRA bomb blasts Brighton's Grand Hotel where Margaret Thatcher is staying; four killed in the attack, including political VIPs.

Downing Street mortar: 1991: IRA sends its love with mortars launched at 10 Downing Street.

By the 1990s, pretty much everybody had had a surfeit of the Troubles: too many had suffered, nothing had been accomplished, there had been far too many funerals, not to mention the occasional attacks on those attending the funerals. Sinn Fein leader Gerry Adams began talking with Irish nationalist John Hume, the IRA declared a ceasefire, the Ulster Boys followed, the United States flew George Mitchell in to help push peace talks. With plenty of stumbling along the way, and plenty of stumbling since, the 1998 Good Friday Agreement was hammered out, and flyers soon were posted through every door across the Irish isle, explaining the treaty and urging voters to come out on the issue. They did in huge numbers: an overwhelming majority voted yes to the Good Friday Agreement, which is at least a hopeful symbol that humans can (maybe, sort of) change.

> In 2001, slightly over half (51 per cent) of the British said London should just cut its losses and slash its ties with Northern Ireland, letting the Irish isle be entirely independent and united. The British government has been slowly giving the six counties more independence and slack, but many think the chains that bind Ulster to Britain will never be fully unlocked. One factor: Northern Ireland industries, including Bushmills and Guinness, pay lots of taxes that London would surely miss. On the other hand, the costs of maintaining police and military there continually drain the British coffers and more and more are viewing Northern Ireland as a liability.

Quick Tour

The history isn't so obvious these days: it's cloaked in the misty hills that fall to the coast like crumpled green velvet, hidden in the grey stone cottages and old country inns with creaking clocks and blazing fires, buried in the graveyards with looped Celtic crosses blackened by time and hard to make out in the caves where walls are scrawled with mysterious ancient languages that nobody knows. Passing the buildings splashed with bright murals that look cheery until you notice their angry slogans, you can still sense it, and if you're looking at the caged and barbed-wire police stations in Northern Ireland, built to withstand rocket-launched grenades, you feel it quite strongly. But wherever you are, the political–religious tension that has so long defined Ireland – never mind all the agreements and the ceasefires and even the healing effects of increased wealth – is still there staring at you, even in the quaintest of the glowing, gas-lit pubs.

> **Celebrating:** *The Irish, always fond of a wee nip of whiskey and a wee bit o' craic, have been hitting the bottle lately, a wee bit too hard, the government fears. According to the* Economist,[2] *not only did incomes jump during the decade between 1989 and 1999, so did alcohol consumption – by a whopping 41 per cent. Now 50 per cent of men frequently toss back more than six drinks before they stumble out of the pub.*

From the way one refers to certain Northern towns – 'Derry' if you're nationalist, 'Londonderry' if you're not – to the whiskey you drink (Bushmills equals Protestant, Jamesons equals Catholic), so much is subtly politicized in Ireland you can utter something offensive by merely opening your mouth. It's understandable: Ireland has been living up to its 'Fighting Irish' reputation since the ninth century – fighting to be united for the past eighty, and for almost all of its existence just fighting to stay alive in a land that was until recently mostly agricultural and subject to weather and bugs.

But if the shadows of an ugly past can still be glimpsed, at least they are not so obvious now, and the chronic feeling of betrayal and playing the role of the underdog is finally gone, more or less. Change has swept across Ireland at an astonishing pace, kicking the rural backwater into the twenty-first century, rolling five decades of modern reforms into one. It's not just the sudden appearance of luxury boutiques and chain stores in Dublin that lends a feeling that Ireland is reconnecting with the rest of the world – and more importantly, the present – and it's not just the immigrants who are suddenly knocking at the door as if Ireland had only just appeared on the map.

Opening the Doors

Ireland shocked the world in 2004, when it – along with Britain, which quickly back-pedalled – welcomed citizens from new EU countries to take up work there. The country of less than four million was already seeing more than 50,000 newcomers in recent years, creating a housing shortfall in Dublin, as well as a skyrocketing of property prices. Nevertheless, Ireland, which now has one of the most educated work forces in the world, needs more workers. Those who came in after 2004, however, will find at least one thing has changed: a child born in Ireland is no longer granted automatic citizenship, unless one of its parents has been living in the country for at least three years.

Immigrants may be saving the Catholic church, say some. While the church – and more so its value system – remains powerful, it is much more in the background with the young Irish, and some priests say they are preaching to churches that are near empty save for a scattering of pensioners. The young immigrants – many from Africa and Asia – are now filling at least a few more rows of pews.[3]

The school system is now secular, being run since the 1970s by the government, not the church, and the agriculture that once employed most of the workers has been shoved aside by industry – Ireland is now the second largest producer of computer software, behind the United States. Society is transforming too. In the land where once you could not buy condoms and where the train to Northern Ireland was nicknamed the 'pill train' because you could get birth control there, contraception is now widely available although it only became legal in 1993.

So tense was the issue of contraception when Mary Robinson first presented it in the Irish parliament in the 1970s that not one parliamentarian supported her move to legalize it.[4]

Divorce is now legal, at least in some circumstances; women – who until two decades ago were forbidden to sit on juries – are now powerful forces organized in voting groups, and the church, while respected, is now taking a back seat.

Sign of the times: *The late-1990s Channel 4 Irish comedy* Father Ted, *about a household of inept priests who are always competing with other clergymen, was a social marker: knocking the sacred cow of religion would have been positively unthinkable not long ago.*

Granted there's a bit of a moral vacuum at the moment, with Ireland finding itself wealthier and with few social constraints. Binge drinking is up, so is heroin use and drug use in general. Marriages are later, the birth rate is dropping, and divorce is on the rise. Well, goodbye banshees and little people: Ireland has finally entered the real modern world.

Religion Matters

Ireland is still very closely aligned with the Roman Catholic church: divorce was not legalized until 1997 – and only in limited circumstances. Ireland also has some of the world's strictest laws on abortion, which in most cases is illegal; since 1982, however, abortion is legal in Ireland if the mother is likely to kill herself; in twenty years there's only been one case – a suicidal teenager pregnant by rape – when the abortion was granted. However, the 1982 law made it legal to go elsewhere for the procedure; it's estimated that every year 7,000 Irish women go to Britain for that purpose. Prime Minister Bertie Ahern thought the existing legislation was too lenient and in 2002 pushed another referendum for a stricter abortion law. It failed. There was a loud din of protest, however, later that year when a Dutch boat pulled in to harbour, offering to provide abortion services just outside Irish territorial waters. One more problem: child-abuse scandals in Ireland (as in Boston, USA) are shaking the foundations of the church.

Future Forecast

The more green Ireland generates, the more it can make a break from its troubles.

Hot Spots

Dublin: A century ago the Republic of Ireland's capital was the site of frequent battles, and a city of mass emigration; now it's hopping and so many immigrants have arrived that housing is extending far into the hinterland. Plenty of computer geeks around here, where the dot.coms have set up and the country's wealth is concentrated.

The countryside: Job possibilities and income levels still lag in rural areas.

The Irish Sea: It's the world's most radioactive, thanks to Britain: nuclear compound Sellafield releases its waste into the waters between Britain and Ireland. Citizens' movements in Ireland – as well as in Norway and Britain – are trying to shut it down.

Northern Ireland (aka Ulster): It's part of Britain politically, but located on the island of Ireland geographically – a situation that gets touchy at times. Wind-carved coasts, stained-glass bars and crumbling castles are lovely, but the history here isn't. Belfast and Derry/Londonderry have been but two epicentres of the anger. Even though it's more peaceful now, tensions still flare occasionally – Catholic schoolchildren walking through a Protestant neighbourhood not long ago set off riots. The winners of the autumn 2003 Northern Ireland Assembly election were Paisley's Unionist party (DUP) and Republican Sinn Fein, a recipe for a lot of yelling and an entirely ineffective government.

Belfast: British-controlled capital of Northern Ireland is experiencing a tourism boom: lots of fancy hotels and restaurants, and salsa dancing is big at the weekends.

Good Friday Specifics

The 1998 agreement has seen some bad weeks, but it's still holding together, more or less. It called for:

- the future political alignment of Northern Ireland to be decided by local vote
- a new legislature to be established that balances Protestant and Catholic powers
- the Republic of Ireland and Sinn Fein to give up demands that Ireland be unified
- the Republic of Ireland to have a say in the Northern Ireland government
- the Irish Republican Army to decommission its weapons

Four months after the signing of the Good Friday Agreement the Real IRA – an offshoot cell – exploded a car bomb at Omagh, killing twenty-nine.

Voting booths: The Irish vote more often than any other member of the EU and, unlike most countries, they vote on EU treaties. If they vote against EU agreements, they can knock them off the table. Not only can they vote via their mobile phones, the Irish can also vote for second choice in political elections.

Not Nice: In 2001 Ireland held a referendum about the Treaty of Nice and whether the EU should accept ten new members from the other

Fetching Ireland: the beauty starts at the coast and rolls in.

side of Europe – the only member state to put the question to its people. The Irish voted against it, raising the ire of many in the EU; after all, Ireland had been in a sorry state when the EU had allowed it to enter in 1978; of any country, it had seen the most dramatic benefit from the EU and its money. The following year a modified Nice treaty was again put to the people and this time they voted to accept it. The whole experience hurt Ireland's reputation at the EU, where they were seen as ingrates. The experience also left the EU wary of referendums put to the people in member states.

Fairy circles: Best not plough up the little people's sacred mounds or you might soon be looking at the Grim Reaper. Those wishing to see leprechauns in action might check out www.irelandseye.com/leprechaun, which shows live shots from a webcam hidden in a magical oak over-looking an Irish glen that's home (supposedly) to a fairy ring. If the leprechauns are boycotting, you can click on the site's Ghost Watch, where a webcam in a Belfast mill is on twenty-four-hour watch for the resident phantoms.

Hot Shots

Mary McAleese: President of Republic of Ireland, 1997 to present. It's a veritable trend: twice in a row women have sat in Ireland's presidential seat. Barrister McAleese, of Fianna Fail, is sharp and looks good on TV. No wonder: she's a former broadcaster.

Here's to you Mrs (Mary) Robinson

No one in modern history has had more of an effect on Ireland than former president Mary Robinson, who led the country into the present. Holding law degrees from Trinity College Dublin and Harvard before she was 25, she won a Labour seat in the Irish Parliament the next year, where she quickly stood out as a reformist. Winning the presidency in 1990, she pushed womens' rights, legalized contraception and divorce, and was so effective in her seven-year term as president – before that mostly a ceremonial role – that she had the approval rate of 97 per cent of the Irish during her term. She hit all kinds of buttons – meeting with Sinn Fein leader Gerry Adams and then the British Queen – and while giving a report after flying to Rwanda, the typically reserved lawyer broke into tears, moving some in her audience to the same. She went from the Irish presidency to head the United Nations High Commission for Human Rights (1997–2002). Pushed out of the position by the United States, who were none too happy about her criticisms of the war in Afghanistan, Robinson was replaced by Brazilian Sergio Vieira de Mello, who was killed several months later in the August 2003 bombing of the UN headquarters in Iraq. Robinson is now president of a new human rights organization based in New York, the Ethical Globalization Initiative, which she founded.

Fianna Fail: Ireland's largest political party, and also the right-leaning party of Prime Minister Ahern. It sprang from the anti-treaty factions of the 1920s. Took a hit in 2004 elections, but still leads the political scene.
Fine Gael: Typically Ireland's second largest party, and also right of centre, they've been losing ground lately; originally were pro-treaty after the 1921 agreement and fought Fianna Fail.
Bertie Ahern: Prime Minister of Republic of Ireland, 1997 to present. The press called him the Teflon Taoiseach because he's been lucky enough to be in the power seat during Ireland's most glorious hour; he's the only

Former President Mary Robinson
brought Ireland up to the present.

prime minister to be elected to two consecutive terms in the republic's history. However, the Fianna Fail politician's popularity is eroding as Ireland's unemployment rate creeps up. President of the EU's Council of Ministers during the first six months of 2004, Ahern was under heavy pressure to get all the EU countries to accept the proposed EU constitution – and he did it. His people apparently didn't care: his party took a blow in the European Parliament elections. Nevertheless, they are still number one.

Gerry Adams: Slick, smart and charismatic – although his charms don't work on Ian Paisley – the head of the IRA's political wing Sinn Fein claims he has no control over the IRA. Sits in the (currently suspended) Northern Ireland Assembly along with Martin McGuinness, former IRA commander, now Minister of Education.

John Hume: Head of Social Democratic and Labour Party (SDLP), the Catholic Nationalist was never keen on the IRA and Sinn Fein; his talks with Gerry Adams, however, pointed the peace process in the right direction.

David Trimble: Head of Ulster Unionist Party (UUP), he too was never a fan of the IRA and Sinn Fein, but he sits in the Assembly with members of the latter. Walks out every so often in disgust.

John Hume and David Trimble won the Nobel Peace Prize in 1998.

George Mitchell: Not that long ago, back when the United States had diplomats and peacemakers, the senator was a shining example: he helped to negotiate the 1998 Good Friday Agreement, and came back in when it started falling apart. Proof that the US isn't always an arms-pushing bully, he too should have been nominated for the 1998 Nobel Peace Prize.

Reverend Ian Paisley: Leader Democratic Unionist Party. Refusing to partake in any peace negotiations, the righteous stick-in-the-mud reverend from Belfast has only helped keep sides angry and divided. Won lots of votes in the 2003 Assembly elections, giving him yet more power.

Irish diaspora: A powerful bunch, particularly in the US, where they are connected with Boston politics and the Kennedys. They helped fund numerous Irish causes, with at least some donating to the IRA. Some estimates put the numbers of Irish emigrants at nearly 60 million, although many are coming back home.

Oscar Wilde (1854–1900)

With drooping almond eyes and long almond-shaped face under a flip of hair, there's a sadness about Oscar Wilde's appearance – even before 1895, when everything went to hell. Until that point, life pretty much had been a gay frolic down the literary lane winning recognition and eliciting laughter along the way. Born in Dublin of a wealthy ear and eye surgeon, Sir William Wilde, young Oscar stood out at Trinity College for his crackling wit, his dandyish appearance and his fondness for decorating with peacock feathers, as well as for his gifts with the pen which brought a slew of awards. Upon completing his studies he sought the hand of his girlfriend Florence Balcombe, but she rejected him for fellow Irishman Bram Stoker, and Wilde slunk from his motherland, rarely to return even for the shortest of visits. Hired as editor for the popular magazine *Women's World*, Wilde married wealthy Constance Lloyd with whom he had two sons and ventured into books, first poetry, then fairy tales, and finally the stinging high-society novels and plays that would be his trademark. *A Picture of Dorian Gray* came out in 1891, to popular acclaim, and in 1895 *The Importance of Being Earnest* was first performed to raves in London. But his high lifestyle soon spiralled downwards: manuscripts he was working on were stolen and, worse, Wilde's double life soon emerged. When the Marquis of Queensberry, who was father of Wilde's young lover Lord Alfred 'Bosie' Douglas, publicly accused him of homosexuality – leaving a note at Wilde's club calling the writer a 'somdomite' (sic) – the playwright sued him for libel, and lost. Having lied to the court about the extent of his dealings with Bosie, Wilde soon was the target of the London prosecutors: found guilty of 'gross indecency' he was sentenced to two years' hard labour in Reading Gaol, his reputation so tarnished that his sons changed their name to Holland. Depressed and sick in prison, he wrote to Bosie possibly the world's longest letter – some 30,000 words – later published as *De Profundis*. Upon his release Wilde slithered off penniless to live in France as Sebastian Melmoth (the name of his favourite literary martyr, from his great-uncle Charles Maturin's novel *Melmoth the Wanderer*). It was here that he wrote *The Ballad of Reading Gaol* and soon died, penniless, of cerebral meningitis. Despite the tragic ending of his personal play, Wilde lives on: his literary works are now among the most cherished of the era.

Charlie McCreevy: European Commissioner 2004 to present. Commissioner for internal market and services.

Bono: Born in 1960 in Dublin as Paul Hewson, the lead singer of U2 brings politics to music and awareness to entertainment: his humanitarian work, much of it focusing on HIV and poverty in Africa, has resulted in the donation of millions of pounds to those causes; has also lobbied rich nations to drop outstanding debts of third world countries and to make their trading practices more fair. In 2000 U2 officially became more popular than the Beatles.

Seamus Heaney: Winner of the 1995 Nobel Prize for Literature, Northern Ireland-born Heaney is a poet, essayist and university professor whose works are motivated by the divide between agricultural and industrial Ireland, as well as the divide between the Six Counties and the Republic. His work is widely regarded as among the greatest modern poetry in English.

Maeve Binchy: Former London correspondent for the *Irish Times*, Binchy hit the big time when she turned to fiction, writing over a dozen novels about everyday Irish life, the family and the victory of courage. Outselling fellow Irish bards Beckett, Yeats and Wilde, the prolific author has seen several of her works, including *Circle of Friends* and *Tara Road*, turned into movies.

7. Spain (España): Living It Up

Fast Facts

Country:	Kingdom of Spain; Reino de España
Capital:	Madrid
Government:	parliamentary monarchy
Independence:	Unified 1492; Franco dictatorship ended 1975
Population:	40,281,000
Leaders:	Head of State: King Juan Carlos (1975)
	Head of Government: Prime Minister José Luis Rodríguez Zapatero (2004)
Elections:	Monarchy is hereditary; leader of majority party or coalition appointed Prime Minister, approved by monarch
Name of Parliament:	Cortes
Ethnicity:	mix of Mediterranean and Nordic
Religion:	99% Roman Catholic, not all of them practising
Language:	74% Castilian Spanish; 17% Catalan; 7% Galician; 2% Basque
Literacy:	97%
Exports:	machinery, cars, food, tourism
Per capita GDP:	$22,000 (2003 estimate)
Unemployment:	11.1% (May 2004 Eurostat figure)
EU status:	founding member (EEC member since 1986)
Currency:	euro
Known for:	fun, sun, sangría

Standout Qualities

Fiestas: Parties for bulls, tomatoes, saints
Siestas: Naps needed
Splits: Regionally divided

Résumé

For a place that was taking a siesta for most of the twentieth century, España – the EU's second-largest country by area and historically one of its poorest – is waking up in grand style. The country swiftly transformed itself from a lumbering, backward dictatorship into a plugged-in liberal democracy in a mere decade and Spaniards keep popping up all across the global board in areas from international politics to the arts.

General Francisco Franco – 'El Caudillo' – lorded over Spain from 1939 to 1975. Upon Franco's death, King Juan Carlos reinvented the country as a parliamentary democracy with a monarch as head of state and a prime minister as head of government.

Since the death of the oppressive Franco, who cut Spain off from Europe, Spaniards seem to be flooding into the world scene. Film-director Pedro Almodóvar recently took two Oscars and was fêted at Cannes while Javier Solana – former General Secretary of NATO – is arguably the EU's most powerful man as de facto foreign minister of the EU. Josep Borrell is the new president of the European Parliament and Judge Baltasar Garzón, who demanded the 1998 extradition of General Pinochet from Britain, summons bigwigs from Kissinger to Berlusconi to his court. (Granted, they rarely show up.) Real Madrid lured Europe's hottest footballers Beckham and Zidane to play for the team, tenor Plácido Domingo is an operatic god, Picasso is hailed as the foremost artist of the last century and Dalí is right behind him. El Bulli chef Ferran Adrià is the toast of the world culinary scene and the stamping of flamenco is now heard in classes from Tokyo to New York.

Tourism rakes in over €33 billion to the Spanish economy[1] and employs about 11 per cent of the population.[2]

Spain is the second most visited destination in the world, with over 50 million tourists each year drinking in its varied architecture from modernist to medieval, and tipping back sherries in tiled bars decorated with hanging hams. Madrid is a hot contender for the 2012 Olympics and Barcelona was site of the event in 1992 – the same year that Seville hosted the World Expo. And Spanish business such as telecom giant Telefonica is spreading out everywhere, including gobbling up Latin America's market.

One of the reasons Spain has perked up and modernized so rapidly: help from the EU, which it joined in 1986. In 2002, for example, Spain received €8 billion in regional funds for infrastructure.

Suddenly Spain matters again, and the country's growing global stature keeps it high in the international news, most notably when less than a year after US-cheering Prime Minister José María Aznar sent Spanish troops into Iraq, Spain's new Prime Minister José Luis Rodríguez Zapatero pulled the troops out.

Nine out of ten Spaniards did not support the 2003 war in Iraq and were against sending Spanish troops there. Prime Minister Aznar ignored the will of his people and shipped off his military for Iraq's post-war reconstruction. The prime minister never explained his actions to Spaniards nor did he broach the topic in parliament before the deployment: he finally mentioned it in the Cortes some eight months after troops had been shipped off.

The country best known for its happy-go-lucky nature rated its biggest headlines, however, over two recent tragedies: the 2002 sinking of the oil tanker *Prestige* off the north-west coast – a spill that blanketed the coast with petrol-goo – and the 2004 bombing in Madrid that killed 191, injured more than 1,400, and caused a political revolution in its wake. A record number of Spaniards – including typically disenfranchised young voters – turned up at the polls three days later and promptly ejected the ruling Popular Party government from power, even though surveys had previously predicted it would win. Some international pundits condemned Spain, saying voters had given in to terrorism. But the truth of the matter was that many Spaniards were fed up with the PP's incessant misinformation and manipulations: the Aznar administration's behaviour during the days leading up to the 14 March 2004 parliamentary election was a perfect illustration of the problem.

'The death squad succeeded in penetrating the crusader European depths and striking one of the pillars of the crusader alliance – Spain – with a painful blow. These bomb attacks were part of settling old scores with the crusader Spain for its war against Islam. Where is America to protect you today Aznar?' – from statement purportedly written by Abu Hafs al-Masri claiming responsibility for Madrid attack on 11 March 2004 in London paper al-Quds al-Arabi.

Political Bombs: 11 March 2004

Terrorism isn't new to Spain: the bombs and bullets of Basque separatist group ETA have killed 800 (mostly police, government officials and journalists) since 1961. However, the country had never experienced anything like what happened that Thursday in March. During Madrid's morning rush hour, ten bombs on three trains carrying the city's workers exploded simultaneously, ripping open the carriages like sardine cans and leaving the tracks strewn with bodies. Within hours, a group affiliated with al-Qaeda – Abu Hafs al-Masri – claimed responsibility for the vicious attack that killed hundreds, but as smoke still billowed out from the trains and emergency workers hauled off the injured and covered the dead, the Aznar administration had already made up its mind: it was ETA. The sophisticated style of the operation – bombs were detonated by calls to explosive-rigged cell phones – didn't fit the Basque group's usual method, and ETA, which typically admits to its deeds, denied all involvement. Investigators quickly discovered evidence pointing to Islamic radicals – a duffel bag with a live bomb, a detonator and an Arabic-configured cell phone, a nearby van loaded with detonators, cell phones and extremist Islamic tapes – but Aznar's Popular Party government wouldn't announce or acknowledge the discoveries. In fact, they pressured state news agencies to quash the reports.[3] Foreign minister Ana Palacio instructed all Spanish embassies to say the Basque separatist group was behind it,[4] the Interior Minister announced it was 'absolutely clear' that the attack was all ETA's doing,[5] and Prime Minister José María Aznar demanded that the UN Security Council immediately condemn ETA for the Madrid attack (which the UN body did that very day). Aznar went on to personally call the heads of all the major media to insist this was a barbarous act of the Basques; his administration continually tried to suppress any information contradicting that view. The reason that Aznar kept up this insistence though absolutely nothing bore out the claims: the parliamentary election was in three days. Aznar's government had always taken a tough line with the separatists, and it was a widely respected stance that helped to keep the Popular Party in power. An ETA attack would ensure victory in the upcoming election. If it was an Islamic attack, perhaps in response to Aznar involving Spain in the war in Iraq – a most unpopular move – then it would be a glaring liability. Despite the government's nonstop chanting of 'ETA, ETA, ETA', word slipped out that it probably was not ETA at all. For their deception, as much as for their unpopular decision of getting Spain involved in Iraq, the Popular Party lost the 2004 parliamentary election as a surprising 77 per cent turned out to vote – the numbers boosted by young voters who put in a rare appearance at the polling booth – with most casting their ballots for the PP alternative, the Socialists.

The Madrid attacks were not the first time that the Popular Party had spouted misinformation. Their handling of the Prestige *oil spill was just as questionable. After the ship broke in two and began gushing heavy fuel oil, Madrid underplayed what was the worst environment debacle to strike Spain. While the international media accurately reported that the oil spill was worse than the* Exxon Valdez, *the Spanish government made it sound like a small trickle: there were a 'few localized slicks' and 'four small threads'. Prime Minister Aznar didn't even bother to visit the disaster site: instead Vice President Mariano Rajoy was shoved in front of the camera to ladle out misinformation while black waves coated the pristine Galician shores in hardening muck. The lack of truth, realistic vision and leadership during the tragedy unnerved the Spanish people, some of whom felt it was like a return of the Franco days, when you had to listen to the foreign press to figure out what was going on in Spain.*

The Socialist government headed by José Luis Rodríguez Zapatero appeared as surprised as anyone else when it won the election in spring 2004, but the new administration quickly made several moves that impressed the public. Zapatero appointed women to half the seats in his cabinet – that's a first – and he made good on promises to end Spain's involvement in Iraq, pulling troops out the next month.

When Defence Minister José Bono informed the US of the decision to bring home Spanish troops there was some serious static over the wire: Donald Rumsfeld reportedly called the pullout 'cowardly', which prompted Bono to yell back that Spain indeed had 'cojones'.[6]

The new government also inherited a few problems: namely, an unemployment rate of 11 per cent, an ill-defined immigration policy and a country of seventeen provinces that is a political jigsaw with identities more wrapped up in regional issues than Madrid. And there's the lingering problem of terrorism: was the March 2004 attack really just a response to Aznar's support for the US and the invasion of Iraq? Or part of an

attempted radical Muslim takeover of Spain to reinstall the Moorish civilization of al-Andalus? Reconquering the lost Muslim empire, after all, was
what Osama bin Laden in an October 2001 missive instructed followers
to do.

> A 17 March 2004 email purportedly from Abu Hafs al-Masri claimed
> that the group would not be targeting Spain in the near future due
> to the election results. However, it's unclear whether the men believed
> to be ringleaders in the Madrid bombing were actually part of Abu
> Hafs al-Masri or a different (although perhaps related) radical organiz-
> ation such as the Moroccan Islamic Combatant Group which also has
> ties to al-Qaeda. Who the North African radicals suspected to be
> behind the attack were working with may never be known: on 3 April
> 2004, after a two-hour standoff with police, a group of suspects in a
> suburban Madrid apartment blew themselves up with explosives that
> were identical to those used in the train bombings. Five of the suspects
> – including a Tunisian and several Moroccans – were killed in the blast,
> although several may have escaped.

History Review

Settled by Romans, Celts and Visigoths, the peninsula of Iberia was a
disorganized mass of scattered kingdoms in the early eighth century when
Muslim Moors invaded, conquering most of the land in a mere seven years
and creating a settlement that was one of the world's most sophisticated.
The weather to the north – the foggy rains of Galicia and the cool wind-
battered east coast – didn't much appeal to the peoples who came from
Syria and North Africa. They moved their headquarters to the parched
terrain of the south, where they made Córdoba the capital of the kingdom
they called al-Andalus, and today is called Andalusia. Working alongside
the natives who lived in these parts, the Moors established a settlement
that rivalled Alexandria and Baghdad in their heydays, would last for
seven centuries and was far more advanced than anything Western Europe
had to offer.

Al-Andalus 711–1492

As word of the new Muslim settlement spread, scientific and philosophical scholars flocked to Córdoba, then Seville and Granada, as did linguists, architects, artisans and scribes who translated lost works of ancient Greeks and Romans, launching a renaissance comparable to the one born in Florence some six centuries later. Marble palaces and elaborate mosques of horseshoe arches appeared across the land; water from mountain snows and rivers was brought to homes via pipes. Irrigation and advanced agricultural practices coaxed forth new crops from the seeds Moors had brought: the perfume of orange blossoms breezed through courtyards and outlying hills burst with trees of almonds, dates, lemons and limes alongside fields thick with rice and sugarcane. While the rest of European civilization was technologically in the dark, the paved streets of Córdoba were lined with lights; markets boasted silks, tapestries, swords, porcelain, and spices. The most popular shops were booksellers, whose trade was made possible by the eighth-century introduction of paper-making techniques and the skills of 'copyists' who produced upwards of 50,000 books every year. Ideas and intellectual explorations flourished as thinkers scratched pens across paper in flowery scrawls of crescents and dots and by the tenth century libraries abounded, including one that contained over 200,000 handwritten tomes – the Koran, Bible and Torah stood alongside books of Ptolemy, ancient histories, scientific treatises and volumes of poetry. Hospitals performed operations for cataracts, schools taught algebra and spherical trigonometry; students also learned Latin, physics, botany and medicine, and studied maps of the seas and the stars. Observatories tracked celestial bodies, and astrolabes guided ships on trade routes to the Far East. Just as impressive as the scientific, architectural and agricultural complexity was the level of civility that typified much of the occupation: women in al-Andalus were doctors, lawyers, librarians and esteemed 'copyists' of books; Christians, Jews and Muslims lived side by side in relative peace, each pursuing their religion in their own places of worship. Non-Muslims enjoyed nearly all rights afforded to Muslims, including working in government and schools; they could also drink alcohol, eat pork and ignore Islamic dictates, but non-believers paid a special tax and males could be conscripted unless they converted. The Moors ushered in an advanced civilization where standards of living were surprisingly high, but little by little Catholics (including the famous Spanish hero El Cid) pushed out the Muslims and the occupiers' territory shrank: retreating from such academic centres as Toledo, the Moors lost Valencia,

Córdoba, then the favoured city of musicians, Seville, until finally all that remained by the 1300s was the southern region of Granada. The long-awaited final moment of the Catholic 'reconquest' occurred in 1492, when the armies of King Ferdinand and Queen Isabella forced out the last Moorish ruler from the spectacular hillside palace of Alhambra; it's said that the sultan, Boabdil, took one final look at the lacy latticework and fine gardens of his home, let out a deep sigh and departed in tears.[7]

Although the armies of Isabella and Ferdinand finally ran the Moors out in 1492, legend has it that before long at least a few of the Moors were invited back. The Spaniards couldn't figure out how to run their elaborate irrigation systems.

Having stitched together their kingdoms and united all of Spain under the strict veil of Catholicism – Muslims and Jews were soon shown the door unless they converted – Isabella and Ferdinand launched the ventures that would make them best known: conquering the New World, and introducing the Spanish Inquisition, both activities that further instilled the Catholic faith. In fact, the voyages to farflung lands were at least partly funded by the riches collected from the poor souls that Inquisitors accused of heresy.

The Spanish inquisition, launched at Isabella's request in 1478, officially lasted until 1808. Initially targeting Jews, it prompted some 200,000 of them to flee Spain, but Catholics were among those accused of heresy as well. The accused, who had no idea who had accused them, lost their property upon being arrested. Subjected to gruelling torture, if they still did not confess they were burned. At least 350,000 accused Spanish 'heretics' died at the stake.

Expanding the Empire via the Seas

Portugal said no, France said no, so did England and Spain, but Christopher Colombus (aka Colón), an explorer from Genoa, would not drop his idea of a western route to the East Indies – nor would he stop pestering monarchs to fund his trip. Finally, after nearly a decade of his whingeing, Isabella – feeling competitive with Portugal, whose sailors kept the sea route to the Indies a secret to themselves – gave Colón his three ships and his funding in 1492. Although Colón kept insisting, from his first voyage to the Caribbean island of Hispaniola to his last trip to the area, that he had found the East Indies, the discoveries and maps of Amerigo Vespucci in the early 1500s showed that Colón had discovered entirely new lands. The race was on to ravage the unexplored world and steal its riches: Ponce de León claimed Puerto Rico for the crown, Velásquez took Cuba, Balboa seized Panama. The mother lode was struck when Hernán Cortés pushed his way into Mexico in 1519, killing Montezuma and claiming the gold of the Aztec kingdom of Tenochtitlán for the Spanish monarchy; four years later, Pizarro conquered the silver-rich Inca civilization of Peru. But the most dramatic and traumatic of any of the voyages was that of Portuguese Magellan, who sailed under the Spanish flag with five ships in a 1519 voyage that sought to find the Spice Islands by heading west. Rounding the southern tip of Chile, where he discovered that his Spanish suppliers had left out a year's worth of food, his ships sailed across the Pacific for three months without spotting land, the sailors eating rodents to stay alive. Finally reaching today's Guam, he continued on to the Philippines, where his pride got the better of him. After converting a local sultan to Christianity, he offered to show the ruler how to fight his enemies the modern, European way. Launching a battle against nearby islanders, Magellan's men were quickly beaten back and Magellan took a fatal poisonous arrow in the heart. The few remaining sailors pushed on, pulling into Seville in 1522 with only 18 of the original 240 crew members remaining to tell the tale of the world's first circumnavigation.

The brutal acts against the native Americans, who died from disease, torture and the slave labour the Spanish inflicted, did not go unnoticed. In 1542 Spanish laws were enacted to protect the locals, although they were mostly ignored. The Spanish priest Bartolomé de Las Casas made the indigenous people's plight widely known in his 1552 book A Short Account of the Destruction of the West Indies. *Still the acts continued until many of the original peoples were wiped out, and Europeans ultimately shipped in African slaves to fill in the labour shortage.*

The Spanish ships, heavy with riches, were raided not only by pirates off Africa's northern coast but by other Europeans, particularly the British, and hundreds of others sank in storms at sea. Enough of the silver and gold made it into Spain's treasury, nevertheless, to make Spanish rulers for a time the world's richest. Under King Philip II, Spain's dominance of the sea didn't last long, particularly as they kept losing ships in wars with the English and French, and in 1587 Sir Francis Drake sneaked into Cádiz and sank all the vessels in port. The most crushing blow, however, was the loss of the mighty Spanish Armada the following year, when Spain's attack on England backfired, and its mighty Armada, thanks to Drake's fighters and a nasty storm, was reduced to splinters on the rocks. New ships were built, new lands – including Naples, Sicily and Portugal – were added to the empire's roster but the problems of corruption and weak leadership continued, and the Spanish empire severely declined in the seventeenth century.

Miguel de Cervantes Saavedra (1547–1616) and his Novel Idea

For a man who was the world's first best-selling novelist, Miguel Cervantes spent rather a lot of time in prison. In 1575 he was captured in Algeria (where he spent five years behind bars until ransom was delivered) and a few other times he was rounded up for his dodgy practices as a tax collector, but for all the discomfort, prison served him well. Some say that he wrote *Don Quixote* behind bars, others say he merely conceived of the idea of a parody of a chivalrous knight there, but most agree the book he produced was Europe's first novel when it appeared in 1605. Readers so adored his book that Part II soon followed, selling equally well, but that only infuriated Cervantes. The 'sequel' was a fake, written by an unknown using both his characters and established plot. The author quickly followed up with his own Part II in 1615. Cervantes also penned plays, poems and collections of tales, but none of the others was apparently worthy of plagiarizing.

The popularity of Don Quixote *was due in part to Cervantes' use of the simple language of Everyman that captured the manners of the times. Among the phrases that Cervantes introduced to the world: 'the pot calling the kettle black'; 'to smell a rat'; 'a wild goose chase'; 'the sky's the limit'; and 'born with a silver spoon in his mouth'.*

Many were the problems faced by weakling Philip IV who reigned from 1621–65: the economy was going to hell, Spain was dragged into the Thirty Years War against France, the Dutch and the Swedes; Catalans on the north-east coast revolted in 1640 and aligned themselves with France; Portugal, irate that Spanish manoeuvres had lost them their lands in the East Indies, shoved off the same year and Naples rebelled against Spain as well. On the positive side, the arts were flourishing. Diego Velázquez became Philip's court painter, the king befriended Peter Paul Rubens, collecting his works, and a few splendid cathedrals, including the one at Granada, were built.

As a result of the Thirty Years War, and its conclusion, the 1648 Treaty of Westphalia, France shoved Spain aside to become the dominant European power and Spain permanently lost its Habsburg claim to the Netherlands.

Spain's situation didn't improve in the 1700s: mentally handicapped Charles II (reigned 1665–1700) died without an heir. At one point Louis XIV of France, who also had claims to the Spanish throne, looked likely to take Spain under his wing: the idea of Spain and France being one was so repulsive to some parties that the War of Spanish Succession – Europe's first big world war – kicked off in 1701, lasting for another thirteen years. As a result of that military devastation, Britain took the rock of Gibraltar off the south of Spain in 1704, British ownership becoming official by the 1713 Treaty of Utrecht, a loss that continues to infuriate Spain to this day.

For all the wealth it brought the Spanish empire, colonization and the country's extreme religiousness ultimately set Spain back. Devout Spaniards were not active in the scientific revolution, nor was this a land that produced many inventors. Like a son raised in wealth who has no need to learn job skills, Spain did not try to evolve with the rest of Europe, mostly ignoring the Industrial Revolution and the changing textile market. By doing so, it set itself back centuries.

The downward spiral continued. The new king Carlos IV, who'd stepped in for his elder imbecilic brother, was inept and unpopular. Catalans in the north-east area around Barcelona and Basques in the north around Bilbao still weren't happy as part of one Spain. Calls for Latin American independence grew louder, and the Spanish ignored them. Independence for

Spanish colonies, however, came about soon – and suddenly – as a result of one thing: Napoleon invaded Spain in 1808. Most of the military in the New World travelled back to Spain to fight in the War of Independence (1808–13), and meanwhile the independence-seekers in Latin America started to fight.

Even if Joseph Bonaparte really had no business being ruler of Spain, he did one thing right: in 1808 Bonaparte abolished the Spanish Inquisition, which had by then been going on for 330 torturous years.

Viva Fernando: The Spanish War of Independence (1808–1813)

Few people liked King Carlos IV (b. 1748, reigned 1788–1808), including his son. And it was while Prince Ferdinand VII (b. 1784, reigned 1813–33) was unsubtly trying to grab the crown off his padre's head – his father had had him arrested in 1807 for attempted murder – that Napoleon saw his chance. In 1808 the French emperor kicked the royal family out, ordered his armies in and placed brother Joseph Bonaparte on the king's chair. That was the easy part. The rest was hell – so hellish that the Bonapartes were shocked, as no other country had reacted the same way. Before Joseph was fully seated on the throne, the people rebelled – from the peasants to the upper classes, launching what the Spanish call the War of Independence, what the British (who dropped in to help) called the Peninsular War, and what the Bonapartes called an *absurdité*. Even if they hadn't liked King Carlos IV, the Spaniards liked less the Frenchman, whom they called Pepe Botellas – 'Joe Bottles' – for his love of wine, and who really annoyed most of them when he diminished the power of the church. Besides, they did like Prince Ferdinand VII – who for about one minute in the confusion had been king – and they wanted Ferdinand back, but he was imprisoned in France. Fighting for his return, the feisty people formed their own government – from the local level to the national – and refused to listen to anything Joe Bottles said, including his orders that church properties be seized. It was the biggest people's war of the day, finally unifying the assorted Spanish peoples who fought it in Ferdinand's name. Their new government, in between fighting off the French, even wrote a liberal constitution that was widely embraced by the Spanish people, or at least those who could read. It took five years before the French finally departed and when they did in 1813, Spain was wiped out economically but poised to be a truly united country for the first time, with all anticipating the return of their beloved new king Ferdinand. Alas, mean-spirited, ruthless Ferdinand came back and ruined the five-year fantasy.

Granted, the new king Ferdinand had a reason to be in a bad mood. He'd been humiliated by Napoleon, who'd invited him to France and then tossed him in jail for five years. But when Ferdinand returned in 1813 he didn't at all appreciate the adoration of his people who'd fought back the French just for him. He appreciated less the little constitution they'd prepared: he ripped it to shreds. That didn't exactly endear him to the masses – nor were they thrilled about what was happening overseas. Spain was losing its New World holdings. One by one they dropped off: first Chile declared independence in 1810, then Argentina, Venezuela, Colombia, Uruguay. Spain waged wars to keep the territories roped in, but fifteen years later only Cuba and Puerto Rico remained of Spain's empire in the Americas. Going downhill before, Spain would plummet to new depths over the next century and a half, as regionalism, value differences and depression worked to rip the country apart.

Linguistic confusion: The strong patriotic feeling in Spain's assorted regions – it runs most fiercely in Catalonia, the Basque country and the north-west corner of Galicia – is called nationalism, even though the area most honoured and beloved is the region. In this book the nationalistic spirit of the regions is called 'regionalism'.

As nationalistic movements spread across Europe in the nineteenth century, the regional differences in Spain became even more pronounced. The original languages of assorted areas were reintroduced with formal grammar rules, and the industrialization in the northern Basque country and Catalonia to the north-east increased populations in those areas leading to an even sharper image of local identity over a national one.

Spain's national identity was further deflated in 1898, known as the year of *el desastre* – the disaster. The United States, which had long been eyeing the Spanish colony of Cuba – and since the days of Thomas Jefferson had made numerous offers to buy it – declared war on Spain after a mysterious explosion on the USS *Maine* which was blamed on the Spanish.

The modern American navy easily blew the Spanish rust buckets out of the water. Spain was devastated after losing its last colonies in the New World as well as the Philippines. Spain sorely missed the income from the colonies and its image as a relevant world power vanished. The national mood was severely downbeat, but at least one person greatly benefited from the Spanish–American War of 1898: Catalan architect Antonio Gaudí. After their foreign investments dried up, the rich in Barcelona decided they had best throw their money into the architectural riches of their own city.

Antoni Gaudí (1852–1926)

Barcelona was always an iconoclastic, flashy kind of town that thumbed its nose at Madrid in any way it could, including with unconventional design that could compete with Madrid's neoclassical splendour. So it was fitting that an eccentric architect imprinted a style that would make Barcelona, a city where anarchists designed utopian neighbourhoods and wealthy eighteenth-century inventors sank fortunes into submarines, stand out as all the more unique. Spiritual Antoni Gaudí drew his inspiration from nature, eschewing right angles and straight lines. His daring creations of swirls and meandering squiggles look like shells or storm-tossed sands, skulls or slayed dragons, candied ice cream cones or icing-heavy cakes, and the strange details – such as dizzying ghostlike figures twirling up from terraces – are as striking as the full-on design. Industrialist Eusebi Güell and the Catholic church were his two most important employers. Güell kept the architect busy for thirty-five years with numerous projects, among them Güell Park, a tile-happy, colour-jumbled park complex of gingerbread house buildings topped with domes amidst gardens and woods, which had originally been planned as a living community for Güell's workers. Another huge project, however, came from the church: the Sagrada Familia took up decades of his life, and during his final twelve years Gaudí worked on nothing but the Swiss-cheese textured cathedral of slender domes, their shapes drafted in reverse – when he weighted threads with ball bearings. His habit of teaching trolley cars to stop for pedestrians did him in one morning in June 1926, when one ran him down. So ragged-looking was the by then impoverished architect that the hospital at first refused to take him in, mistaking him for a bum, but when he died three days later, most of the city turned out to mourn their loss. Now the biggest draw to the Mediterranean city, Gaudí's Sagrada Familia still isn't done –

completion is scheduled for 2023 – but two million visitors in 2002 came to see the work in progress. The man who failed in love and threw himself whole-heartedly into architecture and religion, Gaudí is now in line to be Spain's next saint.

Despite Spain's attempts at keeping itself diverted – the 1929 Ibero-American Expo in Seville for one – regionalism and religion kept splitting the country apart, as did the growing divide between the very wealthy and the working class. Furthermore, many anti-clerical, anti-royalist lib-erals were sick of having a king, particularly when Alfonso XIII installed dictator Miguel Primo de Rivera in 1923. The dictator raised taxes on the rich, created high inflation and was run out of office in 1930. The beleaguered king consented to a democratic vote the next year and the left rallied: ultimately, after workers' strikes and the occasional armed uprising, a rash of anarchists, communists and socialists came into Parlia-ment. Over the protests of royalists – many of whom were rich – Parliament soon declared that Spain was a republic, and the king fled in 1931. The left released all political prisoners, taxed the landed rich and outlawed the fascist party (the Falangists) of General Franco. Before long the country blew up in a heinous civil war.

Spanish Civil War (1936–9)

Even those involved in this military debacle weren't entirely sure what it was about. Some say the Spanish Civil War was a class war; others claimed it was the result of the country's identity crisis – Spain's historical greatness erased after losing its colonial holdings, intellectuals calling the country internationally irrelevant, and the people depressed. Still others claim it was but a violent illustration of that old issue of Spanish regionalism. What led up to it, at least, is clear: after the leftist National Parliament pushed out the king in 1931, a powerful faction of the country was furious, all the more with reports of clergy being attacked by the left. The assassination of a right-wing politician by the leftist police gave the right-leaning army cause to revolt. General Franco and three other officers led a 1936 army uprising in Morocco that spread and brewed into war. The monarchists, fascists, clergy, aristocrats and army rebels fought as

Nationalists battling Republicans, a coalition of socialists, communists, anarchists, anti-monarchists, anti-clerics and assorted liberals. Factions of the Republicans – for whom George Orwell and Ernest Hemingway fought – sometimes battled each other as well. Although most fighters were poorly armed – crooked forty-year-old rifles and rusty bullets were the norm – and military strategy wasn't organized, there was horrific brutality: Republicans lined up priests against church walls and shot them, nuns were gang raped. Nationalists attacked villages by night and left them filled with corpses by morning, and blocked food to Republican-held areas, starving residents to death. Both sides sought outside help: the Republicans sneaked off the treasury's reserves of gold – about €500 million worth – to the Soviet Union for safekeeping and as a credit against arms,[8] although the Soviets supplied them with over-priced second-rate weapons left over from the First World War. Franco invited in Hitler's Nazis and Mussolini's fascists to try out their new weaponry, most famously in the Basque country, where in 1937 they dropped dozens of incendiary bombs on the sacred town of Guernica, wiping out almost all the 7,000 residents in waves of fire and smoke. Nazis and fascists – Italian fighters alone numbered 60,000 – and their modern armies tipped the balance, as they bombed cities from Seville to Madrid. By the time the foreign forces split for their own wars, Spain had pretty much knocked itself out.

The war that more 'happened' than 'began' and more 'stopped' than was 'won', effectively wiped out the country financially and spiritually within three years, and by the time Franco and his Nationalists took power in 1939, millions across the country were starving, war widows walked the streets and villagers set up slums of lean-tos outside the major cities. At least 500,000 died during the war, although some say it was closer to a million, and the killing didn't stop when the war was over. Franco bore a fierce grudge against those who had fought against him, going on to kill at least 100,000 more Republicans, many in the 'traitor' regions of the Basque country and in Catalonia; thousands were deported from the country, thousands were turned into prisoner of war labourers, and thousands are still turning up in mass graves.

Nazis for hire: Picasso's disturbing painting Guernica *is his tribute to the Basque town firebombed by the Nazis' Condor Unit in April 1937. The attack that levelled the town and killed most of the inhabitants in a city-wide blaze is a continuing symbol to the Basque separatist movement of their treatment at the hands of the central government in Madrid. Picasso refused to allow the wall-sized painting to hang in Spain until Franco was dead. In 1981 it finally arrived in Spain, where it is mounted at the Centro de Arte Reina Sofia in Madrid. A tapestry of it hangs outside the meeting room of the UN Security Council.*

The country was on its knees after the Civil War. In fact, its pitiful state and Franco's insistence spared it from being brought into the Second World War, where – had it fought – it would have sided with the Nazis. The place was in such a sorry state that it may have escaped Nazi annexation for the same reason. Although El Caudillo occasionally infuriated the Führer – by making him wait half an hour while the former was taking his siesta, for instance, and refusing to fight in the war – Franco nevertheless continued friendly relations with the Nazis, some of whom were believed to have safe haven in Spain. So cosy was Franco's relationship with Hitler, at least from the Allied perspective, that Spain was slapped with sanctions after the war ended. Among the effects of the economic handcuffs: Spain was not eligible for US-offered Marshall Plan funding that helped pull most of Western Europe out of its postwar slump. As a result, Spain fell under an even worse economic shadow that lingered into the 1960s. One of the few things that kept the country going: loans from Argentina's President Juan Perón.

Some research suggests that Franco and Hitler were not as chummy as the Allies believed. Some say that Franco infuriated Hitler by refusing to cooperate with Hitler's demands to cut through Spain on his way to Gibraltar, and that Franco in fact saved tens of thousands of Jews. Franco did not enact anti-Semitic laws, and according to some reports he offered Spain as a sanctuary to at least 60,000 Jews.[9]

Franco had a vision of one Spain, with one national identity and one political party – his. Other parties were banned under Franco, regional languages and celebrations were prohibited, the media was censored, dissidents and those who had fought on the other side during the Civil War were killed – between 100,000 and 300,000 Republicans were executed once Franco took his seat at the control board. After but a few years of Franco's thirty-six year reign, the country more or less shut down and crawled off from the rest of the world.

Franco so feared rebellion that parties of three or more were not allowed to congregate in public spaces – he made sure there were few public spaces as well – and the Spanish were literally kept under lock and key. Apartment buildings were maintained by doormen who kept the keys to all apartments, and reported to the government on the comings and goings of the residents.

By the 1960s, however, changes were slowly under way, both economic and political. Franco's government, still mostly run by fascist Falangists, although greatly influenced by a conservative and rich Catholic subgroup Opus Dei, was starting to open up to foreign investment and to tinker with economic reform and rapid industrialization, which kicked a little life into the tired system starting in 1961. Before long, Spain was one of the top ten industrialized nations in the world, and its economy was galloping ahead, expanding by 6 per cent or more a year.[10] Meanwhile, the regions that had been deprived of their languages and customs for decades were starting to fight back. By the 1960s, strikes were frequent across Spain, particularly Barcelona; the feisty Catalans, whose language had been outlawed, greeted Franco when he showed up for a concert at Barcelona's Palau de la Musica by singing the banned Catalan anthem to him.[11] The Basques also grew more aggressive in their rebellions. The group known as ETA – Euskadi Ta Askatasuna (Basque Homeland and Freedom) – emerged in 1959 to defy Franco's censure of all that was Basque, and in 1961 the group made headlines when they tried to sabotage a train carrying Francoist supporters. A few years later they made even bigger headlines when they killed the man who had been named as Franco's successor.

One good thing: Franco is given credit for starting the menú del dia, *the multi-course afternoon meal at prices workers could afford. The practice of taking at least a three-course meal with wine continues today, although the prices have gone up considerably since Franco's day: now the lunch goes for around eight or nine euros.*

Waiting on the sidelines sat Prince Juan Carlos, grandson of King Alfonso XIII – who'd left Spain in 1931. Franco had been overseeing his education, and life, in Spain since the prince had arrived there in 1948, without his parents, at the tender age of ten. The Bourbon had to wait twenty-seven years, but when Franco finally died in 1975 – and the streets erupted in joy – Juan Carlos I was handed the baton. Although some dubbed him 'Juan Carlos the Brief' and predicted he wouldn't last more than a few months, the monarch surprised many with his push for an open democracy. The new king called for a nationwide referendum, asking the people what sort of government they wanted. The answer: a parliamentary monarchy with the king as head of state and a premier as leading politico. Understanding the regional divides of his kingdom, Juan Carlos made sure the liberal constitution devolved plenty of power to the seventeen regions.

> *Although Spain's seventeen provinces have their own parliaments and numerous parties, numbers on the national level make elections essentially a vote between two parties: the choice is between the right-leaning Partido Popular and the leftist Socialists.*

In 1981 the king faced his first crisis: an attempted coup. A fanatical group of Spanish soldiers took over the Parliament and held its occupants captive for twenty-four hours, threatening to shoot them one by one if the king didn't step down. Juan Carlos refused to abdicate or to leave the palace: instead he phoned all his generals and talked them out of supporting the power play. Although he initially wasn't well respected, his smooth moves on that day made his reputation soar.

Quick Tour

There's too much to love about Spain, Europe's most festive land: the modernist architecture that swirls in Barcelona, the palm trees that sway in medieval squares, the classical guitar echoing through alleys, the tiled tapas bars, the sunny beaches and kind people. But the biggest draw to Spain and the most compelling reason for some 50 million to swoop down every year is the variety: from the Ireland-green hills of Galicia (home to redheaded bagpipers) and the parched white villages tumbling down the hills of Andalusia (still dotted with palaces of Muslim Moors), to the rugged Mediterranean coast and folded valleys of dairy farms in the north, Spain is a patchwork of different histories, personalities and terrains, each corner possessing its own distinct style and spirit.

Party Time

Nearly stamped out by Franco, the festivals of Spain are now the symbols of an ongoing cultural renaissance. Every region, town and neighbourhood has its own fiestas, some immortalizing historic acts, others tributes to saints, harvest rituals or simply reasons to eat – chestnuts, paella, or grilled leeks dripping in spicy sauce. Geese (or pigs or goats) run through the towns, balls of fire roll down from the hills, locals put on plays lampooning the town's least beloved. Men don branches on their heads and run into a lake, cobblestones are carpeted with bright flower petals and aromatic herbs, statues move or a Madonna is stolen. Some fiestas are mock battles, where goatskin bags transform into wine-shooting artillery or the Moors are driven out by the Catholics or the air is filled with flying tomatoes. A young maiden might be kidnapped and the town searches her out, men might be ceremoniously caked in flour, women might dance around costumed as mules, boys might crawl around looking up dresses, or the streets might be turned over to the white-haired for the famed 'Dance of the Chickens'. But the festival that may be the most dramatic, and the one that certainly makes the most smoke, is the annual spectacle of Valencia – Las Fallas – when hundreds of giant satirical sculptures of political figures (taking a year and thousands of euros to create) are set ablaze in each barrio of the city, the fires flaming eerily through the night, and by morning the disliked figures and sentiments they represent reduced to ashes.

The same crazy quilt of varying cultures is also Spain's greatest weakness. Some call España an artificial country of seventeen disparate regions, first stitched together by power-hungry and religion-driven monarchs and later pounded into one faux nation by Franco's strong arm. Until 2004 – when the country was united by the March 11 train bombings in Madrid and the surprise election of the Socialists – Spain appeared to be severely fraying. Each of Spain's regions has its own parliament and a great deal of autonomy, but regions – Catalonia and the Basque country among them – still want more independence, and sometimes threaten to secede. The new Socialist government is taking the unprecedented step of calling together all the heads of the seventeen provinces, which is certainly hopeful, and Prime Minister Zapatero is trying to hammer together agreements with the Basque country – unlike his predecessor who simply outlawed their political party and refused even to meet Basque moderates.

Socialist Plans

The Zapatero administration marks a shift to the left. Among the issues the Socialists plan to tackle:

* Realign with Europe, deprioritize the US
* Stiffen penalties for domestic abuse: Zapatero says one woman dies every seven days as a result of violence at home[12]
* Legalize all abortions up to three months
* Legalize same-sex marriage
* Allow sex-change operations to be covered on national health care plan
* Resolve problems between Madrid and Basque country
* Address the housing shortages in cities

Regionalism is but one of the historical issues that plague Spain. Another is religion. The country where the Inquisition ran unabated for over three centuries is still nominally Catholic, but nationwide only 40 per cent head to mass on a weekly basis, and among the young the figure is far lower. Liberals have historically loathed the influence of the church on Spain's politics and currently – on the surface at least – the Catholic church stands in one corner and the government in the other; Spaniards, however, can still make donations to the church via their tax forms.

Since 1985 abortion up to twelve weeks has been legal in Spain only if the mental or physical health of the mother is endangered, rape was the cause of the pregnancy or the foetus is deformed. In practice that meant that any woman who was willing to say she might kill herself if the pregnancy continued could get an abortion. Divorce was legalized in 1981. Until 1975 a Spanish wife was not allowed to work, own property or travel without a note from her husband – el permiso marital.

However, there's been plenty of behind the scenes string pulling by the church, particularly in the Popular Party, that remains influential even if it lost in the parliamentary elections. Numerous VIPs in the previous administration are said to be part of the secretive, traditionalist Catholic group Opus Dei. Former defence minister Federico Trillo is a known member; others believed to be involved with Opus Dei include former prime minister José María Aznar and former foreign minister Ana Palacio.

That administration was slammed for allowing Opus Dei to influence government policies in matters from stem-cell research to trying to mandate that the Catholic religion be taught in schools. The problem for many wasn't just that the constitution separates church and state: it was that Catholicism at its most conservative was sneaking in unacknowledged through the back door.

Religion in the Shadows

Started in 1928 by Spaniard Josemaria Escrivá de Balaguer, a fan of pain who encouraged self-flagellations, the right-wing Catholic organization that some call 'a church within the church' sounds like the ultimate do-gooder organization. Operating charities and foundations, Opus Dei ('God's work' in Latin) aims to better the world by 'spreading throughout society a profound awareness of the universal call to holiness'. Opus Dei does so by empowering the lay person. But Opus Dei has its unusual qualities as well, and some call it a cult. One criticism is the manipulative means of recruitment: prospective members, often young high school or college students, aren't fully told what they are getting into, are encouraged to cut ties with their families and old friends, and are told that if they don't join (or if they try to leave) they will lead miserable lives and go to hell. Although quite powerful, Opus Dei members number only 85,000 but those members are said to be the rich and the powerful: politicians, judges, heads of intelligence, newspaper owners, the occasional spy. 'Supernumeraries', as those who are married are called, are encouraged to confess only to Opus Dei priests, attend mass daily, and make very large donations to Opus Dei. A smaller, very devout group are called numeraries: they live in Opus Dei centres (where doors don't have locks), turn over their income to Opus Dei, list Opus Dei as beneficiary of their wills, allow Opus Dei to monitor all mail and communications, take vows of celibacy, attend daily mass, sleep on boards, wear spiked chains (*cilices*) that cut into their thighs for two hours each day, and whip their buttocks with knotted ropes thirty-three times a week – although they typically ask to flagellate themselves more. Pope John Paul II just loved Opus Dei – his press secretary was known to be a member – and in 1982 he made Opus Dei the most powerful Catholic group by raising them to the status of prelate, which means they answer to nobody but the pope. Some say the elevation has to do with Opus Dei's donation of $1 billion to the Vatican Bank the same year, but that rumour like much about Opus Dei is hard to prove (or disprove). The pope was questioned about his move to make Opus Dei founder Escrivá a saint in record time – dying in 1975 he was canonized in 2002 – and that is just one controversial move that has many non-Opus Dei Catholics wondering what is up with this powerful and shadowy group.

Opus Dei is a widely known name these days because of Dan Brown's novel The Da Vinci Code *and because former FBI agent and Russian spy Robert Hanssen was a member. Less widely known is the fact that Opus Dei members in Franco's government are credited with being behind the modernization of Spain's economy and dragging it out of the gutter.*

A final issue that the country faces: foreigners arriving from all corners and hundreds of thousands of illegal immigrants. The problem is entirely new to Spain, which until the past decade had very few immigrants from anywhere except for translators and teachers coming in from the UK. Now they're coming by car, by train, by plane – and increasingly on flimsy rafts or tyres from North Africa. Latin Americans – particularly Argentinians, Ecuadorians and Venezuelans – have arrived by the hundreds, some with Spanish relatives whose existence can help speed along work papers, and some without. Since 2000, over 3 million foreigners have flocked here – 600,000 in 2003 alone.

Blood is thicker: Immigration is a complicated affair in Spain. On the one hand, the Spanish government recently passed a law allowing relatives of Spaniards to gain citizenship more easily, a move that could increase the population by 2 per cent. On the other hand, it is clamping down on South Americans, Central Europeans and Africans who can't claim Spanish relatives: now the government wants flight lists from planes coming in from South America, for instance, so they can search for those who buy a return ticket, but miss the flight back.

Citizens of new EU countries in Central and Eastern Europe officially aren't supposed to work here for at least several more years, but in an economy that frequently employs migrant or unregistered workers there is a market. Most problematic are the Moroccans, with whom Spain has had historical gripes (and vice versa) that go back to the times of the Moors. This is the group that most often faces deportation and limited employment opportunities. In Catalonia, for instance, Moroccan men typically have one of three options: work on construction sites at low wages, pick pockets or sell hash. Spain deports or turns away an average of 300 would-be immigrants a day, and until a new law went into effect it was believed that as many as 1 million were living and working in the country illegally. The new legislation allows immigrants who arrived before June 2004 and have work contracts to get legal papers.

> Despite the figure that per capita GDP is about €18,000 a year, the typical Spaniard – especially the young Spaniard – isn't seeing it. Minimum wages are less than €600 a month, and an educated worker in Barcelona for instance is happy to bring home over €1,000 every four weeks. Meanwhile house prices have skyrocketed – rising about 15 per cent every year – and often one has to put down €5,000 or more as a deposit on apartments.

The land where 'mañana, mañana' is a mantra, where the day revolves around wine and food, and the post-lunch siesta is a national rite, has for decades postponed dealing with its problems. With a new leader at the helm, however, there's hope that at least a few of the headaches can be resolved today. Despite its woes, Spain – with its cultural richness, mind-boggling diversity, happy outlook and let's-party attitude – may be the most alluring place on the planet.

> Spain is one of the few European countries that does not have an anti-immigrant party – yet.

Future Forecast

Regionalism will continue to flare up and may someday lead to a redrawn map of Spain. Until then, *viva la dulce vida!*

Hot Spots

Madrid: Famous for its tapas bars and nightlife, the hopping capital that keeps the country glued together is home to splendid architecture, vast parks and high culture, including the Golden Triangle of museums – the Prado, Reina Sofía (home of *Guernica*) and the Thyssen-Bornemisza Museum. Beautiful Atocha station – part of which is a misty botanical

Ávila: Saint Teresa floated here.

garden – was the site of the March 11 attack that might have been worse if the trains had been running on time: the plan was for them to be side by side when the bombs exploded.

Spanish King Philip II chose Madrid as the capital because it lies in the middle of the country. The exact centre is Plaza del Sol.

Barcelona: The pretty Catalan city on the Mediterranean stays up all night but is best known for Gaudí's melting architecture and its Gothic Quarter where alleys wind past the medieval Cathedral complex. Urban planners rave about the abundance of squares and pedestrian walkways that feel like living rooms in the densely packed city. The Rambla, a main walkway lined with bird cages and flower stalls, is clogged with waddling tourists now, but during the Civil War it was a battleground between Communists and Socialists – and in some of Barcelona's most tranquil courtyards bullet holes in churches leave haunting reminders of the clergy who were lined up and shot nearly seventy years ago.

Barcelona and Madrid are forever competing for power and pre-eminence. Currently Madrid is winning, both on the football field and in transportation. Madrid is the transport hub of the country, but while Seville is two hours away on the high-speed train, it still takes eight hours to go by rail to Barcelona. A high-speed AVE may someday be completed.

Catalonia: Home of the wind-sculpted Mediterranean coast that inspired Dalí, and containing 'Europe's most sophisticated city', Barcelona, eccentric and individualistic Catalonia is a bit smug. Understandably, perhaps: the hilly north-eastern corner that unfurls toward France is the wealthiest of all Spain, thanks to its industry, and one of the country's biggest tourist magnets. Like the residents of the Basque country, Catalans speak their own language – a gruff blend of French, Portuguese and Italian – and it's official: Catalan is the language taught in schools, used on subways and streets signs, and spoken on local TV; often Spanish films in Castilian are dubbed. Catalonia's independent streak, and the substantial contribution the area makes to the country's coffers in Madrid, has given the region political chips: it's Spain's most autonomous.

> *Cadaqués: The spooky, but fetching, village on the Costa Brava where pirates once hid their gold in coves – the locals supposedly stole it and transformed it into the riches of their hilltop church – was Dalí's summer home, and the legends still swirl about the master. When Dalí – a native Catalan – left his estate to the government in Madrid, the regional VIPs were livid. Well, at least Catalonia gets his remains, which lie in the Dalí Museum in nearby Figueres, some say against his dying wish.*

Basque country: Glittering beach getaway town of San Sebastián and the Guggenheim Museum in Bilbao are just two of the many highlights of this northern region of two million people that runs between the jagged Pyrenees and the yacht-dotted Bay of Biscay that hugs France; adjacent areas in that neighbouring country are actually considered Basque territory too. Said to be the culinary capital of Spain, the Basque country boasts hundreds of prestigious cooking clubs – and perhaps only a few dozen radical separatists. Between car bombs and rallies, however, it's hard to overlook some Basques' heated desire for independence, although they might settle for even more autonomy. Big Man on Campus: the regional prime minister Juan José Ibarretxe, whose late 2003 proposal for a new Basque constitution ratcheted up the volume of screaming from José María Aznar in Madrid, who refused even to meet the Basque. New prime minister Zapatero, in contrast, quickly scheduled a meeting, and – who knows? – a deal between Madrid and the Basque country may someday be hammered out.

Rock of Gibraltar: Despite Spanish grumbling and the occasional nearly comical 'invasion' by Spanish troops, who are quickly forced to turn back, this 'rock' that is 19 kilometres from Africa, and 421 metres above the sea, has been legally British territory since 1713. Punctuated by military structures and caves, Gibraltar is home to mostly British residents who still furiously wave the Union Jack, since the Rock is a strategic symbol and one of the last British bases in the Mediterranean; votes consistently show locals want to stay part of the UK. Never mind that Spain won't give up its holdings in Morocco: Spaniards are furious that Brits won't give up and get off the Rock.

Other Important Rocks

Parsley Island (Isla Perejil): When six Moroccan military men 'seized' it in 2002, Spanish warships went in to reclaim this smaller-than-a-city-block rock that's 90 metres off Morocco and home to a few flocks of goats; probable reason: fishing – there's a gold mine of silvery fish in these waters.

Ibiza: This may be the most important rock in all of Spain, at least if you ask partygoers (Elle McPherson and Jade Jagger among them), who descend upon it en masse three months of the year: the locals must just love the two million ravers who stumble through looking for fun and more E. Clubs where you push through oceans of shaving cream and bubbles, and beach parties that go on all day and all night, may be last year's sensations by the time you read this, although the place never seems to go out of style: even during the 1960s it was popular with rich hippies, artists and intellectual sorts, although back then the place didn't have phones or electricity. Now it's turned on and plugged in: the third biggest of the Balearic Islands had its own Chill Out and Rave musical styles, and the Ibiza DJ collections – such as that from Café del Mar and Pacha – defined a recent era. Hippies claim the attraction is Ibiza's energy field, and photographers may pick up strange images in their pictures and nearly everybody who visits talks about the place's good vibes: it was even noted back in ancient times for its welcoming atmosphere and friendly people.

Galicia: In this foggy north-west corner of Spain that hangs over Portugal and is perhaps the least connected to the rest of the country, the ancient Celt settlers left a legacy of red hair, bagpipes, and, some say, magic. Once famous with the Spanish for its fish and beautiful beaches, Galicia is now world-famous for its oil spill. Big Man on Campus used to be Manuel Fraga, but his ineffectiveness with the *Prestige* clean-up has cost him his popularity. Lots of EU money has landed here lately, which is helpful since its tourism industry, a year later, still has not picked up. The Gallego language is entirely different from Castilian, although it shares similarities with the language spoken in northern Portugal. The cathedral in the regional capital Santiago de Compostela marks the destination of a popular pilgrimage across the Pyrenees.

Losing Prestige

When a single-hulled tanker off the north-west coast of Spain sent out an SOS on 13 November 2002, saying it was leaking oil, the administration of José María Aznar didn't follow correct EU procedures, which were to bring it to port and contain the resulting spill. The response from the government was to order the *Prestige* not to come near the shoreline or the Spanish navy would sink it. This was merely the beginning of the ordeal that resulted in over 54,000 tonnes of heavy fuel oil leaking out of the vessel. When the oil slick began hitting the shores, the government response was equally pathetic: the small and ineffective clean-up crews had so little effect on wiping up the black slime that the local fishermen and volunteers bussed in from all over the country took the matter in their hands, while the team in Madrid hemmed and hawwed predicting that the remainder of the oil in the ship would soon solidify: a year later the *Prestige* was still belching up tons of oil, which has since made its way to Portugal, Belgium and France. A new political group quickly showed up on the scene: Nunca Mais (Never Again), a 'platform' whose symbol was the Galician flag – its edges dipped in black – and whose chant (in the local Galician language) to Aznar was '*O de bigote, que limpie o chapapote*' – 'Hey you with the moustache, get over here and clean up the tar.' Aznar, of course, didn't so much as scrape a teaspoon of oil off the tarred coast: he didn't even step foot in Galicia until 16 December – a month after the ship had gone down.[13] When he showed up, however, it was with big bundles of money, which continued, like the oil slicks, to drift towards Galicia. Cynics say that even though Galicia's tourism and fishing industries were knocked out for most of the year, the *Prestige* was the best thing that ever happened to this backward region during the previous regime: it made Aznar finally notice it.

Ceuta and Melilla: These small, prosperous Spanish settlements are actually on the African coast, and Morocco wants them back – but no way, José. In Spanish hands since the 1300s – before Morocco was a country – the Spanish territories have ended up being used as a corridor for illegal migration and drug smuggling into Europe and are also believed to be a hotbed of Muslim radicalism.

Valle de los Caídos (Valley of the Fallen): Rising up in the region of Castilla y León the haunting 150-metre-tall cross atop Valle de los Caídos was an excruciating labour of Republican POWs, who fought against the Nationalists in the Civil War. There was talk of knocking down the towering cross when Franco died, but it still looms, and Spain's two most recent dictators – Franco and José Antonio Primo de Rivera – lie underneath it.

The streets: Spain in general, and Barcelona in particular, have a serious need for outdoor latrines. Locals blame the stinking stone streets on drunk tourists, but whoever is responsible the result is a disgusting assault on the nose. Although there is always talk about installing outdoor facilities, as yet none have been put in, and in the meantime we're awaiting the advent of scratch-n-sniff postcards that will convey the reality of what those romantic back streets are like in July.

Small villages: So many Spaniards have moved away from the small villages that organizations are taking out ads in foreign newspapers offering to fly over families and guaranteeing cheap rent and jobs in rural Spain. Some who arrive from South America and Central Europe are disappointed that the jobs are often manual labour and there's perhaps only one daily bus to the nearest city, hours away, but others feel very much at home in the villages where the population may number a mere 300.

Maternity wards: With one of the lowest birth rates in the world – less than 2 per cent – Spain isn't producing enough babies to maintain its population. Now there are new incentives to induce couples to breed. In Valencia proud parents of a second child are handed a cheque for about €3,000; in rural towns such as Calzadilla they might be presented with a pig. What Spain hasn't yet put into place: a low-cost daycare system that would allow mothers to work.[14]

Alhambra

Peering down from atop Granada, the Alhambra is the final reminder of the era when Muslim Moors ruled much of Spain from the eighth to the fifteenth centuries, a time not favourably recalled by many Spaniards. Begun in the 1100s, the sultans' living quarters-cum-offices-cum-entertainment compound of seven palaces is a labyrinth of scalloped arches, honeycombed domes and glazed tile mosaics surrounded by glassy pools and lush gardens. Each palace had grand baths, heated floors and piped water (a choice of hot, cold and perfumed); private chambers even had flush toilets. Later battered by Napoleon's soldiers and weathered by time, the architectural jewel was crumbling and due for demolition when nineteenth-century American writer Washington Irving became entranced by the stories held within its walls and moved in to write about the place. The resulting book, *Tales of the Alhambra*, so popularized the compound that it was saved from the wrecking ball and refurbished to much of its former grandeur. Now it's one of the country's most popular tourist sites.

The refrigerator: One of the legacies of the Spanish Civil War and Franco's regime is that so much of the older population is tiny, often under 1.5 metres tall, due to the malnutrition that was a way of life for most in that era. Spain's relative wealth may be seen in the new statistic that 53 per cent of Spaniards are overweight. Some 2.5 million cats and dogs are pudgy as well.[15]

Torture chambers? Franco's long gone, but it's said that the torture his regime was notorious for is still being practised in Spain. So many complaints came in from prisoners during the Aznar administration that the EU is investigating the allegations.

Hot Shots

José Luis Rodríguez Zapatero: Prime Minister 2004 to present. He can't seem to get that 'I can't believe I was elected' grin off his face, but the presence of the young Socialist in Madrid is making plenty of Spaniards happy – and may bring the country closer together than it's been in years. A lawyer by training and former member of parliament – in 1986, he was its youngest member, being voted in at age 26 – Zapatero made a U-turn

PM Zapatero: pulled Spain
out of Iraq.

from many of Aznar's controversial policies: the new prime minister immediately recalled troops from Iraq and in 2004 agreed the draft EU constitution that Aznar had blocked. Wants to bring Spain back into the fold of Europe, and is far less Atlanticist and far more liberal in social policies than his predecessor. The only time he felt the people's wrath in his first six months in office was when the women of his cabinet (they represent half of it) modelled for *Vogue*. Some thought it crass.

King Juan Carlos I: Ruling monarch 1975 to present. King Juan Carlos didn't come up the ranks the usual way. His grandfather, Alfonso XIII, correctly fearing a civil war would soon break out, fled the country with the whole family in 1931, although without fully throwing in his key to the monarchy. Born in Italy in 1938, Juan Carlos was raised in Switzerland, while his father, Don Juan (then heir to the throne) waited to be called back, since Franco had promised to restore the king – though he never got around to it. In 1948, Juan Carlos was more or less handed over to Franco, who suddenly showed an interest in educating him; with the prince at close hand, Franco could appear like he might soon restore the monarchy. Juan Carlos was forced to deny his father's accession to the throne, and had to wait almost three decades until Franco finally died before he got a chance to wear the crown. Despite his playboy reputation, he's still respected, as is classy Queen Sofia, a Greek princess, whom he brought to Spain as his wife, with the promise that someday he really would rule it.[16]

Crown Prince Felipe (b. 1968): The man whom *HELLO!* magazine calls a 'royal heartthrob' is best known for whom he's gone out with (a Norwegian model, a German royal, a Greek aristocrat) than anything he's ever done (received a master's degree in law and international relations, trained in the Spanish army, navy and air force). Predictably, he attracted the most ink in his life when he married lovely Letizia Ortiz, a divorcee and a commoner. Surprisingly, given the prince's previous harsh feelings towards the media – which he blamed for ruining a previous love affair – Ortiz was one of Spain's most popular newscasters. The real irony is the couple managed to keep their relationship a secret from the press until plans for the May 2004 wedding were announced the previous autumn.

Javier Solana Madariaga: EU 'foreign minister'. The most powerful *hombre* to step out of España in recent history, Socialist Solana has headed numerous international heavyweight organizations, including NATO where he was Secretary-General for four years starting in 1995; he was the person in charge of the 1999 NATO attack on Kosovo. In 1999 he was selected to be the Secretary-General of the Council of the European Union, which is essentially foreign minister. Now he's the man in charge of security and foreign relations for the EU, and is one of the most quoted men of the Union.

Josep Borrell: President, European Parliament 2004. The Socialist from Catalonia was a former transport minister in Madrid, but the aeronautical engineer is the first President of the European Parliament never to have sat in its chairs as an MEP. Decidedly liberal, we'll see if he can push through Catalonia's demand that the EU list Catalan as one of the official languages. Luckily, he speaks four other tongues.

Baltazar Garzón: Federal Judge. Iron man of the Spanish justice system, judge Garzón banned ETA's alleged political arm Battasuna, went after Spain's Interior Minister (from a previous administration) for his involvement with a political hit squad and tried to extradite international bullies from Chile's Pinochet to the VIPs in Argentina's military junta. One can only hope he will someday take on Telefonica, the Spanish telephone monopoly that apparently bills what it feels you might owe.[17]

ETA – Euskadi Ta Askatasuna (Homeland and Freedom): An equal opportunity separatist group that includes women, ETA wants the Basque region in northern Spain to shake off the rest of Spain, bond with nearby regions in France and start its own country. Started by intellectuals in the 1960s – in part as a delayed reaction to Franco's bombing of Guernica and the gagging of their culture throughout his thirty-six-year regime – the group first showed they were serious when they assassinated the man who was being groomed as Franco's replacement. Since it formed, ETA has split and drastically changed: the intellectual separatists now tend to favour non-violent means, while the main forces of today's ETA, now younger and less educated, are still taking aim at political figures, and blast the occasional bomb to underscore their secessionist wishes. Wounded by recent arrests and the formal banning of their political arm, Batasuna, ETA may limp off into the mountains – or at least so the Aznar government hoped. The ball now bounces to Zapatero who will hopefully be more adept in dealing with the issue than either of his two predecessors: while Aznar tried to gag the group, the previous government of Felipe Gonzalez allegedly attempted to kill off the group's leaders.

> *The Aznar administration requested that the 2003 San Sebastián Film Festival not show* La Pelota Basca, *a documentary about ETA. The film was shown anyway, receiving accolades from across Spain, as presenting an unbiased look at the Basque situation. One of the scandals that plagued the Socialist government of Prime Minister Felipe Gonzalez (1983–96) was the discovery of GAL, a government-linked hit squad that reportedly killed dozens of suspected ETA members in the 1980s. The assassins supposedly made a few mistakes in their targets.*

Ferrán Adrià: The daring Catalan chef who launched a food revolution with his sensory-stimulation restaurant El Bulli – where Rice Krispies show up in the paella, pasta is made from gelatin, and mashed potatoes are flavoured with vanilla – has started up a fast-food restaurant in Madrid. Hamburgers with an olive spread can be had for a mere €8.

Pablo Picasso (1881–1973)

Few artists could pull off as many styles as Pablo Picasso – from neoclassical to modern to the cubism he invented – and no painters have been more popular during their lifetime or left such an indelible mark on popular culture as the Spaniard who studied in Barcelona and headed to France in 1900. In Paris, where his friends were troublemaking anarchists, artists and poets, Picasso was soon under watch by the police who described him as 'a so-called modern artist' who was 'arrogant and stuffy',[18] but his bold works soon attracted the likes of Gertrude Stein who, along with her brother Leo, became his first patrons. By the end of his life, his autograph on a cocktail napkin served as money whenever he went out. Picasso's marriage to Russian ballerina Olga Koklova was only one of a series of bad, maddening relationships, but whenever he chucked one mistress, the short, squat but charismatic creator – 'a raging bull with an insatiable sexual appetite'[19] – soon had another willing victim at his side. His coterie, painting style and even his dog, it's said, would change with every new female acquaintance, but it was a male friend, the poet Casagemas, who inspired his 'Blue Period', when the poet, shortly after lamenting his woes about love to Picasso, pulled out a gun in a café and blew off his head. That was also the method of death used by Picasso's second wife Jacqueline; his lover Marie-Thérèse hanged herself, and his grandson Pablito topped himself by swallowing peroxide. Despite, or perhaps because of, the intensity of his life and those around him, Picasso produced 22,000 works before he died of a heart attack in 1973 in France; Picasso had vowed never to return to Spain while Franco was alive and El Caudillo outlived Picasso by two years.

At the start of the Spanish Civil War, when he was back for a visit, Picasso was made director of the Prado. Since he returned to France when the Republic fell, Picasso was forced to give up the directorship, but that might have been just as well for the Prado's collection. In 1911 the Mona Lisa *mysteriously disappeared from the Louvre. Paris police immediately suspected Picasso, but he didn't do it. He had 'borrowed' a few Roman columns from the museum years before and, with the heat on, decided then was the time to return them.*[20]

General Francisco Franco Bahamonde (aka El Caudillo): Dictator 1939–75. You can still feel his presence, or rather, a reaction to it: now Spain wants to party and forget the nearly four decades it was pinned under his thumb. Born in Galicia, the general who pushed the dominoes that led to the devastating Spanish Civil War, was brave – at 33 he was the youngest man promoted to general since Napoleon. Most of all he was lucky: his two rivals died before the Civil War had ended, he held on to power for a record thirty-six years – and he won two football lotteries. Believed to have killed up to 300,000[21] of the remaining Republicans who had fought against his side in the Civil War, Franco quashed any show of dissent, including shows of regionalism, and kicked his country into the dark ages. He now lies under the giant cross that marks Valle de los Caídos (Valley of the Fallen) that he ordered to be constructed in memory of the Nationalists who fought and died in the Civil War.

Alien Artist: Salvador Dalí (1904–89)

It's hard to understate the importance of his Costa Brava summer home in Cadaqués on the work of Dalí. There, where the tramontana winds whip across boulders and olive groves so fiercely they blow people over and the clouds thick with African dust literally rain red, nature itself takes on a twisted surreal form that Dalí captured on canvas. In the tiny fishing village where stone alleys lace up past tiny white houses stacked upon a hill, time has a way of slipping away, as illustrated in the painter's melting watches. The man known for his peculiar moustache – he saved his clippings from the barbers and elaborately waxed on the upturned tips – also brought oddities he'd found on his annual trips to Paris and Manhattan back to the village, where long after his death, you can still find the remains of his coterie of twins and hermaphrodites. The painter married his muse Gala, after she left her poet husband Paul Éluard, and he paid plenty for that. Gala kept her boyfriends in fine style, buying a castle and yacht for her fave paramour Jeff Fenholt, star of *Jesus Christ Superstar*, but Dalí didn't much care. Those close to him say he never consummated the marriage. The surrealist who amused himself in odd ways – he called agencies to hire models to serve as his doting fans for Parisian events or to prance around like fairies naked in his hotel room – went down in history not just for his strange art, but for being a sell-out. The Catalan lent his name to jewellery, perfume, sheets and ties – and signed blank sheets of paper before they went to the printers. One suspects that the weirdo would get a big kick out of knowing that so many of his works are now considered fakes.

Dalí was not dear friends with Picasso – who regarded the surrealist as a traitor for living in Spain during the time of Franco – but he was close to García Lorca and Luis Buñuel. His first attention-getting creation was the film he made with Buñuel: called Un chien andalou, *it was funded by Buñuel's mother. One can only imagine her reaction at the disgusting opening scene, of a woman's eye being sliced.*

St Teresa of Ávila (1515–82): Reformer of the Carmelite order of nuns and patron saint of the spectacularly walled Ávila – a small town perched on a hill not far from Madrid – Teresa, who was once paralysed for three years, is said to have been able to levitate, and if you feel the unusual energy in the room where she slept you might believe the claim. Franco apparently did, and believed furthermore that she was responsible for his good fortune: he'd come upon a lucky charm of hers during one of the Civil War battles: her severed centuries-old hand. Franco was so superstitious and so attached to the limb that he refused all requests from the nuns of Ávila to get it back. Not until he died was the lucky hand prised out of his and returned to the rest of its corpse and buried.

Pedro Almodóvar: Part of 'La Movida' – the stay-out-all-night, anything-goes arts movement that rose up when Franco finally went down in 1975 – campy film maker Almodóvar brought Penelope Cruz and Antonio Banderas to fame and recently won two Oscars: in 2002 he walked off with Best Original Screenplay for *Talk to Her*; in 2000 he won the Best Foreign Film Award for *All About my Mother*.

Federico García Lorca: Spain's most beloved poet died in the Spanish Civil War.

Javier Marías: The widely acclaimed novelist of *Corazón Tan Blanco* also writes a pithy political column in national newspaper *El País*.

Camilo José Cela and Vicente Aleixandre both won the Nobel Prize for Literature.

Joaquín Cortéz: World's most famous flamenco dancer, Cortéz has stamped across the best-known stages in the world in outfits designed by Armani. Also had steamy love affair with Naomi Campbell.

Noteworthy: Spanish–French rocker Manu Chou is hugely popular in Spain, and in flamenco the late Camerón is the legend. Enrique Morente and his daughter Estrella, however, are taking the art form to new highs. Chambaó seduces with a novel blend of flamenco and electronica; the resulting soulful but smooth rhythms captured the country's heart. Much of the best music comes from the south – and in the caves of Granada the old gypsy flamenco dancers still put on their shows.

Joaquín Almunia: European Commissioner for economic and monetary affairs, 2004 to present.

Media star: *El País*: Spain's finest newspaper is published in Spanish, but at least eight pages are in English through the *International Herald Tribune*: www.int.com/pdfs/elpais/ep1.pdf

8. Portugal (República Portuguesa): Still Sleeping

Fast Facts

Country:	Portuguese Republic; República Portuguesa
Capital:	Lisbon
Government:	parliamentary democracy
Independence:	1143 established; 1910 republic: 1974 overthrew dictatorship
Population:	10,525,000 (2004 estimate)
Leaders:	Head of State: President Jorge Sampaio (1996)
	Head of Government: Prime Minister José Sócrates Carvalho Pinto de Sousa (2005)
Elections:	President elected by popular vote for 5-year term, Prime Minister (usually leader of majority party or coalition) appointed by President
Name of Parliament:	Assembly of the Republic; Assembleia da República
Ethnicity:	Portuguese–Mediterranean; some African, Ukrainian
Religion:	Roman Catholic 94%
Language:	Portuguese
Literacy:	93% (male 95%, female 91%); some figures show 85% literacy or less
Exports:	machinery, manufactures; tourism a major moneymaker
Per capita GDP:	$18,000 (2003)
Unemployment:	6.6% (2004 Eurostat estimate)
EU status:	EEC member since 1986
Currency:	euro
Known for:	sad *fado*, great navigators, port wine

Standout Qualities

Behind: 50 years of dictatorship kept it back
Trailing: Always in shadow of Spain
Lurking: But catching up, well, sort of

Résumé

The most western country of continental Europe shares a peninsula with Spain, but don't confuse stunning Portugal – land of foggy fishing villages and tiny hamlets set deep in cork forests – with the geographical sibling under whose shadow the República Portuguesa has been atrophying for about five centuries. They both came into the EU at the same time – 1986 – but there are plenty of differences, the most obvious being that Atlantic-hugging Portugal has a quarter of Spain's population, is less than a fifth of Spain's geographical size and in Portugal they speak Portuguese. And unlike Spain, now a dynamo in Europe, Portugal has not yet got its act together – despite the many billions of euros the EU has handed the country over the past fifteen years.

Between 2000 and 2006, Portugal was allotted about €23 billion in EU 'structural funds' alone[1] and an additional €700 million or so every year in agricultural subsidies.

Loud, happy Spain is paella and bullfights; gentle, reserved Portugal is the mournful wailing of *fado* and legendary sightings of the Virgin Mary. Spaniards are fiercely proud about their identity – particularly of their regions – which they extol as having the best food, architecture and football team; the slumped Portuguese will tell you that their country is the graveyard of ambition, a kingdom of mediocrity where the national hobby is complaining and the ambitious leave.[2] And if Spain under dictator Franco was missing in action during much of the twentieth century, Portugal under the 40-year dictatorship of António de Oliveira Salazar simply vanished, and in some ways still hasn't fully come back: almost half of the population lives and works outside the country and Portugal is suffering from the continuing brain drain.

In the 1960s, 8 per cent of the Portuguese population moved to France, where along with Belgium, Luxembourg, the United States and Brazil, many still live. Some estimates say that as many as 5 million Portuguese live abroad most of the year.[3]

Twin Brothers of Different Mothers?

While Portugal was deep in its Salazar haze (1928–68) – its press censored, its political system shut down, secret police roaming the streets and thousands of dissenters thrown in jail – neighbour Spain was in its Franco daze (1939–75) under similar repression. Both dictators had the same effect of isolating their countries and transforming their people into impoverished, malnourished masses, although in both countries a privileged elite made out (and still make out) rather well. The two Iberian leaders weren't terribly fond of each other, but each respected the other's territory and both dictators-for-decades flickered out within years of each other in the 1970s.

Kidnapped and driven off into darkness after Salazar grabbed power in 1928, Portugal was absent from the Second World War, and through most of the twentieth century was economically isolated and politically smothered: it wasn't until a military coup in 1974 pulled back the shroud that Portugal emerged, blinking, the poorest and most poorly educated country in Europe. Despite some huge leaps initially, thirty years since democracy was restored, Portugal still isn't fully up to speed: some 13 per cent of women still can't read,[4] less than half the children make it to high school,[5] and Portugal, which entered the European Union almost twenty years ago, remains the low earner of the EU-15. Even new EU entries such as Slovenia have a higher per capita income than Portugal.

The only place Portugal is truly competitive these days is on the football field; the Portuguese are still giddy about Porto winning the Champions League in 2004. Although it didn't win the Euro 2004 Championship played on home turf, at least Portugal made it to the final. The hottest export these days is former Porto manager José Mourinho, currently strategizing for Chelsea.

That the country has come as far as it has – back in the Salazar days about half of the population couldn't read and almost all lived in dire poverty – is partly a result of over €21 billion doled out for educational funds by the European Union since 1989.[6] But many say other outlays of EU money were largely squandered. They point to the newly created 60,000 government jobs – now over 15 per cent of Portuguese workers are employed by the state[7] – which have seemed only to bureaucratize the place further: the court system is clogged with over a million pending cases, tens of thousands are awaiting their time on the operating table in the country's notoriously crowded hospitals and any time anyone needs an official document they must wait in line for hours. Meanwhile, basic infrastructure is in vast need of repair, as evidenced by a bridge that collapsed in 2001 over the Douro river in Porto, killing seventy.

Another controversial expenditure: a new $1.7 billion (€1.37 billion) hydroelectric dam that is Europe's largest. As part of the project, deemed necessary by planners to bring irrigation to southern farms, the government created an exact replica of one village that will soon be under water, a move many saw as just more waste.

More Missteps

Not long ago, former prime minister António Gutierrez (1995–2001) was immensely popular: he helped bring Portugal's unemployment down to 4 per cent, and in 1996, at the beginning of his stint, the economy was growing. He readied the country for the euro – engaging priests to instruct the illiterate in the countryside about the new money – and internationally he was widely respected as the leader who could finally bring Portugal into its own. His administration made a few blunders: a drink-driving law, Portugal's first, was so unpopular that it had to be repealed, planned economic reforms were scrapped and numerous government accounting errors made him look like a buffoon – at one point operating funds for the navy entirely dried up, forcing all ships to return to port. In 2001, after the bridge collapsed in northern Portugal, Gutierrez' popularity sank with it and he was booed and hissed by the crowds. When that year's local elections brought back the Social Democrats, Socialist Gutierrez stepped down after serving only half of his second term, leaving the government in the lurch and forcing the temporary closure of parliament.

'Let us suppose Portugal faced a threat. Who would come to our rescue? The European Commission, France, Germany? It would be the US, no one else would defend us' – Foreign Minister António Martins da Cruz in March 2003 explaining to the Portuguese why the government sent a small number of troops to Iraq despite the majority

of Portuguese being against it.[8] By September 2004 the Portuguese government was talking about pulling its troops out.

Problems abound, including that Portugal – despite its cheap labour, about a fifth of German wages – hasn't exactly enticed foreign investors who could stimulate the lagging economy: Portuguese workers are Europe's least productive, its people get less exercise and take more sick days[9] than anywhere else on the Continent, and it's been called the least attractive place to do business in Western Europe.[10] The previous right-of-centre Social Democrat government of Prime Minister Durão Barroso attempted to make Portugal more attractive to investors with a plan that was ridiculous and widely disparaged: the government proposed slashing the number of sick days, and implementing a sixty-hour working week. The country erupted in strikes; few were sorry when the prime minister – who supported the Iraq war, an unpopular cause here generally seen as unjustified – was shipped off in 2004 to Brussels as the new president of the European Commission.

Nobody had predicted that Barroso would be plucked in summer 2004 to head the European Commission: he wasn't on anybody's shortlist – or long list for that matter – winning as a compromise candidate, since France, Germany and Britain kept bickering over the top contenders and few knew much about quiet Barroso, except that he had supported the war in Iraq and is considered 'Atlanticist'. Barroso's first request as president was that countries send women appointees for the Commission: predictably, the biggest countries didn't heed the call.

Now in the most severe recession of any country in the EU – its economy has been shrinking and the current deficit of more than 3 per cent puts it at risk of penalties from Brussels – Portugal had a new conservative leadership in 2004, which came in bumbling from the start. Given that the new government resulted from a presidential appointment, not an election, perhaps this was no surprise.

So disorganized was the government of former Lisbon mayor Pedro Santana Lopes – a three-time divorcé, seen by his people as Portugal's biggest playboy – that he showed up an hour late for the inauguration, and seemed to be drawing names for cabinet appointments out of a hat. Teresa Caeiro, whom the government had boasted only hours earlier would be the first high-ranking female involved in the country's military matters, was instead appointed as Minister of Arts and Entertainment. Defence Minister Paulo Portas received a second portfolio, being named as Secretary of Maritime Issues, an announcement that, to judge by his televised response, was as surprising to him as anyone else.[11] So dismal were prospects for the new government that Lisbon magazine *Visão* noted that 'expectations are so low that a few intelligent measures . . . can make it look good'.[12]

> *Santana Lopes is known for his bloomers, among them recently writing a fan letter to poet Machado de Assis, who passed away in 1908, and extolling the violin concertos of Chopin, who never wrote concertos for the violin.*[13]

Yet Portugal is rich with potential and a certain backwardness is part of its charm. Some liken the country's rustic undeveloped villages to the Spain of a few decades ago, and many who set eyes upon it fall in love with the fair land that still feels like the final edge of the world. Portugal could use a bit more self-confidence and a lot more marketing of itself. Spain is the second most visited destination in the world, and Portugal, just as lovely, doesn't figure on the top ten list.

But beyond simply low self-esteem and lack of organization, the underlying problem in Portugal is its depressive passivity and dreaminess. So well known is the Portuguese tendency to lose itself in wistful thinking that there is a name for it: Sebastianismo, after sixteenth-century King Sebastião who disappeared and whose reappearance the people have been awaiting ever since. Should Portugal ever fully wake up and learn to harness its potential, Europe could be looking at a powerhouse. A few more strong leaders with coherent policies might also help the country that currently is just stumbling along.

Dom Sebastião (1554–78)

He was sickly, barely educated and mentally disturbed – never three qualities one hopes for in a ruler – but things got worse when 24-year-old King Sebastião developed an obsession about the heathen Muslims. Never mind that previous rulers had already chased Moors off the peninsula, he wanted to fight them, as was the trend, across the Mediterranean in today's Morocco. Setting off with 24,000 soldiers – whom he didn't bother to train or equip terribly well – in 1578, the incompetent leader sailed to North Africa where he unleashed his pathetic army and was promptly defeated in what was the most devastating military disaster in Portugal's history.[14] More than pride or a battered army, decreased in size by one-third, was at stake: the Muslims held hundreds of nobles, demanding huge ransoms that drained the treasury. As for Sebastião, he was probably killed in battle, but the news the Portuguese received had at least a grain of hope: they were told he had merely disappeared. He might have evaporated from memory too except that the throne was empty and he had not left an heir. Spanish king Philip II annexed the country, and the Spanish rulers who followed took away Portugal's autonomy, raised taxes and made the Portuguese miserable. Resistance groups formed out of the hope that the disappeared king would reappear and fix all that had gone wrong – including restoring Portugal to its previous status as the richest kingdom in Europe. Somewhere along the way the hapless Sebastião was transformed into a messianic figure: even as recently as the late 1800s, many seriously awaited his reappearance. Still legend persists that Sebastião will return and make Portugal a great nation, although he messed it up back when he had a real chance.

On several occasions the Portuguese heard news that the king had finally returned. In all cases the 'king' – on one occasion an Italian – was an impostor.

History Review

Some people get fine china as a wedding present, but in 1096 Teresa of León, the illegitimate but adored daughter of the king of the Spanish kingdom of León, did much better: when she wed Henry of Burgundy – a daring knight in the service of the king – the newlyweds were given a future country. Their present was a mixed blessing: the land in the Iberian west was a buffer zone between Muslims, who'd been running the area since the eighth century, and Christians, who were driving them off in the reconquest. Dutiful son-in-law Henry kept the territory secure and loyal to León, but not so his son. Afonso Henriques expanded his parents' patch of land to Portugal's current boundaries and claimed it as an independent and sovereign country in 1143.

Unkind Kin

Poor Teresa: when her husband Henry died in 1112, she was given control of their land, but that lasted about three minutes. The new king in the Spanish territory of León, Teresa's nephew, wanted the land back, and sent out his army in 1127 to reclaim it. Teresa didn't want to give up the wedding present, but then her own son Afonso Henriques put together an army and he too battled her beleaguered army. Damned by the men in her family, Teresa finally relinquished control in 1128 and shuffled off to live in exile in the fishing villages of the north-west.[15]

Given its beginnings as a runaway Spanish territory, Portugal was always looking over its shoulder at the Spanish kingdoms of León and Castile that would soon come together to lead all of Spain. So wary was the Portuguese monarchy of the neighbours that as early as the fourteenth century Portugal formed military and trade bonds with England. The alliance paid off: in 1385, England helped the Portuguese successfully battle the kingdom of Castile, thanks largely to its superior archers. The Portuguese were so grateful that they signed the 1386 Treaty of Windsor, which solidified 'an inviolable, eternal, solid, perpetual and true league of friendship'.[16] The treaty soon led, as so many do, to daughter-swapping: the Duke of Lancaster, who had negotiated the treaty, soon married off his Philippa to Portuguese King João I. But an even more lavish affair – one that further cemented the Portuguese and English bond – was the 1662 wedding of Portuguese King João IV's daughter Catherine of Braganza to King Charles II of England. The Portuguese princess came with an impressive dowry, the contents of which could not fit in one chest: papa sent her off with €500,000 worth of gold, the Indian city of Bombay, the North African city of Tangier and a lifetime supply of tea. Nevertheless Charles quickly tired of her and was always trotting off having affairs.

Portuguese princess Catherine is credited with starting the English tea craze and introducing that breakfast essential, orange marmalade.

The dislike of Spain did more than push Portugal into England's arms. Claustrophobically wedged between its Iberian rival and the ends of the earth – until the 1500s, the waters not far off Portugal were believed to mark the edge of the world – the Portuguese went for the potential suicide mission and headed to sea. The motivation wasn't only their lack of love for the Spanish, who prevented them from acquiring any additional land left in Iberia. The Crusades and resultant hatred between Christians and Muslims was adversely affecting the overland spice trade through Asia: parts of the Silk Road were blocked, attacks were rampant and some Muslims refused to do business with Christians – all problems that required that new routes be explored. A further factor: spreading the word of Christianity. Not only did the Portuguese loathe the Muslims, who had until the twelfth century ruled their land, they also wanted to get on well with the Catholic church, with which Spain was always currying favour.

The Portuguese Age of Discovery officially began with the conquest of Ceuta, a Muslim trading town in North Africa that was stuffed with the riches from Arab and Asian traders who used it as a store house. The Portuguese conquered the settlement in 1415, with English bowmen helping to wipe out the town: less than a dozen Portuguese were killed in the massacre that left much of Ceuta's population piled high as corpses in the streets. Beyond the dead bodies, however, they found spices, tapestries, gold, china and silk. The town would never fill up with such wealth again: once word of the Portuguese conquest got out, Arab traders stopped coming.

Frustrated by the soon-emptied town but intrigued by the possibility of finding others, Prince Henry – who'd been told by an astrologer that he would lead men to discoveries – set up the world's finest maritime school in 1418, pulling together geographers, cartographers, astronomers, Genoese, Venetians and Jews to study the mechanics of the discovery business. They pored over all the world's maps, laying out the known physical geography drawn from Marco Polo, Ptolemy and seafarers' diaries and legends. They devised new instruments to ascertain geographical locations and consulted mapmakers about the best ways to record what was seen. Henry's navigation school even invented a new ship, the caravel, whose manoeuvrability was more suitable for exploration. And then the explorers who'd trained at his school shoved off, first discovering Porto Santo, Madeira (1420) and the Azores (1427).

In Madeira, while clearing the brush, the Portuguese inadvertently started a fire that raged for seven years.[17] The result, once the blaze smouldered out, was soil rich with mineral potash, which was well suited for growing grapes and later used for gunpowder.

Although these learned voyagers possessed the finest of that era's technology, as well as the financial backing and spirit of exploration, superstition still reigned in this period when the compass was viewed as a likely toy of Satan. The most persistent of the folkloric beliefs concerned North Africa's Cape Bojador, a promontory to the south of Morocco, which was seen as the very end of the earth and proved to be a profound psychological barrier. Henry sent out over a dozen explorers with the sole mission of passing it, but crews mutinied and captains buckled under their fear. Even respected navigator Gil Eanes reported upon his return that the cape was impassable – but Henry sent him straight back out. Facing what he believed was certain death, this time Eanes pushed on, only to discover that the ship hadn't plunged off the earth. The door to the rest of the world thus opened, and the rape of West Africa began.

> While there is no debate that the Portuguese were brave souls as they set off to conquer and plunder villages along what would become known as the Gold Coast, Ivory Coast and Grain Coast for the treasures taken from those spots, they were also needlessly brutal, slaughtering people who were fighting their crossbows with stones. The expanding Portuguese empire made the kingdom wealthy from more than just metals, jewels and tusks: the Portuguese also initiated the intercontinental African slave trade, later hauling their victims to the new land of Brazil, discovered in 1500.

Soon the most southern point of Africa, the Cape of Good Hope – another psychological barrier – was rounded by Bartolomeu Dias, whose ship was blown off course, and around the cape, by a storm in 1487; even though the leap had been made, his weary, frightened crew refused to explore further. But no voyage was more profitable than that of Vasco da Gama in 1497. Setting out with three ships and three years' worth of food provided by King Manuel I, he too rounded the cape, then stopped at today's Mozambique and Kenya, searching for one thing: a pilot to lead him to India. He went through quite a few, but finally a Muslim guide (some say he was Arab, some say from India) pointed the way – and sailed with him to Goa. With the arrival of the Portuguese that part of the world would never again be the same.

> Although he gained a reputation as a sage 'problem solver', da Gama will never go down as a statesman or diplomat, often leaving a river of blood wherever his ship dropped anchor. In 1502, passing a boat of

Muslim pilgrims returning from Mecca, he first robbed them, then locked them in the hold and set fire to the ship of 380 men, women and children.[18] His actions at Calicut, India, were even less humane: upon arrival in 1502, he demanded that the leader turn over the sultanate and expel all Muslims. When the leader sent out envoys to try to negotiate peace, da Gama merely killed dozens of nearby fishermen and chopped them into pieces. The boat was sent back heaped with the body parts and a message for the Calicut leader that here were the ingredients for his next curry.[19]

Malacca, the Spice Islands, Timor and Macau soon came under Portuguese rule, and simultaneously the New World was being discovered. Upon hearing what Columbus had found on the other side of the Atlantic – Caribbean islands – King João II demanded that the new lands be ceded to Portugal; after all, they weren't far from the Azores. The Spanish, in whose name Columbus had sailed, didn't see things that way and the Pope was called in to settle the issue. In 1493 Pope Alexander VI drew a line in the Atlantic to demarcate who could take the assorted South American holdings. All to the east would go to Portugal, lands to the west were Spain's. In 1494, perhaps with pressure from the Portuguese, he redrew the line, this time setting the divide 1,000 miles to the east. Under this new so-called Treaty of Tordesillas, Portugal got Brazil out of the deal. It's believed that the Portuguese already knew about the existence of Brazil, which is why they asked the Pope to redraw his previously drawn line in the first place.

Colonial Considerations

The once-mighty Portuguese empire encompassed lands in Africa, Asia and the Americas, but Brazil, where Portuguese royalty often took residence and where rubber barons grew so rich they built opera houses in the jungle and sent their laundry to Portugal to be washed, became independent in 1822. The colonies that remained by the mid twentieth century were mostly liabilities, but Portugal, ignoring a 1960 UN mandate for European countries to give up their colonial holdings, continued to cling on; by the 1970s, military missions in the colonies were eating up almost half of the state budget. Goa was taken by India in 1961, and the African colonies of Cape Verde, Mozambique, Angola, São Tomé e Príncipe, and Portuguese Guinea were liberated after the Revolution of the Carnations in 1974. East Timor proclaimed independence in 1975, which Portugal granted, and one of Portugal's last holdings, Macau, was handed over to China in 1999. The country, however, still keeps hold of Madeira and the Azores. Portugal also had the worst reputation for brutality and doing nothing whatsoever to benefit the locals living in the colonies: in fact, long after the slave trade was outlawed, Portugal was still running slaves out of Africa and into South America to work the sugar plantations.

Having broken the Arab and Chinese hold on the eastern markets, Portugal declared a royal spice trade monopoly in 1505 and held tightly to the secret maps that showed exactly where the lands of nutmeg and cloves, pepper and mace were located. Ships would carry a map specialist, who in addition to updates was charged with guarding the maps, stored under two locks and keys. One of the map keepers was Dutch, busily taking notes on the coveted knowledge and publishing the maps in 1596. From that point on it was war – not just against natives, but Western Europeans.

The battles raged not only on the seas. Portugal, whose king Sebastião was missing in action after an ill-fated Crusade in 1578, was soon under attack from its neighbour – specifically King Philip II, who demanded that Spain and Portugal become one. The next sixty years would be an era that the Portuguese call 'the Spanish captivity'. Not only did Spain overtake the Portuguese monarchy and government, helping itself to the treasury, it dragged Portugal into wars, including against Portuguese ally the English. Meanwhile, the Dutch were busy gobbling up Portuguese lands in the East Indies and Brazil, and the Spanish weren't interested in stopping them. Finally in 1640, when the Spanish region of Catalonia seceded, the Portuguese took advantage of the moment to bolt. They grabbed a new monarch, declared themselves independent, and although the Spanish fought to get Portugal back, Spain's forces were spread too thin. Portugal remained free, although it never fully recovered its previous riches, even after the discovery of gold in Brazil and the expansion of the cotton and sugar industries there. So many Portuguese preferred the life in Brazil and emigrated to the new world that King João V had to ban further moves there.[20]

A chronic fear persists that Spain will reach out and grab Portugal again. As recently as the early twentieth century, the Spanish king Alfonso XIII seriously considered forcibly annexing Portugal. Today Spain is subtly conquering it economically. Spain is the biggest foreign investor in Portugal: in addition to the three thousand Spanish firms operating in Portugal, Spanish companies run about 15 per cent of Portugal's banks.[21]

The eighteenth century was marked by numerous shakeups, from anti-clerical movements to an earthquake that was one of the worst the world has ever experienced.

Lisbon's Disaster

On the morning of 1 November 1755, a sulphurous scent hung in the air and water tasted metallic; the night before the sky had taken on a yellow tinge as a strange smoke rose up from the earth. At 9.30 a.m., the ground shook so violently that entire buildings collapsed, palaces fell, churches crumbled and at the end of six minutes most of Lisbon lay in ruin, its streets ripped open with cracks five metres wide. The earthquake of 1755 pulled back the ocean – exposing the sea bed littered with lost boats, skeletons and treasures – then slammed back with such force that the harbour was destroyed and anyone near the coast drowned. The tsunami pulled back, and hit yet again and again. The city, already reduced to rubble, began smouldering from the candles tossed about in the quake, starting a fire that would rage for seven days. In all, some 90,000 people were killed in Lisbon, where 85 per cent of the city was destroyed, and the tremor shook most of Western Europe and North Africa, its 15-metre-high tidal waves devastating all in their paths.

It is estimated that the Lisbon earthquake would have registered almost 9 on the Richter scale, which jumps by magnitudes of 10 for every level, making it nearly 100 times more powerful than the 7.2 quake that shook Kobe, Japan in 1995.

The royal family survived – they'd left Lisbon the day before for a holy outing at the insistence of one of the princesses – and so did the prime minister, Sebastião José de Carvalho e Melo – later known as the Marquês de Pombal.

The king soon developed a phobia about enclosed buildings and walls after the quake. Henceforth, the royal family lived mostly in tents.

Never was there a cooler head in the face of disaster. The Marquês de Pombal quelled the nerves of the Portuguese who had survived, preventing riots and looting, and ordering rescue teams to 'bury the dead, feed the living'; within a year, the reconstruction of Lisbon was well under way with the Marquês de Pombal overseeing the design. A cool head in times of need, he was, however, a hothead when anyone was in his way. His ideas for modernizing Portugal entailed more than a physical redesign of Lisbon: anti-Catholic, he cut Portugal's ties to the Vatican and ground the Inquisition to a halt; he also banished Jesuits from the land and made education a secular affair – moves that were highly controversial, making him plenty of enemies. After an attempt on the king's life, he used that excuse to imprison anyone who threatened his progress, killing over 1,000 and tossing thousands more behind bars. The Marquês de Pombal also ended slavery, shaped up the wine business in Porto, and reformed Portugal's economy – giving it the shove it needed to compete in the eighteenth century. When religious Queen Maria (1734–1816) came to power in 1777, she reversed all of the prime minister's reforms, released the political prisoners he'd locked up, and banished him to his villa in Pombal.

The Marquês de Pombal also made important contributions to seismology: after the quake he sent out interviewers asking detailed questions about any noticed changes in animals, taste of water or other indicators that the earthquake was approaching.

In the early nineteenth century, Napoleon fixed his gaze on the western strip of Iberia. Having first taken Spain, Napoleon's brother Joseph struck a motivational deal with a Spanish general for the conquest of Portugal: one-third of the country would go to France, one-third to Spain and one-third to the general himself. The Portuguese king fled to Brazil, and Napoleon's forces entered the country in 1807, although with help from the British, the French never fully settled in and were entirely pushed out by 1811. King João, however, was so enjoying his stay in Brazil, where he appointed himself emperor, that he didn't want to come back to Portugal; instead he arranged the future marriage of his daughter Maria Isabel – aged seven – to his brother Miguel, who ruled as her regent. In 1820, a revolution in Portugal prompted João's return, and he left his son Pedro as Brazilian emperor in 1820. Two years later, Pedro made Brazil independent.

The anticlericalism that occasionally brewed would rise again at the turn of the twentieth century, certainly a bad time to be a Portuguese monarch. As happened in Spain after it had lost most of its colonies, Portugal was restless, riots often broke out and in 1911 the parliament wrote a new constitution. Liberals blamed the passive, nonentrepreneurial, 'Sebastianismo' spirit of the Portuguese people on the brainwashing of the king and the church, and slashed the power of both. The new constitution abolished the monarchy and created the separation of church and state, banning religious instruction in schools and forbidding the military from attending church or celebrating religious holidays. The government also sold off all the land held by the king and the church, distributing it to the peasants.

Fátima

In the midst of the anticlerical era, when Catholicism was nearly driven underground, three shepherd children claimed to have had a vision that was as controversial as it was extraordinary. On 13 May 1917, in the village of Fátima, the trio said they saw the Virgin Mary, although only one said she could hear the vision speak. The woman in the vision is said to have shown them hell, and to have told them that the inhabitants were there because none of the living sacrificed themselves enough for these lost souls. Over six months, she is said to have revealed herself six times to the children, revealing three secrets: the first was about the rise of Russia, and how it would cause the death of millions of people. The second concerned another world war. The third was not made public until 2000: in the final secret, a bishop in white is shot and falls, apparently dead. Pope John Paul II, who was keeping the third secret at the time he was shot in 1981, believed that he was the man in the last of the visions.

The legend of the visions is very much a part of the Portuguese belief system and culture, and few would dare question its legitimacy even now. However, the Catholic church did not officially endorse it until 1930.

This great experiment in socialism soon blew up: anarchy prevailed, riots were even more common, and assassination became commonplace. Parliament and leaders rarely lasted two years, and fearing that Portugal's colonies in Africa would be threatened if Germans won the Great War, the prime minister during that era sent Portuguese troops marching into the war in 1916 – a hugely unpopular move. Secret societies of Catholics and monarchists in the north tried to reinstate the king, which led to a brief civil war. Mayhem prevailed as both the economy and the political system collapsed. Even the military was a mess – it kept trying to overthrow the government and failing. If there was ever an hour for Dom Sebastião to return this was it. But instead António de Oliveira Salazar rode centre-stage.

In 1926 the military finally succeeded in taking over the government, but that immediately ended in infighting over which general would run the show and assorted royalists and Catholics battled for control. A year and a half of flying generals later, the situation calmed down enough for a cabinet to be appointed. And that's how a professor of economics at the University of Coimbra by the name of Salazar first entered the government: he was appointed finance minister in 1928. Within two years he had halted the decline of the Portuguese economy and was the hero of the merchant and working class. As his power soared, Salazar publicly outlined his plan to continue Portuguese success: he wanted to start a New State with authoritarian powers that would emphasize Catholic morality, hard work and patriotic duty. Few opposed him, since he was the only leader who seemed to have a vision at all. By 1932, he stepped in as prime minister, a role he'd play for the next sixteen years.

> NATO didn't much mind that Portugal was run by an oppressive dictator, inviting the country to join up as a founding member in 1949. The reason: NATO wanted power over the Portuguese colony of Madeira – seen as crucial to keeping the Western Mediterranean open – and the Portuguese Azores were handy refuelling stations. Portugal, which over the years let NATO set up bases all over its lands, was not at all happy when its rival Spain also signed up in 1982.[22]

Initially, Salazar kicked off public works projects, including a network of paved roads, but before long he had gagged the press, banned opposition parties and settled in to be a self-serving autocrat, albeit one who didn't live a rich lifestyle. He fell out of the power seat in 1968, apparently literally, sustaining head injuries when he slipped out of his chair – some say he suffered a stroke – and dying two years later. Marcello Caetano stepped in to continue the Salazar regime, until 1974, when the military, sick of fighting losing battles in Africa, finally rose up and brought democracy to a people who, outside the cities, were the most backward in Europe.

It was Salazar's obsession with colonies that finally brought his regime down. The rest of Europe was letting their colonial possessions become independent, but Salazar believed that only with its colonies, and the income derived from them, could Portugal ever be great. Starting in the 1960s, he sent 40,000 troops to Mozambique and more to Angola, but the expensive campaigns dragged on year after year without being won. If Salazar – and his successor Caetano – couldn't fathom that it was time to give up, his officers could.

On 25 April 1974, when 'Grândola Vila Morena' played over Lisbon radio few thought it was anything but a pleasant tune. But for a group of young Portuguese officers – the Armed Forces Movement – it was a coded call to overthrow the government, an act accomplished in mere hours and bloodlessly on the rebels' part, although the government killed three people before giving up. As news of the regime's downfall circulated, the Portuguese greeted the revolutionaries with carnations, often climbing on top of their tanks; thousands accompanied them into the villages to inform the peasants that they were at last free. The weeks of jubilant celebration and the common sight of officers walking around with flowers sticking out of their guns gave the overthrow its common name: the Revolution of the Carnations. The rebels disbanded the secret police, restored civilian freedoms, ungagged the press, allowed the return of political parties and, within a year, the new government had set almost all of Portugal's remaining colonies free.

When the Portuguese announced that they wanted to return Macau to mainland China, the Chinese government asked that they wait – until 1999, when indeed the handover took place.

The military ran a liberal transitional government for two years, and a new constitution was hammered out in 1976, when presidential elections took place for the first time in fifty years. Among the additions of the 1976 constitution: women were given the right to vote.

Quick Tour

Edged by 500 miles of coastline, laced by rivers racing towards the Atlantic and divided by mountains rising through its interior, Portugal is strewn with tiny whitewashed towns tumbling down its hills, and villages of twisting narrow streets. The land of port, vinho verde, and two hundred dishes made with cod, Portugal is an eye-pleaser from its train stations wrapped in painted tiles to its hidden bars where one sits around wood barrels, while an old-timer belts out sad ballads late into the night. The capital Lisbon weaves up and down hills, pulls in the tourists but less than a quarter of the population lives here, many Portuguese still living in small towns and mountain hamlets complete with belled goats jingling down dirt roads. Agriculture, much of it in the form of small farms, still employs one-fifth of the population.

> Since the revolution of 1974, and the subsequent realization of the alarming illiteracy in the country, the government has been working with the United Nations and the EU to improve levels of education, which was increased to nine years of mandatory schooling; now 38 per cent attend school for at least nine years, a jump from the 25 per cent who did so in the 1980s.

Portugal is often described as 'the country of the Three Fs' – football, Fátima and *fado*. The description is apt: football is often the only way Portugal keeps its name in the news – with star players such as Figo and Rui Costa, and holding events such as Euro 2004. Fátima – the village where in 1917 three children had visions of the Virgin Mary – is a pilgrimage site that lures millions, vividly illustrating Portugal's continuing bonds with Catholicism, and illustrating why the anticlerical first republic had such a hard time succeeding. The emotional song style known as *fado* – sad songs, originally sung by widows whose husbands were lost at sea and by sailors yearning to set foot on land – may best portray the passive Portuguese spirit that mixes deep yearning and a feeling of betrayal by forces beyond their control.

> What flamenco is to the Spanish, fado is to Portugal. Usually played on a twelve-string guitar, it has two distinct schools in Portugal. In Lisbon, it's more of a sadder wailing, of the sort a sailor's wife might make trying to beckon him back from the ocean, where she fears he's been lost. In Coimbra it's a more straitlaced variety sung only by men.

And lately there's been a fourth F: 'fires' that ravage the country each summer. That too reveals something about Portugal: it's believed that many of the fires are the result of arson, from cork farmers who want disaster relief or developers who want to push out the farmers and buy the land cheap.

Burnt Cork

Cork alone provides almost $1 billion (€810 million) of the GDP, and some 16,000 Portuguese work with the spongy substance made popular by blind French monk Dom Pérignon, who first stuffed a plug of the peeled bark into a champagne bottle in 1650, noting its superior sealing qualities compared with the typical cloth, wax or stopper of bundled twig. From there the industry boomed – Portugal produces over half of the world's cork. A proverb advises, 'Those who care about their grandchildren plant trees of cork,' since the trees can produce for centuries, yielding valuable bark every nine years, but nobody quotes it so much today: farmers who unwrap the cork from oaks, as well as those who transport it to factories and process it, are livid about new changes in the wine industry, which is now using more plastic stoppers and screw tops. The 2003 fires that swept across southern Portugal didn't help the ailing cork industry either: the blazes devastated over 530,000 acres (215,000 hectares), much of it forests of cork oaks.

Although women have had the right to vote for nearly three decades, in Portugal they tend to have a tougher stab at equality than women in other parts of Western Europe. However, Portugal is catching up: its first female minister Maria de Lourdes Pintasilgo was installed in 1974, and she became the country's first, and thus far only, female prime minister in 1979. In 2000 women made up about 20 per cent of members of parliament. However, according to European Database less than 11 per cent of Portuguese women graduate from high school.[23]

Although it emerged in the late twentieth century still locked up in another era, several factors have pushed Portugal closer to the present. Tourism, for one, has soared in recent years, bringing a certain degree of modernization: throngs take to the sandy beaches of the Algarve during summer, the 1998 Expo lured 20 million to Lisbon, almost a mil touched down for Euro 2004 and Porto draws tourists to explore the making of its famous concoction.

Rip-off Exposed

Some say that Lisbon hasn't been quite the same since the 1998 Expo, and that local taxi drivers are now notorious for ripping off tourists. The trip from the airport, which should cost less than €10, may cost 50 or far more for unsuspecting visitors. The problem became so widespread that Vítor Simões, a reporter for a Lisbon newspaper, posed as a tourist on numerous trips from the airport, and was charged outrageous amounts, sometimes over €100; he even convinced the con cabbies to pose with him for pictures. When his cover story came out in 2000 – with a picture of the journalist comically clad as a Russian visitor, arm slung around a taxi driver in front of the taxi – Lisbon's cab drivers were irate: among the angry phone calls taken by the journalist were several hissed death threats.

Another kind of modernization has been brought by the EU: not only has it supplied money for modernization, it also forced Portugal's government into economic reform in order to adopt the euro. The Portuguese media has also triggered change: it has brought corruption and cronyism to the public eye as well as shedding a spotlight on one of the more controversial issues – abortion, which is illegal under most circumstances in Portugal.

Secret Operations

In the Catholic country where contraception was banned until 1976, the issue of abortion was rarely raised, and figures are sketchy as abortion is riddled with guilt and taboo. It is believed that still up to 40,000 women each year head to back alleys, sometimes selling their wedding rings or family heirlooms to hand over bundles of money to end pregnancies; some rely on the use of easily obtained anti-ulcer medication, which doesn't always work. Abortion on demand during the first trimester was almost legalized by Parliament several times, but political pressures intervened; so fiery is the issue that on one occasion, religious Prime Minister Gutierrez put it to a public vote. Only a third of the people turned out at the polling booths, which by law should have nullified the vote: nevertheless, it was regarded as official with 51 per cent voting against and 49 per cent for legalization of abortion up to ten weeks of pregnancy. The issue came back into the spotlight in 2001, when a nurse in the small northern village of Maia was found guilty of performing illegal abortions and sentenced to eight years in prison – a sentence more extreme than for paedophilia or peddling sex slaves; the ruling was subsequently overturned. President Sampaio announced plans to call another referendum about abortion. In the meantime, many Portuguese sneak over to Spain, where legal abortions for reasons of detriment to the mother are easier to obtain.[24]

Even if Portugal doesn't yet have both feet in the twenty-first century – leading Portuguese politicians are among those who call their country 'backward' – it's been slapped by several contemporary woes: immigration, sex slaves and drugs, among them. The irony of the first is that during the Salazar regime, Portugal was largely a country of emigration with people fleeing the poverty and repression: during the 1960s, 8 per cent of the population lived in France. That changed during the 1970s, when the new republic cut loose its African colonies – Angola, Mozambique, Cape Verde and São Tomé e Príncipe – and some 500,000 Africans moved in, partly because it was the only European country where the Portuguese they spoke came in handy. Not all of them stayed, but immigrants from Eastern Europe, including Ukraine, also took up residence in the country: now about 3 per cent of the population is foreign born. A low figure in much of the world, it's alarming to some Portuguese who have always been a homogeneous bunch, even though they are separated among themselves: northern and southern as well as rural and urban populations often live in such different worlds, it's hard to imagine they are part of the same country, and the wealthy 10 per cent of Portuguese who attend college are the country's power elite – that is, if they elect to stay in the country.

The Portuguese People's Party, the country's third most popular, gained popularity with its anti-immigration stance. Bending to the wishes of the PPP, which was then part of the governing coalition, the parliament passed legislation demanding that would-be immigrants submit their application while in their birth countries, and threatening to deport those who just turn up.

Another new issue: the sex trade. Prostitutes operate legally in Portugal, although the act of procuring them is illegal, and so is the trafficking of sex slaves. The country serves as a shipment point for women brought in from Eastern Europe. Heroin, too, is a growing concern: to battle the problem that only added to the backlog in the courts, the government has stopped prosecuting drug users: now they are put into treatment.

Surprisingly Modern

The country is believed to have fewer addicts than most Western European countries, but they did stand out: Lisbon's junkies were known to beg aggressively and camp out in front of hotels as if to advertise the city's underbelly. So severe had the drug problem become that authorities took the radical step of halting their previous method of dealing out legal solutions to users. Instead, anyone found possessing small amounts of illegal drugs is forced to appear before a 'dissuasion committee' — a board of counsellors, social workers and doctors — who talk about drug use and the hazards of the lifestyle, and who guide users into personalized treatment, which must be undertaken to escape time in prison. Thus far, say the authorities, the programme, which marks Europe's most modern approach, appears to be working, with far more becoming clean than when they were simply thrown in prison.

Portugal hasn't yet hit its stride, and despite belonging to NATO and the EU, it still seems to be a peripheral player lost in its own world. Then again, that's one of the charms of the tight-lipped country that still clings to its past like a beloved, moth-eaten blanket.

Future Forecast

Dom Sebastião isn't coming back, but we hope that this beautiful land wakes up from its deep slumber and realizes the many treasures it holds.

Hot Spots

Lisbon: Rebuilt in 1755, the capital city that climbs up and down hills is one of the prettiest of Europe. Too bad the cabbies are corrupt, the restaurants tend to charge you for items you didn't order and the junkies can camp out in a square all day, singing one horrible song for hours. Despite that, though, there's lively nightlife and an ever-present sense of fun.

Porto: Historically the country's wine distribution centre, Portugal's scenic second biggest city straddles the Douro river and is a lively transport hub in part due to its famous export, port. Restaurants, bars and narrow paths are carved into the stone hills at the river's edge. Said to be the most hardworking part of the country, as evidenced by the adage 'Lisbon plays, Porto pays, Coimbra prays.'

Port of Call

Abbots may have created some variations of it long before, but port wine – fortified with brandy or other high-octane alcohol – made its international debut in the seventeenth century. The reason: the British blockaded the French in 1678, thereby cutting off their access to wine. The Brits turned to the Portuguese, but were not impressed by the low-quality vinho of the time and jumped into producing it themselves along the Douro river in north Portugal. To stop fermentation and stabilize the wine for the voyage, brandy was added – thus creating the beginnings of what would become a cult for connoisseurs. By the mid eighteenth century, most port came from Scottish-owned vineyards and producers, but the Portuguese jumped into the scene as well. The British may have the reputation of being the world's biggest fans of port, savoured as an aperitif or as a dessert wine with stilton and fruit, but in fact more French drink rubies, tawnies and vintage ports than anyone else, although the British aren't far behind.[25] There are two basic types: bottle-aged port, which is only briefly aged in wood, retaining both colour and fruitiness, and port aged in casks, which typically becomes tawny in colour. Ruby port is the simplest, youngest and least expensive; produced from black grapes, it is sweeter and spicier. More complex tawnies mature longer in wood casks, and those that have aged a minimum of twenty years are some of the best. Vintage ports, made during outstanding years, age a few years in casks, but mostly come to fruition in bottles. Many ports are at their peak after ageing for a century or more: some of the most valuable ports have been collecting dust since Napoleon's time.[26]

Fátima: Millions descend on the site where three shepherd children saw the Virgin Mary in 1917. Some make pilgrimages from hundreds of miles away to express their faith, but many come requesting miracles. 'If you're sick or your football team isn't winning or you can't make a baby, you go to Fátima,' explains one Portuguese. Some crawl on their knees to the church set up on the site and rarely can you see more old ladies dressed in black.

In many parts of the country, a widow – or a woman who has lost her son – dons black for the rest of her life.

France, Luxembourg, Belgium: Starting in the 1960s, many Portuguese flocked north for work – and many still do.

Alentejo: Cork forests and cork factories are what the southern area is best known for; now it is also the home of burnt stumps and ashes after fires ravaged an area the size of Luxembourg during the summer of 2003.

Palácio da Pena in Sintra: Portugal's sleeping beauty.

Also one of the country's poorest and most illiterate regions, it already had a high exodus rate, which will no doubt be getting higher.

Algarve: Book now to reserve your space on the crowded beaches next summer. Except for the tourist season, the place can be dead.

Football fields: All eyes are upon them in Portugal – which has three stadiums that hold 50,000 and dozens of smaller ones. During Euro 2004 spectators had to travel to eight Portuguese cities, including the little known Aveiro and Braga, to take in all the games – a slick move for tourism.

The umbrella stand: Whatever you do, don't take an umbrella from here and open it inside the house: according to the Portuguese, you're summoning the devil.

Casa Pia: The state-run system of homes for needy children is under investigation after a 2003 scandal rocked the country. Allegations of a paedophilia ring running out of the venerated institution have pointed fingers at a driver, a government minister, a famous TV host and a former Casa Pia director. Many of the alleged child victims are believed to be deaf-mutes.

The TV set: The local version of *Big Brother* may have elicited great ratings when it broadcast racy scenes in 2001, but it also was slapped with a stiff fine from the Portuguese High Council for the Media. More scandalous: Portuguese reality show *O Bar da TV* is set in a Lisbon flat next to a bar. When one episode showed the contestants showering and, later, passing around a vibrator, even some of the contestants, vying for the show's €100,000 prize, were shocked. More appalled were many of the Catholic Portuguese. Lisbon daily *Público* deemed it 'the most vile spectacle ever broadcast on Portuguese airwaves'.[27] So popular is the tube any night, that it's cited as the reason that Portugal is Europe's most sedentary country.

Spain: If only Portugal were snuggled up to a less flashy country – Belgium or Luxembourg perhaps – it probably wouldn't be suffering from such an inferiority complex. But Spain ensures Portugal remains the Iberian underdog as evidenced in the famous James Michener book *Iberia*. The writer doesn't even mention Portugal in the travelogue named after the entire peninsula.

> *Portuguese is the dominant language in Portugal, Brazil, Angola, Mozambique and Macau. Spanish is the second most widely spoken language in the world.*

Historical Hot Spot – The Azores: Flung 1,500 kilometres to the west of Portugal are the Azores, the volcanic islands that Portugal still won't cut loose. Now populated mostly by sheep, and punctuated by the occasional military base, the islands still reflect their glory days as pit stops for navigators between Europe and the New World, who landed here with ships brimming with gold, silver and other stolen treasures. The island of Angra was the biggest beneficiary of the wealth that came through: it still sparkles with stunning palaces, churches and forts that are now on UNESCO's World Heritage list. Part of the reason Portugal still clings to the islands is their strategic value; even though Portugal didn't enter the Second World War, the Salazar government allowed the Allies to run operations from here.

Hot Shots

Pedro Santana Lopes: Prime Minister 2004. What can we say about the appointment of this Social Democrat, previous mayor of Lisbon and former football club owner, except to ask was he the best around? Arriving late and disorganized for the inauguration was not a good sign; the former mayor also left Lisbon's finances in a mess.

José Manuel Durão Barroso: President, European Commission 2004 to present; Prime Minister 2002–4. The former Maoist who several years ago

Durão Barroso: now president of the European Commission.

made a leap to the hard right when he signed on with the right-of-centre Social Democrats has serious luck: it was a fluke when he became prime minister after 2002's surprise election (he promised to trim government spending, attract business and fix the health care system). It was just as statistically improbable that he would be selected as head of the European Commission. Perhaps too few knew his record. As prime minister he was controversial from the start: he clamped down on immigrants, cut workers' rights, and approved a sixty-hour working week.

Jorge Sampaio: President 1996 to present. Kindly Socialist president who dug in when the Socialist government collapsed, Sampaio balanced out the then right-leaning power structure. He wants to hold a referendum on abortion, which the Portuguese Popular Party opposes, and he has taken flak for Portugal's decriminalizing drug policy, but has stood his ground. His appointment of Santana Lopes as PM made little sense, although it may illustrate Portugal's ongoing brain drain.

Paulo Portas: Minister of Defence 2004 to present. The founder of the very right-wing Portuguese Popular Party knows how to work the media effectively and has plenty of experience in it since he started up his own hard-hitting, investigative newspaper in 1988, at the age of 25, that caused several ministers in the Social Democrat administration to flee from office. Makes lots of noise about immigrants from Portugal's former colonies who have, he says, 'a propensity for violence'[28] and has successfully pushed for immigration limits and integration programmes. Anti-abortion, anti-gay marriage, anti-minimum wages for the poor and sceptical of the EU, Portas is slick, rich, ambitious and rather paternalistic: he describes his country as 'backward' and needing 'discipline'[29] – and he clearly thinks he is the one to administer it. One liability: the 40-year-old conservative isn't married. Maybe he can get some tips from the playboy former prime minister Santana Lopes.

Popular Party? They're not that popular, with only 14 seats of the parliament's 230, but they are the anti-immigration party of Portugal and the one most questioning of the powers of the EU. Three other campaign issues for the PPP: they want to keep the ban on abortion, to hear the national anthem sung in schools daily and to allow more young people to be tried as adults and incarcerated.

Sister Lúcia dos Santos: The last survivor of the trio of children who saw Mary at Fátima, the Carmelite nun was so respected that whenever the pope was in Portugal he popped in for a visit.

Poor Francisco Matos – the only boy of the Fátima trio – could see the visions, but could not hear what the angel and Mary said. His companion Lúcia asked if he would go to heaven when he died, and the answer was a qualified yes: he would have to say the rosary many times. Having been told that he would soon die, little nine-year-old Francisco was not at all interested in attending further school. He died within two years of the vision. Little Jacinta Matos, only seven at the time, was the one who blabbed the secret and was most profoundly affected by the vision – particularly that of the souls suffering in hell. She took to making numerous sacrifices – among them wearing knotted rope that abraded her skin as well as giving up water – and within three years, she too had died.[30]

Egas Moniz: Just call him 'Dr Lobotomy': in 1935 the Portuguese physician invented the practice of cutting out parts of the brain to 'cure' schizophrenia and other behavioural problems.

Ferdinand Magellan: Explorer 1480–1521. Portuguese by birth, Magellan was one of the country's original explorers. Fighting in Morocco, he was severely injured and was lame for the rest of his life. Believing that he wasn't adequately compensated for his valour – and later accused of theft – he defected and began sailing for Spain, going on to lead the world's first circumnavigation.

The Moors: The Arab Muslims who landed on Iberia in the eighth century didn't much care for the wetter, cooler northern Portuguese climes and settled into the south around the Algarve. Chased out entirely by the thirteenth century, the Moors nevertheless had helped local agriculture, introducing citrus crops for one, and had shown the Portuguese how to make *azulejos*, the painted tiles for which the country is now famous.

António Gutierrez: Prime Minister 1995–2001. Led the Socialists to their greatest victories with their election in 1994 and re-election in 1999, guided Portugal into the Eurozone and was immensely popular until the economy began to falter and questions arose about the EU and his large-scale use of EU funding. Then a bridge collapsed and the Socialists were dogged by charges of corruption, cronyism and not being able to add up since they kept screwing up the state budgets. He made a few attempts at reorganization – his firing of six ministers in June 2001 made him look desperate and the Douro bridge collapse didn't improve his image. He resigned in December 2001 after local elections brought the Social Democrats in.

Ukrainians and other East and Central Europeans: They are moving into Portuguese blue-collar jobs.

> *General António de Spínola led what may have been history's most democratic and liberating junta in 1974. During his six months heading the government, he brought back the free press and freedom of speech, released political prisoners, restored political parties, fired the secret police force, and negotiated with leaders from Portugal's African colonies to allow their independence.*

Fernando Pessoa (1888–1935): Portugal's most beloved poet was definitely an oddball: not only did the schizophrenic write poetry under different names, using different styles, but his assorted personalities also wrote scathing critiques of the poems written by the others. The good news: almost all of the personalities were indeed talented.

José Saramago: Born in 1922, he is considered among the world's most gifted writers; playwright, travel writer, novelist and journalist, he won the 1998 Nobel Prize for Literature. Tellingly, he lives in Spain.

António de Oliveira Salazar: Finance Minister 1928–32; Prime Minister 1932–68. He was raised as one of the impoverished masses, a group to whom he brought even greater misery during his autocratic rule. Fought against assorted attempted coups – a big one in 1957 – and student demonstrations in the 1960s, by increasing oppression and powers of the secret police. Suffered brain damage in 1968, and stepped down, dying two years later, but his regime carried on until pushed out by army officers in 1974.

Media star: *Portugal News:* www.the-news.net

Last Word: Predictably, Prime Minister Santana Lopes, due to his general ineptness, went flying within months of walking into office. Without a head of government for much of the winter, the Portuguese voted in a Socialist – José Sócrates Carvalho Pinto de Sousa – in mid February. Sócrates, who was against the war in Iraq, plans for Portugal to hold a vote in autumn 2005 on the proposed EU constitution, and daringly says he will float a new referendum on the country's anti-abortion laws. A former parliamentarian who worked on environment issues and prison reform, he is more on the ball than his predecessor, and is far more handsome. Single ladies take note: he's divorced.

> *Portugal, with one of the highest rates of incarceration in Europe, has a prob: its prisons are filled to the gills. Now the country is introducing electronic tagging to keep tabs on those who won't fit behind the bars.*

9. Netherlands (Holland; Nederland): The Thinker

Fast Facts

Country:	Kingdom of the Netherlands; Koninkrijk der Nederlanden
Capital:	Amsterdam; government seat: The Hague
Government:	constitutional monarchy
Independence:	1579 (from Spain)
Population:	16,319,000 (2004 estimate)
Leaders:	Head of State: Queen Beatrix (1980)
	Head of Government: Prime Minister Jan Peter Balkenende (2002)
Elections:	monarchy is hereditary; Prime Minister appointed by monarch
Name of Parliament:	States General; Staaten Generaal
Ethnicity:	83% Dutch; 9% Moroccan, Turk, Surinamese (1999 estimate)
Religion:	31% Roman Catholic; 21% Protestant; 4.4% Muslim; 40% none (1998)
Language:	Dutch, Frisian
Literacy:	99% (2000 estimate)
Exports:	machinery, chemicals, fuels, food
Per capita GDP:	$28,600 (2003 estimate)
Unemployment:	4.9% (April 2004 Eurostat figure)
EU status:	founding member (entered EEC 1957)
Currency:	euro
Known for:	being open-minded and playing by the rules

Standout Qualities

Wood: The famous clogs
Wood: The heady bars
Would: Try to fix the world

Résumé

Don't be fooled by the flower markets awash with colour and the pictur-esque skinny buildings scrunched along canals. The Netherlands is more than just lovely: it's smart, rich and a showcase of sensible planning, a place where every square inch is present, accounted for, and put to good use. The Dutch, it has appeared for decades, had figured out how to run a country that nearly hummed along on its own. Affluent and tolerant, they had seemingly solved their social woes with open minds – euthanasia and gay marriage are legal, prostitution and hash houses are licensed and taxed – and having wrapped up domestic issues they had plenty of time to ponder their role on the planet. Cerebral sorts, fond of debate, the Dutch love nothing more than chatting through the night in candle-flickering restaurants solving all the world's problems, even if nobody's listening.

Global Weight

The Netherlands has found weightiness by casting itself in a new role: global justice centre. The country that is arguably the world's most open-minded and balanced – well, in most respects – is home to the UN International Court of Justice (the UN's judicial organ), the International Criminal Court (a UN-linked court to try war crimes), and assorted international criminal tribunals, including the one that tried Yugoslavia's Slobodan Milosevic. Also to be found in the political capital The Hague: the headquarters for the international EU police force Europol. The Netherlands boasts serious financial muscle as well: it commands serious global attention with Royal Dutch/Shell – a Dutch-Anglo consortium that is the world's second largest petroleum company and one of the most profitable corporations[1] – and it is a major financial and banking player, pulling plenty of strings on Wall Street.

Once a weighty international player – the country was a fearsome seventeenth-century maritime power, not to mention an overzealous colonial force plying the seas – the Netherlands just isn't the global giant it used to be. With a population of 16 million, and a landmass that fits into France fifteen times, the country doesn't have a booming voice in the European Union, despite tossing out hefty dues to the

*club from which it derives little except a sense of belonging. The
country also doles out tons of money for international causes, being
one of the largest foreign-aid donors per capita.*

Much of the Netherlands – or Holland as it is widely known – appears to
be an anachronism, or perhaps a scene from a different, more sensible,
solar system: residents bike down cobbled streets to work, or skate across
icy canals to their jobs in the winter. Dutch cities are architecturally old
world, but with modern public transport, and Dutch towns are homely
pedestrian zones lined with shops selling warm-from-the-roaster coffee
or chutneys bubbling away in a copper pot; shop owners still live upstairs.
And wherever you are, you can always count on one thing: the Dutch put
their rubbish out for collection in an orderly fashion – in the correct bags
and on the right days: that's just how things work around here, or at least
used to.

Geographical Confusion: The Netherlands v. Holland v. The Lowlands

The country that is officially called 'The Netherlands' is often erroneously referred
to as Holland. Actually, there is a Holland in the country – in fact, there are now
two provinces with that name. North Holland holds tourist magnet Amsterdam,
South Holland is home to political headquarters The Hague (Den Haag), but they
are only two of the country's twelve provinces. Back when the Netherlands
was called the United Provinces of the Protestant Netherlands, most maritime
merchants came from Holland, and apparently greatly influenced map makers,
who no doubt found the country name 'Holland' easier to fit on the map. The
area was also at various points referred to as the Lowlands or Low Countries –
so called since part of it is below sea level; until 1830, Belgium and Luxembourg
were included in that geographical package.

But that picture of an evolved, open-minded society where all the
wheels are working together without a snag certainly blew sky high
recently. Now issues from immigration to renegade royals and – what?! –
high-profile murders are shaking up what for centuries has appeared
to be one of Europe's most stable, mellow lands. With mosques and
churches burning, and bombs being planted in elementary schools, the

typically sedate Netherlands has plenty of new debating to do, namely how to defuse a situation that in late 2004 suddenly seemed to hold the makings for Western Europe's first religious war in four centuries. And what struck the match for this time bomb was a most unlikely phenomenon in the permissive Netherlands: being killed for speaking one's mind.

Theo Van Gogh: Unlikely Martyr

Nobody can honestly say that barrel-chested, fleshy-faced filmmaker Theo Van Gogh – great-grandson of Vincent's brother – wasn't pushing it. The director was known for being more than blunt: he was often racist, reportedly known for making such remarks as 'it smells like caramel here – they must be burning diabetic Jews.'[2] But the group that he most disliked were Muslims, whom he'd speared in his newspaper columns and attacked in his mocking book *Allah Knows Best*. But it was Van Gogh's latest work, a forceful ten-minute film called *Submission* that brought rage to a new level. The film, written by parliamentarian Ayaan Hirsi Ali – who, being of Somali descent, was born a Muslim – told of the abuses to women in the name of Islam, the ritual of removing the clitoris being only one. But in filming it, Van Gogh didn't just shockingly make his point. He made it in a manner that was pointedly sacrilegious to Muslims. In the most controversial scene, a Muslim wife describes the abuse by her husband and his family – the brother raped her, for starters – while the screen shows a woman, shrouded in a transparent veil; under it, viewers see her naked body covered in written words, specifically the Koran's many punishments for females. After it was broadcast on Dutch state TV in August 2004, both Van Gogh and Hirsi Ali were bombarded with death threats. Hirsi Ali, who knew she was viewed as an apostate, hired armed security. Van Gogh apparently didn't think he was at risk, at least until 2 November 2004, when a man bicycled up to the filmmaker in East Amsterdam, shot him half a dozen times, slit his throat, stabbed him and slammed a note into his chest with the bloody knife that warned the United States, Europe, the Netherlands and Hirsi Ali that they would all 'go down'.

Within hours, police had arrested a 26-year-old Moroccan Dutchman, Mohammad Bouyeri, believed to be a radical Islamist, who reportedly was carrying a note that foretold Hirsi Ali's death by bullets.

At the news of the heinous slaying of movie-maker Van Gogh – over his right of expression – the Dutch did what they rarely do: they blew up, hitting the streets banging pots and pans, yelling for vindication and mourning the death not only of Van Gogh, but of an era in Dutch society when you could safely express yourself. But the volatile reaction didn't stop at demonstrations. Within days, flames were darting through mosques and a bomb had exploded in a Muslim school. Radical Muslims retaliated as well, burning Christian churches and targeting Dutch schools. The violence continued for weeks, but beyond the arson attempts and homemade explosives, the issue that had been simmering for years came very much back to the forefront: the problem of immigrants in Dutch society who don't want to assimilate, drain the system, resort to crime – and are increasingly becoming scapegoats and the factor prompting an overhaul of immigration policy. And that is where politician Pim Fortuyn, a friend of Van Gogh's, enters the story.

Shooting Turkey

Van Gogh's murder couldn't have taken place at a worse moment: the Netherlands was at that time host country of the revolving six-month EU presidency with Prime Minister Balkenende at the helm. The timing was already unfortunate: many Dutch people are bristling about EU membership, since they pay more dues per capita than any other country, while getting little back in the form of agricultural subsidies, and while the Dutch heed the rules on everything from bread baking to budget balancing, few others take EU regulations so seriously. But what was already a tense presidency turned more so with the brutal killing, which even though it was allegedly committed by a second-generation Dutchman of Moroccan descent was very bad news not only to the million Muslims living in the Netherlands but to another country: Turkey, which was being considered for EU membership during the Dutch presidency. The blood-curdling death and the ominous note appeared likely to darken the chances for Turkey – a secular country where the majority of the 70 million population are Muslim – of being accepted into the club. However, Turkey may get a green light.

'There will be a day when one soul cannot help another soul. A day that goes paired with terrible tortures . . . when the unjust will press horrible screams from their lungs . . . People will be drunk with fear,

*while they are not drunken. Fear will fill the air on the Great Day' –
from the note left on Van Gogh's body*[3]

Given the country's previous non-judgemental attitude and typical sensitivity to ethnic and religious issues – the leading item in the constitution is prohibition of discrimination – the world was agog in 2001 when a shinily bald, openly gay dandy pushed into the Dutch political scene and unleashed a slew of attention-grabbing soundbites and blood-pressure-raising ideas. The Netherlands was 'all full up' – '16 million is enough!' announced Pim Fortuyn, a former sociology professor turned political candidate and controversial columnist from Rotterdam, the city that houses most of the foreign-born population. The country needed to bolt the door to most immigrants, who were responsible for much of the crime, opined Fortuyn; Muslims in particular should be prevented from entering, he said, since he considered Islam 'a backward culture', unkind to women, intolerant of gays. So outrageous were his pronouncements that the 'Livable Netherlands' party which had asked Fortuyn to head it, quickly kicked him out. No problem: Fortuyn simply started his own party, Lijst Fortuyn, with an across-the-board platform that was pro-gay, pro-drugs, pro-euthanasia, anti-crime and against allowing 30,000 asylum seekers into the country each year.

An indication of how much the Dutch people think the government is too compromised and tolerant: two-thirds of respondents in a poll, when asked how the Netherlands would react to Van Gogh's murder, answered, 'as typical for the Netherlands, nothing will happen'.[4]

Pim Fortuyn: Stirring It Up

For decades upon decades, the Dutch government has been known for three things: compromise, compromise, and compromise. Typically none of the country's half-dozen major political parties wins an outright parliamentary majority, so odd coalitions form that compromise themselves right out. So dull and plodding is the Dutch political scene usually that jaws dropped open in 2001 when mouthy professor-turned-politician Pim Fortuyn muscled his way in front of the cameras wearing slick Italian suits, puffing cigars and raising the issue that nobody else dared. The typically PC Dutch squirmed uncomfortably when the parliamentary candidate put the spotlight on those immigrants whom he said were leeches on the system, fuelling a crime wave and not learning the Dutch language that is key to getting a job – ideas too sensitive to discuss before, even if government reports bore out the claims.[5] Fortuyn didn't endorse sending the resident immigrants back – as has France's Jean-Marie Le Pen to whom he was frequently (and perhaps unfairly) likened – but he clearly didn't want many more, and he wanted the Dutch way of life preserved, as was made plain in his book *Against the Islamization of Our Culture*. Through the months leading up to the April 2002 election, few talked of anything but Pim, the country's most colourful candidate – ever. Whatever the Dutch thought of him, and they thought of him often, the camera loved the man whose big shiny head took up nearly the whole lens as he squawked in debates, flounced out of TV interviews, and baited Muslim imams into calling him insulting names. Poised to make a decisive showing in the April 2002 parliamentary elections, the man who had so riled the country was shot down on a Friday afternoon, as he strode out of a radio interview. But Pim talks even from the grave, perhaps more effectively than when he was alive. No one in the past century, besides Hitler, has affected the country more.

'I'm not anti-Muslim, I'm not anti-immigration,' Fortuyn said in April 2002, at the peak of Pim Fever, when the country could talk of little but him. 'I'm saying we've got big problems in our cities. It's not very smart to make the problem bigger by letting in millions more immigrants from rural Muslim cultures that don't assimilate.'[6] But stranger than the emergence of this blunt sociology professor, who was utterly un-PC, was the fact that the Dutch were listening very attentively. After all, plenty of them had been trying to politely ignore the immigration issue for years.

'I am also in favour of a cold war with Islam. I see Islam as an extraordinary threat, as a hostile society' – Pim Fortuyn in August 2001[7]

The most unbelievable part of the Pim phenomenon was how his story ended in 2002: Fortuyn was murdered – in plain daylight at that – something that hadn't happened to a politician in the Netherlands since the seventeenth century. And even that was a surprise: it wasn't a Turk or Moroccan, whom he blamed for crime, who pulled the trigger. It was a home-grown white Dutch man – a young, soft-spoken vegetarian who was most offended by Fortuyn's potential treatment of animals. The politician had promised a slot on his 'list' – in other words a seat in his party

– to a prominent mink farmer, whom the gunman believed mistreated his minks. Volkert Van der Graaf was sentenced to eighteen years in prison for Fortuyn's murder.

Even though Fortuyn was dead, it didn't hurt his political showing in the 2002 election: his party came in with 17 per cent of the vote, and formed a coalition with the big parliamentary winners, the Christian Democrats. That government fell apart within 100 days – the belligerent party members of Lijst Fortuyn successfully prevented anything from being accomplished – and their boisterousness cost them: in January 2003 they lost two-thirds of their seats. Nevertheless, the issues Fortuyn lit up are now burning: the new government under Prime Minister Balkenende slammed the brakes on immigration – in 2003 only half the previous number of typical asylum seekers even bothered to apply; failed asylum seekers are being deported and cities such as Rotterdam are trying to ban any more poor immigrants from living there. And along the way, 'multiculturalism' has become a dirty word – all the more with the death of Van Gogh. Ironically, the director had just finished a film about Pim Fortuyn. Van Gogh did more than memorialize the murdered politician: in his death, Van Gogh became a martyr to Fortuyn's cause.

'The Netherlands does not constitute an aggregation of different cultures' – Prime Minister Jan Peter Balkenende in February 2002

Rotterdam: City of the Future?

Having been flattened by the Nazis during the Second World War, Rotterdam doesn't fit in with the typical quaint image of a Dutch town. In Europe's first city built for the car, the skyline is a modern, glassy assemblage of angles, and its bustling port is the world's biggest. It has also been the Dutch city where most immigrants moved, in part because much of the inner core is council housing; now over 30 per cent of the population is foreign-born. The gangs of immigrant youths and rising street crime were big factors in both Fortuyn's questioning stance and his subsequent popularity. And when a new government study came out in 2004, saying that if current trends continued the city of Rotterdam would have a population that was more than 60 per cent immigrant, the city council responded by enacting new land laws: those moving to Rotterdam now have to have residency permits, granted only to those who are fluent in Dutch and who earn at least 20 per cent over the minimum wage – or more than €9 an hour – a ceiling that many foreign-born workers can't reach. 'We want people to work and we want people to learn Dutch,' said Rotterdam city council member Ronald Sorensen of the Livable Rotterdam party. 'We want Rotterdam to look like any other Dutch city, but at the moment we have more unemployed people and crime than anywhere else . . . If people want to come to Rotterdam they must have a job. If they don't have one, then we don't want them.'[8]

Big issue: A towering mosque – at 50 metres high, it will be Europe's largest – is now rising above Rotterdam, much to the dismay of many residents. 'There's no reason the minarets have to be so high,' protested city council member Ronald Sorensen, who is Rotterdam's new Pim Fortuyn. 'It will not be Rotterdam. It will be Mecca on the Maas [river].'[9]

History Review

For a country that is but a small, soggy triangle bordering the North Sea, the Netherlands has made a huge splash in the world – and much of its power has come from water. It wasn't simply that the Dutch set sail in superior ships to pluck the planet's riches, or that watermills fuelled early Dutch industry or even that North Sea gas finds in the 1970s brought much of its current wealth. Just as important was the sea's role in creating a strong, cohesive society: living in a part of the world long known as the Lowlands – which is exactly what the Netherlands means – the Dutch literally had to pull themselves out of the bog, an activity that fostered a strong cooperative spirit and a preoccupation with every last millimetre of space. That ground-level planning and the scarcity of turf created a highly organized, efficient society where land is valuable, population is dense, everything is planned and everyone has a part and a say.

'God created the world, and the Dutch created the Netherlands' – Dutch saying

Laying the Foundation

The Dutch worked their way up from lowly beginnings, literally. Over a quarter of their ground lies below sea level, and for most of their history they've been obsessed with pushing back water and creating new land. Early settlers built their homes high up on mounds, minimizing chances that they would float away, but in the twelfth century the Dutch launched civil engineering projects that are amazing even today. With a shared enemy in floods and the encroaching sea, common villagers worked together to devise clever schemes to keep water out. They stuck logs into marshes and built their towns up; they designed canals that siphoned high rivers; they built dykes to push back water and constructed windmills to pump water out of bogs and into canals. More astounding than the idea that these were simple medieval folk, who weren't fulfilling the wishes of kings but initiating these clever public works on their own, was the fact that not only did the Dutch come to control the surrounding water, they conquered it. Using pumps and canals to dry out swamps, they filled them in, reclaiming the lost territory for farmland, pastures and houses. For over nine centuries the Dutch have created new land with the fill-in-the-swamp process they call poldering, which is still responsible for the physical growth of the country today.

Oddly, Iberia, the chunk of Europe that contains Portugal and Spain, was nearly as important as water in forming the contemporary Dutch psyche. In the sixteenth century they were all part of the same kingdom, a historical oddity that aptly illustrates how convoluted the Habsburg empire – which contained the assorted pieces of the Holy Roman Empire – had become. But both southern countries presented the Netherlands with something that would profoundly alter its future: one was a zealot, the other a map.

Holy Roman Emperor Charles V was overwhelmed with good fortune: when he became emperor at the age of 19, he inherited the holdings of his father (a Habsburg) and his mother (from Castile), becoming the wealthiest, most powerful person in Europe, and the man lording over the most land.

The Spanish Netherlands

For centuries the Netherlands was part of the grab bag of land called the Holy Roman Empire, which extended from Vienna across the European continent. It wasn't a unified affair: imperial territories were scattered into principalities and duchies; different corners of the Netherlands, for instance, were run by counts, dukes and bishops who didn't pay much heed to the Holy Roman Emperor, who usually sat far off in Austria. That all changed under Charles V, who had a more centralized empire in mind when he inherited the HRE's reins in 1519, lands which now included Spain and Portugal thanks to his mother. Born in today's Belgium, he took a far greater interest in the Netherlands (then including Belgium and Luxembourg) and part of that interest was money: this was the richest region of Europe, thanks to an extensive trade market the Netherlands was building up, transporting grain from the Baltic States and Portuguese wines. Charles, who was forever getting into wars with the French, slapped taxes on the Netherlands to fund his military escapades, which didn't go down well. But that wasn't the only area where Charles and the Netherlands clashed: Charles was Catholic and Martin Luther's anti-Catholic reformation ideas were just having an impact in the provinces. Charles had condemned Luther when he called him to the Diet of Worms, and forbade publication of his writings, but being a kind man (for an emperor) he didn't kill him; besides, he didn't want to fight off Luther-supporting Germans, too. In 1556 Charles divided the unwieldy empire, making his son Philip II, King of Spain, Portugal and the Netherlands as well. Philip moved south to orchestrate the show from Spain, and soon encountered rebellion when he tried to replant the Catholic church in the Protestant provinces of the Netherlands. Believing Catholicism was too iconic, in 1566 Dutch Protestants broke into Catholic churches, looting them, toppling statues of saints and destroying them. Philip dispatched the fervently religious Spanish Duke of Alva to deal with the problem, and he did so a bit too zealously: over seven years Alva killed tens of thousands of Dutch, nailing them to crosses, burning them at stakes, starving them until there was nothing left to eat but weeds. Running out of money, Alva imposed harsh taxes on everything, property, land transfers and 10 per cent on all sales. This ultimately caused the Protestant provinces of the Netherlands – under the leadership of William the Silent, Prince of Orange (ancestor of today's Queen Beatrix) – to announce they were leaving the kingdom, and that triggered a war with the Spanish that would drag on (with intermittent ceasefires) for eighty years. Ultimately, however, the Netherlands got independence out of the deal; first declaring it in 1581, their independence was officially recognized in 1648.

Through General Alva's sadistic attacks and tax hikes, Spain provided the impetus for the Netherlands to declare independence, but Portugal provided something just as important and their contribution would lead to wealth and domination of the seas. The Portuguese accidentally provided the Dutch with directions to the Spice Islands, after a Dutchman stole the secrets of their maps.

> For over a century, the spice trade had been dominated by the Portuguese for a simple reason: only they knew exactly where the Spice Islands (in today's Indonesia) and other Asian trade centres for the aromatics lay, and the Portuguese had no intention of parting with the information. Enter into the picture Dutchman Jan Huygen van Linschoten, who wormed his way into employment on Portuguese trading ships for several years, during which he snooped through the secret archives, copying the treasured Portuguese information little by little. In 1596 a Dutch publisher brought out Itinerario, van Linschoten's map-filled book, which included plenty of detailed navigational charts. He might as well have published a map to El Dorado and Shangri-La. Itinerario launched a trade revolution: not only did every Dutchman and his brother head for the East Indies, so did nearly everybody else, once the book was translated into their language. The English found it quite handy as well.

Initially assorted cities hired crews that raced towards the East Indies, but nutmeg and pepper soon flooded the market bringing the profit down. Again the Dutch spirit of cooperation prevailed: the separate cities bonded together to form the East Indies Trading Company (VOC) in 1602, one of the world's first multinationals. Given powers to acquire land, form colonies, negotiate treaties and run its own army, the VOC was a state within a state. It was such a vicious, murderous and heinous operation that it is surprising the Dutch can talk about that period without wincing. It's not surprising, however, that in 2002, when the Dutch held a celebration of the four hundredth anniversary of the VOC, the Indonesian ambassador opted out, saying the VOC days marked the nadir for Indonesia.

What Price Spice?

Forget all those romantic notions of tropical islands where the breezes are perfumed with nutmeg, cinnamon and cloves. In the seventeenth century, when the Dutch entered the race for the exotic flavours that added zest to desserts and masked rotten meat, they opened up one of the most brutal chapters in human history. The cruelty began on the Dutch boats heading towards the East Indies. Poor sailors were allotted a chunk of bread, a round of cheese and a bottle of water to last them on the voyage that lasted three months, many of them developing scurvy before arrival. And heaven forbid any rowdiness broke out on the ship: whoever instigated a bloody brawl was punished by having his hand nailed to the mast or was pulled under the boat until his head snapped or his skin was peeled off.[10] The Dutch were even more vicious to those Asians who grew the spices they so coveted. Welcoming parties that canoed out to meet them with gifts were blasted to smithereens; the inhabitants who didn't want to play the Dutch way – to accept low pay and trade only with the Dutch – were slaughtered. So much for the teachings of Calvin or humanist philosopher Erasmus, so much for the idea of the evolved Dutch once they left their home turf: the 15,000 inhabitants of the tranquil Banda Islands, the only place where nutmeg then grew, were wiped out when they wouldn't guarantee a monopoly; 10,000 Chinese were eliminated when they threatened a rebellion in Jakarta (Batavia); some 30,000 were killed on Sulawesi and another 100,000 died on the island of Sumatra.[11] They didn't have to massacre the inhabitants of Bali: most killed themselves when the Dutch set foot on their island. The Dutch also ran out the Portuguese and the British, treating them just as savagely to ensure the Dutch retained a monopoly on their aromatic valuables. The islanders had little recourse, since back then there was not an International Criminal Court for war crimes, but the Europeans knew how to make noise: with reports of how the Dutch had tortured British traders in 1623 – boiling them, burning them, blowing off their limbs – several VOC commanders were to be tried. They died mysteriously before the trial, but the Dutch were forced to compensate the victims' families. The spices, silk, textiles and china the Dutch carried back from

South-east Asia did enrich the treasury, but not by that much: some estimates say the VOC contributed as little as 3 per cent of the GDP a year. Far more valuable was their trade of grain from the Balkans and wine from Portugal, which did not entail such butchery. When Queen Beatrix visited Indonesia in 1995 she said she felt 'very sad' for the havoc the VOC had wreaked, but most modern Dutch people still wear blinkers on the matter.

Even after the VOC went belly-up in 1798, the Netherlands just folded most of what is today's Indonesia – and then was called the Dutch East Indies – into its empire. In 1901, three centuries after their first arrival, the Dutch enacted an ethical policy and began to pump a little money back into the Indonesian economy, in addition to providing funding for education and health care.

Few back home in the Netherlands had any idea what the VOC was up to in the East Indies; all they saw were the treasures unloaded from ships and the increasing prosperity of the time. A new wealthy merchant class burgeoned in the seventeenth century and the religious freedom offered in the newly independent country attracted everyone from French Huguenots to Portuguese Jews. Unlike the rest of Europe, the Netherlands was the only place where your station in life wasn't defined solely by birth: more important then, as now, was how much money you had. The booming overseas trade and the rise of the bourgeoisie triggered a golden age in their seventeenth-century society. Dutch women strolled the streets in clothes of the most beautiful fabrics, Indian textiles, chintz, Chinese silk. Ships, which stopped in Japan, China and India on their trips from the Spice Islands, hauled back detailed Oriental screens, tea sets of bone china, delicate Japanese flowers and elaborate sculptures of teak. The fragrant spices – Javanese pepper, Ceylonese cinnamon, sassafras, ginger, nutmeg and mace – were only some of the faraway foods that made the Netherlands the best place to feast: in the land known for chewy breads, creamy cheese, butter and every sort of fruit, vegetable and meat, the Dutch could polish off French wines, German beers, Caribbean coffee, Indian teas sweetened with sugar from Brazil as well as Polish grain, Italian olives, Mediterranean dates, nuts and figs.[12] The University of Leiden, known for its sciences and fine gardens, was attracting brilliant minds from everywhere including famed philosopher René Descartes, astronomer Christian

Huygens who invented the pendulum clock and first identified the rings of Saturn; Anton van Leeuwenhoek who invented cellular biology, after first inventing the microscope to see the wee things; and Dutch scientist Cornelius Drebbel who whipped up a perpetual-motion machine and invented the world's first submarine, which amazed thousands of Brits in 1621 when it emerged from the Thames.[13] But what the Dutch Golden Age is best known for are its elegantly realistic paintings. Wall-sized group portraits of militias and literary clubs showed which member had paid most handsomely by portraying them largest and with the most detail. The religious themes that had dominated art when the Catholic church was the body that commissioned it, were now replaced with paintings of landscapes, domestic interiors and portraits of the nouveau riche. Now the common man could buy art directly from the artist's studio or affordable prints in the public markets – marking the first time that high art could be bought by the masses.

Another Stolen Beginning

The tulip is far more than a flower; to the pragmatic Dutch, it is a bulb. Sure, the countryside of mustard yellows and inky purples is easy on the eyes, as are the markets where the striped and mottled blooms go for a pittance. But the real money comes from the paper-wrapped progenitor, the onion-like bulb, sales of which internationally ring over €600 million a year. The flower that is now a Dutch national symbol didn't originate here: the tulip first poked up in Turkey – ending up in Holland when the Ottoman Empire gave samples to a Viennese ambassador, who brought them to Vienna's Imperial Garden. The head of the garden, botanist Carolus Clusius, arrived at Holland's famous University of Leiden in 1593 and set up a vast horticultural research plot, which soon became the talk of the town. The wealthy were just then beginning to adorn their tables with cut blossoms, but Clusius refused to hand over any of his precious blooms, and he couldn't be bribed or bought. Seeing the commercial value, schemers simply dug up his bulbs from the beds, launching the tulip industry with late-night theft. Because there were so few of the bulbs, a madness overtook the Dutch in their desire to possess them, and the value of the simple tulip bulb shot up, at one point reaching the equivalent of €1,700 a piece. Speculators jumped into the picture, and entire fortunes were made and lost during a few frenzied years in the 1630s now called Tulipmania. When the bottom dropped out of the market, it nearly had the effect of the 1929 stock crash and the tulip was dubbed 'the flower that drove men mad'. Now the Dutch cultivate some 3,500 varieties, selling them at much more reasonable prices.

Of all the so-called Dutch Masters of the Golden Era – a group that includes Flemish artists Rubens, Van Dyck and Pieter Bruegel (see Belgium) – the two who most defined the era as we know it today were Rembrandt and Vermeer, though in lifestyle the two couldn't have been less alike. Rembrandt (1606–69) was flamboyant, well known and wealthy in his day, being commissioned for huge group portraits of militias such as *The Nightwatch* (1642) or portraits of Amsterdam's elite. So famous was Rembrandt that he ran studios with dozens of apprentices, whom he taught to imitate his technique, which led to so many of his works being possible forgeries today. Lesser known, quiet Johannes Vermeer (1632–75), now famous for his *Girl With the Pearl Earring*, lived in Delft, where his main client was a rich merchant, but money was often tight. Both artists, who turned their attention to daily life in the Dutch home – capturing spiritual beauty in the mundane – mixed paints that were heavy on the oil, imparting a sheen, and both played with light. Rembrandt, however, was prolific, leaving some 600 paintings, 300 etchings and numerous drawings. Vermeer worked much more slowly: his collection included at most forty works, perhaps because he was apparently often in bed with his wife, on whom he sired fifteen children. And while Rembrandt ensured that his likeness would be remembered by painting over sixty self-portraits, no one is even sure what Vermeer looked like. But the artists who both died in poverty shared two other qualities: their paintings fetch millions today and their works have been at the heart of forgery scams.

Rembrandt's works were so often copied by his students as well as forgers that the Dutch have an institute devoted to analysing what is and isn't the work of the master. Vermeer too was imitated, but apparently not until the twentieth century: in the 1930s Dutch painter Han van Meegeren suddenly showed up with half a dozen 'lost' Vermeers, previously unseen works that so resembled those of the Delft painter that they fooled all the art experts. Van Meegeren was raking in millions by selling works to museums and when the Germans invaded the Netherlands, Nazi leader Hermann Goering bought a Vermeer as well. The deception might never have been uncovered, except that after the war van Meegeren was charged with the loss of a national treasure. Faced with the prospect of many years of imprisonment, van Meegeren confessed that he had painted the 'Vermeers', illustrating exactly how it was done by painting another fake in court. He still got jail time – this time for forgery – but it was for only a year.[14]

Civil at home – where other religions were free to practise their faith as long as they did so discreetly – the Dutch continued to be overbearing at sea. They were constantly having run-ins with everyone, but particularly the British, with whom they fought two major wars in the 1660s – at one point the Dutch sailed right up the Thames, wreaking havoc along the way. Thousands were killed in the battles over colonies and trades, but the British ultimately ended up with the Dutch settlements in America, including the prosperous colony of New Amsterdam, which the Brits renamed New York. By 1672, everybody was so sick of the Dutch and their high-handed acts on the seas, that England, then France and German territories including Cologne, attacked the Netherlands, forcing them to sign treaties and come to heel. Problems continued however, especially with the British, who at one point temporarily wrested away the Dutch colonies in Asia. A bigger problem was looming on the Dutch horizon, however: the French. Napoleon invaded in 1795, and installed his brother Louis as ruler in 1806. That lasted only four years, but Louis did make some lasting changes, including founding the Rijksmuseum. Another legacy: trade in the port of Amsterdam, temporarily halted during Louis' rule, never really picked back up.

Amsterdam's shipping business really dried up in 1889, when the Dutch built their main train station where the port used to be, and Rotterdam boomed as the country's major port of call.

Once Napoleon fell, the Netherlands put itself back together as a monarchy in 1815, but in 1830 part of the kingdom – namely Belgium and Luxembourg, which remained mostly Catholic – pulled away, with substantial loss of population and land. Not to worry: besides holdings in the Americas, including Surinam and the Dutch Antilles, the Dutch were still clinging to most of the East Indies (Indonesia), an area fifty times bigger than their own. Declaring neutrality in the First World War, the Dutch tried it in the next great conflict, but it didn't work that time. On 10 May 1940 the Nazis attacked, devastating Rotterdam, and occupying the country shortly thereafter. Although the Dutch made valiant efforts to hide Jews, of the 140,000 Jews who lived in the Netherlands at the start of the war only 20,000 survived to its end.

Of all the countries occupied by the Nazis, no country is still more furious than the Netherlands. One sign: the Dutch say there's not a German restaurant to be found in the land.

During the war the Netherlands temporarily lost the Dutch East Indies, when the Japanese occupied it in 1941. The Dutch had assumed that the islands would be coming back into the fold, but the islanders had other ideas: a nationalist movement had grown, and the united islands proclaimed independence as Indonesia in 1945. The Dutch couldn't bear the idea of losing the land they so loved, and whose resources had made them so rich. They shipped out the military in what was called 'the Police Actions' during which they killed an estimated 100,000 islanders over four years.[15] The United States finally stepped in and squeezed where it hurt: the US threatened to cut off all Marshall Plan funding to the Dutch, unless the Netherlands backed down and recognized Indonesian sovereignty, which they finally did in 1949. What happened during the Police Actions is still coming out today.[16]

Another sore point: Srebrenica. When the details of that botched 1995 Bosnian peacekeeping effort emerged in 2002, the shocked Dutch parliament simply walked out.

Srebrenica

It was one of the most sombre and humiliating events in Dutch history. In 1995, while serving as UN peacekeepers in the Bosnian town of Srebrenica, some 100 Dutch soldiers allowed Bosnian Serbs to take away Muslim men and boys, after being given assurances that the Muslims wouldn't be harmed. Instead a slaughter ensued. In 2002 the Dutch government issued its report on the matter, stating that at least 7,000 Muslims were killed, despite being supposedly under Dutch protection. The report faulted both the government for sending in peacekeepers without adequate arms, and the Dutch military, which tried to hush up the affair.

Quick Tour

Except for the weather – which mostly ranges from goosebump grey to bone-numbingly cold – and except for the expense (laying your head anywhere on this densely packed bit of land isn't cheap), and except for that annoying egalitarian habit of splitting every bill down to the last euro cent (alas, there really is such a thing as 'going Dutch') and that ever-present Dutch attitude of 'We're more evolved than you' (well, maybe they are), the Netherlands may be the most ideal place on the planet, except of course that the country of canals and windmills is so frighteningly flat.

Two of the most important EU summits were held in the Netherlands, resulting in hugely important agreements: the Maastricht Treaty of 1992 created the euro (and changed the name of the European Economic Community to the European Union); the 1997 Amsterdam Treaty formalized the desire for European enlargement.

Oh the place has its problems: crime in cities is rising; Amsterdam is clogged with glassy-eyed tourists; the parliament keeps falling apart and even when it functions can make a terminal insomniac snore; the Yugoslav and Russian mobs are moving in with their sex slaves, and newcomers use the wrong bags for the rubbish and put them out on the wrong night. And, as the Dutch love to point out, the train just isn't as punctual now that it's been privatized.

The idea behind the licensed cannabis café that first popped up in the late 1970s was to separate soft drugs from hard ones: better to buy small amounts from a café owner who pays taxes, the Dutch reasoned, than from someone who may be peddling cocaine, crack and heroin on the street. The Dutch say the tolerant approach is effective: relatively few of their youth regularly smoke the herbaceous substances, and the proportion of those who use heroin or cocaine is negligible and far lower than in countries such as the United States where soft drugs are lumped in with the rest.

Besides all that, there's just no place else quite like the land of tall skinny buildings peering over canals, where windmills and pot shops exist side by side, and prostitutes press their bodies against glass not far from museums where tourists press up close to take in the swirls of Vincent Van Gogh. The Netherlands is a rare country where the medieval and modern used to coexist in harmony and liberal notions spring from pragmatic honesty and acknowledgement of the moneymaking potential of vice.

Nederlands: The Language Factor

Gutturally combining about twenty-three letters per word, the Dutch language is neither easy nor romantic ('I love you' comes out 'Ik hou van jou') but without speaking Nederlands – as the language is called – one won't get a job in the country. And while some of the 'guest workers' brought in during the 1960s and 1970s are fluent in the native language, their families often don't speak it. Since 1998, those from other countries who marry a Dutch civilian are required to take year-long language classes to attain proficiency.

Future Forecast

Big problems. The murder of Van Gogh will result in even stricter legislation about immigration and the immigrants who already live there. The lid has blown off this typically coolheaded society and who knows what will happen next, but it's doubtful it will be rational.

In recent Eurobarometer surveys, Public Opinion in the European Union, *the Dutch were the group most likely to say crime was the worst problem the EU faces: 47 per cent answered thus. The Dutch scored highest in saying they had witnessed discrimination on grounds of race or ethnicity: 35 per cent answered affirmatively.*

Hot Spots

Amsterdam: Its ringed canals circle past museums housing works of Rembrandt, Vermeer, Van Gogh, and some of the most eye-pleasing architecture on the planet – the houses built so thin and tall to maximize value from the precious plot of land at their base. The densely packed capital is most associated with vice, given that its popular red-light district is legal, and pot cafés sell small amounts; possession of over 30 grams, however, is actually illegal. The Russian mob is said to be moving in; some unconfirmed reports say over half of Amsterdam's bars and cafés are paying 'protection' to the thugs.

Amsterdam: Dutch victory over the sea.

Rotterdam: Site of the world's biggest port – 80,000 sea-going ships and 110,000 barges call at the port of Rotterdam every year[17] – the Netherlands' second largest city is a major commercial hub – but whereas its most important cargoes were once Indonesian coffee and sweet-smelling spices, incoming ships today may carry drugs and slaves, since it is a major smuggling point into Europe. Home to the highest number of ethnic minorities in the Netherlands – Turks and Moroccans suffer high unemployment particularly among women and youths – Rotterdam also has the Netherlands' highest crime rate.

> *Design-wise: Flattened by the Nazis during the Second World War, Rotterdam pulled itself together with style: the only European city designed for the car is dotted with five dozen parks and is home to assorted architectural oddities including geometric 'cube houses' – diamond-shaped apartments that are perched on stilts; in the Netherlands Architecture Institute you can while away the day in the library browsing through thousands of stunning design books.*

The Hague (Den Haag): Amsterdam is the capital, but politics oozes out of this city not far from the North Sea. It put the Netherlands permanently on the map as the global justice centre, as home for the International Criminal Court, and assorted UN war tribunals.

Does a paper cut qualify: Despite the fact that the Dutch are among the longest living people in the world, working in the Netherlands is apparently extremely hazardous to your health. So one might conclude, given a government finding that 13 per cent of the labour force claimed to be disabled,[18] thus qualifying for compensation.

Friesland: At the north tip of the Netherlands lies the outpost where they speak in a language entirely unintelligible to the rest of the country, where mustard-making is a local art, and where the passion is to trek across the mud flats of the Wadden Sea that pretty much disappears at low tide. Once home to gangs of pirates known as the Sea Beggars, it's still the most secluded and independent of all the Dutch provinces.

Grudge: Germany. Another reason why the Dutch are still resentful of the Germans: Nazis stole all their bicycles at the start of the occupation. In 1974, when the graceful Dutch were poised to win the World Cup, they were beaten off by the efficient, if clunky, Germans. After steaming about it for fourteen years, the Dutch finally beat the Germans in the 1988 European Championship at least. Said the victorious Dutch: 'We finally got our bicycles back.'

Maastricht: The limestone caves that snake underground are also equipped as a wartime civil defence shelter, complete with ovens for baking bread and chapels for breaking it. Above ground, the town and environs are brimming with fantastic medieval architecture and castles. It was here that the Western European leaders agreed on the idea of the common currency, and the treaty that created the euro and the new moniker of the European Union bears the town's name.

Rembrandthuis: Today the lovely home of the master is preserved as a museum, but the five-storey house on the Breestraat was Rembrandt's curse. A bit out of his financial range, the home he'd bought with his beloved wife Saskia was where she died the next year giving birth to his son Titus. House payments ultimately broke his piggy bank: that house is a good part of the reason that the pauper Rembrandt's remains were buried in an unmarked grave.

Squats: The stay-without-pay movement was so strong in the 1980s and 1990s that demonstrations in support of the building takeovers sometimes turned raucous, the most violent being in Amsterdam on Queen Beatrix's

1980 Coronation Day. The prevalence of young people moving into empty buildings and setting up rent-free, anarchistic households actually resulted in an anti-squat movement, when developers moved people into churches, schools and other empty sites designated for future renovation, where they could stay rent-free (having signed a contract that they would move out eventually).

Hot Shots

Jan Peter Balkenende: Prime Minister 2002 (government collapsed); 2003 to present. With round glasses and a perpetual boyishness, the 47-year-old former religious philosophy professor is often likened to Harry Potter, although he has yet to work any magic on the government, which fell apart in 2002 a few months after he entered office. (The problem: constant bickering in the late Pim Fortuyn's party.) That was just the beginning of the problems during his cursed tenure: immigration woes became the talk of the day, the Queen's husband Claus died, Princess Margarita trashed the royal family in print, the fiancée of Prince Johan Friso told a huge lie in parliament, for which she was later nailed, and public sentiment turned against the EU, just before Balkenende took over the EU presidency. A

Pim Fortuyn: shook up the PC.

Christian Democrat, he opposes euthanasia and gay marriage, but says he won't repeal the laws legalizing them; however, he may crack down on hash houses. Leading the country during its most rocky times, the PM now faces the fallout from Van Gogh's murder.

After the United States had insisted it didn't want any UN help on Iraq, it threw Balkenende into the ring in 2004 to announce the US had changed its mind.

Pim Fortuyn: Government administrator, teacher, columnist and Maoist before forming his own right-wing party and creating social uproar with his anti-immigration platform. He may have done the rigidly PC Dutch a favour by raising relevant issues – e.g., immigrants aren't well integrated into society – but he provided few answers and fostered an atmosphere of fear, all the more when in 2002 he was assassinated.

Margarita-Gate

Queen Beatrix, it's said, wasn't fond of many of Crown Prince Willem Alexander's girlfriends – one was rumoured to work for a sex hotline and another modelled lingerie. But the Queen apparently had some real problems with the self-proclaimed baron that her niece Princess Margarita dragged home. Margarita, daughter of the Queen's sister, Princess Irene, caused a royal uproar in 2001 when she announced she would be trotting down the aisle with Edwin de Roy van Zuydewijn, who runs a Dutch personnel agency. When the Queen had him checked out, royal investigations showed he was not a baron as he claimed, but a mere commoner. With his deceit exposed, Margarita's parents protested against the marriage and so did the Queen. The whole royal family was so opposed to Princess Margarita's choice of mate that, except for Margarita's mum, the A-list royal relatives (including Margarita's dad) boycotted her September 2001 wedding, and one imagines Margarita may have been a tad disappointed with the gifts. But that was just the beginning of the scandal surrounding Margarita, who isn't in line for the throne, but nevertheless lives in a spare castle in France. In 2003 she accused the Queen of having ordered Dutch intelligence to check into van Zuydewijn's background (that charge was verified), of bugging her phone (not verified) and of tampering with her husband's business affairs (also not verified). Margarita was so irate, she went on to air all kinds of royal dirty laundry – much of it in a four-part series in a Dutch magazine – claiming among other things that her father had an illegitimate child from their Dominican maid and that her grandfather was a philanderer. But the real blow was when Margarita – charging that Beatrix was way out of line for interfering with her marriage – brought legal charges against her aunt the Queen for tarnishing her husband's professional reputation. Her husband was just as indiscreet, although his royal gossip was much more amusing: van Zuydewijn claimed that whenever he was at a royal dinner party, he was subjected to 'psychological terror'[19] adding that at one bash the Queen got tipsy and took a nap in a chair! What's more, he said the Queen had erased his photo from the family portrait! Maybe the Queen was merely showing foresight with his photo deletion: Margarita's marriage to the faux baron is reportedly on the rocks, although the couple denies it. In the meantime, the world is waiting to see if the Queen will have to fork out that €33 million that Margarita's lawyers are demanding.

Queen Beatrix Wilhelmina Armgard: Monarch 1980 to present. Beloved and benign (well, at least if you're not dating her son), Queen Beatrix of the House of Orange (born 1938) inherited the position passed down from William the Silent, Prince of Orange, who beat back the Spanish and unified the country in the sixteenth century. The richest monarch in the world – she's said to be worth about €2.6 billion[20] – and Dutch head of state, until recently she didn't have much to do except worry about whom her kin plan to marry – and with all the fuss lately, you'd think she'd suggest that they just secretly elope. Well, Beatrix caused a scandal in her day, by marrying Claus von Amsberg, a handsome German diplomat in 1966, when the sting of the war was still fresh. Despite his nationality, Claus, who died in 2002, was quite popular too.

Prince Bernhard (1911–2004): Hubby of former Queen Juliana and father of current Queen Beatrix, German-born Bernhard was a major international player: he founded the influential Bilderberg Group in 1954, and went on to found the World Wildlife Fund. Was involved in scandals as well, most notably in 1976 when he accepted some $1 million from US aircraft manufacturer Lockheed to sway the Dutch government to order from them. Insisted the family wasn't as rich as reported.

Johan Friso (b. 1968): Beatrix's middle son, Johan Friso was long suspected of being homosexual, but he proved otherwise when he began seriously dating a Dutch woman, Mabel Wisse, in 2003. Mum had reason to flip her lid over that too: no sooner had marriage plans been put on the table than the media dished out rumours that Mabel had once been the girlfriend of the biggest drug baron in the Netherlands. To make matters worse, both Johan and Mabel lied about it in Parliament. Now the prince will forgo any shot at the crown since he wed his beloved jewel.

Crown Prince Willem Alexander: Heir apparent. Likeable Prince Willem (born 1967) was a bit of a playboy before he married Argentine beauty Maxima Zorreguieta in 2002. That marriage too caused a furore: Maxima's father was a minister in Argentina's 1970s military junta; Papa wasn't invited to the royal wedding.

Vincent Van Gogh

Everybody knows he was a tortured creator of archetypal proportions who hacked off his ear. Everybody knows about the paint thickly swirled into sunflowers and star-spangled nights and his love of absinthe and how the chemical's green fairy may have been the reason his palette was so verdant and bright. But who knew that Dutchman Vincent Van Gogh signed his works by his first name, because so few could pronounce Gogh (rhymes with loch)?[21] Or that perhaps he had a child with a prostitute whom he wanted to marry?[22] The former preacher whom the church asked to put down his bible because he was thumping it too passionately, actually did have some friends – Toulouse-Lautrec among them – despite his incessant talking that drove many mad. Van Gogh had a dream: to start an artists' colony – the Studio of the South. That's how the painter from Holland ended up in the yellow house in Arles, where Gauguin came to stay for six weeks in 1888, during which Van Gogh whipped up a whopping forty paintings, while Gauguin churned out twenty. So much for the idea of his cheerful colony for creative sorts – cranky Van Gogh wasn't much of a host: he chased after Gauguin with a razor, deciding instead to slash off his own ear. As it was Christmas Eve, he duly presented the bloody ear to his beloved at the nearby brothel – she fainted in response – and from that point on Vincent spent much of his time in a nearby asylum. 'Vincent was hospitalized', wrote Gauguin. 'His state is worse, he wants to sleep with the patients, chases the nurses, and washed himself in the coal-bucket.'[23] His mental health deteriorating, Van Gogh fatally shot himself in 1890; some say that his French physician Dr Gachet was next to his bed, sketching Van Gogh as he passed away, and that Gachet sneaked out carrying several mysterious boxes, which some believe contained Van Gogh's notebooks.[24] Although the artist exhibited in four shows while alive – selling one painting – Van Gogh's posthumous success is mostly the result of his sister-in-law Johanna, devoted wife of his brother and patron Theo, who duly held on to Van Gogh's letters and paintings that during his lifetime were shrugged off as the works of a madman, which, admittedly, they were.

Curiosity: Most of the US flight schools where the September 11 hijackers trained were owned by Dutchmen, who don't know how to fly themselves.

Royal Dutch/Shell: The petroleum bigwig that made over €11 billion in profits in 2003[25] helps to ensure that the Netherlands won't run short on energy – the natural gas fields in the north of the country also help – but it doesn't have a sterling reputation in the countries where it operates, particularly Nigeria.

Shell Game

Royal Dutch/Shell – an Anglo-Dutch enterprise (with US subsidiaries as well) – likes to advertise itself as the jolly green-friendly giant of oil, but lately that is looking more than ever like whitewash. The company's most questionable dealings have centred on Nigeria, which typically provides about 10 per cent of its output, and where the petrol giant's heavily polluting operations leaked almost 10,000 barrels of petroleum in 2003.[26] Royal Dutch/Shell has been accused of bribing local officials,[27] supporting government attacks on whoever threatens the oil biz, and is also allegedly implicated in the 1995 government-ordered hanging of eight activists, including writer Ken Saro-Wiwa, who denounced the oil company's sloppy operations and lack of investment in the community. In 2002 Royal Dutch/Shell's Nigerian operations were temporarily shut down by local women called the Mamas – some of them grandmamas – demanding the company give jobs to their husbands and sons, clean up the petrol-soaked ground and extend electricity across the road to their villages. Shell called in the police and the showdown turned violent: the women's group claims several female protesters disappeared in the round-up and are believed to be dead.

The latest scandal: In January 2004 Royal Dutch/Shell admitted that, whoops, it had overstated its reserves (many in Nigeria) by 20 per cent. Shareholders are furious about the 4.5 billion barrels of oil that apparently aren't really there, the company's heads went flying and assorted international bodies are now breathing down the oil biggie's neck.

Paul Van Buitenen: Founded Transparent Europe; MEP 2004 to present. Many wish that the European Union would stop being so wasteful and corrupt, but when this EU auditor began looking under the rug at the European Commission, the whole twenty-member board was forced to resign. Demanding that the notoriously spendthrift European Parliament reform itself as well, he started up Transparent Europe, which also has an anti-war bent. TE won two seats in the European Parliament in 2004.

Cees Nooteboom: Well-respected travel columnist, novelist, playwright and poet known for such works as *The Roads to Santiago* and *All Souls' Day*, Nooteboom (born 1933) is as adored in Germany and Austria as he is here, winning the 2003 State Award for Literature in Austria. Many reckon he's the Netherlands' best shot for a Nobel prize.

Paul Verhoeven: The Dutch director of some twenty films bounces around in styles: *Soldier of Orange* was an acclaimed historical drama about the Dutch Resistance; *Basic Instinct* was a provocative psychological thriller; *Robocop* was schlock. Now he's delving into mysteries, specifically *One Step Behind* by Henning Mankell, as well as a movie about a Japanese war criminal.

Rescuers: With their maritime know-how, the Dutch were called in to pull up the sunken Russian nuclear submarine Kursk, and to rescue the tanker Prestige when it sank off Spain in November 2002. The latter was a botched mission: the panicky Spanish ordered the ship out to sea, where it broke in two and sank; nearly a year later it still gurgled up petroleum belches.

Desiderius Erasmus: The best-known scholar of the Dutch Renaissance, writer-translator-professor Erasmus (1466–1536) translated the New Testament, wrote assorted books and essays and is often described as a humanist. Sort of hard to tell that in his scathing assessment of his fellow Dutchmen in his 1509 book *The Praise of Folly*: '[Merchants] whenever it is necessary will lie, perjure themselves, steal, cheat and mislead the public.

Nevertheless . . . there is no lack of flattering friars to kowtow to them and call them Right Honourable in public. The motive of the friars is clear: they are after some of the loot . . . After the lawyers come the philosophers, who are reverenced for their beards and the fur on their gowns. They announce that they alone are wise and that the rest of men are only passing shadows . . . Perhaps it would be wise to pass over the theologians in silence. That short-tempered and supercilious crew is unpleasant to deal with . . . they behave as if they are already in heaven; they look down pityingly on other men as so many worms.'[28]

Neelie Kroes: European Commissioner 2004 to present. Former minister of transport in Dutch national government is now in charge of competition policy at the European Commission. No word if there was much competition for the post.

Media Star: The Netherlands has some fantastic papers espousing numerous points of view, but most are only in Dutch. Radio Netherlands runs a site that keeps one abreast of current events – and history – in English: www.mw.nl/cgi-bin/home/NewsEnglish

Hands Off

The Dutch claim that it cures jetlag, knocks the nip out of winter, is a potent aphrodisiac and an alcoholic Viagra. Genever is the sexiest drink in the Netherlands and the libation poured out to celebrate weddings, holidays, births and birthdays. Flavoured with coffee, cinnamon, cocoa, berries, bananas or plums, decorated with rose petals or glittering flakes of real gold and silver, the distilled liqueur that in its young unadulterated form resembles gin is dangerous in any of its fifty-odd varieties. The dazzling colours and high-octane content that gets you woozy fast lend themselves to festivity, as does the centuries-old ritual for drinking genever: you must take the first sip from the overflowing glass – without hands – while bending over the bar.

10. Austria (Österreich): Dancing at the Edge

Fast Facts

Country:	Republic of Austria; Republik Österreich
Capital:	Vienna (Wien)
Government:	federal republic
Independence:	1156 (from Bavaria); pushed out of German Federation 1866
Population:	8,175,000 (2004 estimate)
Leaders:	Head of State: President Heinz Fischer (2004) Head of Government: Chancellor Wolfgang Schüssel (2000)
Elections:	President elected by direct popular vote, 6-year term; Chancellor appointed by president (from majority party)
Name of Parliament:	Federal Assembly; Bundesversammlung
Ethnicity	German 88%; non-nationals 9% (Croat, Slovene, Hungarian, Czech, Slovak, Roma); recent immigrant groups 1.5% (Turks, Bosnians, Serbs, Croats) (2001 estimate)
Religion:	Roman Catholic 74%; Protestant 5%; Muslim 4%; other 17%
Language:	German
Literacy:	98%
Exports:	machinery, vehicles, paper, metal goods, iron, steel, chemicals
Per capita GDP:	$30,000 (2003 estimate)
Unemployment:	4.2% (May 2004 Eurostat figure)
Percentage in poverty:	3.9% (1999 estimate)
EU status:	member since 1995; politically sanctioned for seven months in 2000
Currency:	euro
Known for:	heavenly composers, Freud, the Von Trapps

Standout Qualities

Edgy: Historical borders
Edgy: New EU countries
Edgy: What will happen with EU?

Résumé

The fetching alpine land known for Mozart, Freud and luscious pastries, Austria is still as lovely, regal and cultured as it was in the days when it was the headquarters of the Habsburg monarchy for seven centuries. Today, however, the place is a shadow of its former self: modern Austria holds scarcely a sixth of the imperial territories and its international clout has certainly shrunk as well. Kicking off the First World War with Germany, and siding with Hitler in the next global conflict, Austria has been politically sidelined ever since, often registering on the international radar only when it's done something else that the world sees as wrong.

After the First World War, Austria lost both its monarchy and 87 per cent of what had been the Austrian Empire's land.[1]

Gateway to Western Europe

When Eastern and Central Europe fell under Soviet control after the Second World War, neutral Austria became the door to the free West. Over the past five decades Austria has witnessed a flood of refugees, immigrants and temporary workers from the communist lands. Some 200,000 Hungarians fled here after the Revolution of 1956, and about 162,000 Czechs and Slovaks arrived after 1968's Prague Spring frosted over. When Poland's Solidarity union was banned in 1981–2, some 150,000 Poles ran to Austria and between 1973 and 1989, a quarter of a million Russian Jews came through on their way to Israel. In the early 1990s Austria also took in nearly 100,000 Bosnians fleeing the civil war in the former Yugoslavia. Although many of those who entered here moved on, some stayed: the end result is that some 12 per cent of Austrian citizens are foreign born – one of the highest proportions in Europe – and over 700,000 temporary workers are from other countries.[2]

Now Austria's position in the world is changing again: geographically, it is dead-centre in the expanded EU playing field, a location that may lure plenty of new business and make this rich country even richer. The position, however, makes Austrians jittery: four recent EU entrants sidle up to the country's borders from the East and some Austrians picture their country being caught in a stampede to the West. Even if they don't move in, workers from Slovenia, Hungary, the Czech Republic and Slovakia might commute and compete for Austrian jobs: the five million workers in those countries earn a quarter of a typical Austrian's wages.

> *Fears about Central Europeans nabbing Austrians' jobs appear mis-placed for the moment: members of new EU entrant countries may not be legally allowed to work in most western EU countries until as late as 2012. There could be a big jump, however, in 'under the table' employment.*

Politically, the country's global status is transforming as well. Respected for its impressive postwar economic performance and humanitarian efforts taking in Eastern European refugees – Austria was the first country to notify the UN of the Serbian genocide that began in 1991 – the country entered the European Union in 1995, only to find itself soon thereafter in the EU dog house, collared with political sanctions and kicked around like a stray. The reason: loudmouthed Austrian extremist Jörg Haider, who gave Europe (and Austria) a shock when his ultra-conservative and nationalist Freedom Party gained enough votes in 1999 to join the ruling coalition in Vienna. The vigilante politician, who told immigrants to go back where they came from and on several occasions praised Nazis (words he later recanted), soon ripped his country apart and triggered Austria's (temporary) ostracism by most of the world. By doing so, he only made already isolated Austrians even lonelier.

Haider's Hot Air

Jörg Haider (pronounced HY-der) has never been a wallflower.[3] The Porsche-driving son of two Nazi enthusiasts first captured the attention of former Nazi soldiers when he was a teenager giving political speeches about Austria's Nazi-supporting role during the Second World War. Many Austrians prefer to forget that era – or to portray Austria as a helpless victim – but for Haider, the support for Hitler's cause was a source of pride. He joined up with the Freedom Party – an offshoot of a political party begun by former Nazis – becoming party leader in 1986 and espousing the party's extreme right-wing beliefs. As governor of the southern region of Carinthia, Haider praised Hitler's labour policy (for not rewarding those who didn't work) and in a speech he greeted former members of the Nazi SS as 'dear friends', going on to describe them as 'decent people of good character' who should be awarded 'honour and respect'. He stirred controversy further by referring to concentration camps as 'punishment camps',[4] implying that Holocaust victims had done something for which they should have been punished. For his remarks, which he later retracted, he was forced to resign as governor in 1991, but eight years later he was voted back in as Carinthia's governor, heavily thumping his anti-immigrant idea of 'Austria First'. With Austria's unemployment rate rising to the highest since the war (around 5 per cent), many were listening. The country should shut off its borders to new immigrants, Haider opined, and send those already there back home. France's Jean-Marie Le Pen had said the same, but Haider was the first politician in office to push the idea so loudly and brashly – and given his previous pro-Nazi statements it rang an alarm bell across Europe.

Back-pedalling: *Rising in popularity through the 1990s – one-quarter of Austrians voted for him in 1999 – Haider's sudden popularity portended the rise of the right all over Europe. However, Haider and his Freedom Party have been dropping in popularity ever since.*

'Haider is not Austria. And Austria is not Haider' – Dr Peter Moser, Austrian Ambassador, National Press Club, Washington, DC, 11 February 2000

Since 1955 Austrian politics usually have operated like a well-rehearsed waltz, everything appearing organized and harmonious, as the same steps were repeated every year. Typically the left-leaning Social Democrats (drawing power from trade unions) won the majority of votes and took the more powerful position of chancellor, with the right-leaning People's Party (backed by big business and Catholics) often taking the presidential seat, and the two frequently danced together in a ruling coalition (Social Democrats leading, People's Party following) that never achieved a great deal – except to keep out other parties.

Austria is a big fan of team decision-making: trade unions, corporate heads, economists, thinkers and farmers all sit down together to shape national economic strategy as part of the sozialpartnerschaft *that forms the country's policies.*

So much for snoozy predictability: in 1999, when Jörg Haider cut in to the dance with his anti-immigration, anti-EU, nationalist, ultraconservative Freedom Party, the music stopped and the world looked on in horror as he crashed Austria's exclusive power soirée. Nabbing a whopping 27 per cent of the 1999 parliamentary vote, Haider's Freedom Party kicked the right-leaning People's Party, Austria's traditional number two, to the number three spot. And an unforeseen power shuffle ensued that would alter Austria's image around the world. That year the Social Democrats and the People's Party didn't form their usual coalition. Instead, the leader of the People's Party, Wolfgang Schüssel, formed a coalition with Haider's Freedom Party, and came away from the deal as Austrian chancellor, presiding over Austria's first conservative government in thirty years. The response: outrage, starting in Vienna, where thousands of demonstrators went berserk – an unusual event in a country where public protests rarely occur.

Inauguration days are typically sedate affairs in Austria but that wasn't the case in February 2000 when Chancellor Schüssel stepped forward with new coalition member Jörg Haider in a ceremony in central Vienna. Thousands of Austrians protested against the coalition, pounding on drums as they pushed past the top-hatted bouncers and forced their way into the ultra-refined Sachers Hotel, and then burst into the National Theatre disrupting a performance. Protesters pelted police with eggs and attacked trams, and were so rowdy in their wrath that Schüssel was forced to scurry underground from the ceremony using Vienna's famous tunnels. Every Friday for the next year, thousands marched to show their disgust at the mere existence of Jörg Haider.

The international reaction was just as intense. Israel recalled its ambassador, and the US did as well. Most embarrassing was the admonishment of the countries in the EU, which Austria had joined only four years before. Austria was shamed and rejected: diplomatic ties with all the other fourteen EU countries were officially clipped as part of 'diplomatic sanctions'. The EU 'will not behave with this government as if it were a normal government', declared President Jacques Chirac.[5] So intense was the heat that Haider stepped down as official head of the party, went back to Carinthia and threw in Freedom Party member Susann Riess-Passer in his place, but that didn't appease the EU powers-that-be. Neither did the statement Haider and Schüssel signed denouncing the Nazis and declaring their dedication to human rights. The diplomatic sanctions stayed in place, although they essentially amounted to a collective cold shoulder of Austria, and little more. Austria once again felt alone, its only 'sort-of friend' Germany not about to comment on the matter that hit a little too close to home. Meanwhile Austria became a political dartboard. 'Europe can do without Austria,' sniped the Belgian foreign minister Louis Michel, declaring it 'immoral' to go skiing there.[6]

Among the most worried about the charged atmosphere: those in Austrian tourism who dubbed the international frostiness 'The Haider Effect', as conventions and tour groups cancelled long-held reservations. Tourism typically brings in over €14 billion annually to the country's coffers, representing nearly 7 per cent of GDP.[7] That year it didn't.

Arctic Winds from Brussels

Schüssel's power move did not go down well in Austria's political circles. Even President Thomas Klestil, of Schüssel's party, was furious and did not want to recognize the ruling coalition, although he grudgingly did so. Schüssel should not have been surprised by the harsh reaction from the EU. As foreign minister the year before, he'd been repeatedly warned that Brussels was worried about Haider. So why did Schüssel bond with his party? Could he not resist the idea of the People's Party finally playing first fiddle in the government? Could he not pass up the opportunity for a right-wing government after thirty years? Was he making a statement about what he thought of the EU's meddling in Austrian affairs? His response to the diplomatic sanctions was eloquent when he spoke to the *Economist* that spring: 'I understand there were fears when I invited Jörg Haider's Freedom Party to form a coalition . . . But that should have led to a dialogue, not exclusion. Now we must decide what kind of Europe we want: a hegemonic directorate by a few or a balanced partnership between equals.'[8] With diplomatic relations on ice, Austria threatened to veto important proposals and to withhold its EU dues, but that just led to more barking from Brussels. Finally, seven months later, an EU committee concluded the obvious: sanctions were counterproductive and should be dropped, which they were. The experience, however, left Austria feeling utterly isolated.

'We didn't have a single friend. No one stood up for us' – unnamed Austrian politician in June 2000[9]

The collective finger-wagging turned many Austrians against continuing EU membership, including those who loathed Haider: suddenly only one-third of Austrians approved of being members of the Brussels club. Besides the humiliation of being branded as a racist, neo-Nazi country – because of one coalition member whom three-quarters of the country didn't support – the issue became whether the Union even had the right to tell Austrians whom they could and couldn't democratically vote into office. With Austria's political arena up for international scrutiny, and a matter of lurid fascination to the world's press, Austria did what it had done the last time nearly the same thing had happened – with Kurt Waldheim in 1986. First it got angry. Then it changed.

Re-examination

He had been a source of beaming pride to his compatriots, being the first postwar Austrian to cut such a distinguished presence on the world stage: stately Kurt Waldheim had eloquently represented their country as Secretary-General of the United Nations from 1972 to 1981, during which he unsuccessfully tried to cool down the Iran–Iraq war. After stepping down from the UN, he returned to his homeland to run for president in the mid 1980s, with victory assured on name recognition alone. But it was when he landed back on home turf that the problems began: the press made accusations, never entirely proven, that Waldheim had been far more active with the Nazis than he had let on; some contended that he had served as but a lowly translator. Austrians didn't believe the rumours, or didn't care: in 1986 they voted him in with a landslide victory. The doors to the international community slammed shut the next day. Waldheim, previously the most powerful man in the United Nations, didn't dare set foot in the US where he was listed on the State Department's watch list and barred entry; the only place that welcomed him through his term was the Vatican. Austrians were outraged by the global chill – at first. But anger turned to hushed introspection as many explored what Austria's role really had been during 'Anschluss', as the 1938 annexation of Austria by Nazi Germany was called: it had mostly been a topic to avoid until then. The Waldheim incident triggered a spate of press both at home and abroad and a questioning mood fell over the country. Schools, which had once taught history only up until the First World War, encouraged a more open view, writers suggested a certain complicity and intellectuals pointed out that many Austrians had wanted to bond with Germany after the 1914–18 war, when it was suffering a national identity crisis. Austrian responsibility in the Holocaust was for the first time partially acknowledged, although a broad programme was not set up to compensate concentration-camp survivors and slave labourers for another ten years. And oddly enough, the person who helped to push the programme through, both directly and indirectly, was Jörg Haider.

In August 2000 the Austrian government announced that it would be putting €65 million into a compensation fund for survivors of the Nazi concentration camps. The next month the EU agreed to lift sanctions. Six months later another plan was worked out. This time the Austrian government and state-owned companies would put another €360 million into the fund to compensate Austrian Jews whose lands had been seized during the war. Both programmes were loudly pushed by Haider.

Far from being an isolated phenomenon, Haider, it now seems, was just ahead of the pack. The man who personified the anti-immigrant right was soon joined by others across Europe: Pia Kjaersgaard in Denmark, Pim Fortuyn in the Netherlands, Carl Hagen in Norway and Umberto Bossi in Italy. However, unlike with the others, public sentiment has turned against Haider: furious after a tax cut wasn't passed (and also livid that his 2002 meeting with Saddam Hussein, during which he promised Austria's support, was so controversial), he caused the governing coalition to collapse that year. In the following election, the Freedom Party took only 10 per cent of the vote. Although his party was invited back into the government coalition, Haider was not – the party's chair instead filled by his less volatile sister Ursula Haubner. In the 2004 election for the European Parliament, the party floundered, winning a scanty 6 per cent of the vote and losing four of its five MEPs. Haider remains popular in Carinthia, where he is governor, but as a national leader he now looks like a has-been. And that too may foreshadow trends across Europe.

Another sign that Austria is turning back towards the left: newly elected President Heinz Fischer is of the Social Democrat mould.

Haider was a liability for his country, but a bright star has emerged on Austria's political scene: journalist Hans-Peter Martin, a former Socialist MEP who made international news when he grassed on his colleagues in the notoriously wasteful European Parliament for questionably spending millions of euros. Martin made thousands of tapes of MEPs signing in for Friday's work, and then promptly leaving – but claiming that day's pay and a hefty €270 food allowance. His fellow MEPs were outraged – and his party was so embarrassed that they expelled him. Martin formed his own party, and in the June 2004 parliamentary elections he was the biggest winner, pulling in 14 per cent of the vote. He may be exactly what the country needs just now: an honest hero.

History Review

Lounging against the snow-frosted Alps, Austria is beloved as a scenic skiing gateway and haven for classical music, but it was long the power seat of continental Europe. From the thirteenth century on, Vienna was headquarters of the Holy Roman Empire, the longest-lasting European kingdom – and at times the largest, at points stitching together assorted lands from Portugal to Yugoslavia, Poland to Sicily, Belgium to Venice.

Roman Empire v. Holy Roman Empire v. Austrian Empire

The Roman Empire, during which Romans established military fortresses from Spain to England, Libya to Syria, officially began in 27 BCE; in 476 the last Roman emperor abdicated. The Holy Roman Empire, founded by Charlemagne in 800 with a push from the pope, at various points extended across most of Europe, and for six centuries was usually headed by the Habsburg clan, who for most of their rule fought the rise of both Protestant religions and nationalist movements. Napoleon ended the Holy Roman Empire in 1806, and the termination was made even more official during the Congress of Vienna in 1815, which created a Confederation of 39 German states, with the Austrian Empire being but one. After 1815 the term 'Austrian Empire' was popularly used to describe the Austrian Habsburgs' central and eastern European holdings. In 1867 the Austrian Empire was co-ruled by Hungarians, becoming the Austro-Hungarian Empire. In 1919 the whole kit and kaboodle ceased to exist.

Headed by the Habsburg clan from the late 1200s, the Holy Roman Empire greatly enlarged – mostly through politically motivated marriages – and the riches of Vienna expanded as well. In 1529 and 1683, Turks besieged the opulent city hoping to bring it into the Ottoman Empire. Twice beaten back from the walled kingdom, Turks nevertheless took most of the land leading up to it from the south-east, making Vienna the back door to Europe. Habsburg victories in the following centuries prised Hungary and environs from Ottoman rule, expanding the empire to the East, but Austria still remains a symbolic bridge between East and West.

The lavish imperial capital, known for its baroque architecture, dancing Lippizaner horses and devotion to high culture, was also the site of the most important European summit of the nineteenth century. The 1815 Congress of Vienna was called to redistribute the lands Napoleon had taken and to strategize on how to prevent the French from going on such a territorial rampage again. The congress of European leaders remapped the Napoleonic Empire, creating new kingdoms and confederations and reorganizing the power structure of Europe. Although it was monarchy-heavy, the resulting Europe was much more peaceful through the nineteenth century and the few wars that broke out were typically shorter and less devastating than previous military blowouts.

1815: Congress of Vienna

Headed by charismatic Austrian foreign minister Prince Klemens von Metternich, the conference of international leaders formally erased the Holy Roman Empire (Napoleon had disbanded the messy entity in 1806, after conquering the German lands) and tidied up all the loose ends of Europe. Metternich ensured that Austria came out well with the redistribution of land, and he also pushed an alignment of powers against the upstart France, including the formation of buffer countries. Among the results:

- The creation of the German Confederation, turning 300-odd Germanic principalities into 39 states of which the Austrian Empire, the president of the confederation, was by far the biggest
- The creation of the kingdom of the Netherlands, including Belgium and Luxembourg
- The expansion of Prussia, the second-biggest Germanic state (and Austria's rival) to include most of the nearby Saxon region, land along the Rhine and half of Poland
- The annexation of Lombardy, Venice, Trieste (all in today's Italy) to the Austrian Empire (which also ruled by marriage Florence, Parma, and Naples) as well as the Dalmatian Islands (off today's Croatia)
- The restoration of a Bourbon monarchy in France, which surprisingly was allowed to keep the resource-rich Alsace-Lorraine region that Prussia very much wanted

Of all the results of the Congress of Vienna, the most important was the creation of the German Confederation, which gave a solid outline to that area that long had been a rather amorphous jumble of German-speaking principalities. Essentially it was a geographical tidying-up exercise, the first time organized boundaries were drawn of all the states. The Austrian Empire dwarfed the others, and by size alone, it assumed the role of driving the car.

The Congress of Vienna, however, did not address the main problem facing the Austrian Empire: its unruly mix of peoples. Stretching into Eastern Europe, the Austrian Empire then included today's Hungary, Czech Republic, Slovakia, Ukraine, Slovenia, parts of the Balkans, three states along the north of the Italian peninsula as well as Austria itself – in short a dozen different ethnic groups, all of whom were forced to speak German and heed the archaic Austrian dynasty.

During the nineteenth century most of the empire's various ethnic groups let out loud nationalistic cries. The Magyars (Hungarians) wanted to break away and the different Slavic groups (Czechs, Slovaks, Croats, Serbs and Slovenes among them) also demanded independence from the Austrians. In 1848, revolts broke out across the empire – including in

Vienna. Most were suppressed, but the one in Vienna created a free press, called for parliamentary representation and pushed out the powerful foreign minister Metternich, who fled to London.

But calls for independence weren't the only problem: another party was Prussia, the revved-up Germanic state in the north-east that was tired of Austria puttering along in the express lane. Once Otto von Bismarck stepped in as Prussian chancellor, he solved the problem. After a brief war with Austria in 1866, which Prussia won, he simply kicked the Austrian Empire out of the German Confederation.

> *The remaining German states were soon forged as a united empire, with the Prussian king – the Kaiser – at its head. Austrian leaders and the Kaiser remained on relatively good terms, however, as evidenced by the military support for Austria in the First World War.*

Sensing Austria's weakness, the Magyars pushed their demands. They wanted to run the eastern part of the empire, and decrepit Austria was in no position to resist: Austria's leadership simply shrugged and added a hyphen to the name and the Austrian-Hungarian 'dual monarchy' was born in 1867.

> *Although the Austrian emperor was theoretically Hungary's supreme ruler, the Magyars were running the show in the eastern parts of the empire, which included Hungary, Slovakia, and parts of Yugoslavia, the Ukraine and Romania.*

So many tragedies soon befell the Habsburg family that one wonders if the Hungarians didn't jinx them with a gypsy curse to get them entirely out of the way. Kind-hearted Maximilian, brother of the emperor, hired by Napoleon III to rule France's new colony of Mexico in 1863, was assassinated by a Mexican firing squad and his poor wife Charlotte went insane. In 1889 Crown Prince Rudolf – unhappily married and quarrelling with his father Emperor Franz Joseph – killed himself and his 18-year-old lover at Mayerling, the royal hunting lodge. The emperor's other brother Karl Ludwig, on a pilgrimage to the Holy Land, drank from the Jordan river, and died from the resulting typhoid in 1896. Anorexic Empress Elisabeth, on holiday in Switzerland, was fatally stabbed by an anarchist in 1898. By the time Archduke Franz Ferdinand, who had tuberculosis, became heir to the Austrian Empire's throne a pattern had been established: he too was doomed. But the 1914 assassination of Franz Ferdinand by a Serbian nationalist triggered more than national mourning. The bullet that pierced his jugular launched millions more as the Great War engulfed Europe.

Black Hand, a secret society of Serbian nationalists apparently acting under orders from Serbia's head of intelligence, dispatched at least three would-be assassins from Serbia to Sarajevo. The society wanted Serbian independence and for Serbs to lead the other Slavs. Archduke Franz Ferdinand was considering giving more representation to all Slavic peoples, not just Serbs, an idea Black Hand didn't like. Another motivation for the assassination: all three potential killers, like the archduke, suffered from tuberculosis and believed they would soon die.

Archduke Franz Ferdinand (1863–1914)

Had it not been for a series of unfortunate deaths, Archduke Franz Ferdinand, heir to the Austrian Empire, might have been little more than a distant royal, a role that his uncle Emperor Franz Joseph probably would have preferred. The emperor didn't much care for his rebellious nephew: Franz Ferdinand refused to play by the family rules, which included marrying only Habsburgs or members of high-ranking monarchical clans. Falling in love with a Czech countess Sophie von Chotkovato, regarded as not up to royal snuff, the archduke insisted in 1900 on marrying her despite loud objections from his kin, and by doing so his future children lost all claims to the crown; Sophie wasn't even allowed to ride in the royal coach during state affairs. Franz didn't care: he was mad for his Soph and it is a good thing that he so enjoyed her company: shunned by the class-conscious Austrian upper crust, he was known as the loneliest man in Vienna. Invited to watch military demonstrations in Sarajevo in 1914, the archduke might have said no, had not the invitation (for once) included Sophie, and though the risks of travelling to the region – where secessionist ideas were brewing – was risky, he took up the offer. The murder plot was nearly thwarted thrice: the Serbian prime minister, warned of a possible assassination attempt, ordered the arrest of the three men dispatched to Sarajevo; his order was ignored. The assassins' first attempt at killing the archduke – hurling a hand grenade into the ceremonial parade – missed its target, injuring only those in the following car. The archduke insisted on being taken to the hospital to see the officers who'd been injured:

the general who accompanied the Austrians ordered an alternative route out of the city centre, and upon realizing the driver wasn't going that way demanded that he turn the car around. It was during the slow reversing of the automobile that Serbian extremist Gavrilo Princip ran to the car and fired several bullets, fatally wounding both the archduke and his beloved. 'Sophie dear! Sophie dear! Don't die! Stay alive for our children!' were the archduke's last words, but his wife of fourteen years was already dead. The date, 28 June 1914, was the couple's wedding anniversary.

Kind and loving to his wife and reformist in his ideas, Archduke Franz Ferdinand was brutal to animals: he hunted with a machine gun, and so devastated the bison population in Poland that the beast almost became extinct.[10]

Never mind that Emperor Franz Joseph was said to be relieved at the death of the archduke, and did not attend the funeral. Never mind that German Kaiser Wilhelm, who claimed to be a friend, didn't show up for the ceremony for the dead archduke and his wife either. The assassination provided an excuse for the Austrian emperor to crush the call for independence in Serbia. And the Kaiser was antsy to try out machines. No one thought this military exercise would turn into a world war; everyone thought it would be over in months.

Nine million deaths, and four years later, the 'war to end all wars' had made a wasteland of Europe and resulted in yet another remapping of the Continent. This redrawing of Europe in Paris during 1919 was far more vast than even the Congress of Vienna: it created Czechoslovakia, a new Poland, a new Hungary and the Kingdom of Serbs, Croats and Slovenes, most of the land coming out of the former Austrian Empire. By the time the mapmakers put down their pens, the new republic of Austria was whittled down to but 13 per cent of the nineteenth-century empire's size; it was but a tenth of what it had been during the Holy Roman Empire's sixteenth-century heyday. The population shrank from 60 million to 7 million. Austria was no longer a shining star that guided the destiny of Europe: it was a political has-been that was flickering out.

Painful Words: Treaty of St Germain

The 1919 document signed by the Allied Forces and the Austrian government on 10 September officially dissolved the Austrian-Hungarian Empire. Austria recognized the independence of its former lands in Czechoslovakia, Poland, Hungary and the Kingdom of Serbs, Croats and Slovenes (later to be called Yugoslavia). Austria also lost several of its prized possessions to Italy – namely South Tyrol, Friuli, Trieste and Istria – and the region of Bukovina was handed to Romania. The treaty, which capped the army at 30,000 troops, also prohibited Austria from politically or economically bonding with Germany again – a clause that was ignored by pretty much everybody when Germany annexed the republic in March 1939.

The Great War put the Austrian Empire to bed. Gone was the king, most of the kingdom and the former wealth. After the war Austria, not at all self-sufficient, found itself cut off. The regions of the former empire that had supplied food, energy and raw materials to the Austrian lands now halted their shipments: store shelves were soon bare, factories closed, furnaces lacked fuel. Palaces were looted, trains stopped running, coffee-houses served up weak drinks made from barley, assorted paramilitary groups roamed the streets and everywhere it was cold. Unemployment surged, the government broke down, typhoid swept the city, and the situation was so desperate that fearing a communist takeover the Allies finally sent in food. Still, Austria was broke – so broke that it was deemed absolutely unable to pay war reparations – and it hobbled into the 1920s, a shattered land marked by gloom.

Sigmund Freud (1856–1939)

The inventor of psychotherapy and the 'talking cure' might never have stumbled into the area of mental health had he not been Jewish, which limited him to fields that non-Jews rejected. The medical study of the insane and hysterical was one of the few areas open to Freud, since most physicians abhorred it. Understandably: the mentally ill of the nineteenth century were typically locked up in wards, and treatments, if there were any, usually involved removing sex organs – 'female hysteria' often being treated by slicing off the clitoris. Enter Dr Freud, whose first claim to fame had been finding the sex organs of the eel[11] and whose self-published *Interpretation of Dreams* in 1900 didn't sell well. Nevertheless, the workaholic mapped out new frontiers in psychology, becoming widely respected in his day (particularly outside Austria), and working with such notables as Alfred ('inferiority complex') Adler and Carl ('collective unconscious') Jung – both of whom ditched Freud saying he overemphasized the sex drive. Believing that problematic adult behaviour resulted from unresolved child issues – including repressed desires to sleep with Mummy and kill Daddy or vice versa – that could be brought to the surface by unstifled chatter, Freud developed the theory of the tripartite mind, namely the id (centre of desires), the superego (the conscience) and the ego (the balancer of id and superego). 'Penis envy', 'castration anxiety', and developmental stages oral, anal and phallic were part of the psychoanalytic field that spawned numerous proponents in the first half of the century when patients by the millions stretched out on the psychotherapist's couch. Now, however, it's far more popular to bash Freud, his formulaic ideas and his cold rapport with patients, who during sessions were not to even look at the therapist. One of the most controversial criticisms of Freud is that what he had discovered was not so much childhood sexuality, but the widespread prevalence of child abuse.[12] Some say that when he tried to report that many young girls had experienced incest the response in Austrian society was so explosive that Freud merely repressed the information, and redrew his ideas to state that they were merely experiencing unconscious fantasies.[13]

Freud's daughter, Anna, pioneered the field of child psychology.

The situation didn't improve in the 1930s. Hard hit by the Great Depression, Austria was such a mess that it was relatively easy for Engelbert Dollfuss, of the Christian Socialist party, simply to turn it into a dictatorship: he shut down the parliament, banned other parties, doled out death sentences to political enemies and ultimately prohibited trade unions. Tens of thousands fled Austria after it was stripped of democracy and a brief civil war ensued, but Dollfuss remained in control. The chancellor, a fascist himself, had no desire to bond with Germany, although Hitler's rise to power gave that idea more steam. In fact, Dollfuss tried to stamp out the Nazis. He'd arrested at least seven members of the group that posed a considerable threat: they bombed government sites and set off other terrorist explosions ever since he'd banned their party and Nazis also had printed up plenty of anti-Dollfuss propaganda in an unsuccessful move to sweep him from power. In 1934 they took more drastic means: Nazis dressed as police entered the Chancellery and fatally shot the chancellor; during their coup attempt, they seized Vienna's radio station and announced Dollfuss had resigned. The coup was put down in a few days, and more politicians made promises to eradicate the Nazi threat, although to some Austrians union with Germany appeared the only way out. Even though most Austrians were Catholics and most Germans were Protestants, many – unsure of their national identity and still recovering from the Great War – wanted to hook up with Germany. The full horrors of the Nazi regime had not yet been unleashed, and while Hitler was obviously anti-Semitic, so were some in Austria: the Christian Socialist party had anti-Semitism as one of the party platforms and Vienna's mayor Karl Lüger had continually condemned Jews since he entered office in the 1920s.

Ever since Hitler had come to power in Germany, he'd wanted to annex his homeland. Austria had gold, oil, minerals and labour that he needed to fuel his war machine, plus he had a few hang-ups about the land of his birth: he wanted to come in as a leader to the country from which he had limped, broke and an artistic failure, twenty years before. Austrians weren't given much of a choice in the matter of being annexed as part of Greater Germany even though the Anschluss was opposed by the ruling powers as well as many intellectuals. Chancellor Schuschnigg had been forced to grant Nazis some rights, but he'd tried to avoid the annexation Hitler had in mind by calling for a referendum that would take place on 13 March 1938: the choice before Austrians was whether Austria should remain an independent country with him at the helm. Hitler was furious at the news: he forced Schuschnigg to resign, and sent Nazi troops marching into Austria on 12 March before Austrians had time to vote on Schuschnigg's proposal. There they were greeted by the new Nazi chancellor Artur von Seyss-Inquart – put into office by Hitler – who invited Germany to annex Austria.

Some Austrians responded by leaving the country, some killed themselves, some stayed at home, but tens of thousands cheered Hitler as he entered Vienna and greeted his countrymen. He would later say that in Austria 'there met me such a stream of love as I have never experienced'.[14]

Austria had a new name – Ostmark – only one party, the Nazis, and a new leader in the wings. The Nazis held a vote on whether Austrians accepted the Anschluss and Hitler, and thanks to vote-rigging and threats, 99.7 per cent supposedly gave it a green light.

> *Among those who opposed the idea of the Anschluss: the Habsburgs, but by then they had little say, having been tossed out of Austria and stripped of their land in 1919. The UK, France, the US and the others barely let out a peep. Only Mexico formally opposed the annexation – writing to the League of Nations in March 1938, pointing out the violation of the Treaty of St Germain, the inherent dangers of letting Hitler have the land and warning that if the Great Powers didn't act to prevent the Anschluss, 'the world will regrettably sooner or later be engulfed by a catastrophe far greater'.[15] Mexico was ignored.*

Resistance movements sprang up immediately and some 75,000 Austrian politicians and influential people were rounded up in the first few weeks of the Anschluss. Among those sent to concentration camps: the chancellor, the mayor of Vienna, and assorted Habsburgs, notably the two sons of Archduke Franz Ferdinand. But the group most severely targeted were Jews, who were soon stripped of their rights to almost everything, including the rights to hold property and work. Almost two-thirds of the 220,000 Jewish population in Austria quickly fled,[16] although they often had to pay fees upwards of €100,000 to get out, and any property they sold went for a pittance.

Mauthausen

Hitler had a dream of renovating his home town of Linz, and the granite quarry outside the village of Mauthausen held the materials for his beautification plan. The Nazis bought it weeks after moving in and soon thereafter the first prisoners arrived from Dachau, to build the mother camp of Austria. A grade three facility, it was where prisoners whose status was '*Rückkehr unerwünscht*' – return not desired – were sent for 'extermination by work'. Labourers were split into two groups – those who picked out granite with crude tools or by hand and those who hauled the slabs up 189 precarious stairs from which untold thousands fell. With hundreds of thousands going through it – and sometimes on to its forty-nine subcamps that produced military equipment – Mauthausen, like Auschwitz, was well known for the Nazis' most horrific sadism: the limb-eating Alsatian dogs were let loose on the quarry stairs; Dr Krebsbach experimented with vaccines and lice; SS guards would dress as damsels and hack up hundreds of workers with picks; newcomers chose which two of their group would be sacrificed to save the rest, but they all would ultimately be driven over a cliff; weak prisoners were forced to run with enormous rocks tied to their backs until they collapsed from exhaustion and were shot for 'attempting to escape'. Over 100,000 died in Mauthausen alone.[17] The camp had a broad international mix – Republicans from the Spanish Civil War who'd escaped to France, for instance, ended up here – and Mauthausen was a hotbed for solidarity movements and calls for resistance. When Americans neared the facility in May 1945, the Nazis gave orders to kill the remaining inmates in explosions of the quarries; however, 2,000 survived. Among the survivors: Simon Wiesenthal, who would go on to be one of the great Nazi hunters.

A little late: In November 1943, the UK, United States and Soviet Union reversed their acceptance of the Anschluss, saying they did not recognize Austria as part of the German Reich, calling for Austria's independence to be reinstated and dubbing Austria 'the first victim of Hitlerite aggression'.

How many Austrians willingly complied with the dictates of the Nazi occupiers is a matter of debate, but there is little question that Austria was a vital cog in the Nazi machine, its factories manned by slave labourers churning out ball bearings and explosives, and its camps some of the regime's most cruel. Allied bombing of Austria began in April 1945, and the Soviets marched into Vienna that month. After the war the city was divided into quadrants in the style of Berlin – with the UK, France, US and USSR all taking a corner of the city and keeping them very much separate from one another: during that period Viennese heard different versions of any event, and lacked even a shared newspaper. At least partly due to the Soviets' determination to drain Austria of its oil resources – and their refusal to budge during the Stalin years – Vienna remained occupied until 1955. In that year the State Treaty was signed, forbidding future unions with Germany, banning any return of the Habsburg monarchy and declaring that Austria would henceforth remain neutral. The Allies pulled out in November, an event celebrated by the reopening of Vienna's State Opera House where Beethoven's *Fidelio* rang out for the opening night. Austrians, in a sort of cultural shock, drifted into arias and concertos and mostly went into denial about what had happened in the decades before. Schoolbooks taught history only up to the First World War, there was little discussion of what role Austria had played in the war, and the country hid behind the slogan 'Hitler's first victim'. In fact that slogan had been offered up by the Allies in 1943, when they were trying to stir up an anti-Nazi rebellion – and Austria had merely accepted the part. It was not a perfect fit.

> *At least 80,000 Austrian Jews and others were shipped off to camps during the war. About 7,000 Jews returned, but most found that their homes were occupied, their businesses had been taken over, their savings were depleted and their valuables were gone. Many headed directly to Israel. Jews, such as the Rothschilds, who came to collect their stolen art, were coerced into making substantial 'donations' to Austrian museums in order to export any of their treasures. In 1999 Austria announced it would begin returning the 'donated' art.*

Austria has been slow to accept much responsibility for the Nazi activities of the Second World War. In 1991 Chancellor Franz Vranitzky was the first to admit that Austria had been a partner to Hitler's war programme. In 1996 Austria gave Jewish groups thousands of works of unclaimed art, which raised some €13 million for Holocaust survivors. The previous year Austria made its first payments to victims of the Holocaust, capping each cheque at about €5,700, and in 2001 it added another €400 million to the scheme. In 1998 Austria inaugurated its first public holiday in memory of those who perished during the Holocaust. Despite recent discussions prompted by the scandals surrounding Kurt Waldheim and Jörg Haider, the Second World War, and Austria's role in it, remains a prickly issue.

> *Austrians like to believe Beethoven was an Austrian and Hitler was a German – Austrian saying*

Territorial History

The four new EU countries that rub up against it – Hungary, the Czech Republic, Slovakia and Slovenia – all hold special meaning to Austria. All four were subservient territories in the lasso of the Austrian Empire and all four in some way helped bring about the empire's demise. Hungarians successfully demanded a share in the empire in 1865, directly overseeing about half of the imperial land. Czechs, Slovaks and Slovenes – along with Serbia and Croatia – were hotbeds of Slavic nationalism, the factor that most frayed the imperial ropes from the mid nineteenth century on, and ultimately led to the First World War. After that it was downhill for the Austrian Empire, which lost two-thirds of its territory in 1919 and officially became the Republic of Austria. Where did that lost land go? Mostly to the same EU newcomers, with the exception of Hungary, which actually lost land to Austria. The history alone doesn't make for the smoothest of relations.

Quick Tour

Whether you're talking about Vienna's gleaming baroque buildings layered with sculptures or the folded hills of the Tyrol where church steeples peek up from valleys, Austria is the old world personified. The country often considered to be more German than Germany – even Austria's language is closer to the true Germanic roots – Austria sometimes seems lost in the glorious past. The grand chandeliered coffeehouses with wallsized portraits of royalty, where whipped-cream-slathered concoctions come on a silver tray, are still part of daily Austrian life – despite the incursion of Starbucks; the countryside's wine gardens known as *heurigen* serve the local plonk with sausage and cheese as they have for over 1,000 years. Sunday is the official day when, as has been the habit for centuries, most Austrians stroll in nature; almost any day of the week Mozart recitals can be heard in the hills of his hometown Salzburg or Vienna, and the New Year is not official until tens of thousands waltz to Strauss' *Blue Danube* in public squares.

Wiener Waltzer (aka Viennese Waltz)

It was a simple country dance until the Strauss family got hold of it in the 1800s. Johann II in particular brought his orchestra and the waltz to the royal ballrooms where elegant swaying became the rage, and it is still popular today. The winter in Vienna is filled with nonstop waltzing, with balls every weekend. Now, however, it's best to know how to foxtrot, tango and cha-cha-cha as well.

Austria, however, isn't as stuck in the past as it often seems. Although often considered conservative, until 2000 its governments had been left-leaning for three decades. Its immigration policies, until recently, were quite open, and the country that once ran a multi-ethnic empire saw its first mosque go up in 1887. Austria has long been an environmentally friendly country, and in the land rich in hydropower, nuclear plants were banned in 1978.

> *The Soviets began construction on the controversial Temelin nuclear plant, just over the border in the Czech Republic, and even though Western companies finished the job, it is not up to Western standards. Austrians have frequently demonstrated against Temelin and other Czech reactors with protests that have shut down the border between the two countries. While the reactors are indeed cause for concern, Austria's self-righteousness over the matter is a bit hypocritical since Austria does in fact receive electricity from nuclear power: energy from Hungary's nuclear plants is transmitted via electrical grids.*

Beefs with Czechs

Jörg Haider is one of a few thousand Austrians who has a gripe with the former Czechoslovakia: after the Second World War, Czech president Edvard Beneš issued an order for ethnic Germans (including Austrians) to leave Czechoslovakia. Millions were violently run out and they lost their land as they left, much of it in the Sudetenland, in north-western Czechoslovakia. Now some Sudetenlanders want compensation for their lost lands. It's not a popular cause, but Haider supports it – and he demanded that Chancellor Schüssel block the Czechs' entry into the EU over the issue. When Schüssel refused to do so, Haider couched his demand as an antinuclear campaign: he initiated a petition demanding that the Austrian government veto the Czech Republic's entry unless the Temelin nuclear reactor was closed. A sixth of Austrians signed the petition and tens of thousands demonstrated, but this time the Green Party and many environmentalists weren't supporting the protests. Nor were plenty of others who were actually anti-Temelin, but more opposed to Haider's hijacking of the Temelin cause for his own purposes. The Austrian government ignored the petition, and the People's–Freedom Party coalition nearly broke up over it.

Austria remains a class-conscious society, one that emphasizes strict dress codes and where double standards can apply. While every Austrian is entitled to a roof over their head – provided free by the government if need be – that doesn't apply to immigrants. Migrants in Austria don't qualify for low-income housing, and in fact are routinely charged 20 per cent more.[18] And one in three immigrants lives in substandard housing lacking toilet or running water, a situation that can be found even in modern-seeming Vienna.[19] And in the country that has dragged its feet about compensating Jews who lost their homes, there are growing demands for payments to those who were kicked out of Czechoslovakia after the war. Austrian women are surging ahead in politics yet the plight of the sex slaves brought in by the Russian Mafia is, like the mafia itself, largely ignored. The country is mired in bureaucracy, and the capital that once was brimming with spies, still retains a secretive feel: certain bars broadcast the nationality of foreigners who step in the doors by suddenly playing music from that country.

Encoded Vienna

Wandering around back streets past ornate signs of birds or top-hatted men jutting from café fronts, I find Kumpfgasse, a hidden crescent of cobblestone and the site of Santo Spirito. Beethoven is blasting when I enter the candle-flickering restaurant packed with well-groomed types. Mozart is playing when I take my first sip, leaning against a wall trying to blend into this rather frosty scene. Suddenly paranoid, I suspect the locals are saying unkind things about me – their accents are so harsh people sound like they're telling you off when, in fact, they're uttering a street name. Even the word for the cosy atmosphere – *gemütlichkeit* – sounds deeply hostile. Around mid-glass a new song comes over the speakers: 'I like to be in America, Ev'rthing's free in America . . .' All eyes turn to me. The music switches to Bach, and it hits me: this must be some sort of musical Morse code for spies. The entry of a Frenchman would be signalled by Bizet; an Italian would prompt a Verdi overture; a Russian might be heralded by Tchaikovsky or 'Back in the USSR'. As I plunge deeper into spy logic, everything assumes new meaning. The change on the tray – one schilling up, two down – signifies 'two dead, one lives on'. In a shop window the finger of a glove points to a covert meeting place; the price tag is really the meeting time. And the man scratching his eyebrow as he saunters down the street is subtly revealing state secrets. In that surreal moment, all of Vienna appears a switchboard of veiled signals, and like Freud, I detect subliminal messages in everything. Back in my room, I discover that my earring is missing. After an hour of searching, I pull the mattress off the bed. There's the earring. But there's also something else: a small bound book dated 1992. Inside, its forgotten pages reveal wiry scrawl that, were I to believe its entries, had been penned by a retiree named Irvine. But when I read 'Played golf in the a.m. and discovered my 5 wood was more effective than my #3,' I know what it really means. The crow flies at five before three, Irvine. Or is it three after five?[20]

Austria certainly has its charms – elegant cities, snow-dusted mountains, heart-stirring beauty, shiny chocolates, raisin-stuffed pastries, and thick-layered tortes are but a few as are the musical masterpieces that floated out of these parts. But for all its strengths, Austria seems like a country that is mostly tiptoeing around trying to forget all that is embarrassing. And lately, top of that list is Jörg Haider.

Future Forecast

Given that Austria is still smarting from the sanctions ordeal in 2000, if there is another blowout in the EU, perhaps over lost land in the Sudeten-land, it's not hard to imagine that Austria would blow out of the club where it now knows it has no friends. On the other hand, Austria has the most to gain from being at the threshold of the new EU, and if its business booms as a result, it might swallow its pride and stay put.

Hot Spots

Vienna: Once the pulsating centre of the Habsburg Empire, Vienna still retains its regal air, with plenty of heavily sculpted and chandeliered beauty, and nobles rich enough to still afford it. Moody musicians lug around cellos, apparently composing symphonies in their heads, and the glittering architecture epitomizes the splendour of nineteenth-century Europe. On New Year's Eve they let loose and waltz in the squares, but during the rest of the year the city can feel uptight and dress codes are enforced. Have your credit cards handy for those fabulous suits in the windows bearing price tags in the thousands. On a positive note: you can

Innsbruck: one of Austria's Alpine jewels.

sit for hours reading newspapers in the beautiful cafés for the price of a coffee. Of course in Vienna it isn't that cheap.

> *Subterranean city: Vienna sits over a network of tunnels that served as escape routes in Habsburg times as well as today. The movie of Graham Greene's novel* The Third Man, *set in postwar Vienna when the city was divided in four quadrants, immortalized the underground passages and the furtive dartings of secret agents who vanished like sewer rats. Most tunnels are now bricked up, but some were put to use as recently as 2000, when politicians at the Inaugural Ball dashed through them to avoid the demonstrators clogging the streets.*

Salzburg: The hills are alive with the sound of Mozart here in the composer's birthplace; most tourists, however, pile in to relive *The Sound of Music*, which was filmed here. Whatever the reason that draws them, almost everyone who sets foot here is charmed by the town that made its original wealth from salt mines.

Carinthia: Some tension still exists between Austrians and ethnic Slovenes in the stunning mountainous region that was once part of Yugoslavia, but lately it plays out in street names and road signs. In Haider's stamping ground Slovenes wanted to post street names in Slovenian as well as German. Haider tried to block the move, but the Slovenes took the matter to court. The verdict: in areas where Slovenes are at least 10 per cent of the population, their language can be displayed as well.

On Austrian highways nearing the Czech Republic and Slovakia, sign-posts list how many kilometres away you are from the Czech Temelin plant and the distance to Chernobyl.

Tyrol: Gorgeous if provincial alpine setting, this area was split after the First World War, with some of it going to Italy. This is still a sensitive issue: German-speakers on the Italian side of South Tyrol were promised autonomy which some say hasn't been fully granted.

Fucking: The tiny town in Upper Austria has had the name Fucking since the eleventh century, and they ain't changing it now despite the expense: the street sign with the town's name on it is the most ripped-off sign in the country.[21]

The liver: Who knows why, but Austria has the most deaths from chronic viral hepatitis.[22]

Hot Shots

Wolfgang Schüssel: Chancellor 2000 to present. The eloquent and daring leader of the People's Party gambled by including Haider's Freedom Party in his 2000 coalition, with mixed results. Many politicians, both domestic and international, are still furious that he linked arms with Haider's party, if not Haider himself. But Schüssel did manage to calm down the bunch, so much so that Haider fired several of the party's most visible players. Schüssel pushed through unpopular reforms, and has had to clean up the assorted messes Haider makes; he called Haider's late 2002 Iraq visits 'a serious mistake'.[23] A political pariah now with other Austrian parties who refuse to form coalitions with him, Schüssel is nevertheless fairly popular with the people: he roped in more support for the People's Party than it has seen in decades.

For all the nightmarish scenarios that had been painted, Schüssel's ostensibly very right-wing coalition was in practice fairly moderate and actually got a few things done, which is more than a few previous coalitions could say. Haider stayed off in the sidelines, retaining his gubernatorial position in Carinthia, but having plenty of effect at least initially. Pension plans were reformed – a hugely unpopular, although probably necessary, move – government organization was tweaked, the first major compensation fund for Jews was set up, and although a much more stringent immigration policy was passed, it wasn't as harsh as many had feared it might be. Haider's party campaigned on

MEP whistle-blower
Hans-Peter Martin.

'zero immigration' but did not fully succeed although the numbers dropped drastically: in 2001, for example, over 8,500 foreigners were granted citizenship.[24] The immigration policy was tightened up – now most immigrants must have lived in the country as a foreign worker for ten years and show steady employment – and today's wannabe immigrants must attend integration classes.[25] Previous asylum laws have also been tightened.

Heinz Fischer: President 2004 to present. He's often billed as the first Social Democrat president in eighteen years – the party is usually in the more powerful position of chancellor – but in fact Fischer officially stripped himself of any party membership upon entering office, in the hope of better serving all Austrian people. Former leader of parliament, the even-handed Fischer has a reputation for being diplomatic and moderate. The president is also fluent in Esperanto; that should come in quite handy.

Hans-Peter Martin: MEP 1999 to present. Journalist who was widely published in *Der Spiegel*, Martin also wrote books about globalization (*The Global Trap*) and pharmaceutical giants (*Bitter Pills*), before taking on the corruption at the European Parliament. He was the big winner in the 2004 European Parliament elections, netting 14 per cent of the vote. Proof that Austria has right decent politicians too.

Jörg Haider: Governor of Carinthia 1998 to present: former official, now de facto leader of Freedom Party. The first in-office European politician to make an issue of immigration, he runs marathons, bungee jumps, wears designer clothes, and can charm even a hostile media, but Haider, who was personally the cause of Austria's EU sanctions in 2000, seems to suffer from a variation of Attention Deficit Disorder: when he lacks the spotlight, he does something outrageous to get it back. He grew up in southern Carinthia, a mountainous tourist magnet where the vast 38,000 acre (15,390 ha) estate he inherited from his uncle was reportedly purchased at a very low price from Jews forced to flee when Nazi Germany annexed Austria. Although frequently called a neo-Nazi, Haider gave a big push to a recent plan to provide compensation to survivors of concentration camps. Has some popular ideas – like about how to cut bureaucracy – and some very disturbing ones, including apparently a very nostalgic view of Nazis. What Haider has pointed out, unintentionally, is the continuing unease about Austria's past.

> *Haider jaunted off to Iraq – several times – during 2002. While the US–UK war drums were loudly pounding, there was troublemaker Haider telling Saddam Hussein that Austrians were united behind the Iraqi leader – messages that were quickly contradicted by Schüssel.*

Thomas Klestil: President 1992–2004. The poor man whose blood pressure soared when Schüssel pulled Haider into the governing coalition died of heart failure two days before officially stepping down from office.

Benita Ferrero-Waldner: European Commissioner 2004 to present. Right-leaning former foreign minister of the People's Party, she speaks five languages and wanted to be Austria's first female prez. Instead ended up in Brussels as European Commissioner for external relations and neighbourhood policy.

Karl Renner (1870–1950): Intellectual who not only led the country as chancellor after it was created in 1919, but was the first chancellor after the Second World War. Between the wars he had (controversially) pushed for Austria to be annexed to Germany, including encouraging Austrians to vote yes in Hitler's 1938 referendum.

The Habsburg Rulers: A Few Standouts

The Habsburg clan held assorted titles – a Habsburg was Holy Roman Emperor, usually – and typically made Vienna their home base. Among the most memorable:

- Rudolf I (b. 1218) 1273–91: Started Habsburg rule, conquering Vienna by threatening to destroy vineyards.
- Rudolf II (b. 1552) 1576–1612: Bright but a tad mad and seriously depressed; as Holy Roman Emperor moved capital to Prague, where he invited scientists and magicians to explain the nature of the universe.
- Charles V (b. 1500) 1519–58: As Holy Roman Emperor held so much land it was unworkable; split the empire between his son Philip II (who got Portugal, Spain, Belgium, Luxembourg and Netherlands) and his brother Ferdinand who got the eastern chunk.
- Charles VI (b. 1685) 1711–40: Kept giving away lands so that daughter Maria Theresa would be recognized as legitimate leader without question, but that was for naught.
- Maria Theresa (b. 1717) 1740–80: Her hubby Francis Stephen of Lorraine became Holy Roman Emperor Francis I (1745–65), but Archduchess Maria Theresa held the reins; began reforms of serfdom, initiated public education, abolished torture and was one of the more enlightened monarchs.
- Joseph II (b. 1741) 1780–90: Abolished serfdom and death penalty, allowed total freedom of religion.
- Franz Joseph (b. 1830) 1848–1916: Probably senile by the end of his rule, Emperor Franz Joseph declared war on Serbia in 1914, thereby igniting the First World War.
- Karl I (1887–1922) 1916–18: Poor man came to power during the First World War, tried unsuccessfully to negotiate a separate peace with Allies. Stripped of title in 1918, exiled to Switzerland 1919.

Mrs Bonaparte: Austrian Archduchess Marie Louise married Napoleon in 1810, giving birth to his heir Napoleon Francis Joseph Charles in 1811. Napoleon II, who never got to see much action, being more or less captive in his palace, died of tuberculosis in Austria aged 21.

Theodor (Binyamin Ze'ev) Herzl (1860–1904): He was born in Budapest, but when he was 18 his family moved to Vienna, where he was a journalist, novelist and playwright before heading off to become Paris correspondent for the newspaper *Neue Freie Presse*. Writing such plays as *The Ghetto*, about the difficulties Jews faced in being accepted, Herzl ultimately concluded that Jews are all one people who should have their own state. He proposed the idea to plenty of the day's powermongers – from Baron Rothschild to German Kaiser Wilhelm – but only the British government took him seriously and offered him a potential autonomous Jewish area in Uganda. That idea never went anywhere, but his concept of a Jewish state ultimately led to the creation of Israel forty-four years after his death.

Thomas Bernhard (1931–89): Although his themes were usually depressing – illness and death were high on the list of the writer who suffered from TB and likened his hometown Salzburg to a terminal disease – Bernhard was one of Austria's most famous novelists and playwrights. His most controversial work was his 1989 play *Heldenplatz*, which showed the anti-Semitic side of Austrian life, and was condemned by former President Kurt Waldheim and many critics. Bernhard died several months later, stating in his will that his plays could not again be performed in Austria nor could his books be published. That demand only contributed to his continuing popularity.

Robert Musil (1880–1942): Considered one of the brilliant lights of twentieth-century literature, Musil didn't go down as a lightweight. He wasn't done with his masterpiece – *The Man without Qualities* – even after he'd written three volumes of it. Even if incomplete, the tome elicited raves from heady sorts, despite its frequent straying from any semblance of plot.

The (Vermont) Hills are (Still) Alive with the Sound of Music

The Von Trapp children of Salzburg were indeed talented and hardworking, and at times they were singing slaves to their stepmother Maria who arrived at their villa in 1926 as a tutor and went on to marry their widowed sea captain father. Forget the Julie Andrews image in *The Sound of Music*, which was filmed in their home town. Little outside of 'How do you solve a problem like Maria?' fits the real Mrs Von Trapp. Granted, Maria was determined, well-meaning and motivated, but an abused child herself, she was prone to excesses and violent behaviour. Seeing the potential of the singing family when Von Trapp lost his bank holdings in Austria, she pushed them into music performances, which led to their relocation in the United States – although they didn't have to climb any mountains to do it, taking the train to Italy, and leaving by boat from there. Maria was extremely pushy with the clan: trying to keep them together as long as possible, she discouraged dating, and tried to lock one daughter (Johanna) in her room to prevent her from getting married (Johanna merely jumped out the window). Poor Rosmarie, who hated performing, had to have a nervous break-down before Maria would stop shoving her on to the stage. But with all her overzealousness, Maria did start a relief foundation for Austrians after the war, and she also penned *The Story of the Trapp Family Singers*, the rights to which she foolishly sold to a German producer for a mere €7,500 or so. Luckily, Broadway producers were more generous, and gave her a tiny percentage of the royalties for film and stage performances – but that still brought in millions. Maria died in 1987, but some of the Von Trapps still perform at the Trapp Family Lodge in Vermont. In keeping with the less than Disneyesque story, the kin legally slugged it out over the ownership after Maria died, but most are reportedly on speaking terms now, if not singing ones.[26]

Gustav Klimt (1862–1918): Nobody made romance prettier than Austrian illustrator Klimt, who first came to fame as a mural painter in Viennese museums and theatres. His fluid, gold-infused style best captured in *The Kiss* was quite controversial at the time, and his art was endlessly criticized. Nazis made off with six of his best known paintings, including *The Kiss*, now hanging in the Austrian National Art Gallery. Klimt's 88-year-old niece Maria Altmann, who fled to the United States during the war, says they are rightfully hers and is battling the Austrian government to get them back in the family's embrace.

Wolfgang Amadeus Mozart (1756–91): The Wunderkind was playing min-uets at five, had mastered violin and harpsichord at six, and was writing symphonies and sonatas by nine. He paid (and was paid) for his talents. Papa dragged him around Europe starting in 1762, and he often per-formed for six hours or more a day. The whole family, including 'Amadeus', got deathly ill during the numerous trips on the road, and his mother died during one round of performances in Paris. Before he hit 35, Mozart had written over three dozen symphonies, 27 piano concertos, 6 operas (including *The Magic Flute* and *Don Giovanni*), 17 piano sonatas, and numerous chamber-music compositions. His gifts and his cockiness – he routinely complained he was not paid enough – made him plenty of enemies, and some suspect that his foe Salieri was responsible for his death, which may have been caused by kidney failure or poisoning. Some say, however, that Mozart perished from overdosing on mercury, which he was taking to cure syphilis.[27]

Johann Strauss II (1825–99): His father was also a composer of waltzes but nobody made them more famous than Junior, who became known as 'The Waltz King' for his dozens of heart-stirring creations which brought waltzing to the ballrooms of the Habsburg palaces. Now fiddles in perpetuity as a statue in Stadtpark. Hear *The Blue Danube* at www.aboutvienna.org/composers/strauss jr.htm

Arnold Schwarzenegger (b. 1947): Two-time Mr Universe, the man who made the phrase 'Hasta la vista, baby' famous in *Terminator*, said Hasta la vista to Austria, became a naturalized US citizen in 1983 and fell in behind Ronald Reagan to become the second bad actor to become governor of the state of California.

Russian Mafia: They just love it here so much they've made it the place for annual meetings; Vienna is full of bought women they've hauled in from the East whose plight pretty much goes unnoticed.

11. Greece (Ellas/Hellas): Waking Up

Fast Facts

Country:	Hellenic Republic; Ellinski Dhimokratia
Capital:	Athens
Government:	parliamentary republic (monarchy last rejected 1974)
Independence:	1829 (from Ottoman Empire/Turkey)
Population:	10,648,000 (2004 estimate)
Leaders:	Head of State: President Karolos Papoulias (2005) Head of Government: Prime Minister Costas Karamanlis (2004)
Elections:	President elected by Parliament 5-year term; PM appointed by President 5-year term
Name of Parliament:	Parliament; Vouli ton Ellinon
Ethnicity:	98% Greek; 2% other (officially there is no ethnic breakdown)
Religion:	Greek Orthodox 98%; Muslim 1.3%
Language:	Greek (official) 99%; also English, French
Literacy:	97%
Exports:	food and beverages, petroleum products, chemicals, textiles
Per capita GDP:	$20,000 (2003 estimate)
Unemployment:	9.3% (December 2003 Eurostat figure)
Percentage in poverty:	21% (according to April 2003 Eurostat report)[1]
EU status:	member since 1981
Currency:	euro
Known for:	world's second most famous Homer

Standout Qualities

History continues: Parthenon, Zeus worship, Olympics
Historical problems: Marbles, Turks, world's longest November 17
History repeating: Monarch in, out, in, out, in, out

Résumé

It's not that Greece is no longer great; it just isn't great like it used to be. The birthplace of such civilized concepts as democracy, individual rights and freedom of speech is now best known for line dancing, plate smashing and retsina – certainly festive, though not nearly as lofty. The sun-bleached villages and blissful islands thick with orchids and wild herbs are still as fetching as they were when robed thinkers, not camera-toting tourists, ambled over the hills, and the classical architecture, embodied in the Parthenon gazing down over Athens, still inspires awe even if today it is clouded by smog. However, the culture that has clung to the remnants of its past – from the arenas to the books – has certainly fallen astray from the political path paved by its ancestors: for most of the twentieth century, Greek government seemed a mockery of the very ideas put forth by the Ancients. Civil wars, riots, juntas, occupations and dictatorships defined most of the century leading into the 1980s, making Greece appear more like a Latin American country during a rough stretch than a country that was the cradle of Europe.

Greece used to be the financial weakling of the EU-15 and marked the easternmost boundary of the Union. That changed with the 2004 EU enlargement, which put Greece in the middle of both the economic and geographical planes.

Until recently Greece was so problematic that it was known as the tempestuous child of Europe. On numerous occasions – including in the late 1990s – Greece had to be pulled apart from fellow NATO member Turkey, with whom it nearly started wars over oil-exploration rights, airspace, and uninhabited rocks in the Aegean. Until recently Greece was the weak link in European security – it made little effort to go after the assassination-prone November 17 terrorist group until 2002 – and its airports were seen as so lax that the US, for one, issued travel advisories about going there. After Yugoslavia crumbled, Greece growled at the new republics that had been historical enemies, getting into a serious diplomatic tiff with Macedonia over the use of the name, which is also the name of a nearby region in Greece. On numerous occasions the Hellenic Republic has kicked up problems in Cyprus: it sent guerrillas there in the 1950s to fight for union with Greece and in 1974 tried to annex it by supporting a coup – an event that only ruptured the island where the population is 80 per cent ethnically Greek. So strongly does Greece still feel about Cyprus that it stamped its foot and demanded the island be invited into the EU in 2004 – threatening to veto the other EU entrants if an invitation from Brussels wasn't extended.

Turkey and Greece

Greece and Turkey's problems go back centuries, but they've been really snarling at each other since 1829, when Greece – which had been part of the Ottoman Empire since 1453 – declared independence and launched a decade-long war that ultimately succeeded after it brought much of Western Europe to fight on its side. Greece subsequently fought against Turkey four more times – including in the First World War – and went ballistic when Turkey invaded Cyprus in 1974 and moved in, occupying part of the island ever since. Another major showdown almost took place when Greece was implicated in helping the escape of Kurd leader Abdullah Ocalen, whom Turkish authorities wanted. Every so often, however, diplomatic relations improve and the two foes show a kinder side towards each other: on 17 August 1999 the ground under Izmit in northwestern Turkey rocked with a 7.2-magnitude earthquake that killed 17,000 people. First to arrive on the scene: Greek doctors and emergency teams, bearing medicine, food and blankets, and digging out the people who had been their enemies a few hours before. When Greece was shaken by a quake several weeks later, Turkey returned the favour. Relations between the two countries, if not cuddly, have been considerably warmer ever since. And now instead of trying to block Turkey's application to join the EU, Greece is said to be supporting it.

Turkey and Greece are both strategically important NATO members whose location alone forces the United States and Western Europe to be more lenient with both. The US heavily arms both Greece and Turkey, often simply giving them sophisticated military equipment as gifts, but they both buy plenty of weaponry as well.

Greece may finally be mellowing and simultaneously moving up in the world. Two things pulled this most southern of the Balkan lands out of the gutter it had been wallowing in for almost a century: the first was joining the European Union in 1981, a move which brought it tens of billions of euros in development funds and helped stabilize the country by offering wider economic markets and a watchful eye. The second stimulus was the event that first started in Athens in 776 BCE: the Olympic Games.

> Greece's lagging infrastructure got a boost with over €40 billion in EU funds between 1994 and 2004, much of it used for highways, rail improvements and a bridge from the western mainland to the Peloponnese. The EU says the money it gave to Greece resulted in the creation of some 390,000 new jobs.[2] EU funding has also boosted GDP, says the never bashful EU.

Preparations for the 2004 Olympics catapulted Greece into the twenty-first century, bringing the country fancy new stadiums, an expanded subway, new airport and tram lines. The sporting event did more than kick up a construction flurry and stimulate new development: it gave Greeks a new pride – and an international stature – that they haven't had since about the time Constantinople fell. Some hailed the Athens Olympics as the finest in recent history, but many were simply amazed that the construction for the event was actually done: Greece was so behind in preparations that the International Olympic Committee nearly yanked the future Games away from Athens in 2000, and up until the opening day, construction was an Olympic event in the form of a round-the-clock work-a-thon.

> In the days leading up to the Olympics, when Greece looked hope-lessly behind, a new joke was making the rounds: an Olympic planner runs into a Greek government official. 'Remind me,' says the planner, 'exactly when is the opening day of the Olympics?' The official answers that the event begins on 13 August. 'Oh dear,' says the planner, 'what time does it start?' The official answers that it begins at night. 'Ah,' says the first, 'then there's still plenty of time.'[3]

The 2004 Olympics were not snag-free: prior to the opening, the new tram to the Olympic sites had several crashes since Greeks kept parking their cars on the tracks; drug scandals dominated the news, including some involving red-faced Greece, a guard was killed, a judoist died, an anti-American protest kept US Secretary of State Colin Powell from attending the closing ceremonies and a small earthquake rattled Athens, but only ever so slightly. Carrying a price tag of some €9 billion, the Olympics was more than just a prestigious sporting event however: it also gave Greece new protection. As part of its €1.3 billion security measures, Greece purchased an anti-ballistic missile system and Patriot missiles to defend the event against any attacks.

> **Nude-a-thon:** *The Olympics, that celebration of physical coordination invented by the Ancient Greeks for the mighty god Zeus, started up in the eighth century BCE, with such events as chariot races and discus-throwing wowing the crowds. One event may have been a precursor to today's 'streaking': runners sprinted across fields entirely in the buff. The Games' flames were blown out in 393 CE, but the athletic event-a-thon was revived in 1896 – in Athens – by a French baron, Pierre de Coubertin. In modern Olympics, however, sprinters are required to don clothes.*

Politically stabilized (well, for Greece), with a new popular leadership (on the conservative side), and football champions of Euro 2004, Greece may be on a winning streak with increased tourism and more jobs opening up for the young who are chronically underemployed. The country still has problems to contend with – a lagging educational system and a high poverty rate are but two – but at least now Greece has a reason to hope for the future and can stop dwelling solely on its past.

Good Perspective: The Acropolis

Peering down over Athens from a rocky promontory stands the most potent symbol of the Greek Golden Age: the Acropolis (*akros* = highest, *polis* = city). Palace, fort and temple for Greeks in the fifth century BCE, the site got its most memorable touches under Pericles, who gave it the Parthenon and the curving façade that looks perfectly straight when viewed from below and has inspired architects all over the world for 2,500 years. The forty-six columns of the Parthenon – the high city's most revered structure – are imitated on American one-dollar bills, and replicas stand guard outside Wall Street, the People's Hall in Beijing and at the mausoleums of Mao and Ho Chi Minh.

History Review

The Greek island of Santorini, now a crescent of grey striated rocks topped with small domed churches, may have spelled the end to early Greek civilizations, such as that of the Minoans. When the resident volcano blew its stack around 1650 BCE, it wreaked havoc all along the Mediterranean. So forceful was the explosion that some say it caused the continent of Atlantis to sink.

Was it that the temperate weather fostered outdoor socializing and public speaking or that they could pluck ideas from other lands easily reached by sea? Was it that Ancient Greeks could afford to make the first leap in civilization because few enemies distracted them with invasions or were other cultures doing the same and just neglecting to record their histories and ideas? Or did the thinkers who spent long years studying stars tap an alien vibration that jolted them into a whole new orbit? Who knows, but from the scraps we still have of antiquity the Greeks were latching on to ideas that seem far beyond their time and sometimes weren't proved as the truth for thousands of years.

Today's schools tend to cover Ancient Greece in three days, reducing its 450-year legacy to city-states and Ionic, Doric and Corinthian columns. In other times, however, the wonders of Ancient Greece were exalted. Islamic scholars were the first to translate the works of the ancients, and the classical ideas and designs later went on to inspire the Renaissance. The eighteenth-century American revolutionaries were so adoring of the lost culture that they toyed with the idea of making Greek the official language of the United States.

Differing Philosophies

The creators of philosophy, Socrates, Plato and Aristotle, had different approaches to explaining the world:

Socrates (470–399 BCE): Refusing to write anything down, Socrates believed that 'The life unexamined is not worth living.' He examined everything and everyone so voraciously that there is a word – 'aporia' – for the resulting bewilderment. After a Delphic oracle declared him Athens' wisest, he became arrogant in his 'All I know is that I know nothing' conceit. When two of his students overthrew Athens, he was found guilty of corrupting youth and forced to drink hemlock.

Plato (427–347 BCE): Best known for his written discourses involving Socrates, Plato believed that our perceptions were foggy at best, like shadows flickering on cave walls. True knowledge could only be derived from within, from ideas and a pure soul; the senses merely led one astray.

Aristotle (384–322 BCE): Plato's finest student, Aristotle, who tutored Alexander the Great, believed understanding only came from empirical observation, and laid the basis for the scientific method. Wrote about everything from anatomy to astronomy, politics to poetry. Aristotle is often the most respected of the three.

The civilization of separate city-states such as Athens and Sparta rose up around the sixth century BCE on the islands of the Aegean and on Peloponnesus and later produced a society where not only could citizens vote in their leaders, but thinkers postulated the existence of atoms, calculated the circumference of the planet and correctly portrayed the galaxy as a collection of faraway stars. Fascinated with deities, theatre, politics and wars, Greeks invented coins, pumps, philosophy and democracy and left us with the first written histories. Many of the most memorable works and the best known Greeks emerged in Athens during the fifth century BCE era of Pericles, who pushed democracy, and ushered in the Golden Age.

The Greek city-states expanded their holdings along the coasts of the Mediterranean mostly as a means to secure additional food. They rarely went deep inland, creating a beachfront empire that included Sicily, south Italy, the southern Balkans and North Africa.

Greek Gurus

You may recall that Homer was the blind poet who turned the Trojan War into lyrical epics with the *Iliad* and *Odyssey* – but some historians doubt he existed – and that Sappho (c. 630 BCE) from the island of Lesbos wrote love poems to women, although she threw herself from a cliff over a man. Sophocles (496–406) wrote *Antigone*, General Thucydides (c. 455–395) preserved his battlefield memories in the multi-volume *History of the Peloponnese War*, and superstition-scorning Hippocrates (460–377) is considered the father of medicine, although it is unclear if he actually penned the Hippocratic Oath. Pythagoras (569–475) is best recalled for his formula a^2 plus $b^2 = c^2$ for right-angled triangles, but he also experimented with musical tones (inventing the octave), exalted vegetarianism and ran a philosophical society that reduced everything to numbers; initiates went for five years without talking. A few other memorable Greeks:

- Aeschylus (525–456): The man who wrote tragedies – *The Persians*, *The Suppliants* and the *Oresteia* among them – died comically if painfully: an eagle dropped a huge turtle on his head.
- Eudoxus of Cnidus (408–347): Invented the sundial, classified animals, and taught that planets orbited the sun.
- Eratosthenes of Cyrene (276–195): Calculated the earth's circumference; was off by only a few thousand miles.
- Heraclitus (540–480): 'Everything changes,' said Heraclitus, adding, 'You can't step in the same river twice.'
- Democritus (460–370): Devised the idea that matter is made up of atoms, theorized that stars were far-off planets, and speculated that there were many worlds in the universe, and that life could exist on them.[4]
- Ptolemy (c. 90–168 CE): clever mapmaker, but his universe was geocentric.

Despite occasional claims of being descended from the deity Zeus, and his family of gods, Greeks were mere mortals, and as such entered into the occasional war. Their first known enemies were the Persians – who began conquering lands in the sixth century BCE – but Greeks began successfully regaining many of their lands within decades.

In 479 BCE Persians sacked Athens, destroying among other things the Acropolis. Pericles rebuilt at least part of it, including the Parthenon.

The battles that ultimately rearranged the loosely organized coalitions of city-states, however, were wars between always-dominant Athens and militaristic Sparta. Starting in 431 BCE, the two knocked each other out for twenty-seven years, with Sparta emerging as the victor, though not flexing its muscle for long, as other city-states rose up and shoved it off the stage. The in-fighting made the city-states vulnerable and in 346 Thebes brought in an outsider to help their cause. When Philip II of Macedon showed up on the scene, he changed Ancient Greek society for ever by expanding the territorial holdings and bringing in his son Alexander who would forge even larger boundaries for Greece.

> **Forgotten details:** *the Peloponnesian War between city-states Sparta and Athens ended in 404 BCE. Peace, however, wasn't made official for another two and a half millennia: the mayors of the former city-states Sparta and Athens, now stately cities, finally sat down and signed a formal peace treaty in March 1996.*

Most Greeks weren't happy at first when Philip took control of their cities and proclaimed himself leader, but the Macedonian admired the Greeks and sought to curry favour: he promised return of the Greek lands that had remained under Persian rule. Philip died soon after starting his mission, but his offspring Alexander finished off the quest in grand style. The 20-year-old Alexander the Great (356–323 BCE) not only won back Persian-held Greek cities, he conquered new lands from Egypt to Syria. By the time he died at the age of 33, Greek territories stretched all the way to India. The gem of the Greek acquisitions, however, was on the north coast of Africa: Alexandria.

Alexandria

Founded around 331 BCE, Alexandria (in today's Egypt) was originally a small village which upon Alexander's orders was built into a magnificent metropolis known for its intellectuals, high culture and kinky affairs. Alexander never set foot in the city again while alive, but he left behind a general named Ptolemy (died 283), who eventually proclaimed himself leader – and a dozen subsequent rulers would be called Ptolemy. Palaces shot up alongside temples, theatres, markets and mausoleums – and the lighthouse of Pharos (one of the Seven Wonders of the Ancient World) beamed not far off in the distance. The city was a magnet for scholars and alongside a well-endowed museum filled with temples, gardens, and a zoo, the world's most extensive library was built, where a hundred scholars lived poring over the scrolls that came from across Europe and Asia. Holding half a million documents, the Alexandrian library put even the impressive library in Athens to shame. The collected wisdom of the ancient world, however, went up in flames, although when it caught fire and who is to blame for the blaze that reduced knowledge to ashes is still a mystery (Julius Caesar is an outside contender).

Not as gorgeous as in the movies, Cleopatra (69–30 BCE) – the last of the Pharaohs of Alexandria – still had a zesty social life. Married to her brother (her rival), she got rid of him when Julius Caesar visited her city in 50 BCE. Caesar was impressed with the hospitality: he was presented with a carpet with Cleopatra inside. The two travelled the Nile for months, and soon the pharaoh was pregnant with the emperor's child. Cleopatra married her younger brother, continued sleeping with Caesar until he was murdered, then went for his successor Mark Antony, who handed her Crete, Cyprus and Palestine as gifts. His foe Octavian declared war on Cleopatra, and upon winning, threatened her with death. Rather than chance what method he would devise, Cleopatra came up with her own, and died from the poison of an asp, as befitted the seductress who had a toxic effect on men.

As Ancient Rome ascended in the first century BCE, Greek lands fell into their hands, although Greek was still the spoken language and many of the systems remained, including that of the gods, who were merely given new names. In 330 CE the Roman Empire was split into two parts: the new eastern portion is known as the Byzantine Empire, although back then it was 'New Rome'. Although Venetian interests were tied into it as well, the Byzantine Empire was essentially Greek, and its centre was the grand city of Constantinople.

Constantinople: The Lost City

It was the Queen of Cities, the richest of Christendom, filled with palaces, markets, zoos and the most beautiful churches, including the mosaic-thick, silver-rich Hagia Sofia – Church of Holy Wisdom. Founded by Constantine I in 330 CE, Constantinople spread out along the peninsula formed by the Golden Horn and the azure Marmara Sea. Although it was the capital of the eastern

Roman Empire, Constantinople was a city where, like Constantine himself, most spoke Greek and most of the vestiges of Greek culture lived on. Here, where the Greek Orthodox church grew in power, splitting with the Catholic church in 1054, the city was protected from numerous attempted attacks by two walls connected by a deep moat, the most formidable bastion in Europe. The walls, however, were occasionally penetrated: in 1204 Crusaders sacked the city, looting the churches, raping the women and ultimately establishing Constantinople as a new site of Catholicism for the next fifty-seven years – an event for which the Greek Orthodox church would never forgive the pope. The Greek Orthodox church won back control in 1261, but they would lose it again. In 1453, during one of the most horrifying battles of European history, Constantinople was besieged by Sultan Mehmed II's Islamic warriors for fifty-five days. Byzantines were greatly outnumbered – Mehmed had 200,000 fighters to their 20,000 – but the city held its own. The Ottomans, who were kept on the other side of the wall for weeks, finally gained entry, not through fighting, but a mistake: someone inside Constantinople left open a small gate in the thick wall, and the Ottomans walked right in and claimed the city that had been the crown of the Byzantine Empire.

Under Ottoman rule the Greek Orthodox churches were allowed to remain, and Greeks could freely practise their faith. In fact, the church rulers – seen as shepherds to the flock – were so respected that they were paid as employees working for the Ottoman state. The acknowledgement of the Orthodox religion boosted the church's power, which had been dwindling prior to that. The church, as well as the Greek language, became the symbol for Greeks of their lost culture and their dream that their past lives would be regained.

When the venerable capital of Christendom fell to Islamic fighters in 1453, Constantinople and most of the Byzantine lands were pulled into the Islamic Ottoman Empire, which moved its capital here. And for the next three and a half centuries, Greeks thought of little else but how to get out and restore their previous greatness. Although there were times of relative peace, the period during which Greeks were under the rule of Ottomans was often a violent, unhappy affair. In 1821 Greeks rose up and declared independence – and when luminaries such as Victor Hugo and

Lord Byron took up their cause, Britain and France finally entered into the battles.

> *Ode to a Greek war: Lord Byron was among the many Europeans who fought in the Greek War of Independence that began in 1821. It's said the poet was less concerned with the geopolitics of the day, and died fighting for the ideals of Ancient Greece, which had lured him and other romantics on to the battlefield.*

Greeks successfully shook off the Ottoman hold in 1829, and re-established a much smaller Greece that was little more than the mainland. When Greeks returned to Athens to reclaim the former capital, they found the once-great city was run down and deserted. Notably missing were the sculptures and friezes that had once wrapped the interior of the Parthenon. They'd been shipped off to Britain a few decades before, during the Ottoman rule.

Losing Their Marbles

The Elgin Marbles sound like they should be small colourful orbs that tots shoot across the floor for fun. But they're not. They're marble sculptures and friezes of war scenes and religious ceremonies created in 440 BCE and plucked from the Parthenon in 1799 by the Scottish Earl of Elgin, British Ambassador to the Ottoman Empire. He took the works that Greeks call the Parthenon Marbles for safe keeping, since Greece was then occupied by Turks. He believed he was saving them, although the omens were there that he was making a huge mistake. He had to pay exorbitant fees to get the friezes prised off the wall, and bought his own ship to send them back home. Alas, the vessel sank; it took two years to salvage the pieces, the cost of which came out of the earl's pocket as well. Travelling back to Scotland by land, he and his new bride were captured in France and thrown in prison. The Scot sent to bargain for their release was successful with the Mrs: once he got her out of prison, the two had an affair. When Elgin finally made it to London, the British Museum wanted the marbles but paid less than what he'd paid the workers in Athens. The poor earl died in poverty, first divorcing his wife, but the marbles became the museum's most valued collection. Greece wants the babies back, but the museum won't part with them, despite pleas lodged by tearful Greek politicians (who wanted to at least borrow them for the Olympics) and VIPs from Bill Clinton to Vanessa Redgrave. Pressure continues for Britain to shoot the marbles back to Greece, particularly as some reports have emerged that the museum's caretakers were too thorough in their cleaning and damaged them by stripping their paint.[5]

Since the newly independent Greeks had no ruler, a Bavarian royal was soon shipped in to rule the country, and his construction teams ripped out most of the city's 'barbarian' buildings. The Greeks were not content: after the centuries of dreaming, lands with a majority of Greeks and Greek speakers still weren't part of their fledgling country. Thus was launched '*Megali Idea*', or the great idea to hook all of the former Greeks lands – from Crete and Cyprus to Constantinople (renamed Istanbul by the Turks) – back together with Athens. Although they were ready to tackle the problem right then, they ultimately had to wait nearly a century before they could recover more of the territory that had been theirs during the days of Ancient Greece. After the Balkan War of 1912–13, Greece expanded to the north, bringing in parts of Bulgaria, and later Crete, where struggles had been going on for decades to reunite with the Greek mainland. Still missing were assorted islands, including Cyprus, and their lost capital Constantinople. But when the First World War rolled around, Greeks had renewed hope that Greece could take not only the city, but other important areas in Thrace – the part of Turkey that lies west of Istanbul. And no Greek was more determined to get those territories back than elegant, intellectual and articulate Eleftherios Venizelos, the Greek prime minister, who ran the country with King Constantine I.

> *Monarchy-go-round: In a political version of 'The Hokey-Cokey', Greece has performed a strange dance with its kings. A monarchy was put in when the country became independent in 1832, but was kicked out in 1924, brought back in 1935, booted shortly thereafter, brought back in 1946, ejected again, and nearly brought back in 1967 and 1974. In between monarchs being toppled, one, King George, was assassinated and another died of a monkey bite.*

When Britain and France dangled the prospect of regaining Constantinople, Cyprus and Thrace under his nose, Venizelos quickly signed on Greece to fight the First World War with the Triple Entente (Britain, France and Russia), but there was a problem. King Constantine I didn't want to fight in the Great War, as it created a conflict of interest: his brother-in-law was the German Kaiser Wilhelm II. Constantine wanted to stay neutral, but Venizelos was determined, so determined that the king kicked him out of office. So Venizelos formed another government in Thessaloniki. He didn't have the army's full support, and he wasn't really leading the government, so Britain and France intervened: they gave the king a choice – abdicate or watch Athens be turned into ruins – and they occupied the capital to assure they meant business. The king gave the throne to his son Alexander, Venizelos was reinstated in Athens, and in 1917 Greece was dragged into the war.

> *The split between those who supported the king and his more conservative ideas for Greece and those who supported more worldly and modern Venizelos, caused such a rupturing of the country that it is known as the National Schism. For years after, monarchs and prime ministers competed for power in what would be a revolving door of leadership: the prime minister would come in when the monarch was pushed out and vice versa.*

At the end of the war Venizelos discovered that he wouldn't get all he had been promised. Constantinople was still beyond his grasp, as was Cyprus, but the victors of the war offered up Thrace and the important city that the Greeks called Smyrna and the Turks called Izmir. Venizelos sent Greek troops to take Smyrna in 1919, but it wasn't easy. The port city on the Aegean was home to many Greeks, but it was economically vital to Turkey. The takeover turned violent with hundreds dying in looting and rioting. And in 1922 Turkey took it back even more violently: the Turkish army massacred the mostly Greek population, setting the city ablaze in an inferno that drove many into the sea. Tensions ran so high between Greeks and Turks that the two countries agreed to a mass repatriation: 1.3 million Greeks from western Turkey fled to Greece and 800,000 Turks ran the other way, with thousands dying en route.

> *With its population enlarging by over a million overnight, Athens was overwhelmed in every way, unable to provide jobs or food to the surprise guests: the newcomers were forced to the outlying areas of the city, creating Athens' first suburbs.*

The power struggles and bad news just wouldn't let up: King Alexander died in 1920 from a monkey bite, his father Constantine I returned only to be dethroned in 1922; he was succeeded by his son George II who was himself deposed the following year. Greece was run by a military junta until 1935, when George was restored to the throne by plebiscite. The country was hit hard by the Great Depression, the military brought in new dictator Metaxas in 1936 – and then the Second World War rolled around. Greece did not want to fight. But in 1941 the Axis powers marched into the land – with Nazis, Italians and Bulgarians at their most brutal as they attempted to squash the feisty Greeks. Fierce resistance brewed up immediately, much of it initially coming out of the Communist camp. Rightwingers and royalists joined forces to push out the occupiers, often unleashing as much destruction as the enemy. But in 1944, as the war was drawing to a close, factions within the Resistance began battling each other in a nasty civil war that would last for five years.

During the occupation a million Greeks died – over 8 per cent of the population. Some perished from fighting and many more from starvation, which killed 100,000 during the first occupied winter.

As the civil war raged on in Greece, first the British then the Americans became heavily involved in the internal politics of the country. Their fear was that the Communists, quite popular and the initiators of the Resistance, would lead Greece into the waiting arms of the Soviet Union. So both began purging the country of Communists in a number of ways. The Brits purged the military of Communists, while the Americans, who were mucking around in the background as well, ultimately came through with money: $400 million was doled out to fight Communists as part of the new Truman Doctrine that very much favoured conservatives. They also pushed Greeks to fiddle with the elections – so much for that concept of democracy – to ensure that the right wing could win. Another American demand: Certificates of Political Reliability that ensured that the holder did not harbour left-wing sympathies. Without the certificates – in use until 1962 – Greeks could not vote or get a job.

Some analysts say that Greece was then running under a shadow government with representatives of the monarchy, the Greek Army and the CIA trying to dominate the Greek political show.[6]

But for all their overt and covert manoeuvring to stamp out the left wing in all its forms, the left not only existed, it was popular: in 1964 Socialist George Papandreou was elected prime minister in what was Greece's first victory. His government was immediately under attack by the powers that be and by 1965 he was shoved out of office. He looked poised to re-enter the arena again in April 1967. Two nights before the elections, however, a junta took charge, one that the United States is widely believed to have backed. The coup by three right-wing military colonels was called 'The Glorious Revolution' – by the junta at least. Most Greeks had a few other more colourful terms for the next seven years when miniskirts were banned, long hair was shorn, foreign newspapers disappeared and martial rule was the law. Eight thousand Greeks died in the first week, and even though public congregation was banned, the colonels' rule grew increasingly unpopular.

The United States, however, was quick to recognize the validity of the junta, sending off Vice President Spiro Agnew to meet with them. NATO mumbled unkind things under its breath but didn't do anything: not only was NATO US-dominated, but they didn't want to jeopardize relations with Greece, given its crucial location in fighting the Cold War.

Vocabulary Builder

Oxi: 'No' – the answer to Mussolini who asked to traverse Greece in 1940 on his way to battles. What did Mussolini expect? He was Roman Catholic, this was Greek Orthodox land. Now celebrated as a national holiday.

Katoxi: Brutal occupation by Axis powers during the Second World War.

Enosis: Union (particularly with Greece). A buzzword bandied about on Cyprus, especially in the 1950s and 1960s, it was also used in the nineteenth century when Greece wanted to bond with Crete.

Megali Idea: Great Idea. Name given to an extremely popular plan to reunite Greeks once living in the Ottoman Empire to re-establish Greek greatness, and take back the parts of the former Greek Empire that were then part of Ottoman territory.

Metapolitefsi: the transition from the junta to democracy that started in 1974.

In November 1973 the army stormed a student protest – killing twenty by rolling over them with a tank. Worldwide wrath fell upon the colonels and their popularity plummeted further. Desperate to keep control, the colonels decided to embrace the popular cause of Cyprus, which Greece (with the blessing of most of the Cypriots) had been trying to annex for decades. The junta made a mistake when it backed a coup on that island that was once part of Ancient Greece: the leadership that was supposed to rope Cyprus to Greece lasted only three days, and when it fell, it took the junta down with it.

The tank-rolling incident of 1973 bred such discontent that it led to a small but lethal group who use the date of the uprising – November 17 – as their name. Believing that the junta was backed by the US and UK, which it may well have been, the November 17 group have continued to target VIPs from the West even though the junta's long gone: the assassins have killed at least twenty-one in recent years, a British military attaché and four American diplomats among them. Greece didn't make much effort to crack down on the group until a few months before the 2004 Olympics, when most were rounded up, tried and convicted.

In 1974 democracy was restored, and continuing a pattern established decades before, politics is now dominated mostly by two families: the Socialist Papandreou and the right-leaning Karamanlis, each of whom has for generations led the country. The most obvious changes to Greek society came under Prime Minister Andreas Papandreou in the early 1980s. Not only did he allow civil marriage and liberalize divorce, he abolished the dowry treasure chest that had accompanied women into marriages for centuries. He was also quite anti-West when he strode into office in 1981, disliking anything vaguely connected with Washington, London or Brussels, for that matter. Despite his harsh words and his tendency to show up for warm photo ops with assorted ageing leaders of the Soviet Union, Papandreou didn't pull Greece out of NATO or the European Economic Community – and for all his words condemning America, he even approved a new US naval base. That of course may have had everything to do with his desire to arm Greece: Papandreou insisted that the US give Greece at least 70 per cent of the military aid provided to Turkey – and the US caved in to his demands.

In 1986, when the Reagan administration announced it would give Greece $501 million in aid, which was a mere 63 per cent of the $789 million it was giving Turkey, Papandreou had a tantrum: he threatened to halt Greek participation in NATO military exercises.[7]

Quick Tour

You can see it in the mountain villages cascading white down to the sea or the medieval monasteries wedged so high in the cliffs that basket and ropes are needed to pull visitors up. You can see it in the hilltop ruins or the fields of wild flowers dotted with ancient statues. Greece is deeply lost in its history. The country that trails off the Balkans is obsessed with its spectacular past and that is certainly understandable: it's hard to avoid the connection to Greece's historical greatness since remnants of it are found around nearly every twist in the road, and past every café-lined square. But in the same way as it is hard to be an Onassis or Kennedy, the country's past can be a crippling ball and chain as much as a sparkling crown jewel. The problem is not only that there is so much to live up to: the problem is there are too many reasons to bear a grudge.

Armed to the Hilt

The tensions between Greece and Turkey over everything from Cyprus to maritime boundaries has most benefited one country: the United States, or more specifically that country's arms manufacturers who make a hefty profit in this testy corner of the world. They've been peddling everything from fighter planes to missiles to both Greece and Turkey since the two joined NATO in 1952 – and the US government has given the two plenty of war toys as well; until recently, Turkey and Greece have been the recipients of huge military grants – just behind Israel and Egypt. Now the two are apparently addicted to the latest models from Boeing and Lockheed Martin and both strive to keep up with the other; if Turkey buys tactical missiles with warheads that explode shrapnel, then you can bet Greece will too. Must be hard for Turkey to keep up these days; Greece recently signed up for a $17 billion arms variety pack that includes warships, fighter jets, subs, an AWACS plane, tanks, attack and transport helicopters and assorted missiles and anti-aircraft devices.[8] One of the underlying issues is the size of the armed forces: whereas Greece has an army of 168,000, Turkey's is 693,000.

Israel also supplies arms to Turkey, which supplies water to Israel. Greeks don't like this arrangement at all, and some say it is why Greeks tend to side with Palestinians in the Middle East conflict. A Greek Orthodox official in Jerusalem didn't help diplomatic relations when he recently called Palestinian suicide bombers 'heroes': he was relieved of his church post.

Despite the residents' warm hospitality and easy smiles, Greece, which is Europe's most xenophobic country according to Eurobarometer polls, often appears to be angry with pretty much everybody. Turkey stole Constantinople and its greatness away in the fifteenth century and occupied part of Cyprus in 1974; the Germans, Italians and Bulgarians occupied the country during the Second World War; the Catholic church sent crusaders to sack Constantinople in 1204, and the British effectively prevented union with Cyprus back in the 1950s and continue to hoard the Elgin Marbles. Most Greeks can rapidly tick off the dates and the reasons for rage. And in this country that is Europe's most anti-American, there are plenty who are livid at the United States, which interfered with its postwar politics, suppressed the left, backed the junta, and sold Turkey the weapons that it needed to invade Cyprus in 1974, and which keep Cyprus one of the most highly armed spots in the world. Some are even fed up with the tourists, who are integral to the economy, but bring modernity and change, and strip away Greek tradition; the Orthodox church even has a new prayer to protect Greece from the corrupting outsiders' influence. In fact, in this country where 97 per cent are Greek Orthodox, the powerful church fans the flame.

In May 2001, when Pope John Paul II visited Athens – being the first pope to set foot in Greece in almost 1,200 years – his arrival was treated as a national tragedy: Orthodox clergy had held an all-night pray-a-thon that he wouldn't make it, flags hung at half mast, churches were wrapped in black, bishops led protest demonstrations of the faithful chanting 'Down with the two-horned pope,' and Orthodox Archbishop Christodoulos issued loud statements demanding that the pope repent for harming the Byzantine empire in medieval times. Indeed the pope apologized for past acts, specifically the sacking of Constantinople in 1204, but even after the pope ate crow, Greek clerics still snubbed the repenter; at least Christodoulos came forward to hug him. The rest of the room remained coldly silent, and the anger towards the Catholic church, which among other things recognized the right of the Republic of Macedonia to use that name, burns on.

The Greek Orthodox Church

Currently the official keeper of much of the cultural past – the institution that believes it alone is most Hellenic – is the Greek Orthodox church, the icon-heavy and ritual-rich branch of Christianity that split with Catholicism almost 1,000 years ago. In Greece there is scarcely any separation of church and state: so important is the church that clerics – who are called in for government affairs and christening new buildings – are on the government payroll.[9] More conservative even than the Catholic church – the Orthodox church claims to be the keeper of true Christianity and uses old Byzantine Greek in services – the Greek Orthodox church, based in the former Constantinople (today's Istanbul), is headed by an archbishop and the number two man is the patriarch. The current archbishop appears to have a few secular issues on his mind – like pulling back all of the lands that were once Ancient Greece, even if it takes a war to do it. He has called Turks 'barbarians', wants to block Turkey's entry into the EU, and tried to ban a new mosque from rising in Athens; he also tried to prevent changes to identity cards that would no longer require the card holder to divulge religion. Archbishop Christodoulos is also gunning for Patriarch Bartholomew whom he sees as too moderate, modernizing and too actively patching up problems with Rome.

'Better the Turkish turban than the Cardinal's hat' – Greek saying during the time of Ottoman occupation, reflecting the deep dislike of the Catholic church

While Greece does indeed have plenty of legitimate reasons for anger, that feeling of historical injustice only holds back a country that has already held itself back with inner turmoil for most of the past century. The infrastructure – and the weaponry – now may be twenty-first century in standard but the society lags far behind. Women, given the vote in 1952, saw the dowry abolished in the 1980s, but Greece remains largely a patriarchal society where females may work but are rarely at a high level or in leadership roles. Young Greeks may be well educated, but they often have to go abroad to study since universities are filled to the brim, and a quarter of them don't have a steady job: many shack up with their families until middle age. Poverty runs at around 21 per cent and while the official illiteracy rate is only 3 per cent, some put the figure much higher, particularly in villages; in 1985 female illiteracy was at least 15 per cent. Culturally, modern Greece may have its own Madonna and Elvis equivalents – Anna Vissi (had a smash hit with 'You Are') and Sakis Rouvis (an Elvis-like heart-throb) – but outside the ancients, the most popular Greek writer is Nikos Kazantzakis, author of *Zorba the Greek* – who died in 1957. The most sought-after Greek creator these days is Nia Vardalos – and it is notable that she's Greek Canadian, having grown up not in Athens but Winnipeg.

> *The Greek Orthodox church, whose wealth is estimated to be about €800 million, owns vast amounts of land across Greece: only the government owns more.*[10]

The state of society might not be worthy of comment if this were a country that had little ambition. But, as was made obvious by the national pride generated by the Olympics, Greece longs to be great again and live up to the stature of the Ancient Greeks, who admittedly are a difficult act to follow. Save for the occasional noble statesman – former foreign minister George Papandreou Jr who tried to smooth relations with historical enemies, for one – Greece, land of rugged mountains and secluded beaches lapped by cobalt blue water, has mostly proved itself to be a swell tourist destination, as well as a land of great pride and a deep well of ire. Nevertheless, the situation is slowly changing: Athens has a female mayor, and the Olympics were put back on schedule by Gianna Angelopoulos-Daskalaki. At least it's a start.

> *A new religious group that worships the Twelve Olympians – Zeus and the rest of the Mount Olympus clan – is currently prohibited from doing so under Greek law. They say their members number 100,000.*

Future Forecast

Greece will get their marbles back sooner rather than later. Lord knows what will happen if the Orthodox church comes apart.

Hot Spots

Athens: Adored for its link to the ancients, its dazzling architecture and brainy past, polluted, overcrowded Athens is fun, but until recently hadn't contributed much to the modern age. In fashion, in literature, in art, it

Athens: birthplace of democracy, philosophy and plate-throwing.

coasted on the old glory days – the Acropolis is the most visited site in Greece – but got up to speed with the 2004 Olympics. Home to almost four million – almost a third of Greece's population – the city was designed for only 350,000.

The Aegean: Still fighting with Turks over uninhabited rocks here, and the fish for which Greece is renowned just isn't what it used to be: thanks to overfishing, stocks are depleted.

Islands: More than 1,400 of them trail off the mainland in almost every direction, but only 170 are inhabited, most of those with only a few dozen residents. Superstitions run strong, including that cawing crows bring news of death. The mule trails that once led to the hills of orchids and irises are now covered by asphalt. Buses take tourists up, and often bring villagers down: they're moving to the cities in hordes. Corfu, Mikonos, Santorini and Crete are four islands where you are more likely to meet holidaying Brits and Germans than resident Greeks.

Cafés: A 2002 law banned smoking in them, as well as in railway stations, hospitals, taxis and government buildings. Hasn't been terribly effective: more Greeks puff away than anybody else in Europe.

Crete: Not included in the package when Greece became independent in 1829, Crete triggered one of the Greek–Turkish wars, this one in 1897. Greece lost, but the island became independent of the Ottomans. In 1913, after yet more fighting in the Balkans, it happily became part of Greece and is now its biggest island. Also site of a US naval base.

Araxos: Site of a NATO military base in southern Greece, that held, and may still hold, nuclear weapons.

Imia/Kardak: This tiny uninhabited Greek island in the Aegean almost kicked off a war in 1996: a Turkish boat ran aground here, and when the Greek coastguard arrived to help, the boat owner declined it, saying Imia (called Kardak by the Turks) was a Turkish island. The media had a field day, and Turkish journalists inflamed the issue by sticking a Turkish flag on the 4-hectare rock. Both countries sent out their warships, and fire was in the air, until the international community stepped in and pulled the two apart.

Airports: Don't be taking pictures here! Look what happened to a group of British and Dutch plane spotters in 2001. They'd been snapping shots of planes at military airports, including Araxos, and were arrested as spies. They faced up to twenty years in prison, but were handed over to Britain.

Brothels: Bordellos are legal in Greece, and for the Olympics they wanted to open up a few more. '*Oxi!*' said the church, which blocked the move.

Turkey: Relations are better with Greece's longest-lasting enemy, but so many Greeks and Turks have died in assorted savage conflicts that the bitterness may have seeped into the collective unconscious. Even though both Greece and Turkey are NATO members, the lingering fear of Turkey still keeps Greece well armed, with about 5 per cent of its GDP spent on defence.

> **Ironies:** *The works of the Ancient Greeks were revived, starting in the eighth century, by Islamic scholars and scribes who translated the words of the wise; it wasn't until the Renaissance that much of Europe took any interest in Greece's writings, which might have been dust had not the Muslims preserved the ideas and texts earlier.*

Istanbul/Constantinople: Straddling Asia and Europe, the gorgeous 'Queen of Cities' adored by Byzantine Greeks was snatched away by Turks in 1453, and it's still Turkey's biggest city. Some Greeks still want it back, and many consider Tuesday – the day of the week when Constantinople was conquered by Turks – to be cursed.[11] The city is still the headquarters for the Greek Orthodox church.

Cyprus: For several decades in the mid twentieth century, Greeks wanted to make this island again part of Greece – so much so that Greek guerrilla fighters EOKA went to Cyprus to fight for the cause. When the ruling Greek junta tried to boost its popularity by forcibly bringing Cyprus in, the move blew up in their faces: Turkey invaded, and has been running North Cyprus ever since, causing a schizophrenic divide on that island.

Mount Athos: No women are allowed – and even female livestock are unwelcome – on this northern Greek peninsula that is home to twenty monasteries and hundreds of monks, who are livid about the patriarch of the Orthodox church: the patriarch has been trying to improve relations with the Catholic church, ignoring the fact that even communicating with the Vatican is, according to the Orthodox church, a cardinal sin. When the monks refused to recognize the patriarch in January 2003, he refused to recognize them and ordered them off the island, cutting off their food and fuel. Now they're fighting back – with their prayer beads. They also bought a speedboat in case the beads don't bring food and fuel falling from the sky.[12]

Hot Shots

Costas Karamanlis: Prime Minister 2004 to present. Of the conservative New Democracy party, the nephew of former prime minister Konstantin Karamanlis is the youngest Greek premier ever, and certainly the one with the least experience. His CV, while strong, lacks substance: a lawyer for five years, the professor sat in parliament from 1989 and is also vice-president of the People's Party in the European Parliament. When he ushered in New Democracy, it marked an end to the socialist PASOK government that had ruled Greece for twenty of the previous twenty-three years.

George Papandreou Junior: Foreign Minister 1999–2004. American-born Papandreou of the socialist PASOK party is Greece's finest diplomat and also one of Europe's leading men. Unlike his irascible father (former prime minister Andreas) or his grandfather (former prime minister George Senior), this Papandreou has tried to soothe relations in all of Greece's problem areas – Turkey, Cyprus, Macedonia, Bulgaria – and made at least limited progress. Too bad his party PASOK was voted out in 2004, and his job went with it.

Dora Bakoyianni: First-ever woman to be mayor of Athens, she was hostess of the Olympics, an event that she said left Athens a more 'people-friendly'

PM Karamanlis: a new generation takes the power seat.

place (at least for a country that is Europe's most xenophobic). Despite the chirpy soundbites, the mayor is well attuned to Greek politics: her husband, a senator, was murdered by the November 17 group. She entered the political arena when she successfully campaigned to fill his seat. A welcome sight indeed to see females finally slipping into this man-heavy arena.

Archbishop Christodoulos: Archbishop of Athens and all Greece 1998 to present. Born in 1939, powerful and hotheaded, the archbishop of the Greek Orthodox church is pushing the *Megali Idea* concept again, encouraging Greeks to claim the land lost to the 'barbaric' Turks. May be causing a rift in his own church by trying to steal power from the patriarch.

> *'We are ready, if necessary, to shed blood ... we bless the sacred weapons when the moment demands it'* – Archbishop Christodoulos on possible wars to take back ancient Greek lands[13]

Andreas Papandreou: Prime Minister 1981–9; 1993–6. Son of former prime minister George Papandreou Senior, he was a rebel during the 1930s who, upon being tortured, revealed the names of cohorts, who were subsequently rounded up and killed. Guilt-ridden, he left for the United States, gaining a doctorate in economics from Harvard, and returned to be top aide to his father who'd become prime minister in 1964. Accused of trying to stir up a left-wing movement in the army, Andreas caused the demise of his father's administration within eighteen months. When the junta took over in 1967, he hightailed it to North America, this time becoming a professor in Canada. After the military dictatorship crumbled he returned and started a new political party, the Pan Hellenic Socialist Movement (PASOK), and became prime minister in 1981, working Greece's strategic location to procure free arms from the US. He lost power after two terms amid allegations of bribes, but was re-elected in 1993, and came hobbling in with a new airline hostess wife, Mimi, who loved to pose for the camera and whose naked form was often splashed across the tabloids. Papandreou was actually quite ill – so sick, in fact, that he was ultimately forced to resign while lying in his hospital bed.[14]

Karolos Papoulis: President 2005–present. His is a familiar face: white-haired Karolos Papoulis, 75, has been active in Greek politics since he worked as part of the anti-Nazi resistance during the Second World War. A big boy in PASOK, and foreign minister for four years starting in 1993, popular Papoulis is helping glue the fragmented Balkans back together again: one of his first moves as president was sealing a deal with former foe Bulgaria for a shared 177-mile oil pipeline that will bring Russian oil gurgling into Aegean port Alexandroupolis.

Constantine 'Costas' Simitis: Prime Minister 1996–2004. Considering that he was always the most critical of Andreas Papandreou and led the reform movement of the PASOK party, it was ironic that Simitis was chosen to fill Papandreou's shoes when the prime minister was forced to sign over his power – from his hospital bed. The former lawyer, industry minister and agricultural minister put Greece through tough economic reforms and guided the country into the eurozone then nosedived in popularity.

The Onassis Dynasty

No modern Greek family illustrates the ancient Greek tragedy more vividly than the Onassis clan. Death, jealousy, the depths of loneliness and misery – all set against a backdrop of incredible wealth – are just a few highlights of the shipping family that is still being chronicled in *Vanity Fair*. Patriarch Aristotle Onassis was born poor, but jettisoned his family's tobacco business for an international shipping operation that raked in billions. His ability to attract the fair sex was even more remarkable: opera diva Maria Callas was but one who adored him – and she vowed revenge when Ari dumped her for widow Jackie Kennedy. Maybe

Callas got her wish: the 1968 Kennedy–Onassis marriage, little of which was known outside of paparazzi shots of bikini-clad Jackie on Ari's yacht, was soon crashing on the rocks – Jackie's shopping extravagances being but one problem in the marriage that cost him over $20 million in its first year.[15] Soon the rapport between the two was so icy that when Onassis's only son Alexander died in a freak plane crash in 1973, Onassis sought solace in Callas's loving arms, not his wife's, whose arms were, as usual by then, an ocean away. By the time Onassis died in 1975 – apparently from pneumonia after a gall bladder operation, although details are sketchy – Jackie was out of the will, though she contested it and reportedly shook loose some €20 million. The equivalent of almost half a billion euros went to Christina, daughter from wife number one, and his only living heir. The jetsetter whose life was riddled with drugs and bad marriage choices, she was now even more alluring to high-society pirates, but poor Christina, for all her millions, didn't have glamorous looks (her weight at one point shot up to eighteen stone) and usually appeared out-of-sorts in the in-crowd. In 1985 she gave birth to Athina, by Thierry Roussel, her fourth husband, but that marriage too went the way of all the others. Christina adored the child, dressing Athina up in Chanel and Christian Dior, adorning her dark curly locks with real diamonds and holding up the child as proof that life was worth living, at least for a while. In 1988 Christina died, alone, in Buenos Aires, apparently the result of a heart attack, and perhaps a drug overdose, although details are again blurry; some suspect suicide, others suspect foul play. Toddler Athina, aged three, became heir to the modern world's biggest inheritance. In 2003, Athina – who uses her father's surname – came fully into her fortune, estimated to be around $3 billion, and the vultures are swarming. Far more grounded than her mother, Athina surrounds herself more with four-footed mammals than two-footed party animals. An avid equestrian, Athina now wants to save the whales.[16] Lord knows, with her dough, maybe she can.

November 17 group: Believed to have only a few dozen members, and possibly all part of one clan, the group that rose up to defy the military junta in the 1970s was still assassinating Western diplomats nearly three decades later. The prob: they believe, perhaps correctly, that the US and UK had supported the junta, and every Westerner – including those from the European Union – became a potential target. A round-up may have diminished their force – and they've recently claimed that they are finished. With a dozen behind bars that could be the case.

Tourists: Too often drunk and waddling, they corrupt with their modernizing influence, but their visits kick in some 10 per cent of the Greek GDP – certainly worth a few broken plates.

Nia Vardalos: Writer and star of *My Big Fat Greek Wedding*, the Greek-Canadian from Winnipeg was performing a variation of *MBFGW* as a one-woman show in Los Angeles, when Tom Hanks saw it, loved it and opened doors. Costing a mere €4 million to make it grossed over €200 million at the box office, making it the single most successful indie film (and romantic comedy) of all time.

George Papadopoulous: Dictator 1967–73. Army officer who took over after the 1967 coup, taking assorted titles including prime minister, president and regent. Pushed out in 1973 by a fellow officer, Phaedron Gizikis, who went on to get his junta ousted by backing the ill-fated coup in Cyprus.

The Greek Monarchy

They may be out of power, but they still have their titles and they still have at least some clout. Prince Michael of Greece – a cousin of King Constantine II, the man who would be on Greece's throne if Greece hadn't turned into a republic a few decades ago – moonlights as a writer for *Vanity Fair*. His fifty-seven-page cover story 'The Young and Royal' (Sept. 2003) gives the best overview of European monarchs, including those (like Prince Michael) without a throne, of this century. According to the article, King Constantine (b. 1940) lives with wife Princess Anne Marie of Denmark (b. 1946) in London, where much of the family has put down roots: Crown Prince Pavlos (b. 1967) works at an investment firm, Prince Nikolaus (b. 1969), after a stint at Fox News in New York, now works for his dad.

Media star: Kathimerini. They are on it about everything from politics to soccer: www.ekathimerini.com

Last Word: Orthodox church VIPs suddenly stand accused of lurid crimes – from drug peddling, smuggling and money-laundering to sexually abusing young boys, carousing with prostitutes and bribing judges. It's serious and bishops are flying: the Archbishop presided over the March 2005 swearing-in of President Karolos Papoulis but, says the *Guardian*, Papoulis shunned kissing him. Not a good sign.

12. Scandinavia: Denmark, Sweden, Finland and Norway – Quiet Leaders

Overview

Despite the biting weather and the marauding Viking culture from whence they sprang, Scandinavian countries are seriously civilized, amazingly evolved and rather utopian – from their beautiful, squeaky-clean squares where candle-lit booths flicker in winter to the social welfare system that keeps residents all cosy from cradle to grave. Scandinavia often plays the global peacemaker, with Norway optimistically brokering peace deals with warring factions all over the globe and handing out the prestigious Nobel Peace Prize, and all of them throwing out mountains of money to help out assorted world causes. The three Nordic countries that are in the European Union (Finland, Sweden and Denmark) have also helped out the nearby Baltic States – handing out advice and substantial economic aid – and they've been working to keep Russia happy and involved in the regional family.

Sharing the wealth: Scandinavian countries, along with the Netherlands and Luxembourg, give away more of their wealth to humanitarian causes than anywhere else, being the only countries actually to heed the UN's recommendation to donate 0.8% of total GDP.

Geographic Confusion: Scandinavia v. Nordic Countries

The term Scandinavia is a confusing one: politically, it refers to only Norway, Sweden and Denmark, geographically it is only Norway and Sweden, but in popular usage it often includes Finland and sometimes the far-flung island of

Iceland as well. For the purposes of this section, it refers to the four countries most closely strung together: Norway, Sweden, and Denmark as well as Finland (which was historically part of Sweden). Along with Iceland, they're also sometimes known as the Nordic countries.

Common confusion: The prestigious Nobel Prize, an award that comes with a multi-zeroed cheque and oodles of accolades, is actually a shared two-country venture. Sweden funds the awards and hands out the Nobel Prizes in Literature and assorted scientific areas. The Nobel Peace Prize, however, is actually an award given out by Norway. When Alfred Nobel established the foundation to give out the prize, Sweden and Norway were united as one.

Scandinavians are lucky: they are assured of having a job – the government will educate and train them for free – and they will be very handsomely paid for it. Their corner of the world is stunning in its pristine beauty – filled with thousands of lakes, islands, cliffs and fjords – and the residents are gorgeous, smart and kindly. There is a flipside of course: lunches (perhaps fancy open-faced sandwiches or reindeer stew) are tasty, but they may make three-course dinners in Paris seem really cheap. The welfare state ensures everyone is comfy, but Scandinavians have to hand over up to 60 per cent of their wages to ensure it coddles one and all. And what good is being so evolved and cultured, when for most of the year they have to brave cruel, icy winds to get anywhere? (Well, those ubiquitous Volvos with heated seats help a lot.) For most Scandinavians it's apparently worth it: they may be world travellers, but as far as moving from home, they tend to stay put in their self-made gardens of Eden despite the teeth-chattering cold, although they might escape to holiday homes a few months a year. In fact, these days the problem for Scandinavians is the opposite: immigration. And the issue has also brought to light what might be the only flaw in what is ordinarily an extraordinary advanced people: many really don't want to share their snowy paradise that for so long has been populated by an ethnically homogeneous people. But experts warn that if they want to keep their cushy welfare states rolling along, they'll have to bring in more immigrants – sooner than later.

The Vikings

They will never be remembered for their delicate touch or flowery names, such as Gorm the Old and Harald Bluetooth. But the ninth and tenth century Vikings – that fierce bunch of bandits in handsome ships – were extraordinary in their ability to sail nearly anywhere, plunder without reservation, and set up popular trading posts. Swedish Vikings headed east along rivers, setting up Russia's Novgorod and Ukraine's Kiev, and ultimately rumbling about in Constantinople and Persia.[1] Danish Vikings headed more to the west, sacking Ireland and filling their bags with stolen gold and art from monasteries, and even roping England into the Danish Empire for a while; the French king got so sick of their invasions that he finally handed them the French north-west coast, called Normandy after the Norman warriors. Vikings of Norwegian extraction colonized Iceland and Greenland and first touched down in Vinland – North America – six centuries before Columbus set sail. The Vikings' brutality was so extreme that they threatened to wipe out Western European civilization in the tenth century,[2] but the trading posts they established (Dublin among them) are today bustling cities and the rune stones that they used as divinatory devices are still being pulled out of cloth bags and deciphered. Even the Viking god Odin is making a comeback with a rise in paganism in the Nordic countries, and, in Denmark, Odinist priests can legally perform marriage ceremonies.

Although they are ethnically almost identical (except for Finland), and speak similar languages (except for Finland), Scandinavian countries definitely have their own personalities, quirks, historical rivalries and agendas. Despite the popular perception of them all being one big happy family sitting around the fireplace knitting beautiful mittens, they often roll their eyes at their Nordic neighbours, and historical rivalries still play out, albeit usually in jokes and sometimes in political banter.

Changing Partners

In the eleventh century Denmark, Norway and Sweden were all separate kingdoms, but in 1397 they were united together as one – the Denmark-dominated Kalmar Union. That lasted until 1523, when Sweden broke away, taking the territory now known as Finland with it. Denmark (which for a while had part of England) kept hold of Norway (which at various points included parts of Scotland and Ireland) for nearly four hundred years until Sweden grabbed Norway in 1814, finally setting it free only in 1905. Finland was part of Sweden for centuries, but was lost to Russia in 1809, and proclaimed independence in 1917. The former Danish territory of Iceland, taken by Vikings back in the tenth century, became independent under the Danish Crown in 1918 and a republic in 1944, and Greenland is trying to go the same way; in the meantime Greenland, while having some autonomy, is still technically part of Denmark, as are the Faeroe Islands.

Their best friends aren't on the shared land mass at all: Denmark is (typically) closer in behaviour and outlook to the Netherlands to the south; Finland has a stronger bond with Estonia across the Baltic Sea. Norway has more in common with Iceland off in the Atlantic, although it still has a sweetheart relationship with Denmark, where Norwegians head for shopping sprees. Sweden pretty much sits in its corner alone, although ethnic Swedes, or rather Finnish Swedes, are still wrapped up in Finland, where Swedes are power players in politics and big biz.

However, they do share many qualities, including that their flags are all the same cross design but set against different colours.

The Similarities

- All are wealthy, social welfare states
- All are technologically advanced economies
- All are predominantly Protestant – although typically less than 5 per cent attend church
- All score high on UN Development Surveys (Norway and Sweden topped it in 2004)
- All are worried about maintaining welfare societies, given ageing populations and low birth rates
- All were homogeneous societies until the 1970s and 1980s
- All have low proportions of immigrants, but are clamping down on immigration

- Although not aggressive, they are all heavily militarized
- All have a secret fear of Russia
- All celebrate the summer solstice with a wild midsummer festival that goes on for days
- All score at the top in rate-your-happiness surveys

The similarity that is most the issue of the moment: their shared fear of immigrants. Scandinavians, who weren't big on colonizing (at least since the Viking days), until recently have never lived alongside people from other cultures, unless you count other Scandinavians – and it's very telling that Scandinavians do. Africans, Middle Easterners, Asians or even East Europeans were rarely found living in the Nordic countries until the 1950s, but mostly in the last three decades, and their numbers have been increasing each year since. So uniform was the culture that the first mosque in Scandinavia wasn't erected until 1984, a controversial construction indeed that triggered the formation of anti-immigrant parties. And while the Northerners (and their governments) can rationally conclude that they will need more immigrants to keep the welfare state in place (for one, with declining birth rates they will soon need immigrant taxes to pay for pension payments) and morally have been willing to take in those fleeing danger, at least some don't want to see 'a darkening' of the Scandinavian future. The issue has spawned a number of radical right-wing parties, some of whom wield substantial power, particularly in Denmark. And in the areas where anti-immigrant feelings aren't manifested in the political arena, there's been a swelling of underground racists, particularly in Sweden.

How xenophobia manifests itself is but one of the areas in which Scandinavian countries are different.

The Differences

- Denmark, Sweden and Norway are constitutional monarchies; Finland is a republic
- Denmark entered the EU in 1973, Sweden and Finland entered in 1995; Norway is not in the EU

- Only Finland uses the euro, and Finland is most enthused about being in the EU; the others are sceptics
- Only Denmark and Norway are part of NATO
- Only Sweden is currently allowing entry to many asylum seekers
- Finland was not long ago run by Russia
- Denmark, Sweden and Norway have similar languages; Finnish is in a different branch altogether
- Denmark used to be the most liberal about everything and still is about drink
- Norway is the richest, thanks to its vast oil fields in the North Sea

Perhaps the best way to distinguish the different Scandinavian nationalities is to note where their citizens feel most at peace. It's said the Swedes find happiness in a sailing boat bobbing off the southern islands in the summer. The Danish find it laughing in the pub (called *kro*) – drinking a bitter (beer) and Gammel Dansk (old Danish schnapps). The Finns find their greatest happiness in the home sauna, and then running naked into the snow.[3] The Norwegians find it on top of the mountain, preferably alone.

Mystery: The Sami

Who they are and where they came from nobody really knows. The enigmatic Laplanders – those Mongolian-like bundled-up nomads who call themselves Sami and inhabit the Arctic fringes of Norway, Finland, Sweden and Russia – didn't have a written history and they aren't ethnically linked to anyone on the planet, although some think they may have migrated long ago from Asia. Now only 10 per cent of Sami carry on the tradition of following the reindeer herd on migration; most of the rest stay put and fish. Their numbers have dwindled to 50,000 or so; although their culture and language were nearly obliterated not long ago, since the 1980s efforts have been under way to preserve their mysterious ways. Tourism in their regions is starting to take off, but the Sami still have tenuous relations and limited rights in Scandinavian countries; developments such as dams have infringed both on their livelihoods and lost-in-time culture. In 1986 Sami got another dose of the modern reality: Chernobyl blew over their homelands, contaminating the lichen that reindeer eat and killing off not only the animals, but nearly wiping out their economy when the sale of reindeer meat was banned.

13. Denmark (Danmark): The Bridge

Fast Facts

Country:	Kingdom of Denmark; Kongeriget Danmark
Capital:	Copenhagen (pronounced Ko-pen-HAYG-en)
Government:	constitutional monarchy
Independence:	constitutional monarchy established 1849
Population:	5,414,000 (July 2004)
Leaders:	Head of State: Queen Margrethe II (1972)
	Head of Government: Prime Minister Anders Fogh Rasmussen (2001)
Elections:	monarchy is hereditary; Prime Minister appointed by monarch
Name of Parliament:	Folketing
Ethnicity:	Scandinavian, Inuit, Faeroese, German, Turk, Iranian, Somali
Religion:	95% Lutheran – less than 3% attend church; 3% Muslim
Language:	Danish; English widely spoken; also Faeroese, Greenlandic, German
Literacy:	99%
Exports:	machinery, instruments, meat, fish, ships, beer
Per capita GDP:	$31,100 (2003 estimate)
Unemployment:	6% (April 2004 Eurostat figure)
EU status:	EEC member since 1973
Currency:	Danish krone
Known for:	Isak Dinesen, H. C. Andersen, troublesome mermaid

Standout Qualities:

Close: Nearest to Western Europe
Close: A society that used to feel like a family
Closed: New government says stay out

Résumé

It's delightfully non-judgmental, it's pragmatically liberal, it's joyfully open – oh wait, that's *old* Denmark. In the past four years the Danish government has done a shocking about-face and has swung to the closed-minded, finger-pointing, xenophobic right. What brought about the change? Previously unscheduled elections called immediately after the September 11 attack on the United States brought in immigration-wary Prime Minister Fogh Rasmussen and also handed substantial power to the conservative anti-immigrant Danish People's Party that before was mostly a fringe group. With both political forces at work, this is the most conservative Danish government in seventy-five years. But the deeper reason for the abrupt shift is the attitude towards immigrants: until the 1970s there were barely any at all. Now they make up some 6 per cent of the Danish population. And some Danes think that's far too many.

A Change in Mood

Denmark's sudden shift to the foreigner-fearing right didn't just happen overnight: it is the result of several recent events that threatened the treasured Danish way of life. Until recently, the place was so lacking material for outrage that people still talked about a child who was kidnapped back in the 1960s (from a pram on the pavement), and the time Danny Kaye visited in 1963 and caused a Danish scandal at the Hans Christian Andersen museum (see p. 389). That laid-back feeling began changing in 1993, when some 18,000 Bosnian refugees fled to Denmark during the civil war in Yugoslavia. Turks and Moroccans had been a Danish minority since the 1970s, when they were invited in as guest workers, but this new wave of foreigners was viewed much more suspiciously, especially by right-wingers such as Pia Kjaersgaard of the Danish People's Party. Many of the Bosnians were not employed and often lived in rough refugee settlements outside the cities, relying on state welfare, and sometimes (or so it was feared) marrying Danes to gain full citizenship. Kjaersgaard was already yapping about the refugees, but initially most of the public simply rolled their eyes at her anti-immigrant tirades. In 1999, however, a 14-year-old Danish girl was locked in a shed and gang raped by immigrant teenagers for hours. She pressed charges, and the highly publicized trial in February 2000 resulted in a guilty verdict for seven of the boys. But the group was sentenced to only nine months' imprisonment: since they'd already been imprisoned for that long, they walked free from court. Danish society was outraged – and Kjaersgaard made it her cause célèbre. In the weeks that followed, swarms of anti-immigration protesters marched through the streets, sometimes accompanied by street violence, a most un-Danish phenomenon. With tension already crackling, the final push to full-strength xenophobia resulted after the September 11 attacks on the United States. Foolishly, Prime Minister Poul Nyrop Rasmussen called a snap election, believing that in the panic of the moment the country would stand behind him. He was quite wrong: his Liberal opponent Anders Fogh Rasmussen (no relation) correctly read the mood and campaigned with the slogan 'Time for a Change' plastered across a photo of the convicted Muslim rapists walking out of court. Fogh Rasmussen and the Liberal Party took the election in a landslide. Another big winner: Pia Kjaersgaard, whose anti-immigration Danish People's Party suddenly made sense to at least 12 per cent of the Danish population that voted it in, making it overnight the country's third most powerful party. The stream-shifting 2001 elections also brought the first politician of non-Danish origin – Naser Khader, of Syrian descent – into the Danish parliament, where one hopes he didn't get stuck sitting next to Pia.

'When she retires, Muslims will be a majority in Denmark. The Danish People's Party. Because we're taking the future seriously' – tagline running under picture of wide-eyed blond child in 2001 political poster for Danish People's Party. The United Nations High Commission for Refugees was so horrified by the racist political campaign slogans of 2001 that it issued a statement condemning them.

Doors to foreigners are being slammed shut, minority populations are targets of scorn, the 'social experiment' called Christiania may be closed down, and Denmark bucked the Nordic trend and keenly supported the war in Iraq, sending in troops. Some Danes are just waiting for the next election, hoping to get the place back to what it used to be, although with a flurry of new laws on the books, the effects of the current administration will not easily be erased. Besides, despite a history of liberal Social Democrat governments, the new right-leaning administration might keep a grip on power. Well, at least they probably won't stamp out cigarettes in their conservative zeal to clean up the country: Danish Queen Margrethe is a chain smoker.

Christiania

The most obvious symbol of the formerly tolerant Danish way is the settlement on the outskirts of Copenhagen called Christiania. Students, artists, hippies and others seeking an 'alternative lifestyle' moved into an abandoned army fort in late 1971 transforming it into a self-sufficient 34-hectare village with its own housing, stores, gardens and restaurants, many of them splashed with neon-coloured paint reminiscent of the flower-power era. Initially wary of the well-developed squat, where no one blinked at nudity and the inhabitants endorsed a world without cars or cops, but with free pot, the government, after many threats of closing it down, decided the community was a 'social experiment' and in 1987, turned the land over to the 'Christianites' – requiring only that the community pay taxes. The alternative community of 1,000, including families with children, became a source of pride to many Danes as an illustration of their open-mindedness, and also turned into a huge tourist draw thanks in part to the hash openly sold on Pusher Street – which was illegal, but which the police typically ignored. In 2003, however, the new government began cracking down on hash sales and announced plans to renovate the lushly verdant, lake-dotted hamlet and turn it into a condominium complex; after all, Christiania spreads over what is now some of the most valuable land in Denmark. Thousands of Danes marched across Copenhagen in protest, but the push is on to bring a screeching halt not only to Pusher Street but the whole experiment.

The first of the Nordic countries to join the EU, Denmark has always viewed itself as the physical, mental and political bridge to the rest of Europe. Lately that's even more the case since the 2000 opening of the Öresund bridge that links Malmö, Sweden to Copenhagen, Denmark – from which one can zip down to Germany. The $4 billion (€3.25 billion) double-decker bridge, a joint venture of the Danish and Swedish governments, was predicted to be a heavily used moneymaker, but thus far it hasn't had the intended result: costing about €30 for a one-way crossing by car, it's too steep for many commuters and most are still taking the ferry. All sorts of unexpected side effects have transpired, however: some Danes are simply moving to Malmö, where housing is cheaper (by half) and Danes who have recently married foreigners won't have to go through all the immigration hoops – at least if they trade in their Danish citizenship for Swedish, which some are indeed doing. The bridge also kicked up a new political movement in Skåne, the Swedish region around Malmö, to become one with Denmark, to which it belonged until the seventeenth century. One more effect of the controversial bridge: Danish right-wingers want it closed down to lessen illegal immigration.

Bridge to binge: Some Danes weren't too happy about the new ease with which Swedes could arrive in the Danish capital Copenhagen. With alcohol expensive and much harder to get in Sweden, many Swedes just swing over to Denmark for a serious night of binge drinking.

Eurosceptics

Denmark has been a member of the European Economic Community (the precursor of the European Union) since 1973, but Danes are not thrilled about being part of today's EU: they see the increasingly supranational government as potentially threatening to Denmark's unique identity and, thus far, they don't want to adopt the euro. Danes intensely disliked the ideas of the common currency and a collective EU armed force, which were presented in the 1992 Maastricht Treaty; when Danes voted on approving the treaty in a referendum, they nearly pulled the rug out from under the European Union by giving it a thumbs down (which would have prevented its passage for all of the EU). After killing the euro and mutual defence force requirements for Denmark, the treaty was given a green light in a 1993 vote. Some reckon Danes may some day accept the common currency, but as for the armed forces, the Danish government looks more to the collective defence offered by NATO. Although it's never been a great fan before – partly because of NATO's nuclear arsenal – Denmark is a loud NATO supporter now – another reflection of the times.

Nato-N-Nukes: Until it made the recent sharp turn to the right, Denmark was quite anxious about its membership in NATO, particularly with regards to the alliance's nuclear warheads, which Danes did not want on their soil – or on their faraway territory Greenland, where the US had army bases. In 1985 the Danish parliament voted to keep nuclear energy out of Denmark and to push the idea of a Nordic nuclear-free zone. One problem: Sweden, due to policy enacted in the 1960s, has oodles of nuclear plants, which it will be decommissioning at some time in the future. In the meantime, the plants are yet another source of friction between Denmark and Sweden.

History Review

If there is one word to describe Danish history over the past five hundred years it is 'shrinkage'. Once the power behind the collective Scandinavian kingdom – the Kalmar Union – Denmark lost Sweden (which took Finland with it) in the seventeenth century, lost Norway two hundred years later, and Iceland sixty years ago. Just as painful was when, after a brief war, the duchy of Schleswig-Holstein was ceded to Prussia (Germany) in 1864, thereby costing Denmark a third of its territory and almost half its people. One result of that geographical severing: the new, smaller Denmark was ethnically homogeneous, having lost the part of Denmark that was ethnically German.

Denmark also has had to part with its navy on several occasions. During the Napoleonic Wars, when Denmark sided with France, Britain attacked Copenhagen, and made off with the Danish fleet – taking it back to Britain as war booty. After Germany occupied Denmark in 1940, Brits (after seizing the Danish Faeroe Islands) also made off with more than half of the Danish merchant navy. When Nazis decided to use a heavier hand in running Denmark in 1943, the remaining Danish fleet ended up underwater: rather than serve the Nazis, the Danish navy scuttled all its ships.

Declaring itself neutral during the First World War, Denmark managed to stay out of most of the action, but the same declaration had little effect in the next world conflict. Nazis wanted control of Scandinavian iron ore (much of it in Sweden) and weren't about to risk Allied forces moving in from the west to battle them over it. Germans invaded on 9 April 1940, and the Danes initially didn't resist them: Hitler had threatened to flatten Copenhagen, and the government instead allowed the Nazis to come in without a fight – retaining at least the appearance of an independent, albeit occupied, country in the process. Food and industrial goods were shipped off for the German war effort – and Denmark had to finance the building of Nazi airstrips and fortifications, but the Nazis generally treated the Danes well, as Hitler admired their Aryan good looks, and planned to make Scandinavians part of the German gene pool. Jews, while discriminated against, were not forced to wear stars and were somewhat protected under the collaborating Danish government, at least at first. Resistance flared up in 1941, after Germany attacked the Soviet Union – angering Danish Communists – and by 1942, when Danish politician Christmas Møller escaped to England and began broadcasting calls to resist the occupation, acts of sabotage and riots were kicking up all over the place; Hitler was furious when the Danish government refused German calls to kill resisters. Already fearing that Denmark was slipping out of his grasp, Hitler blew his top when he was snubbed (or so he thought) by King Christian X. In response to a birthday greeting from Hitler, the king had telegrammed back only three words – 'my utmost thanks' – which struck the Führer as curt; apparently the king was supposed to have added 'Love how you're running my country!' or to at least have invited him over for an akvavit. The so-called 'telegram crisis' triggered a power shift. Within weeks the king was given his marching orders, and a new rigid Nazi government kicked the existing government out of Denmark and called a state of emergency. Soon plans were under way to round up Jews, but those plans were thwarted when the Danish Resistance spread the news in advance. Danes helped thousands of Jews flee the country and escape to Sweden.

> In the darkness of night on 1 October 1943 Danish fishermen helped to ferry some 7,900 Jews to safety in Sweden via a secret boatlift – that much is fact. The rest is hard to pin down: some say that Jews had to pay a hefty price for the trip and that some fishermen actually became quite wealthy from what has long been painted solely as a humanitarian effort. Another very touchy bit of wartime history: at the war's end, the Allies were loath to count Denmark as having been on their side, but Danish diplomats struck a deal: Denmark would go down in history as one of the Allies if they offered Greenland as a site for additional US military bases, including the controversial airbase at Thule. Four US military bases shot up on Greenland and Denmark went down in the books as an ally.

Enduring Legacy on Greenland

Allowing the United States to build military bases on Greenland during and after the Second World War was a costly move for the Danish government. Inuit people, forced to relocate during the 1953 construction of the Thule US Air Force base, successfully sued the Danish government for about €55,000. Although Denmark insisted that it didn't want nuclear bombs stored on or transported over Greenland, the US ignored that – as was evident in January 1968 when a B-52 crashed near Thule carrying four hydrogen bombs, releasing at least a pound of plutonium, although some say it was closer to 24 pounds; one bomb never was found. An increase in cancer among those involved in the clean-up led to another settlement from the Danish government, this one in 1995, for about €12 million. And even though most of the bases are now abandoned – at least one is scheduled to reopen as part of the US missile shield defence plan – the military trash left behind has transformed parts of Greenland into a radioactive, PCB-ridden wasteland. That's only one reason the Greenlanders are weary of the Danes and want to secede.

Quick Tour

Denmark may be flat, but it is very pretty – from the thatched-roof cottages of small fishing villages and white-sand coasts where summer throngs flock in thongs to its elegant green-spired capital filled with high-ceilinged cafés, stylish bars and chi-chi design stores and boutiques. Home of what may be the most gorgeous Caucasian race on the planet, Denmark – which is actually a smattering of 400 islands (97 inhabited) kicking back between the North and Baltic Seas – was historically the alpha-dog of the Scandinavian pack, lording over Norway, Sweden and Iceland, but Sweden knocked it down after a few centuries.

Still holding Greenland in its sway, Denmark technically has the most territory of any country in Europe; if you subtract Greenland, which most Greenlanders would prefer, the splatter of 400 Danish islands is the smallest country of the Scandinavian bunch.

In Denmark the pavements nearly glisten, royals stroll through the streets without guards, locals rarely locked their doors (until recently) and Danes leave their swaddled infants in prams on the pavements when they dart into a shop. The country is more like a family that is 5 million strong: Danes speak what is nearly a secret language, barely understood by Swedes (or so say the Danes), and all it takes is a request from the queen – for instance not to litter – for Danes to honour it.

Fairytale Terrorism

A tribute to beloved Hans Christian Andersen, the Little Mermaid statue on Copenhagen's waterfront is the symbol of Denmark – and a target of violence for the past fifteen years. First hoodlums hacked off the tiny lady's head; a couple of years later it was decapitated again, but the local media were implicated in commissioning that sordid deed. Alas, the beheadings didn't stop there, and each time the government faithfully commissioned another *cabeza*, in between cleaning up the red paint that was often splashed upon the wee gal. But in October 2003 the Little Mermaid was a victim of a much more extreme attack: operatives blew the finned female to smithereens. Oddly, al-Qaeda has not so far been implicated in the mermaid attack, nor has the Danish People's Party yet tied the crime to immigrants.

Historically open-minded about almost everything – the country was the first in the world to legalize gay marriage – Denmark is backpedalling; once liberal about immigration, it is now bolting the door. The issue is very much penalizing Danes as well, particularly those who wish to marry non-Danes. Young Danes are simply banned from taking a non-Danish mate until they are 25. Even those over the age limit have a difficult time: the new complicated procedure requires putting down a €7,000 deposit against any draws off the welfare system (which, for immigrants, doesn't provide full benefits until one has been a resident for at least seven years). While the main concern is the foreign-born sponging off the generous welfare state, the unofficial concern is preserving Danish homogeneity. Six per cent of the population is not Danish – an alarming figure to some, although given Denmark's low birth rate, immigrants will have to pick up the slack in employment in the future if the pension system is to survive.

A Danish woman was arrested in New York in 1989 for leaving her baby in its pram on the pavement while she shopped. The New York authorities charged her with child abuse; she pleaded guilty only of being from a country where that was the norm.

It's understandable why Danes so love the country the way it is, which is to say almost entirely Danish. Besides offering social cohesion, programmes that allow residents to take time off from work to study and change careers, and providing the essentials of a generally worry-free life (socialized health and free daycare are a few perks), Denmark is also one of the most environmentally friendly countries in the world, running Europe's biggest solar-energy plant, developing more wind power than anywhere else and even using biomass for electricity; steam from industrial plants is piped out to heat homes, and entrepreneurs are inventing novel ways to illustrate the potential profitability of being green.[1]

Creators such as the writer Isak Dinesen (Karen Blixen) brought Danish insight and gracefulness to their pages, directors such as Gabriel Axel (using a story by Dinesen) captured the lavish art of Danish dining on film with the masterpiece *Babette's Feast*, and the Dogme 95 team made the shakiness of hand-held movie cameras fashionable worldwide. Even if Danish restaurants are painfully expensive, eating in them is an experience to remember (although things get blurry with too much akvavit), and there is no finer holiday meal than duck cooked the Danish way with cardamom, brandy and prunes. In the winter Danes sip *glögg* – spiced wine with slivered almonds – as they shop at candle-lit outdoor booths; in the summer, they frolic along gleaming island waters, where bonfires glow along the shores, and over a thousand festivals are crammed in to those few luxuriously warm days of the year.

Denmark is home to Carlsberg beer, which traditionally kicks off the Christmas holidays with a day of free brews delivered across the country. The beer labels were once adorned with elephants and, prior to the Second World War, swastikas.

So while there's little wonder why Danes so want to preserve their upstanding country, it's nevertheless alarming when a land that's long been synonymous with 'evolved' now stands out for the shrill squawkings of politicians like Pia Kjaersgaard whose racist comments and attitudes do little to solve very real problems. Denmark has been catching plenty of flak for its xenophobic behaviour of late: in 2001, for example, the government temporarily boarded 300 refugees in container units – boxes used for shipping – providing eleven bathrooms for the hundreds to share.[2] The United Nations High Commission for Refugees was only one agency that swiped at Denmark for that move and for that year's parliamentary campaign which was so heavy on racial slurs that it brought to mind the Nazi occupation. Another of Denmark's loudest critics: Sweden, with whom relations for the past century have never been testier. Even Danes themselves are wondering what to do about the political jam they've got themselves in: the big winner of the 2004 European parliamentary elections was former prime minister Poul Nyrop Rasmussen, a Social Democrat, whose more liberal ways some Danes obviously miss.

Future Forecast

Sooner or later, Denmark will revert back to its typically open-minded self and lift immigration bans, but will probably draw its workers from the Eastern European pool, which will be deemed less threatening. The poor Little Mermaid will continue to be a terrorist target.

Hot Spots

Copenhagen: Elegant waterfront capital that is home to the Tivoli Gardens, Christiania and half a million Danes: property prices are rising as land grows scarce, and fear levels are up too in the normally easygoing, pedestrian-oriented and fashionable city. Copenhagen was the site where on 13 December 2002 the EU announced the ten-member shortlist of who would be joining the club.

> *'Today we have closed one of the bloodiest and darkest chapters in European history – Europe is spreading its wings in freedom, in prosperity and in peace' – Prime Minister Anders Fogh Rasmussen in speech at the historic 2002 Copenhagen summit, the political equivalent of a beauty contest, when the 'EU winners' – the countries that would be allowed admission – were announced*

A Peek Behind the Scenes

In an effort to demystify the European Union and elicit a reaction to the EU besides snores, Denmark put forth a novel idea during the six-month European Council presidency of Prime Minister Fogh Rasmussen in 2002. Video cameras would capture the VIPs as they discussed the affairs of the day, including EU enlargement. When it was broadcast in April 2003, the programme was certainly the raciest picture ever viewed of the backstage world of European politics. Russian president Vladimir Putin was caught calling reporters 'bandits'. Germany's foreign minister Joschka Fischer controversially opined that Turkey would never be a full EU member. Assorted leaders (including Rasmussen and European Commission President Romano Prodi) were pushing each other out of the way as they fought for time on the stage. So embarrassing was the ordeal that it's unlikely that the EU will ever again try such a backstage experiment; rumour had it that relations with Denmark suddenly grew rather frosty as a result of the candid camera.[3]

Agricultural lands: The Dutch are buying them up, complain the Danes: more than half of farms recently sold went to the Dutch, who also control some 15 per cent of Danish dairy farms.[4] The Danes are said to be the world's largest exporters of pigs.

Rising above the Danish coastal town of Helsingør, Kronborg Castle was Shakespeare's inspiration for Hamlet's Elsinore.

Danish prisons: Is it that the guards are often women or that the visitors take anger-management courses or that the lodgings don't have bathrooms? Whatever the reasons, those few Danes who end up in prison tend to not stay long (most are in less than a year) and relatively few come back (a 27 per cent return rate).[5]

Hans Christian Andersen's bed: If you've seen the light-hearted musical movie about Hans Christian Andersen (in which Danny Kaye plays the author and the highlight is the singing thumb scene), do yourself a favour and don't mention it while you're in Denmark, or you'll be getting an earful about the outrageous scandal of 1963, which everybody still talks about constantly. When the American actor visited the famous Hans Christian Andersen Museum that year he did the unthinkable, something bordering on criminal: Kaye jumped right into Andersen's bed! Yes, right

Copenhagen: flat, but high-minded, usually.

in his bed, Danes will repeat, incredulously. 'Well, how would you feel,' explained one perturbed Dane to a Brit, 'if a Dane jumped in Churchill's bed?' Ah, yes, see what you mean!

Jutland: A peninsula surrounded by Denmark's 400 islands, Jutland protrudes from north Germany, and is known for white sandy beaches, windsurfing and music festivals. But the biggest draw is Legoland, the fantasy world of snap-together plastic, where the theme park is made entirely of Lego toys, including the train, which happily hasn't suffered the Little Mermaid's fate, yet.

Greenland: When 'home rule' went into effect in 1979, Greenland hastily bowed out of the EU fearing the Union would eat into its fishing industry, which is the main revenue source on the oversized island. Many of the 55,000 residents, mostly Inuits, on Greenland want independence, complete with mineral rights, since there may be lots of oil offshore; while they are looking for petroleum, perhaps they can come across that lost hydrogen bomb lying around somewhere down there since the crash of an American B-52 in 1968. The ice-capped chunk of land holds 10 per cent of the planet's water,[6] and is home to a US airbase at Thule (whence the B-52 was coming). The US wants to make Greenland a strategic part of its missile defence shield, but that idea, understandably, makes many Greenlanders shudder.

Faeroe Islands: The twenty-two islands lying between the Shetlands and Iceland were yanked into the family by Vikings, and they're still populated by sheep herders and fishermen, many of whom want independence, but they might be dreaming: Denmark's subsidies have been a necessary lubricant to keep the place running. On the other hand, oil is gurgling offshore, and they might be able to make it on their own. With limited autonomy, the islands opted not to be part of the EU – worried that the supranational agencies would start dictating rules for their fishing.

Who knew? The Faeroes are home to the longest continuously running parliament in the world, which first started its deliberations back in the tenth century.[7]

Sweden: The countries have been competitive for centuries, but lately the bickering between Denmark and Sweden about everything from energy matters to immigration has grown louder.

Hot Shots

Anders Fogh Rasmussen: Prime Minister 2001 to present. His campaign 'Time for a Change', with billboards showing the infamous Muslim gang rapists in court, was sensationalist but it effectively hit the panic button, getting not only the Liberal leader into office, but also generating votes for the right-wing Danish People's Party, with which Rasmussen formed a coalition. His government has passed a number of laws curtailing immigration, including that refugees will be deported if their countries are deemed safe, limiting the immigration of clerics, banning marriages to foreigners by those under 25 years of age, requiring hefty deposits for marriage to non-EU citizens and denying citizenship to foreign-born people over 60. Rasmussen, who like many Danes uses his middle name (Fogh) as his first, is certainly fickle: earlier in his career he was a free-market-loving libertarian opposed to the welfare state, but has since changed his tune, although doing a strange imitation of a liberal in any sense of the word.

Rasmussen triggered a hushed scandal in 2003, when he became Denmark's first prime minister to denounce the behaviour of the

Housewife Pia Kjaersgaard wants to tidy up Denmark.

Danish government during the Second World War, when it cohabited with the Nazis, a touchy subject indeed.

Poul Nyrop Rasmussen: MEP 2004 to present; Prime Minister 1996–2001. He may be intellectual, but the former prime minister, a Social Democrat, pulled a stupid move when he called a snap election just after the September 11 attacks on the US, thinking that the people would panic and vote for him. That manipulative ploy backfired when the people voted for the right and extreme right. Guess the Danes missed him: he rebounded in the 2004 European Parliament elections, however, with the Social Democrats collecting the majority of the votes.

Prior to the 2001 election, Social Democrats had been running the show for a decade.

The Danish royal family: Head of state Queen Margrethe, famous for tossing back her head in a hearty laugh, is adored and is so trusting of her subjects that she strolls through the centre of Copenhagen alone, shopping sans bodyguard. A respected painter and illustrator of children's books, Margrethe works wonders with her televised talks to her people, which are not only watched but very much taken to heart. Crown Prince Frederik also mingles with the masses: during his playboy years he was known as the 'Turbo Prince' being often spotted dancing in bars with a fetching model draped on his arm. In 2004 he married Mary Donaldson, a lawyer from Tasmania who isn't a model but looks like one; no word on if they too had to pay the new €7,000 marriage-to-a-foreigner fee. Also respected: Prince Joachim and (perhaps even more) his wife, the lovely Princess Alexandra, of Austrian-English-Chinese heritage, who learned decidedly difficult Danish in about six seconds, and soon produced two male heirs, although that took slightly longer.

Princess Alexandra is the first person of Asian extraction to marry into European royalty.

But Really We Love You, Really We Do!

The queen's family is typically very much shielded in the press. So it came as a shock in 2002 when a Danish newspaper published an item saying that Queen Margrethe's hubby Prince Henrik, a French count, wasn't much respected by many Danes. The reason: he hasn't exactly mastered the Danish language, which, granted, is a demanding feat that involves sticking out one's tongue and making strange gagging sounds. At the news that he wasn't as beloved as the rest of the family, Henrik stormed off to his vineyard in France and refused to return to the queen's palace. It wasn't until the Danish public sent off a mountain of letters apologizing for the media's misdeed, and telling him how much they missed him, that Prince Henrik relented and came back. It's not clear whether his Danish has improved, but surely Princess Alexandra can give him some pointers.

Pia Kjaersgaard: Danish People's Party 1995 to present. The impish house-wife who once delivered meals to the elderly is now dishing up plenty of steaming-hot ethnic hatred. Denmark's most rabid anti-immigration spokeswoman and head of the Danish People's Party (Dansk Folkeparti), Kjaersgaard has suggested that Danes stop offering political asylum, shut down the Öresund bridge, and kick up a 'holy war against Islam' – for starters. The press, at least, appreciates her nonstop flood of controversial statements, including that Muslims are 'bringing a medieval mentality to Denmark'. Like you're not, Pia?

Even if the most famous Dane – Hamlet – was the fictional creation of a Brit, there are plenty of other famous Danes and famous Danish inventions, although the Danish pastry is not one of them: in Denmark they call it Vienna bread.

Danish Star: Tycho Brahe (1546–1601)

Nobleman Tycho Brahe was always a rash, passionate sort: in his youth, he duelled with a fellow student over a maths formula, losing part of his nose in the fight. (Being wealthy, he bought a gold prosthesis, but it was a source of humiliation since it frequently fell off.) When he saw a supernova several years later, he became so hooked on astronomy that he talked the Danish king Frederik II into building him a deluxe hilltop observatory, Uraniborg, where he spent years tracking heavenly bodies and fastidiously filling notebooks with Virgoan detail. The next king found his celestial studies boring, so Brahe huffed off to Prague where he became Royal Mathematician for Holy Roman Emperor Rudolf II, and hired a German assistant named Johannes Kepler. While Kepler stayed at home, poring over his planetary studies, Brahe was usually out partying with Rudolf, and, in fact, he died after one particularly rough night of drinking with the emperor. For centuries it was believed that the embarrassing cause of Brahe's death was that his bladder had burst. Recent DNA tests have shown, however, that Brahe died by accidentally poisoning himself with a self-administered substance used to treat a bladder malady. Ironically, the astronomer was killed by mercury.

Brahe died thinking that the universe was geocentric – the earth was in the centre of it all – but in his vastly complicated model, the planets revolved round the sun. Kepler used Brahe's notes to illuminate the motions of heavenly bodies, becoming far more famous, and accurate, than his employer.

Hans Christian Andersen (1805–75): The son of a shoemaker and washerwoman had but a scanty early education, but was soon pulled to the stage. At 14 he headed to Copenhagen where, while trying to make it as a singer-dancer-actor-artist-playwright, he lived on the streets for three years. Ten years later he sold a musical play performed by the Royal Theatre in 1829. Although he wasn't much loved by critics, and was appreciated even less by women, Andersen found a fan in the Danish king, who funded Andersen's travels across Western Europe. Returning from a long journey to Italy, Germany and France, Andersen set about writing what would make him most famous: fairy tales. By the time he died, he'd completed over 150, including *The Ugly Duckling*, *The Emperor's New Clothes*, *Thumbelina*, *The Tinder Box* and *The Princess and the Pea*; Andersen's works are said to be the world's most translated after the Bible. He also applied fictional technique with a heavy hand when writing his fantasy-filled autobiography *The Fairy Tale of My Life*.

Søren Kierkegaard: (1813–55). Wealthy, well read and a wicked wit at parties, philosopher Kierkegaard was secretly tormented by despair, which led to his ideas about the importance of the individual living his own subjective truth – for which he is sometimes called the 'Father of Existentialism'. In the early 1840s he was on a roll, cranking out books that wove together philosophy, psychology, biblical analysis and literary criticism and had such snappy titles as *Fear and Trembling* (1843), *Either/Or* (1843) and *Concluding Unscientific Postscript* (1849), all of which are still widely respected by philosophers today.

Isak Dinesen/Karen Blixen (1885–1962): Born a baroness, the writer of refined sensibilities insisted upon being referred to by her title, although Karen Blixen, who used the pen name Isak Dinesen, hardly lived a life of contained noble boredom. After her father, whom she adored, committed suicide, her life became a long drama: a love affair with a Swedish cousin soured, so she married his twin and traded in her privileged lifestyle to buy a coffee farm in Kenya, an experience that became the basis of *Out of Africa* (published 1937) as well as *Letters from Africa 1914–1931* (published posthumously in 1978). The marriage between the kissing cousins quickly fell apart (the cad gave her syphilis) and then so did the farm, and that bitter period was topped off when her best friend, a British lord, died in a fiery aeroplane crash not far from her coffee plantation. Suffering from an advanced stage of syphilis, Dinesen was forced to return to her family's estate in Denmark that symbolized all from which she'd once wanted to escape. She was shocked that, upon her return, she was a celebrity. A much-touted but gruelling speaking tour of the US in 1959, when she was a sickly 74, nearly killed her, but she held on for another three years. The author of a half dozen books, Dinesen is now pictured on the Danish 50 kroner note and is the only non-royal to have rated a postage stamp. She is buried at the Danish estate, Rungstedlund, which as per her request has been turned into a sanctuary for birds.[8]

Mariann Fischer Boel: European Commissioner for agriculture and rural development 2004 to present.

Media star: *Copenhagen Post* – 'the Danish News in English': www.cphpost.dk

Cut the Crap: Dogme Films

Reacting to the contrived, formulaic scripts and technological slickness that are the hallmarks of Hollywood, Danish filmmakers in a collective called Dogme 95 embarked on a 'rescue action' in 1995: they wrote a list of their own ten commandments – 'The Vow of Chastity' – among them that only handheld cameras could be used and that the films would avoid special effects, artificial lighting, soundtracks, faked actions such as murders: they even shunned makeup for actors. One film that stands out of the three dozen movies made by the Dogme collective: *Festen* ('Celebration') by Thomas Vinterberg, in which a family reunion for the patriarch's birthday transforms into a scandalous forum for airing the clan's filthy laundry. Like others of the underground group's movies it too became a must-see flick. The popularity of Dogme's films rather defeated their revolutionary aim, as other filmmakers took to imitating the style, and even John Travolta and Steven Spielberg signed on as fans. The collective recently announced it is officially dead, but it appears the individual filmmakers haven't really called it a wrap.

14. Sweden (Sverige): Suddenly Unsure

Fast Facts

Country:	Kingdom of Sweden; Konungariket Sverige
Capital:	Stockholm
Government:	constitutional monarchy
Independence:	6 June 1523 (Gustav Vasa elected king)
Population:	8,987,000 (July 2004 estimate)
Leaders:	Head of State: King Carl XVI Gustav (1973)
	Head of Government: Prime Minister Göran Persson (1996)
Elections:	monarch is hereditary; Prime Minister elected by parliament, 4-year term
Name of Parliament:	Riksdag
Ethnicity:	Swedish, Finnish, Sami, other Scandinavian, Yugoslav, Greek, Turk
Religion:	87% Lutheran; Roman Catholic, Orthodox, Baptist, Muslim, Jewish, others
Language:	Swedish; Sami and Finnish
Literacy:	99% (1999)
Exports:	machinery, cars, paper products, pulp, wood, iron, steel products
Per capita GDP:	$26,800 (2003 estimate)
Unemployment:	5.5% (September 2003 Eurostat figure); often 20% among minorities
EU status:	member since 1995
Currency:	Swedish krona
Known for:	being the envy of the neighbourhood

Standout Qualities

Big: Third biggest EU country in area
Big: Generous to third-world countries
Small: Much of population huddled in tiny villages where strange things may happen

Résumé

The largest of the Scandinavian countries, in area, population and ego, sparkling Sweden, land of snow-sprinkled spruce forests and ice-glazed lakes, used to be hailed as a model society. With low crime, high incomes, an economy that was soaring and a government that picked up the tab for healthcare, daycare and education from the first cry of birth to the last gasp of death, Sweden was the most vibrant example of the 'welfare state' that blended the best of socialism and capitalism.

As part of the country's commitment to lifelong education, any Swede can get government funding (and work space) for 'study circles' when five or more learn a new skill, be it mastering a foreign language, putting on a play or learning how to crochet. Another 'Swedish model' benefit: 480-day maternity or paternity leaves with full pay, and each year a parent can take off sixty paid sick days to tend to their kids.

Designed with an egalitarian eye as a 'home for the people', Sweden taxes high – up to 80 per cent in the top income bracket – but the results have been spectacular: cities are well kept, cultural programmes and museums are well funded, strikes are rare, roads are smooth, and everything from urban squares to apartment laundry rooms are planned in an orderly way. The Swedes can't help but feel rather smug, since for decades theirs was the most successful socio-economic experiment in the world, with Europe's lowest infant mortality rate, longest life expectancy (at least for males), and one of the planet's happiest and wealthiest societies.

Contrary to popular belief, the Swedes do not have a high suicide rate. Their neighbours the Finns and the Danes, however, are quite prone to do themselves in, perhaps because it's so hard to keep up with the Swedes. It's even difficult to compete with them on happiness surveys: 96 per cent of Swedes say they are quite happy or very happy.[1]

Swedish Grace

Lean lines, simple shapes, functional decoration and pale, natural colours are the guiding concepts behind Swedish design, which is renowned in areas from furniture and cars to sink fixtures and glass. Predictably, even the design revolution was planned (more or less) when designers geared up for an international home exhibition in Helsingborg in 1955 that showcased many of the ideas now seen as Swedish, including the modern furniture of Bruno Mathsson, a 'functionalist' considered the master designer of Sweden when he was alive. Swedes actually had been known since the 1920s for the fluid styles known as 'Swedish grace' – a term that implied not only simple elegance, but a hand-crafted product, and in the 1940s that grace made its way to the home when a movement sprang up to marry practicality, loveliness and affordability to glorify the common man's castle. Recently, IKEA took the idea further, flat packaging self-assemble products and selling them in warehouses in 131 countries, making its owner Ingvar Kamprad arguably the world's richest man in the process. Even Bjorn Borg has jumped into the scene: he now designs his own underwear line.

The exemplary country that was the object of media coos and the neighbours' envy was knocked off its pedestal around 1986 when Prime Minister Olof Palme was shot down – an event that shook Sweden to its core, all the more since violent crime was until then little known in the land of 9 million. Not only was the popular leader gone, but so was the Midas touch that the Social Democrats – who had formulated the country's economic model – had exerted on the country, as, for a while, were the Social Democrats themselves. Taxes kept increasing, industry stopped expanding, refugees from Yugoslavia, Iran, Iraq and Somalia flooded in and recession hit hard. By 1994 the 'Swedish model' was staggering so badly it appeared to have fallen off the catwalk: the budget deficit was nearly €100 billion,[2] unemployment, typically around 2 per cent, had soared to almost 14 per cent,[3] industries began shutting down and packing up for Asia, and during the period that was Sweden's worst since the Great Depression, there was suddenly a rash of attacks aimed at immigrants, homosexuals and Jews.

Hitting the Panic Button

Sweden welcomed in foreign workers during the economic boom of the postwar years, but many immigrants have come in since the 1970s. Altogether, Sweden has welcomed over 1 million foreign-born people as residents of the country; now first and second generation immigrants account for 20 per cent of the population. Although many are other Scandinavians, at least 12 per cent of those who live here are not of Nordic stock. Initially, there were few problems – and newcomers such as Chileans found themselves quite popular and easily accepted by Swedes – but beginning in the 1990s, when the Swedish economy took a nosedive, the number of racially motivated crimes blew sky high and simultaneously crimes committed by first- and second-generation immigrants also shocked the country. In the year 2000 alone over 2,800 hate crimes were reported (many aren't), with the majority being perpetrated by Swedes against immigrants. A few of the recent incidents:

* 1991: Neo-Nazis shoot and kill Iranian immigrant.
* 1992: Temporary housing for asylum seekers torched 79 times.
* 1993: In Trollhättan, home of Saab, young racists attack two Somalis and burn down a mosque. Neo-Nazi bands begin gigging and selling over €1 million worth of 'white power' recordings a year; some say most 'Aryan' music comes out of Sweden.[4]
* 1997: University of Stockholm report indicates that about one out of three young Swedes expresses doubt about whether the Holocaust occurred; another report says about one in six listens to 'white power' rock.
* 1998: Dance hall packed with young immigrants catches fire, 63 die, hundreds injured, arson by neo-Nazis suspected.
* 1999: Car bomb injures journalist investigating white supremacist activity; neo-Nazis kill union leader, murdered for trying to replace fascist shop steward; three neo-Nazis rob bank, killing two policemen during robbery.
* 2000: Neo-Nazis fatally stab 19-year-old Turk; seven 'Middle Easterners' rape 14-year-old Swedish girl in suburban Stockholm parking garage; immigrants and Swedes kill 17-year-old Swedish skinhead in Stockholm suburb.
* 2002: Enraged Kurdish father shoots his daughter – execution-style, in front of the family – because she refuses to marry the man he has picked for her.
* 2003: Mosque in Malmö set on fire; reports that neo-Nazis are gathering in forests and planning a 'race war'; police raid houses of six neo-Nazis, prompted by intelligence that they are forming a militia; several death threats to reporters investigating neo-Nazi activity; foreign minister fatally stabbed by Serbian immigrant.

During the 1990s, incidents of rape also skyrocketed, with gang rape believed to be at least a sixth of the approximately 2,000 cases reported each year. The government is considering teaching self-defence to girls in schools.

In 2004 Sweden's crime statistics bureau announced a change in policy: previously they had held back the ethnicity of perpetrators of crime, now they will release it – to counter the misconception that immigrants alone were responsible for rising crime.

On paper the situation in Sweden has improved, at least in some respects: the country (controversially) joined the EU in 1995, the unemployment rate is now under 7 per cent, the deficit was slashed and the government has pumped millions into battling xenophobia. But the reality is that the economy, while improved, is still sputtering, leadership is dithering, membership of the EU is a source of debate and the 2003 vote on the euro brought another defiant '*Nej!*' The fatal stabbing of foreign minister Anna Lindh in a department store in 2003 was just one of many bizarre crimes that have Swedes wondering what has happened to the land long believed to hold the secrets of societal success.

Painful Moments

For a country of 9 million people with a relatively low crime rate, Sweden has had a surprising number of political assassinations. Dag Hammarskjöld, UN Secretary-General, died in 1961 when his plane mysteriously crashed over Northern Rhodesia, an event many believe was no accident, although nobody is sure who was responsible. More devastating was the 1986 assassination of Prime Minister Olof Palme when he walked out of a cinema and was shot while strolling down a main pedestrian drag: that sort of thing just didn't happen in civilized Scandinavia, and his death dominated the headlines for the next year. No one claimed responsibility and no one had a clue as to why he was shot, though conspiracy theories abound. The 2003 attack on kindly Anna Lindh was just as baffling: knifed in Sweden's most famous department store NK, she died a few hours later, leaving shocked Swedes to wonder if she had been murdered for being pro-euro. Her killer was at large for months, but when he was caught and tried in 2004, he said that Jesus told him to kill the foreign minister; others say that the second-generation immigrant, of Serbian origin, was outraged that Lindh had supported the 1999 NATO attacks on Kosovo.

As part of social acclimatization, Sweden may be hitting a few bumps in the road lately, but nevertheless it remains a remarkable country that prioritizes the happiness and health of its citizens, including the young. In the 1970s legislation was introduced that protects children: it prohibited adults from spanking or hitting them, set up extensive abuse hotlines and now even advertising to children is banned. In 1999 Sweden introduced a new law to limit prostitution. It didn't go after the prostitute: it hit the customer with a maximum punishment of six months in jail and a minimum fine of fifty days' wages. As the police and judicial system were determined to enforce the new law, Swedish street prostitution dried up. The country is trying to ensure that women, well represented in government, make such a leap in the private world too. And the national government is seeking environmental solutions by working with local governments and communities – asking them how best to meet goals to reduce energy consumption and solid waste and make Sweden even more green-friendly. In short, this is a country that cares, where neither citizens nor foreigners will be thrown out on the street, and everyone is asked to participate in improving the well-being of all.

In Sweden immigrants who are not Swedish citizens can vote in local elections.

History Review

Sweden may sit back today, a neutral country, viewing international developments with aloofness (at least theoretically), but it used to be in the thick of it all. Mostly forgotten now is that Sweden was one of the great powers of Europe in the seventeenth century, when the country ran much of northern Europe's trade, was forever getting in wars and had territories that stretched into Russia and Germany and across the Baltic Sea.

One reason for Swedish military might: the rich iron-ore deposits in the north and an expertise in producing formidable weapons. But as important as the reason for its many victories in battles against Russia, Poland and Denmark were the effects: Sweden was not a feudal society, and under Swedish rule peasants usually were not serfs bound to their lord's tract, but free men, able to buy and sell land. Another important effect: Sweden introduced literacy to the masses in such places as today's Estonia, Latvia and Finland.

By the nineteenth century continual war had bled the country of its vitality – and when Sweden lost a war with Russia in 1809, Finland went along with the victor. That was a crushing blow – Finland comprised nearly half of Sweden's land, and the two had been united for six centuries. So upset were Swedes by the loss that they hired one of Napoleon's generals, Jean-Baptiste Bernadotte, to (ultimately) become their King Charles XIV, hoping he could grab back the last territory. In 1814 Bernadotte showed up with land all right, but it wasn't Finland – he'd taken Norway, which had just won independence from Denmark. The Norwegians, most unhappy with the idea of Swedish leadership, were granted limited autonomy and their own constitution, and were finally made independent in 1905.

> *Ever since 1814, when Sweden tried militarily to lock Norway up in its kingdom, the country hasn't actively fought in a war. Sweden doesn't belong to NATO, but it does have a well-trained military and plenty of arms manufacturers: the world's sixth largest arms industry has sold killing machines everywhere from Singapore to Iran.*

Surprisingly, given its previous clout, Sweden stumbled into the twentieth century mostly an undeveloped and poor agricultural nation. But thanks to its resources of wood, iron ore and abundant water, it galloped through the century, ultimately becoming one of the richest countries in the world. With the aid of cheap hydropower, Sweden became a centre for steel mills producing, among other things, ball bearings (a Swedish invention), and factories producing wooden safety matches (another Swedish invention).

Devising Frameworks and Inventing Thingamajigs

Is it the cold, the vodka, the fact that during long winter nights there's little to do but stay at home and create? Whatever the reason, Swedes are known as inventors, particularly of systems and handy gadgets, from the cream separator to the adjustable wrench.[5] A few of the big names:

- Olof Rudbeck (the Elder) (1630–1702): Identified the workings of the lymphatic system
- Anders Celsius (1701–44): Invented the temperature system that competes with Fahrenheit

- Linnaeus (aka Carl von Linné) (1707–78): Developed classification systems for animals, plants and minerals
- Fredrik Ljungström (1875–1964): Invented steam turbine to produce electricity
- Sven Wingquist (1876–1953): Invented ball bearings
- Alfred Nobel (1833–96): Invented dynamite
- Ruben Rausing (1895–1983): Invented Tetra Pak drinks carton
- Rune Elmquist (1906–96): Invented pacemaker

Another boon to the industrializing economy: Sweden wasn't devastated during the Second World War. Unlike Denmark and Norway, Sweden escaped Nazi occupation. Exactly how Sweden slipped out of the war pretty much unscathed is a matter for future historians to unravel, but it was more than just waving the neutrality flag, an act that proved ineffective almost anywhere else. Germany relied on Sweden's iron ore, and the ball bearings – instrumental in the construction of arms – which Sweden provided to Nazis during the war. Sweden was also in Hitler's good graces for having allowed Germany to practise military exercises and conduct weapons experiments there before the war,[6] actions which flew in the face of the Treaty of Versailles drawn up in the aftermath of the First World War.

Heroes: Several Swedish diplomats including Raoul Wallenberg and Per Anger helped 100,000 Jews in Hungary escape from the fate of concentration camps. Their methods included setting up safe houses in Hungary officially designated as Swedish libraries and research institutions, as well as issuing protective Swedish passports and smuggling people out. The king of Sweden also convinced the Hungarian leader Admiral Horthy to stop the deportation of Jews.

Besides Hitler's fondness for Swedish good looks – tall, blond and blue-eyed, Swedes were the epitome of the Aryan race – another factor may have contributed to his decision to spare Sweden occupation: the Swedish government was running a clandestine eugenics programme, begun in 1935 and greatly expanded in 1941, that would certainly have met with Hitler's approval; whether he knew about it or was involved in it is not clear since the programme itself only recently came to light.[7] Whatever other elements came into play – not the least of which was the simple desire to preserve the country in an era of gruesome insanity – Sweden, while aiding the Nazi war effort with iron and food, remained officially 'neutral' during the war, serving at points as a safe haven for Jews, as in 1943 when 7,900 fled there from Denmark.

Secret Sweden

Sweden is surprisingly open in many ways: for instance, you can read all the prime minister's mail or access anyone's tax returns. But the Swedish government has been hiding a few dark truths from its public. While its placating role with the Nazis is mostly just ignored, the government's Nazi-like eugenics policy was cloaked in total secrecy until 1997 when Polish immigrant and muckraking journalist Maciej Zaremba displayed the skeletons in the closet. Among his shocking findings published in Sweden's largest and most influential newspaper *Dagens Nyheter*: at least 60,000 women (and men) were forcibly sterilized between 1935 and 1976, many simply for showing gypsy-like features or being deemed of a mixed race by Sweden's state-financed Institute of Racial Biology.[8] The Institute, which first studied hereditary diseases, was part of a plan for social engineering of an optimized society. Danes have admitted to the sterilization practice as well: they are believed to have taken 11,000 permanently out of the babymaker pool.[9] (Also an early proponent of eugenics: the United States, where sterilization programmes were set up in such wholesome-seeming places as Vermont.)

A Swedish government commission later investigating the published claims admitted that the sterilizations occurred, but said only 15,000 of them were forced; it awarded about €17,000 to each surviving victim.

How to structure Swedish society in the postwar era became a subject of intellectual debate that gave rise to the so-called 'Swedish Model', largely influenced by Social Democrats (and Nobel Prize winners) Gunnar and Alva Myrdal, who shaped 'social engineering' and racial policies across the world. Heavily taxing the rich – and the poorer not as much – the Swedish government promoted a 'middle way' between communism and capitalism that emphasized equality between citizens and took care of them all from nursery to nursing home. And for much of the last half of the twentieth century at least, it seemed to work, so well, in fact, that other Scandinavian countries eagerly adopted Sweden's model.

'Human beings are good; we can improve conditions through reforms'
– Gunnar Myrdal in his early writings[10]

Meet the Myrdals: Alva (1902–86) and Gunnar (1898–1987)

She pushed disarmament, free daycare and widening education for the masses, he pointed out that white racism in the US held back blacks and that the key to third-world development was land reform. Together social scientists, politicians and diplomats Alva and Gunnar Myrdal (he was also an economist) were the power couple of social engineering, whose reports, books and ideas had dramatic effects all over the globe. After publication of their 1934 book *The Population Crisis*, both were instrumental in designing the Swedish welfare state that pooled its wealth to maximize benefits for all, both served in Swedish government (she was also ambassador to India) and both won Nobel Prizes: his in 1974 for economics, hers in 1982 for peace. Gunnar was profoundly important in race relations, particularly in the United States, where the Carnegie Foundation had given him $300,000 (about €250,000) to investigate the social dynamics of American life. The resulting book *An American Dilemma* documented the shabby treatment of blacks in mid twentieth-century USA: it greatly influenced the landmark court decision to integrate American schools.

'The world is going to hell in every possible way' – Gunnar Myrdal in old age[11]

Postwar Sweden quickly zoomed to the top of the moneyed pack. Absolut Vodka, Saab, Volvo – and more recently furniture manufacturer IKEA and phone-maker Ericsson – are but a few names that made Sweden a global player. Pharmaceuticals are also big biz: Swedish drug-maker Astra hit the mother lode with Losec, an ulcer medication, which is said to be the most prescribed branded remedy on the planet.[12] Politically, Sweden stood out as well, particularly once Olof Palme stepped in as prime minister. He infuriated the United States (by opposing Vietnam) and Israel (by supporting the PLO) and the government in South Africa (by supporting Nelson Mandela and loudly opposing apartheid).

Olof Palme (Prime Minister 1969–86)

Handsome in a hawk-nosed, craggy-faced sort of way, Social Democrat Olof Palme put Sweden smack bang in the middle of the international power map and wasn't afraid to speak out against anyone or anything. He promoted nuclear disarmament and the rights of South African blacks, he thought that Israel was overstepping its borders in the Middle East and when he likened the US bombing of Hanoi to Hitler's persecution of the Jews, Nixon kicked the Swedish ambassador out of Washington. Although a pusher of peace, the Swedish prime minister who came to power in 1969 also pushed arms to plenty of questionable leaders, including the ayatollahs in Iran, and he was chummy with Cuba's Castro and PLO's Arafat to whom he gave financial aid. Friend of the poor and the powerless, Palme took the idea of universal sharing of wealth one step further, welcoming many from the third-world countries as refugees in Sweden – and in 1985 he insisted that Sweden formally adopt the idea of 'multiculturalism'. Adored by some and loathed by others, he would never have been forgotten, but his assassination in February 1986 made him a martyr – and made Swedish detectives look like fools. Nearly two decades and €40 million of investigations later – the manhunt was Sweden's most extensive ever – Palme's killer is still at large, and even the weapon hasn't been recovered. The most likely suspect appears to be Christer Pettersson, whom Palme's wife, Lisbet (who also took a bullet in the 1986 attack) picked out of an identity parade; in 1989 Pettersson was charged with the murder, found guilty and sentenced to life behind bars. Later that year, the courts overturned the verdict, saying the evidence was too scanty and there was no motive. Pettersson reappeared in the picture in 2001, after reportedly writing a letter to a tabloid writer saying 'Sure as hell it was me who shot [Palme], but they can never nail me for it. The weapon is gone.'[13] The writer went to the police, Pettersson came forward and reportedly confessed, but by then – after the government had concluded an investigation damning the fouled-up murder investigation – the case was closed. Besides, said legal experts, Pettersson's confession was questionable: some said he'd been paid by the tabloid to 'fess up.[14]

Before Palme, a Swedish leader hadn't been assassinated since 1792 when King Gustav III attended a masked ball, where he was fatally shot.

Sweden never again found such a strong voice – unless you count Abba – although likeable Anna Lindh showed potential, and it's said Prime Minister Goran Persson was grooming her to take over his spot. That she went down as Palme did – assassinated in public while without a bodyguard – has underscored both the need for additional security, and the changing nature of Sweden.

Quick Tour

Thick with forests, dotted with lakes, ribboned with rivers and capped with mountains, Sverige is a beauty, as are so many of its inhabitants, about half of whom still live in tiny, snowbound villages with populations of 1,000 or less. The glittering capital Stockholm that drapes over fourteen islands is sleepy no more: artistically charged and technologically wired, it is pulsing with new designers and hundreds of Internet companies, and hailed as the 'new Seattle' by *Newsweek*. On the west coast, Gothenburg is the country's major port and home to Volvo, the sturdy car that eschewed assembly-line production, while Malmö to the south-east is the most racially diverse settlement you can find in Scandinavia, with all the issues that come along with it.

Although it now takes in more foreign-born people than any other Scandinavian country, Sweden typically doesn't grant residence simply for workers. Lately, it takes in mostly refugees and asylum seekers, but certainly not all of them. Of some 33,000 who applied for asylum in 2002, for instance, 78 per cent of the cases were rejected.[15] Those given residence in the country are offered financial aid, free education and language lessons, sometimes in the home.

The Malmö Experiment

Malmö, a port city of 265,000 on the Öresund Sound and the shipbuilding capital of Sweden, is the most dynamic, rapidly changing urban area of Scandinavia. One reason is the gleaming bridge that stretches over to Denmark, completed in 2000 and the first land bridge between the countries. This connector kicked up a flurry of change: new universities have sprung up alongside new businesses and high-rises, but that isn't why Malmö sticks out in the minds of many. Rather, it's the melting-pot nature of the city – a mix of Iranians, Iraqis, Somalis, Pakistanis, Turks, Bosnians, Greeks, Poles and more: in all over 130 nationalities, speaking 100 languages, have settled in to make their home here, mostly in the past twenty years. Some are rapidly employed in the work force while some await word on their applications for asylum, a process that can take a year. Many of the poorer immigrants are pushed to Rosengrad, on the outskirts, where over 90 per cent of the population is Arab, Muslim and/or African and unemployment runs as high as 95 per cent.[16] With as few as 5 per cent native Swedes in Malmö's state school classrooms, this was the theory of multiculturalism put into practice: while some of the locals easily accepted the changes – here you can find Swedes laughing it up with Iranians and Poles – others don't like them at all and in the past few years an increasing trend among Swedes here and in other major cities is 'white flight'. Others are staying to fight the population changes, sometimes via anti-immigrant political parties, most of which came into being after 1984 – a landmark year when the first mosque was erected in Malmö, the first in all of Scandinavia. Unlike Copenhagen across the water, most nationalist and right-wing parties don't do well in elections, rarely making it to local government, where they're usually ignored. On one occasion, however, a referendum gave a hint of how uneasy many feel about immigration: in 1988 Sven-Olle Olsson, of the rural-based Centre Party, initiated a poll in a nearby county asking if people wanted to let in more asylum seekers: a whopping 67 per cent voted no. The reaction from the national government was loud anger, followed by a cacophony of cries of racism across the country. Sven-Olle's party was so shamed that they booted him from their group. Despite attempts to stifle the issue, tension still flares up in these parts: one show was in May 1998, when neo-Nazis attacked police breaking up a march. When sixty of the skinheads were rounded up, police found they were carrying nail bombs. As for Malmö's mosque, it was set on fire in 2003.

Denmark's self-appointed immigration expert Pia Kjaersgaard has been hissing criticisms at Sweden's doors-still-open refugee policy. She calls Swedish immigrant communities 'Scandinavian Beiruts', filled with 'gang warfare' and 'gang rapes' and warns that Sweden is facing an 'apocalypse'. In response, Anna Lindh, Sweden's foreign minister, in 2002 called Kjaersgaard an 'embarrassment' to Denmark.[17]

Although its reputation has been bruised in recent years for not effectively dealing with problems, Sweden at least sometimes tries to tackle its problems head-on. One example: responding to the 1997 University of Stockholm study showing high levels of doubt among one in three young Swedes about the existence of the Holocaust, the government launched an aggressive education campaign about the Second World War and the Holocaust, and published a book about the matter, handing it out free to the public and to schools. The government also set up an Internet site and made Stockholm the venue of an international forum about preventing genocide.

> 'Sweden's situation is absurd: the government has spent millions of crowns on printing and distributing a million copies [of the book] about the Holocaust, yet it is unable to recognize, understand and combat present-day Nazism' – Swedish author Anna-Lena Lodenius who writes about the country's ultra-right wing[18]

On the other hand, the government tended to shut its eyes tightly to growing neo-Nazi activity and evidence that Sweden was quite in the middle of it. After a series of murders and bank robberies by neo-Nazis in 1999, the media were gravely concerned: for the first time ever, editors of the country's four competing papers banded together to demand that the Persson administration wake up.[19] Their coverage included pleas that the public, some of whom had been afraid to testify in court cases, come forward with information about racists and fascists. Under the headline 'They threaten democracy' the papers also listed the names and pictures of sixty-two 'active Nazis'. The media efforts were indeed effective: many of those pictured soon found themselves fired, and so intense was the anger directed at them that some left the movement.

White Power

Nobody knows exactly how many active neo-Nazis are living in Sweden, although estimates range from 1,000 to 3,000, which does not sound many. But these young Swedish racists are armed, organized and increasingly dangerous: they killed at least sixteen immigrants, homosexuals and police in the 1990s alone and recently have been sending out nail bombs to politicians. A dozen neo-Nazi groups, most formed in the past ten years, are spread out across Sweden – from

Karlskrona in the south to Stockholm and small villages in the north – and they run Internet sites and put out dozens of magazines, some printing names and photos of police and journalists on the anti-racism beat and others devoted to weapons and extolling the Aryan race. Swedish neo-Nazis have a knack for making money as well: the two biggest 'White Power' record labels – Ragnarock and 88 Musik/Nordland are located here – and Interpol estimates they now make some €3 million a year. Another moneymaker: concerts of neo-Nazi bands. And if all else fails in the financial department, they simply rob banks and post offices. Another of their schemes: joining the Swedish army to get free training and making off with arms. In late 2003 there were persistent rumours, including from Swedish intelligence, that neo-Nazis are running training camps deep in the forest, and are planning to launch a race war. On a brighter note, at least a few neo-Nazi leaders have quit the movement, some of them defecting to Sweden's very active anti-racist groups.

Now neo-Nazis can get counselling too: EXIT is a support project designed to deprogramme those ensnared in far-right propaganda. Started by a neo-Nazi in 2000, the government-funded scheme has so far helped about eighty neo-Nazis. That number may sound paltry, but a similar programme in Germany after a year had failed to attract more than forty.

Perhaps it's no surprise that cities in Sweden are catching up with the times and turning more violent, although the incidence of crime is still much lower here than in most of Europe. But the small settlements are Sweden's most surprising – sometimes for their quirky charms, and sometimes for their dark acts. The best known of these outposts is Knutby, or at least such has been the case since 2004, when it was revealed that this tucked-away settlement was the home of an evangelical cult.

Small Town Living: Take One

Even though the dominant religion is Lutheran (until recently it was the state religion), the pentecostal faith – a fiery take on Christianity spiced up with visions, prophecies and speaking in tongues – has had a foothold in Sweden for the past century, with 1 per cent of the population listing themselves as active members of the evangelical movement. But never have the hellfire and brimstone sermons been linked with being programmed to murder, until 2004, when news of the strange sect of Pastor Helge Fossmo and 'Bride of Christ' Åsa Waldau gripped the country. The Norwegian-born 32-year-old pastor (believed to have prophetic visions) and Waldau (who took her nickname after a vision of her own) were the religious gurus of Knutby, a tiny town of 585 an hour's drive north of Stockholm that is populated largely with software and pharmaceutical execs. Exactly what was going on there and who was doing what with whom are still not clear, but there's been plenty of interest ever since January 2004 when the pastor's wife (who was also Waldau's sister) was found dead, after being bludgeoned with a hammer, then shot while in bed. The murderer: 27-year-old live-in nanny Sara Svensson, with whom the pastor was having an affair. Not only did the 'seer' predict his wife's death, he was also sending the nanny text messages – from God – urging her to kill. The night of the murder – the nanny's hammer attack hadn't worked, and the mysterious text messages advised her to shoot the wife with a gun – the nanny also shot neighbour Daniel Linde, allegedly another target of Fossmo, since the good pastor was also sleeping with Linde's wife. To judge by court testimony, mind control was part of the soap opera: Waldau accused Fossmo of manipulating her; he accused her of having undue influence over him, and the nanny said living with Fossmo had turned her into 'a robot programmed to kill'. The murder of Fossmo's wife, his second, also brought into question the 1999 death of his first wife, who had supposedly fallen in the bathtub and hit her head. Her corpse was exhumed, and found to contain an abnormally high amount of painkillers. Also questionable: the blow on her head, which experts say could not have happened from a fall. The nanny is now in a psychiatric hospital, Fossmo sits in prison and the village faithful are now calling the pastor a new name: 'Satan'.

Small Town Living: Take Two

On the western edge of Sweden, not far from Gothenburg, the village of Uddebo is best known by its 400 residents for two things: the textile factory that makes luxurious bathrobes and the 'chicken incident', when one of the locals went nutty and whacked grocery shoppers with a frozen fryer. Village meetings, well attended since in Uddebo there's not much else to do, had grown boring, and residents wondered aloud how to liven up the place, and simultaneously put their small village on the tourist map. That's when they consulted Mats Theselius, one of Sweden's best-known designers, and that is also why extraterrestrials may soon be hovering in Swedish skies. His idea: an alien landing strip, circular of course, where extraterrestrials can easily touch down. Although Uddebo was never previously on record as a site of UFO sightings, many of the locals' memories have been jarred by the construction of the work known officially as 'the Uddebo Weave'. As part of the project, a book about aliens will be published as well as postcards to publicize Sweden's first strip built to welcome extraterrestrials to the planet. No word on whether, upon arrival, the ETs will be greeted with a gift of one of Uddebo's thick towelling bathrobes.

Sellouts? Saab and Volvo sold their car divisions to American interests and phone-maker Ericsson recently merged with Sony.

In a country that was racing ahead not long ago, suddenly nobody seems to know where Sweden is heading or what it is doing, least of all Sweden. For all its good intentions and its great potential, of all Scandinavian countries Sweden is the most bogged down with distractions and problems, and at the moment it seems to be treading water. So undefined, ineffective and blurry is Swedish foreign policy and general international image that German newspaper *Frankfurter Allgemeine* called the country 'a dwarf that has become so small it is no longer visible'.[20] Ouch.

Future Forecast

Increasing uncertainty. Immigration issues are bound to cause more racist flare-ups, and who knows if the neo-Nazis will rise up or flicker out.

Hot Spots

Stockholm: A tantalizing tangle of streets, stone stairs, ornate castles and floating hotels, Stockholm is the most cosmopolitan of Scandinavian capitals, a magnet for architects and designers who coo about its international style and French flair. The stateliest of all Scandinavia's capitals

Stockholm: Scandinavian beauty.

and the most wired city in Europe, Stockholm was until recently the first Nordic choice for foreign investment, but now it's losing out to the developments around Malmö to the south and Copenhagen, across the sound in Denmark. However, it still draws in the tourists for the summer Water Festival of concerts and theatre along the city's shores, not to mention plenty of Swedes who head to its pretty islands of white wooden houses to catch the sun.

> *Stockholm suburb of Rinkeby is home to the so-called 'New Swedes' – Turks, Kurds, Iraqis, Iranians, Syrians and former Yugoslavs; the main square turns into a colourful market selling exotic goods, and on Sundays it is encircled by Swedish evangelical types, who sing Christian songs and implore the mostly Muslim locals to see the light.*[21]

Malmö: On the Swedish side of the Öresund Sound, and now a fifteen-minute, €30 trip over the bridge to Copenhagen, this is an epicentre of change, and ethnic sparks fly. Also headquarters for the populist Skåne movement, which wants to reunite this area with Denmark, from which it was chopped in the seventeenth century. For all its woes, many love it and the place is creatively charged.

The federal courts: Decidedly liberal, the Swedish national judicial system recently overturned the sentence on Anna Lindh's confessed killer: instead of life imprisonment, he'll head to a psychiatric hospital for an undetermined stay, a ruling that wasn't very popular. Also controversial: the 1989 decision to toss out the guilty verdict on Christer Pettersson, who had been found guilty of murdering Olof Palme: judges said the evidence was too thin.

Internet Bay: Northern Sweden's answer to Silicon Valley, Internet Bay is the technologically savvy area centred on Luleå that nudges the Arctic Circle; the technology for mobile phones was born here, hundreds of tech companies have launched in recent years and the work force is supplied in part by the Luleå University of Technology.

Clouds: Starting in the 1970s, forests, lakes and fish began dying from acid rain that fell from clouds drifting over Sweden from Denmark and Germany. Worse: Sweden got dosed by the Chernobyl cloud that swung over in 1986.

The laundry room: To make the laundry experience a smooth one, there is a special routine for doing one's washing in apartment buildings in Sweden. The ritual involves signing up in advance for the two-hour spot, reserving it with your key, and washing and drying your clothes in private. Swedes take it quite seriously. After reports that some immigrants did not follow these rules, the government provided laundry-instruction classes for foreign-born people and has sometimes hired supervisors to make sure that rules in the laundry room are followed.[22]

Systembolaget: You have to go to these clinical warehouses during weekdays, wait in line, fill up a form and then pay sky-high prices to procure alcohol, since stores in Sweden don't even sell beer. The nearly prohibitionist system is soon to be revamped, promises the government. But perhaps it's effective as a deterrent to alcoholism: Swedes are among the lowest consumers of booze in Europe.[23]

> *Absolut Absurdity: Sweden is home of Absolut Vodka, but for decades it's been absolutely difficult to buy a bottle of the stuff. All liquor is incredibly pricey, and it's sold only through the state liquor outlet, which is closed at the weekend. A beer in Sweden, for example, costs eight times more than in neighbouring Denmark. (But in Norway*

the prices are even more sobering: a pint of ale goes for €8 (£5.30) and up.)

Barsebäck-1: Located near Malmö and just across the water from Copenhagen, the Swedish nuclear reactor so outraged the Danes that one Danish minister suggested that Denmark grab back the lands lost to Sweden in 1658 if the Swedes were going to mismanage the place so.[24] Decommissioned in 2001.

Nuclear Dilemma

Swedish industry blossomed in the early twentieth century thanks to cheap hydropower, but in the 1960s Sweden invested heavily in nuclear power, which was initially viewed as the clean alternative to the fossil fuel plants in neighbouring countries that were killing Swedish forests and damaging lakes with acid rain. In 1976, however, a referendum demanded that all nuclear plants be phased out by the early twenty-first century. Back then it was believed that they had only a 25-year life cycle, but Sweden's plants appear to have a longer lifetime of at least fifty years, or so say proponents. Even though some are urging that the plants – which cost billions of euros to decommission – keep cranking out energy until they croak to make the most of the investment, political promises resulted in the closure of one of the more controversial sites in 2001 and more are scheduled for decommissioning. Now Sweden, which still relies on nuclear power for nearly half of its electricity, has to decide whether to build more hydropower (banned in the 1970s due to environmental damage) or fossil fuel plants (which will fly in the face of the Kyoto Protocol) or satisfy the increased demand for electricity through the Nordic grid, with at least some juice coming from Russia's shoddy nuclear plants.

The nuclear issue was quite heated in the 1970s: Prime Minister Thorbjörn Fälldin was so adamant about closing all the plants that when forced to compromise on his conviction in 1978, he resigned. Nevertheless, he was back the next year. Sentiments for nuclear energy didn't grow any stronger after Chernobyl's radioactive cloud passed over Sweden in 1986, contaminating cattle pasture and causing a temporary ban on Swedish dairy products.

The Ice Hotel: Every winter in Lapland they chisel a fully fledged hotel – with rooms, bars, chairs, tables and beds made of ice – in the district of Jükkasjärvi. Popularized by Versace and Absolut Vodka, the winter accommodation isn't yet an international chain: nothing irritates a Dane more than if you ask directions to the nearest ice hotel in Denmark, where there isn't one. Don't wait too long to check in: by spring, it's just a pool of melted memories. However, now there's an Ice Bar in Stockholm, where you can toss back Absolut from glasses made of ice: open year-round.

Hot Shots

The royal family of the House of Bernadotte: King Carl Gustav, cousin of Denmark's Queen Margrethe, is perennially the most popular man in Sweden, which is pretty impressive since he's been sitting on the throne since 1973, when he was a mere 27 years old. Holds no power, but is seen as a perpetual do-gooder – he was until recently the international president of the Scouts – and he looks good in full regalia when he presents the annual Nobel Prize in December. Met his queen, a lovely German commoner, Silvia Sommerlath, at the 1972 Munich Olympics, where she was a hostess (some Swedes say she worked at a concession stand); they were married in 1976. The royal offspring are jetsetters, but there has been nary a scandal, except for the time Prince Carl Philip reportedly

Olof Palme: a model Swede.

pranced around naked with his classmates at a religious retreat. You might think far worse if you read the German celebrity press, full of rumours of royal riffs, white-powdered noses and illegitimate babies – so many untruths that the royal family charged in via their lawyers, demanding front-page apologies and admission of fabrications. They got them.

Queen Silvia recently became the most popular woman in Sweden, dethroning Pippi Longstocking author the late Astrid Lindgren, who had previously held the seat nearly every year since her book was first published six decades ago. Also rising in the popularity charts: Crown Princess Victoria, who will someday be the first Swedish woman to ascend the throne. She has admitted to suffering previously from bulimia, due to insecurity concerning her public role, and is now a role model for young people.

Göran Persson: Prime Minister 1996 to present; finance minister 1994–5. The only leader of the traditionally strong Social Democrats to keep hold of a government in Scandinavia since the right-wing craze hit, he is the second most popular man in the country, although perhaps not in the eyes of his ex from whom he was divorced in 2002; within mere weeks he was already seriously dating Anitra Steen, who heads the repressive state liquor-store system, and whom he married within a year of his divorce; oh to be a fly on the wall during their wild afternoons (one imagines) of tossing back Virgin Bloody Marys. It's good to know his love life is doing well, because outside his much publicized Holocaust history project his administration really isn't doing much but holding its own. Between neo-Nazis, immigration issues and increasing violence, Sweden has been slammed with problems recently, and Persson hasn't effectively wrestled with them. Many pundits were open-mouthed that Persson managed to get re-elected in 2001; hadn't they seen the popularity polls?

Although historically dominated by Social Democrats, Sweden inched to the right in the 1991 election, with a moderate administration. That government brought Sweden into the EU, a move that isn't widely applauded and helped open the door to the Social Democrats' return in 1996.

Anna Lindh: Foreign minister 1998–2003. Forthright, funny and popular, Foreign Minister Lindh tried to push Sweden towards the euro and away from its traditional stance as a neutral country. Her term ended abruptly

– just before the national vote on the euro – when she was knifed in a department store.

> Lindh was quite friendly with US Secretary of State Colin Powell, who reportedly remarked that the three best things about Sweden were: 'Abba, Volvos and Anna Lindh.' Lindh remarked, 'Am I only third?'[25]

Henning Mankell: Despite living in Africa for much of each year – he's a theatre director and actor in Mozambique – crime-fiction writer Mankell explores how the Swedish Model has gone flabby in a dozen intricately woven mysteries (*The Fifth Woman* and *One Step Behind* among them) solved by overworked, dogged and diabetic Inspector Kurt Wallender. Top Swedish politicians (including the prime minister) are as drawn to the books about Midsummer's Eve murders, Latvian criminals and ethnic clashes in Skåne as everyone else, although hopefully they aren't among the many who write letters to the Inspector asking for advice.

Neo-Nazis: The unlovable bunch is back and in Sweden they often work in a hard-to-trace manner. When they first began targeting ethnic minorities and those who supported them fifteen years ago, the authorities shrugged them off as a bunch of redneck kids. Not so, apparently: Aryan music record labels and bank robberies (complete with executed police) are reportedly funding the neo-Nazis; investigative journalists, union leaders and politicians have been among their recent targets and murder victims. The government's response to neo-Nazi violence through the 1990s was so lacklustre – even Sweden's ban on swastikas and the Hitler 'heil' often wasn't enforced – that the alarmed public took to the streets demonstrating their dismay. At least one neo-Nazi group has recently registered as a bona fide political party: Nationalsocialistisk Front is said to have 1,500 members.

> In 1979 Sweden banned 'smacking' children, making it the first country to outlaw physical punishment of children, and the law was publicized on milk cartons. While some studies have found that those who grew up without corporal punishment tended to be less violent than those who had been spanked or smacked, other studies have found just the opposite.

Maciej Zaremba: Polish-born journalist who became a Swedish citizen in 1978, and whose investigative reporting for *Dagens Nyheter* has left many with gaping laws. He's uncovered dirt on eugenics, judicial improprieties and welfare misdeeds in some of Sweden's most respected institutions.[26]

Alfred Nobel (1833–96)

Born into a previously affluent household where his father had just filed for bankruptcy, Alfred Nobel fancied writing poetry and fiction, so his alarmed parents (then somewhat richer) sent him to Paris to work with a chemist. There he met the man who had invented nitroglycerine, an extremely unstable and dangerous explosive. Nobel brought the chemical back to Stockholm, where his experiments often blew sky high (his brother was killed during one explosion), until local authorities banned nitroglycerine within city limits. Nobel figured out how to contain it effectively when he invented dynamite, from which he grew wealthy, and his fortune increased further from investments in Azerbaijan's oil fields. While his riches went into starting numerous arms manufacturers worldwide – including Sweden's AB Bofors – he was also attuned to the growing push towards disarmament. When he died, Nobel requested his money be used to set up a foundation that would award the world's highest achievers in assorted sciences, literature and world peace (the last category to be handed out by Norway). His relatives hotly contested the will, as did his lover Sophie Hess, who threatened to publish the spicy letters he'd penned to her. She was paid the equivalent of €100,000 to hush up.[27, 28]

August Strindberg (1849–1912): The man who was to Sweden what Ibsen was to Norway wanted to be an actor, but was so untalented in that role that he swallowed opium hoping to end his life. Instead it launched his new career, when the opiate journey resulted in a play cranked out in four days. The playwright, a misogynist, later convinced a pregnant baroness to dump her husband and marry him, and their stormy union was part of the impetus for his many works that revolve around twisted relationships, among them *The Dance of Death* (1901) and *Miss Julie* (1888), in which she starred.

Strindberg despised Norwegian playwright Henrik Ibsen, although it isn't clear whether the hatred started before or after Ibsen parodied him as a boozing poet in *Hedda Gabler*.

Greta Garbo (1905–90): Husky-voiced and mysterious Greta Garbo just vanted to be alone, and the actress known for her roles in *Anna Karenina*,

Grand Hotel and *Flesh and the Devil*, rarely granted interviews to the raving press. At the height of her career in 1941, she called it a wrap and permanently shut the door to the public, becoming a recluse in New York.

Astrid Lindgren (1907–2002): When housebound with a twisted ankle, Astrid Lindgren conjured up a rebellious adventurer named Pippi Long-stocking, writing up her adventures as a book to give as a birthday present to her daughter. The character had universal appeal: Lindgren wrote more than eighty books, selling over 130 million copies, and in 1999 her countrymen voted her 'the most popular Swede of the century', even though she then lived in Norway. Some fans speculate that her relocation was the reason she never won the coveted Nobel prize from the foundation of her fellow Swede Alfred.

Celebrity Confusion: Ingmar Bergman (1918–) v. Ingrid Bergman (1916–82)

Ingmar is the director (*The Seventh Seal, Wild Strawberries, Cries and Whispers*) who captures the pain and torment in daily life and whose trademark is the dialogue-free half-hour scene of a wretched soul looking out a window. Ingrid was the movie star, cast opposite Bogart in *Casablanca*, who played a holy martyr (*Joan of Arc*) and a prudish nun in *The Bells of St Mary's*, but was viewed as something quite the opposite after she had an affair and a child with Italian director Roberto Rossellini, leaving her husband and child to be with him. She and Rossellini later married and had two further children.

Lars Norén: He used to be Sweden's most admired playwright, but the man known for his dark themes lost kudos when he befriended an imprisoned neo-Nazi youth, wrote a play sympathetic to Nazism, and then cast the neo-Nazi in the production when it played at the National Theatre; the inmate was typecast – playing the part of an inmate. While away from prison, said actor was part of a bank heist, during which two policemen were killed. Not only did the play flop, but Noren was forced to resign as the theatre's artistic director.

Lukas Moodysson: A renegade known to chastise those who give him awards and disparage his fans, director Moodysson is Sweden's most celebrated creator. His films, which range from hilarious (*Together* parodied a 1970s Swedish commune) and moving (*Fucking Amal* concerned a teenage lesbian trapped in a small town) to tragic (tearjerker *Lilya 4-ever* focuses on a Russian prostitute bottoming out in Malmö), outsell any other movies showing in Sweden, and have garnered the filmmaker accolades from all corners. Not that he cares.

Abba: Said to be second only to the Beatles in record sales, Abba got their big break from Eurovision, taking top prize in 1974 for 'Waterloo', which became a chart topper, to be followed in the next decade by eight more; their Stockholm studio was so well appointed that Led Zeppelin rented it to record an album. Abba broke up in 1982, but still haven't gone away: the movie *Muriel's Wedding* reinvigorated CD sales, as did the hit musical *Mamma Mia*. In 2000 the band was offered $1 billion for a reunion gig, but turned it down.[29] Definitely not an influence for the White Power movement.

Zvi Mazel: Israeli ambassador to Sweden 2002–4. The career diplomat often lambasted Swedish politicians calling them anti-Semites and 'anti-Israelis', and claimed that 'there are daily agitators in the Swedish media to kill Jews'. He went berserk in January 2004, at an art exhibition in Stockholm: when he saw the piece *Snow White and the Madness of Truth* – a controversial mixed-sculpture piece of a small boat, with a photo of a female Palestinian suicide bomber, crossing a pool of red blood-like liquid – Mazel threw a floodlight into it. Prime Minister Ariel Sharon applauded the move, as did much of the Israeli press, and at least a few Swedes applauded when Mazel retired two months later.

Margot Wallström: Former European Commissioner for the environment, Wallström is now responsible for institutional relations and communications strategy.

15. Finland (Suomi): The Attractive Outsider

Fast Facts

Country:	Republic of Finland; Suomen Tasavalta
Capital:	Helsinki
Government:	republic
Independence:	6 December 1917 (from Russia)
Population:	5,215,000 (July 2004 estimate)
Leaders:	Head of State: President Tarja Halonen (2000)
	Head of Government: Prime Minister Matti Vanhanen (2003)
Elections:	President elected by popular vote, 6-year term; Prime Minister appointed by President
Name of Parliament:	Eduskunta
Ethnicity:	Finnish 93%, Swedish 6%, Sami, Roma, Tatar
Religion:	89% Lutheran; none 9%, Russian Orthodox 1%, other 1%
Language:	Finnish, Swedish (both official); Sami
Literacy:	99% (1980)
Exports:	machinery, cars, paper products, pulp, wood, iron, steel products
Per capita GDP:	$27,400 (2003 estimate)
Unemployment:	9.1% (May 2004 Eurostat figure)
EU status:	member since 1995
Currency:	euro
Known for:	being silent, Linux system, rally drivers

Standout Qualities

Furthest: Most removed
Faraway: Silent dreamers
Fastest: Behind the wheel

Résumé

The most easterly, historically the poorest, and the most distant Scandinavian country[1] in every sense of the word, Finland is the surprise of the

Nordic lands. Now the former wallflower is the region's up-and-comer, the least corrupt place in the world and one of the top three places to do business, according to the Economist Intelligence Unit; the emergence of companies such as mobile telephone outfit Nokia has boosted its international stature as well. The neighbours are open-mouthed that the Finns are finally opening theirs and talking – mobile phones have made them far chattier, say Finns themselves – and are nonchalantly assuming a much more prominent and attractive position in the world. Another shocker: in 2003 Finland became the first European country to have women as both head of government and head of state. That arrangement, however, fell apart before you could say 'grrrl power' and ended in scandal when Prime Minister Annelia Jaatteenmaki was accused of blabbing state secrets.

Finland was the first country in the world to give women the vote and the right to hold office back in 1906, although it took them until 2000 to elect a woman as president. Females are extremely active in the country's political scene now holding over a third of seats in parliament.

Jabberwocky Jaatteenmaki

When former speaker of the parliament Annelia Jaatteenmaki became Finland's first woman prime minister alongside President Tarja Halonen in April 2003, the country made headline news for having females in both of the highest seats of power. Finland made headlines again four months later when Jaatteenmaki resigned over a scandal of publishing and publicizing state secrets. She published a story on her website using classified information (an act that was illegal), about a hush-hush meeting between former Prime Minister Lipponen and President George W. Bush: Lipponen reportedly pledged support for the US-led war on Iraq, a move which Jaatteenmaki said betrayed Finnish neutrality (as well as the will of the Finns). Accused of leaking the information to the press and of actively soliciting the classified documents, she denied that to parliament, implying that the information just fell into her hands; after being caught up in what appeared to be a lie about her role in getting the info, she simply quit.

One of President Halonen's aides zinged the prime minister when the aide testified before parliament that Jaatteenmaki had indeed solicited classified information from him, contradicting Jaatteenmaki's testimony. Some press reports also intimated that she had used the information about Lipponen to secure her premier appointment.[2]

Always wary of international involvement, Finland did not join the EU until 1995, but, surprisingly, for this part of the world, the country is usually a loud EU supporter, to the extent that Finns are loud at all. Finland is the only one of the Nordic bunch to sign up for the euro, and certainly the only one to gush about the benefits of joining up with the Union – well, at least occasionally.

On the Line

Wireless telecom giant Nokia, a firm that used to make toilet paper, now kicks in 4 per cent to the GDP and is responsible for 25 per cent of Finnish exports,[3] 65 per cent of Finns have mobiles, more than any other population – although almost 100 per cent of teenagers do, so many that some school principals have installed metal detectors because of their ringing distractions.[4] Faring better than Sweden's Ericsson, Nokia has also strengthened the country's ties to Estonia, where the Finnish company has set up plants making phone components.

History Review

Finland's location – at the western edge of the landmass that contains Russia, and just across the Baltic Sea from Sweden – has been the single biggest determinant of its history. For six centuries, Finland was mostly a region of Sweden, and from 1809 to 1917 it was an autonomous duchy of Russia, which helped further to instil a fatalistic outlook and a great thirst for vodka. Its location was dangerous: throughout the centuries, Finnish lands were ripped away by the two powerful neighbours who frequently launched territorial pissing matches.

'Closeness without conflict only exists in the cemetery' – old Finnish saying

Pulled into numerous wars, none of which it initiated, Finland developed a strong national identity in the mid 1800s, complete with a push for Finnish, not the traditional Swedish, to be the official language.

The country finally became independent in 1917, when Finland managed to sneak off from Russia during the Bolshevik Revolution; in what is still a national embarrassment, the fledgling country immediately broke into a civil war. The socialists were the Reds, the bourgeoisie were the Whites, and while the latter won, the former was the dominant colour on the land where the bloody battles took place. Only 200,000 fought but at the end of 104 days, some 40,000 Finns were frozen in snow drifts and icy forests, dead from the brutal slap of winter and their countrymen's hands.

Good Names for Bad Things

Finland wins the award for coming up with the best names for wars and other depressing periods, and no wonder – they've had plenty of them. The Long Wrath (1570–95) was the long drawn-out war when Finland and Sweden battled Russia; during the Great Wrath (1713–21) Finns fought to break out of Russia's temporary hold, and during the Lesser Wrath (1741–3) they rose up again against the Russians who'd taken their turf. During the First Era of Oppression (1899–1905), when their country was a Russian duchy, the Finns tried to overthrow Russian rule and during the Second Era of Oppression (1909–17) they (effectively) plotted how to part permanently from the overbearing Bear. In the Winter War (1939–40), independent Finns drove out Soviet troops with no help from anybody, but during the War of Continuation (1941–4), again against the Red Army, Germans joined in the battles. There isn't officially a Third Era of Oppression, but there should be: from the end of the Second World War to the fall of the Soviet Union in 1991, Finland was indeed oppressed by Russia. Living under the Soviet shadow, Finland was prevented from hooking up with the West (or using Marshall Aid reconstruction funds) and was generally forced to keep mum. It's said that Finnish politicians were loath to answer questions from even the timid Finnish press before clearing the answers with Moscow.

Sweden and Russia left deep marks on the country. While now bilingual, with two official languages – Finnish and Swedish – Finland makes a distinction between those who speak Finnish Swedish (it's less melodic than Sweden's Swedish) and those who speak Finnish; while the former comprise only 6 per cent of the population, they often show up in prominent roles of government and industry. One entire part of the country –

the Åland Islands – is so bound to Sweden that Finnish is rarely spoken there, and there is still some chafing between the two language groups, though mostly played out in letters on newspapers' editorial pages.

One situation where it comes in handy to know Swedish: when you wish to talk about a time beyond the present. Finnish has no future tense.

More important in the past century was Finland's relationship with Russia, which historically can be summed up in one word: compromised. After Finland's 1917 independence, Soviet Russia tried to snatch the land back in 1939, only to be utterly shocked that vastly outnumbered Finnish soldiers – dressed in white and fighting on skis – pushed the Red Army back. Finland was thus able to avoid occupation during the Second World War, although just to make sure the Soviets stayed away they handed over 10 per cent of the land and 20 per cent of industry to Russia. That apparently wasn't enough, however: the Soviets returned in 1941, and since the USSR was part of the Allied team, Finland reluctantly asked for help from Nazi Germany. Even though not aligned with the Nazi cause, and battling for its own self-preservation, after the war Finland was forced to pay hefty war reparations and cede yet more land to Russia.

Asking for German help proved to be troublesome in all ways: after the Nazis helped the Finns beat back the Red Army, the Finns had to battle the Germans, driving them out of the Finnish Laplands.

After the war, Finnish–Russian relations were still tricky: as a buffer country between the West and the Soviet Union, Finland had to perform a delicate dance. To maintain peace along the very long mutual border, Finland was pushed into signing a Treaty of Friendship, Cooperation and Mutual Assistance with the Soviet Union that prevented Finland from becoming too friendly with non-Soviet countries. Officially neutral in the Cold War, Finland agreed to fight for the Soviet cause if invaders entered through the Nordic country, but it was able to distance itself from the Soviet alliance, the Warsaw Pact, and from NATO as well. However, it couldn't risk angering Mother Russia next door, and the self-censored Finnish media rarely reported anything critical about the Soviet Union, with whom the country was also tied economically.

The most dramatic part of that tale was what happened when the Soviet Union fell apart: it took Finland's formerly healthy economy down with it. In the early 1990s Finland tumbled into a recession and unemployment shot up to 20 per cent. Finland pulled itself up, however: the Finnish economy is growing and unemployment has dropped to 9 per cent.

Quick Tour

Land of spooky black forests, the darkest winters and ten thousand sparkling lakes, Suomi has always been the off-yonder Nordic country, whose tight-lipped inhabitants rarely let out a peep.

The cliché: *Two Finnish friends, who haven't seen each other in years, celebrate their reunion at a bar. The barman serves them two shots. The first man says, 'Cheers.' The second man says nothing. The barman serves two more shots. The first man says, 'Cheers.' The second man says nothing. The barman serves them two more shots. The first man says, 'Cheers.' The second man says nothing. After a long silence, the second man turns to the first. 'Look, did you come here to drink or just to chit-chat?'*

The land where not long ago barter was the rule, and peas were served as currency, is booming, recently shoving Sweden aside (temporarily) in the GDP department; rich from its wood, Finland is now being hailed as an international innovator in electronics and telecommunications. The country is welcoming in outside investment and almost one-third of Finland's top 500 firms are now foreign-owned.[5] Once-shy Finland is also stepping up as regional leader, acting as big brother to the Baltic States, loaning money, giving advice, and coming in for weekends of riproaring debauchery.

Finns actually drink less than many Europeans, but when they hit the bottle they hit it hard. Sunday mornings in Helsinki are known for the requisite hopscotching across pavements dotted with puke.

Oh, Finns still have their sombre side, especially in dealings with Russia. Long dependent on Russian oil and energy supplies, Finns are trying to slash that demand now, and in 2002 announced plans to put up a fifth nuclear plant – the first plant to be built in Europe since Chernobyl. That didn't go down well with local activists – in Finland there are two dozen active protest groups – and thousands marched on Helsinki. Tough luck:

even most of the local Greens, part of the governing parliamentary coalition, gave the plant the green light, which only elucidates how much Moscow is distrusted here.

> *Privatizing public properties, too much logging and animal rights are some of the hot issues in Finland. So is globalization: when World Bank president James Wolfersohn visited Helsinki in 2001, he was greeted with a cream pie in the face. The culprit, 24-year-old Markus Drake, a vegan and Green Party leader who wants to see marijuana legalized, defended his action as a non-violent protest. 'I would not have thrown a hard pie,' he told the local paper. Apparently, others would: police recently began donning riot gear, and protesters now sometimes show up sporting ice-hockey helmets.*[6]

Serious Problems

Much of the year is bitterly cold, opaquely black, and even if the snow-coated forests are spellbindingly beautiful (when you can see them), there's not a whole lot to do much of the year except get divorced (Finland shares with Sweden the EU's highest divorce rate), take another sauna (almost every house has one), or eat more herring (it's said Finns eat it in 105 ways). Ferry trips to Estonia to stock up on vodka (and take advantage of the nocturnal entertainment industry) are rather nippy during most of the year and how many mobile phone calls can one make or take in a day? In short, things can get pretty depressing around here, especially during winter's polar nights when in the most northern parts the sun doesn't rise, and many of the country's residents suffer Seasonal Affective Disorder (SAD). So it may be little surprise that not only does Finland have one of the highest suicide rates in the EU (just behind Hungary), but that heroin use is also on the rise.

> *'The mightiest enemy of the Finns is the gloom, the sadness, the bottomless apathy . . . The grip of depression is so firm that many Finns see death as their only salvation' – writer Arto Paasilinna in his 1990 book* Collective Suicide[7]

Finland is still the last frontier: only 2 per cent of its population is foreign-born. In fact, with over a million Finns running out of the country over the past century, it has seen net immigration only in the past decade, with many of the immigrants returning Finns (and a few thousand coming from Somalia and Iraq). While immigration problems aren't a huge deal thus far in Finland, the government recently converted a prison to a refugee detention centre, perhaps expecting a future flood.

> *The country's most important role lately is keeping communication open with Russia, which has not happily watched so many of its former Soviet satellites and republics run over to join the EU and NATO, and is now at the back door.*

Historically the bottom-dweller of the Scandinavian bunch, Finland is coming into its own. EU membership, economic reform and a surge in the electronics industry have shined up the place – and it is now totally plugged in: on a per capita basis Finland is more hooked up to the Internet than any other country.[8] Boasting the allure of the new kid on the block, Finland should soon be emerging as a much more powerful player on the global scene. And now that the Finns are finally opening up, maybe the world can share in the jokes that they are supposedly always making.

> *'We knit socks from herring, scrub our backs with herring in the shower, use herring eyes as shirt buttons, sculpt herring into dainty household ornaments, grind up herring scales as an aphrodisiac, and fill our cars with herring liver oil' – daily paper* Helsingin Sanomat *in a tongue-in-cheek piece poking fun at the Finns' attachment to the fish*[9]

Future Forecast

The latecomer to the party, diplomatic, generous and helpful, Finland will end up being the new Nordic star. Another attraction: its vast stands of timber, which will lure more tourists to the forests, and more industry to the north.

Hot Spots

The sauna: Part of the culture for over 2,000 years, there are over 1.6 million saunas across the land,[10] where Finns sit inside beating themselves with sticks. So adored is the ritual of overheating oneself in rooms of pungent wood that apartment buildings often have one on each floor, and these wood-lined ovens are so frequently used that they were the culprit behind an energy crisis in 2003.

Helsinki: hotbed of saunas, tango and wife-carrying contests.

The dance floor: Finns express their hidden passions on the dance floor, which they rip up with the Finnish tango, a distinctly different form from that in Argentina. Finns have such a thing for the dance-floor drama that night-shift workers can swing and swirl in morning tango clubs before heading home.

Helsinki: The pleasant city isn't exactly filled with skyscrapers or a pulsating nightlife, but it is primed to be the next flame for international investment moths. A mix of old and new, including the concert hall – a ruin topped with a glass roof – and some of the traditions are slow to die as well: women still head down to the piers to wash their rugs in the Baltic Sea.

Russian border: It is long (1,000 km) and fraught with bad memories. Recently, Russia closed the border in Salla – after Finland shut off electricity to Russia. The reason: Russia was $30,000 behind on paying the bill.

Tornio/Haparanda: The tiny Finnish town that serves as an entry into Lappland, Tornio should have been named Tornapart since it was geographically ripped in two by Russia: half of it went to Sweden, while half stayed with Finland (then part of Russia); the two are even divided by time, with Tornio being an hour ahead of its Swedish twin Haparanda.

Now Tornio and Haparanda are reuniting (total population 30,000) and are considering taking the less-than-poetic name 'Eurocity' although the names 'Tornaranda' or 'Hapatorn' – which are not being considered – would certainly be more fun to say.[11] No word on how they'll work out the time differences.

> The 6,000 Åland Islands to the north are tourist getaways in the summer, but politicized all year round. Once part of Sweden, they were seized by Russia in the 1800s; now an autonomous Finnish territory their heart still belongs to Sweden: most residents here refuse even to speak the Finns' language.[12] The all-night party boats that run out of here to Sweden sell duty-free booze.

Men's backs: Finns haul their wives around on them every July at Sonka-järvi's wife-carrying contest.

> **Bye-bye Rudolph:** Reindeer is a common Finnish dish served up sautéed, smoked and sliced, cubed in stew or as a slab of reindeer steak. Hurry and get some while you can afford it: the price is soaring.

Gossip-columnists' desks: The pressure must be on anyone who has to dig up a scandal in Finland: since the revelation that MP Pentti Tiusanen was once an informant of the former East German Stasi secret police, news that the ski team was taking a blood-expanding supplement – and not forgetting the cream-pie incident – pretty much nothing outrageous appears to happen around here, but then again who'd have suspected the goings-on in quaint Swedish villages?

Estonia: Finns by the ferryload glide over here to stock up on cheap booze, and Finnish pensioners are moving to Estonia, where the climate may seem relatively balmy.

Hot Shots

Matti Vanhanen: Prime Minister August 2003 to present. Former defence minister Vanhanen was suddenly yanked centre-stage when PM Jaatteen-maki stomped out of office. Maybe it's for the best: the former journalist is an EU-policy expert, and this is certainly the time to be scrutinizing what they're doing in Brussels. The Centre Party politician has a healthy dash of euroscepticism, and has refused to make a definite commitment of Finland's armed forces to any collective EU military operations.

Tarja Halonen: President 2000 to present. Formerly the first woman foreign

President Tarja Halonen: an
independent thinker.

minister, Social Democrat Halonen has been a fixture in Finnish politics
since 1982. The media tend to berate her clothes and handbags – she
will never be accused of being a fashion icon – but she is definitely an
independent thinker: raised her child as a single mother, and it wasn't
until after she stepped into office that she legally married her common-law
husband. She's also known for her 'colourful language'.

Linus Torvalds

The Finn who calls himself 'Benevolent Dictator for Life', and rather resembles
the penguin that is his personal mascot, Linus Torvalds launched a revolution
when he devised the kernel for a new computer operating system, and recruited
more input from computer nerds around the world. The resulting system, Linux,
competes with Microsoft Windows but unlike Windows, you can download it
free. Quite threatening to those money-grabbing capitalists in Seattle.

Aki Kaurismäki: The Finnish director won the Grand Prix at the Cannes
Film Festival in 2002 for *The Man Without a Past*.

Sweden may be best known for its designers, but Finland, it's said, has better design schools. Two Finns of worldwide renown: Alvar Aalto, whose creative touch extends from architecture to furniture, and fashion designer Marimekko.

Jean Sibelius (1865–1957): Finland's most beloved composer known for his original style and his symphonic poems. Also known as a wit: when a countess complaining of the bad behaviour of the young bragged, 'I've been chaste for close to ninety years and who thanks me for it?' Sibelius replied, 'Well I don't, that's for sure.'[13]

Mieskuoro Huutajat: Who knows if it's pent-up rage or too much vodka that fuels them but the male choir known as Mieskuoro is all the rage in Finland. These Finnish singers don't sing as such: they scream. One of their most popular yelled numbers: the Finnish national anthem.[14]

Tove Jansson (1914–2001): Author of the *Moomin* books about big-snouted, heavily furred trolls (she drew the *Moomin* comic strips that appeared in British newspapers until 1975), Jannson also illustrated some editions of *The Hobbit*.[15]

Olli Rehn: Rehn previously worked as the Finnish prime minister's economic adviser. From 2004 he has been the European Commissioner responsible for enlargement. We imagine he comes in for some ribbing over that.

Media star: *Helsingin Sanomat.* The latest scandals in Helsinki, plus good coverage of Estonia and the occasional hilarious humour piece: Helsingin-sanomat.fi

16. Norway (Norge): The Rich Loner

Fast Facts

Country:	Kingdom of Norway; Kongeriket Norge
Capital:	Oslo
Government:	constitutional monarchy
Independence:	7 June 1905 (from Sweden)
Population:	4,547,000 (June 2004 estimate)
Leaders:	Head of State: King Harald V (1991)
	Head of Government: Prime Minister Kjell Magne Bondevik (2001)
Elections:	monarchy is hereditary; Prime Minister appointed by monarch
Name of Parliament:	Storting
Ethnicity:	Norwegian; Sami (20,000)
Religion:	86% Lutheran (state church); none 10%, Catholic 3%, other 1%
Language:	Nynorsk and Bokmäl (and hundreds of dialects)
Literacy:	99%
Exports:	petroleum, machinery, metals, chemicals, ships, fish
Per capita GDP:	$31,800 (2002 estimate)
Unemployment:	3.9% (September 2003 Eurostat figure)
EU status:	not a member
Currency:	Norwegian krone
Known for:	coaxing peace

Standout Qualities

Pax: Awards for peace
Pass: No to EU
Past: Hasn't had a long one as an independent country

Résumé

The most western of the Scandinavia countries, oil-rich Norge is the wealthiest and the most iconoclastic of the Nordic gang, and it continually gives a big nay to EU membership. All of the Scandinavian countries are praised for their humanitarian work, but Norway commands even louder applause. No other country has worked harder to fix all that is broken: Norway has tried to patch things up with Israelis and Palestinians, the Tamil Tigers and Sri Lanka, FARC and Colombia to name but a few.

> *The Oslo Accords of 1993 stemmed out of a political science class at the University of Oslo. As a class project, students contacted Palestinian and Israeli representatives to suggest meeting and discussing a general peace plan. Both Palestinian leader Yasser Arafat and Israeli cabinet member Shimon Peres were interested and secretly met in Oslo to hammer out an agreement. As usual in this conflict, it all came to naught.*

It is ironic then that the land most known for peace is itself fighting new violence on its own turf, with a sudden rise in murders by neo-Nazis and Asian gangs. The country that was once part of Denmark, then Sweden, is dealing with the most dramatic elements of both. Like Denmark, Norway has a loud populist party that stirs up xenophobia; like Sweden, Norway has been hit by neo-Nazis. In short, Norway, too, with about 7 per cent of its residents foreign-born, is grappling with immigration and its effect in a country that has always been homogeneous. But being Norway, the country said to be the most enlightened in the world in its treatment of women, it is trying a novel approach to dealing with the immigration issue: the government is trying to engage immigrant females, and make sure they learn the language and become part of Norwegian society.

> *The recent rise in crime is attributed to roving street gangs of Pakistani and Vietnamese youths, as well as to young Norwegian neo-Nazis, particularly the so-called Boot Boys. And that has only helped right-winger Carl Hagen's cause: his anti-immigrant Progress Party now makes up 15 per cent of Norway's parliament. But the government isn't merely influenced only by his popularist blather. They've hired sociologists to study why some immigrants aren't integrating. Now some immigrant men are in the hot seat: research says they are preventing their wives and daughters from participating in Norwegian*

culture. At least one immigrant husband was recently prosecuted in court when he prohibited his wife from learning the Norwegian language.

The only Scandinavian country that isn't part of the EU, Norway is most tied to the ocean. Therein lies part of the reason it shrinks from full commitment to the Union: Norway doesn't want anyone making waves about its activities on the seas, including whaling. Besides, Norwegians have built up their country on their own – the Protestant work ethic is so ingrained as to be nearly genetic and its unemployment rate is often the lowest in Europe – and while it is happy to help mediate in struggles from Guatemala to Sudan, Norway isn't so keen on other people telling it how to spend its money. Norway, however, is an associate member of the EU. Part of the Schengen zone, Norway has borders without checkpoints, passports from EU countries aren't stamped, certain trade restrictions are eased, and Norwegians can legally work in most EU countries.

Mistaken Geography?

In early 2003 al-Qaeda's number two Ayman al-Zawahiri made a shocking announcement: Norway, the spokesman warned, would be a target for future al-Qaeda attacks. Norway? What had Norway done, Norwegians (and the rest of the world) wondered. Was it the Oslo Accords when they tried and failed to bring peace between Palestinians and Israelis? Was Osama bin Laden angered by Norwegian hunting of whales? Was it that Norway had notified international maritime authorities about two dozen 'phantom ships' – stolen and repainted – that they believed were part of an al-Qaeda fleet? Many believed al-Z was confusing Norway with Denmark and its populist anti-immigrant party that targets Muslims (and that could explain the recent Little Mermaid explosion: see p. 386). Current thought, however, holds that perhaps al-Qaeda's number two was referring to military activity in Afghanistan where Norway had sent troops or perhaps that Norway is a target because it is a member of NATO and was among the very first of that group to sign up in support of the Iraq war.

History Review

Humans may have first entered these parts following food, in the form of the reindeer, but on their arrival here they had the makings of an extended feast, once they mastered the water that pounded the shore. The North Sea moulded the industries for which Norwegians are best known: ship-building and fishing. But in 1969 the choppy waters off Norway's deeply serrated coast yielded another treasure: vast reserves of oil and natural gas.

> *Norway is now the world's third largest petroleum exporter, behind Saudi Arabia and Russia.*

It must be hard to be Norwegian and not look at the neighbours and secretly think, 'Ha, ha, ha.' Because had Norwegian oil been found a century earlier, the money it yielded might be going into somebody else's piggy bank. For most of its history Norway has been chained to Denmark or Sweden, with occasional interlopings by Germans. Denmark politically bagged the territory in the late fourteenth century and held on for over four hundred years. Norwegians shook loose from Denmark in 1814, and the ink had barely dried on their own constitution, when Sweden came pounding at the door, demanding that they join the kingdom. Norwegians fought back and while Sweden won, it was forced to take them in as an autonomous territory with its own constitution intact. By the twentieth century, Norwegian fishing fleets and shipbuilding had given the country enough money and clout that when it declared itself independent in 1905, Sweden conceded the western property.

> *Monarchy, Square One: The first problem before the new country: finding a king. With no royal family of its own, Norway had to borrow a monarch from Denmark, specifically Prince Carl, who changed his name to a more Norwegian one – Haakon VII – when he sat down on the Norwegian throne.*

Declaring neutrality in the First World War, Norway tried that option again in the second, but the Nazis nevertheless invaded in spring 1940. Resistance was fierce; even though the Nazis successfully pushed in after two months, Norwegian resisters kept sabotaging their plans, blowing up bridges, destroying communication lines and even destroying the Nazis' hydrogen-bomb programme at Rjukan. Norwegians also began wearing red hoods and safety pins – both symbols of Norway – during the occupation. Although it was simply a sign of solidarity, the fashion statement drove the Germans nutty as they pondered if it had a deeper, secret meaning.

The royal family fled to Britain, as did nearly all the royal heads of state across Western Europe, and fascist Vidkun Quisling installed himself as head of the Norwegian government. After the war Quisling was tried and executed. Now a traitor is commonly referred to as a Quisling.

For their feistiness, Norwegians paid dearly: Nazis destroyed many of the northern settlements upon their 1945 retreat and by the end of the war over half of the country's ships lay at the bottom of the sea. Germans left another legacy that Norwegians despised: Nazi babies.

War Babies

Sociologists claim that 'whore babies' – as those 12,000 born of Norwegian mothers and Nazi fathers were called – are the European group that has been more victimized than any other since the Second World War: some say they are still as hated today as the day they were born. Branded inferior and assumed to be retarded, many of these children were sent to special institutions and often humiliated in schools; they were frequently shunned by their Norwegian step-fathers and sometimes sent off to orphanages. Now in their late sixties, some of the group are making the government pay for the decades of indignities. In 1999 seven war babies lodged a legal complaint against the Norwegian government for allowing lifelong discrimination, and more are following suit. Compensation is expected. (Norway wasn't alone in despising Nazi babies: stories are also coming out about the same phenomenon in other Western European countries, including France.)

Rebuilding the country with Marshall Plan funding after the war, Norwegians still have an affinity for the US and a feeling of indebtedness, which (some Norwegians say) was a factor in their government showing such quick support for the 2003 war in Iraq. A large proportion of Norwegians, almost one-third of the country, moved to the US during the twentieth century.

Quick Tour

Its geographical shape and rugged terrain is the key to Norwegian identity. A thin tadpole of land that squiggles up to the Arctic, Norway is so long that its southernmost point is halfway between Hammerfest – at Norway's northern tip – and Rome. Only half a million Norwegians reside in the capital – and of those a quarter are immigrants. Most Norwegians prefer to live in small towns – or sometimes villages of a dozen small houses that look like they were sprinkled around a mountain and abandoned to the wild. As a result, Norwegians have a sense of possessing lots of personal space and of being surrounded by nature at its most stunning. Steel-grey mountains tumble down as if from the sky, collapsing into thick forests and fields of wild flowers before splashing into the icy sea. Jagged cliffs are broken by fjords – glacially-gouged inlets of sparkling deep blue water – and the closer one gets to the Arctic, where walruses and polar bears nap on floating icebergs, the longer are the days in the summer and the more vivid the winter's Northern Lights, the storms of helium molecules that race across the sky on cold nights. And whether you're in Bergen – the gateway to the fjords – or Lillehammer, former host of the winter Olympics, you can't turn around without getting a whiff of nature or the salty sea.

Touchy area: *Norwegians are very sensitive about the whaling issue, and many don't support the activity.*

A Whale of a Protest

Is it their 'singing', their strange, blobular shapes or a sense that these creatures are sensitive and smart? Whatever the reason, most humans – even those quick to stick their fork in a beef steak – have an affinity for whales. And nobody knows that more than Norway, which, after abiding by a ten-year ban imposed by the International Whaling Commission, in 1993 began again tossing exploding harpoons at minke whales, which some experts say are no longer at risk. Waves of hate mail were rolling in from all corners of the planet, but Norway protested that they had a right to continue the whaling practised by their ancestors, although it is a far less important industry now. Whale is no longer a popular delicacy in Norway, where steaks can pile up in the supermarket freezers for years;[1] however, blubber is still a favourite appetizer in Iceland and in Japan it commands a hefty price. Although the industry has tried to portray whale meat as healthy, one might question the effects of consuming it, especially the prized blubber: the top of the food chain in increasingly toxic seas, whales are teeming with hazardous waste – autopsies conducted on beached whales show that the poisons collect in the mammal's fat. Yum.

Modern Norwegians, who routinely top the list on surveys of the world's highest quality of life, have blended both liberal and conservative extremes in their lives, making Norway appear a bit contradictory. Norwegians don't blink an eye at the statistics showing that over 50 per cent of Norwegian babies are born out of wedlock, nor does it matter that marriage is much more popular with gay couples, who can legally wed here. Prostitution, however, is a different matter: legal over the water in Denmark, it is outlawed in Norway. Women, given the vote here in 1913, make up at least 40 per cent of the government (as mandated by law), but possession of drugs including cannabis, however, can land one in jail. Alcohol is even harder to find here than in Sweden: until recently, Norwegians ordered it from a desk in the clinical state liquor store, where no bottles were displayed, as if gazing upon them would be too tempting; in some small villages you can't buy booze at all, since a pseudo-prohibition is in effect. Nevertheless, Norwegians are among the world's biggest boozers and are known for making their own high-octane moonshine particularly in the north, where many lace their coffee with the home brew to start the day.

Even with its oil, Norway illustrates its contradictory nature. The petroleum riches that so transformed the place in the 1970s – overnight making it one of the world's wealthiest countries – haven't exactly been showered upon the people. In a country where, even into the twentieth century, Norwegian fishers were often so poor that they wore only woollen socks in the snow, there's still a sense of disbelief that such wealth is rolling in, and a fear that one day it might all vanish as quickly as it appeared. Most of the billions from oil revenues are squirrelled away for future generations in an offshore Government Petroleum Fund, currently valued at about €35 billion.

Norway's petroleum reserves may peter out by the mid twenty-first century, but supplies of natural gas should carry on substantially longer.

The inaccessibility of the Petroleum Fund is a source of exasperation for some, since Norway's hospitals and schools need investment, and increasing numbers of Norwegians are struggling. Some Norwegians use the term 'welfare state' sarcastically these days: despite the high income taxes they cough up, they still must pay for dentists, which, they will quickly point out, are part of the socialized health plan in Sweden; they also must wait for months to get in the hospital and even then wait in long queues. And even if low-key Norwegians supposedly don't show their anger and don't raise their voices, their eyes do darken when they talk about energy, and the electricity bills that have suddenly shot to €2,000 or more a month.

Long reliant on cheap hydropower, Norwegians were shocked during the bitter cold of 2002: water levels were low, and to save on costs, classrooms were so chilly children dared not take off their coats and gloves; factories closed down, and pensioners who were afraid of the next month's bill died from the cold. Norway is now searching out more sources of alternative energy. Among the experiments: harnessing the power of waves.

Besides underscoring their anger that the oil money is locked away, that winter of 2002 pointed once again to the need for Norway to build new electrical plants, an increasingly tricky issue. Additional hydropower would destroy more of Norway's precious wilderness, and would further devastate fishing grounds for the Sami (Lapps), whom Norwegians are suddenly much more keen about. Natural gas plants, as those in Britain and Germany have shown, can create border-crossing acid rain that kills trees and fish. And Norway is not much interested in nuclear power; already the country is bringing a case against British nuclear waste reprocessing plant Sellafield over its effluent – seaweed washing up on the Norwegian coast is radio-active.

And just one more cause for concern: a rise in racism, apparently prompted by the 7 per cent of the population born outside Norway, although in Oslo the percentage of immigrants is closer to 25 per cent. A few hundred Norwegians, many of them young, identify themselves as racists, and the anti-immigration Progress Party has been gaining in power;

2004 opinion polls showed that one in three Norwegians supported them. There's a growing uneasiness about such matters, and in 2001, when a mixed-race teenager – whose father came from Ghana – was fatally stabbed by two neo-Nazis, tens of thousands of people took to the street to protest against the hate crime. Nevertheless, at least some of the immigrant population is isolated, socially and geographically, and to even get job interviews, some take Norwegian names.

> **Fitting in?** Norwegians say that generally the best-integrated immigrant group in Norway are the well-liked Pakistanis, who came as guest workers in the 1970s, and now own many restaurants and stores especially in Oslo's Little Karachi. Now second and third generation, Pakistani-Norwegians are increasingly present in parliament and in local government, although their kids – like those of the Vietnamese – are beginning to show up in violent gangs. Some of the Yugoslav population, say Norwegians, are drifting more into crime, including drugs, prostitution and moving stolen goods.

It may not be perfect, but Norway still shines: it stands out as a model for trying to better the world and for having more promising results than most. Norway's independent streak may prevent it from ever joining the EU – in 1994 the idea was voted down again by a small margin – but there would be one plus to membership: food. With only 3 per cent of Norway's land farmable, most comestibles are imported and subject to steep tariffs. Food is so much pricier here that to cut expenses, some Norwegians shop in Denmark, loading their cars up with nothing but bacon and booze.[2] Beats following reindeer.

> So frequent are the grocery pilgrimages to Denmark – tour buses are filled with price-concerned shoppers – that they have a name: tacky trips (Harrytur). Every time a politician takes a tacky trip, his photo is splashed across the gossip magazines.

Future Forecast

Any successes Norway makes in engaging the female immigrant population will be copied by all and called 'the Norwegian Model'.

Hot Spots

Oslo: The Nobel Peace Prize is handed out here in the city once known as Christiania, and where a quarter of the population is now foreign-born. Locals aren't pleased by the gangs that prowl suburban neighbourhoods. The city shuts down for the summer and by mid July the streets are nearly deserted. By February the snow turns slushy grey and together with the lack of sun the climate seems to breed drug use among the young and alcoholism in all ages.

> **Get real:** The harsh sentences Norwegians hand out for drugs sure don't seem to be a deterrent: much of the young population indulges in everything from cocaine to ecstasy, and there's recently been such a rash of heroin overdoses that some say Oslo has the worst smack problem in Europe. Politicians refuse to fund a methadone treatment programme for most junkies, saying it is unaffordable here in one of the world's richest countries. Prime Minister Bondevik also wants to raise taxes on alcohol.

Laid-back Bergen: Oslo's urban rival.

The Titillating Outdoors: Norwegians claim they have more sex than any-body, and apparently they are having plenty of it in public places. In 2004 couples were noted having sex outside nightclubs and in front of the library and – as part of an art exhibition – in a see-through tent at the outdoor Quart music festival in Kristianland. The hottest act of the festival, however, was when a couple climbed onstage and began fornicating 'in a variety of positions'[3] during one of the musical acts.[4]

Hammerfest: You can see the Technicolor Northern lights streaming over-head here in the world's most northerly city that travel-writer Bill Bryson made even more famous. However, you don't have to go that far: on a crisp January night, you might observe the spectacle even from Oslo.

Bergen: Postcard-pretty Bergen is the entry to the most magnificent of the fjords. The port favoured by the Hanseatic League, it was historically considered more cultured than Oslo. A mountain isn't all that separates it from the capital Oslo: so does a rather superior attitude.

> *Bergen's wealth first came from timber: Amsterdam is built upon logs of Norwegian wood elevating it from the sea. Italian royalty ordered up plenty of another product: honey. It's said that Norway first intro-duced the sweet stuff to the aristocratic palates of France and Italy.*

Rooftops, minarets and bell towers: In March 2000 the Norwegian govern-ment ruled for the first time to allow Muslims to make their call for prayers in Norway. There were a few catches: Muslims could only call out once every Friday – and the call could only be at 60 decibels, a volume some Muslims called 'a whisper'. Some Christians objected to the ruling, and so did atheists. The Heathen Society protested that religious groups, between their Muslim calls and the ringing of Christian church bells, were making too much of a racket. The government therefore gave them the weekly right to shout from rooftops with loudspeakers, 'God does not exist.'[5]

The Christmas tree: Norwegians claim that they invented Santa Claus and the Finns took all the credit.

The dictionary: Better have a few handy, since there are actually two languages in Norway. Bokmäl is derived from Danish and is the historical literary lingo; Nynorsk or New Norse was created from Old Norse. Just to complicate matters, every village of more than three houses has its own dialect.

Hot Shots

The royal family: Norwegians regard down-to-earth King Harald V as kindly, if a bit dull, and not quite as charismatic as his father the beloved King Olav V, who is still recalled for such things as setting an example by taking the tram during the 1973 energy crisis – and for skiing alone with his black poodle, Rex. Harald's son, the club-loving Crown Prince Haakon Magnus, is familiar to young Oslo dwellers and is well liked, although his 2001 wedding was rather controversial. His wife, Mette-Marit Tjessem Höiby, whom he met at a music festival, not only was a commoner and a former barmaid, she also had a four-year-old boy out of wedlock and the child's father was behind bars for possession of cocaine. That she very openly admitted the situation to the public earned her brownie points, and her popularity is on the rise.

Kjell Magne Bondevik: Prime Minister 1997–2000; 2001 to present. First appointed head of government in 1997, Christian Democratic Bondevik was soon overwhelmed by the job. The part-time Lutheran pastor had to take a month off to soothe jittery nerves, a move that made him more popular with some for being honest; edgy TV shows have been lampooning him ever since, portraying him as an anxious, Prozac-addled addict rattling around in his private drug cabinet – parodies for which he demanded an apology, but never got one. He walked out in 2000 over the ongoing problem of generating more cheap energy – he opposed the idea of gas-powered reactors – but walked back in after the 2001 election. Bondevik signed Norway up in support of the 2003 Iraq war.

Carl I. Hagen: Parliament member, leader of Progress Party. Popular with the older, rural population as well as the urban poor, the populist leader of this anti-immigration party is gathering more steam than ever with his calls to limit asylum to 1,000 foreigners a year, welcome newcomers with HIV tests, cut taxes and slash spending for such useless things as libraries. Known as 'King Carl' to fans, he is a magnet for rotten eggs from detractors.

> *The initial platform of the Progress Party used to be reducing taxes, but in the 1990s the rightwingers began harping on about immigration instead, and by 2000 it was showing approval ratings of 35 per cent. Ratings dropped the next year when a senior party member was accused of raping a 16-year-old girl. The next year the Progress Party got the green light from only 14 per cent of voters.*[6]

Carl Hagen: heating up Norway.

Mullah Krekar (aka Najm al-Din Farej Ahmad): The Iraqi Kurd admits to leading the extremist group Ansar al-Islam when he lived in Iraq, but says he gave that all up in 2002 and moved to Norway. The government here has thrown him in jail twice, but released him, and now he's suing the government. Has had lots of set-tos with Carl Hagen.

> *Norwegian cows have legal rights to take vacations: they're not milked (or slaughtered) for several weeks every summer when they freely roam through the countryside nibbling on moist green grass.*

Henrik Ibsen (1828–1906)

With rosy round cheeks and a fluff of white hair, Henrik Ibsen appeared a jolly fellow, but for much of his early life he was miserable: his family lost their fortune while he was a child, and he screwed up his career plan when he dropped out of medical school. Luckily, someone handed him a pen and from the age of 22 until his death he wrote some of the finest stinging commentaries of the time – twenty-six plays in all. *A Doll's House* (1879), about an ideal marriage that breaks apart when wife Nora unties her apron strings, inspired a feminist movement, which made plenty of men hate him. Even more controversial: *Ghosts*, written in 1881, explored the taboo of syphilis passed from parent to child. Some of his earliest works bombed, but when he was 36, Ibsen received a government travel scholarship which allowed him to write from abroad for the next three decades.

Edvard Munch (1863–1944): The painter whose mother and sister died of tuberculosis was obsessed with death and anxiety. Captured a panic attack in *The Scream*, the painting that most makes curators nervous since it is one of the world's most stolen works. Thieves nabbed it again in summer 2004.

Sami: The formerly nomadic tribe that lives in the more northern extremes called Lapland, the Sami speak a language that is as similar to Norwegian as Russian is to Portuguese, which is to say not at all. Although there were many previous attempts to wipe out their culture, they are held in higher esteem since the 1980s, and now are given considerable political control over the happenings in Norwegian Lapland.

Keiko: The star of *Free Willy*, the world's largest celeb, until recently made his home in a Norwegian fjord after escaping from Greenland, where marine biologists had been trying to prepare him for entry into the wild. Norway didn't really want him, however, since he ate all the fjord's fish as well as the tons of food tossed him by tourists. For several years the unofficial state pet of Norway, Keiko passed away in late 2003.

> ***Typically Norwegian:*** *Tore Kjeilen had an unusual college thesis project: he wrote an encyclopedia about the Arab and Muslim worlds. Now his extensive and fascinating 'Encyclopedia of the Orient' can be viewed on the Internet at http://lexicorient.com*

Gro Harlem Brundtland: Prime Minister 1981; 1986–9; 1990–96. Norway's first female prime minister still is one tough cookie, and currently heads the World Health Organization. She vehemently waves the anti-smoking banner but was surprisingly slow to add the initials HIV to her international vocabulary.

> *In 1989 a documentary on the Norwegian seal slaughter had the whole region up in arms over the brutal clubbing and ice-pick stabbing of the marine mammals. Among the most livid: Sweden's King Carl XVI*

Gustav who called upon Norway's Prime Minister Brundtland to halt the practice.

Einar Gerhardsen: Prime Minister 1945–51; 1955–65. Highly respected first leader of government after the Second World War, the Social Democrat is considered the father of modern Norway. He helped build the country with his motto of 'Everybody to work!' The statues of hardworking Norwegians one sees across the country are a testimony to his spirit and inspiration.

Norwegian Trygve Lie was the first Secretary-General of the United Nations.

Marilyn Monroe: Oh, Americans might think she's one of theirs, but the half-Norwegian Norma Jean is still claimed by Norway as theirs.

Ivar Aasen: Nineteenth-century linguist who trekked across Norway collecting hundreds of dialects, most of which still remain. (How those long winter nights jotting down vowel sounds must just fly!) According to some Norwegians he created the language Nynorsk by 'putting them all in the blender and creating a language juice from hell'.[7] Popularly known as the 'Father of Confusion'.

Media star: *Aftenposten.* Sex in public, abused fish, jail breaks and neo-Nazis on the run: read all about them at www.aftenposten.no, where they also show the latest from webcams posted all over the country.

17. Switzerland (Schweizerische Eidgenossenschaft; Confédération Suisse; Confederazione Svizzera): Icy Seclusion

Fast Facts

Country:	Swiss Confederation; Schweizerische Eidgenossenschaft; Confédération Suisse; Confederazione Svizzera
Capital:	Berne
Government:	federal republic
Independence:	1291 (founding of Swiss Confederation)
Population:	7,451,000 (2004 estimate)
Leaders:	Head of State: President Joseph Deiss (2004) Head of Government: President Joseph Deiss (2004)
Elections:	President and Vice President elected by the Federal Assembly for 1-year term
Name of Parliament:	Federal Assembly; Bundesversammlung; Assemblée Fédérale
Ethnicity:	German 65%; French 18%; Italian 10%; Romansch 1%, other 6%
Religion:	Roman Catholic 46%; Protestant 40%; none 9%; other 5%
Language:	German, French, Italian, Romansch (all four official, depending on canton)
Literacy:	99% (1980 estimate)
Exports:	machinery, chemicals, metals, watches, agricultural products; banking and financial services a big moneymaker
Per capita GDP:	$32,800 (2003 estimate)
Unemployment:	3.9% (2003 estimate)
EU status:	not a member
Currency:	Swiss franc
Known for:	secret accounts, watches, fondue

Standout Qualities

Close: Centrally located
Closed: Barricaded by nature
Closing: New party wants immigrants out

Résumé

Hidden behind mountains, approached through dark highway tunnels, geographically in the middle of everything, but living in a secluded world of its own, wealthy Switzerland doesn't much care for the rest of the neighbourhood or the neighbours' activities. It looks down every so often from its snowy, isolated perch, nearly *tsk-tsk*ing as it waves the neutrality flag; nevertheless, Switzerland sends in its groups such as the Red Cross to clean up humanity's messes, which never seemed to climb over its borders.

At least that's how it used to be. Suddenly the world's problems have penetrated the barriered hideaway, its long-cherished silence about Second World War matters has been pierced, its unquestioned benevolence reviewed, its historic ambivalence challenged, and Switzerland, typically the epitome of moderation, is freaking out.

> *Among Switzerland's many humanitarian contributions to the world was the establishment of the Geneva Conventions of humane treatment of war prisoners (the first treaty was drawn up in 1864) as well as the 1864 creation of the Red Cross – an organization founded by Swiss businessman Henri Dunant who'd stumbled across a battlefield where 30,000 injured men cried out for help.[1]*

What else besides societal panic could explain the rise of billionaire businessman Christoph Blocher, and his very right-wing, very racist Swiss People's Party in this egalitarian, democracy-loving land (where everything is put to a vote), except to say that Switzerland is very much under stress and lashing out at invisible monsters? The twitchiness is understandable: recently Switzerland has been smothered in an avalanche of change that has shaken its identity. Blocher simultaneously galloped in pointing out the scapegoats: the immigrants! The EU! Modernity! The press! Now the message echoing through the meadowed valleys seems to be a loud 'Goooo awayyyy!'

> *Blocher's 2003 campaign was a stinker: one poster called Albanians and Africans drug dealers, another showed a drawing of a black person and was captioned 'Switzerland is going to the negroes.' The campaign was so offensive that the UN High Commission for Refugees condemned it. But that didn't stop Blocher or the Swiss People's Party. Just before a vote on asylum they ran a campaign picturing a pile of passports being snatched up by black hands, and weeks before a 2004*

vote easing immigration, an ad appeared in Sunday papers stating (erroneously) that by 2050 the Muslim population in Switzerland would be larger than the entire population of Switzerland today.

Anti-Group

Switzerland has never been big on international groups: like Norway, it refuses to join the European Union; it won't disclose information on banking clients to the global financial community, and for decades it avoided the United Nations like the plague. That independence to operate freely of international dictates is an integral part of the Swiss identity and is one reason it sometimes peers down from its mountaintops with alarm: Switzerland is surrounded by EU countries, most of which are NATO members as well. And it is under increasing pressure in the globalized world to share its financial information. With secret-shielding tax havens like Luxembourg being prised open forcibly, Switzerland fears that it may be next, all the more so when one major show of Luxembourg washing its hands involved a Swiss diplomat: he was imprisoned after being charged with laundering drug money.

The country that shunned international clubs shocked the world when it finally joined the United Nations in 2002, a change that many found threatening to the Swiss mindset of keeping to their own business; the same year, abortion, long a criminal act, was legalized. Simultaneously, the country was slammed with a series of unnerving reports and revelations that poorly portrayed the country during the Second World War.

Reputation Revisited

Nearly all the benevolent and even-handed accomplishments that have made Switzerland stand out have recently come under close scrutiny: the country's neutrality in the Second World War is sketchy, with reports that there were secret dealings with the Nazis to keep from being invaded. The Swiss have always been the epitome of level-headed ownership of guns – all men are required to keep them, but the country's record of violence is so low that America's National Rifle Association holds it up as an example – but that idea was tainted in 2001 when

Friedrich Leibacher blasted into the local parliament building in Zug and killed fourteen politicians in cold blood. The country's symbol of modern efficiency Swissair suffered after a horrible crash – Flight 111 which killed 229 off Nova Scotia in 1998 – and three years later the airline went bankrupt. And its secret-loving banks, long tolerated by the international community, are under increasing pressure to start divulging more details. Switzerland's reputation as a caring nation, as the country that established the Red Cross and pushed humane standards for wartime behaviour (the Geneva Conventions), was tarnished by recent investigations into the treatment of Jews, who were pushed back from the borders even though the fate that awaited them was known. Switzerland didn't look terribly honourable when it dragged its feet for decades in looking for hidden bank accounts of Jews who died in the Holocaust; it looked really pathetic when banks tried to destroy the records, leaving a caretaker to rescue the truth from the shredding machine. Under public pressure, Switzerland finally admitted to finding some inactive accounts dating from before the end of the Second World War and in 1998 forked out $1.25 billion (€1 billion) in compensation to Holocaust victims – a paltry amount, said some recipients, and far too much in the eyes of some Swiss.

A 2001 Swiss government report also blasted Swiss art dealers for running a wartime clearing house for works of art stolen from Jews, often selling directly to Hitler himself.[2]

That Switzerland would acknowledge a politician who is known for racial stereotyping in his campaigns is odd enough; that Blocher's Swiss People's Party is now the country's most popular may strike some as downright peculiar – particularly given that Switzerland is headquarters for the UN High Commission for Refugees and dozens of other humanitarian groups.

Then again, Switzerland is nothing if not a bundle of contradictions. For centuries this rich country has been running in its own quirky way: Swiss financial deals are shrouded in secrecy while small-town elections are quite public – being taken by show of hand; the country that defends human rights didn't give full voting rights to Swiss women until 1971. The country that preached non-violence mandated that all men be part of the Army reserve, and despite playing a high-profile role in global matters from finance to humane standards of war, Switzerland has always acted like it really didn't belong with the rest of humanity – or want to.

Prepared for the worst: Until 2002 Swiss law mandated a bomb shelter in every Swiss home, and as part of national defence requirements every house had a rifle. There are rumours that tunnels have been prepared so that in a state of emergency the country could geographically isolate itself from the rest of the world.

Switzerland's smug superiority has been battered in recent years as has its typical 99 per cent problem-free environment. The usually vibrant economy stagnated and ever so slightly shrank, its unemployment (briefly) rose to new Swiss highs (3.7 per cent), its beloved banks laid off staff and an influx of Yugoslav refugees during the 1990s pushed the number of the foreign-born population up to 20 per cent.

By 2001 the number of foreigners in Switzerland was nearly 1.5 million compared to 5.8 million Swiss. The largest numbers came from Italy and the former Yugoslavia.[3]

The Swiss reacted with alarm to the increase of foreigners in their land, and not just by barring obviously foreign-born men, particularly dark-skinned or Muslim, from entering some cities. They began listening to Christoph Blocher, a man whose answer to all the country's woes seems to be to close the door, and dig in.

History Review

That Switzerland wants to be alone is nothing new: that was the premise that started the whole country. In 1291 three cantons – essentially counties – bonded together and decided to bolt from the Holy Roman Empire run by the Habsburgs, membership of which had never been voluntary. It wasn't that sort of deal. In several fourteenth-century battles, however, the small cantons proved themselves rather formidable opponents when fighting Habsburg armies on the battlefield, and by 1500 they had shaken loose of the imperial bond. The Swiss Confederation, as the new territory was called, kept growing with most of the neighbours wanting to join the club that was free of royal rule.

Although they may be neutral and in modern history have never declared war, the Swiss historically were among Europe's great fighters. So fearsome were the soldiers that in the fifteenth century they established a rent-a-warrior service, namely the Swiss Guards. Among their most prestigious clients: the pope, who formed the first

Swiss Guard of the Vatican in 1505 – and while guarding the Holy See the Swiss Guards still wear the colourful Renaissance clothes of the time. Other commissions weren't so fashionable. Take the one in France, where they were hired to guard the Tuileries in 1789, just months before the French Revolution broke out. Five hundred were slaughtered when the mayhem was unleashed.[4]

The fragile union between the then eleven cantons looked like it might fall apart during the Reformation. While most cantons remained Catholic, Geneva and several others did not – Frenchman John Calvin (1509–64) was one of the Protestant reformers who made the confederation a home. A refuge for persecuted Protestants, particularly the Huguenots, in the sixteenth century, it transformed into an intellectual centre, and 200 years later it again became a magnet for the cerebral sorts of the day, attracting the likes of Rousseau, Voltaire and other Enlightenment luminaries.

Ironically, although the cantons stayed together during the Refor-mation, Switzerland's Catholic and Protestant cantons did slug it out in 1847 during a civil war that lasted four weeks and killed some 100. The following year the country revamped its constitution, giving more powers to the people to vote directly on all issues before the government.

Even if they knew how to fight, the Swiss usually didn't want to – at least unless they were offered mercenary wages. Neutral before neutrality was a recognized option – Napoleon for one didn't seem to understand the term – the Swiss were conquered by Napoleon's army in 1798. The encoun-ter with the little Corsican left a lingering scar. He drafted Swiss men to fight his devastating battles in the brutal snowdrifts of the Russian front, and of the 10,000 Swiss he led to war, only 700 limped home. At the Congress of Vienna in 1815 that divided up the deposed emperor's lands, Switzerland demanded that it be recognized as neutral in perpetuity. And so it has officially remained.

Switzerland declared itself neutral during both world wars.

Dada

With Switzerland's neutral status during the First World War, the rich, the creative and anybody else who could piled into the country, many of them landing up in Zürich. Agreeing that these were absurd, irrational times – as indeed they were when for four years soldiers shot at each other from ditches along fronts that rarely moved – artists launched a sarcastic 'anti-art' and literary movement that reflected the illogical sentiments of the day. Dada, as the movement came to be known, had only one point: not to make one – or rather to illustrate that society was out of its mind to allow life to have become so twisted. Nihilist themes based on dreams, racy performance art, magazines of collage messages and events such as simultaneous reciting of several poems[5] – which didn't make sense alone or together – were part of the movement that unfolded at Zürich's Café Voltaire and soon spread to Germany, France and across the ocean in the form of stamp art, sculptures of urinals, and Dada 'uncommunities' of poets, painters, writers and performers living, or rather not living, together. Marcel Duchamp, Man Ray, André Breton, Guillaume Apollinaire – and other friends of Picasso – were pioneers of the short-lived movement which laid the foundation for surrealism.

As with Sweden, the other country that remained neutral during the Second World War – or rather whose neutrality Hitler recognized – details haven't fully come to light about exactly what dealings went on, but many Swiss would apparently prefer just to keep that information locked up in one of their tidy bank boxes. Some speculated that the rise of Blocher is a reaction to the international humiliation of the recent government reports that don't paint a picture of the Swiss that chimes with their reputation.

Quick Tour

Snow-sugared mountains, chirping cuckoo clocks, and sinfully delicious fondue: the postcard image of Switzerland is the one most deeply lodged in the collective world's head and the one most likely to drive the Swiss batty. Granted Switzerland, with its alpine backdrop and crystalline lakes, may boast more spectacular views than most places, but while some of them are *Heidi* landscapes complete with bleating goats, well-planned cities of grand clock towers, courtyards and fountains, broken up by sleek modern buildings that don't offend the eye, are part of the palette of Swiss scenery as well. Nevertheless the country chiselled into the Alps doesn't always come up to its wholesome dairy-farm billing of blond-haired, yodelling, do-gooder homogeneity – starting with the fact that the country is split up every which way and often doesn't really function as a whole.

> The federal government in Berne is headed by a presidential council of seven ministers, one of whom is the president. The mostly ceremonial presidential position rotates every year. Berne is also home to the Swiss national parliament. Many decisions, however, are made at the canton level, and almost every canton has its own legislature as well. In some of the smaller villages, particularly in the German north, there aren't curtained voting booths: your vote is cast by raising your hand in the air.

The twenty-six states of Switzerland are carved into distinct ethnic regions with the German Swiss in the north, the French Swiss to the west, the Italian Swiss to the south and a small group of Romansh speakers to the east, all of them talking in their own languages, and watching their different TV news, and typically having their own political bents. And now the country is being subdivided again by billionaire Blocher, who has taken advantage of the anxiety of the era and whipped it into xenophobic fear.

> Blocher came out of the north – the German Swiss region – and the popularity of his brand of finger-pointing right-wing racism seemed to be a geographically isolated phenomenon until recently. In 2003, however, his following swelled in the French Swiss region as well, allowing his party to soar ahead in the ratings – taking 26 per cent of the vote and grabbing the lead as Switzerland's number one party. What's fuelled his rise to power: the many referendums he's initiated that seem to match the pulse of the time, even if no one wants to admit it. His previous initiatives opposed EU membership, UN membership, the Swiss troops in UN peacekeeping, and extending asylum; in other words, when it comes to involvement with the outside world, Blocher just says no.

Direct Democracy

The country considered to be among Europe's most stable economically and politically, is also theoretically the most democratic, given that it has been a direct democracy since 1848 (for men at least; women would not get the vote for another 123 years). What that means is that not only can citizens initiate referendums – including those contesting federal laws – but that everyone votes on just about every issue just about every other month. Should the government cut the bicycle brigade (*yes* said the people), should it abolish nuclear power (*no* said the common man – and woman, now that they finally gave the ladies the vote). Whether it's abortion or asylum policy, rights for the disabled or the introduction of 'car-free' Sundays, cuts in the military or lifting the requirement for bomb shelters in every home, the nay or yea of the people is actively solicited. Perhaps too actively, one might suggest, since there are so many elections that typically less than half of the voters turn out, and there are so many issues (sometimes nine heavy-duty ones at a time) that voters are overwhelmed and confused: the Swiss vote nearly always reflects the official government recommendations. And if that's the case, what's the point?

Although in this diverse land it is hard to make generalizations, two things seem clear: Switzerland is changing too fast for many citizens' tastes, and as a result the government is veering sharply to the right. That Blocher bullied his way in as justice minister is raising quite a few eyebrows, particularly at the United Nation's High Commission for Refugees, which frequently delivers Blocher condemnations and warnings about his racist campaigning and more importantly his policies on asylum, which come under his jurisdiction as justice minister. Blocher in turn is now raising the issue of when the UN has the right to butt in – and with regards to Switzerland's membership of the UN, which he opposed back in the 2002 vote, it wouldn't be surprising to see Blocher someday lead Switzerland right out.

In September 2004 Blocher proposed that potential refugees wanting to relocate in Switzerland be shipped to refuge camps abroad – a controversial idea (proposed by other European countries as well) that may violate international law. Under Blocher's scheme the UN would have responsibility for screening refugees and allocating them to

European countries[6] – an idea that perhaps has merit but appeared to be designed simply to give his foes at the UNHCR more work.

As for the EU, don't expect to see the Swiss come on board anytime soon. In this hunker down and bolt the door era, the very concept of taking orders from outside is so anathema that no politician will even publicly mention the possibility of Switzerland ever reaching out towards Brussels. Pundits say that for a politician to use the words 'Switzerland' and 'EU membership' in one sentence is the kiss of death.[7]

Future Forecast

Fortress Switzerland will soon be erected and under Blocher Switzerland won't give a hoot about international law.

Hot Spots

Zürich: In the German part of Switzerland, Zürich – the country's most populous city – is rated the best city to live in in the world and the birthplace of Dada still maintains a lively arts scene.

Geneva: Headquarters for the United Nations High Commission for Refugees and the Red Cross, the lovely lake-nudging city is filled with museums and government types, and parts of it are little changed from the days when Calvin preached here.

Berne: Cradled by mountains and thick with trees, it's easy to forget that bureaucratic affairs are the mainstay of this capital city.

Banks: Blind accounts and banks you can trust with your secrets are just two of the reasons the world's wealthiest and scariest like to hide their money here.

The slopes: Best skiing anywhere, say the rich, who are the only ones who can afford it.

The appointment book: Better use it here. Never call at a Swiss friend's house without first setting up an appointment. Just dropping in is considered quite rude.

The loo: In apartment buildings, it's against the law to flush the toilet after midnight.

Zürich: capital of Dada.

Hot Shots

Christoph Blocher: Billions can't buy you love, but they certainly can help buy you power, as evidenced by several politicians whose names begin with B: Berlusconi, Bush and now, Blocher. The man is definitely skilled at multi-tasking: the passionate orator actually built both his political reputation and his industrial empire simultaneously. He was still in his thirties when elected to the national parliament, and at 43 he bought out EMS, a huge plastics operation that shot him to the top ten list of Switzerland's richest people.

His years of heading companies have created a slick, confident persona, but who knows what really lies underneath: does he really think immigrants are the problem or is he exploiting the times as a part of his rise to power? Whatever his true motives, his popularity has clearly illustrated the fact that, when scared, many run to the black and white answers of the right.

Winning 26 per cent in the 2003 elections, Blocher had enough clout to demand that the seven-person presidential committee give another seat to his party, which already held one. In the process the man who has no legal training became, scarily, Switzerland's justice minister.

The Swiss People's Party was formerly a small farmers' party that Blocher refashioned. The headman pushed aside the more moderate members and leapt to the radical right. The party is now against the UN, against the EU, against immigrants, and against welfare. One thing they are for, however, is giving more power to the shareholder.

Paracelsus (1493–1541): Cranky but brilliant Paracelsus (the name he took because his real one – Theophrastus Bombastus von Hohenheim – was too long) was a profoundly important Swiss physician and alchemist. He thought 'modern medicine' – which believed that disease was the result of bile and phlegm – was bunk: when he became official physician of Basel he made a bonfire of all the current medical books. Instead, he realized that disease occurred because of exposure to outside agents – i.e. viruses and germs. He coined the term alcohol, was obsessed with the curative powers of zinc, and is now considered the father of pharmacology as he

Billionaire Blocher: dreaming of a new, immigrant-free Switzerland.

turned from the direction of alchemy to chemistry and the making of drugs, being the first to add opium to his cures.

The Order of the Solar Temple: Mysterious doomsday cult that was uncovered in 1994 when fifty-three bodies were found in a chalet and a barn in southern Switzerland. At first believed to be a suicide pact, the deaths, or at least some of them, later looked like possible murders given that the bodies had as many as eight bullets in the head.[8] Questions are still unanswered about this bizarre event: cult leader Luc Jouret was among the dead.

Media star: Swissinfo. What Blocher's done this week and the other issues of the day in English at 'Switzerland's news and information platform': www.swissinfo.org

18. Luxembourg: Sleeping Beauty

Fast Facts

Country:	Grand Duchy of Luxembourg; Grand Duché de Luxembourg
Capital:	Luxembourg
Government:	constitutional monarchy
Independence:	1839 (from the Netherlands); full independence 1867
Population:	463,000 (2003 estimate)
Leaders:	Head of State: Grand Duke Henri (2000)
	Head of Government: Prime Minister Jean-Claude Juncker (1995)
Elections:	monarchy is hereditary: Prime Minister appointed by monarch for 5-year term
Name of Parliament:	Chamber of Deputies; Chambre des Députés
Ethnicity:	Celtic base; one-third residents foreign-born, many from Portugal
Religion:	Roman Catholic 86%; Protestant 13%; also Jewish and Muslim
Language:	Luxembourgish (national language); German and French
Literacy:	99% (2003 estimate)
Exports:	machinery, steel products, chemicals, rubber products; most money comes from banking and financial services
Per capita GDP:	$55,100 (2003 estimate)
Unemployment:	4.2% (May 2004 Eurostat figure)
EU status:	founding member EEC
Currency:	euro
Known for:	EU institutions, Radio Luxembourg

Standout Qualities

Little: EU-15's smallest
Big: Financial heavyweight
Invisible: Hidden dealings

Résumé

Home to the European Court of Justice and a half dozen other EU institutions, Luxembourg is easily the most joked-about country in Western Europe: formerly the tiniest Union member (a position now occupied by Malta), the grand duchy that is 32 miles wide and 51 miles long, appears (to those who haven't been there) to be nothing but a big banking machine in a small boring land. But why should Luxembourgers care what the rest of the world thinks: theirs is the richest country in the EU, and Luxembourg with its lush forests and castled hills is one of the prettiest. Luxembourgers are the wealthiest people in the world, and in their fair land you can find the EU's lowest unemployment rate. So what if everybody mixes Luxembourg up with Liechtenstein or the same-named region in Belgium? So what if nobody outside their country speaks their beloved Luxembourgish? So what if few realize how hard it was for the country that is scarcely bigger than London to maintain independence over the centuries? It just makes the place all the more special to the Luxembourgers whose country is more like an exclusive, albeit friendly, club.

Luxembourg leads the world in providing financial aid to developing countries and charities, giving over 0.8% of its GDP to humanitarian causes.

Luxembourg v. Luxembourg v. Luxembourg City v. Liechtenstein

Luxembourg is a rich, independent country, which is one of the world's major financial centres; its capital is Luxembourg City. Just over the Belgian border is a region called Luxembourg: this used to be part of Luxembourg the country, but was lost to Belgium in 1839. Although it is an entirely different entity, Liechtenstein, the principality that lies between Austria and Germany, is also rich, and often confused with Luxembourg. Rosa Luxemburg, the famous socialist, was neither from Luxembourg, Luxembourg nor Liechtenstein: she was born in Poland. As for the famous Luxembourg Garden, that's in Paris.

The land that looks as if it fell out of a fairy tale is not always known for snow-white wholesomeness in the financial department, however. Home to only a dozen banks in the 1950s, Luxembourg transformed into a major financial centre in the 1960s. Now it's the seventh biggest in the world with some two hundred foreign banking institutions operating here: one of the most famous was 'rogue bank' BCCI (a Pakistani–Arab Emirates institution closed in 1991 amid huge international scandal), but there remain plenty of other iffy-sounding banks and businesses that have their overseas headquarters here. High interest rates on savings, low rates on taxes, and bank secrecy laws have made Luxembourg a money-laundering haven and tax-evasion centre, although new laws have been enacted that are sure to prevent that, wink wink.

> **Bank yank:** *In January 2003 the EU forced Luxembourg to agree to certain changes in the order of business. Now the country that holds most of the EU's offshore investments will have to hand over information about the savings accounts of non-EU residents, or impose income tax on interest piled up from savings accounts. The push came from Germany: many Germans hide their money here.*

Banking practices in Luxembourg have raised eyebrows all over the world, and the country has been linked to operations ranging from pretty shady to deeply black. Occasionally new laws are passed, and occasionally they are enforced. But no matter how hard it tries to scrub its hands – and we're not sure how hard it is trying – Luxembourg is so often in the middle of one scandal or another.

Sticky Fingers, Dirty Money and General Grime

Who knows what is really going on in the back rooms of Luxembourg's banks, but a lot seems to be not above-board. Here are but a few of the clues that the business conducted out of the country isn't always squeaky clean:

1991: Important US bank, First American, is found to be controlled by a money-laundering bank in Luxembourg; BCCI closed down after money-laundering scandal involving mujahideen financing and money laundering for Colombian drug cartel.

1994: Employees of KBLux bank steal equivalent of $9 million.

1999: After four years as president of the European Commission, Luxembourg's former prime minister Jacques Santer is forced to resign along with the whole European Commission on charges of corruption.

2000: Pressure from EU to lift banking secrecy laws after more charges that Luxembourg banks are involved in money-laundering and fraudulent operations.

2002: Swiss career diplomat Peter Friederich charged with laundering drug money – proof that Luxembourg does know how to enforce its money-laundering laws; French government denounces Luxembourg as a haven for financial crime – alarming when such accusations come from the less-than-lily-white French.

2003: European Commission's statistical arm, Eurostat, headquartered in Luxembourg, is caught in numerous shady financial dealings, including faked invoices from fake companies to fund an account for volleyball teams and expensive holidays.

As one of the original members of the European Economic Community and the administrative headquarters of the European Coal and Steel Agreement, Luxembourg ended up as a main site for many EEC (and later EU) institutions. It is headquarters for the European Court of Auditors, the Nuclear Safety Administration and the Secretariat of the European Parliament – which oh-so-conveniently holds the library for the parliament that is located in Brussels and Strasbourg.

Despite being a magnet for financial scams and sleight of hand, Luxembourg is just plain smart. Home of some of the EU's most intelligent, popular and diplomatic politicians – current Prime Minister Jean-Claude Juncker among them – Luxembourg figured out early that if it wanted to hold on to its independence, it had to be a team player. While France and Germany were simply talking about perhaps maybe forming a coal and steel agreement, in 1948 Luxembourg was linking up with Belgium and the Netherlands to form Benelux – the name taken from the first letters of their names – which was Europe's first economic-trading bloc that lifted tariffs and allowed easy exchange of workers, goods and resources. Luxembourg was quick to enter the eurozone: in fact, the idea for the euro came out of here.

Luxembourger Pierre Werner – twice the country's prime minister – is called the 'father of the euro', except he called his idea for a common currency the 'euror', which besides not exactly rolling off the tongue, sounds like a combination of 'error' and 'führer' – two words Europeans definitely didn't want connected with their money. Not that it looked like there would be any such currency back in 1960 when he pushed the idea so ferociously that some referred to him as a zealot.[1] The idealist, who saw shared economies as the way to steer postwar European countries back to peace, had to wait quite some time – forty-two years, to be exact – before the idea he planted finally came to fruition. Six months later, at 88, the man who so radically changed Europe's money checked out.

Claiming neutrality through both world wars, and invaded and occupied by Germany during both, Luxembourg ditched that apparently worthless concept after 1945 and signed on as a founding member of the United Nations and NATO. Now it is a partner in a controversial military coalition with Belgium, Germany and France, called the European Security and Defence Union, which the United States sees as threatening to the workings of NATO (and to the American ability to manipulate Europe).

Although Luxembourg's major industrial moneymaker, Arbed, is Europe's biggest steel supplier, the country's leadership also realized that it couldn't rely solely on the riches from its steel plants, whose product was subject to wild market fluctuations. To diversify its economy, the country threw open its doors as a banking centre and sometime financial laundrette.

History Review

It all began with a big rock – an outcropping, actually – in the middle of nowhere, looking out over some pretty woods and hills. Upon that rock, where he found the ruins of an ancient Roman fort, Siegefroid, the Count of Ardennes, began constructing a castle in 963 that would be so heavily fortified over the coming centuries that the triple-walled fortress was known as the 'Gibraltar of the North'. Peering down over what is today the capital, Gibraltar Junior wasn't terribly effective in keeping Luxembourg safe from invasion by the neighbours or from being handed over as a fetching land bonus in treaties. Over the years it was pulled into the Austrian empire, made part of Burgundy, taken over by Napoleonic France, and later given to the king of the Netherlands, although economically and militarily it was tied up with Germany, and later Belgium.

Luxembourg's schizophrenic political history was reflected in the language: half of the country spoke French, the other half German, although most residents in both parts also spoke Luxembourgish.

In 1830, when politically part of the Lowlands, Belgium and Luxembourg rebelled against the ruling Dutch king. As a result Belgium became independent, and Luxembourg was ultimately split in two – with the French-speaking half of its land going to Belgium. Luxembourg gained a measure of autonomy with the little land it had left in 1839. The fledgling country, however, was dirt poor, and the territory that is about the size of Greater London was so lacking in opportunity that a fifth of the population hightailed it over to the United States over the next sixty years. Full independence was at last achieved in 1867.

In 1867 the French wanted Luxembourg so badly that they tried to simply buy it. That led to a treaty that formally recognized Luxembourg as an independent country that wasn't for sale.

Economically linked to Germany, with which it had enjoyed warm relations in the early twentieth century, Luxembourg was rather annoyed when the First World War broke out, and Germany, ignoring Luxembourg's neutrality, invaded and occupied the land. And Germany did exactly the same during the next conflict, initially flooding into the country on the way to Belgium and France. But that occupation was far worse than first time around. The Nazis quickly launched a charm campaign, heavy on the propaganda, about how Luxembourgers were actually ethnic Germans and they should embrace being part of Greater Germany. And then the Nazis held a referendum asking if Luxembourgers wished to join hands geographically as part of the Anschluss. One imagines the propaganda director was soon out of a job: 98 per cent of Luxembourgers voted no, using the phrase that is now the national motto: '*Mir wëlle bleiwe wat mir sin*' – We wish to stay as we are, i.e., independent. The Nazis were furious, annexing Luxembourg anyway, and they unleashed their more brutal side, rounding up the many dissidents and shooting them or sending them off to concentration camps. Luxembourgers were banned from speaking their language, forced to talk only in German and even names that faintly smacked of French were Germanized. Even the name of their country was erased: it became *Gau Moselland*, or the district of Moselle country. The resistance that had sprung up grew stronger with general strikes and railway closures, particularly when the Nazis began calling up Luxembourg boys.[2] But where Luxembourg was really hammered was in the Battle of the Bulge – one of the bloodiest showdowns in European history.

The Battle of the Bulge

Until that December it had been a happy time, or at least happier than it had been for years. The Allies had liberated Paris and Rome, chased the Nazis out of Belgium and Luxembourg and were moving towards Germany. After months of heavy fighting, troops were fatigued, supplies were running low, and the advancing front was at points thinning. Seeing a weakness in the formation as the Allies took a break, Hitler made a last-ditch effort to win the war. His plan was to breach the front – essentially forming a 'bulge' where his tanks would break through – make a run for Antwerp in Belgium, and seize that port city and the land on the way to it. The Allies were caught unawares as some 300,000 Nazis advanced on them starting on 16 December 1944, forcing them to concede some of the liberated territory. General Patton's troops, on their way to the German border, quickly returned to engage in the war's fiercest fighting, made worse by the fact that this was one of the nastiest winters on record. Not only were Allied troops poorly outfitted for the brutal cold, but the snow fell so quickly that fighters often could not see twenty feet away. In the agonizing battle that dragged on for six weeks, American deaths and casualties numbered over 75,000, the British lost over 1,400 and the German casualties were nearly 68,000, until they finally conceded defeat on 27 January 1945.

Quick Tour

The belly button of Western Europe, land-locked Luxembourg is mountainous in its north, lushly forested to its west, and crossed by four rushing rivers. Skiing, hiking and biking are the favoured recreational activities in this 'green heart of Europe' and on weekends out-of-towners descend on the verdant land and clog up the most popular trails. Luxembourgers are quite religious – Catholic festivals come complete with costumed splendour – and they are among Europe's most knowledgeable on political issues, which is handy since voting is compulsory here. They are also the Europeans who travel the most and almost everyone is multilingual, speaking not only Luxembourgish but German, French and often English as well. Lately though you can hear plenty of Portuguese on street corners: much of the foreign labour pool hails from Portugal.

Foreign influence: A third of the country's 400,000 residents are foreign-born and a third of Luxembourg's workforce commutes in from Germany, Belgium or France. And even more out-of-towners bank there: corporations have been drawn by its buttoned-lip banking practices, but so too have the middle class from nearby countries, with Germans in particular fond of Luxembourg's financial services.

What's it like to live in the richest country in Europe? Potentially lucrative, since Luxembourgers take home some of the highest wages in Europe; but it's often tranquil to the point of inducing ennui. Plenty of nice restaurants in Luxembourg City, but the place shutters down too early, say those who like to stay up past eleven. Maybe that's why Luxembourgers are Europe's biggest drinkers, knocking back nearly 12 litres of spirits per person a year.[3]

Radio Luxembourg (1933–92)

For decades the most innovative radio broadcasts heard in Britain and across Europe originated from Luxembourg. The Station of the Stars, Radio Luxembourg – 208 on the AM dial – announced its presence in 1933, and showed its feistiness from the start. Officially assigned a low-power spot on the radio waves, the station owners refused to accept that idea: Radio Luxembourg became the first radio pirate (more or less) by broadcasting at a much stronger, longer wave frequency, and bucking the idea of a standardized format. Travel programmes, fiction readings, quiz shows, live performances and '*reportage à trois faces*' – with news topics presented on radio, in newspapers and on theatre screens simultaneously – were a few of the unusual additions to the radio station, that with its strong transmitter, could be picked up over most of Western Europe. Radio Luxembourg's biggest enemy soon became the BBC, as the tiny station with its huge listenership was cutting into the BBC's audience – and the British network made numerous attempts to shut it down. The Germans effectively did so by broadcasting propaganda during the Nazi occupation, and when it came back on the Allied propaganda team was soon sitting in the DJ's seat. Hugely popular in the 1950s and '60s, Radio Luxembourg stumbled in later years, at one point descending so low that it played only disco music, a move that helped ensure it would not be staying alive for much longer. In 1992 the plug was pulled on the station that had once been the only source of pop music. Rumour has it, however, that the station may make a comeback.

Crime is quite low in this moneyed country, but burglaries are on the rise, averaging about nine a day. One lure for burglars, perhaps, is that so few crimes are solved – only about 3 per cent of the 3,300 or so a year. And while police brutality isn't much of an issue, the police can be bullies, according to the head of the policemen's union. He says police rarely take the paternity leave they are offered because other police harangue them if they do.[4]

> **Shock:** In June 2000 a gunman held two dozen toddlers and their teachers captive in a daycare centre for more than twenty-four hours. He'd poured petrol through the building, and had threatened to ignite it, when a team of journalists arrived to conduct a TV interview that he had requested. As he walked out of the centre, cameras didn't roll. Instead gunshots rang out and he was shot twice in the head. The reporters were actually police. The gunman survived, but the police were soon under fire for their tactics.

For all the financial fun it's offered in the past, Luxembourg's banking allure may be fading: in the continuing waves of EU togetherness and a push to share all that's known, the country is slowly but surely being cleaned up. Well, sort of.

Future Forecast

Widely applauded Jean-Claude Juncker will one day assume a major position in Brussels, but before then he'll probably have to deal with another financial scandal or two coming out of these parts. Not to worry: many people will think that the scandal occurred in Liechtenstein.

Hot Spots

Luxembourg City: Stacked upon a hill, the handsome capital city is brimming with everything needed by the wealthy: banks, fancy restaurants, wine stores, a medieval old town and a modern urban centre, but this city does get plenty of beauty sleep as it locks up early. Siegefroid's castle was dismantled in the 1800s, but parts of the casements – the labyrinthine escape routes that coil around under it – still remain and the pedestrian way that winds down from the hill is known as the most beautiful balcony in Europe.

Ardennes: Low mountains rise above thick woods in this northern region of rolling pastureland, meandering rivers and such attractions as the Valley of the Seven Castles. Known for its romantic inns and for its violent past: much of the Battle of the Bulge played out here.

Luxembourg City: home of the EU's richest citizens.

Luxembourg's vineyards are mostly in the south, which is called 'the good country'.

European Court of Justice: The powerful judicial arm of the European Union, its twenty-five judges (one from each EU country) hear complaints on everything from discrimination to property disputes, taking cases referred to it by assorted EU institutions or member states. Their biggest case lately: whether it was legal to ditch the EU's growth and stability pact, which mandates that countries using the euro keep their budget deficit under 3 per cent. No it was not, ruled the ECJ.

Eurostat building: The place does crank out helpful statistics about EU members – such as monthly unemployment rates – but lately it's been a symbol of embarrassment since a slush fund was uncovered. How about some stats on how many institutions are using dodgy accounting practices?

European Court of Auditors: It has the mission 'to audit independently the collection and spending of European Union funds'. It didn't have to go far to uncover the shenanigans at Eurostat: the two institutions are a stone's throw from each other.

Hot Shots

Grand Duke Henri: Reigning monarch 2000 to present. Bourbon-blooded and handsome Henri has been unofficially running the place since 1998, but his dad, respectable Grand Duke Jean, officially abdicated and handed over the keys just in time for the switchover to the euro; Henri's likeness adorns the one-euro coin. With his wife, Cuban-born Maria Teresa, he is apparently trying to compensate for his country's low birth rate. The royal couple's offspring number five.

Jean-Claude Juncker: Prime Minister 1995 to present. Smart, sweet and slightly nerdy Christian Democrat, Juncker took over Santer's chair, and under pressure from the EU and others, has been pushing through a number of banking changes and new financial laws that are yanking off the country's veil of secrecy. It's a delicate balancing act since what makes Luxembourg rich is its banking attractiveness, but his country is a notably good-spirited team player in the EU, and all the more with Juncker at the helm.

Jacques Santer: Prime Minister 1985–95. Highly regarded when he headed the country, he ran an iffy ship when he ascended to president of the

PM Juncker: popular at home
and within the EU.

European Commission in 1995. Among the charges that prompted Santer
and the whole team to turn in their badges in 1999: total irresponsibility.

*Another important figure born here: Robert Schuman, the French
foreign minister who helped put the whole EU idea into motion when
he announced a coal and steel pooling plan with Germany.*

Jean Nicolas: Editor/writer for Luxembourg weekly *L'Investigateur*, Nicolas
has been kicking up plenty of controversy, particularly in Belgium. His
2001 book *Paedophile Dossier – The Scandal of the Dutroux Case* raises
questions about parties that he claims the Belgian king (then a prince)
once attended – the king denies any misdeeds and has threatened to sue
Nicolas's publisher. In 2000 he provoked more international ink with plans
to publish a list of Belgian paedophiles in *L'Investigateur*. The Belgian
courts were quick to issue an injunction against publication, saying that
such action would harm the rights of the accused paedophiles.

General George S. Patton (1885–1945): Considered a national Luxembourg
hero, the three-star American general helped liberate Luxembourg and
his quick actions in the last months of the war prevented the Nazis from
prevailing at the Battle of the Bulge. In 1945, while in Hamm, Luxembourg,
he was in a gruesome road accident that left him paralysed; he died several

days later. He's buried in Luxembourg, where a George Patton museum was set up to honour him.

Neo-Nazis: Yes, they are here too. But at their only recorded 'march', the participants numbered but four.

Pierre Peters: Head of the anti-immigration National Bewegung, Peters gets his knickers in a twist over the many foreign workers here, especially the Portuguese, although there is little crime associated with immigrants or foreign nationals and the unemployment rate is quite low. Maybe that's why he does so poorly at the polls.

Viviane Reding: Two-time European Commissioner, who previously headed the education and culture commission, right-leaning Reding from 2004 has been the commissioner in charge of the information society and media.

Media star: *352*, a weekly paper in English, also has a free daily website at www.352.lu

Part Two
New Europe

New Europe – Introduction

The ten countries that entered the EU on 1 May 2004 aren't actually 'new' – their histories and cultures go back for centuries, even millennia. To Western Europeans, however, they are all novel indeed – being mysterious places with names like 'Ljubljana' and 'Vilnius' – that for much of the twentieth century lived in a dark parallel universe that the rest of Europe tried to ignore.

Most of 'New Europe' was reborn in the 1990s: when the Soviet Union fell, the three Baltic States (Estonia, Latvia and Lithuania), Poland, and Czechoslovakia re-established independence, with Czechoslovakia going on to divide into two, and Slovenia was born when Yugoslavia fell apart. Cyprus and Malta are the relative elders of the bunch: they've been independent since the 1960s.

New Europe

Poland: Most people
Hungary: Most glum, most Roma
Estonia: Most proud, best behaved
Latvia: Most vulnerable
Lithuania: Most likely to be site of next Chernobyl
Czech Republic: Most eurosceptical
Slovakia: Most likely to be overlooked
Slovenia: Most promising
Cyprus: Most likely to be schizophrenic
Malta: Most likely to bolt

Excluding the Mediterranean islands Cyprus and Malta – both former British colonies – the eight other new EU countries came out of Communism, and except for Slovenia, they were closely bound up with the Soviet Union, being either republics or satellites which spent almost five decades with Moscow panting down their necks. Becoming independent again only in the past decade and a half, these former Communist states are fledglings, filled with energy and hope, but still bearing a few scars from their not-so-distant past. More than simply being repressed under the Soviets, who steamrolled their rebellions, these countries – most of them devastated during the Second World War – didn't have much of a chance to heal: under the Communists, those ugly days were simply swept under the rug. Unlike Western Europe, which had six decades to rebuild itself and forge friendships with former enemies, these countries are still confronting issues that go back to the 1940s, or sometimes even the First World War.

> *1919 was a landmark: Czechoslovakia and the three Baltic States first became independent countries as a result of that year's Treaty of Versailles, which also created the Kingdom of Serbs, Croats and Slovenes that would become Yugoslavia. The treaty brought back an independent Poland and in that time of remapping Europe, Hungary was slashed to a third of its former size.*

These so-called 'accession countries' see the EU as the great equalizer that can shell out the funds for agriculture and infrastructure that many need, and as the provider of opportunity – that can help attract more foreign investment or provide them (some day) with the possibility of new jobs and new homes. They also view the EU as the way to reconnect with their past that was ripped away. And plenty of them eye the EU rather warily, unsure that Brussels won't simply replace Moscow in dictating what they can and can't do.

> *Another feature that most of these countries share is that they are not as wealthy as those in the West, save for Slovenia and Cyprus, both of which have GDP levels around those of Spain and Portugal.*

While there's plenty of excitement about reconnecting with their European kin in the West, some of these new countries are still also peeved at the West, for letting them fall to Communism and despite encouraging them to rebel, not showing up when they defied Moscow. And the one thing that disappoints almost all is that the West seems utterly clueless about who they are, what they've been through, and the history that links them to the rest of Europe. But for all the twitchiness of the moment, all across 'New Europe' there is also a sense of exciting change and regeneration, and a joy at being brought back to the table with the European family.

All of the new 'accession countries' which reside on the Continent have also recently joined NATO, many as a means to protect themselves against Russia, which has threatened at least a few of these countries that it will be back.

New Europe's Gripes

- Poland: No Western help in 1956 uprising against Soviets or in 1944 Warsaw Uprising against German occupation
- Hungary: No Western help in 1956 revolution against Soviets; 1920 Treaty of Trianon cut Hungary's land by two-thirds
- Czech Republic/Slovakia: No Western help during 1968 Prague Spring; Sudetenland handed to Hitler in 1939
- Baltics: Estonia, Latvia, Lithuania: West ignored 50 years of genocide of their people; Molotov-Ribbentrop Pact: invaded by Germany and Russia during Second World War
- Cyprus: Prevented from joining Greece in 1950s; world didn't stop Turkey from invading in 1974
- Malta: the most bombed island in the history of the world and didn't get postwar Marshall Fund aid

19. Poland/Polska:
The Question Mark

Fast Facts

Country:	Republic of Poland; Rzeczpospolita Polska
Capital:	Warsaw
Government:	republic
Independence:	11 November 1918 (founded); 1989 independent from Soviet Union
Population:	38,627,000 (2004 estimate)
Leaders:	Head of State: President Aleksander Kwasniewski (1995, 2000)
	Head of Government: (acting) Prime Minister Marek Belka (appointed by President, May 2004)
Elections:	President through direct public elections every 5 years; Prime Minister appointed by President, approved by Sejm
Name of Parliament:	National Assembly; Zgromadzenie Narodowe (Sejm and Senat)
Ethnicity:	Polish 97%, German 0.4%, Ukrainian and other nationalities 2.6%
Religion:	Roman Catholic 95%; Eastern Orthodox, Protestant 5%
Language:	Polish
Literacy:	99% (2003 estimate); 25% may be functionally illiterate
Exports:	machinery, transport, intermediate manufactures, food, animals
Per capita GDP:	$11,100 (2003)
Unemployment:	18.9% (May 2004 Eurostat figure)
Percentage in poverty:	18% (2002 official estimate); some figures up to 40%
EU status:	joined May 2004
Currency:	Polish zloty
Known for:	being invaded by the neighbours

Standout Qualities

Steel: Was a major producer
Rust: Steel plants falling apart
Gold: Another golden era in sight?

Résumé

The big boy of Central Europe, Poland is the weightiest of all ten EU newcomers in terms of size (almost as big as Germany), people (more populous than the other nine countries combined) and economic output (bigger than the next three countries' GDPs combined) – and the former Soviet satellite is also most likely to rock the Brussels boat, even if it's not trying. Known for steel factories, coal mines, cheap labour and strategic location between Europe's two halves, the fertile land was so alluring in 1989 when it broke out of Communist shackles that Poland was the main reason to fling open the EU door. Ironically, by 2004, when it walked in, Poland appeared the iffiest proposition of all ten entrants. Among the worries: Poland's 20 per cent unemployment, shaky economy, primitive farms and a newfound 'don't mess with us' attitude born from centuries of being knocked around. Another cause for concern: political turmoil that has brought the rise of a radical pig farmer and others who have been threatening to untie the knot with the EU the minute Poland tied it. In 2002, when the official EU invitation list was being finalized, Poland – once the star of the Central European bunch – looked like it might be deleted from the roster. A final push came from Germany: Chancellor Gerhard Schröder was caught on video camera (unawares) saying Germany would toss in extra funding, just let Poland in. Besides cheap labour and an expanded market, two other factors that helped pull open the EU's pearly gates: Western guilt over what happened here and fear that Russia may reach out and grab it again. It isn't happenstance that Poland was the first former satellite to sign up to NATO and is busy bolstering its military.

Does Uncle Sam Have a Deal For You!

Having been kicked around by Russia for centuries, post-Communist Poland was easily wooed by NATO, the US-dominated arms club created during the Cold War to check the Soviet Union; in a move that angered Moscow, Poland joined the club in 1999. It promptly signed on the dotted line on what was the biggest arms sale ever in Central Europe, ordering 48 F-16s for $3.5 billion from Lockheed Martin, not surprisingly the strongest lobbyist for NATO expansion. To sweeten the just-sign-right-here-and-forget-that-your-country-can't-really-afford-this-deal, Lockheed Martin and the United States government promised to lure American companies to Poland as part of a $6.9 billion foreign investment package. Thus far, the US hasn't delivered on its promises, and Poland, pressured to send troops to Iraq as part of the deal, is threatening to pull its military forces back.

No Central European country deserves moneyed Western Europe's help more than historically victimized Poland, even if the place now lacks the spark of the early 1990s when freedom was fresh, Lech Walesa was still popular, the sale of state-owned industries jolted the economy into life and hope crackled in the air. Whatever the method – EU funding or private investment – Poland needs to catapult into the present. Much of the countryside remains stuck in the nineteenth century, and everything from factories to roads is in need of repair. A quarter of all Poles labour on inefficient farms yielding scrappy produce that can't vie with the West's prettified, heavily subsidized food that now floods the foreign-owned supermarkets; steel plants are rusting, coal mines are closing, and a third of Polish miners and mill workers are now out of jobs – as is nearly half of the work force under 30. Older people complain that life was better when the Communists guaranteed housing and food until death; the young say that progress is coming too slowly, and wages are too low. In a country where teachers earn about €200 a month, many of the young hope to move to Western Europe's greener pastures. That dream, however, was stymied when most countries in the EU-15 suddenly announced that residents of the new EU member states would have to wait up to seven years before moving to their countries for work.

Watch Out for Flying Produce

Most Poles (or at least 77 per cent of those who voted in the 2003 referendum) supported EU entry, but the move came with plenty of grumbling. Among the most contentious issues: the EU labour law, which prohibits 2004 EU entrants from working in most Western EU countries until as late as 2012; now the legality of that one-third of Poles who typically work abroad is in question and the unemployed may have to wait seven years before seeking greener pastures. Another cause for snarling: EU subsidies for the ten newcomers' farmers are initially only a quarter of that doled out to farmers in Western Europe. Poles were so steamed up about those EU rules that in 2003, when president of the European Commission Romano Prodi visited Warsaw, they pelted him with tomatoes in greeting. Another issue that gets Poles hot and bothered: a proposed change in the country's voting power within the EU that would lessen Poland's punch. During the EU accession planning talks, Poland had been promised substantial votes reflecting its land size. The proposed EU constitution uses a whole different voting formula and gives Poland fewer votes. Polish President Kwasniewski had a blue fit when it was unveiled in 2003, squawking that if the proposed constitution went through with voting changes intact Poland would veto it. His foot stamping raised plenty of eyebrows in Brussels, where Poland was suddenly seen in a new light: as potential spoiler.

Poland's temper tantrums – legitimate though they may be – are just one demonstration that the country isn't yet slickly presenting itself to the world. The country did not look terribly unified in 2004, when after guiding Poland into the EU on 1 May, Prime Minister Leszek Miller – with an approval rating of under 10 per cent – promptly stepped down from office. The Polish government also forgot to approve a budget to pay its MEPs when they showed up in the European Parliament that year. Oh well, plenty of time to learn the finer points of life in the EU.

The Polish government's friendship with the US is yet another ticklish area. Poland's support of the war in Iraq was met with loud, disapproving clucks from the likes of France's Jacques Chirac; after being heralded as part of 'New Europe' by the US and sending troops into postwar Iraq in 2003 – for which Poland was paid – Poland was branded by Western European media as 'America's Trojan Donkey', alluding to Poland's not exactly knee-shaking military might. For centuries ripped apart by its powerful neighbours, now Poland is pulled between its alliances with the US and the EU, and Polish politicians are feeling the tug between Washington's and Western Europe's interests – a competition evident particularly when Poland was choosing which arms manufacturer to award contracts to for its new fighter planes. According to the *Economist*, one Polish official said that to choose between the US or Europe was like choosing 'between mother and father – and we love them both'.[1] That's sweet, but the bond to the US is a potential liability in an era when the EU is battling trade wars with the US over everything from steel to bananas while building itself up to counter American weight.

> *The bottom line behind Poland's typical devotion to the US: should Russia ever decide to attack, Poland would look to the US – not the EU – to protect it, and the Polish government is unlikely to kiss its across-the-Atlantic friend goodbye, whatever the costs. However, the friendship has been recently tried: President Kwasniewski didn't hide his dismay during a 2004 meeting with President George W. Bush when the Polish president pushed Bush to drop visa and finger-printing requirements for Poles entering the US. And Poland is ticked off that the US is dragging its feet on making good its promises for investment.*

History Review

If Poland sometimes acts all twitchy and defensive, it's understandable. Most of this nation's history can be summed up in two words: Poor Poland. For the two centuries leading up to 1989, when it booted out the Soviet-linked Communist regime, Polska stood out as the textbook victim of geography. Physically trapped between Russia and Germany, Poland has been the local weakling pulled continuously into the violent, exhausting and often horrifying exploits of its powerful neighbours, despite its early military muscle and cultural greatness.

> **High point, low point:** *In one of the most important battles in European history, the armies of King Jan Sobieski pushed Turks away from Vienna's gates in 1683. The regal city was saved from the Ottoman yoke, but shortly afterwards the Polish kingdom went down the tubes.*

That Poland would ever descend to its nineteenth- and twentieth-century lows appeared most unlikely for much of the past millennium. Not that long ago Poland was a powerful and advanced kingdom filled with universities and splendid palaces and headed by a religiously tolerant monarchy that granted previously unknown rights to its subjects, including the right to a parliament that elected the king. Coupled with Lithuania through royal marriage in 1386, the kingdom that spread across Eastern Europe from the Baltic to the Black Sea was Europe's largest state at the time; successfully fighting off German Teutonic Knights, Russian imperialists and Ottoman Turks, the Kingdom of Poland and Lithuania was one of the continent's fiercest powers, at least for a few hundred years. By the fifteenth century, Poland, a literate land where education was valued, was a publishing hotbed, but the sixteenth century was even more enlightened. During this 'golden age' (deeply influenced by Florentines and Venetians with whom Polish royalty was often cavorting and occasionally marrying), architects and mapmakers, poets and painters, scientists and philosophers filled the land that was also the home of Copernicus, whose heliocentric writings would spin the world in a whole new direction.

Source of power: The Federation of Poland and Lithuania (1569–1795), as the joint kingdom was later known, first became wealthy during the fifteenth century from agriculture. Rich in grain, the Federation found a ready market in Europe's booming population. For centuries, Poland continued to be Europe's main bread basket.

Poland's 'renaissance' had fully petered out by the late 1700s, after the country lost half its population to assorted wars, famine and plague. Seizing upon Poland's weaknesses, Russia, Prussia and Austria (and Sweden for a time) all encroached and began annexing Polish lands starting in 1772 – a geographical gnawing that would later be called 'the First Partition', since it didn't stop there. Poles rebelled frequently, and after a particularly heated revolt against Poland's occupiers – Russia, Prussia and Austria – the trio ganged up and split all remaining Polish lands between themselves. What was once Poland was literally erased from the map in 1795, a devastating event known by Poles as 'The Third Partition'.

Napoleon restored recognition and self-governance to Poland in the early nineteenth century, but once he was prised from power, the Poles were once again subject to their Russian, Prussian and Austrian rulers.

Poles never gave up: the violent uprisings, attempts on the tsar's life (one allegedly by future leader Jozef Pilsudski), and assorted furtive acts of

Poland's many secret societies didn't cease, nor did the reprisals. After one bloody 1863 Polish insurrection against Russia, the Russians responded by torching dozens of towns and sending 30,000 rebels to Siberia. Nevertheless, Poland remained essentially 'disappeared' until the First World War, a period that was even more traumatic for Poles. The three countries that had yanked apart Poland lined up on two different sides: not only were Poles forced to fight for countries they didn't support, they often had to fight fellow Poles in battles that killed 1.5 million Polish troops and civilians. But from the misnamed Great War, Poles finally regained independence. When military marshal Jozef Pilsudski, a dashing Pole, took Warsaw in November 1918, he declared Poland an independent, sovereign country; the world powers officially agreed the next year.

> When the victorious Allied powers met in Paris in 1919 to draw the new face of postwar Europe, Poland was well represented. Pilsudski and the country's slickest diplomats very visibly and aggressively presented their plans: Poland would take part of Russia and part of Germany, including the mineral-rich region of Silesia and the port city Germans called Danzig and Poles called Gdansk. Pilsudski wanted all of Lithuania to be drawn within Polish borders as well – he'd sent in the Polish army in 1918 and taken most of Lithuania anyway – but the Allies' mapmakers drew the line at that demand, so to speak.[2]

Known for his handlebar moustache, brilliant military manoeuvres and hot temper, Pilsudski became transitional head of state in 1918, leading Poland into half a dozen wars in the next two years, but by 1922 he left to directly oversee the Polish armed forces, while Poland quickly blew through ten governments. Pilsudski was back in 1926, heading a military coup that killed hundreds, and entrenched him as dictator.

> 'I shit on all of you,' Pilsudski bellowed in 1926 when he burst into parliament, which he was known to call 'The House of Whores'. 'The time has come to treat you like children, because you behave like children.'[3]

Despite his bullish nature, Pilsudski is still revered as the father of Polish independence, and to his credit he somewhat organized the ramshackle republic of assorted ethnicities that used half a dozen currencies and as many languages in a land that was so mismatched that even trains couldn't travel easily since Poland had two different gauges of rail.[4] When Pilsudski died in 1935, Poland disintegrated again, leaving it ripe for attacks from historical foes Russia and Germany. Poland had barely celebrated its twentieth anniversary of independence when its freedom did another vanishing act. The Nazis invaded the western part of the country in September 1939; the Soviets took the east two weeks later. For the next five and a half years, Poland suffered the war's longest continuous fighting, trains rumbled through the countryside carrying millions of civilian prisoners, and an acrid smoke blew from concentration camps, including Auschwitz, Birkenau and Treblinka, where nearly the entire Jewish Polish population of 2 million died, alongside 1.5 million gypsies, gays, Communists and dissidents.

> *Due to the former kingdom's policy of religious tolerance, more Jews lived in Poland than anywhere else in Europe, which is one reason Hitler pounced on the country.*

Germans demolished cities going in – nearly a quarter of Warsaw was in ruin within two weeks – and they devastated them going out – leaving Warsaw a pile of blood-red rocks when they left. But the Russians weren't any kinder. During their occupation, the Soviets hauled off 1.5 million Poles to Siberia and systematically used Polish troops and officers as frontline human shields to absorb Nazi bullets. After killing 4,000 Polish Allied officers in one massacre, despite the fact that the two countries were supposed to be fighting on the same side, the Soviets set up the Poles again in the final battle for Warsaw: the Soviets, who were supposed to back up the Polish Army, didn't show up, watching from the other side of the Vistula river as the Nazis ravaged the outnumbered Poles. Stalin had calculated that he would be ridding himself of many future Polish dissidents. By the end of the war 6 million Poles – over one-sixth of the population – were dead.

> *Painful memory: On 10 July 1941 the residents of the small village of Jedwabne rounded up all the Polish Jews and forced them to the main square. They were then led to a barn which, once all 300 or so were locked in, was set on fire, killing all those trapped inside. President Kwasniewski apologized for the act in 2001, saying it was necessary to uncover the full truth: Poland's Institute of National Remembrance investigated it, finally dropping it in 2003, after concluding: '. . . apart from the persons who . . . had been tried by the Polish administration of justice, no other persons who had committed the crime and were still alive, were found.'*

Relief didn't come when the conflict ceased. Given Allied supervision over the territory after 1945, the Soviet Union yanked Poland into its sphere of influence, which was a diplomatic way of saying that Moscow (usually) put puppets in as leaders and ran the place from afar. Poland remained a Soviet satellite for four depressing, air-polluted decades, when tens of thousands of intellectuals, writers and dissidents – and anybody else considered a threat – were shipped off to Siberian gulags (work camps), locked up or killed, until the trade union turned political movement Solidarity rose up in 1980 and began ripping the Communist power structure down. Independent for only a decade and a half, with a twisted history like that so recently behind it, Poland can't be faulted if it is still reeling.

Clandestine Communication

Across the Soviet satellite states, the underground political movements that sprang up first in the 1940s and went wild in the 1980s relied on small printing presses that cranked out thousands of pamphlets, broadsheets and small books – some political essays and calls for reform, some works of poetry or fiction that could thus escape the censors. The *Samizdat* self-publishing movement, which sometimes used carbon copies, was particularly strong in Poland. So evolved was the subversive communication network in Poland – historically a haven for secret societies – that underground writings could be circulated via a clandestine underground postal system, that operated with its own stamps.[5]

Quick Tour

Poland isn't lost yet . . .
(line from Polish national anthem)

Edged to the north-west by the Bialowieska Forest of ancient oaks where bison roam and bounded to the south-east by the snow-crusted Tatra mountains that peer over thousands of miles of flat plain, Poland has always been the gateway between two worlds. Straddling Russia and Germany – a lethal position for centuries – Poland is likewise pulled between past and present: the landscape of medieval villages and Renaissance castles is broken by smokestacks of Soviet-era steel towns, the donkey-brown carts on two-lane highways are swept aside by trucks and Mercedes, those farmlands that once fed most of Europe are now Europe's most unproductive, and Poland's former greatness is now captured mostly in history books that few outside Poland read.

> *Farming concerns: With some 5 million farmers, Poland's agrarian sector is problematic: it is light years behind agriculture on the other side of the continent, and the process to get it up to twenty-first-century standards will be painful – if indeed modernization and enlargement of farms is the right route to take. Polish farmers looked to the EU to save them, but the Union – which hands over barrels of money to the West's corporate farms – has implied that in the course of evolving into its agricultural scheme, some small farms may die in an economical survival of the fittest. Before Poland even entered the Union, EU grant money was already helping out some educated, form-savvy Polish farmers, who bought shiny new tractors and ploughs. Unfortunately, those over 50 years of age didn't qualify in the first showering of money, and are still using rusty equipment from the 1940s or before. In this largely agricultural country, dominated by small family-run plots, a million or more farms may fold in the near future, unable to compete in the market where rules are dictated by the EU and their simple offerings on the supermarket shelves look shrivelled and pathetic.[6] Another problem: many Polish farmers aren't well educated and the cumbersome EU forms required to receive funding are ridiculously complex; many Polish farmers can't manage the paperwork, and neither Warsaw nor Brussels is rushing in to help them.*

Shut off from the West during its forced experiment with Communism that lasted forty-five years, Poland – the most populous of the Soviet satellites – was arguably the most influential: labour rebellions in 1956, which succeeded in bringing some autonomy, inspired an uprising in Hungary (with disastrous results). The Polish government also helped stall attempts to liberalize Communism elsewhere in Soviet-controlled states: in 1968, fearing that the new freedoms given during Czechoslovakia's 'Prague Spring' – among them the right to criticize the government – would spread to Poland, Polish Communists pushed Moscow to put a forcible end to the Czech experiment in 'opening up'. Polish troops were sent in with the Warsaw Pact forces who violently knocked down the Czechs' recently introduced 'socialism with a human face'.

Bad Year: 1956

Workers in Poznan's locomotive factory wanted more than freedom and a 20 per cent wage hike: during one of Poland's food shortages, they wanted bread. On 28 June 1956 their demands prompted a workers' uprising that saw rioters storm the city jail in a protest that spread countrywide involving some 100,000; it was ultimately quashed by the Polish army that killed up to 100. The protest – the first major uprising in a Soviet-controlled country, except for East Germany in 1953 – had one positive consequence, at least for a while: reform-oriented socialist Wladyslaw Gomulka – a former Communist Party leader who had been imprisoned by the much harsher Stalinists – was brought back to power. Gomulka pushed out Stalinists, cut the powers of the secret police, gave more freedom to the press, lifted requirements for collective farms, tolerated the practice of Catholicism, and kept Moscow at more of a distance in running Polish affairs. There was a price to pay for his (relatively) less oppressive regime which became increasingly hardline: when Czechs broke out of the totalitarian yoke in spring 1968, Gomulka, who by then didn't want to allow any more freedom in his country, was quick to voice his support of a Soviet crackdown and let Moscow borrow Polish troops to accomplish it. That didn't go down well with Polish students, who demonstrated en masse, and Gomulka rounded up student leaders, throwing hundreds in jail. Two years later, when dockworkers protested at Gdansk (foreshadowing the rise of Solidarity in 1980), Gomulka again tried to smother dissent with force; that time, thirty-five died in the showdown. Gomulka was pushed out of power as a result.

Ultimately, however, Poland's most important role in the Soviet era was triggering the fall of Soviet-style Communism. Part of the Poles' feistiness was fuelled by the Catholic church, which like all religions was theoretically banned in all Communist countries (but nevertheless was somewhat accepted in Poland): religious doctrines kept the Communist idea of devotion only to the State from thoroughly sinking in. More important was the man who donned the papal robes in 1978: when Polish Karol Wojtyla, the Bishop of Krakow, had taken the name Pope John Paul II, he triggered a new call for independence that echoed across Poland and spurred more dissent across all the Communist countries. But the most powerful move out of Poland came from the dockers and ship-yard workers in Gdansk, a defiant group who'd staged their first major protest in 1970: when they rose up again in a 1980 protest, a spike was driven into Moscow's heart that a decade later finally would make it stop beating.

Hungry for Change

The soaring cost of meat started it. So furious was the response in July 1980 when the government again responded to food shortages by increasing the price of the staple that much of the country was simply shut down by labour strikes. Most destabilizing was the strike in the Lenin shipyard in Gdansk, where workers had organized an illegal union, *Solidarnosc* (Solidarity). The union chose feisty electrician Lech Walesa as their leader; even though he had been fired from his job, Walesa scaled the fence to join that summer's protests. Backed by workers from twenty other nearby factories, Walesa negotiated an agreement with the Polish Communists that August. Fearing further rebellion, the Communists signed a twenty-one-point agreement giving workers the right to unionize and strike, among other things. Solidarity soon rose as a symbol for more rights to all, and before long a quarter of Poles of all professions rallied behind the banner of Solidarity, which transformed from trade union to political movement. Although Walesa instantly became a celebrity, and initially was able to travel abroad (he immediately went to Rome to meet the pope), the rights extended in August were soon ripped away. By the next winter, Soviet troops were ready in position on Poland's borders; at the end of 1981 Walesa and other leaders were imprisoned, and the country was cloaked by martial law. Curfews remained in effect for a year and a half – those long nights at home triggered a huge baby boom – but under international pressure they were lifted in July 1983 and Walesa, who won the Nobel Peace Prize that year, and hundreds of others were released. As the world looked on – and the Communist regime was continually chastised including by Pope John Paul II and US President Ronald Reagan – Polish Communists were forced to open up the country little by little, a feat helped along in part because the brutal Soviet–Afghanistan war (1979–89) was wearing down both the Soviet army and Soviet coffers. By the time Mikhail Gorbachev, who'd stepped in as premier in 1985, began promoting his ideas for opening up and restructuring the Soviet Union, strong independence movements were already well under way not only in Poland, but in Hungary, Czechoslovakia, East Germany and Romania, all of which had non-Communist leaders in power by the end of 1989. In January 1990 the

Polish Communist Party was dissolved (it was later reformed as the more open Democratic Left Alliance), and in May 1990 Solidarity candidates dominated the country's first free elections in four decades. Lech Walesa was sworn in as president that December.

Another move that blew up in the Communist government's face: in October 1984 government secret security kidnapped and killed Catholic priest Father Jerzy Popieluszko, the chaplain for Solidarity. The death of the religious man, later canonized, only aided Solidarity's cause.

By 1990 the Communist system had entirely crumbled and the newly democratic country euphorically raised independence leader Lech Walesa to the presidential seat. But Poland was soon slapped by uncomfortable political realities.

Party-happy: When the Communists stepped down, dozens of new parties sprang up: over 100 political parties vied for voters' hearts in the first free elections of 1990. At least some of the many political groups explained exactly who they were with their name – the National Party of Old Age and Disability Pensioners for one; among the most popular is the Polish Peasant Party. Despite all the frenzied party-making, in the 1990 election only 40 per cent of Poles even bothered to turn out to vote.

Kindly Walesa had been a fine protest leader, but he had little clue about running a government and faltered in the presidential role: he sacked prime ministers almost annually and his administration was haunted by numerous scandals. Meanwhile, the Catholic church wanted power pay-backs. So influential in pushing for independence and keeping the Soviet indoctrination from seeping under the surface, the church stepped in to reshape Polish life. Among other things, it wanted religious education taught in school and sex education banned, and the religious forces successfully pushed through a 1993 bill to outlaw abortion, legal under the Soviets.

Many Poles were appalled by the law making abortion illegal. Although religion is an important part of their culture and many revere Pope John Paul II, reproductive rights were not questioned under Communist rule. Several subsequent moves to overturn the abortion ban – including one by Prime Minister Leszek Miller in 2004 – were mired in political controversy and thus far the Polish parliament has rejected them. (Miller reportedly dropped his push to legalize abortion, in exchange for the Catholic church supporting EU entry.) Analysts say the church, which pushed through the abortion ban, paid for the move: it isn't nearly as powerful as when it was officially illegal during the Soviet days, and Polish Catholicism has taken a popularity nosedive since 1993.

The good news was that, on paper at least, Poland was vastly improving economically: in the decade between 1989 and 1999, when Poland was selling off many of its state-owned industries, the Polish economy grew by 25 per cent[7] and the international media loudly cooed about the Poles' increased wealth. Many people, however, weren't sharing the enthusiasm: a Polish government study showed that in 1995 a whopping 40 per cent were living in poverty[8] and even now plenty of houses in the countryside don't have running water.

Ouch! In 1995, when he ran for a second presidential term, Lech Walesa lost to the former Communist Aleksander Kwasniewski, who had a better handle on foreign relations and running a government. That race was quite close, but in 2000 when the two faced off again, Kwasniewski was re-elected, while Walesa picked up less than 1 per cent of the vote. One factor behind the return of a Communist: some Poles, particularly the elderly, feel they were better provided for under the Communist system. Kwasniewski is seen as a symbol of that time.

Since 1999 the Polish economy has stumbled, in part because of Russia's own faltering economy, and its debts to Poland going unpaid. The Gdansk shipyard went belly-up, manufacturers fall months behind in paying wages, factories that can't comply with EU-mandated upgrades are shutting their doors, steel mills are being sold off to foreigners, and productivity is down by nearly 50 per cent from the Communist years. Meanwhile, grain imports from Western Europe have shot up, decreasing the prices Polish farmers can command. French and German-owned supermarkets are dotting the land, often shunning local produce, and Polish pork isn't up to EU standards, and isn't sold abroad. In the midst of the faltering economy that saw unemployment shoot up from 12 per cent in 1999 to 20 per cent in 2004, Poland was rocked by a bribery scandal called Rywingate that shook its faith in democratic reform. Movie mogul Lew Rywin, co-producer of *The Pianist*, is now in prison.

Given the sour mood, it was no surprise that the bellowed accusations of farmer Andrzej Lepper rang particularly clear. He'd been screaming for years that the government was corrupt, and filled with 'scoundrels' and 'scumbags' – charges that in Poland qualify as slander, of which he has been found guilty. But Lepper rants about more than just dirty politics; he regularly rails at Polish trade policies that allow the West to dump their surpluses in Poland at the expense of Polish workers and farmers. 'You sold Poland out!' he screamed in parliament in 2000. His polemics about the evils of trade with the EU have only grown louder in the following years, after his Self Defence party gained seats, grabbing 15 per cent of the vote. As Miller was walking out of power in May 2004, Lepper was snatching more of it: by spring 2004, his Self Defence was Poland's most popular party and he was Poland's politician with the highest approval rating. Regarded as an attention-getting buffoon by most of the media, he's nevertheless sending shivers up the spine of the established govern- ment powers. The reason: Lepper is tapping into the growing voice rising up from the rural poor – at least a quarter of the country, many of whom still plough with horses and harvest by hand. To those whose wheat, fresh milk and dusty produce can't compete with goods from Western Europe's intensive agribusiness – and who are facing the prospect of losing their farms – no face shines bright than Lepper's, the pig farmer who nearly lost his own farm in the transition from Communism to a free-market society. And if EU policies further hamper Poland's agricultural community, Lepper has said Poland should quit. By May 2004, at least a third of the country was seriously listening to him.

Poland's Most Famous Camera Hog

In a country marked by a shortage of strong leaders, Lepper stands out. Then again, given his love of stunts, the square-jawed MP with slicked-back hair would stand out anywhere: the fancy-suited pig farmer is a bona fide ham. Forming Self Defence (*Samoobrona*) in 1993, Lepper first grabbed headlines for overturning rail wagons filled with imported wheat and organizing roadblocks of lorries hauling imported grain; soon 20,000 and more showed up for the protests that often turned bloody. The former boxer also sometimes donned the role of Robin Hood, raiding corporate pork farms and making off with the sausages to distribute to the poor, although sometimes he more closely resembled the Godfather whose minions at least once beat to an unrecognizable pulp a civil servant who had come to foreclose a farm. He's stormed the Ministry of Agriculture howling over trade policy, he's pushed hecklers into manure, and he's ordered mobs to toss eggs, potatoes, even firecrackers at politicians supporting sales of Polish industry and land. That his party could show up at the head of the pack in 2004 was a surprise to most Polish politicians, and a sign of how out of touch the establishment is with the non-urban masses. Lepper was laughed off as a loudmouthed nuisance when he ran for president in 2000 – although with over 1.3 per cent of the vote he fared better than former president Lech Walesa – but by 2001, Lepper and his Self Defence party had secured enough votes to take fifty-three seats in the Sejm, the lower chamber of parliament. Then the fun really started as parliamentary speakers were shoved from the podium by Self Defence ministers and Lepper's tirades began; if his microphone was shut off while he was blasting Kwasniewski or his government, he simply picked up a loudhailer and continued. Politicians from Brussels to Warsaw see Lepper as dangerous, but between his hot air that mixes nationalism and the price of bacon, Lepper does make some valid points: namely, he emphasizes the plight of small farmers who can't fight subsidized agribusiness, and he gives a voice to their angst and their anger. So vitriolic were his words hurled in the direction of Brussels that even EU Commissioners launched an anti-Lepper drive in the months before the referendum about coming into the EU. 'Agricultural incomes will rise significantly,' European Commissioner Günter Verheugen promised from his office in Brussels. 'The very small and extremely small farms whose owners produce only for their own needs will for the very first time have a stable income.'[9] Those were empty words to agrarians who can't figure out how to fill out EU subsidy forms: until the Polish government and the EU take small farmers by the hand, Lepper and other loudmouths who prey on fear will continue to be the little man's hero.

'Does anyone think new generations of young Poles will put up with the wretched living conditions on the country's tiny farms?' – European Commissioner in charge of EU enlargement Günter Verheugen[10]

'We are already seeing what the EU has given us, the worst things: deviance, immorality, aggressiveness, increasing crime, unemployment. And if all we do is what the EU wants us to do, and if we continue to adapt our laws to EU laws, then our traditions will disappear. The faith of our forefathers will go away. Our culture will collapse. And my party is trying to preserve it' – Andrzej Lepper[11]

Whether Lepper's words are mere bluster remains to be seen, but he is the only one who's worried about Poland's arrival in the EU. The intelligentsia and major media may applaud EU membership as Poland's symbolic rejoining with Europe and the country's only real option, but fears persist that Poland isn't being treated fairly. Even lawyer Jan Rokita, whose popular Civil Platform appeals to the young, educated professionals, has taken on the issue of Poland's votes in the EU as a personal cause. And there's one concern about EU membership that crosses most party lines: Poles fear that their lands will be gobbled up by foreigners, specifically Germans. At least the EU threw them a bone on that one, agreeing that Poles could prevent foreign land sales until 2016.

'What Bismarck and Hitler didn't seize by force, [German Chancellors] Kohl and Schröder receive for nothing' – Lepper as quoted in Time International, 4 Oct. 1999

Since it came galloping out of the gates in 1989, Poland has mostly been stuck: the great dreams that fuelled independence have faded, Solidarity has sputtered, former leader Lech Walesa is out, the initially promising economic performance stalled and unemployment and fear are spinning out of control. In short, Poland appears to be at its most painful moment in post-Communist history, and nobody yet knows if EU membership will eventually numb or add to the pain.

Future Forecast

Rocky roads. Given that all signs (and the EU's own reports) were screaming 'Not Ready!' months before Poland entered the European Union, it's no surprise if naysayers are screaming 'Wasn't Ready!' since it came in. Some Poles are hopeful, perhaps too hopeful, but mixed with that are feelings of disillusionment. Farmers walked in angry, workers are frustrated about waiting years to look elsewhere for jobs, and Poland's leadership entered on a defensive note – while suffering a lack of domestic support. Symbolically and morally it was right to let Poland in now, but the dear country is seriously needy and loudly demanding. Western companies, however, will find it profitable to take advantage of the relatively cheap and abundant labour market, which may both help Poland's economy and perpetuate its fear of being exploited.

So eager is Poland to join the eurozone that leaders wanted to start using the euro immediately. A panicked EU put the kibosh on that idea as soon as it was floated.

Hot Spots

Warsaw: Hitler ordered the Polish capital along the Vistula river demolished after an uprising in the Jewish ghettos, ordering 'Leave no stone standing atop another'. The Nazis succeeded in the mission all too well, demolishing 85 per cent of Warsaw; it's said that only a few thousand people survived in the city that was formerly home to millions, a third of them Jewish. The Old Town, also demolished during the last days of the war, was (surprisingly) rebuilt by the Soviets: with buildings painted in golds, pinks and reds, and the clomping of horse-drawn carriages (now carrying tourists) across cobblestone squares, it may even be

Krakow: setting for *Schindler's List*.

prettier than it used to be. The Royal Way that stretches from the Royal Palace to the royal summer home is thick with culture – museums, galleries, churches and palaces stretch out along this passageway that would still please a king – and the once-seedy nightlife is slowly giving way to slick clubs and chillout lounges; there's even a growing fashion district. Birthplace of Chopin, Warsaw is still filled with his presence, especially in the summer, when his music floats through the city as thousands spread out in parks and take in free concerts. Like the memories of Communist Russia itself, Soviet-style architecture looms in the background, perpetuating the image of a drab Soviet capital, but it is being gradually torn down.

The Big Screen: *Warsaw is the setting for Roman Polanski's latest film* The Pianist, *about the April 1943 Ghetto Uprising. The film that took the Cannes Film Festival's highest prize and garnered Polanski a Best Director Oscar is based on the true story of pianist Wladyslaw Szpilman (1911–2000), a former house musician for Polish State Radio. Forced into the Warsaw Ghetto, he escaped to the 'Aryan part' of the city, and lived to write* Death of a City, *first published in 1949[12] and later republished as* The Pianist.

The Warsaw Ghetto Uprising: 19 April–16 May 1943[13]

In October 1940 the Nazis forced Warsaw's 500,000 Jewish residents from their homes and pushed them into a ghetto located near a train station. Nearly 300,000 were hauled off to concentration camps over the next two years and another 100,000 ghetto dwellers starved to death or died from disease. In January 1943, when another 5,000 Jews were sent off on trains, a young band of Jews attacked the Nazis, a move that halted deportations for several months. When Nazis returned to continue deportations on 19 April 1943, several hundred young Jews fought back with homemade explosives, while others hunkered down in secretly built tunnels and shelters. The resisters were overwhelmed within a few weeks, and those in hiding were forced out when the Germans torched every building and gassed the tunnels. It's believed only a few hundred of the remaining 60,000 Jews in the ghetto escaped.

Krakow/Cracow: Hub of education, industry and culture, Krakow holds Poland's regal and rebellious past: site of two 1790s rebellions against Russia and Prussia that led to Poland's demise, it's now starring on the tourist map as the setting of *Schindler's List* (and home of the ceramics factory owner who saved the life of one thousand Jews). Thick with legend – it's believed to have been founded after legendary Prince Krak slew the resident subterranean dragon – Krakow is simply one of the prettiest cities of Europe. Nearby salt mines are dripping with elaborate crystalline sculptures, including glimmering chandeliers and even a chapel of salt; some believe the mines were once the home of trolls. No word on how they got along with Prince Krak.

> **Sore spot:** Nowa Huta *(The New Factory)* was the ugliest Soviet addition to the Krakow landscape; this pollutant-spewing steel factory was planned to be a 'workers' paradise' but instead was the site of some of the testiest rebellions in Krakow.[14]

Auschwitz: The most potent symbol of the horrors of the Second World War and the Holocaust, this concentration camp of brick buildings and ovens still sends chills up the spines of the half million people who visit each year. In 1940 the Nazi-occupied Polish village of Oswiecim had its name changed to Auschwitz and its history altered for ever when it became site of a camp that held up to 20,000, usually their last residence before death. First housing Poles, then Russians, then gypsies, then Jews, the original Auschwitz was expanded to include several other sites, including Birkenau (Auschwitz II) a few miles away, where the majority of Jews were sent. Here, in the complex of buildings with room for 90,000, most were gassed and their bodies thrown into crematoria that could incinerate over 300 a day. The exact number of Jews, gypsies, gays, and other Poles who died here isn't really known, but it was at least 1.5 million. In 1996 plans were halted to build a shopping centre right outside its gates.

Shining up the Rust Belt

The smoke-belching factories in Poland that produce low-quality steel, blacken buildings and clog air with brown clouds require major renovation and are often shut down. In 2002 Poland put the bulk of its steel mills up for sale. US Steel was interested in the package to take over 70 per cent of Poland's steel production, but Anglo-Dutch firm LNM Holdings secured a deal. Poland is under the gun to clean up environmental damage lingering from the Communist years; the European Union is being called upon to help the process along.

Gdansk: The port city where Solidarity first rose up in 1980, Gdansk was one of Europe's great cities when it was part of the fifteenth-century marine trading group the Hanseatic League; hard hit during the Second World War, it was rebuilt and today is thick with domed churches, spires and medieval design. Called Danzig by the Germans who held on to it until 1918, Poland snatched it during the post-First World War redesign of Europe. Gdansk isn't rolling in business these days: in 1995 the famed shipyard where Solidarity was born went bust.

> *Poisonous envy: One reason Hitler directed the Nazis into Poland in 1939 was his desire to snatch back the Gdansk/Danzig port as well as mineral-rich Silesia. Another attraction for Hitler: with its history of religious tolerance, Poland was home to most of Europe's Jews. Nearly all were sent to Poland's concentration camps.*

Silesia: Nestling between Poland, the Czech Republic and Germany, coal-rich Silesia was for centuries a centre of mining and industrialization; currently it's best known as a hotbed of discontent, with unemployment hovering around 30 per cent. Running as deep as the mineral is its history of ethnic problems, starting in the 1800s when the Germans were bosses and Poles were workers. Most of Silesia became Poland after the First World War, which infuriated Germans who lived or owned factories there. After the Second World War the Czech Republic took a chunk as well; both countries pushed out the area's Germans in a violent mass deportation in 1946.

Neighbourly Relations

Poland and its neighbours are trying to heal old wounds, but none of these relations could be characterized as happy-go-lucky.

Russia: Poland walks on egg shells with Russia, upon whom it still relies for much of its energy supplies, while it arms itself and joins NATO to ward off any future attacks from the bear. 'Poland wants to be in NATO, not against Russia,' Kwasniewski has emphasized.[15] Sensitive Russia doesn't see it that way.

Germany: Chancellor Schröder opened the doors for Poland in the new EU, but relations are still delicate: a recently proposed investigation into how many people were killed in Nazi-run Polish concentration camps led to prickliness when Germany offered to headquarter the commission in Berlin. Poles are quite worried that Germans, and other Western Europeans, will try to buy up all Poland's land. Germany was livid in 2003, when Poland baulked at the proposed changes in EU voting procedures; rumours floated out of Berlin (and Paris) that Poland would pay by being denied major funding.

Lithuania: There's a forced show of warmth between Poland and Lithuania, a relationship that used to be cuddly, but Lithuanians are still smarting that Poland took most of their land in 1918 (it was returned two decades later) and was slow to recognize Lithuania's hard-won independence in 1991; Poland is also concerned about reports from Poles living in Lithuania who say they are mistreated. Nevertheless, the two share a military force.

Ukraine: Poles feel protective towards Ukrainians, who now need visas to cross into Poland, the country that helps fuel the Ukraine's black markets. Poland has vowed to try to bring the Ukraine – and other former Soviet republics – into the EU in the future.

The podium: Self Defence's favoured tactic in parliament is to swarm the podium during a speech with a theme they don't like – such as announcements of sales of government industry to foreigners – knocking out the speaker. Sometimes they're joined by the Peasant Party as well. Some sessions of parliament are so unruly that President Kwasniewski has threatened to call early elections in the hope that the rowdy parliamentarians would not be voted back.

The radio waves: Radio Maria, a heated political station that claims to reach over 3 million Catholics, was one source of loud EU scepticism. They had to turn down the volume a notch after the pope gave a holy nod to Poland entering the EU, a move reportedly linked to a political compromise: then Prime Minister Leszek Miller stopped pushing his plans to legalize abortion if the church supported Poland's EU accession.[16]

Ambulances and funeral homes: Polish media uncovered a sickening practice in 2002 involving the transport of the desperately ill. Some ambulance crews – generally a poorly-paid group – receive kickbacks of $200 (€160) whenever they deliver a corpse to certain undertakers. The so-called 'skin hunting' is sleazy enough: the scandal emerged from allegations that not only did medics allow patients to die en route, they sometimes snuffed them out to ensure even prompter pay.[17]

Slave markets: Poland is a major node in the Central European sex trade network. Young girls plucked from across the country, as well as Ukraine, Bulgaria and Moldova, are often sold off in Poland's cities en route to Western Europe, where they are sold again as slaves at much higher prices.

A related problem: prostitutes in Amsterdam say new Polish arrivals are often escaping domestic violence, frequently related to alcohol. Poland has a flimsy support system for women battered by their spouses.

Hot Shots

Aleksander 'Olek' Kwasniewski: President 1995 to present. Handsome, smart and charismatic Kwasniewski was sports minister under the Soviet regime, but the former journalist played a key role in engineering the 1989 dissolution of the Communist regime during the Polish transition to democracy. He started his own Social Democratic party, the Democratic Left Alliance, with other reformed Communists, and beat Walesa in the 1995 and 2000 presidential elections, first becoming president at 41. The West-friendly power player in what US Secretary of Defense Donald Rumsfeld termed 'New Europe', Kwasniewski starred as unofficial diplomat of Central Europe after Czech President Vaclav Havel, who'd played that role for a decade, stepped down in 2003; the Pole was even considered for the top job at NATO, which he pushed Poland into in 1999. He alarmed EU politicians when he threatened to block the passage of the draft EU constitution, a move that didn't win him points with Germany and France. Also annoying to the EU's power duo: Kwasniewski, chummy with President Bush, backed the 2003 war in Iraq and sent Polish troops there in the postwar reconstruction. However, even Kwasniewski was annoyed with Bush in 2004 over US visa requirements for Poles entering the United States, as well as unfulfilled promises about Polish business opportunities in Iraq and US investments in Poland. He's still popular, but has felt some heat for sending troops to Iraq and for possibly being connected to the Lew Rywin scandal.

Andrzej Lepper: the farmer's friend.

Papal matters: The Catholic church backed Lech Walesa (who in 1997 founded his own Christian Democrat party) in both the 1995 and 2000 presidential elections; that Walesa got less than 1 per cent of the vote in the latter testifies to the church's shrinking political clout. However, Kwasniewski illustrated that religion still rates in the hearts of some voters: during the 2000 campaign Solidarity showed a clip of Kwasniewski supposedly mocking the pope – and the politician's popularity fell 10 per cent overnight.

Marek Belka: Acting Prime Minister 2004 to present. Former finance minister, the reformed Communist besmirched by corruption scandals was presidentially appointed to fill the Prime Minister's shoes when Leszek Miller stepped out of them in 2004.

The Voting Beef

Poles were already antsy about EU entry, fearing that it could be an excuse for Germany to overtake them again, this time by buying their land. In 2002, when Poland was invited in, the country was offered 27 votes to Germany's 29, a voting system reflecting area and population that's been in place since the Nice Treaty of 2000. The 2003 EU draft constitution, however, revamped the voting system, and made Poland (along with Spain) more of a middleweight, with 80 votes compared to Germany's 170. The Polish government felt that unexpected change was unfair and that it wouldn't play at all well back home. There are rumours that Poland will suffer in the EU funding department as a result of its foot stamping.

Andrzej Lepper: Leader *Samoobrona* (Self Defence) party, Sejm member since 2001. Known for his nationalist and anti-EU views, the farmer and boxer delights in pulling political punches and calling fellow politicians 'scumbags' and 'scoundrels'. His antics range from mildly amusing to violent and obscene, but his championing of the rural poor has done more than win him humanitarian awards from foreign countries: it's also given him new clout. Self Defence won 10 per cent of the vote in 2001 – enough to get them fifty-three seats in the Sejm – but Lepper was so belligerent as deputy speaker of the Sejm that he was ejected from the position, docked pay and stripped of immunity. He was slapped with a jail sentence for slander after calling Kwasniewski a 'layabout', and others are said to be filing charges. Considered highly dangerous by political analysts and most Polish politicians, Lepper nevertheless is a symbol of hope for poor farmers, of whom, at the rate things are going, there will soon be plenty more.

Jan Rokita: Former Solidarity member, he's been MP five times, often jumping parties between elections: party of the month is Platforma Oby-watelska (Civic Platform), which is fiscally liberal and politically conservative. The balding bespectacled lawyer gained mass popularity when part of the government-appointed commission investigating the Rywin Affair; wasn't his fault if the commission, in a 5–4 vote, cleared the SLD government. After all, five of the members had been SLD appointed. Though Rokita is pro-West in attitude, he was so irate about proposed changes in Poland's voting power in the EU that he coined the term 'Nice or death' – referring to the Nice treaty, under which Poland has substantial votes. He may live to regret that dramatic ultimatum, since the constitution will probably spell death to Nice, regardless of what Polish politicians say. Rokita is widely eyed as Poland's next PM: analysts say he's a much better choice than the hotheaded Lepper.

The Bison with Wanderlust

After the First World War, Polish bison were nearly extinct – a result of overhunting by bison-happy Austrian Archduke Franz Ferdinand and others who shot them down with machine guns – but thanks to intervention by animal biologists, the beasts now roam the Carpathian mountains and nearby forests, perhaps too freely in the case of the mammoth beast known as Pulpit, a bison said to stand over two metres high. As a young bull, Pulpit and one of his mates wandered off the reserve, reportedly crossing southern Poland and making it to the Ukraine – where apparently there wasn't much action because the two wisely turned around and came back. Upon their return to the reserve, their friendship was poisoned – over females, as is so often the case. During the mating season, his travelling companion, not wanting competition, pushed Pulpit out of the reserve. On this second trek, which lasted nearly a year, Pulpit's behaviour was indeed beastly. He trampled over fences, destroyed crops, knocked over fruit carts, rammed down shacks and, once, crashed into a funeral, his obnoxious behaviour prompting the horses to shoot off, knocking over the corpse from the wooden hearse, while the bereaved scrambled up trees. A special committee tracked down the bison, and successfully returned him to the reserve, but come the next mating season, he was pushed off again. This time, orders were to shoot him if he posed a threat, and as if sensing the danger, Pulpit was on his best behaviour, so gentle in fact that children fed him sweets and biscuits as he revisited his former haunts. Apparently he was eating far too much sugar; worried about his health (bison, too, have to watch out for tooth decay, obesity and indigestion), the authorities had to intervene. Realizing that, like so many a wayward male, Pulpit needed a female to keep him in line, this time they brought him to a different reserve where apparently he found the love of his life. He never strolled off again.[18] The reserve was fenced in.

Adam Michnik: He railed against Communist rule, and paid for his protests by spending a total of six years in jails, including several during the 1980s when he was an ardent Solidarity supporter. Michnik walked out from behind bars to help negotiate the 'Round Table Talks' that forced the Communists to relinquish power in 1989, and now the celebrated dissident has the last word as editor-in-chief of the first independent, and most popular, Polish daily newspaper *Gazeta Wyborcza*, which he founded in 1989 to follow Poland's first free elections. Ironically, the man who initially supported Solidarity as a political party, changed horses and became one of Lech Walesa's loudest critics. He also triggered Poland's biggest scandal in a decade when he published transcripts of a meeting with Russia's most powerful film producer Lew Rywin, who tried to solicit a hefty bribe – €12 million – to 'fix' a media bill in the works.

Leszek Miller: Prime Minister 2001 to May 2004. He exudes the cool haughtiness of a corporate CEO, and the former hardcore Communist turned Social Democrat wasn't much loved by the masses, partly because of his potential link to Rywingate. His coalition with the Peasant Party – who were always eurosceptics anyway – fell apart in 2003 when he proposed tax increases; Miller stayed afloat, albeit with greatly weakened power. Injured in a helicopter crash shortly after the election, his popularity also crashed during his term: by 2004 less than 10 per cent of Poles approved of his performance, and by March he was shoved out as leader of the Democratic Left Alliance. On 2 May he resigned as Prime Minister, mere hours after Poland joined the EU.

Nearly Forgotten Copernicus (1473–1543)

It was a scandalous, heretical idea at the time, so much so that Renaissance astronomer/mathematician/teacher/doctor/lawyer Nicolaj Kopernik, a devout Catholic, broached it in a handwritten book given only to close friends. In fact *De Revolutionibus Orbium Coelestrium* (On the Revolutions of the Celestial Spheres) might never have seen wide publication had not a German astronomy student, known as Rheticus, become so obsessed with Copernicus that he travelled to Poland and hounded the old man to let him take it to the printers, an act finally accomplished in 1543; Copernicus saw the published book only hours before he died. A graduate of the University of Krakow, Copernicus was actually a lawyer by training, and he did not have a deluxe observatory, often studying celestial movements through specially placed holes in the walls of his house. Although his ideas kick-started the Scientific Revolution, Copernicus was actually not the first to postulate that the sun, not the earth, was the centre of our system; he was, however, the first to widely popularize the notion, and the one who pushed out Ptolemy's theories of the twisting geocentric universe. His book offered valuable theories, but no evidence: it required German astronomer Kepler to prove that Copernicus's theory was right.

Lech Walesa: President 1990–95. He'd been active in worker protests since 1970, but the former electrician emerged as a star in 1980 when he stepped up as leader of Solidarity, the shipyard workers' organization that demanded rights to unionize – a move that snowballed into an independence movement. Incarcerated in 1981, he won the Nobel Peace Prize in 1983 (and wasn't allowed to leave the country to accept it) and in 1990, at 47, he became the first freely elected president of Poland. He immediately donated his $200,000 Nobel Prize money to redeveloping the country. Alas, he had little experience in politics and foreign policy, frequently fought with (and replaced) his prime ministers, once shut down the parliament, appeared erratic and pedantic, and created a political roller-coaster. By 1993 there were calls from all sides for him to step down, but he held on until 1995, when he narrowly lost the presidential election to Kwasniewski. By the 2000 election he was a has-been politically, barely blipping on the voting charts, but he will still go down in history as one of Poland's gutsiest heroes. Walesa now heads his own foundation, and in 2000 was officially cleared of charges that he worked with Soviet intelligence, although conspiracy theories persist.

> *'In 1905, when Poland did not appear on the map of Europe, Henryk Sienkiewicz said when receiving the Nobel prize for literature: "She was pronounced dead – yet here is a proof that She lives on; She was declared incapable to think and to work – and here is proof to the contrary; She was pronounced defeated – and here is proof that She is victorious"' – from Lech Walesa's 1983 Nobel Peace Prize Acceptance Speech, delivered by his wife*

Pope John Paul II: Former Bishop of Krakow, the Polish-born Karol Wojtyla threw his weight behind Solidarity once he stepped up to the Vatican in 1978. Plotted with President Ronald Reagan on how to bring down the Soviets' 'evil empire' as Reagan referred to it, and became quite influential in Polish affairs, albeit less so in the days after independence. (*See* Italy.)

Disco Poles: Name given to some younger Poles who care little for history or politics, but just want to make enough money to afford weekends of clubbing.

Jerzy Kosinski (1933–91): The man who put Polish literature on the English-speaking map isn't much loved by Poles. Born in Lodz, hawk-nosed Jerzy Kosinski, who moved to the US in the 1950s, flapped to fame on the wings of *The Painted Bird*, a hard-hitting novel that casts Polish peasants in a most unflattering light as violent anti-Semites who, like hens in a chicken coop, attack those who stand out. A Polish Jew who escaped Nazi persecution with a birth certificate showing he was Catholic, Kosinski initially palmed off the novel as being based on his Second World War experience, but that claim was later shot down by his many detractors. Dogged by accusations of plagiarism – among them that his popular novel/screenplay *Being There* was a knockoff of a little-known Polish novel – the man who won the National Book Award in 1969 responded by penning a footnote-heavy *The Hermit of 69th Street*, a parody of over-fastidious citation. Brilliant but unstable and noted for lying, Kosinski pulled a plastic bag over his head and suffocated himself in the bathtub in May 1991, leaving a note, 'I am going to put myself to sleep now for a bit longer than usual. Call the time Eternity'.[19] Nobody accused him of plagiarizing that.

Adam Mickiewicz (1798–1855): Born in what is now Lithuania and claimed by Lithuanians too, beloved Mickiewicz is considered by many to be Poland's greatest poet, even though, due to his involvement with secret societies (he formed his own at 19) and protests against the tsar, he was exiled to Russia at 25, and never made it back home. He nevertheless continued to inspire anti-Russian protests, with works such as 'Konrad Wallenrod' – a poem slipped past Russian censors disguised as a battle with Teutonic Knights, although the embedded meaning was about Poland's struggles with the tsar. Befriended by Aleksandr Pushkin in Russia, the poet was later fêted by James Fenimore Cooper, Goethe and Chopin when he travelled across Western Europe, finally settling in Paris. He wrote articles and plays, but his Romantic scribblings (which exalted women, although his own love life was disastrous) and his lyrical poetry that captured the life of Polish peasants set nationalistic hearts beating. Best known for 'Pan Tadeusz' or 'Master Thaddeus', a comical epic poem about a noble feud, and embracing the mystical idea that Poland's sacrifices were part of a messianic struggle of redemption, Mickiewicz died of cholera in Turkey, while fighting in the Crimean War.

Cultural Standout: Chopin (1810–49)

'Poet of the piano' Chopin, considered the world's finest composer for that instrument, is a Polish national hero, despite spending nearly half his life in France. His parents met in the home of a Polish count, where his French father was the tutor and his mother the housekeeper. Frederyk, however, was born outside Warsaw, where his father had risen to be French professor in the Warsaw Lyceum. Chopin began composing his harmonious melodies at 7, performing international concerts at 18, and by 21 was living in Paris, where he hobnobbed with painters and poets. At 27 he entered into a decade-long love affair with female novelist George Sand. Sick with tuberculosis, an illness worsened by an extended winter holiday with Sand in a damp monastery in Majorca, Chopin nevertheless composed several of his greatest works there, including the 24 Preludes and Polonaise in C Minor. The illness soon after killed him: 'the world is suffocating . . .' he said drawing his last breath; 'swear to make them cut me open so that I won't be buried alive.' Most of Chopin's body remained in Paris, but, as requested by his will, his heart went to Poland, the country he hadn't set foot in for eighteen years.

Roman Polanski: Son of a Polish Jew and Russian émigrée, Polanski was actually born in France in 1933, but at the age of three his parents brought him to Krakow, an unfortunate move: during the war both were hauled off to concentration camps, where his mother died; after escaping from the Jewish Ghetto, young Polanski spent the war on the run, sleeping in barns in the countryside. From 1954 he studied at Lodz Film School, made several short films and garnered international recognition for *Knife in the Water*, nominated for an Oscar. In 1968 he moved to California and horrified the world with psycho-thriller *Rosemary's Baby*; shortly thereafter his life became something out of his films when minions of Charles Manson brutally murdered his pregnant wife Sharon Tate. Went on to make *Chinatown* and *Tess* and returned to Poland to film *The Pianist*, which won numerous awards including a 2002 Oscar for Best Director and is considered his finest work.

Other Polish filmmakers of acclaim: Krzysztof Kieslowski, whose morally questioning movies include the *Three Colours* series, *Dekalog* (or *The Ten Commandments*) and *The Double Life of Veronique*, died in 1996. Andrzej Wajda, who cranks out a new film nearly every year, recently won an Oscar for Lifetime Achievement; his early masterpieces include *Kanal* and *Ashes and Diamonds* from the 1950s; he was later celebrated internationally for *Man of Marble* and *Son of Iron*.

Marie Sklodowska Curie (1867–1934): Pioneering scientist who discovered the nature of radioactivity – she coined the term – Madame Curie died of leukaemia as a result. Before doing so, she became one of four people ever to win two Nobel prizes: she shared the 1903 Nobel in Physics with her husband Pierre Curie and colleague Henri Becquerel, and took the 1911 Nobel in Chemistry for discovering two new elements, including polonium, named after her homeland. As her work was done in Paris, the French claim her too.

Others in the Nobel class: Writer Czeslaw Milosz (best known for his essay collection *The Captive Mind*) won the 1980 Nobel Prize for Literature for his works on the twisting of morals in a totalitarian system. Once part of the festive interwar period in Poland when the arts again flourished, Yiddish writer Isaac Bashevis Singer moved to the US, but still wrote of Poland in the passionate parables that won him the Nobel for Literature in 1978; poetess Wislawa Szymborska, known for her ironic touch, achieved the same honour in 1996.

Forgotten Hot Shot: Michel Sedziwoj (aka Sendivogius) (1556–1636)

The life of alchemist Michel Sendivogius is cloaked in legend: depending on who was telling the tale, he was an escapologist (disappearing from flaming towers or dungeon chains) or a form-changing wizard or simply a man of medicine who tended to royals. What does seem certain is that in the late sixteenth century the scientist worked for the Polish king in launching Poland's metallurgical industry. Sendivogius's most important contributions, however, were his books about science and alchemy. *On the Philosophers' Stone* (or *A New Light on Alchemy*) went through dozens of printings in six languages, and was devoured by the thinkers of the day, including Sir Isaac Newton. Sendivogius is the first person credited with writing that air was a mixture of substances, although it wouldn't be until the eighteenth century that anyone could actually figure out what that mixture of substances was.[20]

Jozef Pilsudski: Marshal 1918–35. Tossed into a Siberian prison as a young man for an assassination attempt on Russian tsar Alexander III – oh, those follies of youth – socialist Pilsudski went on to publish his own newspaper *Robotnik* (The Worker). Obsessed with the idea of Poland as an independent country, he became a guerrilla fighter and bandit, robbing banks and trains to fund a private militia to fight Russia, which he saw as the Poles' greatest threat. Fighting in the First World War, he claimed Warsaw in 1918, and hailed all of Poland free and sovereign. The only problem was deciding where exactly Poland was any more. His initial idea was permanently to invite several of the neighbours (Lithuania, Belarus, Ukraine) for Poland's grand reopening, but he settled for most of Lithuania, where he had been born. He was not known for his gentle touch: he pushed Polish troops into half a dozen wars in the country's first two years of existence[21] and by 1926 he was running the place as military dictator. He was propelled to cult status after his death, much to the annoyance of the Soviets,[22] and is still considered the founding father of Poland.[23] Lithuanians don't much like him at all.

Danuta Hübner: European Commissioner for regional policy from 2004 to present.

The World of Spirits

The Polish and the Russians both claim they invented vodka, the spirit with the name that means 'little water'. Whoever started the trend of drinking the alcohol made from potatoes, Poles make the smoothest, say many connoisseurs. Now flavoured with ginger, cinnamon, pepper or jalepeños, the straight, unadulterated stuff is still the fave. One standout: Zubrowka, which comes with a blade of grass floating in it. Some say the secret is that the grass has been subtly flavoured with bison pee.

Closing time?: Many of Poland's vodka distilleries are doing badly and may soon fold.

Media star: There are plenty of interesting papers in Poland, but few in English. One exception: *The Warsaw Voice*: www.warsawvoice.pl

20. Hungary (Magyarorszad): Lost in the Past

Fast Facts

Country:	Republic of Hungary; Magyar Koztarsasag
Capital:	Budapest
Government:	parliamentary democracy
Independence:	1001 (unified); modern Hungary formed 1920; 1989 independence from USSR
Population:	10,033,000 (2004 estimate)
Leaders:	Head of State: Ferenc Madl (2000) Head of Government: Prime Minister Ferenc Gyurcsany (2004)
Elections:	President elected by Parliament for 5-year term; Prime Minister elected by Parliament
Name of Parliament:	National Assembly; Orszaggyules
Ethnicity:	Hungarian 90%, Roma 4%, German 3%, Serb 2%, Slovak less than 1%, Romanian less than 1%
Religion:	Roman Catholic 67.5%; Calvinist 20%, Lutheran 5%, atheist, other 7.5%
Language:	Hungarian
Literacy:	99.4% (2003) (dubious claim)
Exports:	machinery/equipment, manufactures, food, fuel/ electricity
Per capita GDP:	$13,900 (2003)
Unemployment:	5.9% (April 2004 Eurostat figure)
Percentage in poverty:	8.6% (1993 estimate) (dubious claim)
EU status:	entered May 2004
Currency:	Hungarian forint
Known for:	intensity and depression

Standout Qualities

Dark: Sad past
Dark: Gloomy moods
Dark: Strong coffee

Résumé

It's known for cheerful fiddlers, fruit brandies and zesty food, but Hungary often is the most melancholic of all EU countries, a land where the trademark posture is looking down at one's shoe and the national hobby is lamenting the past. Today's Hungarians – a breed united most strongly by their unusual, vowel-heavy language – are haunted by history, and a popular belief that Hungarians are cursed. What else could explain Hungary's fall from greatness and chronic battles to hold on to its language, people and land? What other European country was invaded and occupied five times during the last century alone?

'We know what it is to be losers. We have all been losers for centuries' *– Hungarian psychologist Margot Honti*[1]

Hungary: Suicide Epicentre

Is it the weather – the long winters and frequent grey skies? Is it geology – the thousands of thermal hot springs bubbling up from under the land, or is it history, and centuries of occupiers overshadowing its power? Perhaps the culprit is a lard-happy diet or too much cream or maybe it's a normal reaction to the sight of so many McDonald's and KFCs dotting the horizon. Whatever the reason, Hungarians are a gloomy bunch. Hungarian leaders and writers have often done themselves in: during the last century Hungarians often had the highest suicide rate in the world. It remains abnormally high: among the middle-aged, for instance, only the Japanese kill themselves more. Sociologists attribute the self-destructiveness to pent-up rage; Hungarians say it's genetic – they feel too much. But happiness in a capsule will soon be available, as pills are on the way to the forlorn citizenry: Eli Lilly, the maker of the antidepressant Prozac, announced in 2004 that it will be setting up a research and development arm here. Who knows, maybe future Hungarians will be downright giddy.

Whether it's a curse or a talent for picking losing horses, Hungary still suffers from a few bad decisions that led the wealthy, weighty and splendid nineteenth-century Hungarian empire to its twentieth-century demise, history that still hangs like an albatross from the collective psyche. Clearly lacking soothsaying skills, the country backed the losers in both world wars and paid heftily for the miscalculations. As punishment for siding with Germany in the 1914–18 war, Hungary was whittled down to a third of its former size – an issue that still deeply rankles and politicizes today. Promised return of the lost land, Hungary fell in with Germany again during the Second World War: not only did the former territories stay put on the *other* side of the borders in 1945, but Hungary was also forced to pay war reparations to Russia – which roped it into the Soviet Union and robbed any remaining riches. Yet another lingering wound that people talk about as if it happened only a few hours before: the failed anti-Soviet Revolution of 1956, when nobody helped Hungary in its attempted Communist overthrow, brutally quashed under orders from Moscow. Tens of thousands were killed while the West looked the other way, and the Warsaw Pact forces – soldiers from Soviet bloc countries – stormed in.

Bad Year: 1956

No period of the past fifty years better exemplified the Hungarian plight than the autumn of 1956, when Hungary – pushed by hunger, stirred up by Radio Free Europe and believing that Western powers would come to its aid – stood up to the Soviet Union, alone as it turned out. Suffering under the diktat of Moscow's economic policies, Hungarians were already agitated and unhappy in 1956 when winter hit early – in October – along with drastic shortages of fuel and food. Mimicking Poland's uprising earlier that month, hundreds of thousands of students and workers revolted on 23 October, toppling statues of Stalin and Lenin, smashing out windows and issuing a sixteen-point proclamation, which demanded, among other things, that the USSR cut loose its hold, end the secret police and send in more food. Moscow answered by rolling in tanks, and the already chaotic situation got uglier when the Soviet Warsaw Pact soldiers killed hundreds of demonstrators. Rethinking the plan, Moscow caved in to at least one protest demand and allowed popular Communist, Imre Nagy, a previous Hungarian prime minister known for reforms, back into power. As prime minister again, Nagy first tried to quell the unrest by releasing political prisoners and ordering out the Soviet troops. The troops, however, soon returned, when Nagy announced that Hungary was pulling out of the Warsaw Pact – the Soviets' collective military force – and would become neutral on the world stage; Nagy also notified the United Nations of the desperate situation. Moscow responded by unleashing more Warsaw Pact troops, who killed over 20,000 during ten savage days when tanks dragged corpses through the streets as a warning to protesters.[2] Nagy, whose premiership lasted all of ten days, was kidnapped and hauled off to Romania, where he was imprisoned, later found guilty in a secret trial and executed in 1958. Buried in an unmarked grave, his remains were exhumed in 1989, and Hungarians reburied him as a hero, with the most moving speech given by rising political star Viktor Orbán. Hungarians are still very upset that none of the powers opposed to Communism came to their help in the 1956 Revolution; some believe that the West's lack of support was the result of a secret deal with the Soviet Union not to interfere in the 1956 Suez Canal crisis in Egypt if the West ignored Hungary.[3] Who knows? they could be right.

'To every writer in the world, to all scientists, to all science academies and associations, to the intelligentsia of the world: HELP HUNGARY!' – Message from the Hungarian Writers' Union to the free press during Hungary's 1956 Revolution

'To all those suffering under Communist slavery, let us say you can count on us'[4] – US Secretary of State J. F. Dulles in November 1956, whose words rang hollow considering the US had done nothing but watch while the Soviets regained control

Hungary still hasn't entirely perked up, even in the sixteen years since the Communist regime fell. In the transition from the socialist society – where housing, jobs and food were provided – to a competitive free-market democracy where little is guaranteed, many Hungarians are struggling. The government, meanwhile, keeps tinkering with the economy: wages, while recently boosted, are still low – about a third of those in Western Europe – prices are rising, and many fear that EU entry will only make the cost of living shoot higher. The countryside still isn't fully electrified, and the agricultural sector that employs nearly 20 per cent is rotting: with state subsidies slashed and farmers confused about the EU, look for more farmer-led highway blockades as the impact is felt. Just as alarming is Hungary's deep political fracture, a divide evidenced by a revolving door of governments, none (thus far) voted in for two successive terms as the political mood ping-pongs from left wing to right. The fiery split in voter sentiment – basically between those who support ex-prime minister Viktor

Orbán's populist-tinged leadership, and those who dislike his cocky, self-aggrandizing style – was most obvious in the days after the 2002 elections (between Orbán's Fidesz and the Socialists) when the air was so charged some feared Hungary was peering at civil war.

> *Seventy-one per cent of the electorate voted in the 2002 parliamentary election – the highest turnout since Hungary became democratic – and the race was close, with Orbán's party actually winning more votes: however, due to a proportional voting system, which weights votes from the less populated rural areas, Socialists (who promised wage hikes and payments to pensioners) took the election. It was an emotional day: Orbán cried during his speech conceding defeat, and so did many of his supporters. Fights broke out, and street protests turned so violent that police tear-gassed the crowds. At least seven Hungarians, however, missed the post-election fireworks. They'd died of heart attacks while casting their votes.[5]*

The chasm in the country was immediately acknowledged by the winner, Socialist Peter Medgyessy. 'We must start on reuniting the country,' said the new prime minister in his 2002 acceptance speech. 'I want to be prime minister of [all] 10 million Hungarians, not two times 5 million.'[6] Medgyessy, however, only divided the country further when soon afterwards news broke that he had been a Soviet spy (or counter-spy as he contended) – an announcement that triggered massive protests and caused a popularity slide. By the summer of 2004, his approval rating was hovering at 20 per cent. In August, parliament ousted Medgyessy in a vote of no confidence, appointing millionaire Ferenc Gyurcsany – a former Medgyessy adviser – to fill his place.

Popular with the business crowd, Socialist Gyurcsany's first high-profile move was to announce that, with parliamentary approval, Hungary's 300 troops would be called back from Iraq.

The new prime minister is forced to contend with continuing anxieties about the economy as well as the booming voice of the opposition, led by Viktor Orbán, whom Hungarians are still passionate about in their adoration or deep dislike. Tiger, megalomaniac or Hungary's brave new hero: he's been called all three, and more. One thing is undisputed: nobody is better than Orbán at rattling Hungary's chains, which of course are linked to the past.

Preview of Coming Attractions?: Fidesz also swept the 2004 elections for the European Parliament, taking 48 per cent of the vote. The Socialists took 35 per cent.

History Review

If Hungary's pessimistic streak shows through, it's understandable: in Hungary change typically means 'downturn in standards of living'. Look what happened when the Mongols showed up in the twelfth century: they slaughtered half the Magyar population. Look what happened when the Turks showed up and won the 1526 Battle of Mohács: for a century and a half, Ottoman Turks ran most of the country, taking over beloved capital Budapest, embarking on a depopulation plan and requiring non-Muslims to pay steep taxes. And then when Austrians helped finally push the Turks out in 1699, the Habsburg clan frowned on Hungarian culture, and suppressed the language that so defines the Hungarian people.

During the Ottoman Occupation many wealthy Hungarians fled to today's Slovakia, where they built up the capital Bratislava, attempting to create Budapest, Jr.

Language Lesson

The Hungarian (Magyar) language is a mystery, starting with its forty-four letters, a dozen of them vowels. Officially, Hungarian is part of the Finno-Ugric group, which would make it similar to Finnish and Estonian, but many Hungarians say that was propaganda from the Austrian Empire to link them more closely with Europe; many Estonians and Finns agree. Some point to the Far East as a more important influence, and indeed this land was routinely taken over from that direction starting with Attila the Hun; even Hungary's official founder Chief Arpad rode in from Asia. Hungarians put surnames first – Medgyessy Peter, for example – a custom shared only with the Japanese. But that isn't the only linguistic tie with Asia: villagers in the Himalayan Mountains near Tibet are said to speak a language similar to Hungarian. Wherever it hails from, they love it with a fierce pride, and even in international Budapest, Hungarian often seems the only language spoken anywhere outside hotels, although more and more young people are fluent in English. If you don't speak Magyar, you can sometimes see ice come into a Hungarian's eyes as prices quickly rise. If you speak even a word or two, their eyes brighten with warmth and the price rises aren't quite as steep.

Despite Austrian disapproval, Hungarians clung to their language, and revived it as the language of literature. The revival of Magyar and an accompanying nationalistic spirit fuelled the Revolution of 1848, led largely by writers, who pushed independence from the Austrian Empire with demands called the 'Twelve points' – starting with freedom of the press and lifting of censorship, and going on to call for emancipation of serfs. That uprising against Habsburg rule did bring a brief taste of freedom – after concessions from Austria's Emperor Ferdinand, Hungary ran independently for a whopping six months. However, the move was so unpopular in Vienna that Ferdinand was shoved off the throne: his nephew Franz Joseph succeeded him and unleashed Austrian wrath on Hungary. The plucky Hungarians fought fiercely, and Austrians had to bring in Croatians and Russian Cossacks to successfully return the wayward territory to Austrian rule. In 1867, however, the Magyars rose up against the Austrians again and demanded the eastern chunk of the weakening Habsburg Empire: this time, they got it, and the Austrian Empire became the Austro–Hungarian Empire, with Magyars controlling lands to the north (today's Slovakia), to the east (today's Romania) and the south (today's Serbia and Croatia).

Redefining Europe

Hungarians love to describe Hungary as right in the middle of Europe, but that really depends on what period you're talking about and who's holding the map. The country that now refers to itself as part of Central Europe was called part of Eastern Europe when it was on the far side of the Iron Curtain for five decades. For 150 years, however, Hungary wasn't part of Europe at all. During the sixteenth century – after the 1526 Battle of the Mohács when Hungarians lost to the Turks – most of Hungary was transformed into the north-west frontier of the Ottoman Empire. Back then, Europe ended at the eastern gates of Vienna.

The Hungarian spirit and landscape were remarkably transformed during the so-called Dual Monarchy. Much of the most spectacular architecture that still shimmers in Hungary – from the lacy towers of the parliament building to the ornately decorated town halls in small towns like Kecskemet – is a testimony to that glittering era when Hungary was rolling in dough, and Budapest rivalled Vienna as the grande dame of Central Europe (if not the whole Continent). With its hill-perched castle, thermal springs and fabulous tile-wrapped buildings designed by the likes of Eiffel, the stunning metropolis on the Danube river was one of Europe's cultural capitals, marked by fine music, high literature, provocative theatre and the many intellectual societies and creators who met in grand cafés, where the atmosphere was charged and the clientele beautiful. The political machine was filled with visionaries as well: so thoroughly modern and avant-garde was Budapest of the Belle Europe era that one of Europe's first subway systems was unveiled here in 1896.

Café Society

Vienna may now have the reputation for café society, but coffee – or 'black soup' as it was once known – first caught on here, being introduced by the Turks who occupied Hungary starting in the 1500s. By the 1800s the liquid fuel was exalted by Hungarians in hundreds of ornate, high-ceilinged cafés that were the official meeting spots for prestigious societies and weighty intellectuals; revolutions were plotted and famous magazines born in the cafés, and the heavily wooded hangouts were magnets for writers of all sorts, since scribes were given free paper to capture their caffeine-powered thoughts. An integral part of Hungarian society, the idea-breeding grounds were shut down by the Soviets who for forty years transformed the lovely establishments into warehouses. Since the 1990s, however, many of the history-steeped cafés have reopened and again serve whipped-cream-slathered coffee in antique china cups with cookies, glossy chocolate and a glass of water all on a silver tray.

Budapest's public transit system is still a standout, not only for the fact that one rarely need walk more than two streets to get on it, but for the escalators that descend and ascend to the subway platforms and back to street-level: so steep are some that the common reaction is vertigo.

Long kicked down by their occupiers, Hungarians in the power position were as domineering as their former rulers; while their nationalist aim had been met, they forced other ethnic groups into submission, forcing the ceded territories (today's Slovakia, Romania, Croatia and Serbia among them) to adopt the Magyar language and embrace the Hungarian culture.

Vocabulary Builder

Magyar (pronounced *Mawd-yawr*): Ethnic Hungarian

Greater Hungary: Lands that were part of the Hungarian Empire, and were given up after the 1920 Treaty of Trianon. Weather maps still show the Greater Hungary borders, and lapel badges are worn in support of the controversial cause

Roma: Gypsies

Austria–Hungary: The Austrian Empire that Hungary muscled into in 1867; ended 1918

Paprika: Name given to hundreds of varieties of Hungarian peppers, whether sickly sweet or deathly hot

Transylvania: Beautiful mountainous section of current Romania that was once part of Greater Hungary

At the beginning of the twentieth century Hungary's future looked sweet, but that was apparently a *pálinka*-induced fantasy. Pulled into the First World War on the losing Austrian and German side, Hungary was left in a chaotic state in its aftermath. A 1918 revolution overthrew the king and formed a republic, but the country was soon overrun by outside forces. At the war's end, Czechs, Slovaks and Romanians invaded and looted Hungarian cities, unleashing the pent-up rage that had built up under decades of heavy-handed Magyar rule. The Romanians were the most vicious: when they left after their 1919 occupation, they loaded up most of the country's remaining industrial riches – and even absconded with Hungary's trains.

Dirty Words: Treaty of Trianon

Of all the punches that Hungary endured over the past century, none hurts worse than the Treaty of Trianon, which in these parts is synonymous with ruin. Drawn up by the victorious Allies after the First World War, the peace treaty signed on 4 June 1920 remapped the Austro–Hungarian empire, forcing Hungary to part with two-thirds of its former territory, population and national wealth; even Austria fared better than its eastern partner in what now appears a heavy-handed punishment. When Hungary's physical map shrank – Romania, Slovakia, Ukraine, Croatia, Serbia and Austria all picked up pieces – many Hungarians ended up on the other side of the new borders, living in a different country from their family and past; reuniting the land became a national obsession for decades. Five million ethnic Hungarians – Magyars – now reside in neighbouring countries; after the collapse of the Soviet Union and the rise of Hungarian ethnic nationalism, some began clamouring for reunification.

The Allied victors' redrawing of post-First World War Europe shaved Hungary of most of its land, people and international clout, leaving it merely one-third of its former size and creating a huge diaspora of ethnic Hungarians. The Treaty of Trianon also ushered in one of the lowest points of Hungary's roller-coaster history. Dictators assumed power over the demoralized Hungarian people in the shrunken land: Communist Béla Kun lasted only six months, but the next powermonger, Admiral Miklos Horthy, cracked the whip for twenty-four years, during which he was obsessed with grabbing back the lost lands of the Hungarian Empire. The return of the territories of 'Greater Hungary' was a cause not only for the leader but the people: starting in junior school, children learned about the national tragedy and the necessity of stitching the land back together, and reuniting with the Hungarians who lived in surrounding lands. Posters of the lost lands, shown in black on a map, hung from offices everywhere, with the words 'No, No, Never.'

Admiral Horthy – sometimes called the admiral without a sea – chased out Kun in a violent counter-revolution of 1919 known as 'The White Terror' during which peasants, Communists and Jews were targeted and thousands were killed.

Lured by the return of land, including forested and resource-rich Transylvania, Horthy signed Hungary up with the Axis Powers in the Second World War, another painful error. Horthy tried to pull out of the agreement in 1944 and the Nazis invaded: the Horthy regime was shoved out by the fascist Arrow Cross movement, which deported and killed some 500,000 Jews in the last months of the war. When driven out by the Soviet army in April 1945, the Nazis blew up Budapest's beloved bridges and castle, leaving the city mostly a pile of boulders and dust.

Invasion Central

Hungary claimed the prize as Europe's most invaded country during the twentieth century. In 1919 the French marched in to finish off the First World War; a few months later the Romanians invaded, occupied the capital city and stripped the land of anything remotely valuable. In 1944 the Nazis attacked after Hungary tried to shake loose of its previous war bond with Germany; in 1945 the Russians invaded and drove the Nazis out. Russia invaded again in 1956, this time violently to crush an anti-Soviet revolution.

The Crown of St Stephen, however, which had been presented by the pope in 1001 to the first Hungarian Catholic king, survived the Nazi attack. So worried was the government about the crown's safekeeping that shortly after the war they shipped it off to the American gold repository at Fort Knox.[7]

Saddled by war reparations to Russia, Hungary was forced to turn over industry to the Soviets, and soon the Soviets simply took over, installing hardcore Stalinists in the Hungarian government, who were quick to hang those who questioned their clout. Not only did Hungary lose any remaining wealth, the country was subjected to the planned economies devised by Moscow, including the collectivized farms and the accompanying frequent shortages of food. The weight of defeat coupled with the apparatus of repression were too much for Hungarians to bear: rebellions broke out, and the Soviets displayed their most ruthless side when Hungary tried to loosen their grip. The worst display was the Revolution of 1956: after Soviet troops rolled into Budapest, killing some 20,000 in mere days, another 200,000 Hungarians fled to Austria.

János Kádár, foreign minister under ten-day prime minister Imre Nagy during the 1956 Revolution, left the government in disgust when Nagy pulled Hungary out of the Warsaw Pact. Kádár landed in the power seat when the Soviets steamrollered the uprising and he stayed there until 1988. Kádár initiated his tenure with a show of force, ordering 2,000 Hungarians executed and another 25,000 tossed in jail for their role in the 1956 Revolution. However, soon after he lightened up. Riddled by guilt over Nagy's 1958 execution, Kádár went on to lead a relatively liberal Communist government.

Even after the 1956 slaughter, Hungary still didn't play by all of Moscow's rules. Fearing another disaster, Moscow gave Hungary freer rein: the Catholic church was allowed out of the closet, some political prisoners were released and Hungary's government was allowed to pursue market reforms and loosen state control over the economy. By the 1980s the economy was open to foreign investment and Hungary had even launched a stock market as part of its 'goulash socialism' programme – moves that made the country appear the wealthiest and economically healthiest of all the Soviet bloc countries, although by the end the economy was propped up by billions of dollars in IMF loans.

Hungarians could also travel to Western countries starting in the 1970s.

In those final years of the 1980s when it was obvious the Soviet Union was sinking, Hungarians were quick to jump ship. By 1988, opposition groups had cobbled together the Hungarian Democratic Forum, which ushered in far-reaching political changes. In 1989 a new constitution was penned, allowing such freedoms as a multi-party system, and the right to demonstrate in protest and form trade unions. Sensing there was little that exhausted Moscow could do, Hungary's reform-pushing Communists tore the first big rip in the Iron Curtain in 1989 – literally snipping the barbed wire – and instructed border guards to stop enforcing the shoot-to-kill policy against those who fled into Austria. That summer Hungary was the place for a holiday, as thousands of tourists from East Germany and Romania slipped out. By the end of the year, Hungary, too, effectively had slipped out of thé Soviet hold.

Soviet remnant: Of all the nuclear reactors started by the Soviets (and finished by Western companies), Hungary's four-reactor Paks plant was considered the most modern and, unlike most reactors in Soviet bloc countries, was never seen as cause for concern. In April 2003, however, the plant malfunctioned during cleaning, releasing radio-active gases. The International Atomic Energy Commission swooped in, pointing fingers at poorly trained personnel, and Austria was blushing as well: although neighbouring Austria opposes nuclear power, and screams about the plants in the Czech Republic and Slovakia, the Austrian government buys electricity from the Paks nuclear plant.

Even shaking free of the Soviet system wasn't cause to bring out the plum brandy for long. Hungary was slammed in the early 1990s; the economy stalled, unemployment shot up to 14 per cent, prices doubled and quadrupled, one-third of Hungarians sank into poverty, and depression slunk over the country. This fine freedom that they had been anticipating for forty-four years seemed far worse than the Soviet days. Relationships suffered, divorce became commonplace – some 56 per cent of new Hungarian marriages split up.[8] Indeed, there is now a Hungarian magazine devoted to the subject. But more alarming still was the jump in suicide rates, which became the world's highest. Public outreach, education and suicide hotlines – and the improvement of the economy – helped to slow the trend, but Hungarians are still three times more likely to commit suicide than residents of the US.

The first of the Soviet bloc countries to privatize, Hungary became the private investment magnet of Central and Eastern Europe. Its cheap labour and tax incentives attracted over $23 billion of foreign investments after 1989 and foreign firms control 90 per cent of telecommunications industries, 66 per cent of manufacturing firms and more than half of the energy sector.[9] However, recent surges in wages – incomes of public servants shot up 25 per cent in 2003 alone – are hurting Hungary's drawing power. Now nearby Slovakia, where wages are much lower, is looking rather appealing to those foreigners wanting to set up shop.

Rapid cultural change also contributed to the collective malaise. Hungary quickly embraced all things Western, being the first former Soviet bloc country to open up a McDonald's, which became the most popular in the world. Burger Kings, KFCs, Irish pubs, sports bars and British department stores popped up everywhere as the country began a fast-track programme to reconnect with the West. One of the first to reach out to the

European Union for membership, Hungary was also wooed by NATO; along with Poland and the Czech Republic, Hungary officially signed on with the mutual armed protection club in 1999.

NATO Conflicts

The membership of NATO immediately came under fire: less than two weeks after Hungary signed on the dotted line, NATO began attacking Serbia in response to Slobodan Milosevic's genocidal sweeps in Kosovo. The Hungarians and Serbians are not close, but so many ethnic Hungarians live just over the Serbian border that many felt betrayed by Hungary for supporting the move, fearing that genocide-mad Milosevic would begin persecuting them as well. The NATO problems didn't stop there: so furious were recent protests over erecting NATO radar towers atop a wooded hill in a nature reserve that the project was postponed. Even NATO training in Hungary has brought problems. In February 2004, during a 'Partnership for Peace' exercise with countries planning to join NATO in the future, an Azerbaijani officer beheaded an Armenian officer, causing a huge international flap.

Quick Tour

From Tokaj's sloping vineyards and the slender minarets rising up in Pecs to the flowering apricot orchards unrolling across the great plain, the door is swinging open again for Hungary. With Western Europe's budget airlines swooping in along with hordes of travel writers, capital Budapest is again blipping on the tourist radar, the old-world cafés are reopening, village arts festivals are blooming, and music floats down the streets, escaping from opera houses and tourist restaurants where gypsy bands play. Once prohibited from starting their own businesses, more and more Hungarians are entrepreneurs, and unemployment is a relatively healthy 6 per cent. Fish-rich rivers thread across the fertile land where food is plentiful, soups are rich and creamy and everything is washed down with fine Hungarian wine.

Hungary has twenty wine regions, and a wine industry that could boom. Tokaj, considered the 'king of wines, and the wine of kings', questionably steals all the press (the white wine is an acquired taste),

but many of the reds range from easy-drinking to elegant. Foreigners
are buying up vineyards by the handful.

So, with all the opportunity around the bend, why, besides national temperament, are so many Hungarians utterly glum? At least some Hungarians say that the black hole of sadness comes from a feeling that the past has been ripped away. Not only is the safety net of Soviet-style Communism shredded, but Greater Hungary remains divided, and there's a growing sentiment, especially among the young, that the lost lands should be reclaimed. That's probably an impossible feat – and certainly one that would have vast repercussions; there are plenty of Hungarians who are disturbed by the very notion and who say that the country needs to stop dwelling in the past and look to the future. Nevertheless, the promise of one way or another gluing together the shattered Greater Hungary dream has been dangled by Viktor Orbán, the master manipulator who successfully entangled his image with two of the country's most emotive symbols: the Revolution of 1956 and the Treaty of Trianon.

Greater Hungary

Never mind that Greater Hungary was whittled away eighty-five years ago: the sense of injustice still hangs in the air. You can see it in the wood-shrouded Buda bar where Gabor, a college student, is drawing the outline of old Hungary saying he wants that land back; you can see it in the museums that sell Treaty of Trianon badges and postcards, with the lost lands in black, chastising 'Don't Forget!'; and you can even see it on the TV weather map, which often shows the outline of the pre-1920 empire. Initially the loudest promoters of the idea of a reunited Greater Hungary were radical rightwingers from the Justice and Life Party (MIEP). But the idea got new life recently when Viktor Orbán and his party Fidesz formed a conservative coalition with the agricultural-based Freeholders Union that also pushed the reunited Hungary button. Orbán has been stirring up the Greater Hungary pot since shortly after he strode into office as prime minister in 1998. Relations between Hungarians and their Slovak and Romanian neighbours became tense when Orbán began making noises about bringing together all Magyars, saying that they are one nation, wherever they live; he went on to offer education and employment benefits to ethnic Hungarians who live outside the territory. Although many doubt that a serious effort at physical reunification would happen, there is an unspoken fear that Magyars will rise up and one way or another try to recover the lands ripped away by the much-hated treaty. To do so would be political suicide in a united EU, but tell that to the fervent Greater Hungary supporters, who wear Treaty of Trianon lapel badges, and the tens of thousands who demonstrate on 4 June, the anniversary of the date the land-shaving document was signed.

'Apart from the existing spiritual links, we have been waiting for eighty years for a legal link between the ceded parts of the Hungarian nation [and Hungary itself], a link that could strengthen the ties between those living on both sides of the border and that takes into consideration the large number of Hungarian families that live on either side as citizens of different countries' – Viktor Orbán on Hungarian Radio, 9 January 2002, in a translation supplied by the Hungarian embassy[10]

'At last, after eighty years the Hungarian nation is uniting and is forming Greater Hungary' – Orbán's above statement as translated by Slovakian media[11]

Slick, smart and aggressive, Orbán has a vision for the country that doesn't necessarily stop at its current borders. How far he could or would push the Greater Hungary idea is a matter of debate, but nobody has done more to agitate the whole country and replant the idea that Hungary should reunite with the land and the people lost after the First World War. Critics charge that even to talk about Greater Hungary he and the radical rightwing MIEP are feeding the people a pipe dream, but by doing so Orbán keeps alive the deep-rooted feeling of historical injustice against the Magyars.

The Rise of Viktor

Ruggedly handsome, secretly wealthy and obsessively driven – he believes he is destined to lead the Hungarian people – brash Viktor Orbán rose to fame straight from law school, where he and other political science students put together their own political party – the Federation of Young Democrats (Fidesz). Radically liberal and decidedly young – the party at first wouldn't allow members older than 35 – Fidesz changed directions when Orbán took over the wheel: seeing an opening on the right, he formed Fidesz–Hungarian Civic Alliance, a coalition with the rural Smallholders' Party, and began talking about uniting ethnic Hungarians and closing out foreigners from buying Hungarian land. His first dramatic display was his moving speech at the 1989 reburial of the former Hungarian prime minister Imre Nagy who was unjustly tried and killed after the Revolution of 1956. The event was already rife with emotion, but Orbán made it more so when he demanded that Soviet troops leave Hungary, the first to be brazen enough to say so in a public speech since Nagy. Within nine years he'd climbed to the top of the political mountain – becoming prime minister at 36 – and introduced a number of controversial plans and policies. Loathing Communists, he quickly funded a new museum showcasing their horrors – the House of Terror. Set up in a Budapest mansion previously used as a torture-filled interrogation centre by the Soviet secret police, critics say the museum is propagandistic and Hungarian Socialists (the party that absorbed most of the Hungarian Soviet leaders) claimed it was more about politics and keeping them out of power than documenting history. Orbán blocked opposition voices from the media; he shut down newspapers and weakened public broadcasting, triggering outrage from international media watchdogs. Orbán also stirred up the neighbours. Passing a 'status law' that gave work, healthcare and education benefits to the 5 million Hungarians living in surrounding countries, Orbán triggered fears that he was trying to kick off a pan-Hungarian movement, fears not allayed when he spoke of the 'spiritual and cultural reunification of the Hungarian people'[12] and referred to Transylvania – part of Romania – as 'part of Hungary's living space'.[13] The status law was ultimately watered down and, much to his surprise, Orbán was not re-elected in 2002, losing to the Socialists by a hair's breadth. But not to worry: he's kept busy in European-level politics, as vice-president of the conservative European People's Party (a major force in the European Parliament), and has turned from youthful atheist to hardcore Christian: he was awarded the highest papal decoration in 2004. Besides, with Fidesz 20 per cent ahead in the 2004 polls, he'll probably be back shortly. In the meantime, his family is growing – he now has five children – and he can practise his football: he has a talent for that as well.

Some analysts speculate that Orbán's new-found religion is more about power than seeing the light. He also supports the controversial clause in the proposed EU constitution that states that the EU is a

union of Christian countries. Many see that line as a way of closing out
EU candidate Turkey, a Muslim country and Hungary's historical rival.

Taking over from the Hungarian Socialists who'd come to power in 1994 and initiated economic austerity measures that got them booted out at the next election, Orbán ended up in office, just when the Socialists' changes began coming to fruition in 1998. Orbán, too, juggled the country's finances, including raising real incomes for Hungarian workers. Even though the economy improved, Orbán's megalomania, press censorship and loudly trumpeted vision for Hungarians – and uniting them wherever they lived – became grating, at least to his foes in the urban intelligentsia. His 'status laws' that would welcome out-of-state Magyars back to Hungary for several months a year – giving them benefits for health and education – triggered an avalanche of criticism from the neighbours, particularly Slovakia and Romania, for reawakening the Greater Hungary dream. Nevertheless, Orbán looked likely to win a second term, when his brashness did him in. In the country where it's admitted the left loathes the right and vice versa, Orbán took it too far. 'The trouble is, you're all traitors,' he told Socialists during a session of parliament.[14] His campaign manager echoed the sentiment, when he suggested to Socialists, 'Go find a few thick planks and a stout piece of rope and hang yourselves.'[15] Orbán was haughty in debates with Medgyessy – who came off surprisingly well – and the prime minister alarmed even some fans when he began cuddling up with MIEP, the right-wing extremists who hate Roma and Jews. In a country where typically 50 per cent come out to vote, the high turnout for the elections in April 2002 was seen as a sign: analysts speculated that many Hungarians weren't necessarily voting pro-Socialist, but anti-Orbán.

Another problem for Orbán: charges of cronyism and corruption were
flying by election time. His agriculture minister was better known for
throwing lavish parties than for helping out farmers, and Orbán's
father was alleged to have benefited in a highway development pro-
gramme.

The Socialists, voted back into office in 2002, immediately had to assuage the neighbours' fears triggered by Orbán's Magyar unification drives and Status Laws. Although Orbán saw himself guiding the country into the EU, Prime Minister Medgyessy got that honour, but the transition hasn't been easy. The agriculture minister resigned due to incompetence in explaining to the farmers how EU farming subsidies work, and pessimistic Hungarians are warily eyeing the new union, wondering what fresh hell it will bring.

> *While 84 per cent of Hungarian voters gave a green light to EU accession when they voted in the 2003 referendum, that doesn't mean that most Hungarians are excited about it: only 46 per cent showed up to vote.*

Even though he's out of power, Orbán hasn't shut up or stopped kicking up a furore. He continually blasts the Socialist administration from the sidelines, recently began calling for ethnic Hungarians in Romania to be given autonomy – a charged demand – and in February 2004 gave his own State of the Union address, talking of the 'thickening gloom of economic woe' created by the Medgyessy administration. 'We can only hope no worse period befalls the country,' he admonished, while plugging his own accomplishments nearly every other word. Orbán leaves little doubt that he wants the premiership back. And with the Socialists' popularity sliding, Orbán may well get it.

Radio Roma

Tourists love the festive Roma or gypsy bands whose folk music greets them from street corners, but Hungarians haven't been too fond of the bunch who have been in much more dire straits since the fall of Communism. One of Hungary's EU entry hoops was to ease pressure on the group and fund cultural projects. One such project: the world's first Roma radio station, broadcasting in their language, addressing Roma problems and playing their music; many non-Roma say it's the best station in Budapest. Every so often Roma shut down the station in protest at their continuing struggles with the Magyars.

Future Forecast

With its wine areas, its thermal spas and its architectural riches, Hungary will become even more of a tourist magnet, but more politically polarized. If Orbán makes a comeback – and he'll surely give it his best shot – he'll probably keep pushing the neighbours' panic buttons and dividing his own land.

In a 2002 interview with the Washington Times, *Orbán's appointed ambassador to the United States, Geza Jeszensky, shot down the idea that Hungary had any intention of extending its borders into Romania or Slovakia. 'Elementary logic would say that Hungary on no account could dream of getting back, for instance, the Transylvanian section of Romania, where there are 6 million Romanians and only 1.5 million Hungarians,' Jeszensky is quoted as saying. 'It would lead to confrontations with our neighbours.'[16] Now, that's an understatement.*

Hot Spots

Thermal waters: Thousands of geothermal springs gush up across Hungary and their mineral-rich waters are renowned for their curative effects and ability to soothe aches and pains. Be careful where you're dipping, however: some of the baths that make the skin glow may do so because they're radioactive.

Steam baths: The Turks may have introduced them but the trend is still very hot here.

Budapest (pronounced *Booda-pesht*): The most attacked capital in Europe, and still bearing bullet holes from the 1956 Revolution, regal Budapest is still one of Europe's grand capitals, and has 130 thermal springs

Stately Budapest: once the belle of Eastern Europe.

underneath it; hotels often offer thermal spas, as well as dentists, cardiologists and plastic surgeons on site. Budapest is actually a combo of two former cities – old world Buda, with its wooded hills and seventeenth-century architecture, and more urban, modern, flatter Pest – which sit on opposite sides of the Danube river. The city's beautiful Academy of Music was praised by no less than Stravinsky as having the finest acoustics in the world. May rival Vienna again, if the old beauty ever gets that needed facelift and businesses stop ripping off tourists.

Hotel Gellert: Built during the First World War, the majestic hotel that was Nazi headquarters during the Second World War is the most famous and beautiful place to take a soak: its baths are lined with marble columns and wrapped in stained glass.

The Danube: Forget the idea of being blue, it's usually grey around here. Heavily polluted under the Soviet regime, it is being slowly cleaned up, and the EU has donated over €30 million to help the cause. The river that historically made Hungary's capital an important trade city has been dammed upstream by Slovakia; Hungarians, forced to agree to a joint-dam plan during Soviet times, backed out upon independence, and are screaming mad that Slovakia proceeded. International powers are urging the two countries to sit down and work it out.

The Holocaust Museum: Opened in 2004 at the behest of Prime Minister Medgyessy, Budapest's Holocaust Museum is a memorial to the 600,000 Hungarian Jews killed in 1944. Israeli President Moshe Katsav flew in for the April opening, and several Arab men were arrested in what was believed to have been a foiled assassination plot. Local media report that the museum itself may have been a bombing target.

> Hungary has a tense relationship with Jews. It claims to be the first country to have put Jewish emancipation laws on the books when, among other things, it allowed Jews to live in Pest in the nineteenth century; previously, Jews had been allowed into the city only during holidays. However, Hungary was also the first European country to install anti-Jewish laws – restricting education and marriage among other things – in the twentieth century. Right-wingers MIEP are openly anti-Semitic, but hostile feelings towards Jews – whom some Hungarians link to the Communists – are simply not uncommon in Hungary. Between 600,000 and 800,000 Hungarian Jews were sent to extermination camps from here in 1944; Hungary finally opened a Holocaust Museum sixty years later.

Buda Castle: The hilltop castle that peered down over the Danube from the thirteenth century was supposed to protect Magyars, but over the years mostly helped out the enemies. Turks moved right in, making it their base during their 150-year stay; required demolishing the castle to get them out. The Nazis made themselves at home in the rebuilt structure, using it as a fortress, and showing their thanks by blowing it up when they left. Rebuilt in the 1950s, the castle complex now houses plenty of stately monuments and assorted museums, but no longer a monarch – the last was booted out after the First World War; many tourists miss the labyrinths winding around under it.

It's said that Turks buried treasures in the castle labyrinths; during the Second World War it was a subterranean Nazi town, complete with bomb shelters and hospital.

Pecs: Twenty miles from the field that changed Hungarian history with the Battle of Mohács (the Ottoman Turks won), Pecs exemplifies Hungary's layered past in its main square: there one finds statues of Hungarian warriors, slain during the 1526 battle, and in the background a minaret looms, topped with a cross. The best showcase of the Ottoman occupation.

Eger: Lovely Baroque town, known for the regional red wine called Bull's Blood, a name given after the locals drank copious amounts of it, sloshing it on their shirts, and then beat back the Turks – who attributed their defeat to the alcohol-fuelled fighters drinking bull's blood. The Turks returned a few decades later and took Eger with ease, but the name of the wine sticks. Outside the town, in the Valley of the Nice Lady, wine-tasting cellars are built right into hills; the name of the valley comes from the lady who offered more than Dionysian pleasures in her tasting room.

Balaton: The Hungarian Sea as it's known is Europe's largest fresh-water lake, and several million descend upon it each weekend in good weather.

Refrigerators: In the typical Hungarian fridge you'll find plenty of cream (the base for most soups), whipped cream (slathered on everything) and lard (squirted out of a tube for that popular onion-garnished treat – lard sandwiches). No wonder at least 19 per cent of Hungarians are obese.[17]

Taxicabs: Slimy unaffiliated cabbies bilk the foreigner, charging €20 or more for a five-minute ride. Alas, these scammers are just one form of Budapest's con artists, a group that includes beautiful girls who invite the unsuspecting visitor for a round of drinks that rings up at €500.

Borders: Sharing boundaries with seven countries, Hungary has been a major corridor since the 1990s for drug-running, slave-smuggling, trafficking of arms and stolen cars, and any other activity deemed profitable for the Russian mob. With some of its neighbours, notably Ukraine, Serbia and Croatia, not entering the EU this round, everyone reckons Hungary will be even more the back door to Europe. Tens of thousands of border guards are hoping to reverse that notion.

Wallets: Keep that money handy. In modern Hungary everyone from petrol station attendants to gas meter readers expects a tip.

Neighbourly Relations

Slovakia: Things often heat up between Hungary and Slovakia, where half a million ethnic Hungarians live, right at the common border. Slovaks are still resentful of the days when Hungary bullied them, and Hungarians say Slovaks treat Magyars poorly. Matters worsened when Orbán pushed through his Status Law without consulting any of the affected countries, and Slovaks feared a Magyar uprising. Slovakia's damming of the Danube hasn't helped things a bit. (Note to EU dinner-party planners: don't sit these two side by side.)

Romania: It makes Romanians very jittery when Hungarians start gazing at beautiful Transylvania, once part of Hungary, and which Romania of course doesn't want to give back. Beautiful, resource-rich and several hours away from the current Hungarian border, Transylvania is where the bulk of Romania's ethnic Hungarians live, and where Viktor Orbán is happy to meddle in affairs, whether funding Hungarian-speaking universities or advocating the autonomy of Magyars who live there. But even before Orbán had his finger in the pot, relations between the two countries were tempestuous – Hungarians have not forgotten that Romanians occupied and looted Budapest in 1919. At the moment the situation is actually better. With mutual NATO membership, the Socialist Party in power and with Romania hoping for a 2007 invite from the EU – they are dreaming – the relationship is at least less rocky than usual. Australia also helped, indirectly: when an Australian-owned gold mine in Romania leeched cyanide into rivers first in that country and then downstream into Hungary, both bonded to demand clean-up compensation from the mine's owner.

Austria: Deep historical ties and disputes here, and an unspoken rivalry between Vienna and Budapest, but Austria is a major market for Hungary, including its nuclear-generated electricity, which Austria buys, discreetly, since Austrians voted to ban nuclear energy in their country.

Serbia: Hungary is still cross that it lost land to what is now Serbia, especially the region of Novi Sad, where plenty of Magyars live, and there's occasional unrest.

Croatia: Problems go back for centuries, including when Croatians were called in by the Austrian Habsburgs to crush Hungarian uprisings in the 1800s. Illegal Croatian arms are often smuggled through Hungary.

Ukraine: Lots of Ukrainians sell black-market items to Hungarians; could be problems when Ukraine is cut out of the EU boundaries.

Slovenia: No major problem here.

Hot Shots

Ferenc Gyurcsany: Prime Minister 2004 to present. Young, rich, and charismatic, Gyurcsany might be just what the country needs. Not a hothead like Orbán or bland like Medgyessy, the smooth-talking tycoon – who'd never been in politics before Medgyessy yanked him in as adviser – has urged fellow Socialists to 'dare to be left again' and revamp their image from being dinosaurs left over from the Communist days.

Ferenc Mádl: President 2000 to present. Law professor and former culture minister, Mádl, who is not tied to a party, wrote numerous books about Hungary and its relationship with Europe. Almost everybody but MIEP likes the thinker who mostly stays quiet.

Viktor Orbán: Prime Minister 1998–2002; head of Fidesz. Political chameleon Orbán is the person to watch in Central European politics, if only to see which hat he'll slap on next and which heartstring he'll pull. Formerly an avowed atheist, he's now a devout Christian, and was recently awarded the Vatican's highest honour; his politics shifted from left wing in the 1980s to right wing in the 1990s and experts say he will cater for the middle ground soon. (See The Rise of Viktor, page 535.)

> '[In Hungary] the time-machine does not move forward but backward ... to somewhere where it stopped in 1919' – Nobel laureate Imre Kertész in 2002 interview with writer Margit Koves

Former PM Viktor Orbán fuels Hungary's divide.

Péter Medgyessy (aka Agent D-209): Prime Minister 2002–4. In 2002, Socialist Medgyessy pulled the carpet out from under Fidesz, and immediately had to patch up problems with the neighbours that Orbán had started, and tone down Orbán legislation that offered health benefits to foreign Magyars; also gave himself a hefty pay rise. Approval ratings plummeted after news that he'd been a spy; he says he was a counter-spy, protecting Hungary's financial secrets from Russian eyes, and threatened to sue the paper that broke the story. His handling of the economy, and his unpopular attempt to oust the finance minister, brought him down in 2004.

Budapest is stunning in its beauty but visitors may be stunned by their credit card bills. Some joints add a few more zeroes to the tab. Bands of burgling Roma are another drag.

Historical Hero: Imre Nagy (1895–1958)

Intellectual, earnest and bespectacled, Imre Nagy (pronounced *Eemry Nawdj*) was a Communist in the purist sense of the world, so much so that he didn't get along with the Soviets, who entirely mangled that utopian concept. As Hungary's reform-oriented agricultural minister in the early 1950s, he continually got in hot water, was ejected from the position and forced to reshape his ideas on reform. His ideas of actually involving the people in decision-making made him so popular, that he was called back again to the power arena, replacing Stalin-loving Matyas Rakosi as prime minister in 1953. Nagy's open-minded actions, such as lifting censorship, getting rid of collective farms and holding public forums on economic and agricultural plans, got him tossed out yet again in 1955. In October 1956, however, when Soviet troops killed demonstrators, protesters demanded his return and, in the midst of the violence, he stepped in again as prime minister; his colleague János Kádár became leader of the Communist Party. Ordering Soviet troops to leave, Nagy quickly reordered the Hungarian government, decreasing Moscow's power, releasing political prisoners, abolishing the one-party system, and pulling Hungary out of the Soviet armed forces, the Warsaw Pact. The Soviet Union, led by Nikita Khrushchev, unleashed its ire on 4 November and Nagy was again forced from office. Kidnapped while trying to leave the country, he was shipped to Romania; after a bogus trial there, he was executed in 1958, making Nagy a martyr overnight. In 1989 the Hungarian government announced that Nagy had been set up and falsely tried: the beloved leader of the 1956 Revolution was reburied a hero in 1989; a movie by Márat Mészarós documents his tragic life.

Lászlo Kováks: European Commissioner 2004 to present. A questionable appointment, Kováks was deemed incompetent by the European Parliament that approves European Commissioners, then merely incompetent to hold the energy portfolio. Now in charge of taxation.

János Kádár: General Secretary of the Communist Party 1956–88. Foreign minister during the Revolution in 1956, which he survived. Believed to have betrayed his comrade Nagy, to whom he'd promised safe passage out of the country when the Revolution was flattened by Soviets; it's said the guilt from Nagy's death over trumped-up charges of treason drove Kádár crazy. Kádár died the same day that Nagy was cleared of wrongdoing in 1989.

Pál Teleki: Prime Minister 1939–41. As prime minister at the start of the Second World War, aristocrat and geographer Teleki blocked the Nazis from invading Poland via Hungary, and allowed hundreds of thousands of fleeing Poles to take refuge in Hungary. He was also the architect of what are considered Europe's first anti-Jewish laws, including one formally relegating Jews to second-class citizens. Killed himself in 1941. When Budapest City Council wanted to erect a statue of him at Buda Castle, local Jews had a fit.

Cultural Standout: Béla Bartók (1881–1945)

Franz Liszt may be better known internationally, but no musician strikes more of a chord with Hungarians than Béla Bartók, whose dramatic works were influenced by folk music. Ghostly pale with dark mystic eyes, Bartók's passion was ethnomusicology, a field he pioneered: after overhearing a Slovak peasant singing in 1907, he travelled across the countryside, convincing country dwellers to allow him to record their traditional songs on wax cylinders; fellow composer Zoltán Kodály, also beloved, was equally fascinated by the music of those who worked close to the earth. A pianist, teacher and composer, Bartók's most scandalous composition was the sexually charged ballet *Miraculous Mandarin*, that revolved around crime, prostitution and murder. Upon its debut in 1926 in Budapest, the shocked audience hated it and stormed out; future performances were banned. Bartók won favour shortly afterwards, however, with two violin sonatas and his famous *Dance Suite*. Although his career was soaring, he loathed the interwar ship run by dictator Admiral Horthy and ceased performing during the 1930s. When the Second World War broke out, he moved to New York – and composed for such VIPs as Benny Goodman – before dying there in 1945 of leukaemia.

Hungary has a rich history of literature and theatre, but many works haven't been translated. However, Hungarian novelist and Auschwitz survivor Imre Kertész won the 2002 Nobel Prize for his works (including Fateless *and* Kaddish for a Child not Born*) which capture characters lost under dictatorships. Writer György Konrád is acclaimed for his autobiographical novel* The Case Worker *as well as his work for civil rights. A few other translated masterpieces: Pál Závada's* Jadirga's Pillow *– an epic tale of one Slovak–Hungarian family, and Milan Fust's* The Story of My Wife *about the twisted path of obsession.*

Franz Liszt (1811–86). The Hungarian went down in history as one of the world's finest composers for such works as the *Hungarian Rhapsodies*, but during his life he was Europe's most gifted and passionate pianist, who coaxed an orchestra's worth of sounds from the ivories. Travelling across

Europe on a nine-year concert tour, he worked with numerous composers of the day including young German Richard Wagner, who later married Liszt's daughter. Deeply moved by St Francis of Assisi, Liszt became a priest at age 55 and wrote *St Francis Preaches to the Birds*, a piece capturing the twittering of the swallows to whom Francis was said to often address his homilies.

> *Liszt's influential and complex* Twelve Transcendental Studies *are astoundingly difficult to play and Hungarian pianist George Cziffra (1921–94) was one of the few up to the task; the performer, however, didn't get rich from it – he made most of his money playing for the circus.*[18]

> **Movie makers:** *Hungarians are also known for their cinematic works: they claim the producer Sir Alexander Korda (best known for* The Third Man*) as their own, even though he worked mostly in England (being involved in propaganda and a spy network). Other standouts are directors Miklós Jancsó (*Hungarian Rhapsody*) and István Szabó (who won a 1981 Best Foreign Film Oscar for* Mephisto*).*

Béla Kun: Self-proclaimed leader 1918. Hothead Communist who grabbed the reins after the First World War, kicked off a 133-day (second) Bolshevik Revolution and quickly became hated by everybody for passing numerous laws, including prohibiting alcohol, requiring that children take baths and transforming churches into cinemas.[19] During his six-month regime, Kun seized lands from the rich – but forgot to turn them over to the peasants. The charismatic madman was probably the worst person to have heading the government when the mapmakers were redrawing Europe after 1918: his Communist policies won Hungary absolutely no favours with the Red-fearing Allies.

Out-of-country Magyars: The 1920 Treaty of Trianon left millions of ethnic Hungarians stranded in different countries. Now 1.5 million Magyars live in Romania, Slovakia has 600,000, Serbia 300,000, and Ukraine is home to 200,000 and others are scattered about.

Annettka Fehn: Nutty TV hostess announced her desire to run for the European Parliament in 2004 by baring all – literally – to her TV audience.

Super Hot Shot: George Soros

Hungarian-born billionaire philanthropist George Soros suffered the Nazi occupation in Hungary, then moved to Britain and studied at the London School of
Economics. Jumping to the US in 1956, he became an investment adviser, made
oodles of money, and then as chief adviser for another investment firm, the
Quantum Fund, gave it the world's best record ever. Also has a heart: he has
started up numerous foundations and programmes, including the Open Society
Fund that send blacks to university in South Africa, supports arts and political
projects across Central Europe, founded universities in Budapest, Prague and
Warsaw, and kicked off dozens of other projects to foster less repressed living
situations around the world. The author of eight books, however, has his biases:
he sank a ton into trying to get George W. Bush defeated in the 2004 election,
despite the fact that along with George Bush, Sr, he's part of the questionable
Carlyle group – an investment firm of assorted bigwigs (including the Saudi Royal
Family and, until late 2001, Bin Laden's kin) that is linked to arms sales. Another
black mark: he speculates in foreign currency. 'The Man who Broke the Bank of
England' is also blamed for singlehandedly creating the Asian financial crisis of
the 1990s.

Hungarian Truth and Life Party (MIEP): The good news: they're not very
popular. The bad news: the fact that this openly anti-Semitic, anti-Roma
political party exists.

> *Scary: the rising forces of young skinheads in Hungary. Blood and
> Honour is one group known to stage demonstrations 400 strong in
> Heroes Square in Budapest.*

Media star: The *Budapest Times* gives the news in English: www.buda-
pesttimes.hu

21. Baltic States: Estonia, Latvia and Lithuania – Humming Along

Overview

Lost in that blurry backwater between Poland and Russia, the so-called Baltic States – Lithuania, Latvia and Estonia – are the three most intriguing entries to the EU.[1] The allure is their mystery: these former Soviet republics might as well have dropped in from a different planet, since most of this one has ignored them throughout history. Even now few people can actually find them on a map, but we do know one thing: they can sing.

Geographical Confusion: Baltic States v. The Balkans v. The Slavs

The Baltic States is typically used to mean Lithuania, Latvia and Estonia – three different countries with three different languages and three different ethnicities. Lumped together because of location, the three share little more than a tumultuous past when the neighbours continually invaded. The term Baltic States sometimes includes Finland and Poland, with whom they share history. Another confusion: the Baltic States are often mixed up with the Balkans – Serbia, Croatia, Bosnia, etc. – and that really makes the Balts batty. One more no-no: referring to the Balts, as the people of the three separate countries are sometimes known, as 'Slavic' or 'Russian' unless they indeed are: Lithuanians, Latvians and Estonians are ethnically different from Russians, although some Russians have lived here since the days of the Soviet occupation (1944–91). Even though everyone had to learn Russian back then, since independence it can be iffy to speak '*Russki yazik*' here: for many, it is the sound of oppression.

In these three Baltic-hugging countries song signifies more than just the cheesy Eurovision contest, which both Latvia and Estonia have recently won. Music was also the weapon of their revolt against the Soviet Union. And for centuries song was the vehicle to keep the language and cultures of these often-occupied countries alive.

Neither Europe's largest nor deepest aqueous body, the forked Baltic Sea that divides Scandinavia from Central Europe was once the Continent's most important, being the steely wind-tossed waters upon which medieval trade flourished. The Hanseatic League – a profoundly important fourteenth- and fifteenth-century trading union of merchants that linked ports across northern Europe – made this region Europe's richest, as ships hauled grain from the Baltic States, wood and fish from the Nordic countries, cloth and wool from Germany. For much of the twentieth century, however, the Baltic Sea was less a unifying force and more a symbol of an economic and political divide, cleaving the wealth and freedom of Denmark, Sweden and Finland in the north from the poor, Soviet-occupied republics to the south-east.

History Review

The creation of the Baltic States as separate countries is a recent and remarkable occurrence that for most of their histories just didn't seem to be on the cards. For eight hundred years these northern lands that stretched along the eastern Baltic Sea didn't have their own distinct identities, being but valuable coastal properties that changed occupiers just about every century, with the resident farmers and agricultural land thrown in as part of the holdings. Vikings, Germans, Poles, Danes, Swedes and Russians laid claim to the fertile lands with ice-free access to the sea, each 'owner' passing on the resident serfs when they lost the turf and handed over the keys.

Sweden, which ran Estonia and Latvia until 1721, was the most benevolent master, launching an education and literacy campaign, opening schools, abolishing serfdom and even establishing peasant rights. By the end of the Swedish stay, most of the resident population could read and a printing trade had emerged, further shaping national identities. Russia, however, which took the properties off Sweden's hands, had other ideas and pushed intense Russification, including trying to blot out the national languages.

It wasn't until the First World War ended that the resident populations at last could forge their own countries, and each declared independence in 1918, although apparently nobody heard. While all the neighbourhood bullies were fighting over who would claim the Baltic lands this time, the Baltic leaders slipped off to the 1919 Paris Peace Conference, when the countries of Europe were being redrawn in the Great War's ashes. There they successfully lobbied the powerbrokers and cartographers of the day: in 1920 the boundaries of the Baltic lands were redrawn as three separate, independent countries – Lithuania, Latvia and Estonia – carved from what had once been Russia's western frontiers.

The reason the Baltic lands were up for grabs: Lenin made a slight miscalculation and signed over Russia's western fringes to Germany in 1918, when Russia was still sorting out the Bolshevik Revolution and Lenin was sure that Germany would win the First World War. During the Treaty of Versailles, Germany's holdings were trimmed.

Lithuania was drained by fighting to regain its capital and other territories that Poland had taken after the First World War, but Latvia and Estonia prospered from agriculture after independence, becoming richer than Sweden, the neighbour that had once been the overlord. But the Baltic States enjoyed their long-awaited independence for only twenty years, partly because of their pride. The three new countries had such strong national identities that they refused to unite politically or militarily as a strong Baltic entity; besides, they couldn't communicate other than by using Russian, a language that symbolized the hated centuries of Russian domination. Although the topic was broached occasionally, the three countries didn't forge together as one regional military power and they were seen as easy prey. By 1939 their former 'owners' Russia and Germany were scheming to take over the strategically located lands. They all suffered the same fates: throughout the Second World War, the Baltic States were violently tugged between the two militaristic powers, and ultimately nabbed by Soviet Russia, which held them prisoner by occupying them in the decades that followed.

Dirty Words: Molotov–Ribbentrop Pact

To Balts those words are synonymous with 'ripped-away freedom'. The 1939 'non-aggression pact' between emissaries of Hitler and Stalin had a secret section tacked on: it divided the Baltic States and Poland into German or Russian 'spheres of influence', which was a diplomatic way of saying that Russians or Germans sent in their armies to take over the place. Estonia, Latvia and Lithuania were dished out to the Soviet Russians whose Red Army rolled in during August 1939; Poland, which like the Baltic States wasn't consulted on the matter, was divided between both Germany and Russia. The Soviets denied this reality for decades. During the late 1980s the Baltic independence movement demanded that the Soviets finally admit to the clandestine parts of the pact.

The occupations first started in autumn 1939 when Russia – angered when Estonia helped repair an escaping, but damaged, Polish submarine – moved troops into the Baltic States, shortly after the Germans had invaded western Poland, launching the Second World War. The return of the Russians who'd long dominated them was horrifying for the Baltic peoples, all the more when their occupiers began transporting millions – first intellectuals, aristocrats and politicians, then the commoners, children and farmers – to Siberian work camps. But two years later Hitler declared war on the USSR, and wrested the Baltic States from the Russian yoke. Initially the Germans were greeted as liberators, at least until they too began shipping out dissidents and the region's many Jews. In 1944 the Soviets returned to push out the Germans and forcefully rope in the Balts. As the Red Army rolled into the country yet again, some 500,000 Balts escaped, the Russians bombing and torpedoing their ships as they fled. Another 100,000 Balts ran into the woods.

The Forest Brothers

The thick forests of pine and birch that cover the Baltic States are more than a pretty lumber resource. Long haunted by legends of witches and magic trees, these dense woods also served as home to a brave resistance community, when some 100,000 Lithuanians, Estonians and Latvians fled the Soviets who returned near the end of the Second World War. Some simply preferred nature's hardships to those inflicted by the Russians; others of the so-called 'Forest Brothers' formed a guerrilla force that slipped into urban areas to cut power lines, sabotage government vehicles, write anti-Soviet graffiti and sometimes assassinate local Soviet leaders. Living in crude shacks during brutal winters, most of the Forest Brothers had been captured, killed or had died by the mid 1950s. Those who were caught and survived were packed off to Siberian work camps for terms upwards of fifteen years. Only a few still live on to tell the story.[2]

'Nobody believed that Estonia would, for decades and decades, be left in the hands of the Soviets. That wasn't even a possibility. "It's only a question of time," everybody thought. But after decades went by, the idea about the West coming to their aid disappeared. The fight in the forest became a personal thing. These people fought because they simply wanted to die as free men' – Mart Laar, former Estonian prime minister and author of *War in the Woods* in interview with *City Paper*[3]

The next forty-six years were a tragic rerun as the Russians reoccupied the Baltic States, this time transforming them into Soviet republics complete with centralized planned economies and communal housing where six families crammed into one house, sharing one kitchen and bathroom, in a forced programme of comradely equality.

To much of the world these three republics simply fell off the map when the Soviet Union claimed them. Granted, the United States government, for one, never recognized that the Soviets were in charge of the three countries, but that made little difference to the Balts, who were very clearly informed that Russia was in power; they could be shot on the spot if they questioned it.

Soviet planners soon rearranged the scenery and stamped their communal vision upon the Baltic States: once-productive private farms were collectivized (production plummeted) and once-pristine waters were polluted by rapid industrialization as the three republics were turned into food-processing, electronic and pharmaceutical centres of the Soviet Union.

Farmers who rebelled against collective farms found themselves in Siberia. After the departure of tens of thousands in 1949, most of the remaining agrarians caved in to the idea. Another reason Soviets

wanted to punish the farmers: they'd been helping the Forest Brothers,
bringing them news and food.

Due to emigration and war deaths, the population had dwindled substantially and ethnic Russians were hauled in to accomplish the industrialization task. Just as important was their role in ensuring the populations were no longer homogeneous; the Soviet philosophy was always to keep 'problematic' populations diluted, preferably with their enemies. The Lithuanian, Estonian and Latvian languages were no longer acceptable in business and everyday life: although the local tongue was often taught in schools, to get anywhere in the Soviet world one had to learn Russian. Meanwhile, intellectuals, aristocrats and anyone – including children – who looked like they might raise an eyebrow in protest (or whom the Soviet authorities simply didn't like) was shoved into a cattle truck and moved out to Siberia where they usually starved, froze or were worked to death.

Wanted: War Criminals

Almost the entire Jewish population in the Baltics, some 300,000, was killed by the Nazis during their three-year occupation starting in 1941; the highest numbers were in Lithuania, where a large Jewish community had been living since the 1300s. Although few question that there were some locals involved in Nazi affairs – initially the Nazis had been seen as liberators releasing Balts from Soviet domination – how much complicity there was has never been officially determined, in part because, under the Soviets, the history of the war was swept under the rug. Now Jewish organizations are offering rewards for tips that lead to the trials of Nazi war criminals, but the response has been underwhelming. After several months, only about 200 tips had been called in from all three countries combined, the bulk from Lithuania. What really happened during those dark hours may never be known.

An estimated 2 million Lithuanian, Estonian and Latvian civilians died
during the Soviet occupation of the Second World War.

By 1946 the Baltic Jews were extinct: most had died in camps, some escaped, and those few who remained went into the religious closet. The remaining Balts – by then, between death, deportation and emigration less than a half of the original population was left – were exhausted, and Soviet resistance movements had no effect but to prompt more deportations.

> *'We were behind the Iron Curtain for so many years when the world was completely indifferent to our fate and pretended that the genocide was not going on' – Latvian nominee to the European Commission Sandra Kalniete, a former Latvian foreign minister, born in a Siberian work camp where her family had been sent*[4]

It wasn't until the 1980s, when the second generation came of age, that a defiant, angry spirit rose up again. At the same time the Soviet Union was falling apart: the war in Afghanistan was draining the Union and in 1986 Chernobyl blew up, creating an international furore that had Moscow even more under the gun to reform. New Soviet premier Mikhail Gorbachev had already realized the need for a change, and in 1985 unveiled his ideas for *perestroika* (economic restructuring) and *glasnost* (openness, or freedom of the press). Not fully grasping the deep, if underground, hatred that raged against the Russian machine that had bulldozed the Baltic people and culture, his ideas took a course different from the one he had intended. The younger generation wanted to open up and restructure the place all right – by shoving the occupying Soviet Union right out.

The Singing Revolution

Open demonstrations against the Soviets first took place in 1987 across the Baltics, and by the next year the push for independence was heating up. The Balts stood up to Moscow in typically peaceful demonstrations that were sometimes a million strong. Never has music been more defiant than when they belted out national songs, not in Russian, but in their own secret languages now voiced loudly and with nationalistic pride. Another symbolic, soft revolutionary act: the August 1989 linking of hands across the three countries and over four hundred miles from Estonia to Lithuania on the fiftieth anniversary of the malevolent Molotov–Ribbentrop Pact that had so entirely shredded the Baltics' independence.

Russian rightwinger Vladimir Zhirinovsky called Lithuania 'the republic from which comes the disease that destroyed'.

By 1988 independence movements had sprung up in all three countries. The Estonians sang most often, the Latvians wrote more, the Lithuanians made the most outrageous pronouncements. Whatever their methods – and all three used song, word and political demonstrations – Lithuania, Latvia and Estonia were changing their destinies. Their local governments proclaimed that state law was more powerful than Moscow's dictates as early as 1987, and all three Soviet republics proclaimed full independence from the Soviet Union in August 1991. Their joyous announcements were met with hand-wringing by much of the world. Only Iceland recognized them as independent countries immediately. Nobody else wanted to anger Russia by recognizing independence too hastily, and most waited until the United States gave its official recognition – six weeks later – in the autumn of 1991, shortly after the power regime in Moscow had collapsed.

Home is Where the Vodka is?

Many Russians who'd been forced to move to the Baltic States stayed put after the Soviet Union broke up. Ethnic Russians now make up over a third of the populations in Latvia and Estonia, and in Latvia they are the majority ethnic group in the cities. Some Russians are well integrated into the new societies, and are successful business people, who live in fashionable suburbs. But other Russians are having a much harder time. Since independence the tables have turned: now Russians must learn the local language to get citizenship, and many don't have a passport since they haven't learned the language and aren't legal citizens. Meanwhile, their Soviet passports and citizenship became invalid when the Soviet Union crumbled in 1991. Some 1.5 million of the 8 million residents of the Baltic countries are thus 'stateless'.

In 2004 the human rights organization the Council of Europe blasted Latvia (and Estonia) for not assimilating the Russian population. In Latvia alone an estimated 20,000 children born since 1991 are, like their parents, 'stateless' because of failure to comply with language requirements. The volatile language matter also has the Russian leadership screaming about discrimination, in Russian of course. Many Balts regard Russia's interest in the issue as more political than humanitarian.

The three countries immediately turned their backs to the East and their eyes to the West, revelling in the independence that they had known so briefly between the world wars. If Moscow had hoped they'd soon come crawling back, it was mistaken. The Baltic States turned their backs on Russia: the three countries were the only former Soviet republics who wouldn't even join the Organization of Independent States, the mostly symbolic association of ex-republics. Russia was already furious that the Baltic States – their window to the West and favourite holiday haunts – had left, and Russian politicians such as right-wing nationalist Vladimir Zhirinovsky – who is still a big player in Russia's parliament – demanded revenge: Russia responded to the Baltics' coolness by slapping huge tariffs on Baltic imports and making threats about energy supplies.

> 'I do not breed fish or collect stamps. But I have a special thing for border posts. Let us move those posts out to their old places' – Russian parliamentarian Vladimir Zhirinovsky[5]

Continuing to ignore Russia, the Baltic States presented themselves to the rest of the world, and let it be known they wanted increased defence and greater recognition. By 2002 the three Baltic States were invited into the two clubs that mattered: NATO, the US-dominated arms-buying club that would (theoretically) bolster their defence, and, more importantly, the EU, which will economically, politically and symbolically bring them back into Europe. All three Baltic States entered both NATO and the EU in the spring of 2004, while Russia looked on in anger, a state it's been in for fifteen years now.

Moscow is not celebrating these West-embracing moves. President Vladimir Putin's most obvious worry is Kaliningrad – a separate Russian enclave on the Baltic Sea with an important Russian naval base – which is now surrounded and sealed off by EU countries. He wants Kaliningraders (and Russians) to be able to travel freely through the Baltic States without visas, but that looks most unlikely. More troubling to Putin: Kaliningrad might decide to try to go with the EU too.

> 'The fact that you can go to bed and not worry about somebody knocking on the door and putting you on a train for Siberia' – President Vaira Vike-Freiberga on why Latvia wanted to join NATO[6]

But that's just the beginning of Russia's woes. The government abhors the idea of the Baltics being in NATO in general: in 2004, when NATO planes conducted their first drill in Latvia, Russia asked to observe the exercise – and to its fury was denied. Another serious point of contention: tariffs. Since the three Baltic States joined the EU, those huge duties slapped on Baltic goods coming into Russia must be dropped. The EU has a Partnership and Cooperation Agreement with Russia; goods from EU countries have duties of about one-third of those previously pinned on goods from the Baltics. Russia stalled about signing, and in February 2004 the European Union threatened economic sanctions if Moscow didn't put pen to paper before the new countries came in; Russia says that due to EU expansion and reduced tariffs, it will lose some €150 million a year.[7] Paranoia hangs in the air: Lithuania chucked three Russian diplomats out of Vilnius in early 2004, claiming they were spies, and Estonia booted out several as well. Poor Latvia, always the favoured child of the Soviets, is the target of numerous lambastings from Moscow. Vice-chairman of the Duma Vladimir Zhirinovsky vowed in April 2004 that Latvia and the Latvians would soon cease to exist. Who knows what other mutterings and veiled threats aren't even making headlines, but the situation is potentially volatile. Of course, it's precisely the fear that Russia will pull them back into its suffocating bear hug that prompted the Baltic States to rush into the European Union and NATO in the first place.

NATO-bound: Ka-Ching!

It's understandable why the Baltics would want to enter NATO, the arms club created during the Cold War to flex its muscles at the Soviet Union: even if it appears relatively benign at the moment, Russia is curled up next door, the Baltics' armed forces are flimsy, and NATO carries with it a certain cachet. But why NATO invited the tiny Baltic States into the club in 2002 is another matter. On the one hand, the Baltic States can provide more intelligence about Russian activities. On the other hand, many feel that the militarily-puny Baltics joining NATO is an unnecessary provocation to Russia and some wonder if NATO forces could or would even protect the Baltic States if Russia attacked, despite the Article 5 clause that mandates that NATO do so. What the three incoming countries offer: a bigger market for big-time arms sales, since NATO requires that at least 2 per cent of a country's GDP be thrown at defence spending. The largest arms manufacturer in the United States – Lockheed Martin – was the strongest lobbyist for NATO expansion. And by 2004 Lockheed Martin was ringing in the sales: not only did Poland go with the US arms producers, so did the Baltics when they set up Baltnet, a high-tech air surveillance system with a price tag of $100 million.

Since Lithuanians, Latvians and Estonians all speak different languages, they must speak a lingua franca when together. For older Balts, that common language is typically Russian, but most younger Balts use English.

The irony is that despite the grand breakaway from Russia, the powerful neighbour who for centuries just wouldn't let these lands be, the Baltic States are still best identified because of it. Lithuania has grabbed headlines for its political ties to the Russian Mafia, Estonia for its demands for compensation, and Latvia for its Russian 'aliens' who won't qualify for Latvian citizenship until they learn the local language.

22. Estonia (Eesti): The Elder Sister

Fast Facts

Country:	Republic of Estonia; Eesti Vabariik
Capital:	Tallinn
Government:	parliamentary republic
Independence:	20 August 1991 (from Soviet Union)
Population:	1,342,000 (2004)
Leaders:	Head of State: President Arnold Rüütel (2001)
	Head of Government: Prime Minister Juhan Parts (2003)
Elections:	President elected by Parliament for 5-year term; Prime Minister nominated by President, approved by Parliament
Name of Parliament:	Riigikogu
Ethnicity:	Estonian 65.3%, Russian 28.1%, Ukrainian 2.5%, Belarussian 1.5%, Finn 1%, other 1.6%
Religion:	Evangelical Lutheran; Russian Orthodox, Estonian Orthodox, other Protestant; Catholic, Jewish
Language:	Estonian (official); also Russian, Ukrainian, Finnish
Literacy:	99% (2003)
Exports:	machinery and equipment, wood and paper, textiles, food products, furniture, metals
Per capita GDP:	$12,300 (2003)
Unemployment:	9.1% (May 2004 Eurostat figure)
EU status:	entered May 2004
Currency:	Estonian kroon
Known for:	beautiful women

Standout Qualities

Key bond: Finland
Key love: Music
Key to identity: Language

Résumé

Thoughtful, quiet and proud Estonia – land of fair maidens, rugged coast and tiny villages peeking out from dense forests – is in many ways the unassuming leader of the Baltic bunch; the country of 1.4 million nonchalantly poses in the spotlight of the international press these days, nearly yawning after waiting for so many decades to be noticed. Although it's the smallest, least populated and most northerly of the Baltic countries, it is politically and economically the slickest and, to some, the most attractive. Estonia has the region's flashiest politicians who fluently spell out Estonia's charms in half a dozen languages; the country sparkles with the most vibrant economy in the region and has the highest per capita income of the trio (well, that's not saying much), and has plenty of support from its best friend Finland, including economic investment. Estonia, in fact, was the Baltic country that first rang the doorbell to the West, and helped to pull the other two into the European Union.

Scandinavian countries are quite tied up in Estonia: Finland has opened plants assembling phones, and Sweden is running much of Estonia's banking sector. Finns are also frequent visitors to Estonia: ferries bring them in daily by the thousands, where they can stock up on liquor that's a fraction of the price back home. Finnish pensioners are also starting to move to Estonia en masse.

A Few Quirks

In 1999 Foreign Minister Toomas Ilves blasted the European Union for constantly confusing Estonia with Latvia and Lithuania and lumping them all together as the Baltic States. 'There's no Baltic identity with a common culture, common language, even a common religious tradition,' he was reported as saying. The foreign minister was likewise steamed up about the implicit assumption that since Estonia was in Central Europe then it must be corrupt. Ilves pointed out that in a survey of the world's least corrupt countries, Estonia scored better than Belgium, home of the EU's main headquarters.[1] Not long ago he used to go ballistic when anyone referred to Estonia as 'a former Soviet Republic', suggesting they refer to it instead as 'pre-EU'.[2]

OK, so China it's not, but whatever you do, don't call Estonia 'tiny', a description that really rankles with Estonians. The country, they will point out, is bigger than Denmark, Iceland or the Netherlands; it's downright gigantic when compared with newcomer Malta.[3]

History Review

After becoming an independent country in 1919, Estonia prospered economically, but its democracy didn't stay fully intact.[4] In 1934, just before elections, the acting head of government Konstantin Pät, along with the head of the Estonian Army, seized power in a coup d'état. Hundreds of the country's most powerful people were arrested, the parliament was shut down, political parties were outlawed in what was called the 'Era of Silence'. The dictatorship, however, came to an end when Russia invaded in 1940 and staged faked elections that put Soviet-endorsed politicians in power. Professors, intellectuals, politicians and other powerful and wealthy Estonians were quickly rounded up and shipped off to Siberia.

According to the Estonian government, 60,000 Estonians were killed or deported to Siberia during the first month of Soviet occupation in 1940.

After the war, as the Soviet system was forced into place, Estonians proved to be resistant. Estonians were the least likely to adopt Russian, the language used in business and all official transactions. When someone said something in Russian, Estonians often replied in their native tongue. Estonian dissidents were among the first to make public demands. In 1976, a group of Estonians sent off a formal complaint about the Soviet occupation to the United States Congress, and shortly thereafter, letters were flying – to the Russian press and politicians – protesting against the secondary status of the Estonian language. Before *perestroika* was even in effect, groups of intellectuals were defying Soviet law, forming secret societies and researching Estonian history. Mart Laar, who would later become prime minister, put together the Society of Estonian Heritage, and headed off into farming villages to research the history of the Forest Brothers.

Quick Tour

Physically and spiritually Estonia – or Eesti – seems to have fallen out of a different century. The capital Tallinn is considered the best-preserved Nordic city in Europe even though it's not in Scandinavia, the countryside is dotted with tiny churches that comfortably hold about three, and witches are believed to inhabit the mist-entangled primordial bogs that can be crossed only in canoes.

> *The pagan practices of Estonia's past are still celebrated: the dead are said to return in August when they wander about freely, several holidays are held in honour of ghosts and 23 June is a most mystical night when Estonians prance through fields by moonlight seeking out a rare fern believed to imbue magical powers in those who pluck it.*[5]

Politically, however, Estonia has its feet in the modern world. The country has had plenty of savvy politicians lobbying its causes, including Lennart Meri – its brainy second president who spoke five languages, made documentary films, and should have qualified for a Guinness world record when he outdrank Boris Yeltsin[6] while discussing the withdrawal of Soviet troops (which finally took place in 1994). Estonia's politicians also tend to be youthful: current prime minister Juhan Parts, at 36, became Europe's youngest PM when he was appointed in 2003. Some of his cabinet members are in their twenties.

> **Model politics:** *The Estonian political scene may be getting even more youthful, at least if supermodel Carmen Kass has her way. The golden-haired twenty-something Estonian best known for her Christian Dior 'J'adore' campaign (showing her clad in little more than a gold necklace) has announced she may soon run for parliament on the Res Publica ticket.* Vogue's *Model of the Year 2000 is reported by the* Baltic News *as saying, 'My ideal is to make Estonia younger.' Given that Estonia already has Europe's youngest prime minister and a cabinet of twenty-somethings, one wonders if Kass plans to recruit future politicians from school playgrounds.*

My Bonnie Lies Over the Sea

Estonia's dearest friend lives across the Baltic: Finland, whose capital Helsinki lies a mere 40 miles from Tallinn, is actually closer than the border of the closest Baltic state, Latvia. Finland gave Estonia a boost from the start with money, advice and training – for example in the establishment of a border guard. The Estonians and the Finns actually have a lot in common, including their similar ethnicities and similar languages, which are part of the Finno-Ugric group, in case you were wondering. They also share the same tune for their national anthem (although the words aren't the same) and a love for beating themselves silly with birch branches in the sauna.

While Estonians have a reputation for being reserved – some just call them dour – those who speak the language say they are often making dry jokes. One indication that they're not as uptight as they may seem is their annual 'wife-carrying contest' – when women are slung upside down on the men's back.

All the Baltic States have installed their own language as the official one, but Estonia's national pride runs deeper, perhaps because somehow the country and language survived despite having only a million Estonians. Attempts by Russia entirely to 'Russify' the place failed miserably over two centuries. Now Estonia, like Latvia, is forcing its Russian population to learn the language that the Soviets tried to erase. To be a modern Estonian national, one must speak Estonian and classes in secondary schools are mostly in Estonian.

Estonia was always the most tuned-in of the Soviet republics, or 'pre-EU countries' as former foreign minister Ilves would call them. Estonian TV could pick up Western channels, and such shows as Peyton Place *were hugely popular in the 1960s. Now Estonia is known as one of the most plugged-in, Internet-savvy places on the planet, with a third of the population surfing the net at home.*

Heavenly Inferno

Although Estonia is nominally Lutheran now, early attempts to Christianize the pagan masses largely flopped. Part of the reason: preachers kept threatening that the fires of hell awaited those who didn't convert. Inferno-like temperatures in that frosty part of the world, however, sounded cosy: Estonians are known for their 50°C saunas, finished off by jumping through ice holes into glacially cold lakes.

Estonia, where the leadership considers the Soviet occupation that lasted five decades as 'a terrorist regime', is now seeking financial compensation for damages and loss of life during that time. In a 'White Book' released in 2004, the Estonian government spells out the effects of Russian interference, including the loss of 180,000 Estonian lives during the Second World War, and environmental damage by the Soviet Army alone put at $4 billion (€3.24 billion) according to the White Book, the result of twelve years of research. The Estonian government has said it will push for compensation of $250,000 (€205,000) for persons killed and $77,000 (€63,000) for each person who laboured in the Soviet system. Given the huge total, the Estonian government has said that instead of monetary compensation, it would be happy to accept a timber-rich part of Siberia from Russia.

> 'Attempts to raise damage claims against Russia or demand apologies from it have ... no chance of success' – Russian foreign ministry response to news that Estonia will seek compensation

Estonia is the most organized and promising of the Baltic States, but it isn't as goody-goody as it sounds. Intravenous drug use is on the rise – some point to young Russians who have moved there – and the United Nations shocked the country when it announced in 2004 that Estonia's HIV rate is one of the world's highest. Condom campaigns are kicking in, but promoting 'protected sex' isn't what the new Parts government initially had in mind. The government views the country's number one problem as its plummeting birth rate, and is devising incentives for women to have more kids. Another prob: plenty of illicit goods are smuggled out of lovely Tallinn, and there's an ongoing furore about Finnish heroin addicts who come to Estonia to buy methadone. One more worry to add to the mix: some are anxious that by entering the EU, Estonia will water down its hard-fought cultural identity. The place may not be perfect, but it is attractive in almost every way. The first to lure the EU eye to the region and to qualify for the prestigious EU invitation, Estonia opened the door for its neighbours, who didn't want to be left out in the cold. Ironically, up to the big day, Estonia was suffering pre-marital jitters, and the Cinderella country was the most squeamish about setting foot in the ball.

By spring 2003 less than half were for linking arms with the EU, although a slight majority of Estonians later voted yes on the issue.

Future Forecast

Estonia will date other countries, but will only be serious about Finland.

Hot Spots

Borders: Estonia lost land when it was remapped by the Soviet Union, and Russia still hasn't agreed to the new Estonian-suggested boundaries. Also murky: the border with Latvia.

'[Zhirinovsky] has suggested that . . . he would pile up nuclear waste on our borders and build giant fans to blow it onto us' – former Estonian ambassador to the US, Toomas Henrik Ilves[7]

Tallinn: Like Estonians themselves, Tallinn is striking, but in a quiet, understated way, and its medieval quarter with tiled roofs and candlelit cafés in attics is hauntingly beautiful, like a melody that floats out of a window from an unknown source. Music festivals abound in the Baltic-hugging capital of Russian Orthodox domes, sleek spires and medieval buildings with alarmingly steeply pitched roofs, but any occasion is cause for Estonians to don their traditional white scarves and layered skirts, and sing. Never mind that Finland has helped Estonia with its border security: plenty of contraband still slips out to Helsinki from here.

Estonian saying: *There's really no summer, just three bad months for skiing.*

Tallinn's medieval Old Town.

Tartu: Site of Tartu University, the Baltic States' first when Sweden opened it in 1632 and the alma mater of many Estonian and Latvian VIPs.

Monuments: Illustrating the touchy issue of Estonia's relationship with Nazi Germany, which was seen by many as preferable to that with the Soviet Union, monuments to Estonians who fought on the German side are controversial sites. One plaque commemorating 'Estonian soldiers who died in the second war for the liberation of the fatherland and a free Europe in 1940–1945' was removed in 2002 as the soldier was dressed in German SS uniform. However, other monuments to Estonians who enlisted on the German side keep popping up.

Banks: Sweden controls most of Estonia's financial institutions.

Hot Shots

Juhan Parts: Prime Minister 2003 to present. Europe's youngest PM, Parts is slick, brainy, and business-savvy – and pushing Russia to compensate Estonia for costs incurred during decades of occupation. Of the young Res Publica party, he was formerly auditor-general – a political watchdog attuned to corruption and organized crime. He campaigned on a 'clean-up the system' platform, and surprised everybody when he won. His hope is to get Estonians to have more babies: no word on if he'll be adding aphrodisiacs to the water.[8]

> **Seriously clean:** *Justice minister Ken Marti, who came into office in 2003 at 28 waving the no-corruption flag, recently tried to resign from the post. The reason: he'd been caught speeding in a residential neighbourhood. Parts refused to accept the resignation.*[9]

Arnold Rüütel: President 2001 to present. Former Communist leader who helped push for Estonian independence in the late 1980s, he's an agronomist by formal training, and headed lots of agricultural departments. Now he's leader of the centre-right Estonian People's Union, formerly known as the Rural People's Party. Not quite as worldly as some of the previous leaders, but he's no dummy either.

Lennart Meri: President 1992–2000. Flashy intellectual who helped put the country on the map in Western Europe, he did the impossible: drank Boris Yeltsin under the table (and finally got Soviet troops to roll out). Deported with his family in 1941 to a Soviet work camp, where his father was imprisoned, Meri returned after the war and became an accomplished documentary maker, not to mention ace politician.

Mart Laar: Prime Minister 1992–6; 1999–2002. Only 32 when he took over the job as prime minister, free marketeer and historian Laar, of the

Writer and former PM Mart Laar
helped put Estonia on the map.

Pro Patria Union or Fatherland Party, is an intellectual multilingual sort credited with stabilizing Estonia's flimsy economy by cutting social services, easing business taxes and pushing through a flat 26 per cent income tax rate. Brilliant, if a bit of a hothead, he has lots of ideas about how to promote Estonia. One possibility: selling ethnically pure Estonian genes to science to study disease. He lost a vote of confidence in 1995, but confidence was restored in 1999 when he again walked in as PM, and Estonia's economy took off. Laar got in plenty of hot water in 2001 when news broke that two years before he and other politicos had used a photo of another politician as target practice. He flounced out in 2002 when his coalition fell apart, but is still widely admired. Wrote *War in the Woods*, about the Forest Brothers, guerrillas who went back to nature in 1944 to launch an anti-Soviet resistance movement from the forests, when the Soviets rolled back in.

> *Musical notes: The melodic, vowel-heavy Estonian language is held by some to be the most beautiful in the world. It certainly lends itself to music: Estonia is still beaming over winning the popular Eurovision song contest in 2001. Famous classical composer Arvo Pärt, whose speciality is hauntingly dark 'faith minimalism' derived from medieval music, also hails from these parts.*

Siim Kallas: Appointee to the European Commission, Prime Minister 2002–3. Extremely popular, former Communist Kallas has held just about every position in Estonian politics since independence. Interim prime minister, he was also foreign minister, finance minister, and head of the Central Bank. Tentatively appointed to work with the European Commission on audit, anti-fraud and administrative affairs.[10]

Vodka tourists: Finns by the thousands pour into Estonia to toss back vodka and stock up on the much cheaper booze. Some Estonians are also concerned because Finnish pensioners – whose monthly allotment is several times higher than the typical Estonian's monthly wages – are beginning to buy houses and move there.

Russians: They still aren't fully integrated into Estonian society, and won't get passports until they learn Estonian.

> *'The Russians were immigrants here. They were tools of occupation, tools to liquidate one small nation, tools of a terrorist regime. But the Russian people themselves are not guilty' – Prime Minister Juhan Parts in April 2004 interview with author*

Media stars: Bi-monthly magazine the *City Paper*: www.BalticsWorldwide. com *The Baltic Times*: www.baltictimes.com

23. Latvia (Latvija): The Middle Child

Fast Facts

Country:	Republic of Latvia: Latvijas Republika
Capital:	Riga
Government:	parliamentary democracy
Independence:	21 August 1991 (from Soviet Union)
Population:	2,307,000 (2004 estimate)
Leaders:	Head of State: President Vaira Vike-Freiberga (1999)
	Head of Government: Prime Minister Aigars Kalvitis (2005)
Elections:	President elected by Parliament for 4-year period; Prime Minister appointed by President, approved by Parliament
Name of Parliament:	Saiema
Ethnicity:	Latvian 57.7%, Russian 29.6%, Belarussian 4.1%, Ukrainian 2.7%, Polish 2.5%, Lithuanian 1.4%, other 2%
Religion:	Lutheran, Roman Catholic, Russian Orthodox
Language:	Latvian (official), Lithuanian, Russian
Literacy:	99%
Exports:	wood and wood products, machinery, metals, textiles, foodstuffs
Per capita GDP:	$10,200 (2004)
Unemployment:	10.6% (May 2004 Eurostat figure)
EU status:	entered May 2004
Currency:	Latvian lat
Known for:	fabulous art nouveau architecture

Standout Qualities

Noted Latvians: Dancer Baryshnikov and a famous croc slayer
Noted Leader: Pres is a woman and former Canadian prof
Noted Resource: The continental shelf might be thick with oil; then again, maybe not

Résumé

'If the rest of the world doesn't know we exist, it's for a simple reason: we were an occupied country forcibly incorporated in the Soviet Union. Latvia was kept behind the Iron Curtain with an iron fist – and that iron fist included not being allowed to travel and no people from abroad being allowed to land here. Our contact with the world was rudely cut off for half a century . . . It was a deliberate effort by the Soviet Union to wipe us as a country off the face of the earth' – President Vaira Vike-Freiberga[1]

Closer to Estonia in religion (Lutheran, nominally) and historical 'owner-ship', but closer to Lithuania in language, lovely Latvia – the geographical middle child – is the Baltic States' most vulnerable country for several reasons, all of which concern its angry neighbour to the east. Latvia has the biggest port on the Baltic Sea – Ventspils – and Russia is eyeing it most covetously; some fear that Latvia could be Russia's next attempt at Baltic real estate. Second, native Latvians are barely half of the population (34 per cent are Russian), and complicated problems remain about the status of the 700,000 Russians who were moved here after the Second World War as part of the Soviet industrialization programme. Ethnic friction, which typically shies clear of violence, is at a peak here and at least half of Russians living in Latvia are currently stateless, since most haven't learned the language and can't become Latvian citizens until they do. And words from Russia just keep getting scarier, even though Latvians, by now, just roll their eyes.

'Nothing will be left of Latvia. I promise you this. Nothing at all will be left. Everybody will forget about Latvia and the Latvian language. We will destroy everything if you touch Russians and Russian schools. I promise' – Deputy speaker of Russia's parliament Vladimir Zhirinovsky on Russian TV,[2] *furious about the new requirement forcing Russians in Latvia to take more classes in the Latvian language*

Latvians and Russians: The Beef

Part of the problem Latvians have with Russians is long-term resentment: Russia was an imperial landlord, and then swooped in to snatch Latvia's independence away after the Second World War. The Soviets sent hundreds of thousands to work camps, killed thousands of others, discouraged use of the Latvian language, and treated the locals like second-class citizens as they made the country an agricultural and pharmaceutical cog in the big machine. Latvians are also angry that Russians who have lived there five decades still haven't learned the language (which, granted, wasn't necessary when the Soviets were in power). But the underlying issue is power: if Russians are not granted citizenship, they cannot vote. And there are plenty of Latvians who don't want to give Russians the power to influence their political situation ever again. Nevertheless, the government points out that some 70,000 people (mostly Russians) have been naturalized since the country became independent again. Russians, for their part, feel like second-class citizens in the new Latvia, and are furious that their children don't learn Russian in schools.

Historic grudges play out in the economic world: Russians, favoured under the Soviet system, are now twice as likely as Latvians to be unemployed.

Another issue: Latvia's port at Ventspils. Typically, about 14 per cent of Russia's oil exports run out of this facility on the Baltic, and the transit fees and related income have at times contributed about one-sixth of Latvia's GDP.[3] Not lately: in 2003, when demand for Russian oil was at a peak, Russian pipelines pumped only a trickle here, despite the fact that Russia needs every port to meet demand.

Stinky business: *Something seems fishy in Ventspils. Mayor Aivar Lembergs' salary is officially about €6,000 a year, but according to* Newsweek International *he takes in about €800,000 annually.*[4]

Officially the move was to protest against a March 2003 incident when police roughed up Russians opposing an increase in energy prices, but others have their theories about the boycott of Ventspils. Some say it was a reaction to Latvia joining NATO, but many believed it was more about Russia trying to buy the facility – after driving it to bankruptcy.[5] The company that makes the dosh from oil exports – Ventspils Nafta – was pulling in some $4.5 million (€3.65 million) a year. Since Russia's boycott, the company is crippled, making some $30,000 annually. However, the Ventspils port is diversifying and now getting plenty of business from other sources.

Despite Moscow's manoeuvring, the port is holding its own.

Divided ethnically, Latvia is also divided politically in every way, making coalitions nearly impossible to sustain. Since 1991 the country has changed leadership almost every year. One exception: President Vaira Vike-Freiberga. She's been in the power seat since 1999, remarkable around here. Her prime ministers haven't been so lucky. They seem to resign, like clockwork, every eighteen months.

It may be a little wobbly at the moment but Latvia is going places. The capital Riga is becoming a big tourist draw – you'd never guess the place ever had been part of the Soviet Union – and its handsome Old Town is now crawling with creative sorts from painters and video-makers to poets and fashion designers. Designer hotels are popping up everywhere, alongside numerous galleries, gourmet restaurants abound, and at night, young Latvians are prone to dance in the bars. Here, more than any of the other Baltic States, a spirit of change blows through the air, entwined with a deep love of fun.

History Review

Latvia's current problems with Russia may stem from the fact that this land was a Soviet favourite, and of all the former republics, Russia is most loath to give this one up. Latvia was praised not only for its clothing industry – designs from Riga's Fashion House were worn by Soviet models on international catwalks – Latvian artists were also esteemed, with hundreds given state support for their creative pursuits, and some getting prized commissions from Moscow. Most of all, Soviets loved Jurmala, the white sandy stretch of Baltic coast that is fringed with stands of thick pines: this was a favoured Soviet getaway, and the area is still littered with summer mansions of the Soviet elite, alongside tiny nineteenth-century wooden houses that peek through the woods.

The centre for Soviet radio production and the famed Laima chocolates, Latvia also produced the Soviet Union's finest dancer,

Mikhail Baryshnikov, whom the Soviets often tried to portray as Russian.

Soviets didn't really maintain the capital's fabulous architecture, but they also didn't tear down these buildings dating back to the fourteenth century. More often than not they used the aristocratic homes for the communal-style apartments into which they pushed multiple families of Latvians. New construction, particularly the Soviet block houses – ugly concrete buildings where the elite were given coveted private apartments – was usually built on the west side of the river, far from the high pitched roofs and rounded façades of Old Town. The medieval quarter also holds more than architectural treasures for Latvians: it was the site where hundreds of thousands congregated in January 1990 to prevent Soviet tanks from taking government buildings and the TV station.

'The whole country came to Old Town – some driving their tractors. Everybody made barricades of mattresses, garbage, cars – anything that would keep the tanks from entering and people kept watch all night. And everybody was singing' – Painter Andris Vitolins recollecting January 1990, when Latvians feared that Soviet forces, after destroying the TV tower in Vilnius, would take over the communication centre in Old Town

Quick Tour

'In Soviet times, people didn't go out much. There were only five restaurants and they had long lines outside and you had to bribe the doorman or you'd wait in those lines your whole life. Now there are so many places in Riga, I can't catch up' – Andris Vitolins[6]

The biggest and most cosmopolitan of the Baltic capitals, vibrant Riga is filled with art nouveau design, medieval houses, and beautifully landscaped parks – it wowed even Hemingway – while Latvia's countryside is entwined with the mystical. Amber is thrown up on secluded shores like gifts from underwater gods and the castle-littered land is haunted with legends of wicked gnomes, caves with healing waters and trees that turn those who chant magic words into werewolves during the full moon.

Latvians are obsessed with the eighteenth-century story that puts to paper the legend of the Bear Slayer (part human protector, part furry growler). Also a source of national pride: dainas – ancient folk songs that were an encyclopedia of knowledge telling people everything from when to plant and when to harvest to how to dye wool. Latvia has more recorded folk songs than anywhere in the world.

Latvia's barely touched countryside with scanty dirt roads is one of the country's problems: with poor transport links to the cities, poverty runs rampant in the rural areas, where residents live in a different, albeit beautiful, world.

Even well-educated, professional Latvians say oak trees, which were worshipped by ancient pagans, have curative powers. Many Latvians keep 'grey stones', found at the base of oaks, in their homes and touch them when they want to feel grounded.

Like the typical middle child, Latvia often appears to need the most attention, but is most ignored: Denmark is helping Lithuania, and Finland is linked to Estonia, but Sweden, which is supposed to be giving Latvia a guiding hand, usually just shows up for photo ops. However, Finland has begun to take more interest here. Corruption is also a problem that someone needs to address: in some surveys, in 2003 Latvia scored worse than even Lithuania in terms of bribery and lack of transparency. Yikes.

Latvian joke: *An American, a German and a Latvian are in a field when an elephant comes running out of the forest. The American thinks: 'If only I could harness that great animal's strength, I would be very powerful.' The German thinks, 'If only I could sell the massive animal's meat, I would be very rich.' The Latvian thinks, 'I wonder what that elephant thinks of me.'*

Future Forecast

Latvia will shine as a new tourist destination. Russia will keep a very close eye on everything, and may make a move.

Hot Spots

Riga: The liveliest and biggest of the Baltic capitals (population 800,000), long-forgotten Riga is once again showing up on the world tourist map. The attraction of the port city is its strange architecture, a fanciful blend of colours and richly decorated façades that is part Dutch, part

Riga: once the queen of the Baltic.

Scandinavian, part Dr Seuss. Jugendstil is the name given to the art nouveau style of these buildings, but that's only part of what makes Riga special. Markets are housed in former Zeppelin hangars, the opera is world class, and, thankfully, rarely did the Communist planners meddle with Riga's odd design, where intersections rarely create four right-angle corners. The city that lit the first Christmas tree retains both the feel of the Teutonic Knights who fought for it, believing that 'he who holds Riga, holds the Baltics,' as well as that of its wealthy trading days in the fifteenth-century Hanseatic League when it grew rich from the Western Europe-bound trading ships that stopped here. The nightlife sizzles and the air sometimes crackles with ethnic tension.

It is said that Riga has the highest concentration of art nouveau in the world. Called Jugendstil here, it is most concentrated in the Embassy district – there are sculpted profiles of Victorian beauties whose long flowing hair streams down buildings, and façades studded with stylized dragons and open-mouthed faces, busts of Zeus and heads of space-age knights.

Restaurants: Making up for the dearth over much of the past sixty years, Riga is now bursting with restaurants. They range from cosy eateries heavy with wooden barrels and iron pots serving Latvian food – thick soups and chewy black bread served with hemp butter – to plush high-ceilinged seafood restaurants, perhaps with a waterfall and ponds filled with trout in the main dining hall.

Historic Horrors

Latvians were horribly treated by both the Germans and the Russians. In November 1941 the Nazis rounded up Riga's Jews, marched them to the forest, and forced them to lie in a huge pit atop still warm corpses and shot them in the back of the head. During two days, 30,000 Jews were killed at Rumbali. The Soviets killed or deported an estimated 340,000 Latvians, though Russia still won't give details on the two major deportations in 1941 and 1949, despite continued Latvian pressure to do so.

Baltic coast: Latvia had to negotiate hotly with Lithuania to ensure that the potentially oil-rich shelf was part of Latvian territory. Now a US–Swedish firm is drilling away. Gas lines to Finland and Germany will soon be stretching across the sea.

Latvian saying: We don't have four seasons here, just two winters: white winter and green winter.

Russian border: Still not hammered out.

Schools: The 'language issue' – the requirement of students to take several courses in Latvian – is making schools a high-pressure zone lately. Russia recently donated history books to Latvian schools, in Russian, of course.

The old school: Latvia is also home to the biggest settlement of Old Believers, a Russian orthodox sect that rejects practices and beliefs introduced since the mid 1600s as too modern.

Freedom Boulevard: What else could they name the artery that was once called Hitler Strasse and then Lenin Ulitza?[7]

LATVIA   581

Hot Shots

Vaira Vike-Freiberga: President 1999 to present. Along with her family, Vike-Freiberga ran from the incoming Soviets in 1944, ending up in Canada, where she became a psychology professor in Montreal. She became Latvian president by fluke – the parliament threw her into the ring as a tie-breaker – after she returned to research and promote Latvia's folk songs. She initially wasn't so keen on the EU, telling the *Economist* in 2002, '[Latvia has] had to fight too hard for our nation-state to want to dispense with it now.'[8] Nevertheless, she helped kick Latvia into EU-ready mode, convincing lawmakers to lighten up on some language require-ments and ripping into the judicial system for its injudicious notion of justice. In a country that's blown through four currencies in fifteen years, and where prime ministers go belly-up annually, President Vike-Freiberga is not just greatly admired, she's an anchor.

> *Latvian legend holds that the country would become powerful and prosperous under the guidance of a woman leader. Since Vike-Freiberga stepped in, annual growth of Latvia's economy has been around 5 per cent.*[9]

President Vaira Vike-Freiberga:
smart, powerful, beloved.

Indulis Emsis: Prime Minister (briefly) 2004. Europe's first Green PM, Emsis didn't last six months. There was barely time to memorize his name.

Aigars Kalvitis: Prime Minister 2004–present. In the third change of government in 2004, the PM chair is now filled by Kalvitis of the People's Party. The new leader is said to disagree with his party's wish to repatriate ethnic Russians to Russia. As usual here, don't write his name in stone.

> Some say that the legendary Crocodile Dundee was actually a Latvian
> – Arvids von Blumenfelds, to be precise, from the village of Dundaga
> – who vented the rage pent up from the Second World War by slaying
> crocs in Australia.

Andris Piebalgs: Appointee to European Commission. After Hungary's László Kovács didn't seem up to the job, the mighty energy portfolio was tossed to Piebalgs. He's demanding that Europe figure out what to do with its nuclear waste.

Historical Hero: Kalis Ulmanis

Latvia's first president after the country's first independence in 1920, agronomist Ulmanis disappeared during the Soviet occupation. The inability to find out what happened – an official investigation came up empty-handed – has helped to propel him to cult status.

Alina Lebedeva: Can we say little troublemaker? The ethnic Russian teenager made Latvia front-page news in 2002 when she slapped British Prince Charles with a carnation – protesting against his pro-war stance. She made the local news again in 2004 when she was thrown in jail suspected of torching the ministry of education for its policy of increasing the number of classes in Latvian taught in schools.

Vladimir Zhirinovsky: Russia's radical rightwinger, who typically wins at least 13 per cent of Russians' votes, and is deputy speaker of the Duma, is the symbolic manifestation of Russia's obsession with Latvia. His threats make many Latvians nervous and in 2003 he was blacklisted and denied a visa for entry. He wants Alaska back too.

Media stars: The *City Paper* covers all three Baltic States in English:

www.BalticsWorldwide.com Also newsy: *The Baltic Times*:
www.baltictimes.com

> *It's said that Latvians read more newspapers than anywhere else in the world.*[10]

24. Lithuania (Lietuva): The Wild Child

Fast Facts

Country:	Republic of Lithuania; Lietuvos Respublica
Capital:	Vilnius
Government:	parliamentary democracy
Independence:	11 March 1990 (from Soviet Union)
Population:	3,608,000 (July 2003 estimate)
Leaders:	Head of State: President Valdus Adamkus (2004)
	Head of Government: Prime Minister Algirdas Brazauskas (2002)
Elections:	President elected by popular vote for 5-year term; Prime Minister appointed by President, approved by Parliament
Name of Parliament:	Seima
Ethnicity:	Lithuanian 81%, Russian 9%, Polish 7%, Belarussian 2%
Religion:	Roman Catholic; also Lutheran, Russian Orthodox, Protestant, Baptist, Muslim, Jewish, pagan
Language:	Lithuanian (official), Russian, Polish
Literacy:	99%
Exports:	mineral products, machinery, transport equipment, chemicals, clothing, metals
Per capita GDP:	$11,400 (2003)
Unemployment:	11.5% (May 2004 Eurostat figure)
EU status:	entered May 2004
Currency:	Lithuanian litas
Known for:	being a troublemaker

Standout Qualities

Discordant: Doesn't match with the others
Off key: Crime and nukes grate nerves
Harmonizing: Rushed to pull it together for EU entry

Résumé

The largest, most populous and southerly of the Baltic States, Lithuania is also the feistiest and most intense – the other two regard it as the home of impulsive hotheads. Lithuanians are considered the friendliest, Lithuanian men are the most dashing, and the landscapes – golden dunes swirling around fishing villages for instance – are more dramatic, as are Lithuania's problems. The two biggest headaches facing Lithuania: its creepy Ignalina plant – a Soviet-made ticking time bomb of a nuclear reactor – and the organized crime that is always lurking about. Politically, too, the country is shaky: President Rolandas Paksas was impeached in April 2004, mere weeks before Lithuania entered the EU.

Nuclear Alarm

The eerie Ignalina nuclear plant that provides nearly 80 per cent of Lithuania's electricity and employs 5,000 workers was a Soviet idea, which is to say another really bad one. The same gas-graphite design as the one that blew up at Chernobyl in 1986 – there are a dozen Chernobyl clones scattered across the former Soviet satellite states – Ignalina is so shoddy that after the European Union spent a mountain of money trying to fix it, they concluded it was best just to shut it down – pronto. Not only is the facility unsafe, Ignalina also has been the target of terrorist threats. In 1992 a computer programmer intentionally introduced a virus, and the cooling system shut down. Two years later a Lithuanian national demanded $8 million (€6.4 million) to prevent the plant from being attacked, and the same year the leader of the local Vilnius Brigade – a notorious branch of the Lithuanian mob – threatened to bomb the plant if his son, facing the death penalty, was executed. The son was executed and the plant was shut down, and under high security for several months, especially when German intelligence called up with info that the threat was quite real. Recently an unexploded grenade was also found on the premises. One of Lithuania's EU entry requirements is to shut down the plant, the first reactor in 2005, the second in 2009. Decommissioning price tag: €1.6 billion. Until then: tick, tick, tick.

Lithuania's breakaway from the Soviet Union was more theatrical too: over a dozen Lithuanians were killed in 1991 when the Soviets sent tanks to destroy the communication tower of Vilnius's TV station, and much of the country swarmed in the streets trying to block them. Sajudis, as the independence movement was called, was the nerviest dissident group this side of Poland's Solidarity.

Lithuania was the first Soviet republic to proclaim independence (in March 1990).

History Review

Lithuania's recent past follows the same steps as those for the other Baltic States – twentieth-century independence yanked away by Russia, Germany, Russia – except for one thing: when the Lithuanians collectively blew their top at Moscow they did so much more loudly and intensely than their neighbours, and their rebellion hammered some of the final nails in the Soviet coffin.

The fierce resistance that first rose up in the 1940s was blanketed but never snuffed out. The Soviets shipped thousands of intellectuals to the gulag in that decade; by the 1950s the groups had been mostly disarmed. Dissidence lived on thanks to the small printing presses, which the Soviets could never completely root out. One controversial publication that egged on the resisters: the journal of the local Catholic church, secretly published throughout the Soviet years.

Well, Thanks Neighbour!

Lithuania and Poland once used to be ruled by the same family. The Lithuanian king wed the Polish princess in the fourteenth century, their union launching a three-centuries-long golden period for both: their lands stretched from the Baltic to the Black Sea, the place was thick with thinkers and creators and had a powerful parliament that elected the king. Of all the neighbours, the Poles were always the Lithuanians' closest friends. The Poles, however, forgot all about that at the Paris Peace Conference in 1919: when lobbying for Poland's new boundaries, Polish diplomats tried to snatch Lithuania back, explaining that Lithuanians were just an insignificant little tribe that really belonged to Poland.[1] Lithuanians were furious – more so when the Polish leader Pilsudski sent in his army to claim the capital Vilnius and surroundings. Lithuanians did get their own country from the Paris cartographers – but it was a small patch of their original land. (They promptly snatched some of Germany.) For years they fumed over the matter; nevertheless, most Lithuanians refused to fight the Poles when ordered to do so by the Germans in the Second World War. For the Lithuanians, the war had but one good result: it brought back Vilnius and environs. (Unfortunately, Russia, who returned the lost lands to Lithuania after taking Poland, was also included in the package.) Poland and Lithuania now have a joint army, but there's still an underlying rancour about the Poles' land theft. Another sore point: Poland waited until the US gave the OK before recognizing Lithuanian independence.

Lithuanians had continued rebelling against Soviet occupation long after their weapons had been seized. In 1972 student Romas Kalanta registered his protest against the Soviet regime by setting himself ablaze. His dramatic death by fire led to a mass rebellion in the streets that only the army could quell. Other acts weren't so dramatic, but an underground current of dissidence carried on, encouraged by the banned Catholic church. So when President Mikhail Gorbachev announced his *perestroika* and *glasnost* ideas in the mid 1980s, dissatisfied Lithuanians saw the slender crack that they could rip apart.

Led by plump, soft-voiced music professor Vytautas Landsbergis, the Lithuanian independence movement, Sajudis, grew out of a group of writers, professors and scholars who (the Communists believed) would gather together calmly to discuss ways to reform and modernize the Soviet Union in 1988. Instead, taking advantage of the mood for freer speech, the thinkers quickly and loudly condemned the whole repressive farce they'd been subjected to for decades. Sajudis demanded that the Soviet Union confess to the secret agenda with the Nazis to take over Central Europe under the Molotov–Ribbentrop Pact, and to admit to the mass deportations to gulags – both events that had never been acknowledged by Moscow. Through 1988 and 1989 Sajudis continued to pounce and denounce the Russian occupation during the Second World War, concluding that the Soviet Union had absolutely no claim to Lithuania since its forced annexation was entirely illegal.

Moscow was open-mouthed with horror, then rage, but the Lithuanians wouldn't stop. Taking a cue from the popular momentum that was building up, the Lithuanian parliament proclaimed that Lithuania's laws took precedence over Moscow's and the reform-minded comrade (and current prime minister) Algirdas Brazauskas took over as head of the local Communist Party. He immediately gave the stunning Vilnius Cathedral back to the church authorities (it had been state property) and then caused major fireworks by announcing that the local Communist Party was severing itself from Party headquarters in Moscow.

When Mikhail Gorbachev travelled to Lithuania in January 1990, he was shocked by the loud calls for independence. He responded that Soviets should all work together to improve factories, cities and states. Clearly he wasn't fully comprehending the reality: Gorbachev still thought that even if the matter was put to a vote, Lithuania would want to stay in the Soviet Union.[2]

The Lithuanian parliament welcomed in non-Communist parties and, in an early 1990 election, Sajudis candidates won by a landslide. The movement's leader Landsbergis stepped in as chairman of the parliament and in March 1990 he did what no other leader in a Soviet republic had dared: he declared Lithuania's independence from the Soviet Union, reading the exact same speech that Lithuanian leaders had read back in 1918. Gorbachev hit the roof and issued an embargo. In 1990 oil supplies to Lithuania were cut off, even shipments of paper were banned – as if eliminating the press would eliminate Moscow's problem. It didn't. The demands for independence grew louder. Communist leader Brazauskas tried to make compromises and talk through it with Moscow, but the talks went nowhere. Never fond of Brazauskas, parliament leader Landsbergis reaffirmed Lithuania's independence, stoking up the masses with his speeches on TV and making it clear that Lithuania wouldn't back down.

In January 1991 the Soviet Army attacked, targeting Vilnius's TV station and broadcasting tower, while tens of thousands of Lithuanians tried to block the way; some were beaten back with rifle butts and others crushed by tanks. In that mob scene the Soviet army killed thirteen and injured hundreds in the most violent confrontation of the Baltic States' Singing Revolution. Even when the communication tower was seized, the Lithuanians wouldn't give up. In February the question of independence was put to the people in a referendum, and the vast majority voted to shake loose forever of the Soviet Union. The parliament again announced that Lithuania was a free sovereign country. Only Iceland recognized Lithuania's independence initially, but after a failed coup attempt in Moscow six months later, ultimately resulting in the Soviet Union's break-up,

Russia (and the rest of the world) finally came to the same conclusion in September 1991.

> *Unlike Estonia and Latvia, Lithuania didn't put ethnic Russians through the language hoops. While Lithuanian is the official language, Russians (and pretty much anybody else who wanted it) were immediately granted citizenship in 1991.*

As with any new democracy there were problems, and this being Lithuania, they were more dramatic: unemployment soared as the Soviet machine cranked to a halt. Crime skyrocketed. Banking scandals rocked the country – the two biggest banks folded in 1995 – and corruption ran almost unabated. But Lithuanians who lived abroad began coming back – including a US government policy maker called Valdus Adamkus who'd left five decades before: he became president in 1998. Lithuania began slowly pulling itself together and putting itself back on the map, and by 2002, it was invited into not only NATO but also the EU.

Quick Tour

Lithuania doesn't really fit in with the Baltic crowd. Its history is more wrapped up with Poland, and while citizens in Estonia and Latvia tend to be Protestant (to the extent they're religious at all), Lithuanians are fervently Catholic. While the other two are physically and mentally closer to the wholesome Nordic countries, Lithuania is in the thick of the post-Soviet black-market undercurrent. With Russian enclave (and smuggling centre) Kaliningrad and impoverished Belarus as two of its borders, it's no wonder that Lithuania just can't seem to dust away the illicit activities. In terms of corruption, Latvia may not be lily-white, but Lithuania lives in the darker range of the greys. Despite government crackdowns, the wheels of the country are just hard to scrub squeaky clean, being oiled by Lithuania's mob and offshoots of the Russian Mafia; even President Rolandas Paksas was alleged to have affiliations with the syndicate, and local gangsters encroach into politics and are known to warn off journalists who take a close look.

> *Vitas Lingys, a 27-year-old writer for Lithuanian paper Respublika, was shot down outside his house in 1993 after publishing a piece about local syndicate the Vilnius Brigade. Boris Dekanidze, son of the Brigade's boss, was found guilty of ordering the hit, and executed in*

1994. Headed by editor Vitas Tomkus, said to sleep with a loaded gun next to his bed since the death of his reporter,[3] Respublika is known for its hard-hitting investigative pieces, as well as for its punchy style, highly controversial content and sometimes questionable ethics: leaked documents have a way of showing up here and the paper raised eyebrows when it supported President Rolandas Paksas during his impeachment proceedings in 2004.

Scandal: Paksasgate

When he walked in as president in 2003, two-time Vilnius mayor and former prime minister Rolandas Paksas had plenty of friends and supporters, a few too many said the government by the end of that year. The young stunt pilot had successfully wowed the press (the typically astute *Economist* called him 'honest, modest and down-to-earth')[4] but he had also links with the Russian Mafia, or so said a 2004 government investigation panel that found him guilty of blabbing state secrets and endangering national security. Paksas responded with finger pointing, saying the chairman of the parliament Arturas Paulauskas, who headed the investigation and temporarily stepped in as president when Paksas was ousted, should be impeached for disseminating classified information.[5] Even though Paksas does have his supporters, and some say charges against him were exaggerated, Lithuanians took to the street to protest against him, the panel recommended removing Paksas from the presidential seat, and the parliament voted to impeach him in April 2004. Paksas planned to run again, but legislators changed the law to prevent it.[6]

Had Paksas simply resigned during the brouhaha, he would have retained his presidential pension. Being impeached, he loses it.

The Baltic country with the fewest Russian residents – a mere 10 per cent – Lithuania has the strongest ties to the old Communist Party. Former Party leader Algirdas Brazauskas is now running the place and is often voted the country's most popular politician. While he was never a hard-boiled Russian comrade – he was known blatantly to defy Moscow's orders as Party head in the 1980s – he is neither the multi-lingual slickster nor the well-travelled intellectual that often typifies leadership in the other two Baltic States.

Lithuanian crime exploded in the 1990s after Soviet industry pulled out and unemployment soared. Robberies and car theft were among the most frequent of the 200 or so crimes reported on an average day by the mid 1990s.[7]

Lithuania was formerly the Soviets' ears to the West. Hidden in the thickly forested countryside, Linksmakalnis – a Soviet snooping station – once tapped into Western European communication systems, although so clandestine was the operation that details are still sketchy now.[8]

Sticky Politics

Lithuania's biggest moneymaker and taxpayer, the Mazeikiu oil refinery fuelled a huge controversy in 1999 when it was bought out by US-based Williams Holdings. Then prime minister (and later president) Rolandas Paksas stormed out of office in protest (the *Baltic News* reports he was actually pushed out for alleged bribery). Russia, which controls the pipelines to the refinery, shut off its crude supplies, and effectively shut down the operation. After Williams hooked up with Russian oil company Yukos the spigots were turned back on. However, since President Putin arrested Yukos's former chief executive Mikhail Khodorkovsky, nobody knows how this will all pan out.

Lithuania is beloved by many for its passion and diversity: in the capital's Old Town, filled with ornate Baroque buildings, the religious line up for priestly blessings of juniper twigs that sweep evil spirits away; famous mud spas are set deep in pine forests where artistic communities spring up in old wooden houses; and the curious Curonian Spit, a sixty-mile sand bar that stretches between lagoon and sea, was a magnet for writers, including Thomas Mann, who wrote *The Magic Mountain* while gazing out at the choppy waters. Yet, lovely though it may be, Lithuania is the most backward of the Baltics. By the end of the Soviet era only two-thirds of houses had indoor plumbing and much of the countryside is an undeveloped mess. On a happier note: Lithuania's economy is growing faster than anywhere else in Europe, galloping along at rates around 7.5 per cent a year.

Whether Lithuania is really ready for EU prime time remains to be seen, but of all the countries entering the new union in May 2004,

Lithuania was the most thrilled. When the matter of joining the European Union was put to a vote, a whopping 91 per cent of the electorate said yes.

Future Forecast

Lithuania's tourism will boom as Western Europeans drink in the Amber Coast, the UNESCO World Heritage site capital and the Curonian Spit. The country will also serve as a gateway for illicit goods of all sorts.

Scandal

In 1996 the sleazy Prime Minister Slezivicius refused to step down from office even after he was implicated in a nationwide banking scandal.[9] The year before, Lithuania's two biggest banks had folded, freezing all the accounts. Apparently tipped off about the impending financial disaster, the prime minister allegedly yanked all the money out of his account two days before. He was finally pushed out of office by the irate parliament.

Hot Spots

Borders: The most problematic is Kaliningrad, the Russian enclave and smuggling centre surrounded by EU countries since May 2004, but to the south there's crime-crazy and impoverished Belarus, which has ridiculously porous borders. Plenty of illegal immigrants, arms and radioactive materials are smuggled into Lithuania from almost all sides. Well, at least they have a border agreement with Russia, from 2003, which is more than any of the other Baltic States can say.

Ignalina nuclear plant: Under EU orders, Ignalina is heading towards decommissioning day, with the whole complex to be shut down by 2009. Whether a new nuke plant will replace it or Lithuania will import Russia's natural gas remains to be seen, but in any case the EU will be footing most of the bill.

Should you want to get the latest radiation levels, there's a Geiger counter in the town centre, a mile away from the Ignalina plant.

Vilnius: Capital city of courtyards and church spires against a modern

Hill of Crosses: symbol of Lithuanian resistance.

backdrop, Vilnius is more sedate than the other Baltic capitals, which is part of its attraction. It was once called 'the Jerusalem of the North' due to its high Jewish population, who'd settled there in the fourteenth century at the invitation of a ruling count. Almost the entire group was killed or fled during the Nazi occupation. The few Jews who remain in Vilnius are protesting against plans to renovate the Old Jewish Quarter: they say the money would be better spent educating the population on what happened to the Jews who 'disappeared'.

> *Frankly speaking: In the centre of Vilnius stands a statue of Frank Zappa. As in the Czech Republic, Zappa's radical taboo-targeting music epitomized the anti-authoritarian spirit that led to the break with the Soviet Union.*

Klaipėda: Lithuania's major seaport was once the haunt of Teutonic Knights, and home to a German community. Germany lost it after the First World War, and Lithuania (which had shrunk considerably at Poland's hands during the 1920s) compensated by pinching Klaipėda from France (which had been given supervision of the area after the war). In 1939 Nazi

Germany demanded Klaipėda back, marking the first move into Baltic territory.

Hill of Crosses (Kryziu Kalnas): The spirit (and perhaps spirits) of feisty Lithuanians are embedded in this holy hill covered by a thick jungle of crosses. Over 50,000 crosses stand here – the first dating back to the 1300s. Many, however, appeared during the Soviet era as metaphors of anti-Russian protest and anger. Soviets kept steamrollering them down and they mysteriously kept popping back up. Even today the hill is surreal: it can induce shivers when the many crosses rattle about in the wind.

Curonian Spit: The natural wonder is a UNESCO World Heritage site, and ancient villages are buried underneath its sands. Russia controls some of its sea waters, and Lukoil is now setting up offshore oil rigs. Lithuania is looking for oil on the other side, in the Curonian Lagoon. Environmentalists are shrieking about the potential hazards. Best to get there fast, if you want to know why it's been cooed over for centuries.

Stalin World: 'Disney meets the Gulag' is how the owner, a mushroom mogul, describes his theme park/wannabe tourist magnet. Propaganda blares from loudspeakers, actors dressed as Lenin and Stalin shout orders as they pass barbed wire fences and watchtowers, and everywhere one finds bronzes and marbles heralding Communist leaders in this recreation of the bygone and unmourned Soviet work camp. At least Stalin World provides a home for six dozen toppled Soviet statues that are now somewhat passé. Locals, however, are protesting against the theme park's plans to transport tourists here in cattle wagons that would offer the full deportation experience.

Museum of the Genocide of the Lithuanian People/The KGB Museum: Former inmates of the prison that stood in this previous KGB/Nazi SS headquarters give you all the gory details as they lead you past the grim cells.[10] The so-called 'soft cells' had upholstered walls to muffle the screams of those being tortured. In 1992 it was turned into a museum.

> *Between 1940 and 1958 some 200,000 Lithuanians were sent to work camps, imprisoned or transported to Siberia. Between death and emigration, Lithuania's population shrank by a quarter.*

Hot Shots

Algirdas Brazauskas: President 1993–8; Prime Minister 2001 to present. The former Communist who dared cut ties with Moscow's Communist Party headquarters in 1989 – he later freaked out and tried to backpedal when Russia cut Lithuania's energy supplies – is still in the picture as head of the Democratic Labour Party (the reformed Communist Party) and routinely tops popularity polls. President, then prime minister, burly Brazauskas is fine locally, but may lack the flash that many deem necessary to be a player in the EU. His tycoon buddies who have wealthy connections in Russia are also a bit worrying, but he looks appealing enough compared to former president Paksas, with whom he did not get along.

> *Mr Discreet: Brazauskas secretly slipped off to marry longtime girl-friend Kristina Butamien in 2002, in a location never disclosed. More remarkable: he'd also managed to get divorced from his first wife without anyone noticing. When asked by the media when he'd split from Wife No. 1, Brazauskas replied, 'Some time ago.'*[11]

Valdus Adamkus: President 1998–2001; 2004 to present. A former underground resister, Adamkus left Lithuania for the US, where he worked

Music prof and MEP Landsbergis led Lithuania to independence from the Soviets.

for military intelligence and later became an Environmental Protection Agency policy analyst. Returned to Lithuania in the 1990s and was elected president in 1998, a position in which he wasn't terribly effective, but what does one expect from an EPA bureaucrat? He wasn't quite connected with the local crowd, but was respectable in a grandfatherly way nonetheless; after Paksas was ejected, Lithuanians voted Adamkus in as his replacement in 2004.

> In his first meeting with President Putin, Adamkus pushed for Russia to pay compensation to Lithuania for the five decades of the occupation. The atmosphere quickly turned chilly and Putin refused.

Rolandas Paksas: President 2003–4; Prime Minister 1999, 2000–2001, Vilnius mayor 1999, 2000. The former stunt pilot has been doing a nosedive lately, having been impeached in 2004 from the presidency (association with alleged Russian mob friend/fundraiser brought him down), and forced to resign as prime minister before that (accused of bribing an oil company). Paksas, head of the right-wing Liberal Democrats, is known to change parties, and he also flitted back and forth in his political roles sometimes in the middle of terms: he's been mayor (twice), prime minister (twice), and president.[12] Paksas didn't help Lithuania's already crime-tarnished image when the spotlight was shining upon the new EU country. Even before impeachment he was shunned by the bigwigs, including President Bush, who turned an icy shoulder when Paksas planned an early 2004 visit.

Sajudis 'The Movement': Dissident intellectuals who kick-started the Lithuanian independence movement, the group was headed by Vytautas Landsbergis, a former music professor. Sajudis was elected into a controlling position in the Lithuanian parliament in 1990 but didn't keep hold of the steering wheel for long.

Viktor Uspaskich: Russian-born Uspaskich cashed in when he moved to Lithuania in the 1980s to build a gas pipeline, and invested in profitable projects with Gazprom. His biggest cash cow: his food manufacturing company Vikonda. He's now worth between €40 and 140 million, and Uspaskich has sunk money into his new country, renovating Russian Orthodox churches and funding facelifts to long-neglected towns such as Kedainiai, where dozens of companies are headquartered. The good deeds paid off: the Labour Party he started in 2003 now holds almost a third of the seats in parliament – and Uspaskich sits in one.

Vytautas Landsbergis: De facto President 1998–2000; Head of Parliament

1996–2000. The round-faced, goateed Landsbergis led the Sajudis independence movement, urging protesters to guard the TV tower and not to give up when Russia cut off energy supplies. Emerging as the Lech Walesa of Lithuania, he was de facto president after the country's first free election, when he became head of the parliament; he also served in that role again 1996–2000, but the position at that time wasn't as powerful. Alas, he didn't get on well with anybody from any other party, and after endorsing a TV censorship board and the practice of spying on journalists, public opinion turned against him.[13] The symbol of Lithuania's independence movement, he is still highly regarded, at least outside his country. Author of an autobiography *Lithuania Independent Again* and fourteen other books, he is said to be a maestro at the piano.[14]

Dalia Grybauskaite: European Commissioner 2004 to present. She may be a petite blonde, but few would dare give economist Grybauskaite a hard time – she's also a black belt in karate. Heads the Commission on programming and budget: the chaps may be needed to defend cuts.

Vitas Tomkus: As publisher of the Vilnius newspaper *Respublika*, Tomkus loves to keep the masses riled up. He succeeded particularly well in an April 2004 issue when he reported that Jews run the world. Tomkus himself only hoped to run Lithuania: he registered to stand in the 2004 presidential election, but was disqualified after more than 5,000 of the signatures he collected on the required petition were thrown out as invalid.[15]

Keeping the Language Alive: Bishop Motiejus Valancius

During the 1800s, when Russia imposed Russian as the sole language, valiant Bishop Valancius kept the Lithuanian language alive by having Lithuanian books printed in Germany and smuggling them in. He also started secret schools since nineteenth-century Russians weren't keen on educating the masses.

Vilnius Brigade: Syndicate troublemakers headquartered in the capital and presumably linked to the Russian Mafia, the guys allegedly smuggle pretty much anything from art and slaves to arms and the radioactive ingredients for dirty bombs. Brigade leader Georgi Dekanidze threatened to blow up the Ignalina nuclear plant when his son was executed by the government for killing an investigative journalist prying into their secrets.

Hero: M. K. Ciurlionis (1875–1911)

Composer, painter and amateur hypnotist, Lithuania's favourite creator was nothing if not intense: he excelled in mesmerizing the masses in both artistic fields, becoming best known for his symphony 'In the Forest' and ethereal paintings before dying at the age of 35.[16] He's still beloved, and assorted institutes and museums were opened in his honour.

Media stars: *The City Paper*, a bimonthly publication in English, is stellar: covering all three Baltic States, it is rich with articles about history as well as contemporary culture. Just as amazing, it's written by one person, Michael Tarm, who also reports for Associated Press. Check it out at www.BalticsWorldwide.com For more Baltic news in English, see *The Baltic Times*: www.baltictimes.com

25. Former Czechoslovakia: Czech Republic and Slovakia – Stirring up the 'Hood

Overview

Of all the former Soviet satellites, Czechoslovakia was always the most tantalizing, giving just a wisp of an impression, but an impression nonetheless of the hidden Communist reality. The world first got a glimpse behind the Iron Curtain when Czechoslovak 'New Wave' films trickled out in the 1960s, and Czechoslovakia made news again when the Soviet satellite opened up during the 'Prague Spring'. Then came the televised Soviet reprisals of summer 1968 and images of crying Czechoslovakians throwing themselves onto incoming Russian tanks, followed by blackness as the communication system was unplugged.

> **Prague Spring:** *The six months in 1968, when Czechoslovakia's government allowed liberties never before seen in a Soviet-controlled country (including freedom of the press), was the only time Czechoslovakia under Communism cold-shouldered Moscow's prescribed way of life. In general, Czechoslovakia was one of the Soviet bloc's most docile countries, which was why the Soviet leadership in Russia was dumbfounded when Czechoslovak Communists made the move to reform the country without a thumbs-up from them.*

For the next twenty years, Czechoslovakia pretty much dropped out of Western view, its memory kept alive only by the occasional smuggled-out book that spoke of secret lives and depression. But then in 1989 the picture of Czechoslovakia blipped across the TV screen again, this time with images of hundreds of thousands in the streets during the Velvet Revolution demanding that the Soviet handcuffs be unlocked.

> *As with other Soviet satellites, Czechoslovakia was a buffer zone that protected the Soviet Union from Western military advancement; Czechoslovakia was also of paramount importance because of its*

borders that hugged West Germany and Austria. Fearing NATO would attack if there was a break in the chain, Soviets kept a watchful eye here, all the more after the Prague Spring, when the Soviet army bolstered its presence.

In the 1990s Czech president and former dissident playwright Vaclav Havel rose up as symbol of the revitalized country (that privatized its economy quicker than any other in the Soviet bloc) and post-Communist Prague suddenly became internationally chic as the world discovered its enchanting beauty: silver-spooned American twenty-somethings swaggered in and bought up entire buildings and the printing presses that once cranked out underground writing churned out hip weeklies for ex-pats. Of all the former Communist capitals, Western travellers descended here first, cooing about the statue-lined Charles Bridge and the charming architecture that seemed to have dropped out of a seventeenth-century picture book. While this was an era of happiness, there were plenty of problems including old ethnic grudges working their way to the surface: in 1993 Czechoslovakia broke apart in what was called the Velvet Divorce.

Vocabulary Review

Munich Pact: 1938 agreement between Britain, France and Germany that Hitler could have part of Czechoslovakia if he'd just shut up and calm down and stop making people nervous about war.

Prague Spring: The period in 1968 when the local Communist party opened up the country for eight months until the Soviets cracked down.

Velvet Revolution: Czechoslovakia's November 1989 uprising against the Soviet Union that cut loose the ropes.

Velvet Divorce: The amicable 1993 split of Czechoslovakia into the Czech Republic and Slovakia was sudden, but the fabric had been fraying for decades.

Where once stood a united country now stands two: the Czech Republic and Slovakia, both recent entries into NATO and the EU. The Czech Republic and Slovakia are now a study in contrasts: the Czech Republic's capital is mysterious Prague, whose castled beauty lures 6 million tourists a year; Slovakia's capital is little Bratislava (where the Castle District is pretty) that has barely blipped on the tourist charts. The Czech Republic has a strong but cold leader, Prime Minister Vaclav Klaus, an EU-critical economist who wouldn't mind leading his country out of the Union; Slovakia has a kind but anaemic leader, Prime Minister Mikulas Dzurinda, whose greatest achievement was convincing Brussels to take his country in. Czechs are grumbling because prices have shot up, Slovaks are down in the mouth because 18 per cent can't find jobs.

When the Czech Republic came into the EU, it changed the structure of its Value-Added Tax; suddenly restaurant bills and goods such as nappies and imported food soared in price as VAT jumped from the 5 per cent to 19 per cent bracket.

Geographical Confusion: Czechoslovakia v. Czech Republic v. Slovakia v. Sudetenland

Czechoslovakia: (1919–92): A geographical experiment doomed to failure, or so some predicted when the ink was drying on the post-First World War maps. Czechoslovakia was cobbled together from parts of the former Austro–Hungarian empire, roping in several ethnic groups that never did get along. Three key pieces: Bohemia (mostly Czech), Slovakia (mostly Slovak), and Sudetenland (mostly German). Nazi-occupied during the Second World War, Czechoslovakia was pulled into the Soviet bloc in 1948. Following the 1989 'Velvet Revolution' – the independence movement led by play-wright Vaclav Havel – Czechoslovakia officially cut ties to Russia in 1990. Following the Velvet Divorce – caused by a rift between Czech and Slovak leaders – the country officially fractured into Czech Republic and Slovakia in 1993.

Czech Republic (formed 1993): Always the flashier, dominant and richer western half of Czechoslovakia, today's Czech Republic includes Bohemia (and capital Prague), industrial Sudetenland and agricultural Moravia. More secular than Slovakia and historically entangled with Austrians and Germans.

Slovak Republic/Slovakia (formed 1993): Always the country cousin, sweet Slovakia is catching up, well, sort of. One reason it lagged in the Czech Republic's shadow: former nationalist Prime Minister Vladimir Meciar, a press-censoring, Russia-loving authoritarian, who ticked off nearly everybody and made the place look unstable and possibly dangerous to potential foreign investors; his antics (including beating up reporters) nearly kept Slovakia out of the European Union. New leadership, however, shaped up Slovakia at the last minute. Heavily Catholic, Slovakia was historically tied up with Hungary.

Sudetenland: Historically home to ethnic Germans, this strategic north-west corner, known for its breweries and sugar factories, was tossed to Hitler in 1938 in the hope that if he was given what had been Germany's 'Southern Land' he would stop his march to war – a slight miscalculation. Returned to Czechoslovakia after the war, the Sudetenland became the site of violence, when Germans were ordered out. Still a very sore point with many of the neighbours, including Austria, Hungary and Germany.

Despite their differences, the Czech Republic and former sidekick Slovakia do share plenty of intense, painful history given the seventy-four years the two spent together as one Central European country – fifty years of them under Communist control. Theirs was the land first sacrificed in the days leading up to the Second World War, when the British and French handed over the Sudetenland to Hitler under the 1938 Munich Pact. Czechoslovakia was also the birthplace of an issue that continues to be one of Europe's thorniest: the Beneš Decrees, a Second World War hangover that is still not resolved.

Festering Wound: The Beneš Decrees

Named after Czech President Edvard Beneš, who led the country after the Second World War, these Allied-approved decrees expelled 3 million Czech Germans from Czechoslovakia and authorized the seizure of their lands, mostly in the Sudetenland; some 250,000 Hungarians were sent packing from eastern Slovak territory as well. The 1945–6 exodus was as horrifying as Nazi deportation: 300,000 died along the way, many killed in mass violence. During the past fifteen years, many of the expelled Germans (and to a lesser extent Hungarians) began pushing for apologies, financial compensation and/or their land back. The topic has only become more heated with time, and assorted rightwingers have taken the issue on as a cause: Austria's Jörg Haider is just one who demands that the decrees be reversed, as does Hungary's Viktor Orbán, and the German government is withholding payments to Czech victims of the war until the matter is settled. For many Czechs, however, it is a done deal; they don't want to negotiate any return of land, they don't want to hand out compensation, or even talk about the Beneš Decrees, and find the importance placed on the matter absurd given the devastation and loss of life they suffered at the hands of the Nazis. The heat is on, however, as former Sudetenlanders are organizing: in 2003 a Sudetenland rights group took up offices in Prague to push the issue that was already rearing its ugly head at the EU round table before the new countries were even on board. Austria's Haider and Hungary's Orbán were among those calling for the Czech Republic and Slovakia to be barred from EU entry until seized land was returned or deportees had been paid for their losses.

The Beneš Decrees, and the Czech and Slovak tendency to avoid the murky issue, are only one reason why the Czech Republic and Slovakia are the troublemakers of the neighbourhood. Both also have reputations for slapping together questionable nuclear plants, and making other energy decisions which have Austria and Hungary screaming.

The Austrian highways crossing to the Czech Republic and Slovakia are lined with signs indicating how many kilometres you are from Chernobyl – and from the Czech and Slovak nuclear plants.

Austria, which banned nuclear power in 1978, is shrieking about the Czechs' newly revved up Temelin plant, a Soviet design, that sits a mere 65 kilometres from the Austrian border – and may be manned by Homer Simpson since it breaks down every few months. The Slovaks' Bohunice plant – an older Soviet design built to 1950s standards and lacking containment domes to trap leaking radioactive gases – isn't any better, and in 1998 Slovakia also fired up the Soviet-initiated Mochovce plant, ignoring vehement Austrian protests (led by rightwinger Jörg Haider) that blocked the highway between the two countries. (Never mind that loudly anti-nuclear Austria quietly buys electricity from Hungary's nuclear plant.)

Not in my backyard, but yours is fine: *How did all these half-finished Soviet plants begin operating despite not being up to scratch and missing assorted vital safety parts? American and Western European companies finished the jobs, while admitting that the standards for reactors were much slacker in Central Europe. The Czech Republic* *doesn't currently even need all the electricity that its plants generate. Therein lies one explanation for why Western European countries got the plants up and running: Central Europe's nukes can unobtrusively deliver electricity to Western European countries where consumers often oppose nuclear plants. Plently of Czechs are against them too, and the Temelin plant in particular is an ongoing issue both domestically and abroad, all the more since the Czech government is talking about bringing yet another reactor on line there.*

Hungary is hopping mad as well. In the 1970s the Soviets unveiled a grand plan for generating electricity by damming the Danube river that runs through Slovakia to Hungary, and providing energy for both countries. But when the Soviet Union fell apart, Hungary ditched the plan for their dam, because of its environmental impact. Slovakia, however, ignoring Hungarian protests, went through with the dam on the Slovakian part of the river. Slovakia now has more electricity, but Hungary now sees lowered water levels, destroyed habitats and fewer fish.

The dam matter was taken to the International Court of Justice in 1997. The court supported Slovakia, and chastised Hungary for backing out of the deal.

'There's not a drop of water in sight today. To our right there's an outcropping of earth that used to be an island. It's crowned by the bare branches of dead trees, a ghostly reminder of a river that's disappeared' – Dan Charles, National Public Radio reporter describing the effects of the Slovakian dam on marshlands in Hungary

Both the Czech and Slovak Republics also entered the European Union with governments that weren't a perfect fit: Czech President Vaclav Klaus regularly badmouths the EU, while Slovak Prime Minister Dzurinda is dwindling in popularity and dipping below the 10 per cent approval mark. A few more commonalities: both countries are riddled with corruption and both have a problem with illegal arms that just seem to walk out on their own.

Arms Sale! Prices Slashed! Come on Down!

Under the Soviet regime, Czechoslovakia was transformed into weapons-and-explosives central, best known for cheap rifles and Semtex, an explosive that is still a favourite of guerrillas. (So singularly Czech is the product, that Semtex is the name of a popular Czech energy drink.) Czechs and Slovaks had little say in the matter back then, but the arms industry (both legal and illegal) is still thriving today. Since independence, the two countries have supplied arms to China, Cuba, India, Iran, Vietnam and Libya[1] among others (Soviet back orders), and also produce weapons for and run guns to assorted questionable governments and radical groups, including those in Yemen, Eritrea and Sri Lanka. With the Czech Republic now part of NATO, Czech arms manufacturers hope their alliance colleagues will call in even more orders. And who knows what they're doing in Slovakia? Apparently not the government, which seems to have little idea who's making what or what's slipping over the borders. Reports persist that Slovak arms are ending up everywhere from Angola to Burma.

In 2004 the Czech authorities cracked down on a company illegally sending ammunition to Iraq.

History Review

Czechoslovakia was born of a pipe dream. In the mid nineteenth century, as nationalistic awakenings sprang up across the Austrian Empire, idealistic intellectuals – sick of Austrian domination in everything from culture to language – envisaged a land that would unite Czechs and Slovaks who'd for centuries lived side by side in the region atop today's Austria and Hungary. While their fantasy may have looked good on paper, it was a shaky proposition once it was actually hammered into reality at the Paris Peace Conference of 1919. After all, Czechs and Slovaks had never exactly been good mates: even in 1918, as the First World War drew to a close, the two kept battling with each other, despite fighting on the same side.[2]

The two groups even had different histories, particularly in the nineteenth century: while Czechs had been part of the Austrian Empire, Slovaks had been part of the Hungarian half.

That Czechoslovakia actually did emerge as a country was a result of two things: the territorial reshuffling of Europe after the First World War and the relentless work of Czech scholar Tomas Masaryk, who had been travelling across the United States and Europe even before 1914, pushing for the independence of this Central European region. When the Great War victors met in Paris to redistribute the losers' lands, smooth-talking Masaryk saw his chance. Along with Czech intellectual Edvard Beneš, he skilfully lobbied for a new country that would bring together Czechs and Slovaks, as well as the resident Ruthenes (Ukrainians) and the Germans, Austrians and Hungarians left over from the days of the Austro-Hungarian Empire. Considering that Masaryk was famous for his work on suicide and that Beneš was a sociologist, you'd think they might have realized that the country they were creating would have self-destructive tendencies due to its volatile ethnic mix.

It might not have had the same ring, but if only they'd called the country 'Slovakoczechia' maybe things would have been different. After all, the big gripe of the Slovaks was that Czechs, with less than half of Czechoslovakia's population, always came first, starting with the name.

As leader of the new land with its capital in Prague, President Masaryk set about rearranging the place, embarking on radical redistribution and democratization programmes. All residents of Czechoslovakia were forced to hand over a start-up tax of 20 per cent of their cash holdings – a tax that hit the wealthy (mostly German) particularly hard. Land tracts held by German nobles were divvied up and handed over to peasants. The international community hailed the 1920 constitution that the new government devised as progressive, but non-Czechs who lived in the country complained that it was mostly Czechs who had penned it. Another snag: Slovaks and Ruthenes, who had been promised autonomy back when Czechoslovakia was on the drawing board, soon growled that Czechs weren't living up to their word – since autonomy hadn't materialized; resident Hungarians and Poles were also peeved about how Czechs were always top dog.

The royal family of Liechtenstein is pushing for the return of lands seized during the 1919 land redistribution. Their claim stretches over 1,600 sq. kilometres of Czech land.

Even angrier: the ethnic Germans living in the Sudetenland, whose tracts had shrunk to provide the peasant lands and who had been slammed by the country's start-up tax. Given no say in the writing of the constitution, and deprived of political power, Germans became yet another dissatisfied group. Already on the verge of geographical fissure due to ethnic strife, the country fell apart when Hitler showed up on the scene.

The Lords Giveth, The Lords Taketh Away

The Big Four (Britain, France, Russia and the US) had approved the 1919 creation of Czechoslovakia, but two of them (Britain and France) went on to carve it up twenty years later, hoping to appease Nazi Germany with a geographical bone. In the infamous 1938 Munich Pact the British prime minister Neville Chamberlain and France's premier Edouard Daladier gave a troubled nod to Hitler, who wanted to annex the Sudetenland, which held an ethnic German majority as well as Czechoslovakia's most valuable industry. The Czechoslovakian leadership, not consulted on the matter, was livid. Forced to sign the pact, President Edvard Beneš promptly resigned, pointing out (correctly) that Hitler would just take the whole country. Stalin was also furious that he wasn't in the loop: in response he secretly arranged for the Russian–German meeting that created the Ribbentrop–Molotov Non-Aggression Pact. Meanwhile, Poland and Hungary swooped in to claim a few territories in the country that suddenly seemed up for grabs.

When Hitler began making noises about uniting all ethnic Germans in his new world plan, some Germans in Czechoslovakia welcomed the chance for a split – and they were given that geographical break by the Munich Pact of 1938. That handout didn't appease Hitler for long, and when Nazis went on to invade Czechoslovakia six month later, they found little resistance and some outright support. Slovak leader Monsignor Jozef Tiso, who had opposed the 1919 formation of Czechoslovakia in the first place, quickly made a deal: Slovakia would be made an independent region, and Tiso would be in charge, although supporting the Nazis. The Czech government (then under President Emil Hacha) simply let the Germans roll in: Hitler had threatened to pummel Prague with the Luftwaffe, and then-president Hacha did not want to risk it. As promised, Nazis did not mar Prague's well-preserved beauty: they wanted the city as the site for a new museum they were planning about Jews to be called the Museum of an Extinct Race.

> *Some German Czechs, however, strongly opposed the Munich Pact that gave Hitler the Sudetenland; they organized resistance groups (and escape routes for Jews) when Nazis took the rest of the country the following spring. Among them: Count Joachim von Zedtwitz, a wealthy German Czech who was a one-man resistance force, helping transport Jews and other political targets out of the country, as he sped along in his sports car; the Nazis assumed that with his Aryan looks and German ethnicity he was on their side. He was tried by the Nazis, but pretended to be insane and was released; he was tried by the Czechoslovaks after the war, and was nearly run out by the Beneš Decrees, but numerous Czechoslovaks testified to his valiant anti-Nazi efforts. When the Communists came to power, however, he sped off again – this time to Switzerland.[3]*

During the Nazi occupation over 250,000 Czechoslovak Jews died along-side another 100,000 Czechs. Few Slovaks were killed, except those who were Jewish, since the government of Monsignor Tiso supported the Nazis, and allowed them to build arms plants and work camps. Initially, many Slovaks were unaware of the priest's collusion with the Germans, but resistance groups eventually grew from a 'whispering campaign'. In 1944 the angry Slovaks rebelled against Tiso in the Slovak National Uprising, which Germans easily crushed.

> **Tragically late for the liberation:** *Thousands of Czechoslovaks were killed in the very last hours of the war, even though the Allies weren't far away. The Western troops, however, were forced to wait three days for the tardy Russians, who'd been promised the honour of liberating Prague.*

Edvard Beneš, who'd been living in London during the war, returned as president in 1945, just as the Sudetenland was returned to Czechoslovakia. Furious that so many ethnic Germans still lived there, he ordered them to be shipped out by issuing the so-called Beneš Decrees: 3 million former German-speaking Czechoslovakians were pushed out by several hundred thousand ethnic Hungarians. Beneš, however, was soon pushed out him-self: by February 1948 the Communists had wrested control in a coup, and promptly scribbled out a new Lenin-loving constitution. Beneš refused to endorse it and resigned as president, this time for good.

In 1948 Jan Masaryk, who opposed the Communists' hitching the Czech wagon to Moscow, toppled out of a window. Some said the foreign minister, son of founder Tomas Masaryk, had committed suicide, but most believed he had a helping hand from the comrades. In 2004 a Czech investigation concluded that he was indeed murdered.

By the 1950s Czechoslovakia was powerless as the Soviet machine eased into top gear: intellectuals, Jews, even Communist Party members who weren't Stalinist enough were killed after mock trials for treason. Dissidents disappeared. Workers' protests were stamped out as Communists pushed 'normalization' – the submission of personal will for the supposed greater common good.

'For fear of losing his job, the schoolteacher teaches things he does not believe; fearing for his future, the pupil repeats them after him; for fear of not being allowed to continue his studies, the young man joins the Youth League and participates in whatever of its activities are necessary; fear that under the monstrous system of political credits, his son or daughter will not acquire the necessary total of points for enrolment at a school, leads the father to take on all manner of responsibilities and "voluntarily" to do everything required' – Dissident Czech writer Vaclav Havel in a 1975 letter to President Husak protesting against normalization. The letter got Havel imprisoned.

Upon Stalin's death in 1953, the doors began to creak open a little and in the early 1960s some theatre groups and movie makers were permitted to travel. But it wasn't until a new Communist leader in Czechoslovakia really gave the doors a push in spring 1968 that Czechs had a close brush with freedom. Predictably, Moscow went bonkers.

'We shall have to remove everything that strangles artistic and scientific creativeness' – Alexander Dubcek in the 1968 speech to Czechoslovaks that led to the 'Prague Spring'

Prague Spring

When Czechoslovakia's economy slumped in 1968, the Communist Party brought in fresh leadership to give it a lift. New Communist Party head Alexander Dubcek unveiled a new radical reform plan that lifted much more than the economy: Dubcek boosted the Czechoslovak mood. As part of his programme that he dubbed 'socialism with a human face', he ripped away press censorship, allowed freedom of expression, made trade-union reforms and, being a Slovak, he also created an autonomous state for Slovakia. The Soviets in Moscow were dumbfounded, but President Leonid Brezhnev liked Dubcek and did little except call him screaming every day. But Dubcek wasn't trying to make a break, simply to brighten the outlook: to Brezhnev's relief, the reformer continued to keep Czechoslovakia in the Soviet military collective – the Warsaw Pact – that Moscow saw as necessary defence against NATO, and Dubcek also toed most of the Communist Party line. But unlike anywhere else in the Soviet bloc, that spring – dubbed the Prague Spring – Czechoslovakians could soon listen to criticisms of the Soviet regime via radio and TV, and read accurate news of the West while revelling in their newly found freedom to say whatever they wished, wherever they wished. For eight months the country opened up and appeared to wake from the collective Communist slumber. But when Dubcek went so far as to open up parliament and welcome non-Communists into politics, Brezhnev blew his stack. On 20 August Czechs awoke to the sight of their dreams being smashed. Tanks of Soviet troops – Poles, Hungarians, East Germans, Russians and Bulgarians – rolled into Prague, the soldiers ignoring the pleas of those who climbed atop their tanks begging them to stop. An estimated 120 died over the next two days, including thirteen killed while trying to prevent the Soviets from taking the radio station. By 22 August it was over: a Soviet-style black-out had once again descended as the free press was shut down, Soviet troops permanently moved in and Czechoslovakia transformed from the most open of the satellite states to the most repressed. Dubcek, kidnapped during the ordeal and hauled off to Moscow, was soon fired as party head: he survived the ordeal, but spent the rest of his career tending to trees for the Slovak forestry service. More rigid Communists soon took power and ripped away all the rights he had given.

'You may think Czechs behaved like cowards when they did not fight. But you can't go against tanks with empty hands ... The only way you can help us is this: Don't forget Czechoslovakia. Don't forget

Czechoslovakia ... even when Czechoslovakia ceases to be news in the paper' – Unidentified 22-year-old Czech student in a message to the world on 23 August 1968, as the Prague Spring experiment was going down[4]

The Prague Spring is not much celebrated in the Czech Republic, where there's a sense of sadness and guilt that the Czechoslovakians caved in (as if they had a choice). In Russia, however, it's often a much bigger to-do with leaders apologizing for stamping out what they now say was necessary reform. Mikhail Gorbachev, who initiated glasnost and perestroika nearly two decades later, said he drew his inspiration from Prague's happiest spring.

The mood in Czechoslovakia was gloomy as the Soviets erased former rights, fired thousands, and tossed even more out of the Communist Party; in response, some 150,000 Czechs soon fled the country. Suspected and known dissidents, such as Vaclav Havel, were forced to work as janitors and street sweepers, and the arts scene that had blossomed under the Prague Spring now withered under heavy censorship rules. In January 1969 student Jan Palach, livid that Czechoslovakia was again wrapped in Soviet chains, set himself on fire, dying in his protest at the Soviet occupation, and blackening spirits further.

'What was important about the events of 1968 was that immediately after the occupation, people – to their own surprise – did not forget their civic and national self-awareness, the feeling of pride and self-determination. The country was under military occupation, the country's leadership was backing off, but civil society managed to mobilize itself. Although it was at moments so tragic ...' – Vaclav Havel in a speech to the French Senate in 1998

Enter the last person you would expect in the picture: Frank Zappa, the American musician whose experimental music – often long-winded, drugged-out rambles – lodged stinging social criticism and tackled every taboo including masturbation. Or rather enter the title of his song, 'Plastic People of the Universe', which inspired a 1970s Czech rock band to take that name and write music that struck out at the system. Refusing to take the test required of all performing artists – a propaganda quiz asking such things as when Lenin was born – the group was banned from playing; being an officially underground band, they of course gigged around anyway, cranking up the volume defiantly. In 1977, when Plastic People of the Universe members were arrested and thrown into prison, local writers and artists formed a protest group, Charter 77, to fight censorship and promote human rights. Known for his biting plays about Communist bureaucrats (and for coining the name 'Absurdistan' to describe life under the Soviets), Vaclav Havel rose up as the dissidents' leader. So frequently and loudly did he protest at the oppression that he carried a toothbrush in his pocket, expecting to be arrested yet again.[5] Officially banned from writing, Havel didn't stop making noise, even from prison where he spent nearly four years – of course with a pen in his hand.

Havel and members of Charter 77 frequently wrote letters to Amnesty International and the New York Times *publicizing the dehumanizing acts of the Communists, and continually airing the dirty laundry in the Western press.*

While the dissidents grew louder, the spirit in Moscow was weakening, as it was drained on several fronts: the Soviet–Afghanistan war dragged on, while protests in Poland, Hungary and the Baltic States in the 1980s grew more heated, and the thousand-member Charter 77 pushed even harder. When the Berlin Wall fell in 1989, Charter 77 – along with the Slovak dissidents in Public Against Violence – seized the moment to finish off the Communist chapter in Czechoslovakian history.

The Velvet Revolution

When the Berlin Wall fell in November 1989, a group of protesters took to the streets of Prague, calling for independence. The peaceful march might have been ignored had not the police roughed up a hundred or so: the next day, the country rose en masse and marched through the streets. During the next twenty-four days, hundreds of thousands showed up in Wenceslas Square, rattling key chains, chanting slogans, singing songs, burning candles, as they rallied around playwright Vaclav Havel, demanding that the Communist government step down and the Soviet troops roll out. Their slogan was corny – 'Truth and love will win over hatred and lies' – but it did the trick. In December the Communist Party stepped down, and the new democratic government of Vaclav Havel stepped in. In 1990 Czechoslovakia regained independence.

Vaclav Havel called the break with Communism 'the Velvet Revolution' because it was soft and while hundreds were injured, nobody was killed.

By the end of December the Communist leaders had stood aside, and Havel's party, Civic Forum, along with Public Against Violence, had marched into parliament with Havel as their head. Dissidents and others who'd risked their lives to return the freedom first known during the Prague Spring filled the offices of Prague Castle, now Havel's presidential headquarters, where officials zipped through stone corridors on scooters. The new government flew in Frank Zappa and gave the singer a new role as honorary consultant to the Ministry of Culture.

'All I knew about Czechoslovakia before I got there was what I had seen on Cable News Network: people walking around in dingy, gray streets and having a revolution. I had no idea how pretty and quiet it is . . . What they don't want [Czechoslovakia to become] can be summed up by the comment urgently made by one of the many kids who trailed me throughout my visit: "Frankie, Frankie, please don't bring me Las Vegas"[6] *– Frank Zappa in a 1990 interview with* The Nation

Havel, whose trademark was the heart that trailed his signature, switched on a big pink neon valentine atop the castle, a symbol visible across the city. But while the international media cooed, and the international masses applauded the return of independence, all wasn't as cheery as it seemed.

One headache in Czechoslovakia's early days came from the east: namely, Slovakia. An autonomous region under the new constitution, Slovakia had its own prime minister who worked in tandem with the Czech prime minister in Prague, or at least that was the theory. When former Communist-turned-Slovak-nationalist Vladimir Meciar stomped into the Slovak premiership in 1992, Czechoslovakia started to crumble. Meciar's first meeting with his Czech counterpart Vaclav Klaus turned nasty: Meciar threatened to pull Slovakia out of the union if Czechoslovakia continued its rapid pace of privatization; Klaus urged him to do it. Within months the two countries were formally split.

From 1 January 1993 the former country had two passports, two currencies and, with Slovakia under Meciar, two different ways of life. Slovakia leaned towards Moscow, the Czech Republic grabbed on to the West. Another difference: while Slovakia gave citizenship to

Czech-born residents, the Czech Republic didn't automatically offer citizenship to those who lived there but had been born in Slovakia.

The so-called Velvet Divorce of 1993 was partly about Czech dominance, but neither Czechs nor Slovaks wanted the country to split. But the two prime ministers decided the country's fate, without bothering to put the important matter to a vote. Even Vaclav Havel was not consulted in the matter: he was so livid over the split that he quit as president. A few months later, however, he resumed the presidential post; now almost everybody, including Havel, believes the break-up was a good thing.

26. Czech Republic (Ceska Republika): Jaded Loveliness

Fast Facts

Country:	Czech Republic; Ceska Republika
Capital:	Prague
Government:	parliamentary democracy
Independence:	1 January 1993 (created as separate state from Czechoslovakia)
Population:	10,247,000 (2004 estimate)
Leaders:	Head of State: President Vaclav Klaus (2003) Head of Government: Prime Minister Stanislav Gross (2004)
Elections:	President elected by Parliament, 5-year term Prime Minister appointed by President, 5-year term
Name of Parliament:	Parliament or Senat
Ethnicity:	Czech 81%; Moravian 13%; Slovak 3%; Polish, German, Roma, Hungarian
Religion:	Roman Catholic 39%; atheist 39%; Protestant 5%; Orthodox 3%; others 13%
Language:	Czech; also Slovak, German, Polish, Hungarian spoken by minorities
Literacy:	99.9% (1999 estimate)
Exports:	machinery 44%; manufacture including arms 25%; chemicals 7%; fuel 7%
Per capita GDP:	$15,700 (2003)
Unemployment:	8.4% (May 2004 Eurostat figure)
EU status:	entered May 2004
Currency:	Czech koruna
Known for:	Prague Spring, Velvet Revolution

Standout Qualities

Czech-out: Vaclav Havel's gone and so are some dreams

Czech-in: President Vaclav Klaus is in and soaring in popularity

Czech-point: Vaclav Klaus keeps loudly making the same one about the EU: it's bad

Vaclav v. Vaclav

The two most powerful men in the Czech Republic share a first name and little else; in fact they appear to loathe each other. Former president Vaclav Havel, who stepped down in 2003, was for much of his tenure the hero of the common man. Current president Vaclav Klaus is a tightly wound economist who campaigned on becoming the 'People's President' but insists that the people call him 'Professor'. Havel is warm, Klaus is haughty, and the two were unabashed foes back when Havel was president and Klaus was prime minister; they still hiss at each other even though Havel is no longer in office. After Havel stepped down, right-leaning Klaus climbed into his chair.

Résumé

The Czech Republic is wealthier than most former Communist countries, but these days it's appearing rather jaded. The recent EU bonding with Western Europe, once viewed as synonymous with success, is now eyed quite warily. Less than half of Czechs bothered to vote in the referendum about EU entry; now that they're in, only 10 per cent think EU membership will make their lives better; 40 per cent think it will only make their life worse. But no wonder Czechs are feeling so downbeat. From the start President Vaclav Klaus was telling them what a drag being in the EU was going to be.

Biting the Hand that Feeds You

Unlike the other Central European leaders, Eurosceptic President Vaclav Klaus (who describes himself as a 'Eurorealist') never waved pom-poms at the idea of EU entry. He has no use for the euro, loathes the proposed constitution, rejects the idea of a supranational power and isn't thrilled about the entry conditions, particularly the reduced agricultural subsidies for Czech farmers. He'd already raised eyebrows in Brussels in 2001 with his comments about 'the creeping, silent unification of the continent', and by suggesting that the EU put the brakes on enlargement back then. When he took over as president in 2003, he duly encouraged Czechs to vote in that year's EU referendum, although naturally he didn't encourage them to vote yes. But the one-man EU-sniping machine pulled out all stops as the 1 May 2004 entry date drew nearer. 'In a few days, our state will cease to exist as an independent and sovereign entity', Klaus wrote in the Czech newspaper *Mlada Fronta Dnes* ten days before the Czech Republic joined the EU. His opinion piece, titled 'Let Us Not Lose Ourselves in the Union', went on to forecast that the Czech people might be wiped out. 'We must do everything we can so that our unique existence over 1,000 years will not crumble and be lost', he wrote, as though the country was facing an invasion of aliens or a close brush with Ebola. Klaus trashed the EU's haste in expanding their Union, and the less than democratic EU decision-making process, and as the minutes until 1 May ticked by, he told reporters he had no intention of flying the EU flag over Prague Castle. From whence came his killjoy attitude nobody knows, and it's all the more mystifying since Klaus's government first launched the EU accession process back in 1996. Is it a ploy to win support from a Eurosceptic public or simply a way to stand out amid Europe's gushing politicians? Perhaps it's about the Beneš Decrees, which Klaus had wanted hammered into the country's EU accession agreement so they couldn't be changed, or maybe it's a signal to Europe's big boys that his little country won't be bossed around. Certainly some of Klaus's criticisms are valid: the enlargement process thus far has already been rocky and Brussels *is* sneaky, often keeping the public in the dark about its decisions and plans. But his bristly attitude and caustic remarks aren't making the Czech politician any friends in an era when the country might benefit from having a few more in the 'hood. Domestically, however, his outbursts against the EU, the war in Iraq, and the newly increased Value Added Tax – he unsuccessfully vetoed the VAT bill – are working: his approval rating was only 35 per cent in his first year in office, but now he's got over two-thirds of Czechs whistling his tune.

It wasn't the first time Klaus had shaken up the Czech crowd. As the country's first finance minister, he kicked up a storm with the ultra-fast rate of privatization, which made his country a shining example for Central Europe, although the transformation was fraught with scandal, shady backroom deals and charges of corruption. As prime minister he engineered the 1993 Czech–Slovak split. Four years later he stepped down over charges of inappropriate campaign funding: news leaked out that one of his two biggest campaign donors was actually dead and the other one lived in an African village and had never heard of Vaclav Klaus. In 2003, however, he was back – this time in the presidential palace, which he runs with characteristic brusque efficiency. Like a coach who bets on the other team, Klaus may be the worst choice as an EU leader since he seems to do nothing but badmouth the institution. Nevertheless, in a time when most Central Europe leaders are wimpy, at least Klaus has some 'umpf'.

Quick Tour

From its fetching high-towered castles, where officials of yore oft tumbled out of windows, to Prague's elaborate astronomical clock, the country now called the Czech Republic is stunning, surreal and tinged with the macabre.

One of Prague's most beloved sights is the beautiful Apostle Clock on the main square: every hour elaborately sculpted saints and skeletons come out for a mechanical spin. Legend has it that in the fifteenth century when the work was created, Prague's Town Council so adored their unique time-telling marvel that they blinded the clockmaker to prevent him from ever making such a masterpiece for anyone else.

Hard to imagine a prettier place than this castled land that has more royal structures per acre than anywhere in the world: flowering orchards and lush vineyards carpet soft hills and the heavily spired architecture is straight out of a fairy tale. But Ceska Republika has a dark, brooding side, and has long been a magnet for the strange and the sinister. In Prague, a centre for alchemy, astrology and magic in the sixteenth century during the reign of the Habsburg emperor Rudolph II, there's still an undercurrent of secrecy, and a hint of malevolence that seeps out of the Vltava river (some say it holds evil water sprites). The once-common fear of Mother Russia returning may have been conquered (joining NATO helped), but the place lives in shadows: Russian and Ukrainian mobs have moved in, along with the Chinese, Yugoslav and Chechen; kidnapping is one means to recruit sex slaves for international rings, and one never knows what long-buried secret will be unearthed in the woods.

One Soviet-era secret presented itself in the 2002 floods: the north's Spolana Neratovice chemical plant's hidden hoard of toxic chemicals came floating out and streamed into the Elbe river – source of drinking water downstream in Germany. The factory's ill-stored by-products, long kept hidden from the public, may be the cause for the mysteriously high number of miscarriages in the area.

Although the place has loads of potential, the Czech Republic had several enemies in waiting before it even walked into the new EU. When the official acceptance of the ten candidate countries was put to a vote in the European Parliament, the Czech Republic received the most nays. The reason: those troubling Beneš Decrees, an issue that still burns.

'Once I counted the changes of political regimes in my mother's life and there have been eight during her 78 years. Britons have never experienced as many changes during their whole history, so no wonder we are a nation that doesn't show too much enthusiasm. We are sceptical optimists' – Prime Minister Vladimir Spidla in 2004 interview with UPI,[1] two months before resigning

Many once-idealistic Czechs are disillusioned with the democracy that finally has materialized and cynicism has crept in since the innocent days when peace and truth could win over war and lies. Wages are now higher but so is the price of everything from beer to rent; many Czechs can no longer afford living in housing-short Prague. The once dimly lit city flashes with neon, the arteries that were nearly void of cars are now clogged with traffic, and the stores that lacked variety are today crammed with slow-moving tourists. Nothing in this land has ever turned out as it was imagined, and even former President Vaclav Havel, like his neon heart, was little more than a highly visible icon with limited power. In 1999 the feeling of discontent was so strong that 250,000 Czechs launched a 'Thank you, now leave' campaign, calling upon Klaus and other powerful politicians to step down. That didn't turn out as envisaged either: the politicians stayed – Klaus grabbing more power – and after a few years the movement flickered out. So perhaps it's easier to understand that, with Czechs fully back in the driver's seat for little more than fifteen years, many fret about letting the EU hold the map.

'The most important thing is that new generations are maturing, generations of people who grew up free and are not deformed by life under Communist rule. These are the first Czechs of our times who inherently consider freedom normal and natural' – Vaclav Havel in 2003

Future Forecast

Klaus will be a combative force in the EU and the Sudetenland issue and the Beneš Decrees will stir up even more trouble.

Hot Spots

Prague: Gorgeous and vaguely eerie capital Prague is the most visited city in Central Europe. Best known for Kafka, revolts, beer and the statue-lined Charles Bridge – which survived six centuries of wars, but was nearly washed away in the 2002 floods – the place is also getting a reputation for its prostitutes. It's said that over 15,000 of the gals work here.[2]

Prague Castle: Built on a pagan sacrificial ground, spired Hradcany Castle looks more like a Gothic church and serves as the Presidential Palace.

> *Unsolved mystery: The building in Prague that houses the US-funded Radio Free Europe was reportedly an Iraqi target in 1998; the Iraqi diplomat who was believed to have been assigned the task of blowing it up was forced to leave the Czech Republic – and did so with 150*

Fairytale pretty: Prague's Charles Bridge.

suitcases, whose contents weren't revealed to the media.[3] *Mementoes? Semtex? Bottles of absinthe for Saddam?*

Sudetenland: When the post-First World War mapmakers were drawing new boundaries, the Sudetenland was originally intended to be part of Germany because of its then high population of Germans; however, this mountainous and industrial region was instead made the north-west border of Czechoslovakia after 1919. The reason: Czech Edvard Beneš disagreed with the census figures showing that more Germans lived there than Czechs. Annexed by Hitler in 1938, it went back to Czechoslovakia after the war, and Beneš ensured that Germans were no longer a majority, when he expelled the resident Germans in 1946.

In 1999 the small Czech town of Usti nad Labem used city funds to build a wall that separated Roma (gypsies) from the Czechs, a move that elicited wagging fingers and loud lectures from the EU. Since then the Czech government has received EU funding to promote understanding of Roma culture, including publishing Roma poems.

Temelin: The Soviets started construction of this controversial nuclear plant located 190 kilometres outside Prague and 65 kilometres from the Austrian border, and it's brought up just about every time Czechs and Austrians meet. Plenty of Czechs protested against it too, and they absolutely detest the proposed plan for dealing with the radioactive waste: the government is considering burying it in nearby villages.

Moravia: Hilly land of orchards and vineyards in the south that was once a powerful dynasty and is now the location of the Czech Republic's second biggest city Brno. Pretty Moravia used to get ignored by the tourists, but now some are unlocking the secrets of this misty agricultural region, known for fine wines and plum brandy.

The skies: The Czech Republic joined NATO in 1999, but Czechs themselves say the current military equipment is not a huge asset. Czech-made helicopters frequently crash and recently, on its way to a nearby airport, a Czech-made trainer plane fell apart in mid air. The Czech government plans to spend a few billion to buy Swedish fighter planes; other aggressive bidders for that juicy deal, such as Lockheed Martin, withdrew their offers over the government's alleged financial misdealing and possible bribery.

Under EU requirements, bars now must have hot water and paper towels in the loo; many owners, says Radio Prague, are resisting the upgrade.

Bars: Tourists are typically the only ones who dare knock back the absinthe (complete with wormwood) that can be ordered in the bars here – the high-octane, mildly hallucinogenic 'green fairy' is outlawed in most of Europe – but almost everyone tipples it. It's said that Czechs drink more beer – over half a litre daily – than anyone else in the world, and the country is home to the world's oldest working microbrewery, the world's first Pilsner, and the world's first 'Budweiser' (the local manufacturer has been fighting with Anheuser-Busch over the name for more than a century, sometimes winning its cases, so to speak).

Historical Hot Spot: Windows

Czechs have an odd history with windows: for centuries dismay in Bohemia was expressed by shoving people out of them. The most famous case was in 1618 when two Catholic officials were pushed from Prague Castle's tower by Protestants who didn't want to convert. That event came to be known as 'The Defenestration [from the window-ization] of Prague.' Fortunately, the two men who fell out of the castle landed in a soft, smelly pile of manure[4] and survived. Unfortunately, the tossing launched the Thirty Years War, which stripped Bohemia of its power, prestige and language for the next three hundred years. Czechs wouldn't have much of a say in the world again until 1919.

Hot Shots

Vaclav Havel: President of Czechoslovakia 1990–92; President of the Czech Republic 1993–2003. Dissident writer whose incredulousness with the Soviet situation helped finally to free Czechoslovakia from Moscow's hold when he led the Velvet Revolution of 1989, Havel – like Lech Walesa – was frustrated by his lack of real power; unlike the Pole, Havel lasted thirteen years. He wielded great clout with the masses, and was the unofficial diplomat of Central Europe to the West, but did a few political about-turns: he said he wouldn't support NATO, but changed his mind and became a major NATO booster; mouths really dropped open when Havel backed the 2003 invasion of Iraq, for which President George W. Bush awarded him the Medal of Freedom as a supporter of US policy. His wife Olga was as popular with Czechs as he was; within a year of her 1996 death from cancer, he married flirtatious actress Dagmar Veskrnova twenty years

Vaclav Klaus: the professor is a
Eurosceptic.

his junior (she's in her late forties), causing a scandal and a drop in popularity; many still love him anyway. Sick with cancer, the playwright who was a brewery caretaker during the Soviet days (his punishment for lashing out at the system) lost half a lung in 1996 and has nearly died several times since. Havel is now working on his memoirs and lives part of the year in Portugal.

> Besides plays, Havel wrote essays, manifestos, and provocative letters. His 1978 essay 'The Power of the Powerless', analysing the Soviet brainwashing techniques employed to create a passive society, was one of his most influential works. Also notable were his critical letters to Communist leaders, factors which led to his three prison terms during their regime.

Vaclav Klaus: Czech Republic Prime Minister 1993–7; President 2003 to present. The EU's loudest and most articulate critic, the icy-eyed economist Klaus is driven and known to run over whoever or whatever is in his way. As finance minister 'the Professor' pushed Czechoslovakia onto the free-market fast track, which led to the Velvet Divorce with Slovakia; accusations of corruption trailed him through the transition. He stepped down as prime minister in 1997 after being accused of misusing political funding for his essentially one-man Civic Democratic Party; when he did not secure the required votes for the prime ministerial position in 2002, he suffered a nervous breakdown. When Havel stepped down as president in 2003, Klaus was not a dead-cert: it took three voting rounds in parliament for him finally to nab the presidential seat. Some like him, and some really, really don't, and many are just plain shocked that despite the protests and scandals Klaus still looms large on the political scene. His cocky, brusque style is legendary, prompting the joke, 'What's the difference between God and Klaus? God doesn't think he's Klaus.'[5]

> Klaus condemned Havel's surprising support of the Iraq invasion. He has also posed probing and relevant questions about the increasingly 'supranational' nature of the EU. Both factors have helped boost his popularity at home.

Stanislav Gross: Social Democrat, 34, filled in when Spidla resigned in June 2004 to take up a post at the European Commission.

Vladimir Spidla: Prime Minister 2002–4; European Commissioner 2004 to present. Prime ministers usually hold the most power, but Social Democrat Spidla's premiership was weak due to a very thin, compromise-heavy coalition; besides, he's so bland and full of innocuous soundbites that the *Prague Post* described him as 'personality-free'. Between his loose hold and Klaus's scepticism, Spidla's government was really not the ideal one for guiding the Czech Republic into the EU, but at least he didn't snap at the EU hosts when the Czech Republic walked in to their enlargement party. Spidla stepped off his PM's pedestal in 2004 and headed off to Brussels to pick up the post as Commissioner for employment, social affairs and equal opportunities.

Creative Hero: Franz Kafka (1883–1924)

Born in 1883, coal-eyed, heavily uni-browed Franz Kafka studied law, sold insurance, lived with his parents, and regarded Prague as his curse. The combo created some of the strangest fiction ever to see the ink of the printing presses, which thankfully they did since Max Brod, the friend to whom he bequeathed his writing, refused to destroy it as directed. Although he lived before Czechoslovakia was forced into the Soviet Union (for most of his life it was part of the Austrian Empire), Kafka painfully captured the terrible anonymity of being a powerless cog in the machine. That sentiment of worthlessness is best expressed in *The Metamorphosis*, in which a worker wakes up as a giant insect – a state which also captured Kafka's chronic feeling of being a wimp in his overbearing father's eyes. The insurance seller who spent his nights writing (and sometimes cavorting with prostitutes) had few of his works published during his lifetime and never could marry, despite being engaged numerous times to several women. This problem, too, he blamed on his father, to whom Kafka, upon learning he was dying of tuberculosis, wrote a forty-five page tell-off letter that Dad never read. His disturbing fiction best captures the mysterious, malevolent part of Prague, but it is not without humour: in *The Trial*, for instance, the judges who are perpetually reading thick books, presumably about legal matters, are at last revealed to be delving deep into porn. The writer who is so tied to Prague that he is nearly a cliché, finally received public recognition in 2004, when a statue of his likeness was erected in the square outside the Jewish Quarter apartment where he first scratched pen across paper and brought his nightmares alive. His eerie writing endures and he's said to influence numerous creators from composer Philip Glass to novelist Gabriel García Márquez. Can't say the same for his dad.

Milena Jesenská: Journalist and translator with whom Kafka fell in love, writing her daily letters (though only meeting her in person twice), Jesenská wrote critically of the Nazis, was instrumental in the resistance movement, and died in a concentration camp.

Creators: A Short Czech List

Milan Kundera, exiled to France, opened the door to modern Czech writers with *Unbearable Lightness of Being*, which kept the memory of Czechoslovakia alive internationally, but he lost cachet with Czechs for writing in French. Ivan Klima's absurdist novels were hugely popular when his books were banned; now that you can buy them at every bookstore, he's nearly passé. Many vibrant Czech works are not translated, but Vladislav Vancura's avant-garde novels are. The best known of the 1960s Czech 'New Wave' film movement is director Milos Forman (*One Flew over the Cuckoo's Nest, The People Versus Larry Flynt*). Forman now works in Hollywood, but in the 1980s returned to Czechoslovakia to film

Amadeus in Prague. The nineteenth-century historian Frantisek Palacky was never known for haiku: his *History of the Czech People* filled five volumes, and helped to spur on the dream of creating a country of Czechs.

Noteworthy: *The divine works of Czech classical composer Antonin Dvořák might never have fallen on modern ears had he continued in his original line of work as a butcher.*

Historical Hotshot: King Rudy (1552–1612)

Holy Roman Emperor Rudolph II, an Austrian Habsburg who moved his kingdom from Vienna to Prague in 1577, wasn't content with material riches. He sought spiritual wealth as well, and hoped to unlock the keys to the universe. Rudolph kicked off a renaissance in Prague when he invited in Europe's most wise to uncover the true nature of Godliness and the mysteries of life. They arrived from all corners: magicians and musicians, artists and astrologers, alchemists and architects; respected scientific men – astronomers Tycho Brahe and Johannes Kepler, and Queen Elizabeth I of England's personal physician from London – were likewise drawn to the quest in Prague. In between boozy nights at long dinners with Rudy, they all toiled to explain the inexplicable: whether trying to transform lead into gold, calculate celestial movements, decipher ancient texts, or discover the restorative qualities of beer, they attempted to demystify the mysteries, find eternal life and divine what lay ahead. Hundreds of spiritual seekers were lodged in Prague Castle; in the dungeons below the corpses of those cast off as charlatans rotted.

Media stars: Broadcasting for sixty-six years, Radio Prague has a story of its own, including being censored by the Soviets and airing broadcasts from hidden locations. Now it's the best one-stop source for history, culture and news, which can be accessed in six languages on their remarkable website: www.radioprague.cz Also notable: the weekly *Prague Post*.

Last word: These are shaky times for the Czech Republic's youthful prime minister Stanislav Gross, who stepped into the power seat in mid 2004 and is now dodging political bullets. The left-of-centre leader's Social

Democrat party still dominates parliament by a hair, but Gross – once seen as an energizing force – is now draining the country's confidence as he has a bit of financial accounting to do. The Czech leading newspaper is but one source grilling him about how in 1999 he could afford to buy a new ritzy flat, complete with covered pool, that carries a price tag of some €150,000. He says he borrowed the money from a relative, but some remain unconvinced. Another headache: his wife, an estate agent, reportedly rented out a building which houses a brothel – bringing to mind, for some, possible connections with the shadowy underworld, which Gross hotly denies. Whether his problems are enough to bring him down remains to be seen, but his integrity is definitely on the line: according to the *New York Times*, Gross was the source of the erroneous report that Mohammad Atta, ringleader of the September 11 attacks on the US, had previously come to Prague to meet Iraqi intelligence.

27. Slovak Republic
(Slovakia; Slovenska Republika):
The Forgotten Slav

Fast Facts

Country:	Slovak Republic/Slovakia; Slovenska Republika
Capital:	Bratislava
Government:	parliamentary democracy
Independence:	1 January 1993 (created as separate state from Czechoslovakia)
Population:	5,424,000 (2003 estimate)
Leaders:	Head of State: President Ivan Gasparovik (2004) Head of Government: Prime Minister Mikulas Dzurinda (1998)
Elections:	President elected by direct, popular vote, 5-year term; Prime Minister appointed by President, 5-year term
Name of Parliament:	National Council; Narodna Rada
Ethnicity:	Slovak 86%, Hungarian 11%, Roma 2%, Czech–Moravian 1%
Religion:	Roman Catholic 60%, atheist 10%, Protestant 9%, Orthodox 4%; others 17%
Language:	Slovak (official), Hungarian
Literacy:	not available
Exports:	machinery 33%, intermediate manufacture 28%, miscellaneous manufacture (including arms) 13%, chemicals 8%
Per capita GDP:	$13,300 (2002)
Unemployment:	15.9% (September 2003 Eurostat estimate)
EU status:	entered May 2004
Currency:	Slovakian korun
Known for:	being overlooked

Standout Qualities

Confused: With Slovenia
Confused: With Czech Republic
Confused: Future unclear

Résumé

Slovenly thinking: When asked by a journalist what he thought of the Slovak Republic, President George W. Bush replied that all he knew of it was what he had learned during a visit from Slovakia's foreign minister. Turns out that the Slovakian foreign minister had never dropped by: Bush had met a VIP from Slovenia.[1]

It's rather a bore always playing second fiddle and nobody knows better than Slovakia, the Czech Republic's mostly agricultural ex who didn't get much in the divorce, except a chance to come out from Prague's shadow. Too bad that in 1993 when the spotlight was first shining on the newly formed country, the stage was dominated by Prime Minister Vladimir Meciar whose undemocratic actions, dodgy economic practices and general belligerence sidetracked the country from any reunion with the West. The new government of Mikulas Dzurinda has had to sprint to meet EU entry requirements; even though Meciar's out of power (at least temporarily) the place is still suffering from his indelicate touch. The Slovak Republic enters the EU as the most dubious of the new kids bringing with it the most woes – not least its high unemployment rate of 16 per cent, which is the second worst in the EU, after Poland.

When the Slovak government cut back on social welfare in 2004, the group most affected – the Roma – protested against the move by looting supermarkets and stores. Romany people are the group most discriminated against in Slovakia, and have a high unemployment rate. The British government issued a report in 2004, warning that some 13,000 residents of new EU countries would probably move to the United Kingdom, many of them Roma; however, Slovak Roma experts say that number is grossly inflated.

Quick Tour

You could talk about the friendly people and the bright, idea-filled students, the loveliness of Bratislava's old town that embraces its castle, how you can hear world-class opera at low prices, or how you could walk to Vienna if you grew really bored. But say Slovak Republic and it's pretty hard not to think 'Vladimir Meciar' followed by a long groan.

Well then, I'll take my republic and go home! The 1992 Meciar blow-up with Czech Prime Minister Klaus was theoretically about economic matters, but it seems likely that deeply nationalist Meciar planned to break up from the start. His people didn't want to split Slovakia from Czechoslovakia back then, but some now think it was for the best: relations between Czechs and Slovaks have definitely improved.

Nationalist, Moscow-linked Meciar does have his supporters – mainly businessmen who benefited from his friendship, older country folk apparently ignorant of the shadow he cast on Slovakia, and former Soviet apparatchiks who are still his cronies. The man who sawed off Slovakia from Czechoslovakia made a shambles of the economy; he handed huge low-interest loans to his chums, while ignoring the rising unemployment and the screaming need to make some reforms.

During his six years as prime minister he turned at least one TV station into a Meciar-controlled vanity channel, tried to fine others who weren't rah-rahing his questionable moves, and he threatened to raise the newspaper tax and cut supplies of newsprint to journals that lodged criticism of his wacky leadership. The former Communist stayed buddy-buddy with Russia and negotiated cheap energy deals, while assuring the EU he wanted to be part of their union, but rarely getting around to the changes they demanded. His foreign relations were prickly – he offended Hungary's leaders by making a joke about the expulsion of Hungarians after the Second World War – and his domestic politics were shadowy: head of the secret service, he may have been linked to a political kidnapping, but the witness, who was about to spill the beans, mysteriously died.

It's still not clear what role Meciar played (or did not play) in the strange 1995 abduction of Michael Kovak, Jr – son of President Michael Kovak who was a Meciar foe. Michael Jr, whom the German authorities wanted to question about a fraud scandal, was nabbed by masked men and dumped across the Austrian border, perhaps more easily to facilitate questioning by German police. A supposed witness to the kidnapping fingered Meciar's secret service and was about to tell all when his car exploded with him in it.

In short, Meciar appeared to be marching the country into a dictatorship, when the European Union and the United States noticed and began having a fit. Letting it be known that if Meciar returned to power the doors to NATO and the EU would slam shut, the US government was so worried about Meciar returning in the 1998 elections that it funded an ad campaign urging people to vote. Slovak voters brought Meciar back anyway, but his bid for power was blocked from within. Although his party actually garnered the most votes – 20 per cent – none of the other parties would join his to form a coalition, so he was barred from the prime minister's chair.

> *An amateur boxer, Meciar punched a reporter during the last election after being asked about the recent million-dollar renovation to his home. When the same question was posed during an in-studio television interview, Meciar stormed out, restraining himself from decking the interviewer.*

The good news (for many) was that Meciar was shoved away from the control board, but the bad news was that the coalition that blocked him wasn't exactly sturdy: the four parties from both sides of the spectrum are weakly united only in their dislike of Meciar. Prime Minister Dzurinda's government somehow managed quickly to tighten the financial belt and slap the place into some semblance of working order so that the EU gave it the green light for entry in 2002.

> *Another factor: if Slovakia hadn't been approved it would have been a minor nightmare to cross the country that would have been surrounded by EU states, since within the Union borders are no-stop drive-throughs and Slovakia would have slammed the brakes on the flow.*

There are still plenty of problems rearing their heads around almost every corner and one benefit of the EU is that it throws the money around to bring all its members up to the same speed (more or less). Slovakia may be the perfect test case for the EU to work its wonders, starting with fixing up the bridge that served as a strong economic link to Hungary – it's been broken for almost sixty years. When the EU offered to help repair it a few years ago, Meciar – wary of EU ties and no friend to Hungarians – said no.

At least one thing that the EU's politically weakest country has going for it: Meciar didn't win the 2004 presidential elections. The position was nabbed by another populist, but analysts say that anything is better than Meciar back in the driver's seat.

Pass the Tippex, Please

The Catholic church, horribly persecuted under the Soviet regime, has traditionally had a strong hand in politics in this religious country: the first calls for an independent Slovakia came from a priest (Andrej Hlinka, who put together Slovakia's first powerful political party in 1918), and the Second World War government was led by another priest (Jozef Tiso, who co-operated with the Nazis). More recently, a priest wrote the official Slovak history textbook for schools – and kicked off a huge scandal. *History of Slovakia and the Slovaks*, written by Father Milan Durica, is riddled with errors and thick with whitewashing: he made Tiso's work camps sound like health spas, even praising the fine dentists on hand and their use of gold fillings, and skipping over such facts as some 65,000 Slovakian Jews perishing after being 'resettled' to other parts of Europe. Also missing from his happy-go-lucky rendition: that Tiso's government was charging Jews for their transport to death camps. Although the Catholic church reportedly stood by the book when it was released in 1997, the Jewish community was furious, as were others, though no group was more red-faced than the EU: they had commissioned the book, paying a reported €69,000 for the historical mistake.[2]

Future Forecast

Meciar will make another grab for the reins.

Hot Spots

Bratislava: OK so it's not Prague, but the tourist board is sure trying. Mostly built by Hungarians when they moved here en masse to escape the sixteenth-century rule of Turks in their country, the old town surrounding the hilltop castle is very lively, and students who crowd into the bars have plenty of ideas about how to turn Slovakia around, including bringing in more light industry. The city was subjected to bomb threats in 2004 when it hosted a NATO meeting.

Slovakian border with Hungary: Tension here runs particularly high between Slovaks and Hungarians, who make up about 10 per cent of the Slovakian population.

Castle Hill in Bratislava.

A Goulash of Resentment

Slovak history is deeply entangled with that of the Hungarians. When the Turks took over Hungary in the sixteenth century, many Hungarians left for Slovakia, turning the capital Bratislava into a Budapest substitute, where the Hungarians became the power elite until Budapest was returned some 150 years later. In the 1870s Slovakia fell under Hungarian (Magyar) rule when the Austrian Empire added 'Hungary' to its name. Slovaks, forced to learn German under Austrian rule, were now forced to learn Hungarian, and the Magyars, on a nationalistic roll, were heavy handed about the so-called Magyarization. The fact that Hungarians tried to stamp out Slovakian culture has never been forgiven; Czechoslovakia's expulsion of Hungarians after the Second World War (they were actually exchanged for Slovaks living in Hungary) just increased the tension between the two. The recent Slovak damming of the Danube had Hungarians damning Slovaks from downstream. Against that historical simmering, former Hungarian Prime Minister Orbán's 'status law' inviting ethnic Hungarians to work in Hungary for a few months a year stirred up more confusion and ethnic ire. Hungarians frequently complain about their treatment by Slovaks, and vice versa. With all the hissing and snarling, it will take expert marriage counsellors to untie this gnarled knot.

Slovaks and Hungarians share more than the Danube river, they also have one social issue in common: the Roma, more popularly known as gypsies, who to some are synonymous with petty crime.

Eastern and north-eastern Slovakia: Most Roma live here, sometimes in leaking shacks. This was the scene of looting when social welfare was halved, and is Slovakia's most impoverished region.

Bohunice nuclear plant: Austrians have every right to be worried about this hazardous Soviet-era plant that was supposed to have been shut down when the newer – but still not up to Western standards – Mochovce plant went online.

Hot Shots

Alexander Dubcek: Head of Czechoslovakian Communist Party 1968. The reform-minded Communist initiated the Prague Spring in 1968 when he pushed the idea of 'socialism with a human face'. The only change he made that stuck was to give Slovakia more autonomy. He was forced into the forestry service after Soviet troops stamped out the freedom-giving movement. Died in a 1992 car crash (some suspect foul play), which is tragic, since Dubcek, the most beloved Slovak, might have successfully filled the necessary role of strong, likeable leader.

Ivan Gasparovik: President 2004 to present. The good news – the lawyer is not Meciar, who had been predicted to win the 2004 presidential election. The bad news – since he used to be Meciar's right-hand man, he may turn out to be essentially a Meciar clone. Meciar, however, didn't see it that way when he was defeated that spring: he refused to shake his former mate's hand. No doubt Meciar feels doubly betrayed: not only did Gasparovik win, he defected to SMER, Slovakia's new populist party, which is also the country's most popular.

Vladimir Meciar: Prime Minister 1992–8. Fills a void for those who miss the days of totalitarian dictatorship. He may have ultimately helped his country by splitting off, but certainly didn't start it on the right foot. He was arrested on corruption charges in 2000, but the man who led the right-wing Movement for Democratic Slovakia party is still practising his lines in the wings.

Late for the ball: The Slovaks arrived a bit late for the 1919 mapmaking marathon in Paris – the Czechs had held them back – and by the time they showed up in France, Czech leader Beneš had already convinced

PM Dzurinda: EU loves him,
people not so sure.

the powers-that-be that the two regions should be combined. Despite the Slovaks' intense lobbying to make Slovakia separate, Czechoslovakia was a done deal.

Mikulas Dzurinda: Prime Minister 1998 to present. Who knows how he did it, but earnest Dzurinda definitely wasn't dawdling when he started reforming the place, whipping it into shape (or close enough) to earn an EU invitation for 2004 entry. Although he is of centre-right Christian Democrat inclinations himself, he has liberalized the country greatly. Plenty of hurdles lie ahead, including making his people like him. Admired by the international community, Dzurinda was slapped by results from a late 2003 confidence poll: Slovaks gave him an approval rating of – ouch! – a mere 5 per cent.

Prime Minister Mikulas Dzurinda's cabinet included Hungarian politicians, a laudable step in helping soothe the historically tense relations.

Jan Figel: European Commissioner for education, training, culture and multilingualism from 2004 to present.
Roma: They can be found all over Central Europe, but Roma are a particularly thorny issue in Slovakia, where they often live in trashy villages where

the shacks have holes in the roofs. With near universal unemployment – few are willing to hire them – they were the group most affected when the government cut welfare payments, and they responded by looting supermarkets. Numerous organizations are trying to address this ongoing social problem, but few have made much progress. One sign of hope: Roma music is all the rage across Central Europe, and Roma literature (sometimes published with EU funds) is increasingly popular too.

The Band Formerly Known as the Gypsies

Their culture is rich, their history tragic, and Roma have never been embraced by any European society. With their large families (women often have six children or more) and little education (the policy was often to send all Roma to schools for the retarded), the group that long ago hiked over from India has usually been left out in the cold; pickpocketing bands of mothers and children have done little to polish their image. The situation is worse since the fall of Communism, leaving Roma without any socialized safety net, and few employment opportunities. Some Romanies have headed West; a band of them made headline news by camping in a Viennese park and eating the resident swans. Now some Western European countries require special visas from Slovaks, believed to be a method to keep Roma out. The EU is funding cultural awareness projects all over the place, but the truth of the matter is the Roma are Europe's unloved and efforts to integrate them successfully will be daunting. Suffering from high unemployment in conventional jobs, Roma have a harder time of it in Slovakia where more than two-thirds are unemployed, the worst rate in Europe. In this country of high overall unemployment, Roma are increasingly targets of violence – recently a gang of Slovak teenagers broke into the house of a 50-year-old Romany woman and beat her to death. International women's rights groups are publicizing cases of Romany women in Slovakia who say they're subjected to sterilization without their consent.

Traditional Romany music influenced numerous composers, including Bartók and Liszt.

Andy Warhol's mother: She was born around here, well, actually it was Ruthenia, now part of the Ukraine, but Slovaks claim her anyway since it's slim pickings for celebrities in Slovakia.

Historical Hotshot: Jozef Tiso (1887–1947)

Opponent of the 1919 linking of the Czech part of the region with the land held by Slovaks, Monsignor Tiso was quick to convince the Nazis he'd support them if they gave him the keys and granted Slovakia independence from Czechs. Tens of thousands of Slovak Jews were deported from Slovakia during his regime, with Auschwitz as their destination, but the man of the cloth told his people they were bound for a special homeland for Jews. The priest was tried by the Czechoslovak government in 1947, after it had returned to power and pulled Slovakia back into its loop. Tiso was found guilty of treason and collaboration with the Nazis, and that same year he was executed by hanging. Some Slovaks still regard him as the true father of their country, since he first put Slovakia on the map without the 'Czecho' before it, but others find his memory repulsive. A move to erect a public statue of his likeness in 2000 blew up; thus far the man stands in storage without his pedestal.

Media star: *Slovak Spectator*, slovakspectator.slc
Last Word: Little by little, people are figuring out that Slovakia exists. Capital Bratislava was the site for a Bush–Putin summit in 2005: there's no better publicity than that.

28. Slovenia (Slovenija): Most Likely to Succeed

Fast Facts

Country:	Republic of Slovenia; Republika Slovenija
Capital:	Ljubljana
Government:	parliamentary democracy
Independence:	1991 (from Yugoslavia)
Population:	2,012,000 (July 2004 estimate)
Leaders:	Head of State: President Janez Drnovsek (2002)
	Head of Government: Prime Minister Anton Rop (2002)
Elections:	President elected by popular vote, 5-year term;
	PM elected by Parliament
Name of Parliament:	National Assembly; Državni zbor
Ethnicity:	Slovene 88%, Croat 6%, Serb 2%, Bosniak 1%,
	also Yugoslav and Hungarian minorities
Religion:	Roman Catholic 71%, atheist 4%, Lutheran 1%,
	Muslim 1%, other 23% (1991)
Language:	Slovenian 91%, Serbo-Croatian 6%, other 3%
Literacy:	99%
Exports:	manufactured goods, machinery, transport
	equipment, chemicals, food
Per capita GDP:	$19,000 (2003)
Unemployment:	6.4% (May 2004 Eurostat figure)
EU status:	entered May 2004
Currency:	Slovenian tolar
Known for:	not being Slovakia

Standout Qualities

Hot: Ljubljana's artists
Warm: Good foreign relations
Cool: Gotta love a place with a festival for cows

Résumé

Slovenia – the forested land that spills down from the Alps and snuggles up between Italy, Austria, Croatia and Hungary – may be easy on the eye but it has an international identity problem. For one thing, it's always confused with Slovakia, with which it has little in common, except a similar sounding name. For another thing, for centuries now few have been able to find it. If you're looking for Slovenia on a pre-1991 map, the country, as an independent entity, doesn't exist. For a while (1945–91) it was part of Yugoslavia, before that (1918–45) it finished last in the Kingdom of Serbs, Croats and Slovenes (renamed the Kingdom of Yugoslavia). And prior to that everyone from Austrians to Romans, Germans to Turks, Venetians to Hungarians sank their flags here. That's the price Slovenia has paid for being the resource-endowed country that straddles the Adriatic and the Alps, the Balkans and the West: for most of its existence the neighbourhood toughs kept roping it in.

Geographic Confusion: Slovenia v. Slovakia

They do have a few things in common besides identical starting letters. Both Slovenia and Slovakia entered the EU and NATO in 2004 and both their languages have the same Slavic roots. Beyond that, Slovenia and Slovakia have as much in common as do Spain and Estonia – which is to say not much at all. Slovenia was once part of Communist Yugoslavia, a relatively relaxed socialist federation that stayed out of the Soviet Union (Yugoslavian dictator Josip Broz Tito kept Yugoslavia 'non-aligned' during the Cold War); after the Second World War Slovenia was a prosperous state – the richest of Yugoslavia – and usually got on quite well with the neighbours. Slovakia was one half of the former Czechoslovakia, a Soviet satellite, and suffered harsher Moscow-dictated Communism. Highly agricultural, Slovakia is still relatively poor and has plenty of problems, including relations with neighbouring Austria and Hungary. Slovenia, with a stable government, strong economy and low unemployment, was the ideal candidate for EU admission; Slovakia, with its wavering government, iffy economy and high unemployment rate, was a big EU gamble.

Now Slovenia, independent from Yugoslavia since 1991, is the youngest of all the Big Bangers, all of which, except Slovenia, had been sovereign nations at least once before. But despite its young age, Slovenia is outshining its elders. Here's the gem everyone's suddenly looking at; here's the country that is overnight the most popular holiday destination on the Continent for Brits and the one the EU thinks will be first to make the economic changes needed to adopt the euro. The wealthiest of all the

EU entries is, by nearly every measuring stick, the healthiest. With few historical hang-ups, a well-oiled economic machine and a contented society, technologically-savvy Slovenia, of all the EU newcomers, is the most likely to soar.

> Don't worry about Slovenians flooding the Western European job market: even when offered pay rises to work in foreign offices of Slovenian firms, most refuse to budge from their beloved home-land.

The country does have a reputation, however, for being a bit smug and elitist. A 2004 election confirmed that image internationally when Slovenians denied citizenship and basic rights to some 130,000 Bosnians, Croats, Serbs and other former Yugoslavians who fled there during Yugoslavia's civil war in the 1990s. President Drnovsek unsuccessfully tried to overturn the vote.

> 'We cancelled the law that would make non-Slovenes equal to Slovenes' – Ultra-right Social Democrat party leader Janez Jansa, who had introduced the bill, celebrating its 2004 passage[1]

History Review

'Yugoslavia is a façade. We've got three religious faiths and at least three different cultures. There are very few people who would say they feel Yugoslav' – Former journalist and defence minister Janez Jansa in 1991, just prior to Slovenian independence[2]

The Balkans v. Yugoslavia v. Slovenia

Slovenes cringe whenever their country is referred to as one of the Balkans, which geographically is debatable. Slovenia lies at the most north-western edge of the Balkan peninsula that swells between the Adriatic and Black Seas and contains Greece, Albania, Macedonia, Romania and Bulgaria as well as the other countries of the former Yugoslavia – Croatia, Bosnia, Herzegovina, Serbia and Montenegro. The mellow Slovenes never had too much in common with the groups that live to the south, except for language similarities with the Slavs:

geographically, Slovenia is much closer to Venice than it is to Belgrade or Sarajevo. Nevertheless, along with the other five republics in the former Yugoslavia, it was governed by Communist Josip Broz Tito, who kept it bound to Yugoslavia even if it didn't really fit in.

Yugoslavia, or the Socialist Federal Republic of Yugoslavia as it was formally known, was a real mix: under Tito it pulled together six republics, three religions, two alphabets and a dozen ethnic minorities. After Tito's death, ethnic tensions flared, with President Slobodan Milosevic pushing for Serbian dominance that ultimately led to civil war in the 1990s. By that time, however, Slovenia was independent.

Lassoed by the Austrian Empire from the fourteenth century, Slovenians made a geographical departure when that German-speaking kingdom was shattered after the First World War. Hoping they'd have more in common with groups who spoke similar languages, in 1920 Slovenians opted to sign on in a new country with the Serbs and Croats to the south. In name alone the Kingdom of Serbs, Croats and Slovenes illustrated the power structure in the newly mapped land, not to mention the assorted groups' enthusiasm about being part of it. Even the Slovenian language – different from Serbo-Croat – wasn't officially recognized, and Slovenes were often seen as third-class citizens in the country ruled by a Serbian king. Some Slovenes wanted to secede from the start, but a small country is a vulnerable country, and by the time the Second World War broke out it was too late: their land was seized first by fascist Italy, then the Nazis, with tens of thousands of Slovenes soon deported to Mussolini's Italian concentration camps. Leading the resistance movement that rose up to fight back at the fascists was locksmith turned military man Josip Broz Tito, who after the war nailed the former kingdom of Serbs, Croats and Slovenes back together again (with a few additions) as the Socialist Federal Republic of Yugoslavia, which he ruled first as prime minister, then 'president for life'. An avowed Communist, he nevertheless did not like Stalin and kept Moscow at arm's length.

Historians still wonder why the Soviets didn't invade and take Yugoslavia by force, but Tito certainly rattled the Soviet Union. Whenever Soviet politicians wanted to have one of their colleagues executed, all

they had to do was whisper he sided with Tito – a charge synonymous
with treason.

Istrian Peninsula

The toe of land dangling off Slovenia's south-west and dipping into the bay of
Venice is heartbreakingly beautiful, which is why, like the rest of Slovenia, this
land and its many nearby islands, have been fought over for centuries, being
snatched by Austrians, Venetians and Napoleon. Now divided into Slovenian,
Italian and Croatian sections, all of Istria (aka Istra) was claimed by Italy after
the First World War. In 1946 Tito annexed part of the area driving out 300,000
Italians and killing 20,000 more in his anti-fascist sweeps. During the postwar
years there was so much hatred between Italians and Slovenians in the border
city of Nova Gorica (known as Gorizia on the Italian side) that a wall was erected
cutting right through it. Part of the divider came down in 2004, when Slovenia
entered the EU, but resentment still lingers on both sides. Ongoing issue: the
return of houses to Italians who ran from here after the Second World War.

There wasn't much chance to break from the country when Tito was alive
– and while the dictator looked warm and cuddly compared to Stalin, he
nevertheless ruled with an iron fist and the frequent help of his secret
police. He wasn't about to bid farewell to resource-laden Slovenia, Yugoslavia's industrial motor, which with just 8 per cent of Yugoslavia's population contributed 20 per cent of the country's national income. After he
died in 1980 the Communist machine likewise kept wealthy Slovenia
locked in its hold, although dissent was simmering. Calls for autonomy
grew to a movement for independence, which the Yugoslav government
successfully resisted. Until, that is, a group of smart-aleck Slovenes hacked
away at their handcuffs in an innovative way: by mocking the Communist
machine.

Yanking the Chains[3]

Shortly after Marshal Josip Tito finally loosened his 35-year-long grasp on
Yugoslavia by dying, a group of young Slovenes in the tiny mining town of

Trbovlje devised a powerful way to illustrate the absurdity of living in the country that refused to let them go. Instead of protesting, they parodied the totalitarian system, saying it just wasn't totalitarian enough. Called *Neuer Kollektivismus* (New Collectivism), the group began their subversive attack with art that propelled nationalism and leader worship to an absurd extreme. In 1987 NK entered a prestigious Yugoslavian poster contest – a serious annual competition for a design to commemorate national Youth Day. NK's submission wasn't exactly original: it was an old Nazi poster of a patriotic-looking youth – with the Yugoslav flag waving where the swastika used to be. Their submission won, with the Socialist selectors lavishing praise on the design for 'expressing the highest ideals of the Yugoslav State'. The poster was just about to be plastered across the country when its origins were revealed. So red-faced was the government over the ordeal that Youth Day – one of the most important holidays during the Tito era – was quickly erased from the calendar and never celebrated again. Taking advantage of the resulting scandal called 'the Poster Affair', NK formed a band, well, sort of – it was more of a politicized, musical, experimental theatre group that played loud industrial noise. Taking the German name for Ljubljana – Laibach – a pointedly sensitive move considering Slovenia was Nazi-occupied during the Second World War – the four-man group goose-stepped across the stage in black uniforms and blasted speeches from Tito, Mussolini and Hitler mixed with sound effects that made 'Let It Be' and 'Maggie May' sound like military marches with their lyrics barked like orders. The authorities quickly shut down Laibach's performances and banned NK's art shows, which made the group so infamous that even out-of-touch peasants knew who they were and the threat that they supposedly posed. Laibach moved to the capital Ljubljana and continued pushing the censors' buttons with art shows of political posters calling for the death of political posters and ridiculing the propaganda machine, which infuriated the government more. Now tens of thousands were pouring in to see their edgy exhibits and performances. So controversial was the group that they were tried on charges of disseminating propaganda (the liberal Slovenian court let them off) and at one point a TV commentator implored the public to kill them. Realizing that the more they condemned NK and Laibach the more power they gave them, the Slovenian censorship board broke down and gave up and let them do pretty much whatever they wished. With the general lifting of censorship, the whole country opened up and calls for independence grew louder.

When the art collective NK and their offshoot band Laibach turned censorship on its ear, the media too ventured to be more brazen: with politically provocative publications flying around and a new spark of discussion and hope in the air, this season of 1988 was soon dubbed the 'Slovenian Spring'. One magazine dared to devote an entire issue to the proposition of an independent Slovenia; the national government became apoplectic as it debated how to fight against this new Slovenian 'secret war'. Another publication went further: *Mladina*, formerly the propagandistic magazine for Socialist youth, suddenly turned into a Slovenian version of magazines such as *Spy* or *Private Eye*. Part investigative, part humour, the ballsy publication began targeting the national government in general, and skewering the defence minister Branko Mamula in particular. Publicizing his arms sales to Libya and famine-ridden Ethiopia – for which Mamula was dubbed a 'salesman of death' – *Mladina* humiliated him further with an inflammatory article about how the defence minister had used Yugoslav soldiers as slaves to build his grand villa on the Adriatic coast.

The article didn't play well: Mamula was forced to resign, and the military decided the magazine's writers should pay. Further infuriating the military, one of *Mladina*'s star journalists, Janez Jansa, got his hands on a document showing that federal Yugoslavia was planning to militarily suppress Slovenia's move towards independence. In 1988 Jansa, along with another *Mladina* journalist, its editor-in-chief and the soldier who had leaked the information were hauled off to a military trial. So serious was the 'Trial of the Ljubljana Four' that it was closed to the public and the media, and conducted in Serbo-Croat.

> '[It] was the best thing they could have done for us. Suddenly, it was we [Slovenes] versus them [the Yugoslav state]' – Mladina *editor Franci Zavrl in 1993 looking back on the 'Trial of the Ljubljana Four', in which he was tried*[4]

Of all the writers, Jansa was targeted most fiercely, and the public rallied around the 29-year-old, demanding he be found innocent. When Jansa, along with the other journalist and the army man were found guilty and sentenced to prison, Slovenians erupted in anger and demanded independence in demonstrations of 30,000 and more. Petitions were signed, more articles written, the Slovenian legislature passed laws affirming the right to determine Slovenia's future, and Slovenia held its first multi-party elections, which pro-independence parties handily won.

After a few weeks in prison the writers and the army man were released. In December 1990 Slovenians voted in a referendum about whether their country should break away from Yugoslavia and become its own sovereign state: 88 per cent voted yes.

> 'For more than a thousand years we were waiting to have our own independence, and we have had it now for ten years. People see it as very precious' – Ernest Petric, Slovenian Representative to the United Nations[5]

In 1991 Slovenes took over manning their borders, and the Slovenian government declared Slovenia independent. The Yugoslav armed forces briefly disagreed, showering Ljubljana with bombs from above and then marching in. Sixty-six died in the resulting ten-day War of Independence, but Slovenian leader Drnovsek, who was voted in to continue running the country after independence, quickly negotiated their (generally) peaceful retreat. The Slovenian departure from Yugoslavia compelled Croatia, then Bosnia, to try the same and, before long, the secessionist mood and Serbia's attempt at domination had kicked off an ugly Balkan war. Slovenia didn't enter into the fighting, which never crossed over the borders, although plenty of fleeing Yugoslavs did.

> Resource-happy Slovenia could afford to secede: oil, steel, iron, coal and mercury are but a few of its natural treasures, and agriculturally it can hold its own. The country also has a fine wine industry, harking back millennia to the days when it was run by the Romans.

However, the ten-day war wasn't as cut and dried as it is sometimes portrayed. Several years later a news story broke reporting that the Slovenian army had shot several unarmed Yugoslav soldiers who were retreating. As leader of the country at the time as well, current President Drnovsek is being called to trial for war crimes in The Hague. Also to stand trial: Janez Jansa, the former *Mladina* journalist. Rabidly anti-military as a reporter, he was appointed minister of defence when Slovenia gained independence, becoming a power-crazed arms nut.

Quick Tour

Who knows why this fetching gem of a country was barely noticed for its first decade of independence, but the holiday secret long held by Italians and Croatians is out. Now millions are swooping in, and tourism accounts for over 10 per cent of GDP, and is growing fast. Understandably so, because Slovenia has a little bit of everything: the Adriatic washes its shores, there's skiing in the mountains, hiking in the forests and plenty of traditional festivals in the villages that spring up between the wheat fields and vineyards, not to mention that the place is crawling with subterranean caves that lead to thermal springs, gorges and underground rivers filled with strange creatures, like the rare 'human fish'. But what will soon put Slovenia on the world map in bold colours is the capital Ljubljana, where beyond the pretty domed buildings and steeply angled red-tiled roofs lies one of Europe's most creative scenes.

Language lesson: In Slovenian, 'j' has the sound of a 'y' – so the capital is pronounced 'lyoo-blya-na'.

Long the closely held treasure of alternative types, Ljubljana is awash with art, artists and politically driven art collectives, such as Alkatraz – a former army barracks converted into a village of artists' studios, galleries, newspaper office and performance spaces. Here science meets creativity with, say, twirling robotized bugs programmed with electrical neural-like systems that respond to touch, or multi-media installations broadcasting the dangers of the media and advertising the crassness of commercialization.[6] That the Slovenian art scene is supported by the national government – which spends nearly 1 per cent of GDP on the arts, commissioning and subsidizing projects and even sending artists to New York and across Europe to open their exhibitions – is one indication of how much the country embraces those types who splash colours and sculpt words.

Here creativity is regarded as a national treasure: after all, it was really Slovenia's creators who, by pushing the envelope, pushed open the doors to independence.

Nineteenth-century poet France Preseren and twentieth-century architect Joze Plecnik adorn Slovenian paper money.

Predictably, the post-independence economy initially went into shock having lost its Yugoslav markets, but Slovenia gracefully changed gear, partially as the result of the work of former finance minister and current prime minister Anton Rop. Western Europe quickly picked up the slack, buying two-thirds of Slovenia's exports; many Slovenian workers became co-owners of the firms that employed them under Communism. The computer industry boomed: over two hundred software companies operate in Slovenia, and Ljubljana, with its university population of 35,000, has plenty of young, educated entrepreneurs.

Slovenia is considered one of the most 'connected' countries on the planet, since nearly the entire country uses the Internet.

There have been a few snags in recent years as well: Slovenia has had to pay off some of the former Yugoslavia's foreign debt, while Slovenia hasn't yet received its share of the money left in the collective coffers when Yugoslavia crumbled. Janez Jansa was booted out as defence minister in 1994, amid allegations of roughing up citizens, tapping phones and tailing journalists. A first bid for NATO membership was rejected in 1997, causing such a furore that the foreign minister was forced to resign. And even Slovenia's initial stab at becoming an EU associate was blocked in 1996 by Italy, which was still furious about the status of Italians' homes in the Slovenian part of Istria. Slovenians worked out a deal with Italians, offering compensation and the right of first refusal of all houses that go on the market to Italians who were forced to flee after the war. Slovenia also created a special minority status for those Italians living in Slovenia, who are now represented in parliament. But the status of the 'erased' – those 130,000 refugees who came to newly independent Slovenia to avoid Slobodan Milosevic's ethnic cleansing – is still an issue hanging heavy in the air. The 2004 referendum to prevent their citizenship was a black mark on Slovenia's generally shining record.

'I am dismayed by elements of intolerance in [Slovenian] society' – President Drnovsek in a 2003 radio address referring to the upcoming vote on the 'erased'[7]

Neighbourly Relations

Slovenes generally get on well with the neighbours, although there is the occasional squawking. Austria, which once lorded over the area that was part of its empire, is now a major trading partner, but there's some friction in southern Carinthia, where Slovenes are the majority of the population and want the government to put up street signs in Slovenian too – an issue which makes right-wing nationalist leader Jörg Haider, governor of these parts, go ballistic. Relations with Croats, with whom Slovenes always had more in common than with Serbs, are usually warm, although tinged with competition, especially when it comes to fishing territories, which are poorly defined between the two countries. Italians, along with Austrians, are the biggest supporters of the local tourism industry. Dealings with sometimes prickly Hungary, however, are generally smooth.

Future Forecast

Let the festivities begin. With its success all but guaranteed, Slovenia will soon be dubbed 'the next Ireland'. However, Slovenes will soon get sick of being called 'the next' anything and Laibach may seize the moment and start calling the country 'the next Slovenia', which will make everyone scratch their heads wondering what that means.

Future issue: Slovenia co-owns a nuclear power plant with Croatia. Built in the 1980s, the plant is located in Krsko, Slovenia, but Croatia is responsible for dealing with the radioactive wastes. Lately Croatia has been grumbling loudly about the arrangement.

Hot Spots

Ljubljana: Many hadn't heard of it before US President George W. Bush and Russian President Vladimir Putin met here to discuss arms in June 2001, and most still can't spell it, but this beautiful capital shines with culture and should soon be a magnet for those searching for neo-bohemia. Some liken it to Paris of the 1920s, Prague in the 1980s or Seattle of the 1990s, the difference being that here the people are still welcoming and friendly, as long as you don't start a chain restaurant or buy up their land.
The Balkans: Things have cooled off since Serb leader Slobodan Milosevic was put out of the picture, but who knows how long that will last? Serbs were not thrilled when Slovenia approved of the NATO bombing of Serbia in 1999, and Slovenia's blocking of citizenship to Yugoslav refugees will only add to the country's dire image.

The United States blamed Germany for helping to spark off the Bosnian War. The reason? Germany was quick to recognize Slovenia's 1991 independence, which inspired Croatia and Bosnia to secede from

Ljubljana: new tourist hotspot.

Yugoslavia. The US didn't recognize Slovenia as a sovereign state until 1992, much to Slovenian chagrin.

Italian border: Italians flood into the region of Istria at weekends, drawn by the casinos and the prostitutes. The bridge between Italy and the Balkans, this boundary is well crossed by smugglers, carrying everything from tobacco to slaves.

Piran Bay: Croat and Slovene fishermen sometimes snipe at each other in this disputed zone that is Slovenia's only maritime access to the Adriatic Sea.

Napoleon conquered this area, calling it the Illyrian Provinces, and planning to run it as a naval base on the Adriatic. Even after it was returned to the Austrian Empire, Slovenia continued many of the practices Napoleon initiated, including free schools for the masses.

Bohinj: Slovenia may be a thoroughly modern and Internet-connected country, but they still celebrate the *Kravji Bal* (Cow's Ball), a festive, old-time bash in the alpine meadows that marks the annual change of cattle pastures.[8]

Hot Shots

Janez Drnovsek: Prime Minister 1992–2002; President 2002 to present. They just can't get the guy out of the power seat, but lately they've been voting him in. The reform-minded Communist of the Liberal Democratic Party (LDS) has been leading Slovenia since the 1980s, when he was elected as the country's president in Yugoslavia's collective and rotating presidential council. Never a hardcore comrade – he was said to cut out of policy meetings to head to the slopes – the economist isn't flashy or lovable, but he is a well-travelled polyglot, who (along with popular former president Milan Kucan) got Slovenia into the clubs that matter. Leading Slovenia, pre- and post-independence, he was constitutionally banned from being prime minister for a third term, so he instead ran for president. Some Europeans are annoyed that he is frosty to the idea of selling off Slovenia's profitable firms to foreigners, and others complain that he has been running the place, in one role or another, for too long. But most Slovenes seem to like him just fine, despite the charges of corruption that are always being lodged against his party.

Slovenia joined NATO in 2002, but to do so it had to change its maritime law that had prevented nuclear-powered vessels from travelling through Slovenian waters.

Anton Rop: Prime Minister 2002 to present. The handsome former finance minister, also of the Liberal Democrat Party, got a boost when former prime minister Drnovsek switched seats and became president. Although the prime minister theoretically has more power, with Drnovsek in the picture, Rop is merely co-pilot.

Janez Jansa: Parliamentarian, leader of (misnamed) Social Democrat Party; Defence Minister 1990–94. As military-loathing investigative reporter in the 1980s, he harpooned the defence minister for iffy arms sales and corrupt practices; his reports landed him in jail and helped to spur Slovenia to independence. As defence minister himself, Jansa was accused of illegal arms sales, using his position for political influence, tailing journalists and being linked to nefarious activities. Jansa turned ultra-conservative after he stepped up as leader of the Social Democrats in the mid-1990s: routinely tries to knock the current leaders out of power, and he introduced the legislation barring citizenship for refugees. Now opposition leader in the National Assembly, he is definitely Slovenia's number one man to watch, and will certainly make a stab at running the place himself.

Janez Jansa: leftish journalist turned hard-right politician.

Josip Broz Tito (1892–1980): Yugoslavia Prime Minister 1945 onwards; President for life 1953–80. Tito went down as the world's most beloved dictator: he reduced ethnic tensions to a dull roar and also kept Yugoslavia out of the Soviet Union. In fact, his dislike of Stalin was good for Yugoslavia's economic health since the Communist country was forced to trade in Western markets. Tito also unleashed his secret police, carted political prisoners off to an Adriatic island and gagged the press. Some still mourn his 1980 death.

Laibach: Musical offshoot of artists' collective Neue Slowenische Kunst (NSK)/Neuer Kollektivismus (NK), they helped kick-start independence with their totalitarian-swiping industrial band. Even though they're now targeting NATO and the EU, they played a concert at the EU Accession festivities in Dublin and they are so respected that even the official website of the Slovenian government describes Laibach as 'absolutely pivotal in the field of music'. Propelled to cult status, they gig everywhere these days.

Laibach also formed its own republic – complete with real passports. The documents reportedly work, and those friends of Laibach with the VIP versions are said to have received VIP treatment from passport controllers who aren't quite sure just where the country is.

Other creative hotshots: Architect Joze Plecnik (1872–1957) left his unique mark and mix of styles on Ljubljana, Vienna and Prague. Besides the Alkatraz bunch and architect–sculptor Marjetica Potrc – who had a solo show at New York City's Guggenheim – another big name is Irwin, a collective of anonymous artists. In theatre the playwright Ivan Cankar is most influential, but let us not forget perhaps the world's most famous Slovenian-American, the late Frankie Yankovic, best known for his fancy footwork as 'the Polka King'.

Barbara Brezigar: State prosecutor who led government's anti-corruption campaign and ran against Drnovsek in 2002 presidential race. That she got 43 per cent of the vote suggests that next time the presidential doors might open.

Janez Potočnic: European Commissioner for science and research 2004 to present.

Creative Standout

Of all the Slovenes who ever picked up a pen (or quill as the case may be), none is more revered than France Preseren (1800–1849), whose lyric poems held high lofty ideals, and were often quoted during the independence struggle. Writing in the mid 1800s, when nationalism was on the rise and Austria tried to suppress all non-German languages, he used poetry as a vehicle for politics, demanding freedom and more rights for the Slovenian people. Like Laibach, he too raised the censors' hackles, with one collection withdrawn from sale in 1847. Like Laibach, it only made him more famous (and his works were published in a newspaper the following year). His words have been quoted in Slovenians' most trying times including during the 'Slovenian Spring'. In 1989 his poem '*Zdraylijica*' ('The Toast') was set to music as the country's national anthem.

'The Toast'

God's blessings on all nations,
Who long and work for that bright day,
When o'er earth's habitations
No war, no strife shall hold sway;
Who long to see

That all men free
No more shall foes, but neighbours be.[9]

Media star: *Slovenian News*, http://slonews.sta.si

29. Cyprus: Adding Division

Mediterranean Sea

Rizokarpaso

Kyrenia

UN buffer zone

Turkish Cypriot–administered area

Morphou · **Nicosia**

Strovolos

Polis

▲ *Mount Olympus*

Larnaca

Famagusta

UN buffer zone

Area controlled by Cyprus Government
(Greek Cypriot area)

Dhekelia
Sovereign Base Area
(UK)

Paphos

Vasilikos

Limassol

C Y P R U S

Akrotiri
Sovereign Base Area
(UK)

Mediterranean Sea

0   20 km
0   20 mi

Fast Facts

Country:	Republic of Cyprus (aka Greek Cyprus)
Capital:	Nicosia (divided with Turkish Republic of Northern Cyprus)
Government:	republic
Independence:	16 August 1960 (from United Kingdom)
Population:	606,000 (not including 170,000 in North Cyprus) (2003 estimate)*
Leaders:	Head of State and Head of Government: President Tassos Papadopoulos (2003)
Elections:	President elected by popular vote for 5-year term
Name of Parliament:	House of Representatives; Vouli Antiprosopon
Ethnicity:	almost entirely Greek*
Religion:	almost entirely Greek Orthodox†
Language:	Greek, English, Turkish
Literacy:	male 99%, female 97% (2003 estimate)
Exports:	both: citrus, potatoes, textiles, cement, pharmaceuticals, cigarettes
Per capita GDP:	$19,000 (2003)
Unemployment:	4.4% (September 2003 Eurostat figure)
EU status:	member since 2004
Currency:	Cypriot pound
Known for:	being divided

* If both parts of Cyprus are counted together, the total population is 776,000 and the ethnic breakdown is 85% Greek, 14% Turk, 1% other.
† Religion breakdown for all of Cyprus is Greek Orthodox 78%, Muslim 18%, Maronite and Armenian Apost. 4%. (Source: *CIA World Factbook 2004* and *Columbia Encyclopedia*.)

Fast Facts

Country:	The Turkish Republic of Northern Cyprus (TRNC) (aka Turkish Cyprus) – not recognized as a country by anybody except Turkey
Capital:	Nicosia (divided with Republic of Cyprus)
Government:	republic
Independence:	formed separate 'republic' in 1983
Population:	170,000 (2003 estimate)
Leaders:	Head of State: Rauf Denktash (1975)
	Head of Government: Mehmet Ali Talat (2004)
Elections:	President elected by popular vote for 5-year term
Name of Parliament:	Assembly
Ethnicity:	almost entirely Turk
Religion:	almost entirely Muslim
Language:	Turkish, Greek, English
Literacy:	not available
Exports:	citrus, potatoes, textiles
Per capita GDP:	$5,600 (2003)
Unemployment:	not available
EU status:	Although Cyprus as a whole entered the EU, political problems of recognition mean that the Turkish Republic of Northern Cyprus is not effectively a working member
Currency:	Turkish lira
Known for:	being divided

Standout Qualities

Divided: By the Green Line into two parts
Divided: Only Greek Cyprus effectively entered EU
Divided: Greece and Turkey helped pull it apart

Résumé

The third largest island in the Mediterranean and the third smallest country in the EU, Cyprus is the most baffling country to enter the European Union – ever. Among the numerous reasons to scratch one's head is trying to pin down exactly what Cyprus is, since the very definition of the island is fraught with political ambiguities and political correctness. On maps the island that dangles 65 kilometres off Turkey looks like one country. But look more closely and you can see the 180 kilometre Green Line that runs through the capital Nicosia and cleaves the country, effectively creating two Cypruses – one ethnic Greek and the other ethnic Turkish, although most of the world formally acknowledges only one Cyprus: the government run by Cypriots who are ethnically Greek.

> The Green Line became the dividing boundary of the country after a July 1974 coup, sponsored by Greece, took over the government for eight days. Believing that ethnic Turks living on Cyprus were threatened in the political turmoil, Turkey invaded and occupied the northern part of the island, and pushed Greek Cypriots out. Overseen by UN peacekeeping forces, the Green Line now separates the Greek sector from the Turkish. Until 2003 neither Greek Cypriots nor Turkish Cypriots could cross over the Green Line to the other part of the island.

The southern two-thirds of the island, with an ethnic Greek majority, is the gloating Republic of Cyprus: this is the Cyprus that is internationally regarded as the only legitimate governing authority of the whole island. The much poorer northern third of the island holds a Turkish majority: in 1983 it proclaimed itself an independent republic – the Turkish Republic of Northern Cyprus. Only Turkey recognizes it as a legitimate country and most of the world – including not surprisingly the Greek Cypriots in the south – regards that northern third of the island as Turkish-occupied land. The northern Turkish part of Cyprus does not recognize the southern Greek part of Cyprus as legitimate either, while the Greek Cypriots call the land to the north the 'pseudo-state' and always put terms such as 'president' and 'prime minister' in quotes. So neither part of the island thinks the other one is legit, and that's just the beginning of the complicated tangle of issues that define volatile Cyprus, the only country in the world where the capital is divided.

Although Cyprus as a theoretical whole entered the EU, practically speaking only the internationally accepted Republic of Cyprus can participate in the Union, since the legitimacy of the Turkish-dominated Republic of the north is not recognized by any country in the EU.

Cyprus is the oddball of the European Union, a misfit in the Brussels club for several reasons. First of all, the island that is located closer to Syria and Israel than to any EU country doesn't even really fit in the conventional definition of Europe; until recently it was often lumped together with Asia. Second, Cyprus is the EU country where racial tensions run highest: while not as volatile as the Middle East, Cyprus is a potential powderkeg with plenty of hatred between ethnic Greek Cypriots and ethnic Turkish Cypriots; it is heavily armed with about 35,000 Turkish soldiers in the north and 12,000 Greek troops in the south. Third, Cyprus is physically schizophrenic and dysfunctional, running as two separate republics.

Since 1960, Britain has run military bases on Cyprus at Akrotiri and Episkopi. Cyprus is not a member of NATO, although both of its two mother countries – Greece and Turkey – are members of that powerful defence club. Even outside the British bases, Cyprus has plenty of missiles of its own, thanks to sales from the US (which went to the Turkish side) and sales from Russia (which went to the Greek side). In fact, Cyprus is considered 'the most militarized country in the world'[1] outside North and South Korea.

In short, this Siamese twin of a country is definitely the problem child of the new EU, bringing with it drama and confusion not witnessed anywhere else in today's European Union. Until reunification – or acknowledgement of its legitimacy – the northern third of Cyprus remains out in the cold.

Given the ethnic tensions on the heavily militarized island and the physical and governmental divide, why was Cyprus even invited into the European Union at this time? One big factor was Greece's insistence: the Greek government – which tried to make Cyprus a part of Greece during the twentieth century – threatened to veto the candidacy of all the other countries if Cyprus wasn't on the invitation list. Another influencing factor was its strategic location: now the boundaries of the EU stretch nearly to the Middle East. A third possible factor: military considerations. With the EU military forces getting more meat, Cyprus might provide a handy location to launch any exercises into the Balkans or Middle East; it also lends a good location for keeping Mediterranean traffic lanes running smoothly.

Numerous attempts have been made to glue the two chunks of the island back together again. The most recent was a hard-pushed UN-devised peace plan – called the Annan Plan – which was a detailed proposal to redistribute lands lost by Greek and Turkish Cypriots in 1974, to repatriate people who have been in limbo since 1974, and most important to bring the two governments back together as one confederation, with Turkish Cypriots getting less land, but more power out of the deal.

There are certainly criticisms to be lodged about the plan as well, including that it was wrapped in secrecy. Since the 9,000-page plan wasn't actually published, some of the details were sketchy, which only fuelled anxiety and rumours about the plan among Cypriots. What was known was that it would call for a public vote on reunification, that it would create a united island with two zones, and it would reduce Turkish Cypriot land while giving Turkish Cypriots legislative representation. Between the presentation and the power plays, Annan's Plan was far from perfect but it was the best hope for Cypriot peace launched thus far.

In April 2004 – a few weeks before Cyprus was to enter the EU – both Greek Cypriots in the south and Turkish Cypriots in the north were asked whether they would accept it. The Turkish north – which wanted to enjoy the benefits of EU membership – said yes, overwhelmingly; the Greek south – which did not want Turkish Cypriots to have access to funds allocated to the island – said no, overwhelmingly. Thus, the island stayed divided: when Cyprus came into the EU, the Turkish north was locked out. And that's only one illustration of the tension that lingers on this island where time does not heal wounds.

'Our great joy at joining the European Union is overshadowed by our sorrow because we cannot celebrate this moment together with our Turkish Cypriot compatriots' – Greek Cypriot President of the Republic of Cyprus Tassos Papadopoulos in his May 2004 EU accession speech. The words were not at all convincing considering that two weeks before Papadopoulos had urged Greek Cypriots to vote no on the referendum to accept the UN peace plan to unite the island – and that would have allowed Turkish Cyprus to enter the EU.

'Turkish Cypriots have very clearly proved to the world that they want a united Cyprus. It is the Greek Cypriots who have pushed this chance away' – Turkish Cypriot Prime Minister Talat in 2004, when it became obvious yet again that Cyprus would not be united.

Although the Turkish north was shut out, the 2004 referendum resulted in some relief for that part of the island: the EU lifted sanctions against it that have long hurt that economy. Furthermore, since the Turkish Cypriots accepted the UN compromises, the EU promised some €259 million in outside funding and the US vowed to chip in as well.

The referendum had other consequences: it heated up criticism of the Greek-dominant Republic of Cyprus. The UN and the US were frustrated that the years of work ended in failure because of the ethnic Greek vote, and both snubbed the Greek-dominant Republic of Cyprus. UN Secretary-General Kofi Annan blamed the failure on the Greek community and called for the long-sanctioned Turkish part of the island to be brought back into the international community – greatly angering Republic of Cyprus President Papadopoulos by the mere suggestion. Papadopoulous really lost it, however, when US Secretary of State Colin Powell paid a visit to the Turkish north: he referred to Mehmet Ali Talat – the new Turkish Cypriot head of government who campaigned for reunification and a 'yes' vote on the referendum – as 'Prime Minister', which infuriated the Greek Cypriots who maintain that the whole Turkish Cypriot government is illegal. What's more, US State Department spokesman Richard Boucher had only days before called the Republic of Cyprus 'the Greek Cypriot government' – when ordinarily the international community regards the government as the only government of Cyprus.

'I think if these acts were intentional mistakes and not a slip of the tongue they must be deemed by us as being very hostile acts' – Republic of Cyprus President Tassos Papadopoulos referring to the American comments in May 2004. The president also snapped that the island's 'foreign friends' were acting more like 'censors and overlords' than mediators.[2]

Numerous issues continue to rankle on both sides: thousands of Greek Cypriots lost their land, businesses and homes when they were run out of the north in 1974, and Turkish Cypriots lost theirs as well when they were pushed out of the south. Furthermore, there is still mystery about what happened to thousands of Cypriots on both sides during 1974: their families want their remains or at least to know their fates. Other issues for Greek Cypriots: they are mad that Turkish Cypriots, with only 15 per cent of the population, control over a third of the Island, and Turks have damaged many historical sites.

You can blame almost all of today's tensions – and the 'Green Line' that slices Cyprus – on its two most influential past owners, Greece and Turkey; both of whom still pull Cypriot strings. With both countries behind the power plays and military actions in 1974 that divided the island, Greece and Turkey have more to do with the current condition than do Cypriots themselves. When handing out blame though it is very hard not to ladle some up for Britain, which ran Cyprus as a crown colony from 1925 until 1960. When the British refused to let Cyprus unite with Greece in the mid twentieth century, they unleashed a violent anger that still simmers today. If Cyprus as an independent country is alarmingly dysfunctional it's largely because most Cypriots never wanted the independence that the British foisted upon them in the first place. One more place to point in assigning blame: the United States, which keeps arming Turkey (and thus Turkish Cypriots) as well as Greece, so creating a localized arms race. Russia and Israel – both of whom provide arms as well – aren't helping matters either.

Vocabulary Builder

The already complex situation in Cyprus is further complicated by terms that are tossed about as though they are everyday language. A few to know:

Enosis: Political union with Greece; popular with most Greek Cypriots well into the 1960s

Taksim: The Turkish Cypriot preference of politically dividing the island

T-Cypriot or T/C: A person who lives in the northern, Turkish part of Cyprus

G-Cypriot or G/C: A person who lives in the southern, Greek part of Cyprus

The Green Line: UN-patrolled boundary between north and south

EOKA: The major Greek Cypriot guerrilla group fighting for *enosis* in the 1950s

TMT: The main Turkish Cypriot guerrilla group fighting against *enosis* in the 1950s

History Review

The Greeks who settled on Cyprus back in 333 BCE did more than introduce pagan gods, mosaic-covered walls and statue-lined temples to the Mediterranean-lapped island of dusty mountains and cypress trees. They also brought the ethnic bloodline that is still the most common one on the island; for all of the island's existence since then, most Cypriots have been ethnically Greek and spoke the Hellenic language. The Ancient Greeks were ejected by Romans in 58 CE, but their descendants who stayed on saw a flurry of governments as everyone from Byzantines, Franks and Venetians to Richard the Lionheart and the Knights Templar took turns running the place.

> Richard the Lionheart, on his way to the Crusades, conquered the island in 1191, staying long enough to take a bride. He did not have a blissful honeymoon. Villagers killed his prized hawks, so he knocked down a few villages in response.[3] With things not starting so well, he handed the island to the Knights Templar, whose pigheaded, boisterous rule made them among the most hated of the occupiers: they'd barely unpacked their bags when the Cypriot masses revolted, driving them out in 1192.

The most influential group ever to show up on the island, besides the Ancient Greeks themselves, were the Ottoman Turks, who conquered the island in 1571. In some ways extraordinarily advanced, Ottoman rulers, who were Muslim, allowed the religions of whatever lands they took to continue, and officially recognized the church's highest leaders as the tenders of the local flock.

> By acknowledging the Eastern Orthodox church – which had been losing influence ever since the Great Schism that split it from the Roman Catholic church in 1054 (one of their disagreements was over whether sacramental bread should be leavened) – the Ottomans not only helped establish it as one of the great powers of Cyprus, but also re-legitimized the church.

For the religious tolerance, there was a price to pay, literally: non-Muslims were slapped with high taxes, and the taxes kept rising during the three centuries of Ottoman rule. While some Christians converted to Islam to avoid the annual dues – some dressed as Muslim by day, but practised as Christians by night – those who didn't convert found it difficult to pay the taxman, who began using any method necessary to extract payment. Violence, desecration of churches and rape were becoming increasingly common. By the 1800s the situation was intolerable, and when Greece won back its independence in 1829, some Cypriots longed to fight off the Turks and join up with Greece.

Russia ultimately and inadvertently brought freedom from the Ottomans for Cyprus: emerging victorious from the Crimean War against the Ottoman Empire in 1878, Russia laid claim to the Ottoman territories, including Cyprus. The British, however, blocked any Russian move for Cyprus, fearing it would compromise British dominance in the Mediterranean and future ambitions in the Middle East. Seeing what would lie ahead, British negotiators had signed a secret agreement with the Ottoman sultan the year before: the sultan gave the British rights to run the country, with the implicit agreement that it was still officially Ottoman territory. Most of the Turks who had lived in Cyprus before simply stayed.

> In 1915 the British government offered Cyprus to Greece: all Greece had to do was fall in behind Britain in the Great War. However, the Greek king – a German by descent and a brother-in-law of Kaiser Wilhelm – refused to bite. Greece was eventually dragged into the war in 1917, but by then the offer was null and void.

Cyprus was a fetching complement to Britain's strategically important Rock of Gibraltar off Spain, since it gave the Royal Navy dominance over the entire Mediterranean. Displacing the Turkish Ottoman Empire in 1878, the British officially annexed the island and took charge in 1914, securing the land during the First World War when the Ottomans sided with Germany and Austria. When it officially became a British colony in 1925, the situation heated up – all the more when Britain, which had granted independence for most of its other colonial holdings, clung on to Cyprus through the 1950s. Cyprus was for long a crackling bundle of ethnic and political tensions, but under British rule the sparks really started flying, particularly after the Second World War, when sentiments towards the British changed. The foreign presence kicked off not only an independence movement, it started a guerrilla war as militant Greek Cypriots pushed for a political bond with Greece and to get the Brits off the island, even if it required shipping them off as corpses.

Unity with Greece: Enosis

Through the twentieth century, and particularly after the Second World War, most Greek Cypriots wanted only one thing: *enosis*, or union with motherland Greece. The calls grew ferociously loud in the 1950s when the slogan 'Enosis, and only enosis' was plastered across the island, written on posters hanging from windows, and scribbled on walls. Never mind that most Cypriots hadn't visited Greece, and seemed blissfully ignorant of the poverty in the Hellenic state that was more often than not run by a dictator. Never mind that the call for enosis was actually planted and orchestrated by Greece, where Radio Athens (which could be picked up on Cyprus) blared propaganda extolling the joys of being back together, or that Greece's motives were as much militaristic as familial – Greece wouldn't have minded having a foot in the waters off Turkey, long their mortal enemy. Even if they were mostly being manipulated by powers in Athens – which also shipped over guerrillas to help the cause – the Cypriots saw reuniting with Greece as a step into the great promised land. But while nearly 80 per cent of the islanders wanted to be part of the national Greek family, at least 20 per cent did not – they were the Turkish Cypriots, many of whom feared the repercussions of living in an even more Hellenized state; they preferred that the island be politically partitioned with the British staying in control. Turkey itself, like Greece a new NATO member, was adamant: they didn't want Greece in their backyard at all. Assessing the options – allow Cyprus to be united with Greece (a move that would infuriate Turkish Cypriots and Turkey), or divide the island and keep it as a crown colony (which would infuriate Greek Cypriots) – the British authorities came up with a daft solution: make Cyprus free. While dozens of countries were crying out for independence, Cyprus had to be pushed into declaring itself a sovereign country in 1960. As part of the independence deal, Britain was allowed to keep two military bases on the island.

The signs of an impending clash were there all right: in Orthodox churches – the strongest campaigners for the enosis idea – numerous petitions were signed demanding union with the motherland. In a referendum organized by the head of the Orthodox church, Archbishop Makarios, Cypriots were asked if they want to be part of Greece; the result was an overwhelming yes, and in 1954 Greece asked the United Nations General Assembly to endorse the union of Cyprus with Greece. After the Turks and British had given their thoughts on the matter, the UN decided not to take a formal stand. At that news, Cypriots blew up, calling a general strike. Britain responded by saying enosis supporters could be jailed for up to five years. But still the British didn't grasp how the grass-roots enosis movement was snowballing.

The British who taught in the schools – including the writer Lawrence Durrell – didn't take seriously the petitions for enosis that their old pupils presented them with – nor did others note the increasing fervour in the masses of Archbishop Makarios. So on 1 April 1955 there was wide-spread shock when the typically sleepy island was racked by violence. Granted, the bombs that went off in a police-station letter box and a radio station were crude, and the flyers that blew down the streets were almost comical, being signed by Dighenic, the Cypriot mythological superhero who could bound across whole islands and always addressed the needs of the poor. Some even thought that first attack was an isolated incident. It wasn't.

EOKA: The Fight for Union

The arrival of 40,000 British troops on Cyprus, the UN's lack of action, and the British announcement that Cyprus would never control its own fate all occurred in 1954.[4] And the effect was explosive. EOKA – Ethniki Organosis Kyprion Agoniston, or the National Organization of Cypriot Fighters – had been planning actions since 1951, when Colonel George Grivas, a former anti-Nazi guerrilla leader in Greece, took on the enosis cause at the behest of the Greek government. He'd met Archbishop Makarios – a staunch supporter of enosis – but initially Makarios had advocated that Cyprus use peaceful methods to achieve union with Greece. After the events of 1954, few wanted to wait any more. Grivas set about moulding young minds, recruiting from schools where often the entire student body would sign up with the secret society. At first they merely collected signatures on petitions and showed up at rallies. But by summer 1955 their anger was unleashed, with numerous attacks – against the British, against Turkish Cypriots, against any Greek Cypriot who didn't loudly support enosis. Twelve-year-old girls attacked police with soda bottles, groups of laughing boys on bikes tossed bombs into crowds, students beat up teachers and principals believed to be against union with Greece. Soon the flags of EOKA and Greece fluttered over the schools, but the British demanded they be taken down. Petrified, the school board simply shut the schools down, and thousands of school kids followed

Grivas, the pied piper of EOKA, into the woods, where the group ran paramilitary training camps and made raids on Turkish Cypriot villages. But EOKA was more than a youth group. It had members everywhere – from the newspapers to the government. And EOKA's attacks over the next four years became bloodier and more organized. Turkish Cypriots' homes were torched, and they were run out of Greek Cypriot villages. Murders were everyday events: a British officer was shot down in a Nicosia street while holding his toddler's hand, Turkish Cypriot women and children were slaughtered in their homes, Greek Cypriots who didn't make enosis their life cause were seen as traitors, their houses and workplaces bombed.

Even Greek Cypriots whose only crime was riding on the same bus with Turkish Cypriots were threatened with death. In fact, during EOKA's four-year reign of terror, which killed an estimated 600, more Greek Cypriots died than anyone else.

By November 1955 the situation was so charged that the British governor declared a state of emergency. Strikes were outlawed, public assembly was banned, the new crime of carrying a weapon carried the risk of the death penalty, and towns shut down at dusk. As a vocal supporter of enosis, Archbishop Makarios was seen as a threat and exiled in 1956, the same year that two EOKA militants were found guilty of terrorist activities and executed. Demonstrations against their deaths turned so frenzied that seven were killed. Over the next few years the attacks against the British, Turkish Cypriots and those Greek Cypriots not viewed as sufficiently pro-enosis only heightened, and Nicosia's main drag Ledra Street was so frequently coated in blood that it became known as Murder Mile.

Insider info: During the 1950s Greek Cypriot attacks on the British police were so routine that at least one reporter, Nicos Sampson, made a career out of them. No wonder Sampson always had a nose about such things: he was a militant member of EOKA, and later admitted to killing at least fifteen of the cops (and British civilians) himself, although that was probably an understatement.[5]

Disinclined to cede Cyprus to Greece previously, the British weren't about to bow to terrorism now. They instead allowed – a nice way of saying 'suggested' – the creation of a Turkish resistance group. Formed by Rauf

Denktash, TMT (Türk Mukauemet Teskilati) was every bit as brutal as EOKA, if not more.

More guerilla groups entered into the picture. When Turkish Cypriots targeted the Greeks, the militant Greek Cypriots answered by attacking Turks and burning down villages. Boycotts were launched and ambassadors withdrawn as more bombs exploded in the streets, along with more acts of sabotage and calls for enosis. There were high-level multilateral meetings, plans for partitions, letters to the UN, pleas to the US, numerous threats, and little progress. Finally, Britain recalled Archbishop Makarios from exile, and he reluctantly agreed to their new plan: the majority of Greek Cypriots still wanted union with Greece, most Turkish Cypriots wanted partition and the British had the solution: Cyprus would instead be made free. And as part of the constitution that the British had drawn up, enosis with Greece was outlawed.

> *The reasons that Britain forced Cypriot freedom: naval bases and NATO. With anti-British violence rising, Britain wanted to shake loose of the island, but couldn't afford the risk that Greece might turn its ships away and close down its bases. More importantly, Britain could not afford to alienate Turkey – a strategically vital part of NATO's defensive bulwark against the Soviet Union. If Cyprus was handed over to Greece, Turkey might pull out of the military alliance. Worse, if fellow NATO members Turkey and Greece went to war with each other over enosis, a serious hole would emerge in the alliance's geographical fortress.*

On 16 August 1960 Cyprus dejectedly proclaimed independence. The hastily drawn plan for governing the island was a power share between Greek and Turkish Cypriots: the president would be Greek, the vice-president Turkish, and both would have veto power. Parliamentary representation was broken down by ethnicity, with roughly 70 per cent of the seats going to Greeks, and the remainder to Turks. The two groups didn't get along; Turks were resentful that Greeks had the upper hand, and many Greeks resented that Turks had any power at all.

> *Makarios wielded a bit too much power for some people's tastes: not only was he president of Cyprus, he was also the head – essentially pope – of the Greek Orthodox church. The island's first president, Archbishop Makarios had been a loud voice initially in the call for enosis. He soon found himself attacked from all sides: the G-Cypriots*

who'd demanded enosis hated him for not linking with Greece, the
T-Cypriots hated him for ignoring Turkish rights granted in the 1960
constitution and further pushing them to the margins.

Whatever his intentions were, Makarios certainly slammed on the brakes in 1963, when he issued a thirteen-point constitutional amendment that began with dropping Turkish Cypriots' veto power. Infuriated, they walked out of government, and never came back. Ever since the vice-presidential chair has been empty.

The atmosphere was so charged in 1964 that when EOKA attacked a Turkish Cypriot village, massacring dozens, and shoving the Turkish Cypriot population up to the north, Turkey nearly sent in its air force. War was narrowly averted when US President Lyndon Johnson talked Turkey out of striking, threatening to cancel military contracts. UN peacekeepers came in, but violence continued for another four years, and in 1968 Turkish Cypriots formed their own separate administrative government. The country already wasn't functioning as one, but Cyprus fragmented further when Greece backed a 1974 coup, in the hopes of forcibly uniting Cyprus with Greece. That idea not only blew up, it physically divided the island after Turkey invaded.

The 1974 Split

Greek Cypriots and Turkish Cypriots occasionally recall that for much of the three-century Ottoman reign the two groups got along, or at least got along better than they have done for the past five decades – when Greece and Turkey both tugged at Cyprus so hard it began to rip. The latest additions to the tapestry of discontent on Cyprus were woven in July 1974. Greece, which had long been trying to bring Cyprus back, was then run by a heavy-handed military junta, which was losing power fast. Trying to gain popular support, the junta backed a coup in Cyprus, with the goal of finally uniting the island with Greece. EOKA member and journalist Nicos Sampson stepped in and President Makarios fled. The resulting bloody rampage killed up to 3,000 Greek and Turkish Cypriots alike. The coup was aborted five days later when 30,000 Turkish troops dropped out of the skies and marched in from the coast avenging previous atrocities. In the 1950s and 1960s, when pro-Enosis paramilitaries were running amok killing thousands, Turks had been pushed up to the northern part of the island;

in 1974 Turkish soldiers ran nearly 200,000 of the Greek Cypriots out, killing some 5,000 in the process. In the ensuing weeks, Turkish Cypriots were forced to the north, and the Turkish forces occupied the area, splitting the island into two ethnic parts, with a barbed-wire Green Line making the separation official.

The failed coup not only fractured the island – it pushed the junta in Greece out of power as well, and made union with Greece less appealing to many. When Makarios was brought back from exile, he vowed he would not let Cyprus be split into two separate parts. When he died in 1977 the island was indeed divided, and the fragmentation has endured. Until 2003 neither group could cross into the other section. Now, Greek Cypriots can enter Turkish Northern Cyprus for day trips – and vice versa – but the two societies remain almost entirely estranged.

'We will not forget' seems to be the official motto for both sides in this ethnic conflict that at least at the moment is mostly a war of words. Turkish Cypriots don't forget when they were the target of violent anti-Turkish round-ups in 1964 and pushed out of their houses during the coup ten years later. Greek Cypriots don't forget that they were occupied by the Turkish Ottoman Empire for three centuries until 1878 and that the 1974 invasion by Turkey (in response to the coup) killed thousands. And neither side forgets that tens of thousands of their homes are now on the other side of the island-splitting Green Line.

Quick Tour

For over nine thousand years the rocky outpost of jagged mountains surrounded by crystal waters has been luring just about everybody who set an eye upon it to move on in. Phoenicians, Egyptians, Greeks, Persians, Romans, Venetians and the Turkish Ottomans were but a few who planted their figurative flags in this island that was valued for its beauty but even more for its strategic location between Europe and Asia. A trading post for much of its past, Cyprus is now littered with ruins and history. Here you can find eleventh-century monasteries nudging Roman amphitheatres, temples to Dionysus along with lavish Orthodox churches, Crusader castles standing guard over citrus groves, slender minarets peering over hills thick with vineyards, and mosaic masterpieces set against a backdrop of deep blue. The contrasts are more than its historical monuments: the busy pace of the capital city is forgotten in tiny mountain villages where wine is served straight from the barrel and the common form of transport for many is still the mule.

> *Legend holds that history-entangled Cyprus is where the love goddess Aphrodite washed up in seafoam, spreading cheeriness and amour as she flitted through woods and plunged into cool pools, with laughing Adonis (and hundreds of others) hot on her trail. These days, however, it's more fitting to recall that it was also the stamping ground of battle-prone Greek god Ares than of carefree 'your cloud or mine?' Aphrodite.*

If you could ignore the barbed-wire posts at the Green Line, or fail to notice the tens of thousands of Turkish and Greek troops that patrol the different sides of the island, then you might be happy just to sit in a taverna sipping the retsina that has a hint of pine, or delving into huge portions of overbaked lamb. Lapped by cobalt waters, Cyprus still – for days at a time – can feel like a festive land, of folk dances and wine festivals, where you can lounge at seaside resorts or go scuba diving or hunting for turtles. And now the Cyprus tourist board claims that the missing continent of Atlantis might be lodged under the island – yet another draw to the place that likes to call itself 'the island of love'.

> *In 2003 a new pro-unification Turkish Cypriot candidate entered the scene: Mehmet Ali Talat. President Denktash appointed him as prime minister of Northern Cyprus in 2004, and he helped push through the yes vote on the Annan peace plan.*

It wasn't just the no vote in April 2004 that gave the Republic of Cyprus a black mark. The Greek Cypriot government has also nearly started wars with Turkey over arms purchases – most recently with a 1998 order for some €250 million of anti-ballistic missiles from Russia, which Turkey said it would eliminate if they were deployed. At the last minute the order was cancelled – or rather it was apparently rerouted to Greece, which used exactly such weapons as part of its 2004 Olympics security. Should Turkey or Greece ever invade again, whatever the reason, it will probably turn into a major confrontation: while Turkey protects the Turkish Republic of Northern Cyprus, Greece since 1993 has a pact with the Republic of Cyprus. If Turkey attacks, this time Greece will come to its aid.

Another cause for concern: The new leader of the Greek Orthodox church, Archbishop Christodoulos is loudly encouraging Greeks to reclaim old lands taken by Turks.

In this land where the common language appears to be disagreement, it's encouraging to note that most Cypriots – whether Greek or Turkish – agree on one thing: they are sick of the schizophrenic lifestyle. Who knows how long they will have to wait for a solution to appear. But the sooner the better: this island is an overarmed powderkeg, just waiting for a spark.

Yet another division: Greek Cypriots earn nearly three times as much as Turkish Cypriots, and get the lion's share of the three million tourists who touch down each year.

Future Forecast

The EU may come to regret bringing in a divided Cyprus. With too many arms, too much bad history, and too many outside forces interfering, there will be a military showdown here sooner or later. And if anybody listens to Greek Orthodox Archbishop Christodoulos's calls to Greek Cypriots to seize Turkish-owned lands, it will be sooner.

Hot Spots

The Green Line: Stretching from Pyla through Nicosia and into Famagusta, the Green Line effectively created two worlds, one Greek, one Turkish, one economically stable, one poor. Until recently only tourists could cross the line but only from the Greek Cyprus part, only for a few hours during the day, and without taking luggage. If they were late crossing back over to the Greek side, they were blacklisted from future entry. Turkish Cypriots and tourists from that side were banned from entering at all until restrictions eased in 2003, despite the opposition of the Turkish Cypriot leader Denktash. When both parliaments lifted the ban, a total of 17,000 from both sides made the trip in the first three days.

Ledra Street: During the 1950s Nicosia's main drag was so notoriously dangerous for Britons that it was known as Murder Mile. Since 1974, when the Turks took over the northern part of the isle, it has become the main checkpoint in the city.

Tranquil Kyrenia harbour: is Atlantis hidden underneath?

Northern Cyprus aka Turkish Cyprus aka the Turkish Republic of Northern Cyprus (TRNC): Created by President Denktash in 1983, the much poorer and less developed part of the island is a haven for criminals and a base for some 30,000 Turkish troops, although at least it's been spared the slapped-together tourist resorts and eyesores that dot Greek Cyprus. Turkish Cypriots are getting sick of the division that has kept them penned in for three decades and has brought most to a near poverty level, worsened by the fact that international aid can come in only through Greek Cyprus, whose government is not recognized in Turkish Cyprus. Human rights and freedom of speech are a concern here too; some of the most interesting political developments in Northern Cyprus are broadcast to Turkish Cypriots via illegal Bayrak radio. Greek Cypriots call Turkish Cyprus 'the pseudostate'.

> In recent years many of the icon-rich Greek Orthodox churches in the Turkish north of the island have been demolished, ransacked, looted and otherwise stripped of their treasures. While some of this is believed to be vandalism, many of the robberies are thought to be the work of smugglers, who have even peeled frescoes from the walls.

Southern Cyprus aka Greek Cyprus aka the Republic of Cyprus: Tourist honeypot complete with tacky resorts, it still has its charms, not the least of which are its churches, beaches and monuments attesting to the isle's rich past. Archaeological digs turn up lost cities and palaces every few years, including what is believed to have been the home of Dionysus; no word on the state of the wine cellar. Economically, Greek Cyprus has made huge progress in recent years – Greek Cypriots are among the wealthier of the new EU citizens. Some 12,000 Greek troops are deployed here, and it is also home to British military bases.

> *Change of heart: President Teyyip Erdogan, Turkey's most charismatic leader in decades, would love to see his country become part of the EU. Since 2002 Turkey has taken a pro-negotiation stance on Cyprus.*

Mass graves: Their locations are secret – and are said to be on both sides – but Cypriot leaders sometimes mumble about revealing the whereabouts of the skeletons from 1974 battles, including at least some of the two thousand or more Cypriots who have been missing (and are presumed dead) for three decades. There's talk of using DNA testing on the bones when the mass graves are finally revealed.

Aphrodite's Love Rock: Temples to Aphrodite are scattered across Cyprus (and the Mediterranean), but the huge black rock found about 65 kilometres from Paphos must have been supercharged. When the area around it was excavated in the 1950s, it revealed the existence of a love cult who had moved there and dedicated their lives to the goddess, imitating her wanton ways before the coal-black boulder. Local Cypriots flocked there when the rock's role was uncovered, leaving shreds of their knickers in front of it as a modern sex sacrifice, hoping for an aphrodisiacal effect.

Geographical Confusion: Cyprus v. Crete

It's understandable why Cyprus and Crete are so often confused: they are both Mediterranean islands with majority Greek populations, both were conquered by Ottoman Turks and both fought to get back together with Mother Greece. Among their differences: Crete, more to the west, is the biggest island in the Mediterranean, and unlike Cyprus, succeeded in its enosis quest; it is now part of Greece.

When Ireland recently unveiled a new stamp of all 25 EU countries, stamp collectors were mystified. The country that was apparently supposed to be Cyprus was in the geographic location of Crete, and also highly resembled that island in shape. The stamp designers maintained that they just had to change Cyprus's relative location given the small size of the stamp.[6]

Hot Shots

Tassos Papadopoulos: President of the Republic of Cyprus since 2003. When he beat Glafcos Clerides in 2003, many thought he was the perfect man to reunify Cyprus, but many were apparently dreaming. The centre-right head of the Diko Party admittedly had a big job before him: guiding the country into the EU in May 2004, and trying to bring it together as one prior to EU entry. He failed miserably on the second point, when he encouraged Greek Cypriots to vote against the Annan peace plan in the April 2004 referendum. Tarnished his reputation in the process, and now the EU is much more sympathetic to Turkish Cyprus than previously.

Glafcos Clerides: President of Greek Cyprus 1993–2003. Never got anywhere with the Cyprus divide issue, but did successfully ready his part of

Makarios: flip-flopped on enosis.

the country for the EU. He nearly provoked an ugly showdown in 1998 when he signed on for a Russian-made anti-aircraft defence system, but under international pressure – and threats of an attack from Turkey in response – wisely opted not to deploy it.

Parallel Lives

Leaders of both parts of the divided island have met at assorted points since 1974 to try to hammer out something, but no two had more UN pressure heaped on them than Glafcos Clerides and Rauf Denktash, who like the others before them got stuck in diplomatic limbo. Their meetings in 1997 and 2002 weren't the first time the two had met on opposing sides of the table. Both were trained in England as lawyers, and both had worked in the highest Cyprus courts in the 1950s, when Clerides defended militants charged with attacks on the British and Denktash was on the prosecuting team. It's said that despite their spitfire dance in public, the two have some warm regard for each other.

Rauf Denktash: Vice-President of (united) Cyprus 1973–4; President of Turkish Federated State 1974–83; President/Founder of the Turkish Republic of Northern Cyprus 1983 to present. One of the first to publicize the plight of Turkish Cypriots to the international community in the 1960s when they were being stripped of their lands and rights, Denktash has been a driven leader for four decades, including helping to launch an anti-enosis paramilitary group back in the 1950s. He hasn't done Turkish Cyprus any favours lately by dragging his feet on reunification and letting international criminal fugitives and drug traffickers move in without fear of extradition. He is the target of many pointing fingers whenever the topic of Cyprus's continuing conflict comes up. Sidelined (slightly) by the 2004 election which brought pro-EU Mehmet Ali Talat to power – but Talat has been forced into a coalition with Denktash's son.

Mehmet Ali Talat: 'Prime Minister' 2004 to present. Theoretically leader of the Turkish Cypriot government – which Greek Cypriots will remind you doesn't really exist – Talat was seen as the key to unifying the island. His appointment as prime minister by his foe Denktash – whom he has loudly badmouthed for a decade – gives an idea of how much the international community was pressuring Denktash to bring Talat into the equation: the 'prime minister' title did not exist previously, but it was the means to get around Denktash's refusal to deal. Denktash acceded to their wishes, but made sure that Talat had his hands tied: Talat heads a coalition with Denktash's son Serdar who holds most of the same views as his father. Talat, however, managed to push through a yes vote on the referendum issue – and he emerged as the island's hero. Just like everybody else in this scenario, he's a pain in the neck: when the EU offered him €259 million in aid, even though the Turkish North wasn't even really part of the EU, Talat sniffed that it just wasn't enough.

Archbishop Makarios: President of (unified) Cyprus 1960–77. Born in 1913, Makarios – as head of church and state – was not only a walking conflict of interest, but the most powerful man on the island, and in the Orthodox world. His motives were not always clear – a major supporter of enosis, he later dropped the idea – and the man who was the church's most holy was said to be quite a womanizer. Always clad in black robes, his chest was so heavy with pendants that he often looked like a jewellery display, but he definitely had a certain charisma and a photogenic way, and was able to keep Cyprus from entirely disintegrating in its most troubling times.

Markos Kyprianou: European Commissioner for health and consumer protection 2004 to present.

Media stars: Lots of top-notch press here including *Cyprus Mail* (www.cyprus-mail.com/news) and *Cyprus Weekly* (www.cyprusweekly.com.cy)

30. Malta: Most Likely to Secede

Fast Facts

Country:	Republic of Malta; Repubblika ta' Malta
Capital:	Valletta
Government:	republic
Independence:	21 September 1964 (from UK)
Population:	397,000 (2004 estimate)
Leaders:	Head of State: President Eddie Fenech Adami (2003)
	Head of Government: Prime Minister Lawrence Gonzi (2003)
Elections:	President appointed by House of Representatives, 5-year term; Prime Minister appointed by President, 5-year term
Name of Parliament:	House of Representatives
Ethnicity:	Maltese (descendants of ancient Carthaginians, Phoenicians)
Religion:	Roman Catholic 98%
Language:	Maltese and English (both official)
Literacy:	93%
Exports:	machinery, manufactures; tourism a major moneymaker
Per capita GDP:	$17,700 (2003)
Unemployment:	8.9% (May 2004 Eurostat figure)
EU status:	entered May 2004
Currency:	Maltese lira
Known for:	grilled songbird, old rocks, great views

Standout Qualities

Small: EU's new midget
Minuscule: Slim majority favoured EU entry
Tiny: Roasted finch anyone?

Résumé

It's best to have a microscope handy should you wish to find Malta on a world map: the five sun-drenched islets stretch out for a total of 240 kilometres between Africa and Europe, making the archipelago appear to be a speck with a star. But these beautiful Mediterranean rocks – best known as the historical home of the Knights of Malta – were the most difficult to coax into joining the EU. The reason: local power players, known for creating political earthquakes, kept the islanders rattled and confused, making the question of EU entry one of the most explosive issues ever to hit Malta since the Second World War. And birds were right in the thick of it.

Geographical Confusions: Malta v. Malta

Malta is both the name of the five-island 'archipelago' and the name of the largest island. The other islands are Gozo and Comino; Comminotto and Filfla are virtually uninhabited pebbles in the Mediterranean.

Hitting almost every quirk the Maltese have known – from the vulnerability of being a 'frontier fortress' to being abused when a British crown colony – the issue of EU enlargement scored particularly high on Malta's political Richter Scale. The ruling right-of-centre Nationalists were all for it, left-wing Labour was against joining, and the Catholic church was wary.

A Flap Over Birds: Part One

There are about three trees on the islands, hence Malta has few native birds. Twice a year, however, the sky is thick with huge flocks of thrushes, turtle doves, quail, woodcock and hundreds of others species winging from Africa to Europe and back six months later. You'd think the birds might have figured out an alternative route, because every time they pass over Malta, hunters are waiting and tens of thousands of the feathered creatures drop out of the sky to become that night's dinner or next week's mounted wall piece. Some four million birds are shot or captured while flying over Malta each year, a practice that has environmentalists furious about the fate of the migratory birds, and the European Parliament is also expressing concern. Hunting, however, is a time-honoured activity on the food-short island, and fear of EU-imposed hunting bans nearly prevented Malta from joining up.

The Swan Affair: It was a lovely Sunday afternoon at the seashore, with families relishing Malta's balmy January weather, when a flock of swans – and awkward cygnets – alighted on the waters of St Thomas's Bay. As the children ran out to feed them and parents held their toddlers up for a better view, a speedboat suddenly skimmed across the water. Shots rang out as the boat's occupants – three masked men – took aim with rifles, and killed all but one of the swans. After hastily retrieving the booty, the boat sped off. The 2002 swan massacre outraged many locals, and cast Malta in a bad light: international wildlife organizations demanded that the EU rescind Malta's invitation to join.

With the numbers of pro-EU and anti-EU voters running neck and neck, hunters and trappers – some 18,000 of the population – became Malta's most important special-interest group. In a country where winning with 2 per cent of the vote constitutes a landslide victory, their votes were crucial – and they were among the most fretful about how EU entry would change Maltese life. Knowing that a loss of the hunters' votes would result in a no in the 2003 referendum, the Nationalist government lobbied hard with the EU to keep hunting rights intact. The result was a compromise: while there would be little change in autumn hunting practices, when pretty much anything with wings was game, in the spring only quail and turtle dove could be shot, and the controversial practice of shooting birds from speedboats was allowed to continue.

Malta was granted seventy-seven exemptions from EU regulations – more than any of the nine other new EU countries. Among the pages of Malta's accession document was also the guarantee that the EU would not interfere with Maltese laws on abortion or divorce. Another clause prevented EU nationals from buying Maltese homes.

Even with the exemptions, the likelihood of a yes vote looked so slim that Brussels pushed the Maltese government to postpone any vote until the next round of enlargement, fearing that a no from Malta – the first of the invited countries to put the issue to a public vote in January 2003 – would have a ripple effect on the other eight countries holding referendums about joining up.

A Flap Over Birds: Part Two

In 1999 a Maltese pet-shop owner was arrested in London in a songbird smuggling racket. According to the *Independent*, the man was believed to have exported up to 60,000 wild birds, mostly finches, to Malta, after clipping counterfeit rings on the birds to certify they had been bred in captivity. The Maltese are mad about songbirds: they've been a part of the culture since the Middle Ages – although some say they are more fond of the birds' taste than their songs. In any case, the birds captured in the wild typically aren't long for the world. If kept in cages, they usually stop singing permanently within three months.

With a nod from the EU, Maltese law still allows for the trapping of seven types of songbirds.

Surprisingly, given all the confusion and high-pitched anxiety, Malta's voters gave the nod to EU entry with 53 per cent voting yea in the March 2003 election. Noting that voter turnout was 91 per cent – low for Malta, where 96 per cent usually show up at the polls – Labour refused to accept the result, and pressured the government to hold an early general election.

A Flap Over Birds: Part Three

Although Malta is most associated with the movie *The Maltese Falcon*, which really has nothing to do with the islands, the hunting birds do feature in the area's history; the Knights of Malta were first given run of the place in 1530 by Holy Roman Emperor Charles V, who leased it out in exchange for annual rental of two trained falcons. The last falcons on the island were shot by hunters in 1987.

The hope that Labour would win – and derail EU membership – was shot down when Nationalists took the 2003 election with 52 per cent of votes. While the victories in both polls were substantial for Malta, they illustrate the division and queasiness with which the islands stepped into the EU, and the very real possibility that if all doesn't go well with the EU, Malta will fly off in the night.

> *Curiosity: Is the EU interested in the oil that might lie off Malta's coast? Did they want to extend their borders and get nearer to Africa? Do they feel guilty for Malta being pummelled during the Second World War? Or is this a matter of the military and transport: are the EU planners thinking that sometime in the future it might be handy to use it as a fortress again or as a site to control western Mediterranean sea lanes? Why would the EU care so much about letting Malta, a far yonder rock that has few natural resources, join the EU that they would offer more exemptions here than anywhere else? One thing you can be sure of: they don't plan on tapping the island for its timber, of which there is barely enough to construct a toothpick.*

Church Matters

The Maltese are among the most devout Catholics in the world: almost everyone claims affiliation with the church and every week over 70 per cent head to mass, where women still don black shawls; the traditional head covering bonnet was customary until a few decades ago, and some Maltese still ritualistically kiss loaves of bread before slicing it. Due to strict religious beliefs, Malta is the only European country where residents can't get a divorce; abortion is also illegal. The church is a strong political force, and was so heavy-handed in the 1960s in 'guiding' islanders' votes that the pope himself told the local bishop to give it a break.

History Review

Never mind that it has scarce water, poor soil and that its only bountiful resource is limestone: with its boulder-strewn beauty, Malta – the only pitstop between today's Libya and Sicily – has beckoned to just about everybody who sailed by over the past seven thousand years. Neolithic peoples who worshipped fertility goddesses were among the first inhabitants who climbed up and began rearranging the rocks: some of the dozens of temples are crude, Stonehenge-like assemblages; others, such as the Hypogeum, are elaborate subterranean affairs that have archaeologists baffled about their creation with crude tools.

Believed to have been excavated with obsidian and flint, the 500-square-metre Hypogeum – discovered in 1902 – was a place of worship and burial ground that may have taken centuries to construct. Few clues are left about exactly who created the temple, but whoever it was, they mysteriously disappeared around 2500 BCE.

Home to Phoenicians, Carthaginians, Romans, Vandals, Goths, Sicilian Normans, Arabs and Genoese over the next few thousand years, Malta was also the site where St Paul was shipwrecked in 60 CE – another reason why some regard the land as divine.

Spiritual seekers and religious pilgrims say that Malta is one of the world's centres of cosmic power.

Winding up in the hands of the Aragonese and Castilians (today's Spanish) by the fourteenth century, geographical hand-me-down Malta was passed on to Emperor Charles V, who was then running Spain. He changed the island's history when he gave the island to Knights Hospitallers in 1530 hoping they could calm the pirate-plagued waters that were threatening Spain's gold-filled ships. The sixteenth-century Knights Hospitallers (aka Knights of Malta) left the most indelible mark on the land: the capital Valletta is dense with their Renaissance and Baroque palaces, and they spread the faith around just as thickly. All of Malta is heaving with churches – over 320 of them – some lavishly decorated, some tucked away in limestone caves.

Although the knights were Catholic, they were none too happy to find that Malta had an Inquisition Board established on the island, and the two groups had numerous run-ins. Inquisitors looked askance at the Knights' possession of banned books and general amnesia about their vows of poverty and chastity. Nevertheless, the Inquisition typically took aim at the locals: Muslim slaves were among those believed to invoke Satan with magical spells, but even the man who dared to eat meat on Fridays might be hauled before the board and flogged.

The Days of the Knights of Malta

Although the Knights Hospitallers became legendary for their battles with Arabs, the original charge of the chivalrous group – most of them European aristocrats – was to tend to pilgrims who fell ill on their trek to the Holy Land. Running hospitals in Jerusalem for seventy-four years, the Knights were ousted in 1187, when Saladin's Arabs took the city. The Knights then dropped anchor on the island of Rhodes, which they fortified so heavily that they remained there for two centuries. In 1522, however, Suleyman the Magnificent unleashed 200,000 of his Ottoman fighters, who so ravaged the Knights' population that the few survivors were given free passage, with the promise they'd stopped attacking Muslims – a false promise as it turned out. The homeless knights wandered about the Mediterranean until 1530, when Holy Roman Emperor (and King of Spain) Charles V waved a tempting offer under their noses: they could move to Malta if they battled pirates, particularly the Berbers who plundered ships nearing North African waters. On Malta the Knights held their ground well – too well thought Suleyman, who sent out his warriors again in 1565. This time the Knights, with the help of the locals, Spanish militia, and the limestone caves that served as shelters from cannon balls, successfully fought back the invaders; when the Ottoman warriors tried to break into villages, they were greeted not only with swords and muskets but vats of hot grease. When the Ottoman ships sailed back to Turkey after four months, the Knights rebuilt and refortified the islands splendidly thanks to their aristocratic tastes and the bags of gold that Charles' successor, Philip II, paid them as reward. The pope sent over his chief engineer, who designed a grid system for Valletta, and Europe's finest architects and artisans were shipped in to create the most sumptuous palaces of the day. Poets, artists, musicians and thousands of courtesans turned up as well, as Malta launched its rollicking Golden Age. Before long, however, the brave Knights had degenerated: rather than battling pirates, the Knights became pirates themselves, plucking not only riches from passing ships but running a slave trade of the passengers taken captive. By the late eighteenth century the sodden, bloated Knights couldn't even hold down their fort. So worthless were the island's defenders that when Napoleon swaggered in in 1798, his forces captured Malta without firing a shot.

Napoleon booted out the Knights and the Inquisitors in 1798, but his fondness for looting the gold and silver-laden churches ensured the French wouldn't last long. The religious Maltese people were so distraught at the theft of the holy riches that they called for British help. The French were sent packing in 1800 and Britain kept control of the island – a key port in the Mediterranean – with Malta a crown colony for a century and a half.

Britain, too, profoundly shaped the small island chain that became a colony starting in 1814. Headquarters for the Mediterranean fleet, Malta was a 'fortress economy' for most of the nineteenth and twentieth centuries, when it was almost entirely dependent on British military bases to pump up its coffers and provide jobs. The Maltese paid dearly for that allegiance to Britain: key to manoeuvres in North Africa during the Second World War, the archipelago was pummelled by German bombs for two and a half years without a break.

At the start of the Second World War, some Maltese wanted to side with Italy. They were quickly shipped off and interned in Uganda.

Bad Year: 1941

Britain ran it, Italy wanted it, and Germany knew that if Allied forces continued to use Malta as a naval base, North Africa could never be taken. The attacks on the Mediterranean islands started in June 1940, within a day of Italy entering the Second World War, but the most vicious siege began on 16 January 1941 after Hitler ordered that Malta be 'neutralized'. For the next five months, air-raid sirens blared nonstop and the sky rained with bombs and mines in the longest continuous daily bombardment of the war. With Nazis soaring down to drop their payload in half a dozen sorties a day, the red flag that alerted islanders to another incoming enemy plane was almost constantly flying over the Governor's Palace and the skyline of domed churches was soon crumbling. The pitifully armed Maltese tried to fight back using the island's three decrepit biplanes – locals named them Faith, Hope and Charity. Shelters were hastily created in the colony that wasn't at all prepared for the siege: moats were transformed into ditches, caves became homes and hundreds of bomb shelters were chiselled out of the limestone hills. Thousands died in the bombings, food supplies ran out, and many of the islanders nearly starved to death since food-carrying convoys were routinely sunk en route to Malta. British forces took many weeks to show up and take their place next to the fighting Maltese. Initially, the Allies, whose bases had made the island a target, did not consider Malta worth saving.

'Under repeated fire from the skies, Malta stood alone but unafraid in the centre of the sea, one tiny bright flame in the darkness – a beacon of hope for the clearer days which have come. Malta's bright story of human fortitude and courage will be read by posterity with wonder and with gratitude through all the ages' – Franklin D. Roosevelt in speech on Malta, 7 December 1943

In 1942 Britain presented the George Cross for heroism to Malta – 'the most heavily bombed place on earth'[1] – marking the first time the medal was ever presented to a nation. The United States gave Malta a plaque, and both King George VI and President Roosevelt arrived on 'Siren Island' to personally honour the Maltese whom they'd nearly abandoned during the siege. Despite the show of support, Britain refused to turn over Marshall Aid funding to heavily damaged Malta for postwar reconstruction, a move that ultimately led to Malta declaring independence. The archipelago has bounced along a bumpy road ever since.

Quick Tour

Gold-glowing palaces and square-shouldered forts peer down over glistening water, brightly coloured buses bounce along cliff-hugging roads, restaurants serve up fish caught mere minutes before and nearly half the year is a religious holiday: Malta's festive nature, honey-hued beauty and balmy weather are just a few of the reasons that so many crowd onto such a small rock.

Malta is one of the most densely populated countries in the world.

Tourism is now the number one moneymaker on these islands – and has been since 1979, when Prime Minister Dom Mintoff so severely raised rents at the resident Royal Navy base that he effectively gave the British the heave-ho, and was forced to devise another way to rev up the economy.

Mintoff memorialized the removal of British troops by declaring 31 March 'Freedom Day' – one of Malta's five national holidays.

Granted, apart from exploring ancient temples, strolling through courtyards, touring palaces, and flopping around on the beach, there's not much to do on sleepy Malta, where 'Empty Wasp Nest is Found in Attic' is literally headline news. Or at least so it appears at first glance in the land known for its friendly inhabitants, all of whom speak English, as well as Maltese, and most of whom are related.

Maltese, an Arabic-derived language peppered with Italian, is believed to be a remnant of the Phoenician settlers who arrived here from the Lebanon. Almost every village in Malta has its own dialect of the language.

Despite an outward appearance of happy homogeneity, the Maltese are a deeply divided people. And much of that division stems from the land's most infamous politician Dom Mintoff, whom some Maltese worship and some out-and-out despise. Beak-nosed and bespectacled, Rhodes scholar Mintoff flew to fame in the 1950s when he grabbed control of the Labour party becoming prime minister in 1955. Furious that Britain had denied Marshall funds to Malta – which after all had been devastated because of its association with the British – he had another idea: become part of Britain, and get funding that way. The Maltese people supported the idea in a referendum; however the British didn't. Mintoff stormed out of office – the prime minister's seat remained vacant for the next five years – and hatched a new plan: independence. He stood for the premiership again in 1962, but this time he was not voted in, having formed a fierce enemy: the Catholic church. And what they did in the 1960s not only divided the island as never before, it also was such an abuse of power that religious scholars still cite it today.

A Different Sort of Inquisition

Marriage outside the church is not such a fiery issue now, but in 1960s Malta the all-powerful church viewed it as just about as bad as signing your soul to the devil. When Dom Mintoff campaigned with a promise to allow civil marriage, he might as well have sprouted horns in the view of the Catholic church, particularly its archbishop Sir Michael Gonzi. Worried that the unpredictable socialist might next snatch up their land, Gonzi took the extreme step of excommunicating not only Mintoff, but the whole Labour party. Gonzi – soon called the Iron Archbishop – did not stop there. Voting Labour – or even reading the party's newspaper – he declared a mortal sin. The archbishop forced priests to follow his lead and not only devote sermons to the evils of Labour, but to use the confessional to discover how parishioners planned to vote in 1962's election; those voting Labour were not absolved and were told they would be damned to eternal hell if they cast a vote for Mintoff's party. Even children were pushed by priests to spy on their parents and confess the adults' political affiliations. Whenever Mintoff gave a public speech, the church drowned it out with the ringing of bells. Catholics were given whistles to blow to disrupt Labour gatherings, and directed to chant, throw stones, or do whatever was required (murder was hinted at) to ensure Labour did not win the election. The archbishop won that round at least: Mintoff came into the House of Representatives as opposition leader, only to see the Nationalists, under his foe, Prime Minister Borg Olivier, lead the country to the independence he'd campaigned for. But the archbishop's actions had raised plenty of eyebrows in Rome; the pope finally shipped over a replacement in 1969.

Mintoff finally snatched back the premiership in 1971, and went on a rampage. He charged exorbitant amounts for the use of British bases – about \$40 million (€32 million) a year, initially used to fund education – but finally just pushed the British out of port, along with NATO. Disgusted by the supposed white knights of the Cold War, he befriended Libya's Muammar Qaddafi (who gave him great prices on oil) as well as North Korea's Kim il-Sung, all the while making an international reputation as a loose cannon. He let Soviet ships refuel at the facilities NATO had built, signed a multi-million-dollar trade agreement with Russia, and nearly derailed a 1975 US–Soviet global arms agreement because he wouldn't sign. Increasingly autocratic, Mintoff took on the church – seizing property, barring priests from visiting prisons, outlawing religious tuition in state schools – and his alleged henchmen made high-profile appearances on Malta's streets. Many of Mintoff's political foes soon disappeared – some fled, and at least one turned up dead. The Mintoff administration began talking of making Malta a one-party country, and there was little dissent in the House of Representatives, at least in 1981: that year the Nationalist party won the majority of votes, but Labour took the most seats – and the Nationalists walked out in protest. By 1984 Malta was a mess: tourism was down, foreign investors had pulled out, and unemployment shot up to 20 per cent. Mintoff, under pressure, finally pushed back his chair from the prime minister's desk.

Mintoff made Malta stand out for all the wrong reasons, and when he stood down as prime minister in 1984, many heaved a sigh of relief.

(However, he wasn't done with politics: he simply took a place in Malta's House of Representatives.) When the Nationalists, with Eddie Fenech Adami at the helm, took over running the country in 1987, they sought to undo almost all that Mintoff had done. Adami welcomed NATO ships back into port, and signed Malta up for NATO's Partnership for Peace programme. The prime minister also reached out to Europe, and in the early 1990s began negotiating for Malta's entry into the EU. That move blew up in his face: in 1996 voters threw the Nationalists out of power. The new Labour government, under Alfred Sant, pulled Malta out of the NATO group and immediately told Brussels 'Never Mind', freezing plans to enter the EU. The appearance of Malta in the 2004 enlargement looked most unlikely – until, that is, Mintoff rattled the country again.

By then 72 years of age, Mintoff, who was rabidly against joining the EU, apparently didn't see what he was doing that tumultuous day in 1998, when he ripped the carpet from under his own party. Mintoff had made no secret that he had little respect for Labour's new leader, Prime Minister Alfred Sant, who was Harvard educated and modern and set to raise the country's utility charges by 200 per cent, an admittedly unpopular move. When parliament was voting on giving the Knights of Malta their own sovereign state on a Maltese fort, Mintoff snapped. Not only did he not like the idea, he didn't like Sant, and he so ripped the prime minister to pieces over the next hour that the House of Representatives fell apart. Sant was forced to call early elections when he lost a no-confidence vote, and the ousted prime minister – disliked for his proposed electricity rate hikes – did not resume power. Prime Minister Adami was soon back on the phone to Brussels putting Malta back on the road for EU entry, assuring the enlargement commissioner that yes, this time, Malta's application would stick.

'We would be on the frontier of the European Union and would be once again prized for our fortress role on the frontier. And we don't want to be a frontier fortress any more' – Labour leader and former Prime Minister Alfred Sant in 2003[2]

'Upon membership, one of the twenty-five European Commissioners will be Maltese, giving us the same representation in that body as the largest member state, Germany' – Then-Prime Minister Eddie Fenech Adami assuring voters in 2003 that Malta wouldn't be swallowed up in the Brussels Sea[3]

EU Worries

Nationalists promised EU subsidies, more tourism, increased foreign investment, and the symbolic importance of linking arms with Europe. But the Maltese had plenty of concerns. Since Malta has to import almost everything – including 70 per cent of its food – some worried about the effects of Brussels setting the prices; others worried that EU nationals would buy up the land. The church didn't want the EU to interfere with divorce and abortion laws, and the Labour Party – the loudest of the anti-EU groups – talked about the loss of sovereignty and the security risk of officially becoming Europe's south-western frontier. But much of the to-do that so thoroughly split the island was about political power.

Tugged back and forth in hard-fought billboard wars and TV campaigns, voters approved EU entry in the March 2003 referendum. Malta walked into the EU in May the next year, not only the smallest of the twenty-five members, but the country least likely to be there. And it's also the least likely country to stay.

Future Forecast

Labour will rise up and divide the island again.

Hot Spots

Valletta: The sixteenth-century palaces shimmer as the sun drops into the red bay in this fortress city that was built up by Malta's Knights. Renowned as one of the world's finest showcases of the Baroque, capital Valletta was also one of the first European cities designed on a grid. Space is getting tight in Grand Harbour, where cruise ships vie for moorage with NATO warships.

> Bombed during the Second World War, Valletta's opera house still hasn't been repaired.

Mdina: The walled city on the island of Gozo is a tumble of garden-wrapped squares and sixteenth-century cathedrals and palaces (still owned by nobles) housing valuable Renaissance paintings, including the famous *Beheading of St John* by Caravaggio.

Golden-hued Valletta: once a city of knights.

Second island Gozo claims that it was made famous by Homer's Odyssey: *it was here, Gozans claim, that the sea nymph Calypso nursed Ulysses back to health, keeping him captive for seven years, but never convincing him to marry. Homer called the island Ogygia.*

Birds' balconies: Back in the 1500s, when respectable women were forced to stay at home (making lace, one supposes) while the menfolk went out cavorting, the gals could watch the movements of their guys from balconies with far-reaching views (and potential consequences), considering the place was choc-a-bloc with courtesans.

Summer homes: With Malta already one of the most densely populated chunks of land in the world, the Maltese government negotiated EU waivers to prevent Europeans from buying second homes on their island. After Malta became independent in 1964, the British kept hanging around for another decade, until the Maltese pressured many out of their summer cottages.

The media: Both major parties own their own newspapers, TV and radio stations in which they air the dirty laundry of the other party's politicians.

Freemason lodges: Never mind that none is officially registered with the police, freemasons and secret societies are rumoured to run rampant on the island.

> *Although it's part of Malta mythology – 10 February is the Feast of St Paul's Shipwreck – some religious scholars say Paul's ship did not hit the rocks here, but in Greece.*[4]

Maltese territorial waters: When the Maltese government recently sent out a team to survey the coastal shelf for petroleum, the Libyan navy blocked the move, and sent the ship packing back to Malta. Now Libya is muscling into Malta's oil exploration.

Hot Shots

Eddie Fenech Adami: President 2003 to present; Prime Minister 1987–95; 1998–2004. Devout Catholic and Nationalist Adami is a man of his word: he vowed to get Malta into the EU (succeeding in 2004), and vowed to resign from the premiership when he turned 70 (doing both in 2003). However, he simply walked into the presidential role instead.

Lawrence Gonzi: Prime Minister 2003 to present. Nationalist Gonzi may have a cigarette hanging out of his mouth most of the time, but that

Adami led the Malta flock into the EU.

doesn't mean he isn't deeply religious. It may be in his genes: his uncle Sir Michael Gonzi was 'the Iron Archbishop' who led the anti-Labour movement of the 1960s.

Dom Mintoff: Prime Minister 1955–8; 1971–84. A diehard socialist and former leader of the Maltese Labour Party, Malta's most outrageous politician started out trying to address valid grievances, but ended up driving Malta over the cliff. Even many of his former fans are still mad that his antics brought down the Labour government in 1998: at recent public appearances, he's been booed from the stage.

Alfred Sant: Labour Party leader, Prime Minister 1996–8. Poor Sant was tossed out on his ear only two years into his term as premier, but he still snipes loudly from the sidelines. Will be sure to point out everything wrong with membership of the EU – and can do so at close range: Eurosceptic Labour won three seats in the European Parliament to the Nationalists' two.

The Catholic church: It may be more powerful here than it is in Rome, but even Rome had to intervene in the 1960s when Malta's archbishop, Sir Michael Gonzi, jumped into politics, dictating how his flock voted.

Joe Borg: European Commissioner for fisheries and maritime protection 2004 to present.

Birdlife Malta: The organization that tends to wounded winged creatures, and campaigns for bird rights, is itself often under fire from hunters. Some active members have received death threats.

Knights of Malta: They once brought hospitals, churches and palaces to Malta, along with plenty of prostitutes. Now a do-gooder group, they number in the tens of thousands, and are considering starting their own mini-country – complete with passports, stamps and postal system – in the same Maltese fort where they fought off Ottoman invaders in 1565. The organization also plays a starring role in numerous conspiracy theories.

Glossary

Accession country: Those countries approved to come into the European Union, but not in it yet: e.g. until 1 May 2004, Latvia, Poland and Malta were among the ten accession countries.

Acquis Communitaire: All of the laws, amendments, treaties, regulations and requirements of the European Union combined in one long document that runs to 80,000 pages.

Amsterdam Treaty: 1997 treaty that formally adopted use of the Schengen zone (creating open borders for most of Western Europe). The treaty increased collective policing powers of the European Union and called for an integrated approach to immigration. It gave more power to the European Parliament, did away with the requirement for unanimous approval in many areas and also guaranteed certain human rights of EU citizens, including equal opportunity for men and women.

Asylum: An area of freedom, security and justice in another country for an individual in fear of death or persecution in their country of nationality. (*See also* Refugee.)

Atlanticist: Typically used derogatorily, it refers to a European country that is closely allied with the United States, e.g. Britain.

Austrian Empire: Term used after the 1815 Congress of Vienna to designate the area under Habsburg dynastic control, which extended across today's Austria into Eastern and Central Europe. After 1867, when Hungarians demanded the running of half the empire, it became the Austro-Hungarian Empire. After the First World War, when the empire fought on the losing side, the holdings of land were reduced by two-thirds and new countries including Czechoslovakia and Slovenia were formed out of the land.

Benelux: Shorthand for the former 'Low Countries' – Belgium, the

Netherlands and Luxembourg – when talking about them collectively and as a region.

Beneš Decrees: 1947 Laws of Czechoslovakian President Edvard Beneš calling for Germans to get out of Czechoslovakia and forfeit their land: millions were kicked out. Now a source of debate: some who lost their land want it back or compensation.

Brussels: The 'capital of Europe', often used as shorthand for the European Union since most EU institutions are headquartered there.

Candidate country: A country that is negotiating with the EU about the possibility of joining. As of 2004, Bulgaria, Romania and Turkey are all candidate countries.

Coal and Steel Agreement: 1951 agreement to pool coal and steel resources. Initiated by France with regards to West Germany, the agreement was signed by both countries as well as Italy and the Benelux countries.

Council of European Union v. Council of Ministers v. European Council v. Council of Europe

In that 'let's make matters more complicated than need be' style that is emblematic of the EU, there are so many councils that few can recognize them apart. For the record:

The Council of the European Union is the same as the **Council of Ministers**: it is the EU's main decision-making body. If the Council of Ministers is discussing money matters, it is a meeting of finance ministers from EU countries; if they are discussing farming matters, then the Council of Ministers is a meeting of agricultural ministers from EU countries. However, if the Council of Ministers is having one of its biannual meetings with leaders of EU states, then the meeting is called the **European Council** or **European Council of Ministers**. The **Council of Europe** is a non-profit organization that is not part of the EU. Most European countries belong to this group concerned with protecting human rights.

Common Agricultural Policy: Created after the food shortages resulting from the Second World War, this policy aimed to increase production, and provide dependable food sources at affordable prices in a stable market. Part of that was provision of huge subsidies, of which France always takes the most. CAP subsidies eat up almost half of the EU budget and are hugely controversial.

Common Foreign and Security Policy: 1992 agreement that the EU should have a collective military as well as cooperative policing.

Congress of Vienna: 1815 meeting of Western European leaders to redistribute the lands taken by Napoleon and set up new borders and buffer countries. The Congress of Vienna tidied up boundaries that had become messy during the centuries when much of Europe was part of the Holy Roman Empire. Among other things, it created the German Confederation of thirty-nine states, remapped the Low Countries – putting Belgium, Netherlands and Luxembourg together – and gave Austria control of northern Italian states.

Copenhagen summit: 2002 meeting at which the names of those countries accepted as European Union members in 2004 were announced.

Council of Ministers: Executive board of the EU that makes laws and directs policy. (*See* Box.)

Court of Auditors: Watchdogs of the EU budget.

Dual Monarchy: From 1867 to 1919 the Austrian Empire became the Austro-Hungarian Empire, with royals heading both halves. It is sometimes called the Dual Monarchy.

EMU: European Monetary Union. The bringing together of EU countries' economies so that they could use the common currency, the euro.

Enlargement: Typically refers to the 2004 enlargement of the EU, when ten countries from East and Central Europe joined the fifteen Western European countries that were already on board; geographical expansion that is sometimes called the Big Bang.

EU-15: The fifteen member states that were part of the EU prior to the 2004 EU enlargement. The EU-15 are Austria, Belgium, Denmark, Finland, France, Germany, Greece, Ireland, Italy, Luxembourg, the Netherlands, Portugal, Spain, Sweden and the UK (Britain).

EU-25: The EU-15 member states plus Poland, Hungary, Estonia, Latvia, Lithuania, Czech Republic, Slovakia, Slovenia, Cyprus and Malta.

Euro: Common currency that resulted from the Maastricht Treaty of 1992. It became the sole currency of 12 EU member states on 2 January 2002.

European Commission: Policy-making arm of the EU with twenty-five commissioners who recommend policy on everything from energy and transportation to fisheries and trade. Each member state has its own commissioner.

European Commissioner: Appointed representative from each member state who oversees policy areas such as food safety and environmental issues. Commissioners are appointed for five-year terms.

European Constitutional Treaty: This massive, controversial undertaking of 2003–4 was an attempt to bring all the treaties and laws into one document approved by all member governments. It also establishes human rights for EU citizens and changes the voting weight of member states. It was supposed to make the EU easier for citizens to understand but failed in that mission. Will be voted on by citizens in several EU countries in 2005; if they don't pass it, the treaty could get binned.

European Council of Ministers/European Council: The summit when all the heads of state or government of EU members meet and hammer out laws and priorities over expensive meals and numerous bottles of wine. Typically takes place at least twice a year.

European Court of Justice: Headquartered in Luxembourg, this is the EU's main judicial arm, where member states might be called if they don't play by the rules. Each member state has a judge in the court.

European Parliament: Headquartered in Brussels, the parliament is the only place where EU citizens can elect their representatives. The legislative body now has 732 members and is currently filled with Eurosceptics. Once a month they jaunt off to Strasbourg for a plenary session. Travel costs of the parliament amount to €155 million a year; with the newly admitted countries this could rise to €185 million.

Eurosceptic: Person who takes a critical stance regarding the EU; often refers to someone who questions the benefits of EU membership for their country.

Eurostat: Statistical arm of the EU.

Eurozone: Those countries that use the European single currency, the euro.

Ever-closer union: Phrase from the 1957 Treaty of Rome that is one of the main goals of the European Union – to bring member states closer and hence less likely to be in a state of chronic war.

Federalism: In the EU the idea that more laws should come out of Brussels; some federalists want to see a strengthening of the powers of Europe's parliament.

Franco-German axis: Power moves of France (with most land) and Germany (with the biggest economy and highest population) in the EU.

Growth and Stability Pact: To be part of the eurozone, countries are supposed to limit their national deficits to less than 3 per cent. This pact that limits borrowing is, to quote Hamlet, 'more honoured in the breach than the observance', particularly by France and Germany which pushed it in the first place.

Holy Roman Empire v. Roman Empire

The Holy Roman Empire, begun in 800 CE by Charlemagne, pulled much of Europe, particularly the western sectors, under the rule of a Catholic emperor. Headed by the Habsburg clan of Vienna for the last six centuries of its thousand-year existence, it was a loose network for much of that time: rulers of different principalities often paid little attention to the Holy Roman Emperor. Was officially put to bed by Napoleon in 1806. The Roman Empire began in the first century BCE and continued into the fifth century CE. It was begun by Romans whose military forces expanded as far as England and from Germany to Syria and North Africa. They pulled together the empire mostly with paved roads, Latin language and later Christian belief. The Vandals and Visigoths ultimately pushed them out of power.

IGC: Intergovernmental Conference is a protracted affair at which heads of government and numerous ministers of all the EU member states meet to cobble together a treaty.

International Criminal Court: Located in The Hague, Netherlands, this court is not an EU institution. Linked to the United Nations, which recommended it be started, the ICC tries international war criminals. The US hates it and often demands that any country that enters into a contract with the US sign a contract saying that that country won't try any US citizen in this court.

Maastricht: a lovely town in the south-east of the Netherlands; used to refer to the Maastricht Treaty (below).

Maastricht Treaty aka Maastricht: 1992 treaty signed in the above Dutch town that created the basis for the new European Union: changed the name from the European Community to European Union, created its common currency the euro and allowed EU citizens to move freely and work in other EU countries. It also called for the creation of a European Union military force.

MEP: Member of European Parliament – sits in the EU Parliament in Brussels and Strasbourg.

NATO: A mighty military alliance, the North Atlantic Treaty Organization was created in 1949 to ward off the Soviet threat to Western Europe. It never fought Communists, but its muscle was indeed a threat to the Soviet Union, which formed the Warsaw Pact military alliance of

Communist countries in response. NATO was mostly a way to sell huge amounts of arms – members must spend 2 per cent of GDP on arms acquisitions. The only time NATO forces fought was in Yugoslavia in 1999 against Slobodan Milosevic in Kosovo and they made a big mess of it, bombing a civilian train on a bridge and the Chinese embassy in Belgrade among other blunders. Many Eastern and Central European countries have signed on since the mid 1990s, mostly as a means of protecting themselves against Russia, but they usually deny that to the Russians. Article Five of the NATO charter says that if one member is attacked all will respond to defend that member. The **26 NATO members** as of 2004: Belgium, Bulgaria, Canada, Czech Republic, Denmark, Estonia, France, Germany, Greece, Hungary, Iceland, Italy, Latvia, Lithuania, Luxembourg, the Netherlands, Norway, Poland, Portugal, Romania, Slovakia, Slovenia, Spain, Turkey, United Kingdom (Britain) and United States.

New Europe: The poorer, younger countries mostly of Eastern and Central Europe (and the Mediterranean), most of whom were under Communist control after the Second World War up to the early 1990s. Many countries of 'New Europe' were formed in 1919 or even the 1990s: now many are joining NATO and ten 'New Europe' countries joined the EU in 2004. US Defense Secretary Donald Rumsfeld coined this term when he was talking about how these countries supported the US on the 2003 invasion of Iraq.

Nice, Treaty of: Controversial 2000 treaty finally pounded out in Nice that altered the number of votes for EU member states.

Old Europe: Another vocabulary creation of US Defense Secretary Donald Rumsfeld who meant it as out-of-date, boring Europe (much of which wouldn't back the American invasion of Iraq) but that is not how the term is used here. In this book it refers to the Western European countries which avoided Communist rule after the Second World War.

Ottoman Empire: Headquartered in Istanbul, Turkey, and founded around 1300 by Sultan Osman I, the Ottoman Empire was the rule of Muslim Turks which at points spread as far east as today's Iraq, as far west as Algeria, and as far north as Hungary, including most of the Balkans.

Paris, Treaty of: 1951 treaty signed by France, Germany, Italy and the Benelux countries, that formalized the pooling of coal and steel and created the main bodies: the Council of Ministers, European Commission, Parliament and Court of Justice, although initially they had different names.

Rapid Reaction Force: The EU armed force of 60,000 that is designed to work with NATO in areas requiring 'peace keeping'.

Refugee: A foreigner with a well-founded fear of being persecuted because of their race, religion, creed, political beliefs, etc., and who is outside their country of origin and believes that country cannot help them. (*See also* Asylum.)

Schengen Agreement: Zone created in 1995 in which border checks in most EU-15 countries are lifted, allowing people to drive through without stopping or showing their passports.

Soviet republic: a country that was officially part of the Soviet Union: e.g. Estonia, Latvia and Lithuania.

Soviet satellite: a country that was controlled and very much affected by the Soviet Union, which gave it aid and quashed rebellions: e.g. Hungary, Poland, Czechoslovakia.

Steel and Coal Agreement: 1951 agreement to pool coal and steel resources between six European countries, namely France, Germany, Italy and Benelux.

Strasbourg: City in eastern France where the European Parliament holds monthly plenary sessions.

Subsidiarity: Decision making at the lowest level of government.

Sudetenland: North-west corner of the Czech Republic (formerly Czechoslovakia) which used to be home to many Germans. Hitler annexed it in 1939, and the Czechoslovakian president ordered Germans out of here after the Second World War.

Supranational: An institution, such as the EU, that affects more than one country but is not controlled by the affected countries' governments.

Treaty of Rome: 1957 treaty signed by France, Germany, Italy, Belgium, Netherlands and Luxembourg, this was the grand-daddy of all treaties which called for 'ever closer union' between the countries. It formed the European Economic Community and Euratom, the European Atomic Energy Commission (which is not a part of the EU).

Treaty of Trianon: 1920 treaty signed between the victors of the First World War and the new state of Hungary, which was reduced to about a third of its pre-war size.

Treaty of Versailles: 1919 treaty drawn up between Germany and the allied victors of the First World War that rearranged Central and

Eastern Europe, creating such countries as Czechoslovakia and the Kingdom of Serbs, Croats and Slovenes out of what had been part of the Austro-Hungarian Empire. One of the guiding points was to form new countries based on ethnicity and language.

Warsaw Pact: The Soviet Union's answer to NATO, the 1949 Warsaw Pact created a military alliance of the Soviet satellites and republics. They were called upon to stamp out any uprisings in Eastern bloc countries.

Notes

Introduction

1 Q and A: Opinion of the Commission on the draft European Constitution, 17/09/2003, DN: MEMO/03/177, available on http://europa.eu.int.
2 *Economist*, 18 Sept. 2004.
3 So said former French president Valéry Giscard d'Estaing, who oversaw the drafting of the proposed EU constitution.
4 'Après EU, le déluge?' *Economist*, 3 July 2003.

Part One: Old Europe
Chapter 1: France

1 Source: EU: *Financial Report of European Agricultural Guidance and Guarantee Fund*, Annexe 11, Évolution des Dépenses du Feoga – garantie par état membre.
2 Source: EU: *Financial Report of European Agricultural Guidance and Guarantee Fund*, Annexe 11, Évolution des Dépenses du Feoga – garantie par état membre.
3 Among those with that theory: Adam Gopnick, columnist for *The New Yorker*.
4 Source: BBC.
5 Bruce Crumley and Adam Smith, 'Sisters in Hell', *Time International*, 2 Dec. 2002.
6 Barry James, 'Le Pen based appeal on fears about crimes', *International Herald Tribune*, 23 Apr. 2002.
7 Source: BBC, 'Profile: Jean-Marie Le Pen', 23 Apr. 2002.
8 Lowell Ponte, 'France's Rising Right', *FrontPageMagazine*, 23 Apr. 2002.
9 Paul Webster, 'Le Pen: populist who rose from ashes', *Guardian*, 22 Apr. 2002.
10 According to the *Economist*, citing 2004 surveys by CSA/*Le Parisien* and *Elle*.
11 Elaine Ganley, 'Second explosive device in a month found . . .' AP, 25 Mar. 2004.

12 James Graff and Bruce Crumley, 'France is not a Pacifist Country', *Time*, 16 Feb. 2003.

13 CNN interview with Christiane Amanpour, 16 Mar. 2003.

14 Declaration of Jacques Chirac posted on French government's presidential website.

15 So sniffed US State Department spokesman Richard Boucher.

16 So admonished Christopher Hitchens in the *Wall Street Journal*, 'The Rat that tried to roar', 6 Feb. 2003.

17 So estimates *Napoleon* author Paul Johnson, as noted in Stephen Goode, 'Napoleon's Legacy leads to Gulag . . .', *Insight Magazine*, 12 Sept. 2003.

18 Rashid Tlemcani, 'Islam in France: The French have themselves to blame', *Middle East Quarterly*, Mar. 1997.

19 Source: *Library of Congress Country Studies: Algeria*, 'France in Algeria, 1830–1862'.

20 'Franco-Prussian War', Microsoft™ Encarta™ Online Encyclopedia 2004.

21 As noted by Ruth Franklin, 'Arse Poetica', *The New Yorker*, 17 Nov. 2003.

22 Arthur Rimbaud letter to Paul Demeny.

23 Figure according to www.Globalsecurity.org.

24 'Pétain's crimes still split French', *Jerusalem Post*-AP, 2 Aug. 1995.

25 Richard Cavendish, 'Months Past: Death of Marshal Pétain', *History Today*, 1 July 2001.

26 Information drawn from numerous sources, including *Library of Congress Country Studies: Algeria* and Robert Rinehart, *Countries of the World: Algeria*.

27 Alan Riding, 'Paris intellectuals in ramparts', *New York Times*, 28 Feb. 2004.

28 'France's Autumn Blues', *Economist*, 4 Oct. 2003.

29 Charlene Crabb, 'Ailing French healthcare system to go under the knife', *Bulletin of the World Health Organization*, Mar. 2004.

30 'A shuffle offshore', *Economist*, 30 Jan. 2003.

31 Dominique Pobel and Jean-Francois Viel, 'Case-Control Study of leukaemia among young people near La Hague nuclear reprocessing plant . . .', *British Medical Journal*, 11 Jan. 1997.

32 As noted on 'About France': www.ambafrance-au.org/aboutfrance/home.en.htm.

33 'Apathy Contest', *Economist*, 20 June 2004.

34 Nanette van de Laan, 'French campaign takes on crime', *Christian Science Monitor*, 26 Feb. 2002.

35 Source: BBC.

36 James Graff and Bruce Crumley, 'France is not a Pacifist Country', *Time*, 16 Feb. 2003.

37 'Turkey entry "would destroy EU"', BBC News (from website news.bbc.co.uk), 8 Nov. 2002.

38 According to Nostradamus biographer John Hogue in *The Essential Nostradamus*.

39 Robert Hughes, 'Sublime windbag: writer, lover, national hero, Victor Hugo . . .', *Time*, 27 Apr. 1998.
40 Sources: Wikipedia, *New Statesman and Society*, *Economist*.

Chapter 2: Germany

1   See: 'Background Notes', www.germany-info.org.
2   Christopher Booker and Richard North, *The Great Deception: The Secret History of the European Union*, London: Continuum, 2003.
3   Tony Czuczka, 'Berlin Wall Opened in Chaos', AP, 9 Nov. 1989.
4   'Interview of the Emperor Wilhelm II', *Daily Telegraph*, 28 Oct. 1908.
5   Margaret McMillan, *Paris 1919: Six Months that Changed the World*, New York: Random House, 2001, p. 161.
6   Ibid., p. 480.
7   Ibid.
8   Source: www.en.wikipedia.org.
9   Ibid.
10 Ibid.
11 Source: 'Adolf Hitler', www.en.wikipedia.org.
12 Dorothea von Schwanenfluegel Lawson, 'World War Memories', www.germanculture.com.
13 Matthew White's war-death statistics website: http://users.erols.com/mwhite28/warstat1.htm.
14 Jeevan Vasager, 'Churchill "betrayed East German rising" ', 17 June 2003.
15 Source: the *Economist*.
16 'Germans should retire later . . .', AP Worldstream, 6 Sept. 2003.
17 Gerhard Schröder, 'We can do more, but only all together', *New York Times*, 19 Sept. 2003.
18 'Germany's Deadly Legacy', *German Life*, 31 July 1997.
19 Jacob Hellbrunn, 'Springtime: Germany's newfound strength', *New Republic*, 16 Oct. 1995.
20 Charles Wallace, 'European Newsmaker 2002: Gerhard Schröder', *Time Europe*, 30 Dec. 2002.
21 'President slams "greedy" Germans', BBC, 23 May 2004.
22 'No frau after Rau', *Economist*, 13 Aug. 2003.
23 Matthew Schofield, 'Germany's cannibal trial reveals perverse intimacy . . .', *Knight-Ridder News*, 18 Jan. 2004; also includes information from assorted CNN reports.
24 'History of the Federal Republic of Germany': www.en.wikipedia.org.
25 'Willy Brandt', CNN Cold War Profile, www.cnn.com/SPECIALS/cold.war/kbank/profiles/brandt.

Chapter 3: United Kingdom

1 Lance Morrow, 'Isaac Newton: 1642–1727 . . .', *Time*, 31 Dec. 1999.

2 'Sir Isaac Newton,' BBC History, www.bbc.co.uk/history/historic_figures/newton_isaac.shtml.

3 Some information derived from Scotland's University of St Andrews, School of Mathematics and Statistics, profile of Isaac Newton: www-history.mcs.st-andrews.ac.uk/Mathematics/Newton.html.

4 'United Kingdom: Unemployment', European Foundation for the Improvement of Living and Working Conditions, www.eurofound.eu.int.

5 Mark Oliver, 'An "extreme and political" preacher', *Guardian*, 20 Jan. 2003.

6 Tapes of his calls to 'loot and shoot' were aired on BBC2 in December 2002, as reported by Mark Oliver, ibid.

7 In interview with *The Radical*, 13 Sept. 2001, as noted by Yotam Feldner in 'Radical Islamist Profile: London – Abu Hamza al-Masri', *MEMRI*, Inquiry and Analysis Series, No. 72, 16 Oct. 2001.

8 'Anti–EU faction surges in British polls', *EU Business*, 14 June 2004.

9 'Britain's eurosceptics vow to "wreck" EU parliament', Agence France Presse, 14 June 2004.

10 Martin Wainwright, 'Ukip's bloomer over women's rights', *Guardian*, 21 July 2004.

11 Alan Travis, 'Blunkett law will free UK's domestic slaves', *Guardian*, 11 Nov. 2004.

12 Source: UK Parliament, 'Beyond the myths of immigration', www.publications.parliament.uk/pa/cm200304/cmselect/cmintdev/79/7901.gif.   Also: Refugee Council (www.refugeecouncil.org.uk) and Steve Silver, 'Asylum in Britain: setting the record straight,' *Searchlight*, Aug. 2002.

13 Some information drawn from www.EnchantedLearning.com – 'Explorers' series. *See* also 'Hot Shots' below.

14 Jeffrey Lee, 'Great Geographers: Charles Darwin and Thomas Henry Huxley', *Focus on Geography*, 22 Mar. 2004.

15 Diana Muir, 'The man who dared to climb the family tree . . .', *Christian Science Monitor*, 26 Sept. 2002.

16 Source on Galton: Nicholas W. Gillham, 'Sir Francis Galton and the birth of eugenics', *Annual Review of Genetics*, 1 Jan. 2001.

17 'Inventors from the British Isles', www.EnchantedLearning.com.

18 Professor Martin Daunton, 'London's "Great Stink": The Sour Smell of Success', BBC History, www.bbc.co.uk.

19 Source: 'Is the British loo down the pan?' BBC News.

20 'The Great Exhibition at the Crystal Palace', The Great Exhibition of 1851, www.Victorianstation.com.

21 As noted in 'The Rhodes Scholarships: A Giant Step for White World Domination', *The Conscious Observer Newsletter*, October 1995.

22 As noted on 'Queen Victoria's Empire: Cecil Rhodes', www.pbs.org.

23 Sources include: Matthew Sweet, 'A Bad Man in Africa', *Independent*, 16 Mar. 2002 and James North, 'The Randlords', *New Republic*, 19 May 1986.

24 Source: www.en.wikipedia.org.

25 Nigel Slater, 'Natural born thrillers', *Observer*, 4 July 2004.

26 The 2001 report by Professor David Warburton of the University of Reading is discussed by Richard Alleyne, 'Celebrity chefs dish up dinner party neurosis', *Daily Telegraph*, 4 Dec. 2001.

27 Figures for 2003.

28 Internet observation reported by Natalya Predtechenskaya, 'Newspapers in Britain', *Life There*.

29 Assorted organizations, including UN Development Program, International Adult Literacy Survey and Organization for Economic Cooperation and Development.

30 Source: Literacy Trust, using information from Book Marketing Ltd, which conducted surveys in 2001.

31 'Britain a "racist" society', BBC News, 20 May 2002.

32 'Q and A: Fighting gun crime', 16 Sept. 2003; http://news.bbc.co.uk/go/pr/fr/-/hi/uk/3112818.stm.

33 Nick Lowles, 'BNP kicked off Oldham riots', *Searchlight*, July 2003.

34 Robert Verkaik, 'Race in Britain: Immigration lawyers face campaign of fire-bombing and death threats', 12 Apr. 2004.

35 Information derived from reports from thinktank Bellano and University of Bremen, Greenpeace, and the *Guardian* among other sources.

36 Peter Oborne, 'The End of the Affair', *Spectator*, 2002.

37 Some information here derived from article written by Prince Michael of Greece, 'To Be Young and Royal', *Vanity Fair*, September 2003.

38 Ibid.

Chapter 4: Italy

1   'Why al-Qaeda targets Italy', United Press International, 19 July 2004.

2   Jeff Israely, 'The Berlusconi Channel', *Time*, 3 Mar. 2003.

3   Germans usually spend over €6 billion a year in Italy.

4   Constant Brand, 'Berlusconi Nazi Comment Triggers Outrage', 2 July 2003.

5   James Hardy, 'Fury over PM Muslim Slur', *Mirror*, 28 Sept. 2001.

6   'Berlusconi in his own words', BBC, 20 Dec. 2003.

7   Frederika Randall, 'The irresistible rise of Berlusconi', *Nation*, 21 June 2004.

8   Jessie Grimond, *Independent*, 30 Sept. 2002.

9   Peter Popham, 'Odyssey of despair', *Independent*, 19 June 2003.

10 Bossi's office later released the following statement: 'The content of the interview published this morning by *Corriere della Sera*, headlined "Cannon-shots to stop illegal immigrants", does by no means reflect my

thoughts, nor the meaning of my replies in what has been only a quick exchange of just two remarks. In fact, my thoughts on dealing with the major phenomenon of clandestine immigration are identical to those laid down by the Palermo Treaty which our government has not yet signed, as many other countries have done. The treaty equates the trafficking of clandestine immigrants with the slave trade, faced with which the possible boarding of these boats by the navy is not considered an act of piracy.'

11 Charles Raw, 'Mani Puliti', *The European*, 29 Aug. 1996.

12 Some information draws on Norman Davies, *Europe, A History*, 1997 and H. A. L. Fisher, *A History of Europe*, 1970.

13 Author Margherita Marchione is source of some info.

14 Peter Stalker, *Oxford Handbook of the World*, 2000, p. 154.

15 Robert P. Libbon, *Instant European History*, 1996, pp. 76–7.

16 Benito Mussolini, *The Cardinal's Mistress*, English translation: Hiram Motherwell, 1929, as noted on www.oddbooks.co.uk.

17 Margaret McMillan, *Paris 1919*, p. 280.

18 Statistic from Datamonitor: 'Young cannot afford to leave home', BBC, 12 Mar. 2003.

19 Source: William T. Grant Foundation: 'Adolescence not just for kids', *Washington Post*, 2 Jan. 2002.

20 'Foreign Relations of Albania': www.wikipedia.org.

Chapter 5: Belgium

1 So claims Belgian businessman Jean-Michel Nihoul, a defendant in the case of Marc Dutroux, the paedophile and murderer. Dutroux keeps insisting he was securing his victims as part of a ring, and that the government is not investigating his leads.

2 Bart Crols, 'Hungarian pastor found guilty of killing family', Reuters, 5 Mar. 2002.

3 Ambrose Evans-Pritchard, 'Jews suffer surge of hate on streets of Belgium', *Daily Telegraph*, 30 May 2003.

4 Jennifer Ehrlich and Tom Vandyck, 'Belgian Malcolm X seeks office', *Christian Science Monitor*, 16 May 2003.

5 Some information in this section derived from the fascinating and beautifully written book by Thomas Pakenham, *The Scramble for Africa*, New York, Random House, 1991. Another source: Adam Hochschild, *King Leopold's Ghost*, New York, Houghton Mifflin, 1998.

6 Ambrose Evans-Pritchard, 'Belgian fury at film on Leopold's Congo terror', *Daily Telegraph*, 4 July 2004.

7 Information in this section derived from interviews, the Belgian Tourism Board, the *Economist* and *Lonely Planet World Guide: Belgium*.

8 'New government to amend war crimes legislation in attempt to avert crisis within NATO', AP Worldstream, 8 July 2003.

9 Glenn Frankel, 'Belgian war crimes law undone by its global reach . . .' *Washington Post*, 30 Sept. 2003. Additional information derived from AP and the *Economist*.

10 'EU's soulless capital', United Press International, 15 Aug. 2003.

11 Barry James, 'Eurocapital in search of a human dimension', *International Herald Tribune*, 23 Oct. 1998.

12 'Al-Qaeda plotters sentenced', BBC News, 30 Sept. 2003.

13 Andrew Osborn, 'EU buys back "Berlaymonster" headquarters', *Guardian*, 24 Oct. 2002.

14 Information from *Economist*, *Washington Post*, AP.

15 Liz Kelly, 'Confronting an Atrocity', *Trouble and Strife*, Vol. 36, 1998: http://cwasu.org/confrontingatrocity1.htm.

16 Sebastian Lapaque, 'Simenon the myth in seven legends', *Le Figaro Littéraire*, 9 Jan. 2003.

Chapter 6: Ireland

1 According to the *Economist*'s 'World in 2005' survey.

2 'Slainte', *Economist*, 1 May 2003.

3 Niall Moonan, 'Immigrants are saving the Church', *Daily Mirror*, 17 June 2004.

4 Source: www.wikipedia.org.

Chapter 7: Spain

1 Source: World Tourism Organization, June 2004.

2 Source: BBC.

3 'Spanish Reporters: Government Silenced the Truth About the Attacks,' Inter Press Service, 18 Mar. 2004: www.commondreams.org/headlines04/318-10.htm.

4 Source: *El País*.

5 '11 March 2004 Madrid attacks', Wikipedia: www.wikipedia.org.

6 Elaine Sciolino, 'Spain is firm: troops won't return,' *New York Times*, 7 May 2004.

7 Some information from David Gilmour, *Cities of Spain*, Chicago: Ivan R. Dee, 1992 and John A. Crow, *Spain: The Root and the Flower*, Berkeley: University of California Press, 1985.

8 James Townsend, 'Tracking Spain's Gold to Moscow', *Wall Street Journal*, 4 Aug. 1994.

9 *Newsweek*, 2 March 1970. See http://hitlerstoppebyfranco.com/franco_jews.htm.

10 John Hopper, *The New Spaniards*, London: Penguin Group, 1995.

11 Ibid.

12 Keith B. Richburg, 'Spain Engulfed in Vast Social Change', *Washington Post*, 12 June 2004.

13 Some information drawn from Tom Lappin's excellent article 'Turning on the black tide', *New Scotsman*, 13 Feb. 2003 and from the insightful article in Spanish daily *El País* 'El Gobierno nose amenazó con hundir el "Prestige" si lo acercábamos a la costa', *El País*, 15 Nov. 2003.

14 Dale Fuchs, 'Spain labors to bring home baby – and the bacon', *Christian Science Monitor*, 26 June 2003.

15 Patricia Cazón, 'Un problema de peso', *El País Semanal*, 26 Oct. 2003.

16 T. D. Allman, 'The King Who Saved His Country', *Vanity Fair*, August 1992. (Interesting article, although Allman is out to lunch to claim that siestas are a thing of the past, and that Spaniards often holiday in Switzerland because it's cheaper.)

17 Bringing that lot to heel could be his toughest challenge yet.

18 Alan Riding, 'Picasso flunked French citizenship', *International Herald Tribune*, 28 May 2003.

19 Jackie McGlone, 'Picasso's Women', *Scotsman*, 9 Aug. 2000.

20 Riding, 'Picasso flunked French citizenship'.

21 So said Martha Gellhorn, author of *The Undefeated* (1945), as noted on www.spartacus.schoolnet.co.uk/2WWfranco.htm.

Chapter 8: Portugal

1 Source: UK Trade and Investment: 'Portugal: Setting Up'.

2 Based on interviews with Portuguese.

3 'Links between Europeans living abroad and their countries of origin', Council of Europe Parliamentary Assembly, 5 Mar. 1999.

4 Source: *The World Factbook*, International Planned Parenthood Federation; some studies say closer to 20 per cent of the women can't read.

5 Between 1991 and 2001, 38 per cent of Portuguese finished mandatory nine years of schooling, according to a 2 April 2003 statement by Portuguese UN Ambassador Gonçalo de Santa Clara Gomes to the Commission on Population and Development.

6 'Victory in Portugal lifts European right', *International Herald Tribune*, 19 Mar. 2002.

7 'Portuguese stocks surge after conservatives take power', AP Worldstream, 18 Mar. 2002.

8 'Portugal: U.S. "best way" to have security', UPI, 10 Mar. 2003; Martins da Cruz was speaking on RDP Antena 1 Rádio.

9   A 2003 law allows employers to fire those taking off more than four days.

10 'Portugal seeks to revive economy', Associated Press, 18 Mar. 2002.

11 Barry Hatton, 'After shaky start, Portugal's new prime minister still looking for chance to prove himself', Associated Press, 8 Aug. 2004.

12 Ibid.

13 Source: www.en.wikipedia.org.

14 Source: *Library of Congress Country Studies: Portugal*.

15 Source: ibid.

16 Source: www.Manorhouses.com: 'Portugal – The Treaty of Windsor'.

17 Source: Daniel J. Boorstin, *The Discoverers: A History of Man's Search to Know His World and Himself*, New York: Random House, 1983 – using a journal of one of da Gama's crew as the source.

18 Source: ibid.

19 Ibid.

20 Source: 'History of Portugal': www.wikipedia.org.

21 'Europe: Those big boys next door; Portugal and Spain', *Economist*, 25 Jan. 2003.

22 Source: *Library of Congress Country Studies: Portugal*.

23 Isabel Romão, 'Country Report: Portugal', European Database: www.db-decision.de/CoRe/Portugal.htm.

24 Some information from 'Abortion: the Portuguese Case', *2002 Reproductive Health Matters*, Elsevier Science Ltd.

25 According to M2 Wine Education Center: www.intowine.com/port.html.

26 Some information from Wine Spectation as well as M2 Wine Education Center.

27 'Portugal clamps down on reality TV', BBC News, 23 May 2001: http://news.bbc.co.uk/1/hi/entertainment/tv_and_radio/1346736.stm.

28 'Portugal's Popular Party a thorn in the side of the centre-right', Agence France Presse English, 21 Mar. 2002.

29 'Portuguese stocks surge after conservatives take power', AP Worldstream, 18 Mar. 2002.

30 Source for all above information: www.Fatima.org.

Chapter 9: Netherlands

1   Source: 'Global Five Hundred Ranked by Performance,' *Fortune*, 26 July 2004.

2   As reported by Manfred Gerstenfeld, 'How Dutch tolerance boomeranged,' *Jerusalem Post*, 9 Nov. 2004

3   As reported by Associated Press on 11 May 2004.

4   *Algemeen Dagblad*, as reported by *Jerusalem Post*.

5   Many immigrants and foreign-born workers are well-integrated in Dutch society; however, the proportion of those leaning on the welfare system is

far higher among immigrants, and the rate of unemployment and crime is often linked to not learning the language. The problem is at a peak in Rotterdam.

6 'Holland's high-camp hero of new politics,' *Daily Telegraph*, 5 Apr. 2002.

7 Interview with *Rotterdams Dagblad*, as noted by Wikipedia.

8 Andrew Osborn, 'Rotterdam plans to ban poor immigrants . . .', *Guardian*, 2 Dec. 2003.

9 Jennifer Ehrlich, 'Liberal Netherlands grown less so on immigration', *Christian Science Monitor*, 19 Dec. 2003.

10 Giles Milton, *Nathaniel's Nutmeg*, New York: Farrar, Straus and Giroux, 1999.

11 'Aceh backgrounder', Indonesia Alert, www.indonesiaalert.org; 'The Dark Side of Power', Radio Netherlands, www2.rnw.nl/rnw/en.

12 'Matters of Taste: Foodways of the Dutch Golden Age', Albany Institute: www.albanyinstitute.org.

13 Zbigniew Szydio, and Richard Brzezinki, 'A New Light on Alchemy', *History Today*, 1 Jan. 1997.

14 'The art and craft of Han van Meegeren', Radio Netherlands, 22 Jan. 2004.

15 Paul Doolan, 'Time for Dutch courage in Indonesia', *History Today*, 1 Mar. 1997.

16 Ibid.

17 Source: Port of Rotterdam website.

18 'By Invitation: The high road that leads out of the Low Countries', *Economist*, 22 May 1999.

19 Stephen Castle and Leyla Linton, 'Sex, spies, smears and vendettas: a royal family tears itself', *Independent*, 12 Mar. 2003.

20 Source: *Forbes Magazine*.

21 Some say it was the French who bungled the name; some say the Brits.

22 Van Gogh lived with the prostitute Sien Hoornik in 1882–3.

23 As noted by John McEwen, 'The odd couple with an ear for painting', *Sunday Telegraph*, 14 Apr. 2002.

24 Richard Edmonds, 'Van Gogh, the Good Dr', *Birmingham Post*, 23 Oct. 1999.

25 'Global Five Hundred Ranked by Performance', *Fortune*, 26 July 2004.

26 According to Friends of the Earth.

27 So alleged former Nigerian oil minister Dauzia Loya Etete as reported by *Forbes*: Sansoni, Silvia, 'Dirty Oil', *Forbes*, 28 Apr. 2003.

28 Excerpts from *The Praise of Folly*, noted on www.historyguide.org/intellect/erasmus.html.

Chapter 10: Austria

1 'Austria: The First Republic 1918–1935', Library of Congress *Country Studies: Austria*, 1 Jan. 1991. Note: the figure 264,453 sq. miles (425,505 sq. km.) –

given as the area over which Habsburg emperors ruled – includes lands that ultimately became part of the Hungarian Empire in the late nineteenth century. Current Austria covers about 33,000 sq. miles (53,000 sq. km.).

2 Michael Jandl and Albert Kraler, 'Austria: A Country of Immigration?', Migration Policy Institute, March 2003: www.migrationinformation.org.

3 This section draws on information in *Newsweek International*, *Economist*, AP, Reuters and BBC.

4 Thomas Fields-Meyer, 'Alpine Uproar', *Time*, Feb. 2000.

5 Joshua Hammer, 'Austria's Power Player', *Newsweek International*, 14 Feb. 2000.

6 Ibid.

7 Source: Statistics Austria: www.statistik.at.

8 'Wolfgang Schüssel, Austria's steely chancellor', *Economist*, 6 June 2000.

9 Ibid.

10 Norman Davies, *Europe: A History*, London: Pimlico, 1997.

11 Gyles Brandreth, 'Everything you wanted to know about Freud but were afraid to ask . . .', *Sunday Telegraph*, 12 May 2002.

12 'Sigmund Freud', Internet Encyclopedia of Philosophy, www.iep.utm.edu/f/freud/htm.

13 J. Masson, *The Assault on Truth: Freud's Suppression of the Seduction Theory*, London: Faber & Faber, 1984; A. C. MacIntyre, *The Unconscious: A Conceptual Analysis*, London: Routledge & Kegan Paul, 1958.

14 Adolf Hitler speech at Koenigsberg 25 Mar. 1938: www.spartacus.school net.co.uk/2WWanschluss.htm.

15 Letter of Mexican envoy Isidro Fabela to League of Nations Secretary-General Joseph Avenol, dated 19 Mar. 1938; *Library of Congress Country Studies: Austria*, Appendix, 1 Jan. 1991, Federal Press Service.

16 Source: *Library of Congress Country Studies: Austria*.

17 'Austria: Nazi terror in the wake of the "Anschluss" ', *Library of Congress Country Studies: Austria*, 1 Jan. 1991, Federal Press Service.

18 Johannes Pflegerl, 'Living in migration in Austria', *Journal of Comparative Family Studies*, 22 Sept. 2001.

19 Ibid.

20 Melissa Rossi, 'To Catch a Spy', *National Geographic Traveler*, Sept. 1999.

21 Source: www.nationmaster.com.

22 Ibid.

23 'Austria's Haider in Iraq Visit Flap', AP Online, 4 Nov. 2003.

24 Source: Magal Perrault, 'Austria', *Central Europe Review*, 20 Jan. 2001: www.ce-review.org.

25 Some information also derived from *Library of Congress Country Studies: Austria*.

26 Much information derived from Eric Myers, 'A problem like Maria . . .', *Opera News*, 1 May 2003.

27 'Wolfgang Amadeus Mozart', Wikipedia.

Chapter 11: Greece

1 'Poverty and Social Exclusion: Population at Risk of Poverty . . .', Eurostat press release, 7 Apr. 2003.
2 'European Structural Funds contribute to higher growth . . .', Europa press release, 17 June 2003.
3 Coral Davenport, 'Olympic feat: modernizing Athens', *Christian Science Monitor*, 6 Aug. 2004.
4 Source: Wikipedia: www.en.wikipedia.org.
5 So says William St Clair in his book *Lord Elgin and the Marbles*.
6 Among those who contend thus: William Blum, author of *Killing Hope*. Also see: 'The Greeks Choose', *The Nation*, 30 Mar. 1985.
7 'Maverick in Moscow', *Time*, 1985.
8 Source: Federation of American Scientists Fund, 'U.S. Arms Clients Profiles – Greece': www.fas.org/asmp/profiles/greece.htm.
9 Source: *Guardian*.
10 Patrick Quinn, Associated Press, 29 Aug. 1998.
11 'Trouble with Turkey', *Economist*, 31 Dec. 1999.
12 'Besieged Monks to Fight', *Independent*, 18 Jan. 2003.
13 Patrick Quinn, Associated Press, 29 Aug. 1998.
14 Ted Clark, 'All Things Considered', report on National Public Radio, 24 June 1999.
15 Source: *Forbes*.
16 Some information from 'Very Happy Birthday', ABC News, 29 Jan. 2003.

Chapter 12: Scandinavia

1 H. A. L. Fisher, *A History of Europe*, London: Fontana, Vol. 1, p. 191.
2 Ibid. p. 193.
3 Insights provided by Anne Katarine Paulsen, interview November 2003.

Chapter 13: Denmark

1 Colin Woodard, 'A Scandinavian Pioneer Shows that Sustainability Can Be Profitable', *E Magazine*, 1 July 2001.
2 'UN criticizes national immigration policy', *Copenhagen Post*, 29 May 2001.
3 Source: 'Fogh pas', *Economist*, 24 Apr. 2003.
4 Charles Wallace, 'Exploring the North', *Time*, 2001.
5 Dan Damon, 'Lessons from Danish prisons', 2 July 2003, BBC: http://news.bbc.co.uk/2/hi/europe/3036450.stm.

6   Peter Stalker, *Oxford Handbook of the World*, New York: Oxford University Press, 2000, p. 364.

7   Ibid., p. 362.

8   'Karen Blixen', *Library of Congress Countries of the World*: Denmark, 1 Jan. 1991.

Chapter 14: Sweden

1   Source: OECD Social Cohesion Data.

2   According to Sveriges Riksbank.

3   According to European Foundation of the Improvement of Living and Working Conditions, EMIRE.

4   Kai R. Lofthus, 'Swedish biz decries racist music', *Billboard*, 24 Jan. 1998.

5   Source: Sweden and Swedes, 'In Ingenuity We Trust': www.Sweden.se.com.

6   J. M. Roberts, *Twentieth Century: History of the World 1901 to 2000*, New York: Penguin, 1999, p. 388.

7   'Sweden's Shameful Eugenics Policies', *McCleans*, 8 Sept. 1997.

8   Paul Gallagher, 'The man who told the secret', *Columbia Journalism Review*, Jan/Feb 1998.

9   'Nordic Eugenics: Here, of all places', *Economist*, 30 Aug. 1997.

10   As noted in *Time*, 'Died: Gunnar Myrdal', 1 June 1987.

11   Ibid.

12   'Too good to be true', *Economist*, 21 Jan. 1999.

13   'Cleared suspect "admits" Palme murder', BBC, 28 Oct. 2001.

14   'Experts doubt Palme case to reopen', BBC, 29 Oct. 2001.

15   Source: US Committee for Refugees.

16   'Mix and Match', *Economist*, 24 June 2003.

17   'Danish far-right leader Pia Kjaersgaard', Agence France Presse, 23 May 2002.

18   Lodenius wrote this in *Frankfurter Allgemeine Zeitung*.

19   'Sweden: Dark Shadows', *Economist*, 13 Nov. 1999.

20   Quoted in 'Too good to be true', *Economist*, 21 Jan. 1999.

21   'The Swedish Way of Laundering', Ian Taylor, *Contemporary Review*, 1997.

22   Information drawn from Taylor, 'The Swedish Way of Laundering'.

23   Source: Scandinavian Studies.

24   'A nuclear waste', *Economist*, 9 July 1998.

25   'A Nordic and European Tragedy', *Economist*, 13 Sept. 2003.

26   Gallagher, 'The man who told the secret'.

27   Sarah Gold, 'Letters to his mistress shed light on Nobel' (review of *Alfred Nobel* by Kenne Fant), *Publishers' Weekly*, 19 July 1993.

28   Some information drawn from 'Alfred Nobel: the Man Behind the Prizes', *Los Angeles Business Journal*, 8 Oct. 2001.

29   Sources: *Billboard* magazine and Wikipedia: www.en.wikipedia.org.

Chapter 15: Finland

1 Finland is not always considered a part of Scandinavia, but given its historical links with Sweden as well as its geographical location, for the purposes
   of this book, it is.
2 'General Notes: Finland', *The European Legal 500*.
3 Paija Ali-Yrkkö and Ylä-Anttila Reilly, 'Nokia: A Big Company in a Small
   Country', ETLA Series B 162, Taloustieto Oy, Helsinki; as noted in 'Finnfacts'.
4 Morley Safer, and Bob Simon, 'Finland 2000', *Sixty Minutes* (CBS), 19
   Dec. 1999.
5 Source: 'Finnfacts'.
6 Source: Saska Snellman, 'The pies have it', *Helsingin Sanomat*, 10 Apr. 2001.
7 Source: 'Finland battles high suicide rate', Reuters, 8 Dec. 2003.
8 Peter Stalker, *Oxford Handbook of the World*, Oxford: Oxford University
   Press, 2000.
9 'You Know You Have Been in Finland Too Long, When . . .', *Helsingin
   Sanomat* website: www.helsingensanomat.fi/english/estras/toolong.
10 Source: Finnish Sauna Society: www.sauna.fin.
11 'Finland and Sweden play Eurocity', BBC, 8 July 2002: http://news.bbc.co.uk/
   1/hi/world/english/2115938.stm.
12 Jeremy Atiyah, '192-Part Guide to the World. Part 60: Finland', *Independent
   on Sunday*, 30 July 2002.
13 Source: Mario De Biasi, *Meet the Finns*, as noted by Finnish Foreign Ministry's Virtual Finland website.
14 Source: 'Shouting men of Finland perform ice break,' BBC News, 2 Mar.
   2004.
15 Source: Wikipedia: www.en.wikipedia.org.

Chapter 16: Norway

1 Alistair Doyle, 'Norway sees whaling ban extended by IWC', Reuters, 26
   Apr. 1999.
2 'Edging Closer', *Economist*, 24 June 2003.
3 'Sparks fly after sex on stage', *Aftenposten*, 7 July 2004.
4 All information from assorted *Aftenposten* reports.
5 'Muslims, atheists to slug it out in Oslo via loudspeakers', Reuters, 29 Mar.
   2000.
6 Source: Mikael Widmark, 'Race in Scandinavia', *American Renaissance*,
   Dec. 2003.
7 So say Mrs A. K. Paulsen and Mrs Elin Läkken.

Chapter 17: Switzerland

1 Deborah Shapley, 'Tending to the Wounded' (review of *Dunant's Dream* by Caroline Moorehead, Carroll & Graf, 1999) *Washington Post*, 4 July 1999.
2 Alexander G. Higgins, 'Nazis bought stolen art via Switzerland', AP, 31 Aug. 2001.
3 Source: Switzerland Bureau of Statistics.
4 Source: Columbia Electronic Dictionary.
5 'Dada': www.tiscali.co.uk.
6 Christian Raaflaub and Barbara Speziali, 'Blocher proposes setting up refugee camps abroad', Swissinfo, 3 Sept. 2004: www.swissinfo.org.
7 Graham Turner, 'The EU? It's political suicide . . .', *Daily Telegraph*, 8 May 2004.
8 Michael S. Serrill, 'Remains of the Day', *Time*, 24 Oct. 1994.

Chapter 18: Luxembourg

1 'Pierre Werner', *Economist*, 4 July 2002.
2 Much information in this section draws upon 'Brief Historical Survey of the war years in Luxembourg' by Roland Gaul published on the Luxembourg tourism website: www.luxembourg.co.uk.
3 'Alcohol consumption', *Economist*, 1 July 2004.
4 'Q and A about Luxembourg's police', May 2004, www.station.lu.

Chapter 19: Poland

1 'A nervous new arrival on the European Union's block', *Economist*, 30 Aug. 2003.
2 Margaret McMillan, *Paris 1919: Six Months that Changed the World*, New York: Random House, 2001.
3 Robert Pearce, 'Josef Klemenis Pilsudski: Robert Pearce introduces the man who has been called "the George Washington of Poland".' *History Review*, 1 Sept. 2003.
4 Ibid.
5 Jan Stopasal, 'Creative Bloc', *Time International*, 20 May 2002.
6 Oana Lungescu, 'Poland weighs EU pros and cons', BBC News, 5 June 2003: http://news.bbc.co.uk/2/hi/europe/2967116.stm.
7 Peter Stalker, *Oxford Handbook of the World*, Oxford: Oxford University Press, 2000, p. 255.
8 The report, the PAN 'Committee of Prognosis – Poland in the 21st century', is discussed in depth by Czeslaw Mojsiewicz, 'Fears and Doubts in Poland:

internal obstacles to European integration', *World Affairs*, Vol. 158, 1 Sept. 1995.

9   As quoted in *European Report*, 13 July 2002.

10 Ibid.

11 Lepper interpreted by a translator, quoted in 'Populist politician in Poland embarrasses Poland's political establishment,' *All Things Considered*, US National Public Radio, 20 Mar. 2002.

12 Source: United States Holocaust Memorial Center.

13 Source: Holocaust Learning Center.

14 Source: *In Your Pocket: Krakow*.

15 In interview 'Model of Transition', Jim Lehrer, *NewsHour*, PBS, 8 July 1996.

16 David Ost, 'Letter from Poland', *Nation*, 25 Nov. 2002.

17 Beata Pasek, 'As reports on cash-for-corpses scheme stuns Poland, police probe whether ambulance crews let patients die', AP Worldstream, 11 Feb. 2002.

18 Source: *Kaleidoscope* magazine, Sept. 1994; also see www.polishvodka.com.pl/bisons.htm.

19 'Death of a mythmaker', *Newsweek*, 13 May 1991.

20 Information mostly derived from the article by Szydlo Zbigniew and Richard Brzezinski, 'A New Light on Alchemy', *History Today*, Vol. 47, 1 Jan. 1997.

21 Margaret McMillan, *Paris 1919*.

22 'Poland's disputed past: The nation's hero was no democrat', *Economist*, 21 Nov. 1998.

23 Some information from Robert Pearce, 'Josef Klemens Pilsudski'.

Chapter 20: Hungary

1   F. Branfman, 'In Search of the Hungarian Soul', *Budapest Week*, 2 June 1992.

2   'Hungary 1956', History Learning Site: www.historylearningsite.co.uk/hungary_1956.htm.

3   So believe some Hungarian journalists who prefer to remain unnamed.

4   As quoted on historylearningsite.co.uk/hungary_1956.htm.

5   Helen Connolly, 'Hungary for new leadership', *Guardian*, 10 Apr. 2002.

6   George Kahn, 'Socialists Triumph . . .', AP Worldstream, 21 Apr. 2002.

7   Brook Peters, 'Bittersweet Budapest', *Opera News*, 1 May 1999.

8   Michael Kovrig, 'Splitsville in Old Hungary', *US News and World Report*, 7 Aug. 2000.

9   According to US Commercial Service: www.BuyUSA.gov.

10 As reported by Radio Free Europe, 18 Jan. 2002.

11 Ibid.

12 'Viktor Orbán, an assertive Hungarian', *Economist*, 28 Feb. 2002.

13 Ibid.

14 Radio Netherlands, 8 Apr. 2002.

15 Ibid.
16 'No border changes sought, envoy says', *Washington Times*, 7 Apr. 2002.
17 OECD figures for 2000; OECD notes that the percentage of obesity might be even higher.
18 'Romanticism in France and Spain', Culture Kiosque.
19 Margaret McMillan, *Paris 1919: Six Months that Changed the World*, New York: Random House, p. 265.

Chapter 21: Baltic States

1 Information in this section was drawn from a variety of sources including interviews, *City Paper – the Baltic States*, *The Baltic Times*, *Helsingin Sanomat*, the *Economist*, *EU Observer*, *Central Europe Review*, *Library of Congress Country Studies: Estonia, Latvia and Lithuania*, *Lonely Planet World Guides*, *Newsweek*, *Reuters*, *Time*, Margaret McMillan's *Paris 1919*, BBC, Associated Press, the *Guardian*, the *Independent*, the *New York Times*, the *Washington Post*, *International Herald Tribune*, Itar-Tass, Pravda, UPI and assorted government and NGO documents.
2 Michael Tarm, 'The Forgotten War', *City Paper – the Baltic States*, 1996: http://www.balticsww.com/forgotten.htm.
3 Ibid.
4 'Latvia Braced for EU Minus Russian Aliens', UPI, 14 Apr. 2004.
5 'Zhirinovsky beat', *Time*, 11 Apr. 1994.
6 Susan B. Glasser, 'Tensions With Russia Propel Baltic States Toward NATO', *Washington Post*, 7 Oct. 2002.
7 Andrew Beatty, 'Russia may face threat of EU sanctions', *EU Observer*, 17 Apr. 2004.

Chapter 22: Estonia

1 'Estonia minister rails against West's arrogance', Reuters, 14 Dec. 1999.
2 Estonia Guide, *City Paper – the Baltic States*.
3 'The Top Ten Misconceptions about Estonia', *City Paper – the Baltic States*.
4 Some information in this section derived from www.Estonia.org and *City Paper*.
5 Lonely Planet World Guide: *Destination* Estonia, www.lonelyplanet.com/destinations/europe/estonia/htm.
6 'The Baltic bobsleigh', *Economist*, 5 Feb. 1998.
7 1993 interview with American National Public Radio.
8 Kaja Grünthal, assorted articles in *Helsingin Sanomat*.
9 Source: *Helsingin Sanomat*.
10 Sources: *City Paper* and BBC.

Chapter 23: Latvia

1   April 2004 interview with author.
2   Timothy Jacobs, AP Worldstream, 29 Mar. 2004.
3   So says Frank Brown, *Newsweek International*, 3 Nov. 2003.
4   Ibid.
5   One source of this thinking: Vladimir Socor, 'Have Oil, Won't Let it Travel Via Latvia', *Wall Street Journal Europe*, Feb. 2003.
6   May 2004 interview with author.
7   *International Herald Tribune*.
8   'Conventional Wisdom', *Economist*, 28 Feb. 2002.
9   'Latvia History: A Brief Chronology', *City Paper – the Baltic States*: www.balticsww.com/tourist/latvia/history.htm.
10 Clare Thomson, 'The Complete Guide to the Baltics', *Independent*, 2 June 2001.

Chapter 24: Lithuania

1   Margaret McMillan, *Paris 1919: Six Months that Changed the World*, New York: Random House, 1991.
2   Jean Smolowe, Ann Blackman, John Kohan and Strobe Talbott, 'And now, divorce?', *Time*, 22 Jan. 1990.
3   Ina Navazelskis, 'Lithuania: a killing and a crusade', *Columbia Journalism Review*, July/August 1995.
4   'Small wonder', *Economist*, 12 Oct. 2000.
5   Steven Paulikas, 'Doomed Paksas launches feeble counter attack', *The Baltic Times*, 26 Feb. 2004.
6   Information derived from assorted sources including *The Baltic Times*, the *Economist*, and *World Press Review*.
7   'Lithuanian government declares war against rampaging crime', Itar-Tass, 18 Jan. 1997.
8   'Knocking at the clubhouse door', *Economist*, 30 Aug. 2001.
9   *Library of Congress Country Studies: Estonia, Latvia, Lithuania*.
10 *Lonely Planet World Guide: Destination Lithuania*: www.lonelyplanet.com/destinations/europe/lithuania.htm.
11 'Lithuanian Prime Minister marries in secret ceremony', AP Worldstream, 24 Apr. 2004.
12 Niall Green, 'Report Exposes Criminal Connections of Lithuanian President', 25 Nov. 2003.
13 Liudas Dapkas, 'Lithuanians are tired of outspoken leader . . .', Associated Press, 26 July 1998.

14 Mel Huang, 'Lithuania Independent Again', *Central Europe Review*, 15 Feb. 2001.
15 'Forced signatures cancel candidates', *The Baltic Times*, 13 May 2004.
16 Lithuania Guide, *City Paper – the Baltic States*.

Chapter 25: Former Czechoslovakia – Introduction

1 Kenneth Banta, 'In a secluded wood 55 miles east of Prague . . .', *Time International*, 26 Mar. 1990.
2 Margaret McMillan, *Paris 1919: Six Months that Shook the World*, New York: Random House, 1991.
3 George Gibian, 'Germans, Czechs and one brave man . . .', *The New Leader*, 3 June 1996.
4 BBC: 'On this Day – 1968: Russia brings winter to Prague Spring'.
5 Source: BBC News.
6 David Corn, 'Frank Zappa: Trading partner', *The Nation*, 19 Mar. 1990.

Chapter 26: Czech Republic

1 Gareth Harding, 'Proud Czechs refuse to be EU pawns', 23 Apr. 2004.
2 Francis Harris, 'Czech gangs kidnap women as sex slaves', *Sunday Telegraph*, 8 Mar. 1998.
3 Peter S. Green, 'Prague Spy Scandal Raises Concerns over Czech Entry into NATO', *International Herald Tribune*, 5 Feb. 1999.
4 Birdall Viault, *Modern European History*, New York: McGraw-Hill, 1990, p. 73.
5 Jan Stojaspal, 'In Winning Form? . . .', *Time International*, 17 June 2002.

Chapter 27: Slovak Republic

1 Sam Thorne, 'The Brighter Side of New-look Bratislava', *St Petersburg Times*, 29 Aug. 2003.
2 Peter Green, 'School Text Glorifies Slovakia's Role as Nazi Puppet', *International Herald Tribune*, 13 Aug. 1997; 'Skewed book on Holocaust to remain in Slovak schools', *Jewish Telegraphic Agency*, 11 July 1997.

Chapter 28: Slovenia

1 Vesna Peric Zimonjic, 'New EU member says non to minorities', Inter Press Service, 5 Apr. 2004.

2 As reported by Joe Treen, 'The Mouse that roared . . .', *People Weekly*, 15 July 1991.

3 Some information in this section came from 'Laibach: Biography'. www. mute.com/mute/laibach/laibach.htm, and Louis Menashe and Jasminka Udovicki, 'Art, history and politics in the former Yugoslavia: An interview with Michael Benson', *Cineaste*, Vol. 22, 1 Jan. 1996.

4 Chandler Rosenberger, 'The Efficient Cause: The Trial of the Ljubljana Four and the End of Yugoslavia', *Institute of Current World Affairs*, Nov. 1993.

5 Samantha Henry, 'The Art of the Possible', *Newsday*, 17 Feb. 2002.

6 Ibid.

7 As reported by Ali Zerdin, 'Slovene President lambasts lack of tolerance . . .', AP, 31 Dec. 2003.

8 Information from *Lonely Planet World Guide: Destination Slovenia*: www.lonelyplanet.com.

9 Thanks to Jaka Bartolj.

Chapter 29: Cyprus

1 Scott Peterson, 'Greek–Turkish conflict gets a quiet UN hand', *Christian Science Monitor*, 3 Feb. 1999.

2 Source: 'Papadopoulos critical of US comments . . .', and 'Cyprus President rebukes "foreign friends"', Athens News Agency, 7 July, 2004: *www.hri.org.*

3 Source: *Lonely Planet World Guide: Destination Cyprus*: www.lonelyplanet-.com/destinations/europe/cyprus/htm.

4 Some information in this section derived from *Bitter Lemons* by Lawrence Durrell as well as *Library of Congress Country Studies: Cyprus*.

5 'Nicos Sampson', *Economist*, 17 May 2001.

6 Source: BBC.

Chapter 30: Malta

1 So called by the George Cross Data collection board.

2 Broughton, Philip Delves, 'Malta buzzing with anxiety . . .', *Daily Telegraph*, 8 Mar. 2003.

3 Ibid.

4 Some information in this section drawn from *Lonely Planet World Guide: Destination Malta*: www.lonelyplanet.com/destinations/europe/malta.htm.

Bibliography

Books

Blainey, Geoffrey, *A Very Short History of the World*, London: Penguin, 2004

Booker, Christopher and Richard North, The *Great Deception: The Secret History of the European Union*, London: Continuum, 2003

Boorstin, Daniel J., *The Discoverers: A History of Man's Search to Know His World and Himself*, New York: Random House, 1983

Cirlot, Juan-Eduardo, *Gaudí: an Introduction to his Architecture*, New York: Triangle, 2002

Crow, John A., *Spain: The Root and the Flower*, Berkeley: University of California Press, 1985

Davies, Norman, *Europe: A History*, London: Pimlico, 1997

Evans, Graham and Jeffrey Newnham, *The Penguin Dictionary of International Relations*, London: Penguin, 1998

Ferguson, Niall, *Empire: How Britain Made the World*, London: Penguin, 2003

Fisher, H. A. L., *A History of Europe, Vols. I and II*, London: Fontana, 1970

Gilmour, David, *Cities of Spain*, Chicago: Ivan R. Dee, 1992

Hochschild, Adam, *King Leopold's Ghost: A Story of Greed, Terror, and Heroism in Colonial Africa*, New York: Houghton Mifflin, 1999

Hooper, John, *The New Spaniards*, London: Penguin, 1995

Libbon, Robert P., *Instant European History*, New York: Fawcett, 1996

Library of Congress Country Studies for all countries

Martin, Russell, *Picasso's War: The Destruction of Guernica and the Masterpiece that Changed the World*, New York: Plume, 2003

McCauley, Lucy (ed.), *Spain: Travelers' Tales Guides*, San Francisco: Travelers' Tales, 1998

McEvedy, Colin, *The Penguin Atlas of Recent History*, New York: Penguin, 2000

McMillan, Margaret, *Paris 1919: Six Months that Changed the World*, New York: Random House, 2001

Nadeau, Jean-Benoit and Julie Barlow, *Sixty Million Frenchman Can't Be Wrong*, London: Robson Books, 2004

Norman, Peter, *The Accidental Constitution*, Brussels: Eurocomment, 2003

Orwell, George, *Orwell in Spain*, London: Penguin, 2001

Roberts, J. M., *The Penguin History of Europe*, New York: Penguin, 1999
Stalker, Peter, *Oxford Handbook of the World*, New York: Oxford University Press, 2000
Viault, Birdsall, *Modern European History*, New York: McGraw-Hill, 1990

Newspapers, Magazines, Broadcast Media and Online Resources

Baltic Times
Budapest Week
Christian Science Monitor
City Paper – the Baltic States
Columbia Journalism Review
Contemporary Review
Daily Telegraph
Der Spiegel
Economist
El País
EU Business
EU Observer
The European
Forbes
Guardian
Helsingin Sanomat
History Review
Independent
International Herald Tribune
Jakarta Post
Jerusalem Post
Le Monde Diplomatique
Lonely Planet Country Guides
The Nation
National Geographic
New Republic
New Scotsman
Newsweek
New York Times
New Yorker
Observer
Searchlight
Time US News and World Report
Wall Street Journal
Washington Post

ABC News
Associated Press
BBC
CBS News: *60 Minutes*
CNN
National Public Radio
PBS
Radio Free Europe
Radio Netherlands
Radio Prague
Reuters

Columbia Encyclopedia
Common Dreams: www.commondreams.org
Enchantedlearning.com
EU site: http://europa.eu.int
Europe Direct: http://europa.eu.int/europedirect
Lonely Planet: www.lonelyplanet.com
Microsoft Encarta
Wikipedia online encyclopedia
Government websites for all countries
Tourism sites for all countries

Photo Credits

The author warmly thanks those tourism boards, organizations, governments and photographers who kindly donated their photos. Catherine Juckler and the Photo Department of the European Parliament were particularly helpful.

Page 363: Athens, Greece. Courtesy of the Greek National Tourism Organization

Page 366: Greek Prime Minister Costas Karamanlis. Photo by Takis Diamantopoulos. Courtesy of the Greek Government Press Office

Page 390: Copenhagen, Denmark. Courtesy of the Danish Tourism Board

Page 392: Danish politician Pia Kjaersgaard. Courtesy of the Danish People's Party

Page 415: Stockholm, Sweden. Photo by R. Ryan. Courtesy of Image Bank Sweden. Copyright Stockholm Visitors Board

Page 418: Assassinated Swedish Prime Minister Olof Palme. Courtesy of Image Bank Sweden

Page 433: Helsinki, Finland. Photo by Paul Williams. Courtesy of Helsinki City Tourist and Conventions Bureau

Page 435: Finnish President Tarja Halonen. Courtesy of the Office of the President of the Republic of Finland

Page 447: Bergen, Norway. Photo by Olaug Eiksund

Page 450: Norwegian politician Carl Hagen. Courtesy of Norway's Fremskrittspartiet

Page 464: Zurich, Switzerland. Courtesy of Switzerland Tourism

Page 465: Swiss politician and billionaire Christoph Blocher. Photo: Corbis

Page 477: Luxembourg City, Luxembourg. Luxembourg City Tourist Office

Page 479: Luxembourg Prime Minister Jean-Claude Juncker. Courtesy of Luxembourg Office of the Prime Minister

Page 504: Kraków, Poland. Polish National Tourism Office, London

Page 510: Polish politician Andrzej Lepper. Courtesy of Samoobrona Party of Poland

Page 539: Budapest, Hungary. Courtesy of Tourism Office of Budapest

Page 544: Former Hungarian Prime Minister Viktor Orbán. Photo: Corbis

Page 568: Tallinn, Estonia. Courtesy of Tallinn City Tourist Office and Convention Bureau

Page 569: Former Estonian Prime Minister Mart Laar. Photo by Tiit Koha. Courtesy of Ismaalit Party of Estonia

Page 579: Riga, Latvia. Photo by Vitaly Titov

Page 581: Latvian President Vaira Vike-Freiberga. Courtesy of Presidential Office Latvia

Page 594: Hill of Crosses, Lithuania. Courtesy of Lithuania State Department of Tourism

Page 596: Lithuanian MEP Vytautas Landsbergis. Courtesy of European Parliament, Photo Dept

Page 622: Prague, Czech Republic. Courtesy of Czech Tourism

Page 625: Czech President Vaclav Klaus. Photo by Petr Skvrne. Courtesy of the Office of the President of the Czech Republic, Press Dept

Page 636: Bratislava, Slovakia. Courtesy of Slovak Embassy, UK

Page 638: Slovakian PM Mikulas Dzurinda. Courtesy of the Slovak Republic Government Office

Page 653: Ljubljana, Slovenia. Courtesy of Ljobljana Tourism

Page 655: Slovenian politician Janez Jansa. Courtesy of the Social Democratic Party of Slovenia

Page 676: Kyrenia harbour, Cyprus. Photo by Dawn Blundell
Page 678: Former Cypriot leader Archbishop Makarios. Courtesy of Photo Department of Press and Information Office of the Republic of Cyprus
Page 695: Valletta, Malta. Courtesy of Malta Tourist Office
Page 696: Maltese President Eddie Fenech Adami. Courtesy of Government of Malta

Index